The Changing Continuity of Christian Ethics Vol 2

THE INSIGHTS OF HISTORY

The Changing Continuity of Christian Ethics
Vol 2

R. E. O. White

THE INSIGHTS OF HISTORY

PATERNOSTER PRESS

The Paternoster Press
Exeter

AUSTRALIA:
Bookhouse Australia Ltd.,
3-7 Richmond Road, Homebush West, N.S.W. 2140

SOUTH AFRICA:
Oxford University Press,
P.O. Box 1141, Cape Town

British Library Cataloguing in Publication Data

White, Reginald Ernest Oscar
The changing continuity of Christian ethics.
Vol. 2: Insights of history
1. Christian ethics
I. Title
241'.09 BJ1201

ISBN 0-85364-282-6
ISBN 0-85364-283-4 Pbk

Typeset by Photoprint, Paignton
and Printed in Great Britain for The Paternoster Press,
Paternoster House, 3 Mount Radford Crescent, Exeter, Devon
by Butler & Tanner Ltd., Frome, Somerset

CONTENTS

The Question is . . .

THE QUESTION THAT HAS confronted Christian ethics through nineteen hundred years is easy to frame: "How is it possible to change, so continuing to be relevant, while remaining the same, so continuing to be Christian?"[1] But it demands a lengthy answer, for the changes have been immense, far-reaching, radical and unceasing.

Histories of Christian ethics have passed somewhat out of fashion. This is, doubtless, partly because of a conviction that each age must do its own moralising, finding its way for itself among new situations by such light as it possesses. Precedents, rules, inherited insights, custom and tradition seem wholly irrelevant to new moral issues raised by a rate of change more rapid than the world has ever seen. Partly, too, the history of Christian ethics is depreciated by a suspicion that the church has been mainly wrong, divided, disloyal, compromised, or otherwise deprived of authority to teach the present — the only hope for a Christian ethic today lying in a return directly to the Bible.

It has been argued in the first volume of this survey[2] that although new circumstances, unprecedented situations demanding original moral decisions, must provide the content and occasion of each generation's ethical judgements, yet in form and direction, in presuppositions and approach, in nature and in quality, those judgements — if they are Christian at all — derive from a paradosis of history, scripture, tradition, and accumulated experience, of a clearly defined pattern. Only when any response to a given situation is informed by a vision of the good life historically based in the life and teaching of Jesus, and an experience of divine grace historically mediated through Christ and the church, can it justly be characterised as "Christian".

For all that (it was further contended) for the modern Christian biblical ethics is *not* enough. There are many reasons why this is so. The changing place and function of the church in society through the centuries; the unquestionable influence upon Christian thought of nineteen hundred years of "accommodations, developments, debates, disappointments, new insights, experiments, and unresolved questions"; the emergence of modern science, and the new problems posed for ethics by the modern world, affecting industrial morality, economics, contraception, nuclear warfare, genetic engineering and the like, on which the Scriptures offer at best only very indirect advice; and the continuing ministry of the Holy Spirit within the church, taking of the things of Christ in each generation and leading believers progressively into all the truth — any one of these considerations would justify an earnest appeal, on any moral problem, to the history of Christian ethics as well as to scripture. Taken together, they constitute an unanswerable case for the constant re-examination of biblical principles, precepts, examples and ideals in the light of the changing needs and advancing knowledge of the growing church.

Nor can the modern Christian, in any case, afford to dispense with the accumulated wisdom and insight of the Christian generations, even though some of it may have been purchased by error and contention. In truth, the story to be told contains a great deal more light than shade, and at least as much of courage, earnestness, flexibility, faith, and fidelity, as most modern Christians can summon to their aid.

As we set forward upon that story it is not possible to recapitulate adequately so exceedingly rich and varied a heritage of moral wisdom and divine truth as the Bible contains. One notable feature was the constant interweaving of ethics with theology and religious experience, so that precepts, incentives, and resources are never separated. Another feature was the assumption everywhere that moral law and judgements are objective — not human opinion — and obligatory, whether expressed as the divine sovereignty, in messianic terms, as the kingdom of God, the Lordship of Christ, or the supreme law of love. A third feature was the discovery that the law of love is in fact the fundamental law of human nature as God created it, and so of human society; so that obedience to it is at the same time the highest self-fulfilment, the condition of human welfare, and the most perfect freedom. The close inter-relation of ethics in the Bible with basic truths of creation, incarnation, moral redemption, the family and the church, lent to Christian ethics a corporateness which effectually balances its individual inwardness; at the same time, by the same truths, the ethical ideal was rooted in the soil of humanity and could never consistently become totally world-renouncing. Central to all else in biblical ethics was the incarnation of the ideal in the Person of Christ, uniting ideal and incentive, obligation and grateful love, in a single relationship with Him who is at once Lord and Saviour, Master and Friend. By the same identification of the ideal with the Saviour of the world, the biblical ethic is shown to be *unique* in offering not only ethical insights and directives for the righteously-inclined, but effective moral salvation for the sinful and despairing.

It was this last feature of biblical ethics, the profound and complex notion of the imitation of Christ, already within the New Testament period variously understood, and still further enriched by the continuing presence of the Spirit of Christ in the church in succeeding ages, that explained the flexibility, the capacity for apparently endless adaptation and development, shown by Christian ethical teaching as the centuries passed. A coded law, an abstract moral philosophy, a closely regulated ethical institution — even with the help of skilful casuistry — could not have provided the vision, faith and guidance to peoples of every race, culture and age, that men and women have found in the Person of Christ, accepted as the embodiment of conscience, the expression of the ideal, the living Word of God on all matters of conduct and character. Just because the Christian ethic is ultimately expressed, not in words, definitions, principles or regulations, but in loyalty to a Person entirely worthy to be trusted, worshipped and obeyed, it has been possible for successive generations, in circumstances vastly different from those of Palestine in the first century, to transplant the ideal into their own land and time and culture, and "follow Christ" wherever God and history have placed them.

It is the story of this process, with all its successes and its failures, its insights and confusions, its experiments and its conservatism, its few central affirmations and its many disagreements, that makes up the history of Christian ethics. The value of its study may be defined by adding slightly to words already used:[3] "to know the Christian heritage, and to discern what is permanent, what transitory, in its developing formulations, is a necessary foundation for Christian ethical investigation still. To set the student at the point where, with informed mind and matured judgement, he may enter scripturally *and historically* prepared into that contemporary enquiry, is our immediate purpose."

(*Additional Note:* An extended treatment of certain complex and insistent current ethical problems was carefully considered, but decided against for several reasons. (a) Such a treatment would occupy enormous space since the topics included would call for consideration from so many angles — legal, medical, social and even denominational. (b) The available material changes every year with the appearance of fresh books, pamphlets, pronouncements and even legislation. (c) On most questions of this kind expert knowledge is required beyond what is provided by skill in biblical exegesis and a knowledge of Christian history. For these reasons it was decided that this volume should attempt only *to bring the student reasonably equipped to the threshold of the current debate.* For the rest, he must have recourse to more specialised sources.)

1

Into a Pagan Context

THE MOVEMENT OF THE CHURCH out of Jewry into the pagan world, complete by the beginning of the second century, saw the Christian institution, hierarchy, ritual and Scriptures replace the living apostolic memory and fervour; intensified hostility by the State evoke a new Christian heroism; and an increasing use of pagan terms, given Christian overtones, initiate the process of assimilation by which the church strove to make herself more widely intelligible.

(1) THE SOCIAL MILIEU

(i) Lecky's fearful picture of the prevailing tone of Roman society is based upon the nature of the public games, the gladiatorial shows, the prevalence of cultivated sensuality and of idleness, the wide-spread decay of moral faith and of the old religions. Among its causes, he mentions loss of military training and discipline, decline in human dignity due to slavery, change from rural and agricultural society to urban and commercial life, and decline in national aspiration due to the settlement of the Empire.[1] In his detailed study of the literature of the age*, William Barclay remarks that despite the recent fashion to play down the evidence of Tacitus, Suetonius, Juvenal and Seneca, "the fact remains that in Graeco-Roman society the general atmosphere was one of vicious immorality". Barclay instances the worship of wealth, "fantastic luxury", the search for ever new pleasures, cruelty, the cheapening of life involved in the public shows, the vanishing of purity and chastity, and the feeling of moral helplessness. "In a situation like this, philosophy, if it was to have any relevance . . . had to become moral philosophy."[2] Henson considered that the surviving literature is on the whole of the better type, and that a wide gulf existed between moral teaching and popular standards of conduct. He cites as symptomatic "slavery, infanticide, sexual perversion, religious prostitution, widespread suicide

*Beginners in patristic study should find the notes to this and the following chapters especially helpful.

and the bloody shows of the arena" — a moral corruption "prevailing, penetrating, and subtly pervasive."[3]

There were splendid exceptions to this indictment but Scott confirms the "simple historical fact that pagan society . . . was steadily deteriorating . . . The pagan ethic glorified brute force, made egoism a virtue, sins of the body venial and indifferent. Errors of such a kind were bound to vitiate all moral judgements." Beside, the pagan ethic had no means of asserting itself: "it depended on traditions that were steadily growing weaker, or philosophic doctrines that were all in conflict and might be changed."[4]

Even more inimical to Christian standards was the full fruition and ascendancy of gnosticism, that strange amalgam of high thinking, unbridled imagination and specious ethics which had already infiltrated Judaism and the infant churches of Asia. In the second century, "gnostic antinomianism reached its unblushing climax".[5]

Few generalisations are true of every gnostic sect: superstition, philosophic speculation, eastern mysticism, magic, ritualism, deep emotion, even "a wild, fanatical, and obscene cultus," were mixed in varying proportions. Salvation was by knowledge, whether arising from philosophic insight or ritual initiation. The saved formed an intellectual aristocracy not subject to the moral disciplines required of ordinary Christians. Matter being incurably evil, spirit essentially good, ethics is dualistic. Evidence already cited (on 1 John) from Irenaeus,[6] Clement,[7] and Ignatius,[8] for gnosticism's moral indifferentism, lovelessness, and sensual excesses, might be extended — Clement of Alexandria says the Nicolaitans pervert an adage of Nicolaus, "the flesh must be abused", and abandon themselves to pleasure like goats, leading a life of self-indulgence;[9] Hippolytus says that followers of Simon Magus "even congratulate themselves upon this indiscriminate intercourse, asserting that this is perfect love. For (they would have us believe) they are not overcome by the supposed vice, because they have been redeemed . . . They do whatsoever they please as persons free, for they allege that they are saved by grace."[10] Caius of Rome[11] is frequently quoted for the extremely sensual millenial hopes of the gnostic Cerinthus; Dionysius of Alexandria says Cerinthus was a voluptuary. The Ophite sect reversed the story of Eden to make the serpent hero, the defender of the knowledge of God and of evil, to whom therefore mankind is eternally indebted; while the Cainites reversed all the moral judgements of the Old Testament, making the heroes villains and the sinners saints.

When all allowance is made for exaggeration by reporters zealous to defend orthodox Christology from gnostic denial, the gnostic influence within the churches obviously presented a serious challenge to Christian ethics. The whole of the writings of Irenaeus, most of Tertullian[12] and of Hippolytus, and some by Clement of Alexandria, were devoted to its refutation.

One effect of the prevailing atmosphere was a Christian recoil into austerity. Says Inge: "In the main, Christian asceticism rested not on any philosophical belief consciously held, but on the desire to escape from a social environment at once corrupt and miserable";[13] and Marshall, "The licentiousness of the times . . . strengthened what ascetic tendencies there were in Christianity, and associated them with ascetic tendencies which were not properly Christian at all."[14] Henson remarks that "the non-Jewish environment shaped Christian morality mainly by the reactions it evoked: the pervading licentiousness strengthened the ascetic tendency."[15]

A second effect of social permissiveness was the church's increasing authoritarianism. The firm discipline of moral instruction required of catechumens, the development of a strict moral code alongside the prescribed creed, the emergence of an elaborate penitential system, and the fearful threat of excommunication, are all symptoms of a protective hardening of the Christian conscience. "Sub-apostolic discipline" is now carried much further, in an institutional ethic imposed on pain of punishment. Luthardt spoke of a third effect, the strengthened tendency to moralise and legalise the gospel. Paul had answered incipient antinomianism by asserting a moral transformation by faith-union with Christ and the rule of the Spirit of holiness; in reply to gnostic antinomianism the church fell back upon Jewish legalism and stoic self-sufficiency. Eventually, a doctrine of good works made its appearance, merit was ascribed to fasting and prayer, and expiatory power to almsgiving. Thus evangelical truth became obscured, though the intention was sound — to fight at all costs the moral infection of pagan society in general and the gnostic ethical heresy in particular.[16]

(ii) Christian intolerance of idolatry, and refusal to conform to public opinion, led to two-and-a-half centuries of hostility. Tacitus[17] explains that Christians were a class "hated for their abominations", and convicted of "hatred of the human race". With some bewilderment, Celsus contrasted the respectability of the religious Mysteries with the invitation of Christianity:

> "Those who summon men to the other initiations and offer purification from sins, proclaim 'Whosoever has clean hands and is wise of speech. . .' or 'Whosoever is pure from defilement, whose soul is conscious of no guilt, who has lived well and righteously. . .' But let us hear what sort the Christians invite: 'Whosoever is a sinner, or unintelligent, or a fool — in a word, Whosoever is God-forsaken, him will the kingdom of God receive.'"[18]

Christians, having no visible god, were considered atheists, while the custom of *private* worship (for theological reasons and because of political pressure) led to charges of ritual incest and of cannibalism. In such a climate of opinion, intensified official repression found popular support.

The moral effects of persecution were varied. Demonstrably false charges tend to foster a sense of superiority over one's accusers, and to obscure real faults. This may have contributed to the continued exaltation of martyrdom as an incontrovertible vindication of sincerity, and of righteousness in the face of calumny.

"To the confessor was granted in the church a great and venerable authority . . . To the martyr, besides the fruition of heaven, belonged the highest glory on earth. By winning that bloodstained crown, the meanest Christian slave might gain a reputation as glorious as that of a Decius or a Regulus. His body was laid to rest with sumptuous splendour; his relics . . . were venerated with an almost idolatrous homage. The anniversary of his birth into another life was commemorated . . . and . . . his heroic sufferings were recounted . . . By the 'baptism of blood' the sins of a life had been in a moment effaced . . . Men seemed indeed to be in love with death" (Lecky[19]). Believing, with Ignatius, that they were "the wheat of God" they panted for the day when they should be "ground by the teeth of wild beasts into the pure bread of Christ." As a boy, Origen[20] had to be restrained from voluntary martyrdom. For many, all family ties succumbed to this burning enthusiasm: "the desire for martyrdom became at times a form of madness, a kind of epidemic of suicide" which far-seeing Christian leaders had to check. Said Epictetus,[21] "there are some whom madness, there are others like the Galileans whom custom, makes indifferent to death." Marcus Aurelius[22] ascribes it to the Christians' "pure obstinacy"; Lucian explains it by the conviction of immortality.[23]

Henson hints at darker consequences.[24] Persecuting intolerance bred in the church a kindred temper. When in turn the church herself became persecutor, the methods, the plea of social necessity, and much of their spirit and ruthlessness, were borrowed from her tormentors. No doubt the church's self-protection as a powerful political institution, and her involvement with the State, lie behind "Christian" persecution, but the use of torture, violence, and death to enforce religious conformity is so entirely alien to original Christianity that some deep spiritual wound, utterly distorting the church's judgement, seems necessary to explain it. Perhaps her remembered agony, possibly even some long cherished corporate desire for revenge, supplies the key: even in Christian hearts violence breeds violence.

On the other hand, the years of persecution strengthened within the Christian tradition the theme of conflict, steadfast endurance, and dauntless courage. Christlikeness became again a literal sharing in the experience of the cross, not only a sacramental, or emotional, identification with Christ's attitude. Christ in conflict, Christ in agony and Christ the Victor, kindled Christian imagination; perhaps for the first time, Christians became heroes. The years of suffering bred also a deeper sense of fraternity. Though some sought refuge in secrecy, and some in desertion, the maintenance of Christian fellowship in the catacombs and other hiding places, the readiness to share in suffering, to strengthen the resolution of those threatened with death and to care for the bereaved, show that persecution helped to consolidate the Christian brotherhood. The blood of the martyrs proved the seed of a more stubbornly united church.

(iii) A third factor in the church's new environment was what Inge[25] calls a "widespread religious revival". "The stoics still preached the moral virtures" says T. R. Glover, "and it was well that they did. The *Letters* of Seneca and the *Discourses* of Epictetus show us the better side of that age and introduce us to men of real moral earnestness, about whom gathered anxious disciple souls, troubled with the sense of failure, conscience stricken . . ."[26] James Orr, too, speaks of "a powerful religious and ethical revival" when rhetoricians, philosophers, preachers, teachers, declaimers, were everywhere. Vespasian arranged support for such lecturers, while "towards the end of the first and during the course of the second centuries, a certain glow of moral enthusiasm began to spread itself through the Empire". Itinerant homilists "began from the Flavian period to go about proclaiming moral truths, collecting groups of hearers, and sowing the seeds of spiritual wisdom and knowledge on every soil that would receive it": Apollonius of Tyana, Dion Chrysostom, Epictetus, are examples.[27] J. S. Stewart remarks that "in the streets and market-places of Asia Minor and of Europe the stoic evangelist was a familiar figure. Wendland compares him to the Salvation Army missioner in the towns and villages of Great Britain . . ."[28] According to the Trajan-Pliny correspondence, temples which had been well-nigh abandoned were beginning to be frequented again, while the market for fodder for sacrificial animals was rising.[29]

One consequence of this "spiritual awakening" was the considerable infiltration of higher ranks of society by the gospel, lending to Christianity a new interest in culture, art and learning. Although since its intrusion into the gentile world the new faith had made its major appeal to more obscure sections of society, there had always been some of the educated, commercial, professional and official classes who heard the gospel gladly — a centurion, a president of the synagogue, Lydia, the city treasurer of Corinth, the Ethiopian chamberlain, Dionysius the Areopagite, his excellency

Theophilus, and others. Increasing ethical and social concern led to many more such converts, wealthy, educated, with moral insight and purpose.

The Roman catacombs illustrate the wealth, social standing, high imperial connections, and artistic awareness, upon which Christians of the second century could call. With wealth of detail, Orr[30] confirms the report of Pliny that many "of all ranks" were being converted, and the warning of Tertullian to the persecuting proconsul of Carthage, that he would find many "men of your own order, and noble ladies, and all the leading persons of the city" brought before him. Valerian's edict was directed expressly against Christian senators, men of rank, knights, and those in Caesar's household. Minucius Felix[31] declares that Christians were no longer "a dumb folk muttering in corners" but emboldened to present their case in the open court of public opinion, and that through the writings of men trained as philosophers, rhetoricians, lawyers, with the skill of learning, art, the dialectic of the schools and the gift of the forensic pleader. Appollonius the martyr was a Roman senator renowned for learning and philosophy; Aristides[32] and Athenagoras[33] were philosophers of Athens; Justin Martyr[34] and Tatian[35] were likewise men of wide learning and deep culture; Tertullian and Minucius were lawyers of great gifts. The cultivated Celsus[36] thought it necessary to combat with considerable care the influence of Christianity among his own class.

The new ethical and religious concern which opened the way into such circles also evoked deliberate emphasis upon the moral effects of salvation. Christian propaganda became especially a moral apologetic addressed to those eager for illumination and a new ideal. As we shall see, it is exaggeration to say that the apologists "reduced Christianity to a rational moral theology", but it is true that the gospel was offered as a prescription for the good life. Lecky says, "the Christian notion of the enormity of little sins, the particularity of the coming judgement, and the reality of eternal life, exercised altogether new influence" in creating a moral earnestness that appealed strongly to those who shared Christian dismay at prevailing social conditions.[37] Philosophy undoubtedly attracted to virtue those capable of feeling such attraction: Christianity proved effective in actual regeneration of the vicious. For many, therefore, the moral argument for the new faith took precedence over all other recommendations.

(2) THE CHRISTIAN IMPACT

The background, and evidence, for the literary apologetic was, however, the distinctive quality of the Christians' daily life:

"To the profligacy of that effete heathen world Christianity opposed its own fresh young life and glowing spiritual ideals; to its pride, the proclamation of a common fall and a common salvation; to its selfish egoism, the demand for a universal charity; to its denial of the rights of humanity, the doctrine of the love of God and of the spiritual dignity of man . . .; to its degradation of woman, the assertion that in Christ Jesus there is neither male nor female; to its contempt for labour, the recollection of the Carpenter . . . Opposed at nearly every point to the existing pagan order, it yet . . . implanted within it the seeds of emancipation and renewal. If it did not save the old Roman empire, it at least laid within it the foundations on which the rearing of a new order could proceed . . ." (Orr[38]).

Evidence supporting that idealist picture must inevitably be selective, though not all is Christian. Pliny[39] testifies that Christians could not be made to curse Christ, and bound themselves with an oath not to commit theft, robbery, adultery, to break their word, or to deny a deposit when demanded. Describing Christian conversion, Justin Martyr emphasises the change from fornication to chastity, from magical arts to God, from acquisitiveness to sharing of goods, from hatred and exclusiveness to hospitality, prayer for enemies, and the wish to persuade those who are hostile to participate in Christian hope and joy.[40] Many have been led to "change their violent and tyrannical disposition" and become Christians, "being overcome either by the constancy which they have witnessed in their neighbours' lives, or by the extraordinary forbearance they have observed in their fellow-travellers when defrauded, or by the honesty of those with whom they transacted business."[41] Justin is partial, but his argument would lose all force unless supported, generally, by the Christians' social reputation.

Aristides[42] testifies that Christian life was marked by freedom from adultery, from false witness, covetousness, denying of deposit, idolatry, unchastity. If slaves are converted, they are called brethren. Christian women are pure, the men honest in business; they prove to be humble, kind, truthful, loving, hospitable, "communist", sober, ever giving thanks, or else weeping over the lost; generous to all in need and concealing their generosity. If this picture be idealised, it at least delineates the character which the church sought to cultivate and present to the world. No less can be said of the moving description of Christian life in "Diognetus"[43] —

"Christians are distinguished from other men neither by country, nor language, nor the customs which they observe . . . following the customs of the natives in respect to clothing, food, and the rest of their ordinary conduct, they display to us their wonderful and confessedly striking (lit. 'paradoxical') method of life. They dwell in their own countries, but simply as sojourners. As citizens they share in all things with others, and yet endure all things as if foreigners. Every foreign land is to them as their native country, and every land of their birh as a land of strangers. They marry, as do all; they beget children; but they do not destroy their offspring. They have a common table, but not a common bed. They are in the flesh, but they do not live after the flesh. They pass their days on earth, but they are citizens of heaven. They obey the prescribed laws, and at the same time surpass the laws by their lives. They love all men, and are persecuted by all. They are unknown and condemned . . . They are poor, yet make many rich . . . they are dishonoured, and yet in their very dishonour are glorified. They are evil spoken of, and yet are justified; they are reviled and bless; they are insulted, and repay the insult with honour; they do good, yet are punished as evil-doers . . . To sum up all in one word — *what the soul is in the body, that are Christians in the world.* The soul is dispersed through all the members of the body, and Christians are scattered through all the cities of the world. The soul dwells in the body, yet is not of the body; and Christians dwell in the world, yet are not of the world . . . The flesh hates the soul . . . the world also hates Christians: the soul loves the flesh that hates it, Christians likewise love those that hate them. The soul is imprisoned in the body, yet preserves ("keeps together") that very body, and Christians are confined in the world as in a prison, and *yet they are the preservers of the world* . . ."

Lecky remarks that noble lives, crowned by heroic deaths, were the best arguments of the infant church, and their enemies themselves not unfrequently acknowledged it: "the love shown by the early Christians to their suffering brethren has never been more emphatically attested than by Lucian, or the beautiful simplicity of their worship than by Pliny, or their ardent charity than by Julian. There was, it is true, another side to the picture; but even when the moral standard of Christians was greatly lowered, it was lowered only to that of the community about them."[44] Lucian (described by Inge as "the Voltaire of antiquity") said scornfully of Christians "their original lawgiver had taught them that they were all brethren one of another . . . They become incredibly alert when anything happens which affects their common interests; on such occasions, no expense is grudged."[45] In the dialogue "Octavius", Minucius Felix makes Caecilius the critic say, "Christians recognise each other by means of secret marks and signs, and love one another almost before they are acquainted." Minucius himself speaks of the Christians' justice, honesty, and love, as constituting true sacrifices, in contrast to those offered by idolaters; he extols the Christians' attitude towards pain, their courage in martyrdom. "It is we who do not show wisdom in our dress but in our hearts, who do not proclaim great things but live them, who are proud of having obtained what philosophers have sought in their utmost efforts but failed to find."[46]

Tertullian, contrasting the private and public morality of believers with the foul conduct of pagans, like a good lawyer challenges his opponents to produce from the long lists of those committed to prison for crime, any instances of Christians so convicted. He appeals to the pagans' own testimony: "You are accustomed in conversation yourselves to say, 'Why is so-and-so so deceitful, when the Christians are so self-denying? Why merciless, when Christians are so merciful?' " On Tertullian's account of the organisation of Christian charity in his day, Inge comments that the church "must have resembled a large benefit society with very liberal management. The authorities exerted themselves to find work for those who were able to work, and gave doles to the unemployed."[47] Around 250 AD the church at Rome supported more than fifteen hundred widows and poor or suffering Christians.[48]

Marshall's summary of the evidence for the quality of Christian living in the second and third centuries adds further details. "In contrast to their pagan neighbours, it was not their practice to expose children to death, for they never regarded any child born to them as 'unwanted' but deemed child-life a sacred thing; fellow-believers of every people and language were one; the new position of women was distinctive; special care was taken for the proper burial of the poor."[49] Later, this social concern of the church won high praise, especially during uncontrollable epidemics. Julian wrote, "the godless Galileans nourish our poor in addition to their own, while ours get no care from us."[50] Eusebius says, concerning a time of plague,

> "Christians showed themselves at that time to all the heathen in the most brilliant light; for the Christians were the only people who, in the midst of so much and so great tribulation, proved by deeds their sympathy and love of their kind. Some busied themselves day after day with the care and burial fo dead bodies (they were without number, and no one else bothered about them); others gathered together into one place all who were tortured by hunger and supplied them with food. When this became known, people glorified the God of the Christians, and confessed that they alone were the truly pious and God-fearing people, because they gave proof of it by their deeds."[51]

Dionysius tells a similar story concerning plague in Alexandria: after unsparing affection and fearless visitation of the sick, many of the Christians died; "quite the reverse was it with the heathen, who fled from their dearest friends and threw out their sick half-dead . . ." Cyprian repeats the story, concerning Carthage.[52]

"The gospel," says Harnack "thus became a social message", and he illustrates fully the immense range of Christian benevolence. "From the apostolic counsels down to Cyprian . . . ever-increasing stress is laid upon the importance of alms to the religious position of the donor, and upon the prospect of a future recompense." Cyprian develops alms into a formal means of grace, but "with Clement of Alexandria the motive of love for men is kept steadily in the front rank." "A great deal, a very great deal, of alms is given away privately throughout the Christian churches;" one frequent recommendation was, to fast in order to be able to give.[53]

Various motives for almsgiving were urged: Didache: "Blessed is he that gives according to the commandment, for he is guiltless . . . give with thine hands a ransom for thy sins."[54] Polycarp recommends almsgiving as "redeeming from death", quoting as do other early Christian writers, Tobit 12:9, cf. 4:10 — "charity delivers from death and keeps you from entering the darkness."[55] Barnabas: love of one's neighbour holds nothing to be an exclusive possession, but "communicates" in all things; love gives alms, which work a ransom for sin.[56] Hermas: the rich must help the poor and the poor must pray for the rich — suggesting a direct reward for almsgiving through the grateful prayers of the recipients.[57] For "2 Clement" almsgiving is 'beautiful' even as repentance for sin; fasting is better than prayer, but almsgiving is better than both . . . for almsgiving removes the burden of sin.[58] Cyprian's special treatise on almsgiving describes it as a divinely appointed means of cancelling sins, a complement of baptism, offering cleansing to souls who have lost their baptismal purity; almsgiving can make prayers efficacious, and free souls from death; "by means of alms, we can wash off any stains contracted after baptism. Cyprian can even compare the ostentatious bestowing of gifts in the presence of emperors with Christians alms bestowed while God looks on with approval.[59] For Ambrose, too, almsgiving cancels sins: "Thou hast money — ransom thy sins. God is not purchaseable, but you are: purchase the ransom of thy sins with thy works; buy thyself off with thy money"; baptism promises forgiveness once, almsgiving as often as given — "a second bath of the soul".[60] Doubtless such appeals tend to make love for others a higher kind of selfishness; but the importance attached to almsgiving is plain, and so is the real intention — to use the longing for assurance to enforce benevolence.

The expression of Christian charity is manifold. Orphans — especially abandoned children — and "old folk unable now to go about"[61] share the church's care of the poor with an immense number of widows, supported mainly to avoid necessity for immoral employment or remarriage. The sick are cured, consoled, visited, maintained; innocent prisoners, those persecuted or imprisoned for debt, are also visited, comforted, assisted; where possible they are ransomed, even at risk. Those sentenced to the mines were recorded, visited and sometimes ransomed; in the mines at Phaeno a church was organised. Hermas urges, "Instead of fields, buy souls in trouble"; Clement of Rome says, "many have given themselves up to be captives in order to ransom others; many have sold themselves into slavery to feed others." Eventually, a law was aimed directly at Christians, forbidding such ministry to prisoners, on pain of sharing the prisoners' lot.

Tertullian speaks of burial of the dead as an organised church-charity; Aristides, as a private act. In part, this expressed human feeling shared equally by pagans, but other motives prompted it too: Lactantius says, "We cannot bear that the image and workmanship of God should be exposed as prey to wild beasts and birds, but we restore it to the earth from which it was taken, and do this office of relatives even to the body of a person whom we do not know, since in their room humanity must step in." The care and ransoming of slaves was another avenue of charity; and where a man for conscience' sake could no longer follow his employment, the obligation to support him or find him work was accepted. Already in the Didache it was laid down that a man without work must be helped, but not in idleness — work should be provided, and he must do it; so Cyprian, and the pseudo-Clementine homilies — "For those able to work, provide work; to those incapable, be charitable." Hospitality to the travelling stranger, and widespread concern for Christians in trouble in other districts (as Cyprian's collection of ransom money for Christians captured in Numidia) may be a "domestic" charity, but it illustrates the brotherly-love which knit the church together. Harnack concludes: "The excellence of the church's charitable system, the deep impression made by it, and the numbers that it won over to the faith, find their best voucher in the action of Julian the apostate, who attempted an exact reproduction of it in that artificial creation of his, the State-church, in order to deprive the Christians of this very weapon."[62]

If such a picture of the church's impact upon paganism appears too favourable to be probable, it must be remembered that in an atmosphere of hostility, under extreme social pressure, those who remained loyal to Christ were inevitably above average in conduct and devotion — the weak and insincere were weeded out by circumstances. Moreover, another aspect of the picture has still to be described, a serious moral aberration, and a lamentable failure to leaven society when opportunity fell into the church's hands. But that will not contradict the testimonies offered of the church's quality of life and the attractiveness of her example. Justin declares it was the steadfastness of Christians that convinced him of their purity of motive. Tatian names as the main reason for his conversion, "the excellence of Christianity's moral doctrines". Cyprian says it was the moral power of the gospel that won him; Tertullian and Origen speak in similar terms — in each case, of course, an impression made upon an *unconverted* man.[63]

Rejecting vigorously all "miraculous" explanations of the conversion of the Roman Empire, the critical Lecky lists — the appeal of Christianity to the affections, which Stoicism starved; "the charm of a sympathetic worship"; the dignity and comfort offered to the slave; the hope kindled by a moral faith; the heroism evoked by martyrdom. He declares "never before was a religious transformation so inevitable". The church's discipline was rigorous, evoking a devotion very like patriotism. Her penitential system was strong enough to impose sexual abstinence, public confession, humiliation, loss of all Christian friendships, fear of eternal damnation; most offences, from neglecting worship to unchastity, adopting the profession of actor or gladiator, betraying Christians, homosexuality, had prescribed penalties. But on the other hand, her moral training, close-knit fellowship, sacramental means of grace, and lofty faith, offered a still more effective, because positive, moral inspiration.[64]

Behind all else lay the constant memory and appeal of the words and the Figure of Jesus. Against Harnack's view that imitation of Christ played no part in Christian aspiration in this period, Inge says "the Apologists and Irenaeus speak of the human Jesus as a model for our imitation, and Cyprian says, 'In Christ there is given to us an exemplar of life'."[65] Harnack's dictum is strange, based perhaps upon a restricted view of 'imitation'. Polycarp had said, "Let us then be imitators of His patience . . . for He has set us this example in himself"; Irenaeus declared "(He) did through His transcendent love become what we are that He might bring us to be even what He is in himself . . . that having become imitators of His works as well as doers of His words, we may have communion with Him."[66]

With Clement of Alexandria, "assimilation to God" as known in Christ becomes a constant theme — usually with the qualifying phrase, "as far as possible", or "as far as allowed to men".

Christians "believe Christ to be God's image and likeness, (they) having become . . . by Jesus Christ so far already like God"; "It is incumbent . . . to perform the works of the Master according to His similitude, and so to fulfil what scripture says as to our being made in His image and likeness"; Jesus "draws for us the model of the true life"; "Better far to become the imitator . . . of the best of all beings." "God formed man . . . regenerated him . . . made him grow . . . trained him . . . directing him . . . in order that . . . He might fulfil to the utmost that divine utterance — 'Let us make man in our own image and likeness . . .' "; "In truth, Christ became the perfect realisation of what God spake . . . 'Let us take on the impress of the truly saving life of our Saviour . . .' ": "He is the gnostic (mature Christian) who is after the image and likeness of God as far as possible . . ." "Openly and expressly the apostle says 'Be ye followers of me as I am of Christ' . . . Assimilation to God, then, he lays down as the aim of faith . . ."; "He who is made like the Saviour is also devoted to saving . . ."; "the perfect inheritance belongs to those who attain to 'a perfect man' — the image of the Lord . . . To the likeness of God, then, he that is introduced into adoption and the friendship of God . . . is brought." "He is to us a spotless image; to him we are to try with all our might to assimiliate our souls."[67]

Ambrose declares, "the scripture wills that the Spirit of the Son of Man should be in us"; and appeals to the misguided to "cast out of the kingdom of thy soul the likeness of the devil, and raise up the likeness of Christ. Let this shine forth in thee; let this glow brightly in thy kingdom, that is, thy soul . . ." "If then any one wishes to please all, he must strive in everything to do, not what is useful for himself but what is useful for many . . . For this is to 'be conformed to the image of Christ' . . ."[68]

Glover quotes from Horace "and less amusing authors" the Stoic's question, "What would Socrates have done in such a case, or Zeno?" "You ought to live as one who wishes to be a Socrates" — "Go away to Socrates . . . Think what a victory he won over himself."[69] Epictetus urged his disciples to set before themselves some man of surpassing excellence, and to imagine him continually near them.[70] Such personalised idealism illustrates the appeal to example when philosophic doctrines lack conviction, but as Lecky remarks, stoicism could not press beyond admiration to affection.

The final explanation of Christianity's triumph, even in a pagan milieu, lay in the fact that whereas "the Platonist exhorted men to imitate God; the Stoic, to follow reason; the Christian called men to the love of Christ." The moral enthusiasm kindled by devotion to Jesus was a transfiguring, creative, and sustaining dynamic that outlived the ancient world. As Aristides said, "Christians trace their origin from the Lord Jesus Christ . . . They have the commands of the Lord Jesus Christ Himself graven upon their hearts."[71]

2

Moral Apologetics

THE PREOCCUPATION OF THE first Christian centuries with ethics finds expression in literature addressed to those *outside* the church as a moral apologetic; to those *inside*, as a moral training for church membership. R. A. Norris[1] remarks in these writings a deep hostility to Roman society, plus a rigorous perfectionism. In the west, a legal and moralistic conformity to church standards marks the Christian, to be rewarded by salvation in the day of judgement. One major problem was the right discipline of the baptised who fell from Christian ways. In the east, the emphasis was upon mystical and ascetic purification; the goal was the vision of God; the means, monasticism. While throughout the church, rejection and pessimism governed the attitude of most towards the outside world, until Augustine and Ambrose worked out afresh the relation of Christians to sinful human society.

Our purpose is not the historical one of understanding each man in his own time, but the practical one of discovering the changing continuity that links numerous writers in growing insight. Some distillation of leading themes is therefore unavoidable, even though the result does less than justice to individual leaders. So very different from our own time, the second and third centuries were also very different from the first, and some of the questions which exercised the apologists set the pattern for Christian ethical thought, either to follow or to reject, for centuries afterwards. The first impact of Christianity upon the Roman world provides immediate illustration of the church's perennial problem in ethics: the application of a given and final revelation to continually changing situations.

(1) THE RELATION OF ETHICS TO THE GOSPEL

The "sub-apostolic" decline from the high confidence of the apostolic age, that true faith and genuine salvation-experience *would* find expression in Christlike character, to earnest exhortations that they *ought* to find such expression, continued into the post-apostolic period. Patristic ethics "create the impression that the Christian becomes such not by the grace of God but by his own effort, by bringing his conduct into line with Christian standards." In defining such standards, the major emphases were: the superiority of simplicity over luxury, of love over hate, of harmony over division and anger; the importance of truth as against falsehood and pretence; sexual temperance and the rejection of fornication, paederasty and exposure of infants.[2]

(a) The Didache directly *infers* moral obligation from saving faith, understood as essentially obedience to the preached word.

Describing that obedience, Didache gives chief place to the two great commandments, to the negative form of the golden rule ("Whatsoever you would not have done to you, neither do you"), to the Christian fast-days, and to the Decalogue, extended to prohibit corrupting boys, fornication, witchcraft, abortion, infanticide, malice and being double-minded or double-tongued.

The tone is plainly moralistic: "a lifetime of faith will be of no advantage unless you prove perfect at the last moment."[3] Cool, commonsense moral endeavour contrasts with the exuberant joy and victory of apostolic experience: "If unable to bear the whole yoke, do what thou canst."

(b) Clement of Rome appears to set justification by faith and Christian morality *side-by-side*, not relating them in any inward way, or deducing one from the other. "We are blessed if we perform the orders of God in the name of love, unto the forgiveness — through love — of our sins."[4] God's benefits turn into judgements if we fail in virtuous deeds. Listing the wonderful gifts of God — immortality, joy, confidence, trust — Clement urges that we strive to share them, by faith in God, performing His faultless will, following the path of truth, casting from us all injustice, wickedness, covetousness, strife, malice, deceit, gossiping and evil speaking, hatred of God, arrogance, boasting, vainglory and inhospitality.

F. L. Cross thinks that Clement "hardly understood" Paul's teaching on justification, since he can say that Rahab was justified by "faith and hospitality".[5] Woolley, too, remarks Clement's lack of comprehension of the grace of God — he lays much stress on repentance and good deeds, but very little on the work of Christ.[6]

Nevertheless, Clement can speak with equal clearness of God's "magnificent and surpassing gifts of peace and kindness"; of the "refuge we have found in His mercies through our Lord Jesus Christ; of "the Lord Jesus, whose blood was given for us". He says, "We also, having been called through His will in Christ Jesus, are not justified by ourselves, or by our own wisdom or understanding or piety or the works we have done in holiness of heart, but through the faith by which the Almighty God has justified all men . . ." Further, "in charity the Lord received us; out of the charity which He had for us, Jesus Christ our Lord gave His blood for us by the will of God, and His flesh for our flesh, and His life for our lives."[7] Clement's so-called "blunting of Paulinism" merely illustrates the difficulty, which Christianity ever faces, of urging those who receive grace without merit nevertheless to merit the grace they have received.

(c) Sometimes the gospel is almost *lost in moralising*, until a salvation by "evangelical good works" emerges, as in the "self-ransoming" motive sometimes mingled with altruism in the emphasis upon almsgiving.

"2 Clement" leaves Paul's gospel behind in its treatment of repentance: our confessing Christ, fulfilling His commands in good works and in love, is a kind of reward we offer Him, a "return" for what Christ has done for us; so we attain salvation.[8] Justin Martyr says, God "accepts those only who imitate the excellences which reside in Him".[9] Hermas' primary mission was to preach repentance: the "Shepherd" is a long conversation on the duty of penance. The new life is the gift of God; salvation is received through baptism; but security lies in unceasing repentance, moralistically conceived. Of those who sin repeatedly, and repeatedly repent, "it is not profitable for such a man, for hardly shall he live."[10] Woolley says that in Tertullian, too, ascetic and benevolent practices supplemented the work of Christ in making satisfaction for sins.[11]

(d) The relation of ethics to the gospel is sometimes primarily a question of *church discipline*. Clement of Rome emphasises obedience to leaders, the divine spirit of "order"; Ignatius held that the new life realises itself when the Christian is introduced to the Christian community, whose unity regulates all. Here, Christian conduct becomes church-centred: marriage, for example, is to be contracted only with the consent of the bishop. After enlistment by baptism into the church, Christians are told "Let none of you be found a deserter. Let your baptism endure as your arms, your faith as your helmet, your love as your spear, your patience as a complete panoply. Let your works be the (military) commission assigned to you . . ."[12] Christian morals have become church orders.

Within such church-orientated ethics, post-baptismal sin becomes a serious problem. The prevailing rigorism denied all comfort to those who fell from the purity conferred by baptismal washing. *Hermas* does defend the possibility of restoration through repentance — *once.*[13] Tertullian's earlier view was that "canonical penance" might be prescribed for the baptised who became guilty of serious sins, but only once; in his later, Montanist, period Tertullian distinguished sins which are remissable for the baptised from those (adultery, fornication, murder, idolatry) for which there is neither penance nor pardon.[14] The implicit distinction between mortal and venial sins remained a feature of ecclesiastical discipline from Tertullian's time. The *Didascalia Apostolorum* held that all sins may be remitted except that proscribed in the Gospels, the sin against the Holy Spirit. Cyprian, Hippolytus, held the more rigorist view.[15]

For Tertullian, too, the believer is rescued from Satan and set within the church, where God's will is known, where the good is what God commands in the church's scriptures and the church's tradition of apostolic discipline. The new life in Christ derives from regular faith and regular discipline: by observing that discipline, the man forgiven in baptism maintains himself in God's favour against the day of judgement — "a legal note from a legal mind". Ambrose represents a still more vigorous ecclesiastical discipline. He saw the church as school and guardian of morality, an arm of God's judgement; though his total doctrine of Christian morality went far deeper than conformity to church rules.

This general and persistent notion of Christian ethics as the ethos of the institution, theory and explanation being left to experts while ordinary Christians conformed to the church's directions, was first clearly defined in these centuries, when the church was made forcibly aware of her separateness from a culture superficially alluring but in fact deeply hostile to her faith.

(e) Closer to the apostolic gospel of a salvation experience that itself transfigures character were —

Polycarp: the new life proceeds from faith in Him "who endured all things for us, that we might live in Him;" — "the strong root of your faith brings forth fruit to our Lord Jesus Christ . . . By grace ye are saved, not of works but by the will of God through Jesus Christ." Love to God and man, all righteousness and obedience, follow from salvation. Grace originates salvation — despite the promise that almsgiving will redeem from death.[16]

Barnabas: Remission is effected by Christ's blood: the Lord endured to suffer for our souls. He chose apostles from those who were sinners that He might show He came not to call the righteous but sinners to repentance. The new law of Christ is inward, free, based upon knowledge and insight. Christian "fasting" means the practice of true compassion, generosity, tenderness, justice, freedom for others, humility. "The habitation of our heart is a holy temple to the Lord" when we have received forgiveness and placed our trust in the name of the Lord; then we have become new creatures . . . God truly dwells in us. "The way of light is — love Him that created thee, glorify Him that redeemed thee from death . . ."[17]

"Diognetus": God sent from heaven Him who is the truth: He came in clemency and meekness, as Saviour, as seeking to persuade, not to compel — "for violence has no place in the character of God" — as calling us, not as vengefully pursuing us, as loving us and not as judging us. Faith in this Christ is a moral power that inwardly renovates the soul, elevating the Christian above the world.[18]

Justin Martyr: Men are made new through Christ by becoming persuaded, undertaking to live accordingly, having been in baptism regenerated, forgiven, illumined. The basis of the Christian's new conduct is his conviction of the truth, his washing in baptism, remission, regeneration, and "living as Christ has enjoined": — a total change of moral attitude, especially towards idolatry, sorcery, and lust.[19]

Tatian: Regeneration corrects the disorder introduced into man's nature by the misuse of freedom, and unites the soul with the Holy Spirit. Man must die to the world and live unto God: the Spirit takes up His abode with those who live justly, "intimately combining with the soul".[20]

Irenaeus: Christian living is "following the only true and steadfast Teacher, our Lord Jesus Christ, who did through His transcendent love become what we are, that He might bring us to be even what He is Himself." Christ redeems us by His own blood, imparting God to men by means of the Spirit. We are made alive, saved, only by the operation of the Spirit. The work of Christ is fundamental: "but He did not set us free that we should depart from Him, but that the more we receive His grace, the more we should love Him."[21]

Clement of Alexandria: "Our Instructor is Son, sinless, Lord, the expiator of sin, the Word of truth that regenerates man by bringing him back to the truth." The music of the Word can win over the hardest heart. "Christ is the Bridle of colts untamed." All depends upon faith — "the first movement towards salvation, after which fear, hope, repentance, advancing in company with temperance, patience, lead us to love and knowledge." The foundation of such moral salvation is firmly set in the action of God: "the Lord pities, instructs, exhorts, admonishes, saves, shields, and of His bounty promises us the kingdom of heaven . . ." Beach says that Clement has something of the Hebrew-Christian sense of the divine initiative and grace: "the hand of God is present at every point of moral advance. After all, he says, 'the ball-player cannot catch the ball unless it is thrown to him'."[22]

Origen: None are able "apart from the aid of the word to become free from sin". The wicked are invited to be saved through repentance and reformation of heart, before they will participate in knowledge of God and fellowship with Him. To change human nature is difficult yet possible: numbers of sinners whom no one could have reformed by punishment were changed by the preached word "which moulded and transformed them according to its pleasure". Those who have condemned themselves are received by God on account of their repentance, virtue taking up her abode in them, expelling the wickedness. So-called fools and slaves no sooner accept the teaching of Jesus, than they keep themselves in a state of virgin purity; they are preserved by God, well-pleasing to Him, filled with all righteousness and goodness. Even those not well educated exhibit a high degree of gravity, purity, and integrity. Right conduct, moreover, is closely related to prayer. With Tertullian and Cyprian, Origen saw in the Lord's Prayer an epitome of Christian life. Discussing "forgive us our debts", he lists the Christian's obligations — to his brethren (natural and spiritual), to citizens, strangers, the aged, all men, to himself (body and soul), to God in maintaining a right mood, to Christ who redeemed us, to the Spirit Whom we are not to grieve, and to our personal guardian-angels.[23]

Even so brief samples of the Apologists' work may illustrate the variety and vigour of their exposition of Christian morals. Clearly, the apostolic understanding of ethical obedience as the fruit, rather than the pre-condition, of salvation persisted through the patristic period, despite more moralistic, legalistic, and ecclesiastical views. The tension so produced was to last throughout Christian history.

(2) THE RELATION OF CHRISTIAN TO JEWISH ETHICS

The church's relation to Judaism was always ambivalent, asserting both continuity and difference; the new faith claimed for itself all that gentiles admired in the Jewish heritage, while repudiating what they disliked (circumcision, sacrifices, nationalism). From the first, Christianity appealed to synagogue audiences by emphasising its loyalty to the high ethic of Judaism, while advancing to a non-legal, non-racial ideal. The inclusion of the Old Testament in Christian scripture and of the Decalogue within early catechesis, later within the Eucharist, made the relation of Christian to Jewish ethics a permanent issue for the church.

The Jewish atmosphere of the *Didache* may be deliberate archaism, but the doctrine of the Two Ways, the negative golden rule, and the exposition of the Decalogue, show Jewish teaching being adapted to cover gentile sins. By stressing the change to Christian fast-days, the *Didache*, like the later *Didascalia Apostolorum*. appeals to traditional Jewish piety while asserting Christian distinctiveness. F. L. Cross[24] finds in Book II of *Hermas* and the first five of his Similitudes, "a Christianised . . . development of the Old Testament moral code"; this may be true of the form of the writing, but its content makes no direct allusion to the Old Testament.

On one side of his thought, *Justin Martyr* presents[25] Christianity as the fulfilment of the Jewish law — its abrogation and its replacement. The new covenant replaced the old, and the eternal, universal law of God which Israel failed to understand is found in the precepts of the gospel, in which the true meaning of Jewish sabbath, purification, and fasting, is revealed in

Christian repentance, baptism, and obedience. Christians possess the true righteousness, which Israel so long sought and failed to find. *Barnabas*[26] similarly sees the inward, free law of Christ as replacing the Old Testament law; true sabbath-keeping is to sanctify oneself; the true temple is the cleansed and indwelt soul.

It was, however, Irenaeus who developed the most fruitful concept of this relation to Jewish ethics. He saw one morality advancing steadily through the moral code of nature possessed by the ancient patriarchs; through the Decalogue; enlarged (through Israel's disobedience) to a fuller "yoke of bondage" (in the Torah?); and through Christianity's new law of genuine *love* (in contrast with Judaism's externality) and of true *liberty* (in contrast with Judaism's legal system). "That this is the first and greatest commandment, and that the next (is) love towards our neighbour, the Lord has taught, when He says that the entire law and the prophets hang upon these two commandments. Moreover He did not Himself bring down any other commandment greater than this one, but renewed this very same one . . ."

"The precepts of an absolutely perfect life . . . are the same in each Testament." "He did not teach us these things as being opposed to the law, but as fulfilling the law, and implanting in us the varied righteousness of the law . . . This which He did command us is not . . . the utterance of one destroying the law, but of one fulfilling, extending, and affording greater scope to it." The law drew men to God as by a bond, "but the word set free the soul . . . that men should follow God without fetters . . . inasmuch as the working of liberty is greater and more glorious than that obedience which is rendered in slavery." "Inasmuch then as all natural precepts are common to us and (the Jews) they had in them indeed the beginning and origin; but in us they have received growth and completion . . ." "These things therefore which were given for bondage and for a sign to them, He cancelled by the new covenant of liberty. But He has increased and widened those laws which are natural, noble, and common to all . . ."[27]

Tertullian, also, sees one morality increasingly informing the law of nature, the law of the Old Testament, the teaching of Christ, the leading of the Paraclete, and the inspiration of the Spirit who disciplines the church:

"Why should God, the Founder of the Universe, the Governor of the whole world . . . be believed to have given a law through Moses to one people, and not to all nations?" In the law given to Israel we recognise in embryo precepts . . . being fulfilled in Christian piety. "After all these precepts had been given carnally, in time preceding, to the people of Israel, there was to supervene a time whereat the precepts of the ancient law . . . would cease, and the issue of the new law, with the recognition of spiritual sacrifices and the promise of the New Testament, supervene . . ." The law of justice has given way to the law of love. It is significant for Tertullian's view of the relation of Christianity to Judaism, that he sees the great distinction — "the difference between us" — to lie only in the doctrine of the Trinity: ethically, one law and one ideal run through both faiths.[28]

The whole of Origen's work presupposes the Old Testament as "scripture", setting forth truths and ideals that flowered in Christianity. Mainly theological rather than ethical, his treatise against Celsus is a sustained argument for Christian faith and practice resting upon Judaist premises; he holds, as clearly as did Irenaeus and Tertullian, that one increasingly clear moral law runs through Old Testament and New:

"Unless all men had naturally impressed upon their minds sound ideas of morality, the punishment of sinners would have been excluded . . . It is not therefore matter of surprise that the same God should have set in the hearts of all men those truths which He taught by the prophets and the Saviour." Origen agrees with Celsus that it is the same divine Spirit who today has announced divine things (the gospel) and formerly made known many important truths.

Clement of Alexandria, likewise holds that the Mosaic law is the foundation of all ethics and expounds the Old Testament laws, including the Decalogue, to find therein Greek and Christian ethical ideals.[29]

Christianity early adopted Jewish fasting and with it a tendency towards austerity; almsgiving as a duty towards God and with it a real concern for the poor. It preserved also the Judaist emphasis upon prayer, sexual purity, domestic fidelity and home training. The conception of the good in terms of the divine will expressed in commandments remained an element in Christian moral theory, as did a certain ethical rigour, fostered by the expectation of divine judgement and reward. Both the legalist bias and the eschatological dimension, present in Christian ethics from the first, arise from this Judaist matrix.

On the other hand, Novatian[30] argues against the Jewish food laws: all foods, being God's creation, are good and lawful — except when dedicated to idols. A more radical distinction lay in the insistence that the Christian law is inward, and developing; for a *revealed* code ought to be perfect, and unchangeable. By holding that the content and inner meaning of Jewish law are progressively unfolded and superseded, the older codification is being steadily set aside; direction by the living Spirit in the growing conscience is replacing "the written commandment contained in ordinances". The breach with Judaism which Christian theology and mission had begun was completed by the moral logic of the gospel.

(3) THE RELATION OF CHRISTIAN TO PAGAN ETHICS

To present the Christian ethic as rival to prevailing pagan codes was more difficult. "Amid its numerous forms and variations — the Platonic pursuit of absolute values, the Aristotelian rational ethics of moderation, the Stoic principle of apathy, the Epicurean enjoyment of refined pleasures — there was a single moral temper that warrants the use of the term 'Greek' " says Professor Beach[31]: "its ideal of the highest good was that of rational discipline, moderation, and self-restraint in a balanced and well-rounded life." Other keynotes were, individualism in face of the sprawling State and impersonal natural law; and a resolute fortitude, a cultivated unconcern, attaining relative peace of mind. Confronted with this ethical tradition, Christian apologists took up varied positions.

Hermas may have imitated the Platonic "cardinal virtues" when he listed Christian excellences, but the first clear assertion of the *continuity* of the Christian ethic with Greek teaching was made by Justin, whose Judaist background was supplemented by thorough philosophic enquiry:

"Philosophy is . . . most honourable before God, to whom it leads us and alone commends us; and these are truly holy men who have bestowed attention on philosophy." All truth is one: Justin recounts his pilgrimage through the schools, finding all unsatisfactory; but "there existed long before this time certain men . . . both righteous and beloved by God, who spoke by the divine Spirit . . . they are called prophets; he who has read them is very much helped in his knowledge of those matters which the philosopher ought to know."[32]

Justin saw Christian morality as the universal reason ("Word"), previously only partially known but now fully revealed in Christ to faith — "gnosis", truth inwardly recognised. Those baptised are illumined as well as regenerated, and so put in possession of the wisdom which Greek philosophers had sought in vain.

Whatever either lawgivers or philosophers uttered well, they elaborated by finding and contemplating some part of the Word. But since they did not know the whole of the Word, which is Christ, they often contradicted themselves. In Christ, who was partially known even by Socrates (for He was and is the Word who is in every man . . .), not only philosophers and scholars believed, but also artisans and people entirely uneducated. "Each (philosopher) spoke well in proportion to the share he had of the spermatic Word (the divine Word or reason disseminated amongst men) . . . Whatever things were rightly said among all men, are the property of us Christians. For next to God, we worship and love the Word . . . All the writers were able to see realities darkly through the sowing of the implanted Word that was in them."[33]

Justin's pupil, Tatian, took the opposite view, *rejecting all contact* with pagan philosophy, delighting to call Christianity "the barbarian philosophy", and emphasising not illumination or knowledge but regeneration.

Tatian ridicules Diogenes, Plato, Aristotle, Zeno: "the reading of your books is like walking through a labyrinth . . . you discourse like the blind with the deaf." "Retiring I sought to discover the truth. I happened to meet with certain barbaric writings . . . and I was led to put faith in these by . . . the excellent quality of the precepts . . . My soul being taught of God, I discerned that the former class of writings lead to condemnation, but that these put an end to the slavery that is in the world . . . Our philosophy is older than the system of the Greeks . . . So, bidding farewell to the arrogance of Romans and the idle talk of Athenians, and all their ill-connected opinions, I embraced our barbaric philosophy."[34]

The first systematic attempt to show the Christian ideal as the *fulfilment* of pagan aspiration was made by Clement, addressing himself to educated and liberal-minded enquirers in academic Alexandria:

"Before the advent of the Lord, philosophy was necessary to the Greeks for righteousness. And now it becomes conducive to piety, being a kind of preparatory training . . . till the Lord should call the Greeks . . . a schoolmaster to bring 'the Hellenic mind' . . . to Christ, a preparation, paving the way for him who is perfected in Christ." We who have become disciples of God have received the only true wisdom; that which the chiefs of philosophy only guessed at, the disciples of Christ have both apprehended and proclaimed . . ." "Truth is one: falsehood has ten thousand by-paths"; each philosophic sect "vaunts as the whole truth the portion which has fallen to its lot. But all, in my opinion, are illuminated by the dawn of Light . . . So, the barbarian and Hellenic philosophy has torn off a fragment of eternal truth . . . from the theology of the ever-living Word." "If the Hellenic philosophy comprehends not the whole extent of the truth, and besides is destitute of strength to perform the commandments of the Lord, yet it prepares the way for the truly royal teaching . . . There is then in philosophy, a trace of wisdom and an impulse from God."[35]

Nevertheless, the knowledge of God can be attained only through faith; Clement devotes eight chapters to expounding faith's meaning, excellence and value:

" 'Now my just one shall live by faith' the prophet said, and another prophet also says, 'Except ye believe, neither shall ye understand.' For how ever could the soul admit the transcendental contemplation of such themes, while unbelief respecting what was to be learned struggled within? . . . The exercise of faith directly becomes knowledge . . ."[36]

The first stage, simple faith under the discipline of the church, leads to knowledge, love, and the imitation of God — the life of the true Christian "gnostic". To the description of this advanced level of Christian experience, Clement gives many pages:

"This is the true athlete — he who in the great stadium, the fair world, is crowned for the true victory over all the passions. He who obtains the mastery . . . wins immortality." "He is the gnostic who is after the image and likeness of God, who imitates God as far as possible . . . practising self-restraint, and endurance, living righteously, reigning over the passions, bestowing what he has . . ." What are called "the preparatory exercises of gnostic discipline" include abstention from evil, comprehending and surpassing the law, faithful profession, patience in all affliction, and full manhood in Christ. The gnostic "graduates" from doing good out of fear to doing it out of love, for its own excellence. He will do good by habit, not for advantage, reputation, glory, or reward, "but so as to pass life after the image and likeness of the Lord."

"Assimilation to the divine" is a frequent phrase in Clement. He can speak even of its being possible for the gnostic already to have "become God". Much is said, too, of the contemplation of the divine, of "embracing the divine vision . . . which is the privilege of intensely loving souls." This is the function of the gnostic, to have converse with God through the great High Priest — "His whole life is prayer and converse with God." Again, the gnostic "is subject only to the affections that exist for the maintenance of the body, such as hunger, thirst, and the like." Jesus Himself was "entirely impassible (apathes), inaccessible to any movement of feeling, either of pleasure or of pain; while the apostles were not liable to even such of the movements of feeling as seem good, such as courage, zeal, joy, desire." So the gnostic is free of all perturbations of soul, showing neither fear, courage, cheerfulness, anger, envy, or desire; even his love is a changeless unvarying state. "Though disease, accident, death, come upon the gnostic, he remains inflexible in soul . . . not disturbed by anything that happens . . ." "Fit objects of admiration are the Stoics."[37]

On the Epicurean and Stoic stress on "undisturbedness", or "freedom from emotion" Glover comments, "the Greek word was and is, letter for letter, *apathy*." It was no ideal of Christ's; He was *pathetos*, liable to feeling; a tremendous battle had to be fought over that word, the antithesis of apathy. "How is a Christian negating himself, if he fortifies himself like a Stoic against all that his Master felt — and chose to feel? Like the Master he must expose himself to feel what wretches feel."[38]

Beach[39] isolates four Greek strands in Clement's thought: the strong tendency towards individualism (the perfection of the single gnostic is all-important); the place given to rational apprehension of moral truth; the principle of balance — the rational mean, moderation, avoidance of excess and fanaticism; the teleological view of Christian conduct as determined by a foreseen end — the vision of God. The emphasis upon imperturbability makes a fifth strand, more

Roman than Greek, but like the others relating the Christian ideal closely to pagan values. One effect of Clement's philosophic apologetic was, that the contemplative life of reflection, imitation, and love of God, was idealised; withdrawal into God-like freedom from passion or concern became part of the goal of Godlikeness. As Norris[40] says, "This marks the beginnings of the ascetic-mystical tradition in Christian morals." Moreover, since all cannot attain to the contemplative life, Christianity comes to possess a double morality, corresponding to Clement's two stages of Christian development, which was to haunt Christian ethics for centuries.

Nevertheless, with Clement, faith, hope, and love remain the ground and goal of *gnosis*; and such knowledge is a moral *energy*, a spiritual power, expressed (in biblical fashion) in well-doing, self-discipline, and Godlike love.

In fact, Clement would have agreed with Pfleiderer's summary: "The primitive Christian and the Stoic morality had certain features in common from the outset: withdrawal from the outer world into one's inner life, the enfranchisement of the soul from the fetters of the material, the conquest of the passions, the low estimate of external good and evil, cosmopolitanism, the recognition of the common worth of humanity, and of mutual obligation, the encouragement of gentleness and good will, philanthropy and humanity. But that which was pure theory in the schools of the Stoics became power and life in the communities of the Christians."[41]

Tertullian, however, met all such arguments as Clement's with a fine impatience: Paul's warning against philosophy was due to acquaintance with "that human wisdom which pretends to know the truth whilst it only corrupts it . . . What indeed has Athens to do with Jerusalem? . . . Away with all attempts to produce a mottled Christianity of Stoic, Platonic, and dialectic composition!"[42] The church alone possesses truth: philosophy is "the rash interpreter of the nature and the dispensation of God. Indeed heresies are themselves instigated by philosophy . . ."[43] "The truth which philosophers . . . affect to hold, and in so doing deprave . . . Christians intensely long for and maintain . . . The divine writings are the treasure-source whence all later wisdom has been taken. What poet or sophist has not drunk at the fountain of the prophets? . . . Even that which they had discovered degenerated into uncertainty, and there arose from one or two drops of truth a perfect flood of argumentation."[44] So far from Christian ideals fulfilling pagan thought, Tertullian sees pagan teaching as mere distant borrowing from original divine truth, now more clearly seen in Christ. For all that, on more theological topics, Tertullian is quite ready to use philosophic terms and methods of discussion; and even to appeal to the universal, intuitive witness of the unspoilt "soul by nature Christian".[45]

Origen's *Contra Celsum* reveals the wide range of his philosophic knowledge. F. L. Cross[46] remarks that while Origen is usually ranked with neo-Platonists, Chadwick has shown how extensively he was affected by Stoic influences. Origen applies to philosophers Paul's words concerning vain imagination, foolish and darkened hearts: "those who accounted themselves wise gave proofs of great folly," turning from "grand arguments" to idols, and living unworthily of the knowledge they had received from God.[47] But he will nevertheless appeal, for evidence of the changeableness of human nature, to the moral conversion of pagan heroes and thinkers by philosophic reflection.[48] Two characteristics illustrate the influence of Greek dualism. Though Origen is said to have regretted his early self-mutilation, he continued to practise severe austerities — a strict regimen of prayer, fasting, voluntary poverty, world-renunciation, mortifying of the flesh; living "monastically" with his disciples, he strongly emphasised virginity, and believed that by abstinence and discipline the experience of communion with God, prophecy and other "spiritual gifts" could be attained. On Romans 12:1 Origen commends three kinds of "living, holy, God-pleasing sacrifice" — a martyr death, voluntary celibacy and abstinence from sexual intercourse by married persons.[49] Origen's other "Greek" characteristic was his emphasis upon the rational soul's enjoyment of the contemplation of God. He often distinguishes the two lives, of action and of contemplation ("which he was possibly the first to compare with Martha and Mary"); and he as often speaks of rising above sense, figures and shadows, to one mystical, unspeakable vision.

"Those among us who are teachers . . . strive in every way to raise the soul to the Creator . . . and show that we ought to despise things sensible, temporal, visible, and to do our utmost to reach communion with God, and the contemplation of things intelligent and invisible . . ." Celsus "is not aware that (a) reference to the two eyes, of the body and of the mind, which he has borrowed from the Greeks, was in use among our own writers; this twofold kind of vision in us was familiar to our Saviour . . . All true Christians therefore have the eye of the mind sharpened, and the eye of sense closed: each sees and knows the supreme God and His Son." Elsewhere, Origen eloquently describes the spiritual conflict with the flesh, the demons, and the devil, which constitutes Christian life — a conflict only finally resolved in heaven.[50]

In Origen, it is clear, Greek thought has become acclimatised in biblical exegesis. In Lactantius and Ambrose it is Roman thought which provides the mould for the refashioning of the Christian ethic.

Lactantius devotes Book III of *The Divine Institutes* to detailed criticism of "the false wisdom of philosophers", including Cicero and Plato: yet in Book IV (ii, iii) he holds that righteousness and religion are the true wisdom:

Philosophy was not able to conceive the truth . . . But where wisdom is joined with religion, both must necessarily be true . . . where one God is worshipped, where life and every action is referred to one source, and to one supreme authority: in short, the teachers of wisdom are the same, who are also the priests of God.

And when Lactantius finds the essence of the Christian ethic in righteousness and social justice, he is following Cicero's principle ("man is made for justice"), as numerous allusions confirm, and also challenging comparison with Plato's *Republic*:

"Justice is either the greatest virtue, or the fountain of virtue, which not only philosophers sought but poets also. These feigned that justice, being offended with the vices of men, withdrew to heaven. The worship of God being taken away, men lost the knowledge of good and evil. Thus the bond of human society was destroyed: they began to contend, to plot, to acquire for themselves glory from the shedding of human blood . . . justice being banished, and drawing with her the truth, left to men error, ignorance, blindness . . . The expulsion of justice is . . . the laying aside of divine religion, which alone effects that man should esteem man dear, bound to him by the tie of brotherhood, since God is Father to all, so as to share the bounties of the common God with those who do not possess them; to injure no one, oppress no one, not to close his door against a stranger, nor his ear against a suppliant, but to be bountiful, beneficient, and liberal. But God . . . sent a messenger to bring back that old age . . . and justice was restored to the earth, but assigned to a few; this justice is nothing else than the pious and religious worship of the one God."[51]

The excellence of Christian "justice" is then shown in the piety, virtue, fortitude, and equity of Christians. Justice rests upon the equality of common sonship:

"Kindness is the greatest bond of human society . . . For if we all derive our origins from one man, whom God created, we are plainly of one blood; and it must be considered the greatest wickedness to hate a man, even though guilty . . . Likewise, if we are all inspired and animated by one God, what else are we than brothers? . . . For God, since He is kind, wished us to be social . . ."[52]

Such a statement of the gospel clearly owes more, as to its *form*, to the philosophic tradition than to the New Testament, though the truth expressed is, in the end, none other than the message of the kingdom of God.

To exercise righteousness in all human relationships is to worship God, whose righteousness is seen in the punishment of crime. Yet, although happiness belongs to man, justice has in this life to endure suffering. The *summum bonum* therefore lies not in this unjust life, nor in virtue itself, but in the immortality which Christ offers, in which justice and happiness coincide. Immortality is argued, indeed, upon philosophic rather than theological grounds, though there is no doubt that Lactantius' thought centres in Christ, "He is the door of the greatest temple, He the way of light, He the guide to salvation, He the gate of life."[53] But Lactantius' whole approach, manner, language, show the issues of Christian apologetic defined, and the lines of discussion determined, by pagan philosophic interests.

This is even more true of Ambrose, whose major work on ethics — *The Duties of the Clergy* — is explicitly a Christian commentary upon Cicero's *De Officiis*.

Cicero is named five or six times, his title discussed, his definition of good rejected.[54] Romestin's footnotes make 136 direct references to *De Officiis*, usually at each fresh development of thought. Typical is the discussion of happiness, where the views of eight philosophers are first cited, then the scriptures;[55] but "Let no one think that . . . it was spoken of by the philosophers before it was mentioned in the gospel. For the philosophers . . . certainly lived before the time of the gospel; but they came after the prophets . . ." Elsewhere, Ambrose can say concerning heresy, "we must cite the scripture, 'Take heed that no man make spoil of you by philosophy . . .' It was not by dialectic that it pleased God to save His people."[56]

Despite such caution, Ambrose is thoroughly philosophic in his constant appeal to "nature", another idea which perpetually haunts Christian ethics.

"It is seemly to live in accordance with nature . . . whatever is contrary to nature is shameful." "The piety of justice, is in accordance with nature . . . It is ingrained in all creatures to preserve their own safety . . . to strive for what is advantageous . . . to herd together . . ." (illustrating prudence and justice). The rule to seek the good also of others, is taught by interdependence of eye, hand, mouth, mind. Nature, likewise, teaches common property, "for nature has poured forth all things for all men for common use." Nature teaches us to avoid excessive grief; that reincarnation in animal form is unthinkable; and to be grateful . . ."[57]

In the same way, Ambrose frequently echoes the philosophic appeal to moderation:

"We must keep the mean, so that calm countenance, quiet speech, may show there is no vice in our lives." ". . . as regards moderation, order, the right timing of things, I think that everything should be open and straightforward." "What moderation so true (as Jacob's); and when he entered the ark, with what moderation (Noah) passed the time!"[58]

Most of all, Ambrose reveals his assimilation of Christian to pagan ethical thought in his elaborate treatment of the cardinal virtues. All the apologists tended to multiply the virtues: Hermas names at least, eleven, and Clement of Alexandria twelve, among them faith, hope, and love (the later so-called theological virtues) as "the indissoluble bonds of salvation".[59] Ambrose, following Cicero, explicitly borrows the stoic scheme:

Of the Old Testament heroes, "What duty connected with the chief virtues was wanting in these men? . . . They showed prudence, which is exercised in the search of the truth; next, justice, which assigns each man his own and disregards its own advantage; thirdly, fortitude, which is conspicuous in greatness of mind and in the strength of the body; fourthly, temperance, which preserves right method and order in all things." "The different classes of duties are derived from these four virtues . . ."[60]

Scripture first presented these insights and made faith fundamental to all virtues — "the fountain is Christ". Both scripture and nature teach prudence and justice. "Justice is first directed towards God; secondly towards one's country; next, towards parents; lastly towards all." That which holds society together "is divided into two parts, justice and goodwill, which also is called liberality and kindness."

Ambrose thinks Christian justice higher than the pagans', avoiding harm even to those who wrong us, and holding all God's gifts for common use. Justice exists rather for the good of others than for self, "an aid to . . . fellowship". Fortitude is expressed at war, at home, in martyrdom, in protecting others, in self-conquest, and in an even mind armed against adversity and temptation. Temperance is "seemliness", the bloom upon moral health, with tranquility, moderation. The issue of a virtuous life is happiness. Here too the Christian ethic is superior; for it rests not on worldly circumstances but on inward blessedness, and looks ever to eternal life for ultimate reward. Virtue is also identified with the "useful" — not the merely advantageous, but that which is just, virtuous; "the same thing is both useful and virtuous". Ambrose seems here to be feeling after the modern concept of "value". Usefulness is then discussed as love, goodwill, good counsel, liberality, hospitality.[61]

Ambrose evidently strove to be loyal to the uniqueness of revelation while presenting the Christian ideal in philosophic terms. In the whole discussion of the relation of Christian to pagan ethics, the immediate issue was how to be distinctive yet remain intelligible to pagans. But a deeper question emerged: can there *be* a distinctive Christian ethic, exclusive to believers, not binding upon all; or is the Christian ethic essentially the natural, universal moral obligation, common to mankind but finding various forms and degrees of clarity in differing religions and cultures? In the Graeco-Roman world the church tried to say both *No* and *Yes*: that the Christian ethic is a distinctive, given, revealed ideal of life — but also the full flowering of the "natural law" inherent in rational creation in all ages.

(4) CHRISTIAN ETHICAL THEORY AND THE TONE OF SOCIETY

If the prevailing corruption and distress evoked the positive, practical impact described by Aristides, "Diognetus" and other sources, it led also to surprising changes of emphasis in Christian moral doctrines.

(i) The self-protective separation from the world urged upon vulnerable converts by Paul and John deepened into a more rigid exclusiveness, a stricter non-conformity. Christians became increasingly aware of belonging to "a new self-conscious community . . . over against 'the world', with a common memory, a common mission, and a common destiny."[62] Tertullian insisted,

"We are a body knit together by a common religious profession, by unity of discipline, and by the bond of a common hope . . . It is mainly (our) deeds of love that lead many to put a brand upon us. 'See' they say, 'how they love one another . . . how they are ready even to die for one another.' And they are wroth with us too, because we call each other brethren." We recall Lucian: "they become incredibly alert when anything happens which affects their common interests."[63]

The "sectarian" ethic first met in the Psalms, the Remnant doctrine, Qumran and John the Baptist, is here strengthened by popular hostility and official persecution; by the belief that the world lay under Satan's control; and by the conviction that the State represented demonic power, pride, and peril. An additional, eschatological motive is suggested by Tertullian's phrase, "the bond of a common hope . . ."

Tertullian refers elsewhere to Christians as "candidates for angelhood"; to Christian prayer as yearning for Christ's coming and "for the world (age) also to pass away at the great Day of the Lord"; to the Christians' gaze fixed on spectacles "holy, everlasting, free. Count of these as *your* Circus games, fix your eyes on the courses of the world, the gliding seasons, reckon up the periods of time, long for the goal of the final consummation. Our banquets, our nuptial joys, are yet to come." 2 Clement declares that this world and the next are two enemies: "this world speaks of adultery . . . that world bids those things farewell . . . Let us reckon that it is better to hate the things present, since they are trifling, transient, and corruptible; and to love those (which are to come) as being good and incorruptible." Patristic millenarianism, expecting "a complete renovation of the earth", the hope of the resurrection of the *body*, and emphasis upon Christ's ascension *in the flesh*, all show, similarly, that at this early stage the moral recoil was against the usages of the age rather than against the material world itself. Later, Clement of Alexandria still argues for continence within marriage as the obvious preparation for the brother-sister relationship of the life to come.[64]

For such mutually supporting reasons Christians abstained not only from their former gross sins and from emperor-worship, but from participation in public office, amusements and manners.

Thus an explicitly non-conformist ethic underlined every difference between Christian and non-Christian:

Didache warns against corruption of boys, fornication, magic, sorcery, infanticide, abortion, astrology, idolatry; *Barnabas* urges, "Let us hate the error of the present time. Let us not give loose reins to our soul . . . to run with sinners and the wicked . . ."[65] *Athenagoras* contrasts the immoral tales about the gods with the purity required of Christians "to whom a wanton look is adultery . . . called to account for their very thoughts." Just as "the harlot reproves the chaste" so pagan adulterers and paederasts themselves "set up a market for fornication" while they defame the pure. Christians abjure gladiatorial spectacles, and account abortion, infanticide, plain murder.[66] *Clement of Alexandria* regulates Christian behaviour in satirical contrast with prevailing luxury, effeminacy, sensuality, idleness, gambling, theatre-going.[67] *Tertullian* castigates luxury, drunkenness, vice, providing names, places, details: "Blush for your vile ways before the Christians . . ." He makes great play with immoralities recounted of the gods and enacted in sacred rites. He urges catechumens to abstain from "circus, theatre, combat, or show" because of their association with idolatry, deception, passion, immodesty, rivalries ("What an aggregation of idolatries you see in the decoration of the place!") — and from racecourse, wrestling, amphitheatre, because of their cruelty ("With such dainties let the devil's guests be feasted!").[68]

The tract ascribed to *Novatian* condemns "debasing" theatre spectacles, compares their disorderly scenes with the beauties of nature, analyses their idolatry, cruelty, lewdness, and demands "What does a faithful Christian do among these, since he may not even think upon wickedness? He is learning to do while he is becoming accustomed to see . . ."[69] *Cyprian* asks of the games and theatres "Can he who looks upon such things be healthy-minded, or modest?" and appeals to Donatus to appreciate his Christian security and enrichment, "loosed from the snares of this entangling world . . . purged from earthly dregs . . ."[70]

Lactantius thus explains persecution: "he who sins wishes to have free scope . . . Why should any be unseasonably good, who when the public morals are corrupted should censure them by living well? Why should not all be equally wicked, rapacious, unchaste, adulterers, perjured . . . They are not of our number but of theirs, who beseige the roads in arms, practise piracy . . . mix poisons, kill their wives that they may gain dowries, or their husbands that they may marry adulterers, strangle their sons . . . or if they are too pious, expose them; who restrain their incestuous passions neither from daughter, sister, mother nor priestess; who conspire against their country, commit sacrilege, forge wills, prostitute their own persons to lust, take bribes, grasp at heaven by sorceries . . . But which of these things can be laid to the charge of our people, with whom the whole of religion consists in living without guilt and without spot?" Lactantius protests against the "public homicide" of the arena, by which "just and pious men have lost their humanity;" against the strangling of the newborn, "the greatest impiety," and the exposure of children to dogs, to slavery, to the brothel, or to incest; against the stage for its unchaste themes and representations and the games for their idolatrous associations.[71]

A tendency to reject the good things of life, to repress "the enjoying nature", to live in anxious suspicion of all pleasure and at a distance from non-Christian neighbours, has infected Christian ethical thought over many centuries. In the biblical ethic, the doctrines of creation and incarnation, and the sociable, out-going character of Jesus, had set another key; and despite the protective counsel enjoined upon catechumens, the freedom of the "strong" conscience was still maintained. The apologists' more severe reaction against the permissiveness of Greek and Roman manners suggests that perhaps Christian freedom must always be exercised in inverse proportion to the licentiousness of society.

(ii) A second new theme in the apologists' moral theory was a growing antipathy towards marriage and procreation, an attitude which few Jews would understand, and which most of the first Christians would condemn.

Recall Colossians 2:20,21, Hebrews 13:4, 1 Timothy 4:3, 5:14. Inge remarks that "the ancient world saw something demoniacal in the act of generation. Sometimes, as in the cults of Astarte and Aphrodite, it was deified; sometimes it was held to be a pollution." In Egypt, the priests of Isis were celibate. Cynics, and Epictetus, counselled chastity for those who could attain it. Pythagoreans advised periods of sexual continence; the priestesses of Delphi, like the Roman Vestals, were bound to strict virginity. Celibacy came to be expected of pagan philosophers: Porphyry, for example, apologises elaborately for his marriage.[72]

Ascetic Jewish sects had encouraged celibacy, and one trace of such influence has been seen in Revelation 14:4 (cf. Matthew 19:12). Paul, and Peter, argued for common sense and consideration within marriage, strict sexual abstinence outside it. Ignatius advised that "It becomes both men and women who marry to form their union with the approval of the bishop, that their marriage may be 'according to God', and not after their own lust.''[73] This caution is heard again in Justin Martyr, who condemns polygamy and incontinence, regarding marriage as simply a means to procreation: "either we do not marry at all, unless to nourish children, or rejecting marriage we are perfectly continent."[74] Athenagoras, too, recognised marriage only as intended for procreation; otherwise the Christian will abstain from sexual intercourse, counting celibacy, and the deeper fellowship of God, a higher end.[75] This tendency found a climax in Tatian, in his Encratite days, who condemned marriage altogether, and in Marcion, also an Encratite, who made celibacy a condition of church membership.[76]

Clement of Alexandria thought sexual intercourse for any other end than procreation a wrong against nature, and he enjoins upon Christians "not to treat their wives as mistresses".[77] *Origen* mentions Christians who "from a desire of exceeding chastity, to worship God with greater purity, abstain even from permitted indulgences of (lawful) love;" and those who provide evidence of the keeping power of God by "maintaining a perpetual virginity" and "keeping themselves in virgin purity". "God has allowed us to marry, because all are not fit for the higher, that is the perfectly pure, life; and God would have us bring up all our children . . ." Yet (as we have seen) Origen also extols virginity as elevating the soul above sensuous existence, and names virginity, and sexual abstention in marriage, with martyrdom as elements in the sacrificial life commended in Romans 12:1.[78]

Tertullian declares "The Creator bestowed His blessing on matrimony as on an honourable estate, for the increase of the human race . . . Matrimony is not to be refused because, enjoyed without moderation, it is fanned into voluptuous flame . . . " "If any limitation is set to marrying — such as the spiritual rule which prescribes but one marriage — it will be His prerogative to fix the limit . . ." On 1 Thessalonians 4:3,4 Tertullian argues that "we should abstain from fornication, not from marriage." The law of nature does not forbid connubial intercourse, but concupiscence, which honourable matrimony takes care of; nevertheless, Tertullian maintains "the superiority of the higher sanctity, preferring continence and virginity to marriage." He quotes Paul (1 Corinthians 7) as *permitting* marriage but preferring abstinence — "how far better it is neither to marry nor to burn." A whole treatise argues monogamy; most of another is against second marriages, and mixed marriages, closing with a moving description of Christian marriage as "a church in miniature". Nevertheless, "How many there are who from their baptism set the seal of virginity upon their flesh!" Virgins shall have the nearest vision of the face of God; In *"Exhortation to Chastity"*, appealing to a widower to remain chaste, Tertullian identifies "sanctification" with three species of virginity: that from birth, of happiness and innocence; that from second birth, from the font — the virginity of virtue (either marriage *precluding* sexual intercourse or preserving widowhood from choice); and a third grade, monogamy (but *renouncing* sexual intercourse) — the virginity of moderation.[79]

Some of this teaching may be held to be little more than realistic appreciation of the dangers and excesses of sex. With Cyprian a new note creeps in, with the description of consecrated virgins as "the flower of ecclesiastical seed, the grace and ornament of spiritual endowment, God's image answering to God's holiness, the wholesome and uncorrupted portion of Christ's flock, the joy of the Master." "Continency follows Christ; virginity is destined for the kingdom of God." Cyprian speaks constantly of the advantage, reward, honour, of virginity; and assembles many scriptures by which he thinks to prove "the benefit of virginity and of continency".[80] Gradually, as Harnack says, the cult of virginity came to be "the specifically Christian virtue, the essence of all the virtues."[81]

Methodius, imitating Plato's dialogue on love (*eros*), expounded the excellence of virginity, "supernaturally great, wonderful, glorious, the root of immortality . . . walking indeed on earth but reaching up to heaven." Ten virgins in turn sing the merits of chastity, the honour of virgins "betrothed and given in marriage" to Christ, the gift, contest, martyrdom, abiding glory, of virginity — sure way into the Kingdom, image of the virgin Christ; virginity *is* divinity (but for one Greek letter) and "superior to ten thousand other advantages of virtue." An elaborate antiphonal hymn celebrates Christ the Bridegroom of virgins, of the church His Bride.[82] A tract attributed to *Novatian* grades Christian chastity: "the first rank in virgins, the second those who are continent" (in marriage), the third — even to maintain marriage-faith is a matter of praise. In all, chastity is "glorious"; "before all things maintain the barriers of chastity"; the church is "given in marriage as a betrothed virgin" to Christ. The writer could set forth "abundant laudations of chastity," but contents himself with fourteen paragraphs and two scriptural examples, Joseph and Susannah.[83] *Lactantius*, also, exalts "Godlike celibacy" above marriage.[84]

With *Ambrose*, the anti-sexual trend becomes a serious distortion. Virginity and celibacy are preferable to marriage, though virginity is not a matter of commandment prescribed to those in subjection but a counsel of grace given to God's friends, the way of "perfection". Repeatedly Ambrose insists that he is "not discouraging marriage, but enlarging on the benefits of virginity — the former is not reproved, but the latter is praised." Nevertheless he lists with enjoyment the disadvantages of marriage, misapplying many scripture verses to extol virginity.

"Marriage is honourable, chastity more honourable" — a "principal virtue'' which ''brought from heaven that which it may imitate on earth — virgins are as angels''. Virginity is the feature original in Christian morality: ''I certainly have not this in common with the heathen, nor . . . with barbarians, nor . . . other animals, with whom (although we . . . differ not in mode of generation) in this point alone we nevertheless avoid the reproach of likeness, that virginity is aimed at by the heathen, but when consecrated it is violated, . . . and is unknown to others.'' ''Each may walk along the path which he prefers . . . so long as he can reach the camp. The path of virginity is good, but being high and steep requires the stronger wayfarers. Good also is that of widowhood, not so difficult as the former, but being rocky and rough, it requires more cautious travellers. Good too is that of marriage; being smooth and even it reaches the camp of the saints by a longer circuit. There are then rewards for virginity, there are merits of widowhood, there is also a place for conjugal modesty.''

For Ambrose, marriage disqualified a man for ordination: ''ye know that the ministerial office must be kept pure and unspotted, and must not be defiled by conjugal intercourse.'' Even more significant was his adoption of Methodius' thought, that individual virgins represent to perfection the church, the virgin Bride of Christ: ''Christ was before the Virgin, of the Virgin, Himself immaculate, the Spouse of the virgin church, Himself the Virgin who bare us . . . You who with unspotted chastity keep the couch of the Lord holy . . . the Bride of God . . . A virgin conceived the salvation of the world, a virgin brought forth the life of all, . . . our flesh joined to God by a virgin . . .'' And all are exhorted to follow in detail the example of Mary, ''Mother of God''.[85] As Inge says, ''the notion of the soul as the bride of Christ, to be kept spotless from any other love . . . emphasised by Ambrose . . . became the favourite dream of countless virgins of the cloister, whose meditations have often been quoted by modern psychologists as examples of transferred or sublimated eroticism.''[86]

In the fourth century and afterwards, the social and religious aspects of marriage fall out of sight behind the individualist and sensual; physical details are dwelt upon to arouse disgust; and Christianity adopts a prevailing idea that sexual intercourse is so defiling as to preclude participation in religious festivals and worship.[87] Eusebius thinks the higher Christian life does not admit marriage; the lower, more humble and human, ''permits pure marriage and children . . .''[88] *Jerome* writes with zest on all misfortunes and discomforts of married life, and the incorrigible misbehaviour of wives, though he acknowledges the place of marriage — ''the church does not condemn marriage, but makes it subordinate, . . . regulates it''. Nevertheless, all who have not preserved virginity are, in comparison with angelic chastity and our Lord Jesus Christ, defiled. ''I praise wedlock, marriage, but because they give me virgins; I gather the rose from the thorns, the pearl from the shell." Beach quotes, "marriage populates the earth, virginity populates heaven." Virginity appears necessary to diligent prayer; of once consecrated virgins now married, Jerome can say, "Shall she come to this after the bridal-chamber of God the Son, after the kisses of Him who is her kinsman and spouse!" A virgin is "my Lord's bride", "a King's wife"; "assuredly no gold or silver vessel was ever so dear to God as the temple of a virgin's body . . . Ever let the privacy of your chamber guard you, ever let the Bridegroom sport with you within" — with amorous phrases from the Song of Songs to elaborate the sexual fantasy. Instructions to virgins written thirty years later are said to be less fanatical; but Jerome still speaks of consecrating his correspondent to "eternal" chastity, and describes with extravagant hyperbole the *world-rejoicings* at her dedication to virginity.[89]

In time, "to take the yoke of the Lord" came to be but a name for voluntary sexual abstention. For Athanasius, virginity is angelic and unsurpassed, the holy "unearthly way", bearing perfect fruit one-hundred-fold.[90] There were a few protesting voices: the third-century *Didascalia Apostolorum* assumed the married state to be normal for Christians, and nowhere praised celibacy or virginity, while *Helvidius* in the fourth century denied the perpetual virginity of Mary.[91] But clearly by this time marriage has largely lost its biblical significance. The angelic sexlessness which Christ described as man's post-resurrection destiny is made the ideal for this world and for sexual natures. To this extent, and on this theme, the Christian ethic succumbed to that unbalanced and unnatural asceticism which was to affect its vision for a thousand years.

(iii) A third new element in Christian moral theory provoked by the prevailing tone of society, was the deliberate adoption of a double standard of Christian morality. The pressure not to conform, and the increasing austerity, created serious problems for Christians with existing family relationships to maintain and their livelihood to earn in the pagan world. That there will always be among Christians differences of moral strength and of dedication, is plain. The *Didache's* "If thou art able to bear the whole yoke of the Lord, thou wilt be perfect; but if thou art not able, do what thou canst"[92] merely acknowledges human weakness. *Hermas'* "If you do any good beyond what is commanded by God, you will gain for yourself more abundant glory . . . if therefore in keeping the commandments of God you do in addition these services, you will have joy . . ."[93] implies little more than an encouragement to greater zeal. Clement of Alexandria, acknowledging that all cannot attain to the life of contemplation which he extols, recognises as valid Christian callings both the middle way of faith and the perfect way of knowledge.[94] Origen, too, takes account of intellectual differences between

Christians; because "simpler brethren", "babes", "the plain Christian man who has little capacity for subtleties of thought",[95] may be shocked by speculative and allegorical theology, Origen exercises a reserve, or economy, of truth:

"It ought to be known that the holy apostles . . . delivered themselves with utmost clearness on certain points which they believed to be necessary to everyone, leaving however the grounds of their statements to be examined into by those . . . more zealous, lovers of wisdom."[96]

But from such intellectual discrimination arises "the tendency towards two religions, the one of freedom for the intellectual elite, the other of bondage for the masses."[97] Commenting upon Romans, for example, Origen says "In so far as anyone does only what he ought, that is, those things which are commands, he is an unprofitable servant; but if you add anything to the (mere) commands, then indeed you will be a servant not unprofitable."[98] Discussing marriage, Tertullian distinguishes rules which are "prescribed" from "the better state" which is "recommended", and argues from Paul's *permission* to marry, that marriage is less good than abstaining from marriage, a state not merely permitted but *preferred* as intrinsically good. Elsewhere, Tertullian distinguishes *advice* to remain single from the *bidding* to marry (if at all) "only in the Lord". "One may with more impunity neglect an 'advice' than an 'order', in that the former springs from counsel, proposed for voluntary acceptance or rejection, while the latter descends from authority, and is bound to necessity." To disregard *advice* is to exercise one's liberty; to disregard an *order*, is rebellion. Paul is said to profess "that he has granted marriage by way of indulgence, not of command"; marriage being a matter of permission, by way of sparing the Corinthians, but "the counsels of continence" are commended as divine.[99]

This distinction of alternative standards is strengthened in Ambrose as a middle way of "precepts" and a perfect way of "counsels". Every duty is either "ordinary" or "perfect", having to do either with the "commandments" which the rich young ruler had already kept, or with the "counsels" which would have led him to perfection. For example, to be perfect as the Father in heaven is a "perfect duty". Paul says, "Not as though I am already perfect . . . As many of us as are perfect . . .", indicating "a twofold form of perfection, the one having but ordinary, and the other the highest, worth; the one availing here, the other hereafter; the one in accordance with human powers, the other with the perfection of the world to come." On Paul's refusal to give commandment concerning marriage, but willingness to offer counsel, Ambrose says: "a command is given to those who are subject; counsel is given to friends. You will see the difference between precept and counsel if you remember him to whom it is first commanded to do no murder, a commandment which has penalty; then a counsel that he should sell all and follow the Lord . . . For there are two ways of commanding things, one by way of precept, the other by way of counsel: he is not bound by a commandment, to whom the choice is left whether to obey."[100]

The "commandments" were gospel precepts binding upon all who would be Christians at all; the "counsels" were binding upon all who sought the higher life of Christian "perfection". So developed the distinction of "religious" and "lay" Christians; of expert, "professional" obedience from that of ordinary Christians whose second-class discipleship must be content to fulfil, in family life and the work of the world, the simple basic precepts of the Gospels; while those favoured with a "vocation" to perfection can alone hope to attain the evangelical counsels of the higher life.

Christian ethics has plainly moved some way from the New Testament when a double standard of morality is explicitly taught. Paul's distinction is really a difference of authority, distinguishing counsel for which he had a word of the Lord from counsel which was merely his own best thought on the subject — not a distinction in the standard of obedience required of different Christians. The rich young ruler was not yet a disciple at all: he was certainly not a Christian hesitating between two levels of dedication. And Christ's word concerning "unprofitable servants" has nothing to do with double standards of behaviour.

Nevertheless, on such bases a full-time "withdrawal into holiness" — mainly of virginity, austerity, and contemplation — introduced a new concept into Christian ethics, at an opposite extreme from the positive involvement in the world's need described by "Diognetus". A Christianity which could not come to terms with pagan ideals, nor redeem pagan society, *could* only flee from it in total rejection: the Encratite and monastic movements were to this extent logical enough. The thought that "What the soul is to the body, Christians are to the world" deserved wider acceptance, but the trend was towards defensive, even self-righteous, separateness. By the fourth century, Eusebius can say —

"Two ways of life were given by Christ to His church. The one is above nature and common human living; it admits not marriage, property, nor wealth, but wholly separate from the customary life of man devotes itself to service of God alone in heavenly love. They who enter upon this course seem to die to the life of mortals; to bear nothing earthly but the body; in mind and spirit to have passed to heaven. Like superior beings they gaze on human life, and discharge the office of priests for the whole race. The other life, more humble and more human, permits men to marry, have children, undertake office, command soldiers fighting in a good cause, attend to farming, trade, and other secondary interests . . . a kind of secondary piety . . . giving such help as their lives require . . .''[101]

One feels that Eusebius has faithfully represented the accepted Christian views of his own time, but that his own sympathies lie with the ''more humble and more human'' and more useful expression of Christian loyalty.

It is evident that in confrontation with Jewish and pagan thought, and with the tone of social life, Christian moral theory has suffered powerful pressures and made far-reaching adjustments. But not in theory only: similar adjustments were called for in conduct and attitude, as Christians faced wholly new moral situations and urgent but unprecedented moral problems for which inherited biblical directives were scarcely sufficient.

3

Unprecedented Problems

IN VIEW OF THE GREAT CHANGES that confronted the church as she moved into the second and third centuries it is scarcely possible to assume "the early church . . . (is) best qualified to interpret the mind of the New Testament"[1]: but its ethical conclusions, and still more its methods of ethical debate, are important for another reason. Just because the problems faced were unprecedented, finding at best only equivocal scriptural guidance, with little in Christian tradition that was relevant, and with very diverse social pressures and inward impulses to be reconciled, the ethical procedures of the first three centuries illuminate the initial attempts of the church to discover the mind of Christ upon unexplored issues. We see the Christian "situation ethic" at its beginning. It is possible, indeed, to conduct an ethics "workshop" — a practical demonstration of Christian moral theory at work, by making a selection of the new problems and watching the Christian conscience in formation, analysing the process by which the ethic of the New Testament became the ethic of the later church.

Four or five examples must suffice.

(1) WEALTH

Despite the wry comment of Ambrose, "riches are hardly to be found among the saints of the Lord"[2] it is evident from the attention given to it that wealth and its responsibilities were no longer just a hindrance to entering the kingdom, or an opportunity for charity, but had begun to pose real questions for conscientious converts. Property, says Troeltsch,[3] was "the first social problem with which the church had to deal."

Scriptural exhortations to "sit light" to possessions, to be generous in stewardship, were not forgotten. *Didache* recalls "the Father wishes a share of His gifts to be given to all": yet because some take without need, "Let your alms sweat in your hands until you know to whom you are giving. Do not hold your hands open for receiving and closed for giving. If you possess something by the labour of your hands, give it for the redemption of your sins. Do not be reluctant in giving, nor murmur when you give, for you will know who He is who gives a good reward. Do not turn away from the needy but share all with your brother and *do not claim that it is your own*. For if you are sharers in immortal things, how much more in mortal."[4]

That renunciation of personal claim, along with the ideal of sharing, persist throughout the period:

To *Barnabas*, love reckons nothing an exclusive possession, but "communicates" — makes common cause — in all things.[5] *Hermas* included among impulses "never to be restrained" helping widows, looking after orphans and the needy, rescuing the servants of God from necessities, being hospitable, and "having fewer needs than all men". Fasting is "perfect" only if "having reckoned up the price of the dishes which you intended to have eaten, you will give it to a widow or an orphan, or to some person in want." "You who are servants of God dwell in a strange land, for your city is far away from this one . . . Why (then) do ye here provide lands and make expensive preparations and accumulate dwellings and useless buildings? As one living in a foreign land, make no provision for thyself further than may be merely sufficient. Instead of lands, therefore, buy afflicted souls . . . visit widows and orphans . . . For to this end did the Master make you rich, that you might perform these services unto Him."[6] Similarly, *Justin Martyr* instances among evidences of conversion, the convert's coming to regard possessions as "common", to be fully shared.[7]

Lactantius is more radical: "riches do not render men illustrious, except . . . by good works . . . and they who seem to be poor . . . are rich because they are not in want, desiring nothing." Lactantius contrasts sharply the amount spent on pleasure, the games, public buildings, with that spent on relieving distress. He scorns the hope of gain which prompts some to be generous for "utilitarian reasons". True "justice" looks for no profit, but gives to anyone — "blind, feeble, lame, destitute, dying" — because he is a man, valuable to God, given life and light by God. "He who is able to succour one on the point of perishing, and fails to do so, kills him."

"This is the chief and true advantage of riches . . . the welfare of many; the reward must be expected from God alone . . . Hospitality is a principal virtue, though if the benefit be returned it is destroyed; the ransoming of captives is a noble exercise of justice; (so) to protect and defend widows and orphans . . . the care and support of the sick; the last and greatest office of piety is the burying of strangers and the poor, upon which other teachers of virtue touch not at all."

To those who say, "If I do all these things I shall have no

possessions", Lactantius replies, first, that philosophers themselves testify that to be poor is to be safe from accident, robbery, taxation, plundering. Secondly, that to use wealth well is to "entrust treasures to God . . . He who is rich towards God can never be poor . . ." God judges men by their own principles, being merciful to the merciful, hearing the prayers of those who hear the cries of others.[8]

The fullest treatment of wealth is the homily by Clement of Alexandria entitled "The Rich Man's Salvation", which Troeltsch describes as one of the most sensible works, filled with fine and tender piety.[9] Beach says it is an effort to calm the fears of well-to-do Christians — to reckon with the rigour of the gospel command in an urbane and prosperous environment.[10]

"Some, hearing in an off-hand way that it is easier for a camel to go through the eye of a needle than for a rich man to enter the kingdom, despair of themselves, no longer enquiring either whom the Lord calls rich, or how what is impossible to man becomes possible to God. Others attaching slight importance to the works which tend to salvation, do not make the requisite preparation. 'Sell thy possessions' does not bid him abandon his property; but bids him banish from his soul his notions about wealth, his excitement and morbid feeling, the anxieties, the thorns of existence, which choke the seed of life." It is neither great, nor desirable, to be destitute, else destitute beggars . . . on the streets, who know not God, . . . would be most blessed, sole possessors of everlasting life! Nor was renunciation and almsgiving a new thing . . . Why then command, as alone life-giving, what did not save those of former days?

What is it the Son of God teaches? Not the outward renunciation, but more Godlike, more perfect, the stripping off of the passions from the soul, the disposition. After ridding himself of wealth, one may none-the-less have still the lust and desire for money, and may doubly grieve. It is impossible that those in want of the necessities should not be hindered from better things in the endeavour to provide them: how much more beneficial, by possessing a competency, not to be in straits, and to give help to others. If no one had anything, what room would be left for giving? . . . for "making friends by means of the mammon of unrighteousness" . . . "acquiring treasures in heaven", "giving food to the hungry, clothing the naked"? Jesus does not bid Zaccheus, Matthew to part with their property . . . Riches, then, which benefit also our neighbours, are not to be thrown away. They are instruments for good. That which of itself has neither good nor evil, ought not to be blamed, but that which uses it well, or ill — the mind and judgement of man. The renunciation, then, and "selling of all possessions", is to be understood as spoken of the passions of the soul, which hinder the good use of wealth. For he who holds possessions as the gifts of God; and ministers from them to the God who gives them, and knows that he possesses them more for the sake of the brethren than his own; and is superior to the possession of them, not the slave of the things he possesses; and does not carry them about in his soul, nor blind and circumscribe his life within them, but is ever labouring at some divine work, is able with cheerful mind to bear their removal equally with their abundance. This is he who is blessed by the Lord, and called poor in spirit, heir of the kingdom of heaven, *not one who could not live rich.*[11]

The case for wealthy Christians remaining wealthy has probably never been better argued. Beach comments, "To what extent this . . . is . . . an evasion of the gospel and a compromise . . . have been matters of continued debate . . . Radical monasticism found such an answer false, whereas an American Protestant business man might express his resolution of the problem in much the same terms as did Clement."[12] But this is not all that Clement has to say:

"Riches, then, are to be partaken of rationally, bestowed lovingly, not pompously; nor is the love of the beautiful to be turned into self-love and ostentation, lest some one say, 'His horse, or land, or slave, or gold, is worth fifteen talents; but the man himself is dear at three coppers' . . . Wealth seems to me to be like a serpent, which will twist and bite, unless one knows to lay hold by the point of the tail. It is not he who has and keeps, but he who gives away, that is rich; it is giving away, not possession, which renders a man happy."[13]

For Ambrose, too, wealth poses problems. Sometimes he merely moralises: on the ancient, powerful vice of the love of money, deadly, seductive, defiling; on the fortitude that "flies from avarice as from a plague that destroys all virtue"; on the freedom conferred by contempt of riches; on the sharp word of Christ, "Take neither gold nor silver nor money", whereby "as with a sickle He cuts off the love of money that is ever growing up in human hearts."[14]

Ambrose counsels the rich not to expect deference: "in the church, he is rich who is rich in faith." He misquotes Colossians 3:11 to emphasise equality: "we, both rich and poor, bond and free, Greek and Scythian, noble and common, are all one in Christ Jesus." "Riches are left here; faith alone will accompany you." Despise not the poor man — he has made you rich; Christ, when He was rich became poor for you; if you will be rich you must be poor in spirit. The more a man gains, the more he thirsts for gain. Riches in themselves are not blameable: 'the ransom of a man's life are his riches' (Proverbs 13:8), since he that gives to the poor redeems his soul." The rich are often without real friends; a poor man's friendship is free from envy. Caution, shrewdness, are necessary in giving; yet "we must take care lest in our money chests we bury the life of the poor in a sepulchre." Benefits should be conferred especially on those who cannot return them. The highest liberality lies in redeeming captives, assuming others' debts, providing dowries for maidens (rescuing them from shame), and relieving widows.[15]

But behind such moralising lies a more radical belief, that "charity is the partial adjustment of a *wrong*, and as such is able to cancel sin."[16] "Philosophers considered it consonant with justice that one should treat common (that is, public) property as public, and private as private. But this is not even in accord with nature; . . . God has ordered . . . food in common to all, and that the earth should be a common possession for all. Nature produced a common right for all, but greed has made it a right for a few."[17] How far such a declaration against any natural right of private property implies a Christian "communism", was (and is) much debated:

(i) Almsgiving, as Clement showed, presupposes private property and the presence of the poor. Lactantius writes: "Some one will say, Are there not among you poor, rich, servants and masters? Is there not some difference? There is none: nor any other cause why we bestow upon each other the name of brethren, except that we believe ourselves equal." The expression in Didache "share all . . . and do not claim that it is your own" (which Harnack said became a common formula); and that in Acts 4:32 about "having all things common", which Justin Martyr asserts also of all converts, and which Barnabas repeats ("thou shalt communicate in all things with thy neighbour; thou shalt not call things thine own"), are usually interpreted (as by Troeltsch and Harnack) as simply challenges to "energetic charitable activity". But Tertullian's words, "Being thus incorporated by love, we Christians can never dispute what we are to bestow upon our own members. Accordingly, among us all things are in common — excepting wives!" have a different ring. It is true that "the example of the Essenes was never followed"; whatever sharing of surplus wealth took place remained voluntary, family life was rigidly preserved. Lactantius argues against Plato's communism in goods and ("in consequence") in wives, as destroying all chastity, fidelity, affection, honour towards parents, frugality, abstinence, temperance, self-respect, and virtue. As to possession of all things in common, "how impossible and how unjust it is I could show by many things . . ." Inge remarks, "There has always been a slight tendency in Christianity to regard community of goods as the ideal, but the only serious attempt to carry it into effect was in the monasteries . . . Communism is possible only under two conditions — a religious basis, and celibacy."[18]

(ii) But if communism was not forcibly imposed, the taking of usury was strictly forbidden. Traditional Jewish antipathy to profiting by distress, reinforced by Christian compassion, pressed the words of Jesus — "If you lend to those from whom you hope to receive, what credit is that to you? Even sinners lend to sinners, to receive as much again. But love your enemies, and do good, and lend, expecting nothing in return" — into an absolute prohibition of usury, which few Christians questioned for a thousand years. This had far-reaching results.[19]

Tertullian expounds the case against usury to illustrate how the law prepared for the gospel's generosity. Clement of Alexandria says roundly: "the law prohibits a brother from taking usury, designating as a brother not only one born of the same parents, but one of the same race, and sentiments, and a participator in the same word." So Lactantius: The true worshipper "if he have lent money, will not receive interest, that the benefit which succours necessity may be unimpaired . . . To receive more than he has given is unjust, gaining booty from another's necessity." Ambrose, too, considered the taking of interest unconditionally forbidden — robbery, plunder ("rapina"). Augustine held it a "crime"; Cyprian proves from the Old Testament "that we must not take usury". Thereafter, the prohibitions recur, as Dow said, "with a rising vehemence that suggests the evil was increasing."[20]

All in all, the early church dealt realistically, but also generously, with the issue of wealth in Christian hands, when changed circumstances called for revised attitudes. The gospel sayings; Old Testament traditions about almsgiving and usury; awareness of pagan moral teaching, especially about justice, communism, and the reward due to charity; and some appeal also to "nature" as a source of natural law (or at least of natural conditions), all went to the shaping of the church's judgement. Subsequent generations have not added greatly to the insights then attained.

(2) SLAVERY

Since slavery has for many reasons — economic, sociological, and political as well as ethical — moved from the centre of Christian concern, it is not necessary to rehearse in detail the early church's thought concerning it, except to illustrate the factors that formed Christian opinion. This problem was not new; but with her increasing numbers including many from the slave-population, and confronted with liberal attitudes in Diaspora Judaism and in pagan society, the church found her earlier reactions insufficient.

Slavery within Jewry was never as cruel as it became among her neighbours. The slave was part of the household, sharing sabbath rest and religious festivals, able to inherit, and to marry into the family, so far protected that severe ill-treatment entitled him to freedom; consideration towards him constituted a religious merit.[21] Philo, in Alexandria, says of the Essenes: "There is not a single slave among them. They condemn the position of master, not only as unjust, being a breach of equality, but as impious, since it violates the order of Mother Nature, which gives birth to all alike and rears them as genuine brothers; whereas crafty covetousness disorganises this natural kinship . . ."[22] Beyond Jewry, treatment of slaves varied widely: many became doctors, lawyers, scribes, business managers, teachers, and could earn freedom by outstanding service. Barbarous ill-usage was possible, but inhibited by a slave's economic value. Though Seneca, Pliny, Plutarch, and the later Stoics, challenged the worst excesses of the system, "heathenism had no concept of the natural rights of man; only the free-born were men in the full sense, not foreigners, labourers, the poor, or slaves. Barbarians were captured in thousands, and sold as cheap as horses."[23] Especially did denial of the right of marriage and of ownership — even of his or her own body — rob the slave of human dignity, in ways abhorrent to the Christian spirit.

Within her own circle, the church continued (in Troeltsch's phrase) to "neutralise the slave relationship". Harnack remarks that the designation never occurs in Christian sepulchral inscriptions,[24] suggesting that the condition was not named among Christians — at any rate in death. To the challenge, "Are there not among you slaves?" Lactantius retorts, "We believe ourselves equal; we measure all not by the body but by the spirit, although the condition of bodies is different, yet we have no slaves, but regard them as brothers in spirit, in religion as fellow-servants."[25]

Ignatius had charged that Christians "despise not male or female slaves; yet let not these be puffed up, let them be the better sevants to the glory of God, that they may obtain from God a better freedom." The Didache urges masters to treat slaves kindly, slaves to obey their masters "as a type of God". Aristides: "Slaves, male and female, are instructed so that they become Christians, on account of love felt for them by their masters; when this takes place they call them brethren without any distinction whatever." Irenaeus found in the story of Jacob a promise that "Christ should raise up sons of God both from free men and from slaves, bestowing upon all the gift of the spirit."[26]

More significantly, the same honour and virtues were expected of slaves as of free Christians — the same courage, and heroism. Tertullian sternly charges that the slave attending upon his master when sacrificing — "if he hand the wine, or if by any single word necessary to the offering of the sacrifice he shall have aided him, he will be held to be a minister of idolatry."[27] Schaff lists nine known slaves who are commemorated as martyrs without distinction from free men.[28]

Euelpistes, questioned as to his condition, replied "I am a slave of the emperor, but I have received liberty from Jesus Christ; by His grace I have the same hope as my brethren." Of the high-born martyr, Perpetua,

Gwatkin remarks, "from the first to the last she never dreams that Revocatus and Felicitas are less than her equals . . . the deepest social division of the ancient world is utterly forgotten." Origen sees the raising of the status of slaves as one of the excellences of the new faith; and the consecration of Pius (at least brother to a slave) in mid-second century, and the ex-slaves Callistus (AD 218-223), Evaristus and Anicetus, as bishops of Rome illustrates his point. Some of the implications here are hinted at in the expedient rule that slaves shall not be promoted in church without their masters' permission; and in the Edict of Elvira (300 AD) forbidding any to hinder freedmen from becoming ministers simply because their former owners were still alive. But the same canons reveal that some "revolting harshness" towards slaves still required to be condemned.[29]

It is clear that Christian households continued to contain slaves, but sought to treat them well, and Christians among them as equals. At the same time, the church encouraged manumission. Ignatius appears to imply that slaves might be ransomed with church wealth, though no *claim* to such liberation was admitted: "Let them not crave to be freed out of the common fund, lest they be found to be 'slaves' of lust."[30] Ambrose declares it to be the highest kind of liberality to redeem captives, to "snatch men from death, and most of all, women from shame, to restore children to their parents . . . and to give back a citizen to his country." He recounts "vast numbers" of slaves sold after the Thessalonian war: "yet there were some who would have sent back into slavery those whom the church had redeemed. They themselves were harder than slavery itself, to look askance at another's mercy" — adding sharp comment upon those who say that if they had been sold into slavery, *they* would have accepted the situation.[31]

Ambrose spiritedly defends his own action: "I once brought odium on myself because I broke up the sacred vessels to redeem captives. Who can be so hard, cruel, iron-hearted, as to be displeased because a man is redeemed from death, or a woman from barbaric impurity, or boys and girls and infants from the pollution of idols? . . . Far better to preserve souls than gold for the Lord . . . it had been better to preserve living vessels (for the Master) than gold ones."[32]

Later, the manumission of slaves became a solemn act, superintended by the clergy, a "document of emancipation" being read at the altar (especially at festivals) that the congregation might ratify a slave's freedom. Figures of liberations by great Christian houses — from 1,250 to 8,000 — show the compromise with slavery to which the church after Constantine has succumbed, when wealthy families joined her membership. But they also illustrate, even if grossly exaggerating the piety of "saints", the spirit which animated the church, and the legend-writers, at the time such records were circulated.[33]

As to motives, wealthy converts freed slaves and bestowed munificent gifts upon the church as thanksgiving for their own baptism; or, having baptised slaves, they argued that "their sonship with God put an end to their servitude to man."[34] Clement of Alexandria argued that slaves, like women, barbarians, the old, the young, are equally capable of philosophy, self-control, "the same nature, the same virtue, the same martyrdom . . . to live faithfully . . . and to reach the highest excellence." He repeats at length Paul's advice to masters and slaves as the final Christian word on the relationship.[35] Ambrose declares "one Nature mother of all men, and by the same token we all are brothers."[36]

Norris says that Ambrose regarded slavery, property, and social inequality, as products of sin, not part of the natural constitution of things. This is the view of Augustine, too: "This is why we do not find the word 'slave' in scripture until righteous Noah branded the sin of his son with this name — a name introduced by sin and not by nature" — contradicting Aristotle's opinion, that some were born slaves. The concept of natural equality remained the church's view. Jerome says: "We are all born equal, both emperors and slaves, and equally all die. Equality is our natural condition." Schaff says that Chrysostom was the first to discuss the social issues involved in this principle, and to recommend, cautiously, a gradual emancipation.[37]

Compassion, New Testament exhortations, and the principle of equality (of spiritual experience and status conferred through Christ) were to be expected in the church's judgement upon slavery. But we might not have anticipated the appeal to a broader, natural equality, prior to Christ and to conversion. Here again the influence of the best contemporary pagan thought is seen. But the church as a whole, which when weak, poor and without political power had protested against slavery, in her social prosperity came to terms with it, seeking to control and ameliorate but not to destroy, until in the west slavery gave place to serfdom. When eventually Christian concern was again directed intensively upon the problem, early Christian motives and arguments revived, and in changed conditions bore belated fruit in abolition.

(3) THE STATE

In years of intermittent persecution, the church's attitude to the State continued to vacillate between conscientious support, on the one hand, following Paul and the Old Testament theocractic ideal, and on the other, following Revelation, courageous resistance to any encroachment upon conscience.

The Didache still urges that Christians bless those who curse them and pray for their enemies; "love those that hate you, and you shall not have an enemy." Clement of Rome can frame the prayer (as Marshall says, after persecution by Nero and Domitian): "To our princes and rulers on earth, Thou O Lord didst give royal power . . . that we . . . may submit . . . in no way resisting Thy will. Give to them, O Lord, health, peace, harmony, prosperity, that they may exercise the authority bestowed upon them without stumbling . . . Direct their counsel . . . that they may share Thy favour." But Ignatius, by encouragement and example, commends the martyr-spirit; while Polycarp, though he asks intercession for kings, all in authority, persecutors, accepts the likelihood of persecution, exhorts to all endurance, and finds chains "the fitting ornaments of saints". He seals the exhortation with heroic death, rather than submit conscience to State control.[38]

But the Christian's relation to the State presented two new aspects as the church began to infiltrate the higher ranks of society, and as she began to think of herself as a new, "semi-political" people.

There had always been some Christians from wealthier classes; during second and third centuries, many people of culture and influence were attracted, at first at the cost of their social position, but later retaining their privileges, so carrying Christianity into places of power in official administration — the high-born Pomponia, the consul Titus Flavius Clemens and his wife, members of the gens Annaea, and others. Ignatius fears influential Christians at Rome might hinder his martyrdom. Hermas complains of Christians "absorbed in business, wealth, friendship with pagans, the affairs of this world"; Tertullian claims that Christianity had filled "all the places you frequent, cities, lodging houses, villages, townships, markets, the camp itself, the tribes, town-councils, the palace, the senate and the forum — all we have left to you are your temples". Clement of Alexandria speaks to converts of culture, writes a treatise for the wealthy. Origen speaks of "the multitude of Christian rich men, persons of rank, delicate and high-born ladies". Eusebius mentions that the faith had spread through all classes by the time of Commodius, and that Diocletian's wife and daughter were Christians; Dionysius of Alexandria mentions Christians in government service; Minucius Felix refers to the Christian dialogue proceeding between cultivated lawyers. Irenaeus refers to believers in the royal palace. Ambrose can claim "the senate is now made up with a majority of Christians".[39]

With the changed position inevitably arose new tensions and obligations not very different from those facing modern Christians holding rank and responsibility in our secular world. In addition, a change came over the church's conception of herself and of her place within society, as not merely a religious sect but as the "new people", the "original people", the "people of the future". Deriving from Peter's "holy nation, peculiar people", from Paul's idea of the second Adam, Head of a new humanity, and from the whole doctrine of the church as the New Israel, substituted for the Israel after the flesh, this new historical and political self-consciousness brought to the church a considerable sense of unity, solidarity, of immunity from political criticism, and of superiority over the world. Harnack assembles numerous references to "the Christian race", the new "succession", the "race of the pious", "the third people" (beside Greeks, i.e. gentiles, and Jews), in Origen's phrase "the divine nation, that is the church". Hermas speaks of "the old woman, the church, created first of all — for her sake the world was made"; Barnabas, of Christ's preparing for Himself the new people, offering Himself for the sins of the new people. Aristides divides mankind into four races, Barbarians, Greeks, Jews and Christians, and says of the church "this people is a new people, and there is something divine mingled with it". Justin declares that God delays the judgement of the world "because of the seed of the Christians, who know that they are the cause of preservation in nature".[40]

The fall of the Jewish State left the way open for the church to inherit the political consciousness of Judaism, and to take the place of Jewry as the messianic community upon which the destiny of the Roman world was to depend. Persecution strengthened this sense of solidarity over against the empire, so helping to create the "church-State problem". The positive evaluation of the State expressed by Luke and Paul continues in Justin's confident plea for a fair trial, before regular courts. He continues:

> "When you hear that we look for a kingdom . . . we speak of that which is with God . . . If we looked for a human kingdom, we should deny Christ . . . More than all other men are we your helpers and allies in promoting peace"; "We who hated and destroyed one another, and would not live with men of a different tribe, now since the coming of Christ live familiarly with them, and pray for our enemies. Everywhere, more readily than all men, we endeavour to pay the taxes, as we have been taught by (Jesus). To God alone we render worship but in other things we gladly serve you, acknowledging you as kings and rulers of men and praying that with your kingly power you may be found to possess also sound judgement . . . We reckon that no evil can be done us unless we be convicted as evil-doers . . . you can kill, but not hurt us.'[41]

Melito of Sardis, addressing Marcus Aurelius, goes yet further in allying church and State —

"This philosophy of ours brought rich blessings to thine empire in particular. For ever since then the power of Rome has increased in size and splendour; the most convincing proof is this — that the empire has suffered no mishap since the reign of Augustus, but on the contrary, everything has increased its splendour and fame, in accordance with the general prayer" —

the empire and the church being, in Harnack's words, "foster-sisters".[42]

Origen, too, argued that "God prepared the nations for Christ's teaching, that they might be under one prince, the king of the Romans, and that it might not be more difficult for the apostles of Jesus to accomplish their task . . . The existence of many kingdoms would have been a hindrance to the spread of the doctrine of Jesus . . . Righteousness has arisen in (Christ's) days, and there is an abundance of peace, which took its commencement at His birth."

"Kings are appointed by God . . . The king will not inflict deserved punishment upon us if we say that not the son of crafty Saturn gave him his kingdom, but he who removeth and setteth up kings . . . Would that all were to follow our example in maintaining the divine origin of the kingdom and observing the precept to 'Honour the King' . . . For men of God are assuredly the salt of the earth: they preserve the order of the world: and society is held together as long as the salt in uncorrupted . . . The more anyone excels in piety, the more effective help does he render to kings . . . And we take our part in public affairs, when along with righteous prayers we join self-denying exercises and meditations, which teach us to despise pleasures . . . none fight better for the king than we do (in such ways). Christians are benefactors of their country more than others. For they train up citizens, and inculcate piety to the supreme Being; and they promote those whose lives in the smallest cities have been good and worthy, to a divine and heavenly city."

(As to holding civil office) "We recognise in each State the existence of another 'national organisation' (or, 'patriotic system') founded by the Word of God, and we exhort those who are mighty in word and of blameless life to rule over churches . . . and those who rule over us well are under the constraining influence of the great King . . . It is not for the purpose of escaping public duties that Christians decline public offices, but that they may reserve themselves for a diviner and more necessary service in the church of God — for the salvation of men. And this service is at once necessary and right . . ."[43]

On this theme, that Christians "preserve the order of the world" and "are benefactors of their country more than others", Origen challenges comparison, with unexpected boldness. "The churches of God which are instructed by Christ, when carefully contrasted with the assemblies in the districts in which they are situated, are as beacons in the world; for who would not admit that even the inferior members of the church are nevertheless more excellent than many of those who belong to the assemblies . . . The church of God, for example, which is at Athens, is a meek and stable body, one which desires to please God . . . whereas the assembly of the Athenians is given to sedition . . . And you may say the same thing of the church of God at Corinth and of the assembly of the Corinthian people; and also of the church of God at Alexandria and of the assembly of the people of Alexandria . . . In comparing the council of the church of God with the council in any city, you would find that certain councillors of the church are worthy to rule in the city of God . . . whereas the councillors in all other places exhibit in their characters no quality worthy of the superiority which they enjoy . . ." The church exhibits "a general superiority in what relates to the progress of virtue . . ."[44]

For the future of the State, Origen expects that "every form of worship will be destroyed except the religion of Christ, which will alone prevail . . . will one day triumph, as its principles take possession of the minds of men more and more every day . . . All who are endowed with reason will come under one law . . . Our belief is that the Word shall prevail over the entire rational creation, and change every soul into His own perfection, in which state everyone will . . . choose what he desires and obtain what he chooses. There is no evil so strong that it cannot be overcome by the Supreme Word and God . . . The consummation of all things is the destruction of evil . . . All shall call upon the name of the Lord, and serve Him with one consent."[45]

Clement of Alexandria, includes no duties to the State among the instructions of the Christian's Paedagogue, in accord with his general emphasis upon a withdrawn and contemplative life, yet he fully acknowledges that martyrdom may well be the lot of the righteous, and of the confessor who endures for the truth. The "contemplative" is not entirely submissive to an alien rule:

> God does not will such suffering, but He does not prevent it, and overrules it for good. Witness to the Lord by blood is the beginning of the true life. The church is full of those who have courted death. Moreover, the free, though threatened with death at the tyrant's hands, and brought before the tribunals, and all his substance imperilled, will by no means abandon piety: though Clement deprecates failure to avoid persecution when opportunity is offered.[46]

Tertullian, in his enthusiastic loyalty to the State, almost outdoes Paul:

> "For we, on behalf of the safety of the emperors, invoke the living God, whom the emperors themselves prefer to have propitious to them beyond all

other gods . . . Christians . . . pray for them a long life, a secure rule, a safe home, brave armies, a faithful senate, an honest people, a quiet world — and everything for which a man and a Caesar can pray. All this I cannot ask of any other but only of Him . . . " Christians are bidden to pray (Tertullian says) for their enemies, for persecutors, for kings; and he continues, "We know that the great force which threatens the whole world, the end of the age itself, with its menace of hideous suffering, is delayed by the respite which the Roman empire means for us. We do not wish to experience all that; and when we pray for its postponement we are helping forward the continuance of Rome.[47]

This almost reverses the attitude of the Apocalypse, as the second reason Tertullian offers carries Paul's thought to an extreme conclusion: "Why need I say more of the religious awe, the piety, of Christians, where the emperor is concerned? We must needs respect him as the chosen of our Lord. So I have a right to say, Caesar is more ours than yours, appointed as he is by our God."[48]

"A Christian is enemy to none, least of all to the emperor of Rome, whom he knows to be appointed by his God . . . and whose well-being, moreover, he must needs desire, with that of the empire over which he reigns so long as the world shall stand — for so long as that shall Rome continue. To the emperor, therefore, we render such reverential homage as is lawful for us and good for him, regarding him as the human being next to God . . . and less than God alone."[49]

Ambrose holds that Christians should obey the (now nominally Christian) State, except where it transgresses divine law — in practice, the law of the bishop. Ambrose is always ready to meet such transgression with passive resistance — "our weakness is our power" — but knowing that he has the populace behind him. On its part, the Christian State, as ally of the church, should protect without interfering. Church and State are co-operative, but independent, authorities — though the ultimate sanctions, the salvation or the judgement of God, are clearly on the side of the church.

Ambrose remonstrated with Valentinian I, and with Theodosius; to warn Valentinian II he withheld mass; he refused to surrender a Christian basilica at Milan — "By no right can you violate the house of a private person, and do you think that the house of God may be taken away? It is asserted that everything is lawful for the emperor, that all things are his. My answer is, Do not, O emperor, lay on yourself the burden of such a thought as that you have any imperial power over those things which belong to God. If you desire to reign long, submit yourself to God. It is written, The things which are God's to God, those which are Caesar's to Caesar: the palaces belong to the emperor, the churches to the bishop. Authority is committed to you over public, not over sacred buildings . . ." On matters of faith, and charges against the character of bishops, priests should judge priests, and bishops judge bishops. "Bishops are wont to judge of Christian emperors, not emperors of bishops." Again, "Who will dare to tell you the truth," he asks Theodosius, "if the priest dare not?"[50]

Yet the church loyally supports the State: "It is part of the guidance of nature, to love our country". The emperor Gratian is complimented on his "devout and loving keeping of the faith" and addressed repeatedly as "your sacred Majesty", "Christ's loyal servant and defender of the faith". The young Valentinian II is "the most blessed prince, a veteran in the power of faith." "What is more full of respect than that the emperor (Valentinian) should be called the son of the church . . . The emperor is within the church, not above it. For a good emperor seeks the aid of the church and does not refuse it."[51]

Addressing Gratian, Ambrose urges the emperor to go forth to war with the Goths "sheltered indeed under the shield of faith and girt with the sword of the Spirit" to victory promised by Ezekiel, "with the aid of the catholic faith that is strong in you". The Roman State could not be safe with heretic defenders: this is no land of unbelievers, but the land whose custom it is to send forth confessors. Occasionally, loyal support descends to sycophantic eulogy: "In truth, the Lord is propitious to the Roman empire, since he has chosen such a prince and father of princes, whose virtue and power, established on such a triumphant height of dominion, rests on such humility, that in valour he has surpassed emperors, and priests in humility . . ."[52]

Expounding this new relation of Christians to the State, Ambrose makes much of the Old Testament doctrine of "limited monarchy", by which kings were plainly subject to both law and prophets; and of the words and example of Christ, and of the counsel of Paul, on right attitudes to the ruling power. The hostility of the Apocalypse is left behind: among all these early writers, it finds echo only in Lactantius, who describes with much lurid detail the horrible deaths suffered by the great persecutors.[53] But even here, the purpose is rather to illustrate the theme of divine justice, than to nourish hatred or stiffen resistance. On church-State relations, it is scarcely possible to understand later attitudes without measuring accurately the distance which separates Patmos from Milan.

It is evident that the Christian mind could find ample warrant in the scriptures — New or Old — for either pietistic withdrawal from the affairs of State, for resistance, for active support, or for the assertion of spiritual over civil authority, as circumstances required and opportunity offered. The sense of being a distinct, growing, and increasingly influential group within society contributed greatly to Christian independence, that threatened to degenerate occasionally into political ambition. But awareness that the church must continue to contribute, positively and powerfully, to the welfare of society and the cohesion of the State, saved the Christian attitude from mere opportunism and a cynical lust for power.

(4) MILITARY SERVICE

One perennial tension between Christian conscience and civic duty turns upon the ethics of military service, concerning which, in the new situation of the second and third centuries, both facts and attitudes are keenly debated.

(i) Moffatt illustrates fully the use in early Christian literature of military metaphors, frequent in pacifist as in non-pacifist writers, and indicating the attitude of the church towards war no more than Paul's illustrations from slavery or harlotry imply moral approval.[54]

(ii) Exhortations, as by Justin Martyr and Irenaeus, to peaceableness, the turning of swords into ploughshares, love of enemies, avoidance of strife and revenge, must not be mistaken for decisions upon the issue of military duty; in the years before the wars of Marcus Aurelius (circa AD 170) the *problem* did not confront the conscience of the church.[55]

(iii) Whether Christians served in the Roman army in the second century is controverted. Bainton, Ferguson, hold there is no evidence that they did, and that this, with the absence of conscription and the rejection of slaves or freedmen, means that the church withheld her members. Origen does not deny a rebuke by Celsus against Christian "pacificism" — abandoning the State to lawless barbarians. Against this ambiguous silence must be set the precedent of the New Testament: soldiers receiving instruction from the Baptist, Jesus' allusion to a king preparing for a war, the enigmatic saying about disciples buying swords, approval of a centurion's faith, and that of Cornelius — all without a hint that either should demit service. Clement of Alexandria expects that as the Christian seafarer will listen to the Heavenly Pilot, so the converted soldier will listen to "the Commander who orders what is right", again with no suggestion that he resign. By 172 AD, the 12th (Melitene) Legion certainly had numbers of Christians in its ranks — not, surely, all new recruits; others were in the army at Lambese. Moffatt remarks that there was no *escape* for the soldier, save incapacity, disease, completion of service, or desertion. *Enlistment* by men already Christians is another matter: Tertullian is sure no convert could think of enlisting, but (as Bainton remarks) "his stern rebuke to voluntary enlistment is a witness to the practice which he condemned".[56]

(iv) From the beginning of the third century, there is less doubt. Tertullian boasts of Christians "in . . . your fortresses . . . the very camp . . . We sojourn with you, sail with you, fight with you"; the refusal of one soldier to wear the military chaplet singled him out as "a soldier of God, more steadfast than the rest of his brethren who imagined they could serve two masters". Tertullian deals at length with the self-justification of these compromisers. By AD 202, a king of Odessa made Christianity the religion of a frontier province — hardly possible if the faith implied universal pacificism. Eusebius holds that renewal of persecution "began with the brethren in the army". Among instances contested are — the soldier martyr Basilides (Alexandria AD 203); Besas, Laurentius, Egnatius, soldier martyrs under Decius (AD 250); five others, encouraging a Christian on trial and apparently themselves martyred with him; others possibly under Valerian but probably under Decius; Marinus, centurion at Caesarea (before AD 262); under Diocletian soldiers were forced to sacrifice or be discharged. Harnack thinks such purging shows how numerous were Christian soldiers, citing Eusebius, "a vast number". Cadoux, Bainton, Ferguson, argue no sovereign would deprive himself of a tenth or even a twentieth of his forces (not even if they were unreliable?). Licinius, and Galerius, also purged Christians from their armies. Harnack lists with caution a further thirteen named Christian soldiers. Bainton admits that the church did not prohibit recording military service in epitaphs. Stories of Christians dramatically defying military orders and suffering for it naturally overshadow the greater number who "compromised".[57]

(v) From early fourth century, the progressive accession of Constantine "terminated the pacifist period in church history" as Bainton holds. The church henceforth saw no impropriety in the cross on the military labarum. The Council of Arles (AD 314) condemned Christians who in peace deserted the colours. Eventually, Ambrose (as we have seen) urges Gratian to war sheltered under the shield of faith, "no military eagles, no flight of birds (of omen) here lead the van of our army, but Thy Name, Lord Jesus, and Thy worship . . ." Bishop James of Nisibis inspired the military defence against the Persians; Christians in Armenia took to arms against persecution. Protests of course continued: Martin of Tours declined to shed blood and was excused (AD 336); Basil of Caesarea (AD 370) still discouraged militarism — retired soldiers should wait three years for communion, intentional homicides must wait twenty years (Basil seems to have thought that at times soldiers must kill, but at other times Christian soldiers could avoid bloodshed, leaving it to others). Ferguson says, of the fourth century, "at the beginning, Diocletian purges the army of Christians; at the end Theodosius purges the army of pagans." At mid-century, Firmicus Maternus calls for a holy war, holding that an army which has been putting down idolatry needs no purification. Later church Councils still forbade the clergy to fight, but the church herself was soon at war with Moslems, heretics and Jews. According to St. Louis of France, the best answer a layman can give to a contentious Jew is to run his sword into him: from that to the Crusades and papal armies is no military march at all.[58]

Only against the background of this changing practice can the varying opinions of early Christian writers be understood. Since it is their reasoning, rather than their conclusions, which remains illuminating, it is necessary to set out typical statements with some fullness.

Ignatius: "Nothing is better than peace, by which all war of those in heaven and those on earth, is abolished."[59]

Justin Martyr: "We who were filled with war and mutual slaughter . . . have changed our warlike weapons, our swords into ploughshares, our spears into instruments of tillage . . . We who formerly used to murder one another now refrain from making war upon our enemies."[60]

Tatian: "I have no desire to rule . . . I decline military command."[61]

Athenagoras: "How could anyone accuse of murder and cannibalism men who cannot bear to see a man killed . . . thinking that to watch men being killed is practically equivalent to taking life."[62]

Clement of Alexandria: "It is not in war but in peace that we are trained" . . . "If thou enrol as one of God's people, heaven is thy country, God thy lawgiver. And what are the laws? Thou shalt not kill . . . thou shalt love thy neighbour as thyself; to him who strikes thee on the cheek, present also the other"; "Let us arm ourselves with the armour of peace."[63]

Minucius Felix: "It is not right for us even to see or hear of a man being killed."[64]

It is, however, Origen and Tertullian who as Moffatt says are "the protagonists of the extreme section in the church which now frankly disavowed the military profession":[65]

Origen: "How then was it possible for the gospel doctrine of peace, which does not permit men to take vengeance even upon enemies, to prevail throughout the world unless at the advent of Jesus a milder spirit had been everywhere introduced into the conduct of things?" The Christian Lawgiver nowhere teaches that it is right for his own disciples to offer violence to any one, however wicked (or) to allow the killing of any individual whatever. Christians have adopted laws of so exceedingly mild a character as not to allow them to resist their persecutors." "For we no longer take up 'sword against nation' nor do we 'learn war any more', having become children of peace." In the case of the ancient Jews, who had a land and a form of government of their own, to take from them the right of fighting for their country . . . would be to subject them to sudden and utter destruction . . . And that same Providence which of old gave the law . . . has now given the gospel of Jesus Christ . . ." On Celsus' charge that if all were to do as Christians do, the emperor would be deserted and affairs of earth fall into barbarian hands: "If they do as I do, even the barbarians will become most humane . . . If all the Romans . . . embrace the Christian faith, they will not war at all, being guarded by divine power . . . Do not those who are priests at certain shrines . . . keep their hands from blood? Even when war is upon you, you never enlist the priests . . . How much more so, that while others are engaged in battle these (Christians) too should engage as the priests and ministers of God, keeping their hands pure and wrestling in prayers to God on behalf of those who are fighting in a righteous cause . . . We do not indeed fight under the king, although he require it, but we fight on his behalf, forming a special army by offering our prayers to God."[66]

Tertullian insists that Christ is no warrior. His sword is the "allegorical one" of truth: "The patience of the Lord was wounded in the person of Malchus, and so He cursed for all time the works of the sword . . ." "If we are enjoined then to love our enemies . . . whom have we to hate? If injured, we are forbidden to retaliate, lest we become as bad ourselves . . . In our religion it (is) counted better to be slain than to slay." "We must first enquire whether warfare is proper at all for Christians . . . Do we believe it lawful for a human oath to be superadded to one divine? . . . to come under promise to another master after Christ? . . . to abjure father and mother, whom even the law has commanded us to honour and love next to God Himself? . . . to make an occupation of the sword, when the Lord proclaims that he who uses the sword shall perish by the sword? Shall the son of peace take part in the battle when it does not become him even to sue at law? And shall he apply chain, prison, torture, punishment, who is not the avenger even of his own wrongs? Shall he keep watch-service for others more than for Christ? . . . on the Lord's Day, when he does not even do it for Christ Himself? Shall he keep guard before temples he has renounced? — leaning meanwhile on the spear with which Christ's side was pierced!"

"Of course, if faith comes later, and finds any preoccupied with military services, their case is different, (as with) the soldiers who came to John, the centurion Christ approves, the centurion Peter instructs. Yet when a man has become a believer . . . there must be either an immediate abandonment of it, as with many; or all sorts of quibbling will have to be resorted to; or . . . the punishment must be endured". But how will (a Christian) war, nay, how will he serve even in peace, without a sword which the Lord has taken away? For albeit soldiers had come unto John (and) a centurion had believed, (still) the Lord afterward, in disarming Peter, unbelted every soldier."[67]

This antagonism to military service found support in Cyprian, in "Hippolytus" (to whom are ascribed certain canons thought to preserve 2nd and 3rd century material, with various church orders formerly thought to be from Egypt and Syria[68]), in Arnobius, and especially in Lactantius.

Cyprian: "After the Eucharist has been carried in it, no hand is to be spotted with the sword and blood"; "God willed iron for the tilling of the earth, not the killing of men". Murder, which in the case of an individual is admitted to be a crime, is called a virtue when it is committed wholesale. Impunity is claimed . . . because the cruelty is perpetrated on a grand scale."[69]

"Hippolytus": "No Christian should become a soldier, unless a commander, who has a sword, compels him; let him not draw any guilt of

bloodshed upon himself"; "A catechumen or believer who wishes to become a soldier shall be rejected, because it is far from God"; "They shall not receive into the church one of the emperor's soldiers. If they have received him, he shall refuse to kill if commanded; if he does not refrain, he shall be rejected"; Ferguson cites with these another rule from the Syrian "Testament of Our Lord" — "if soldiers wish to be baptised to the Lord, let them cease from military service, or from the position of authority." (Moffatt thinks some versions of these rules show later modifications).[70]

Arnobius: "After the name of Christ was heard wars were in great measure diminished . . . For since we . . . have learned from his teaching . . . that evil ought not to be requited for evil; that it is better to suffer wrong than to inflict it; that we should rather shed our own blood than stain our hands and our consciences with that of another, an ungrateful world is now for a long period enjoying a benefit from Christ, inasmuch as by His means the rage of savage ferocity has been softened . . . If all would lend an ear to His peaceful rules, the whole world would now be living in placid tranquillity."[71]

Lactantius: (Our countrymen) so admire valour "as to imagine that brave and warlike generals are admitted to the assembly of the gods, and that there is no other way to immortality than to lead armies, to lay waste the territory of others, to destroy cities, to overthrow towns, to put to death or enslave free peoples . . . If one has slain a single man, he is regarded as contaminated and wicked. But he who has slaughtered countless thousands of men, has inundated plains with blood, and infected rivers, is not only admitted into the temple but even into heaven . . . If this is the virtue which renders us immortal, I for my part would prefer to die . . ." "When God forbids us to kill . . . it will be neither lawful for a just man to engage in warfare — since his warfare is justice itself — nor to accuse any one of a capital charge . . . since it is the act of putting to death, itself, which is prohibited. With regard to this precept there ought to be no exception at all; it is always unlawful to put to death a man, whom God willed to be a sacred animal." "For if you wish to defend religion by bloodshed, tortures, it will no longer be defended, but will be polluted and profaned."[72]

It might seem impossible to reverse an ethical tradition so passionately argued: yet the historic church has not in fact been preponderantly pacifist in outlook. To a large extent, this was due to Ambrose, who in adjusting the Christian ethic to the changed situation in a nominally Christian State, accepted the need for war, provided it be just, and reserved pacificism for private individuals and priests.

"Our fathers, as Joshua, Jerubbaal, Samson, David, gained great glory in war." "How brave was Joshua, who in one battle laid low five kings with their people . . . Gideon . . . Jonathan . . . the Maccabees, ready to fight for the temple of God and for their rights, . . . Here is fortitude in war, which bears no light impress of what is virtuous and seemly, for it prefers death to slavery and disgrace." "Justice . . . must even be preserved in all dealings with enemies. For instance, if the day or the spot for a battle has been agreed upon, it would be . . . against justice to occupy the spot beforehand or to anticipate the time . . . A deeper vengeance is taken on fiercer foes and . . . false (as Moses exterminated Midianites, but Joshua spared Gibeonites)." Elisha gained peace by insisting the Syrian captives be well treated (an incident referred to again as an outstanding act of virtue). "Fortitude without justice is the source of wickedness . . . ready to crush the weaker. One ought to see whether (any) war is just or unjust. David never waged war unless he was driven to it, (nor) without seeking counsel of the Lord. Thus he was victorious". Ambrose pleads boldly with Theodosius for clemency towards the conquered; after the massacre at Thessalonica he writes "I dare not offer the sacrifice (mass) if you intend to be present. Is that which is not allowed after shedding the blood of one innocent person, allowed after shedding the blood of many?"

As to the participation of priests: "The thought of warlike matters seems to be foreign to the duty of our office, nor is it our business to look to arms." "If force is used, I cannot meet it. I shall be able to grieve, to weep, to groan; against weapons, soldiers, Goths, my tears are my weapons, for these are a priest's defence. I ought not, I cannot resist it any other way . . ." "It is not bodily guardianship but the Lord's providence that is wont to fence in the servant of Christ". And for individuals: "I do not think that a Christian . . . ought to save his own life by the death of another; just as when he meets with an armed robber, he cannot return his blows lest in defending his life he should stain his love towards his neighbour. The verdict on this question is plain and clear in the books of the gospel: 'Put up thy sword, for everyone that taketh the sword shall perish with the sword'."[73]

"What Ambrose thus sketched, Augustine amplified" writes Bainton.[74] This is true especially of the concept of the "just war", of the idea that defence of the Christian State is defence of the faith, and the rule that the private citizen, even if attacked, must like the priest accept the pacifist principle. In evaluating this variety of moral judgement within a church confessing allegiance to one law and one Lord, several qualifications need attention. Harnack suggests that "a rigorous party" objected to military service, though for a time the church as a whole "closed her eyes" to the issue, except when the soldier's renewal of his oath on the emperor's birthday, or the offer of promotion, or distribution of bounties requiring wearing of the laurel, sharpened the moral challenge. Moffatt denies the existence of such a party in the earlier period: later, at any rate, the double standard was the church's solution. Eusebius[75] allows that the lower "more humble and more human" way of Christian life permits men to command soldiers who are fighting in a good cause; "superior"

Christians are forbidden military service. So Ambrose: ordinary Christians may fight when need arises, but not monks or priests.

A wider differentiation of function allotted military service to pagans while Christians confined themselves to prayer and good works — thus benefitting by war while condemning it. So Origen: if all Romans are converted safety will come through prayer. Christians have the better way to conquer the world — the supreme and healing word, and God.[76] Similarly, Tertullian would leave the running of the empire, and its defence, to unbelievers: "we have no pressing inducement to take part in your public meetings; nor is there aught more entirely foreign to us than affairs of State"; forbidding Christians to fight, he offers prayer "for the safety of our princes . . . for security to the empire, *for brave armies* . . ."[77] This raises the question, whether the real source of such quietism was withdrawal from contamination, or merely impotence.

A different explanation of the varied views appeals to the ambiguity of "military service". Tertullian distinguishes between officers and the "inferior grades" who need not share in sacrifices or capital punishment. Eusebius records an action of Licinius against 'soldiers of the cities". Harnack defines these as police, guardians of the peace, a superior civil service. Bainton mentions "a soldier of civil authority", fire fighters, "beneficiarii" (aids to administration) and "protectores" (guards of the emperor's person, and of prisoners) and other soldiers in charge of public transport, the mails, and secretarial duties. These are the soldiers (in the Hippolytan canon) who might be "taught not to kill" — and those whom the Council of Arles would punish for unnecessarily laying down their commission *in peacetime*. There was obviously room for varied judgements about the fitness for Christians of tasks so different. Bainton persuasively links this consideration with the geographical distribution of the varying opinions. The greatest objections to military service came from the east, where in wilder and more vulnerable provinces, actual combat would be frequent; opinion in quieter north Africa was divided; least objection arose at Rome, where security, and so civilian soldiering, were greatest.[78]

One further confusing factor was the difference of attitude among Christians to the empire itself. Some condemned its sins, and said with Tertullian "all the powers and dignities of this world are enemies of God". Others appreciated its advantages to the gospel — the open roads and seas (Irenaeus), the peace of the world (Origen), the tranquillity of Carthage (Tertullian). Their prayers for the empire showed that Christians did not wish to see its rule ended: the advent hope had receded — Bainton says Hippolytus expected three hundred years, and Tertullian could pray for "the delay of the end." Mixed feelings towards the empire naturally created varied attitudes towards its defence. Above all, the "Christianising" of the empire was bound to affect the Christian moral stance, striving to remain relevant, and to translate timeless principles into an "adjustment ethic". It may be said that this implied "an increasing tendency to accommodation with the world . . . persecution could not destroy the church's witness, but worldly power went far towards doing so" (Ferguson). Or such adaptation may represent a necessary enlargement of Christian responsibility, beyond a minority's pietistic quietism, without which Christian aims cannot be fulfilled nor Christian obligations discharged. That the change of circumstances deeply modified the Christian ethical outlook, is beyond question.[79]

Thus on another moral issue, unprecedented, complex, and immediately relevant, earnest, able and eloquent men sought the mind of Christ. By what means? Nothing has so far been said of the influence of divergent scriptural exegesis: the selection and interpretation of appropriate passages served more to illustrate views already held than to explain how such views arose. A brief review of the statements summarised reveals, first, how far the need for scriptural justification helped to form the Christian conscience. Isaiah's vision of a world of peace, learning war no more, was an essential element in the messianic "testimonia" to which the church appealed, and it is cited or echoed (as we have seen) in Justin Martyr, Origen (who so defines "counsels of Jesus"), Cyprian, Arnobius; it may shape Lactantius' phrase "people *ignorant* of wars" and Clement's "trained in peace". Ambrose ignores Isaiah, and turns instead to Ezekial's prophecy of victory and the military prowess of ancient heroes. Acceptance of the Old Testament as Christian scripture might seem thus to have distorted Christian thinking; but pacifists could always discard unwelcome precedents by denying the Old Testament outright (Marcion), by allegorising it (Origen), by relegating its principles to an earlier stage of God's purpose (Origen on Jewish nationhood), or by ridicule (Tertullian). One Old Testament principle that carried greater authority was "Thou shalt not kill", which Clement of Alexandria, Origen, and Lactantius repeatedly quote.

New Testament directives, especially the command to love enemies and not to retaliate, are remembered by Clement, Tertullian, Arnobius, Lactantius and even Ambrose (applying them to priests and private persons): and they carry considerable weight in the discussion. Tertullian mentions the soldiers who came to the Baptist, the centurion Christ approved, and him whom Peter converted, but he sees in them no precedent for Christians remaining in the army ("albeit . . . still the Lord afterward . . ."). The saying "Put up thy sword . . ." is determinative for Tertullian ("Christ unbelted every soldier henceforth"). It occurs again in Ambrose, and possibly underlies Cyprian's phrase "the hand spotted with the sword". More argumentative are Tertullian's appeal to precepts about not serving two masters, not going to war with an enemy ("much less to battle"), and not taking meals in idol temples, as the temple guard presumably did. Recurrent expressions in Hippolytus and the Egyptian Church Orders ("guilt of bloodshed"), Clement of Alexandria (the "bloodless host"), Cyprian ("hand spotted with blood"), Arnobius ("the blood of a fellow creature"), Lactantius ("inundated plains with blood . . . defend religion by bloodshed" . . . "will be polluted"), and Ambrose ("the shedding of blood") seem more than coincidental and suggest a horror of bloodshed itself. This could owe something to the ancient Jewish blood-tabu; or to the western text of the Jerusalem Council's decree (Acts 15), on which Tertullian says[80] "the interdict upon 'blood' we shall understand to be an interdict much more upon *human* blood", and concludes that the three foremost sins, not to be remitted, are adultery, idolatry, and *bloodshed.* Though probably local and indefensible, this interpretation might yet have been influential: Cyprian's "adultery, fraud, manslaughter are mortal crimes" may reflect the same exegesis.

The appeal to scripture being thus inconclusive, reference is made to assumed "natural law" on the Stoic model — the notion of natural justice which even war should observe, as with Origen ("praying for those fighting in a just cause . . . wars should be waged in a just and orderly way . . . as among bees"). Clement, tracing the rudiments of pagan ethics to a prior revelation through Moses, cites as deserving universal approval the provisions of Deuteronomy on treatment of enemies:

> ". . . not to bear malice; . . . no grudge against those who have done ill . . . And enemies, although drawn up before the walls attempting to take the city, are not regarded as enemies until they are by the voice of the herald summoned to peace" (and have refused it)[81]

Ambrose's theory of the just war is but a Christian version, step by step, of Cicero's "natural justice" and the Stoic idea that war itself must be "justified" by a just cause. Lactantius' remarkable phrase about man as a "sacred animal" ("sacrosanct creature") is likewise an appeal to natural morality. Of the same kind, basically, are the reiterated references to the "humanising" influence of Christianity —

Origen's "barbarians become most humane"; Tertullian's "war is no way to truth, meekness, righteousness"; Cyprian's heartsick description of the world drenched with internecine bloodshed and speciously defended mass-murder; Arnobius' "rage of savage ferocity softened"; and Lactantius' strong protest against admiring and deifying the savage, the brutalised, the ruthless —

as though the new faith restored something *natural* to man but hitherto lost. Some universal, moralist standard, superior to religion itself, is being applied, too, when Lactantius argues that to "defend" religion by violence, only profanes and pollutes religion.

Tertullian's very different objection to military service concerns the moral danger in which the Christian soldier is placed, by an oath, a loyalty, a uniform, crown, banner, and watchword that are not of Christ. Similar is Origen's reason for pious disengagement from the world's affairs; Tatian shares Tertullian's conviction that military service cannot be divorced from idolatry.[82] Dacius' martyrdom arose from his objection against the dissolute behaviour of the army, especially the celebration of the Saturnalia.[83] This argument, of course, is not against military service itself, and fails entirely when the army becomes "Christian".

However, in neither of the foregoing "reasons" for Christian objection to war do we hear the true ring of Christian conviction or feel the pulse of the Christian heart, as we do in the early Christian writing taken as a whole. The deep and passionate assumptions of the believer are not entirely analysable. We feel this in Ignatius' assertion of the moral value of peace ("nothing is better . . ."); in Justin's naive claim that, being converted, we henceforth naturally are men of peace; in the recurrent references to "the gospel of peace" (Clement's remarks about Christ's "trumpet of peace . . . the strain of peace . . . the armour of peace"; Origen's "the gospel doctrine of peace" . . . "a milder spirit, children of peace"; Tertullian's "the son of peace"; Arnobius' "peaceful occupations and placid tranquillity" and Lactantius' "mind engaged in perpetual peace with men"). We discern too the cultivation of a certain Christian good taste, a moral sensitiveness, in the reiteration that Christians cannot bear, or are forbidden, to "look upon" the killing of a fellow-man (Athenagoras, Minucius, Lactantius). The immediate reference may well be to "enjoying" the sight in the arena. Something intuitive and inarguably Christian gleams in phrases like "better to be slain than to slay" (Tertullian); "it is far from God" (Egyptian Church Order); and clearest of all in "If we are enjoined to love our enemies, whom have we to hate?" (also Tertullian). The persistent echoes of the sermon on the mount and of Christ's law of love, show that the deepest intuition of the church feared something irreconciliable between military service and the law of Christ. As Moffatt says, "the spirit of Jesus still controlled the church . . . the ideal was that of the beatitudes"[84]; or as Justin Martyr expressed it, "Of our love to all, He taught thus: 'If you love them that love you, what do ye that is new?' "[85]

How very close that appeal brought the church to the beloved Figure of the Master may be demonstrated through three details in the discussion. Marinus at Caesarea, challenged by a rival for the position of centurion to confess himself a Christian, is given time to visit the bishop, who before the altar offered him the single choice — a sword, or the book of the Gospels.[86] Even Ambrose says (for the private soul) "the verdict is plain and clear in the books of the gospel . . ." Secondly, Cyprian, ("neither after the Eucharist has been carried in it (may) the hand be spotted with blood"), Ambrose ("I dare not offer mass . . . after the shedding of blood"), and Basil ("Let soldiers wait three years for communion"), make the direct link between taking life and the Life given for us, between the shedding of blood and the blood shed for us, and found them incompatible. Thirdly, men as widely apart as Tertullian and Ambrose bring the question explicitly to the presence of the Master: the confessing soldier gave up the sword "which was not necessary, either, for the protection of our Lord"; "Put up thy sword . . . Christ would not be defended from the wounds of the persecutor." The Gospels, the Eucharist, the memory of the Master — here the church's heart truly lay.

Thus, on yet another issue, changing circumstances, traditional and prevailing ethical insights, moral expediency, Christian conviction, feeling, and devotion, all contribute in varying degrees to form in the church "the mind of Christ".

(5) CAPITAL PUNISHMENT

The church for long bore no responsibility concerning capital punishment, but the question did arise academically in connection with officership in the army. Athenagoras said "we cannot bear to see a man put to death, even justly". Origen argues that Christians, not being a nation like the Jews, "could not condemn to be burned or stoned them that had broken the law". Tertullian mentions the duty of capital punishment as another reason why Christian service in higher ranks is impossible; and Lactantius declares "He who reckons it is a pleasure that a man, though justly condemned, should be slain in his sight, pollutes his conscience as much as if he should have become a spectator and a sharer in a secret homicide". It is not "lawful . . . to accuse any one of a capital charge because it makes no difference whether you put a man to death by word or by the sword, since it is the act of putting to death, itself, which is prohibited." With the State's recognition of the church, Ambrose is "embarrassed" by the appointment of Christian judges, his general attitude being averse to capital punishment. In time, the death penalty was accepted as a necessary sanction of social order, Old Testament precedents and Paul's words about the ruler being "a terror to the evil and not bearing the sword in vain", yielding scriptural support. As Troeltsch points out, in the Donatist controversy, the church herself demanded the death penalty for certain heretics.[87]

No Christian theory of crime and punishment is here in sight; Christians faced no necessity to propose alternative sanctions for serious offences against society. To appeal to the ancient commandment against "killing" is superficial and inconsistent, since the Mosaic law certainly did not prohibit the death penalty. The church's reaction is almost wholly one of feeling and of moral "taste".

Whether we consider the Christian impact upon society, the moral apologetic offered in Christian literature, or the practice of the church in her new situation, one outstanding feature is the absence of any fixed rule, code or law, the lack even of any consistent, determinative appeal to scripture. Instead, the scriptures — Jewish and Christian — are *used to provide justification* for ethical attitudes fashioned by other influences. Christian ethics in these centuries is matter of discussion, open-minded, flexible, changing with changing circumstances, often confused. A second general feature was the recoil from the moral condition of society towards a world-renouncing ethic, withdrawn from public life, suspicious of the natural impulses of marriage and parenthood, tending increasingly towards asceticism. The "double standard" made extreme renunciation practicable for the few, and increased the veneration it inspired; while the compromise involved in becoming the church of a "Christian" State itself helped to polarise Christianity into *both* a fiercer, world-renouncing ascetism on the one hand and an ever more powerful, wealthy, world-affirming political institution on the other. Responding to the "spiritual awakening" by emphasising her ethical achievements, the church faced the temptation to fall from the apostolic gospel of redemption by grace through faith to mere moralism in a religious context: but on the whole her writers kept the balance true.

As in the New Testament period the Christian ethic struggled for both support and definition against a background of Jewish moral tradition, so in the early church the contention that one ethical ideal persists through Jewish, pagan and Christian teaching leads on to a similar struggle to show the Christian ideal at once confirmed by the best in paganism, and yet distinctive and superior. This unexpected borrowing of current ethical language and thought, began with the appeal to the Stoics' "natural law" in the discussion of wealth, slavery, the State, and the just war. It produced what Inge describes as the position finally adopted by the church — the Stoic principle, "All are by nature equal", plus the Christian adaptation "because of the Fall, to punish and remedy sin, God has sanctioned the civil power, with its hierarchy of authorities".[88]

This significant appeal to natural law is sometimes made to rest upon scripture. Tertullian quotes Paul's "does not nature itself teach you . . .?" and "When gentiles . . . do by nature what the law requires, they are a law to themselves . . . they show that what the law requires is written on their hearts", as suggesting "both natural law, and law-revealing nature . . . We first of all, indeed, know God Himself by the teaching of nature."[89] But sometimes the appeal stands by its own right, as in Tertullian: "the appeal for Christian practices becomes all the stronger when also nature, *which is the first rule of all*, supports them . . . Ours is the God of nature: everything which is against nature deserves to be branded as monstrous among all men, but with us it is to be condemned also as sacrilege against God, the Lord and Creator of nature."[90] Ambrose, too finds in nature's laws the essence of Christian morality:

> Nature teaches care for others, modesty, gratitude to God; "what is so contrary to nature as to injure another for our own benefit? The natural feelings of our hearts urge us to keep on the watch, undergo trouble, do work, for all . . . There is one law of nature for all; we are bound by the law of nature to act for the good of all." "What is so contrary to nature as not to be content? . . . If a virtuous life is in accordance with nature — for God made all things very good — then shameful living must be opposed to it . . ." citing Corinthians xi 13, 14. "Nature arranges for us both character and appearance, and we ought to observe her directions."[91]

This appeal to traditional ethical concepts of paganism (like the earlier appeal to traditional Jewish concepts) considerably modifies the autonomy of Christian ethics. But Christian insight is still necessary to complement nature — "We are obliged" (in pursuing our subject, Tertullian means) "to turn from the rule of nature which we share with mankind in general, that we may maintain the whole peculiarity of our Christian discipline . . ."[92]

So, Christian ethics remain Christian. The "instinct" of the church held her to what was native and distinctive in the faith. As we have seen, the words, and spirit, and memory of Jesus still exercised their fascination, even though at times the real explanation of Christian feeling could not be analysed intellectually. Immediately the Christian ethic has left Palestine and the direct authority wielded by eye-wtinesses of Christ and by apostles, every new problem has to be *situationally* resolved in open discussion. But amid all the persuasions, pressures and novelty, there lingers an ideal, a vision, a spirit: scripture, eucharist and the Figure of the Master continue to exert the greatest influence of all. The central moral conviction which nourished all that is distinctive in Christian ethics was best expressed by Lactantius — "The most religious worship is, to imitate."[93]

4

Asceticism: Monasticism: Mysticism

DETAILED SURVEY OF THE DEVELOPMENT of mediaeval Christianity is not necessary in seeking the factors that shape the modern Christian conscience, but two main emphases must be noted. One, ascetic-monastic, ultimately mystic, was fundamentally world-renouncing in the sense of retrieving ethics from the compromises involved in wielding power. The other, that of moral philosophy and theology, of ecclesiastical statesmanship, was world-affirming in the sense of applying ethics to problems of life in new political conditions. The difference corresponds roughly to the double standard of Christian morality. "The combination of the control of the world and the negation of the world determines the attitude of the mediaeval church."[1]

The church of the east, in Luthardt's phrase, "passed out of the historic movement," at least temporarily. Western Christendom faced the problem of educating the new Germanic peoples in Christian morality, and developed for that purpose, beside a considerable moral philosophy, a system of canon law and of penitential discipline. Canon law expressed Christian ethics again as the rules of the Christian society. As eventually summarised by Gratian (12th century) it reveals a low state of morality among clergy and laity. Among the former, profligacy, drunkenness, concubinage, ignorance, have to be disciplined; nunneries too have frequently to be reformed. Among the laity, superstitious offerings to the dead, before trees and at wells, social intercourse with Jews, toleration of heretics, arson, forgery, duelling, tournaments, all call for penalties — sometimes unexpectedly mild for infanticide compared with full excommunication for celebrating Easter on the Jewish date. Perjury before a consecrated cross earned three years' penance; committed before an unconsecrated cross it deserved only one year. Criminals, suicides, those executed, were denied Christian burial. The clergy's duty to educate the young, defend the poor, care for widows, orphans, the needy and slaves, is often recalled. Inevitably, canon law suffered the limitations of all enforceable ethical systems — legalism, externalism, and an evasive casuistry.

The penitential system, seeking to apply canon law to individual lives, offered instruction, and where required, absolution, on condition that the penitent showed contrition, confessed and performed works of "satisfaction". Originally, "doing penance" meant exhibiting proof of repentance; later, and popularly, it became a "compensation for doing wrong by doing right". Books of "cases of conscience" and alphabetic moral lexicons fed the ethical casuistry which was the staple of popular religious education. The substitution of ritual tasks, and fines, for true acts of repentance "did more harm than the church's teaching could undo". Almsgiving, for example, was discussed as an element not of Christian love but of penance. Innocent could say that alms purify, redeem, protect, make perfect, justify, awaken new life and save; its merit lay not in the help given but in the renunciation it implied.[2]

Some protests were voiced, as by Alcuin, who demanded true penitence and sincere love for God. Jonas, bishop of Orleans, denied the purchase of remission and emphasised right disposition. Hincmar of Rheims insisted that works of mercy could not wipe away guilt without repentance and abstinence from sin.[3] Those who craved a deeper relationship with God than conformity to church law afforded, generally turned inward — sometimes in guilt and self-castigation, leading to asceticism; sometimes seeking comradeship in self-discipline, through monasticism; sometimes seeking the perfection of Christian experience in unity with God, in mysticism of several kinds.

(1) ASCETICISM

The positive athleticism of the New Testament occasionally gave place, in the early church, to a negative, even masochistic austerity. Increasing devotion to the Crucified, nourished in part by artistic representation of an emaciated and bleeding Figure; the Pauline dichotomy of flesh and spirit, seriously distorted by Platonic and later gnostic dualism; scriptural references to fasting and celibacy — these, combined with revulsion against coarser social mores, encouraged more and more intense self-mortification. Some Jewish, and some gnostic sects too, practised an asceticism which certain in the church did not wish to fall below. The early fathers therefore were quite prepared to call believers to austere and costly discipleship —

The counsel of *Didache*, to abstain from fleshly lusts and fast regularly, is continued in *Hermas* and *Didascalia* (though Barnabas, Justin Martyr, Hermas, and Clement of Alexandria, warn against attaching to fasting itself, without a pure heart, any religious merit[4]). *"2 Clement"* treats of the moral combat with weapons of penitence, fasting, almsgiving and love. *Clement of Alexandria* urges self-discipline and restraint in enjoyment. *Origen's* counsel is darkened by increasing rigour, voluntary poverty, stricter abstinence, to regain a lost heavenly existence. *Tertullian* later became more rigorist, insisting upon a "perfectionist" church. *Lactantius* sounds almost "Puritan" in his evaluation of moral conflict as bringing out the best in self-discipline, preparing the soul for eternal life.

But there is nothing in these ealier writings of the self-torturing asceticism which distorted Christian morality so violently that it must be counted an aberration rather than a development. St. Simeon Stylites, living at the top of a pillar for forty years, must be as unlike Jesus as it is possible to be. Jerome, praising the monk uncombed, unwashed ("since washed by Christ"), in rags, denying all natural feeling within the family, admiring only virginity, reveals the fanatic mind that could contribute nothing permanent to Christian ethics save the salutary warning that is the self-refutation of asceticism —

"In my youth, when the desert walled me in I was still unable to endure the promptings of sin and the natural heat of my blood; my mind still surged with evil thoughts . . . I used to sit alone . . . filled with bitterness . . . my skin from long neglect black. Tears and groans my portion . . . nothing but cold water . . . in fear of hell . . . no companions but scorpions and wild beasts, I often found myself amid bevies of girls, the fires of lust bubbling up . . . Helpless, I cast myself at the feet of Jesus . . . and subdued my rebellious body with weeks of abstinence."[5]

Lecky protests: "A sordid, emaciated maniac, without knowledge, patriotism, natural affection, passing his life in useless self-torture, quailing before the ghastly phantoms of his delirious brain, had become the ideal of nations which had known the writings of Plato and Cicero, and the lives of Socrates and Cato."[6] Solitude, idleness, violent self-mortification, dragging of weights, walling oneself up for years, living at the bottom of a well, wallowing in a mosquito-infested marsh, going about on all fours — all are mentioned by Inge as ways in which individuals have shown devotion to Christ. "Augustine, who was a gentleman and a cultivated man, advises some nuns not to wash frequently, but at the usual intervals, that is to say once a month."[7] One persistent form of self-infliction was flagellation, connected either with extreme penitence, or with hysterical mob-reaction to plague.

Wilful self-deprivation and self-torture is irreconcilable with a gospel of abundant life, freedom and joy. Obviously, more lies behind such an aberration than recoil from sexual permissiveness. Pathological guilt, refusing to accept in penitence and faith a free divine pardon, turned instead to self-punishment and mingled inverted pride with self-loathing — both entirely unchristian. Masochistic delight in self-inflicted pain is likewise no part of Christian trust in the loving goodness and compassion of God. The desire for self-mastery, to crush sin, is a better motive for the subjugation of unlawful desires, but when so practised as to concentrate all attention upon self-conquest, instead of upon self-understanding and positive self-fulfilment, it actually stimulates the passion it aims to crush. The philosophic dualism that underlay some asceticism has no place in the Christian view of the material world as created by God and redeemed by Christ. Mania for things ugly and repulsive is again no evidence of devotion, but the symptom of an unhealthy mind. One deeper motive for extreme asceticism was the desire to induce a sense of God's nearer presence in the mystic trance: fasting, prayer, and mental concentration, could help stimulate a sense of "blessedness"; where these failed, it was natural to intensify the process, at any cost, even though the desired reward became ever more remote. So Augustine held that ascetic principles are only means to an end: they do not become good because they are unpleasant, or because they crucify the flesh, but as ways in which more perfectly to serve God. For that end, moderation is often *better* than complete abstinence.[8]

A more sympathetic "explanation" of Christianity's divergence into fanatical asceticism suggests catharsis:

"That pagan civilisation had discovered . . . the mistake of nature-worship . . . inevitably producing things that are against nature . . . Sadism sat on a throne, brazen in broad daylight. The whole world was coloured by dangerous and rapidly deteriorating passions; by natural passions becoming unnatural passions . . . These people needed a new heaven and a new earth, for they had really defiled their own earth and even their own heaven . . . erotic legends were scrawled in stars . . . Let anyone who knows a little Latin poetry recall what would have stood in place of the sundial or the fountain, obscene and monstrous in the sun . . . Nothing could purge this obsession but a religion that was literally unearthly . . . Nothing but the stark supernatural stood up for its salvation. It was no good to preach natural religion to people to whom nature had grown unnatural . . . they knew what sort of demons tempted and tormented them; and they wrote across that great space of history the text, 'This sort goeth not out but by prayer and fasting . . .' The end of the era of asceticism was therefore the end of a penance; or if it be preferred, a purgation . . . A certain spiritual expiation had been finally worked out . . ."[9]

Allowing for Chesterton's rhetoric, that view of asceticism as a reaction from a defiled social imagination, the exorcism of inhuman vices by inhuman discipline, an exaggerated protest against exaggerated evils (a principle often exemplified in the history of morals), offers some excuse, not wholly devoid of truth, for a deplorable distortion of the Christian ethical tradition.

(2) MONASTICISM

Monasticism too, of course, was essentially an ascetic movement, but its asceticism was far more healthy than the solitary self-affliction so far described, if only because it was socially organised, more rational than pathological, and on the whole positively useful both to its devotees and to society. Those who despaired of civilising the new alien and violent peoples; those who reacted against the worldliness, political power, legalism, and discipline of the ecclesiastical system; those disillusioned by the vanity of the world and all earthly ambitions, or who feared the pressures of a decaying culture — all such sought refuge in the piety, brotherhood, and security of monastic retreat. For such, austerity and asceticism were a reasonable price for spiritual freedom, deeper experience, concentration upon supreme values, the vision of God. "The *summum bonum* of the monk was spiritual perfection in the contemplation and love of God, to be achieved by renunciation of the world and the uncompromising imitation of Christ."[10] In the west, as for Bernard of Clairvaux, "monasticism is the true Christianity, the monk the perfect Christian", and the monkish vow was sometimes put on a level with baptism.[11] R. A. Norris[12] considers that for the eastern church, too, the whole end of Christian life was the vision of God and the attainment of His image through purification and illumination. In consequence, he suggests, the eastern church turned away from the attempt to "baptise the social and political ideals of the Constantine empire", and sought separation.

For the monk, the call to self-denial and Christlikeness took the specific forms of poverty, chastity, and obedience. Private ownership was prohibited — "If a man calleth aught his own he maketh himself a stranger to God" wrote Basil.[13] A man would always be "possessed by his possessions", tied by them to the world's system of values, deflected by them from his spiritual vocation, tempted to seek security elsewhere than in faith. The vow of poverty implied also a protest against an age obsessed with luxury. Under Benedict's rule, corporate labour provided corporate food and clothing, "so that there may be no need for monks to go beyond the gates" — economics and immunity combining to make labour a form of piety. When this system made the monasteries affluent, Francis attacked it, committing his followers to corporate poverty also. The ideal was imitation of the Christ who had no where to lay His head, who called disciples to provide "no purse, no scrip, nor two coats . . ."

The free, gay spirit of this vow is well caught in Chesterton's description of the wealthy soldier-about-town, Francis, stripped to his hair-shirt, tossing all he possessed on the top of his discarded finery, and going out "penniless, parentless, to all appearance without a trade or a plan or a hope in the world; and as he went . . . he burst suddenly into song." Said a later Franciscan, "A monk should own nothing but his harp."[14]

The vow of chastity implied, beside renunciation of the flesh, the renunciation of domestic love as distracting from divine love, from ultimate satisfaction in God. Benedict assumed celibacy, and the need to keep this healthy provided another reason for manual labour. Here, too, the earthly example of Jesus provided the pattern; but some feeling that sex involves exploitation, and again the need for protest against prevailing laxity, underlay the vow. Equally strong was reverence for one's own psychical nature — the will to keep mind and spirit clear of passion, that the vision of God might be unclouded. Hence not sexual purity alone, but abstemiousness in food, drink, talk, comfort, sleep, were included in monastic "chastity".

The vow of obedience renounced self will — important in a community bound in closest intimacy for life, but also the road to humility and the antidote to self-assertive pride, the origin of all sin. Said Thomas à Kempis "It is more beneficial to live in subjection than in authority; to obey is much safer than to command."[15] Those who are tempted to add "and much easier" have probably never tried it. Once more the example of Jesus, living under a constant sense of divine compulsion, provides the motive; the "kingdom" of God and the Lordship of Christ plainly imply such surrender. But Benedict speaks also of the "bright and all-conquering *weapons* of obedience".[16] A man seeking refuge from his own weakness, wilfulness, and folly, might in some hour of dedication surrender to the direction of a superior he could trust, feeling that he was imitating Christ's obedience, and placing himself in a secure way to salvation. It was no small attraction of the threefold vow that it rendered a man practically invulnerable.

In the east, asceticism tended to preserve individuality, giving more attention to art, liturgy, and pilgrimage, than to community organisation. In the west, Basil made the religious community the sphere of Christian virtue; monastic settlements became centres of culture, education and evangelism — work, study and worship being the daily programme. The rule of Benedict emphasised precisely those aims — celibacy, poverty, communism, intellectual and liturgical concentration — which could only be pursued in specialised communities. These necessarily tended to become parasitic, minority-groups following their vocation to seek the perfect Christian way. The monk held that "God hath called us into this holy religion for the salvation of the world, and has made this compact between the world and us, that we should give it good example and it should provide for our necessities,"[17] So long as this "compact" worked, the monasteries remained living examples of how one form of the Christian ideal could be followed in wholly religious communities, providing refuges for the hard-pressed, centres of education for leadership, protests against materialism and sensuality, and offering intercession for the world "outside", which they renounced but did not despise. In a curious way, the *eschatological* dualism of the apostolic church (living between two ages), which had given place to the *metaphysical* dualism of the ascetics (living between two worlds), now gave place again to a *social* dualism — living between two types of society, one wholly religious, the other wholly secular.

The Christian monastic movement arose in flight from the Decian persecution (late 3rd century) and grew in power throughout the Middle Ages, being repeatedly reformed and developed, by Benedict (6th century), "Augustinians" and Cluniacs (10th), Cistercians (12th), Dominicans (13th), and largely transformed into a mobile preaching crusade by Francis (13th). *Benedict's* all-embracing *Rule* enjoined labour, reading, moderate asceticism, and forbade social distinctions. His high standard made the monasteries homes of learning, and treasuries of precious manuscripts. *Gregory* saw monastic life as one long penance. God forgives our sin, but we must expiate the punishment, making satisfaction for doing what was *not* allowed by abstaining from what *is* allowed — compensating for sin by prayer, fasting, almsgiving, celibacy, poverty. Diligent imitation of Christ becomes the crux of personal salvation. *Francis d'Assisi* renewed the movement, returning to Benedict and the Gospels. Again the ideal is "what Jesus did". Inge speaks of Francis' "nature-mysticism" (itself recalling Jesus — the pure soul rejoicing in the Father's world). Hardy speaks of Francis' vocation to follow "the naked Christ" in poverty and joy, going among the poor preaching peace, love and gladness. The enclosed monastery gave place to open pilgrimage, the "imitation of Christ" emerging from the cloisters as a "simplification of life". Friar Giles summarised the Franciscan ideal as "that which follows more closely than any other the footsteps and the ways of . . . our Lord Jesus Christ."[18]

To evaluate monastic ethics (apart from its flowering in mysticism) it is necessary to remember how the inner values of the movement persist in both Catholic and Protestant churches. The impulse towards communal expression of Christian life, the ascetic note of self-discipline and self-denial, the longing for a clearer vision of God, and the imitation of Christ, are not confined to any one Christian tradition. Lutheran deaconess-societies (such as Kaiserswerth), the Zoe Brotherhood in the Greek Orthodox Church, the various Anglican Church Orders and Abbey communities, the Bohemian Brethren and the Moravian Brethren in their rural settlements, the austere and close-knit groups of Puritans, modern communities at Taizé (Burgundy) and Iona, and even (in form, discipline, and public service) the Salvation Army, all preserve in varying form and degree values which the monastic movement strove to express. "History seems to show," says E. R. Hardy, "that the special monastic response to the call to leave all and take up the cross is, in one form or another, a permanent feature of the Christian life"; though, as Beach emphasises, a wide gulf separates the mediaeval concept of a "religious" society, isolated from the secular world as an end in itself, from the modern activist, socialised, worldly, democratic spirit.[19]

(3) MYSTICISM

The monastic life was never intended, however, to be an end in itself, but only (in Benedict's phrase) the beginning of conversion. The monastic rules were designed to cultivate inward self-denial, purity, and love for God; outward poverty, chastity, obedience were but symbols of a total inner approximation to the likeness of Christ, itself an element in the inner apprehension of His divine life. In this sense, mystic idealism continually inspired, reformed, and renewed monastic practice.

The monastics' aspiration centred in the soul's deep intimacy with God. Moral purification, purgation ("the dark night of the soul"), and surrender, were steps toward indentification of the will with God, and ecstatic absorption in the love of God. Such identification and absorption never (in truly Christian mysticism) led to loss of self-identity in God, but to a unity of wills, and a joy of soul, that remained conscious, moral, fully personal. Sometimes more intellectual and contemplative, as in the eastern church, sometimes more moral and emotional, as in the west, Christian mysticism ever retained a clear ethical impulse and vision.

Augustine included knowledge with love in the way to God; Benedict and Cassiodorus furthered this intellectual emphasis. Hugo of St. Victor also counselled contemplative discipline. Richard of St. Victor analysed contemplation into "enlargement, elevation, ecstasy" — and this "rapture" loses touch with historic salvation; the spirit forgets all, including its moral task in the world; "reason dies in giving birth to ecstasy". Bonaventura moves on to "immersion in God, a mental and spiritual ecstasy . . . possible only to the higher Christian life." Bernard, on the other hand, declares: "only by the movement of my heart have I been aware of Him. In the reformation and renovation of my mind and spirit . . . I have seen the fashion of His beauty."[20]

The mystics' goal is that the soul "might look at God without anything in between . . . unconscious of the knowing-process, or love, or anything else" (Eckhart).[21] The mystic is sure that God is there, and is good; that the spiritual order is prior to the material, sensible world, and can be achieved only by negation of the world of sense. He believes that encounter with God is meanwhile transient, alternating between eternal and temporal worlds; and that the means to the beatific vision are not sense, or reason, but intuition, perceptiveness, spiritual sensibility, faith. Tinsley well summarises, "The teaching of mainstream Christian mysticism has been . . . that what we are speaking about is the life of prayer in which *all* may engage . . . There is an authentic mysticism . . . which plays an important role in preventing religion from being reduced to a moralism."[22]

Bernard of Clairvaux, held the earthly life of Jesus to be the object of most devoted study, alongside the immediate mystical relation of the soul to Christ, the heavenly Bridegroom. Humility (the way to purgation and to charity) and love (analysed in four stages, leading to unity of will with God) are the appointed ways of communion with God. The reason for loving God is God Himself; the way to love Him is beyond measure; the highest of all love for Him is *disinterested* — seeking nothing in return — an important contrast to monastic theories of meritorious penance.

Anselm's inward devotion to God and to "dulcis Jesu" were based upon Christ's humility and self-surrender as our Example (more than upon forgiveness through His death). The divine love shown in His life evokes an answering love, that imitates His life, especially in mystic contemplation. Moral tasks, the worth of this life, fall into the background; a subjective state of feeling ("grace of tears") becomes an end in itself. Ascetic self-denial must compensate for constant interruptions in our communion with God.

Eckhart, "greatest of all speculative mystics", held that final appeal must always be not to history but to the deepest part of my own being. The "apex of the mind", akin to God, is a power, an uncreated light, a divine spark, by which God reveals Himself to us, and unites Himself with us.

"Reasonable knowledge is eternal life", but "how can external revelation help unless it be verified by inner experience?" When Eckhart speaks of the imitation of Christ, "he distinguishes between 'the way of the manhood' (including imitation of the earthly life of Christ) which has to be followed by all, an elementary stage; and 'the way of the Godhead', for the mystic only. "Imitation of Christ" is here changing from emulation of the Galilean Example to an inward experience of the living Christ within the soul — "God begets His Son in me". Nevertheless, "it is better to feed the hungry than to see even such visions as Paul saw". Eckhart insists on the importance of the good will — "If your will is right you cannot go wrong" — so moving from the merit of the thing done to the personal worth of the doer.

Renunciation of the world is, first and last, an inward matter; if a monk has truly overcome the world within himself, his observance of vows is of minor importance. "Disinterest" (detachment) is the highest virtue: God comes to perpetual birth in the soul only as men first empty themselves of all temporal, sensual love, willing nothing, desiring nothing, knowing nothing.[23]

With Thomas à Kempis this "spiritualised" imitation of Christ reaches full self-consciousness. *The Imitation of Christ* "the best known classic of monastic spirituality" (Hardy), (reputedly by à Kempis) contains counsel on interior dispositions, and on Holy Communion, expressed mainly through dialogue with the Christ of inner experience, instead of resting upon emulation of the earthly Example. Self-denial, renunciation, prayer meditation, humility, and purity are the road to joy and peace. Though the cross of Christ is kept in view, there is evident an indifference towards human affairs, a shunning of society, which evades confrontation and makes little contribution to the service of men. Inge's verdict, "the book cannot safely be taken as a guide to the Christian life" shows how far "imitation of Christ" could depart from the divine Example.[24]

Tauler emphasised the need of grace and of forgiveness but held that progress depends on "being loosed from all selfness," being submerged, "melting" in God — a position close to pantheistic mysticism, which loses the creature in the Absolute Being. So, Suso called Christians, by the repetition of Christ's sufferings, to rise above sense, natural powers, desire, and imagination. "All perfection ends where the soul is received with all its powers into the Only One, which is God"; where God is known *immediately*, not mediately through historical salvation.[25]

In evaluating the ethics of mysticism (i) the contrast between mystic and activist must not be overdrawn. The suspicion perseveres that mysticism is self-centred, "noticeably feeble in its social ethic". Tinsley assembles judgements like Oman's "it has no message for the toiler" and Richard Niebuhr's "unavailable for the burden-bearers of the world".[26] Yet others speak eloquently of the mystics' social concern. Bernard, "one of the busiest executives of twelfth-century Europe," held that prayers without deeds of mercy are inane idleness, breaking the true rhythm embracing sacred repose and necessary action. Work and worship are diverse expressions of a single will, a single love.[27] Says Inge, "All the great mystics have been energetic and influential, and their business capacity is specially noted in a curiously large number of cases", citing Plotinus, often in request as guardian and trustee; Bernard, a gifted organiser; Teresa, founder of convents and extraordinarily practical administrator; as was Juan of the Cross. John Smith was an excellent bursar of his college; Fénelon ruled his diocese extremely well; Madame Guyon showed surprising aptitude for affairs; Henry More was offered posts of high responsibility.[28] Tinsley adds to the list of socially active mystics, Catherine of Siena, Francis d'Assisi, Ignatius Loyola. Beach says that Eckhart was much in demand as preacher as well as vicar of a large province, quoting: "What a man takes in contemplation he must pour out in love . . ." and "If a person were in such a rapturous state as St. Paul once entered, and he knew of a sick man who wanted a cup of soup, it would be far better to withdraw from the rapture for love's sake and serve him who is in need."[29]

Here again, post-Reformation developments have often preserved some of the values of pre-Reformation experience. The emphasis of the Society of Friends upon the Inner Light, "the Christ within", making ministry and sacraments superfluous, is the Protestant heir to mediaeval mysticism. Eckhart's "When a person has a true spiritual experience, he may boldly drop external disciplines"[30] is the very text of Quakerism. But side by side with it has persisted a social concern for prisoners, the poor, the wounded, and for world peace, that has been an inspiration to the whole church. The truth is, that Christian mysticism may best be judged precisely by the measure in which the intellectual insights and emotional energies which it generates are seen to nourish ethical endeavour and social achievement.

(ii) To evaluate the ethics of mysticism (and of monasticism) it is necessary also to appreciate fully the mediaeval passion for the imitation of Christ. Taking up this formulation of the ideal from the New Testament ("following the example", "having the mind of Christ"), from the early fathers (the remembered Figure whose word still has authority and whose portrait fascinates), from the ascetics (who emulated mainly Christ's renunciation and suffering) and the monasteries (who sought an outward likeness to Christ's chastity, poverty, and obedience), the mystics intensified the idea and re-interpreted it yet again. As Luthardt expresses it, "the imitation of Christ became the catchword of the Middle Ages": we have heard that catchword in Gregory, Francis, Bernard, Anselm, Eckhart, à Kempis. On the whole, western mystics turned to the example of Christ in suffering, humility, poverty, purity, wisdom; to the Leader, to whom we must be grateful; and to the Perfect One who "goes before us in the way of the virtues".

Plainly, the meaning of "imitation of Christ" varies as either inward or outward likeness is aspired to, and also as one or another feature of Christ's earthly life is selected for emulation. In Bernard, study of that earthly life alongside the inward relation of the soul to the heavenly Bridegroom shows the "imitation" concept in process of retranslation once again. Anselm sees Christ saving men through His example; but Eckhart sees imitation of the earthly Christ as only the first stage towards assimilation of the living Christ within the soul. That inward assimilation is then paramount in à Kempis — "in the life of Christ to meditate . . . and be conformed." Bernard, Abelard, Suso, and indeed most of the church, focused reverent imagination especially upon the sufferings of Christ, to evoke "the devotion of compassion". More broadly, one Franciscan eulogy traces no less than forty resemblances between Francis and Christ.

Thus, variously interpreted, "the Christian constant" — imitation of Christ — persisted through the Middle Ages when so much else in Christian ethics was changed. Unexpectedly, despite the sharp separation of sacred from secular, there persisted also that practical compassion for the poor, defenceless and oppressed which had been as prominent in the first three centuries as in the Gospels. Perhaps in no era, save that of the apostles, have men so striven to live the Christian life at its highest excellence as in the Middle Ages. The manifold tensions which then developed — between the perils of the world and the claims of the world; between withdrawal from men and the service of men; between renunciation of life and longing for fullness of life; between outward conformity to rigid rules and inward contemplation, the vision of God; between conformity to the historical Galilean pattern and inward imagination of the living Christ; between corporate, organised obedience and individual freedom — would all appear to be native to the many-sided Christian ideal. "Imitation of Christ" clearly does *not* solve every Christian moral problem. But it is both fascinating and forbidding, rigorous and ecstatic, imperative and impossible. And so long as men trust, love and worship Christ, they will go on trying in some sense to resemble Him.

5

Augustine: Christian Moral Philosophy

A MODERN HISTORIAN SPEAKS of the sixteen centuries that *unite* us to Augustine, centuries "penetrated through and through with Augustine's presence, his glory, and influence."[1] Though he has been called "the greatest of the early moralists"[2], his thought is so far-ranging, that to isolate his teaching upon morality is inevitably to oversimplify; while it is always necessary to keep in mind the circumstances, and the controversies, amidst which his thought took shape.

Thus Augustine's preoccupation with evil, grace, the processes of salvation, and the place of the city of God within the social milieu springs from "the troubles of the dying empire" — widespread corruption, suffering and death. Superstition, and sometimes violent strife, marked the church, and both people and clergy needed severe warning against sorcery, immoral shows, abortion, adultery, usury, magic, perjury, amulets, gluttony, abduction and paederasty.[3] To understand Augustine's approach to ethical questions, and especially his argument by definitions and the examination of all logical possibilities, it must be remembered that he came to Christianity by way of Latin philosophy and rhetoric, with its ethical concern in Cicero and Porphyry, strengthened by the Christian Platonism of Ambrose.

Similarly, it was ascetic Christianity that determined the pattern of Augustine's conversion. His fifteen years' faithfulness to one mistress was meritorious, rather than outrageous, by pagan standards; his stealing pears is more a prank than a step to perdition. Yet "the moral crisis of his conversion was a struggle between his sexual passions and the shaming examples of Christian asceticism";[4] its apparently miraculous circumstances emphasised the supernatural nature of divine grace; while salvation clearly involved for him fleeing "from all that is bodily" — "the only thing that held him back (from becoming a Christian) was his inability to live in continence."[5] It is not surprising that a soul so conditioned should interpret the challenge of Christianity as a call to "make no provision for the flesh, but put on the Lord Jesus Christ". Almost immediately, Augustine founded a small monastic group observing moderate asceticism, voluntary poverty, and chastity. This context of conflict and sexual renunciation in which his Christian life began, undoubtedly coloured all of Augustine's thought about morality, the inheritance of original sin through concupiscence, and the need for overwhelming, invading grace if any man is to be saved.

Controversy affected Augustine's thought by hardening his theological positions, sharpening his definitions, sometimes driving him to extreme positions; it also determined the areas of his most vigorous thinking — sin, free will, grace, predestination, the nature of God, the purpose of God in history — so providing the theological and religious background of his ethical teaching.

(1) CONTROVERSY

Augustine was deeply involved in three major contentions, each affecting his ethical outlook.

(A) Against Manicheism, which attempted to solve the problem of evil by positing an evil agency eternally opposed to the good and to God, so that the only hope of extrication from evil was by an ascetic life, Augustine offered two replies. (i) He asserted the essential goodness of all creation, made and sustained by the good God. This conflicted, as Burnaby shows,[6] with Augustine's tendency to regard the flesh and material existence as evil in itself, but the Creator being identified with goodness, everything must be good as existing in Him. Creation exhibits a *graded* order of being and goodness: inanimate things, living creatures, the mind in man above the body, the human soul at its purest — the image and likeness of God, by taking our stand on which we may discover at the summit the Being who alone is supreme, God Himself.[7] This view not only moulds Augustine's ethics, it underlies his own delight — so alien to dualism — in the world about him.

Augustine often descants eloquently on man's wisdom, reason, art, weaving, building, agriculture, pottery, painting, sculpture, theatres, cookery, rhetoric, literature, song and physical beauty.[8] While renouncing the world, he reveals his pleasure in lovely things — "What do I love, when I love you O God? Not a beautiful body, nor a fine climate, nor the clear light which — just look! — is so dear to these eyes, nor the lively tunes of songs and ditties, nor the sweet smells of flowers and perfumes and spices, nor manna, nor honey, nor limbs it is agreeable to take in close embrace . . ." — "the music of his words," says Marrou, "conveys the thrill of his emotions in face of these earthly joys, so appealing to the frail heart of man."[9]

Yet nothing must distract from love for God: "no part of our life is to afford room to enjoy some other object."[10] "On our way to our happy fatherland, we have no right to linger, enjoying the beauty of the country we pass through, nor the charm of the journey", nor knowledge, nor aesthetics, for their own sake. The convert "remembers that he has sinned. Because he had for too long wandered, estranged from God, he now violently exorcises the love of those far-winding ways." Having once loved music too much, he now reproaches himself for savouring too pleasurably the liturgical chants! In part too, Augustine's rejection is of a culture in decadence. But all this is far removed from the typical dualist rejection of the world of the senses as evil in itself. A man may be distracted by the beauty of the world from the love of God, but it is beautiful, and God's creation, for all that.[11]

(ii) Augustine also replies to the Manichean doctrine of a positive evil principle, that evil is essentially the *privation* of some good that ought to be. Physical evil is *absence* of perfection in mere creatures; moral evil arises from man's *failure* to choose rightly. Since everything that exists is made by God, evil can have no positive existence; it has no substance, but is a hole (as it were) in the tissue of being, something missing — as blindness is lack of sight, so vice is lack of virtue. The privation of good is a real fact, with serious consequences: but "the good alone has reality; the evil is measured by the absence of the good."[12]

Evil is not a substance; if it were, it would be good. All things that exist, seeing that their Creator is supremely good, are themselves good: but their good may be diminished. However diminished, it is necessary that *some* good should remain, to constitute its being — the good which makes it a being cannot be destroyed without destroying the being itself. If it should be completely consumed by corruption, there will then be no good left because there will be no being . . . Every being therefore is a good; a great good if it cannot be corrupted, a little good if it can.[13]

This relieves God of having created evil. But, as Wheeler Robinson says, the privative theory of evil does not do justice to the positive character of evil in human experience. Augustine virtually passes to a positive conception in his doctrine of the evil *will*. "I asked what wickedness was; and I found that it was no substance, but a perversity of will, which turns aside from Thee, O God, the supreme substance, to desire the lowest."[14]

"If it be asked, What was the cause of their evil will? — there is none . . . When the will abandons what is above itself and turns to what is lower, it becomes evil — not because that is evil to which it turns, but because the turning itself is wicked. Therefore it is not (some) inferior thing which has made the will evil; it is itself which has become so, by wickedly desiring an inferior thing."[15]

Henceforth "the fallen will can produce nothing but evil from a religious standpoint; it remains free to express its evil nature, and always does so."[16] Thus *man* is responsible for evil. The power of intelligent choice, in which man shows likeness to God, also makes possible the negation of good, the turning from God to the inferior good, and the enslavement to the flesh, in pursuit of *enjoyment* of physical goods which God intended only for *use* — an important distinction for Augustine.

Illustration, and proof, of this enslavement lies for Augustine in the *compulsiveness* of sexual desire. "Instead of maintaining the goodness of the sexual instinct . . . his own experience of it as uncontrollable passion led Augustine to pronounce it . . . an evil, only to be converted into good when treated not as an end, for the pleasure it gives, but as the means of procreation." (Burnaby)[17]

The resulting ambivalence — creation is good, to be enjoyed in passing, but yet by man's choice of lesser good becomes (in one whole area of experience) an evil, not to be enjoyed but only used — is doubtless the result of thinking in controversy.

(B) Against Pelagius, Augustine pursued the analysis of will and responsibility, so central to Christian ethics; and also, the entire dependence of all good upon the free, prevenient, operating and co-operating grace of God.

Pelagius, "a British monk of high character and earnest morality," emphasised the need for virtuous effort, the truth of human freedom and responsibility, as the basis of Christian morality. For this reason Pelagius often wins the sympathy of Christian moralists, and the difference between his position and Augustine's is ethically important.[18]

Here, eastern emphasis on human freedom comes into conflict with western emphasis on human sinfulness, the need for divine grace. Pelagius stood for freedom, the possibility at any given moment of choosing either evil or good: "We have implanted in us by God a possibility (of action) in both directions."[19] This seemed essential to any real virtue or freedom: "to be able to do good is the vestibule of virtue, and to be able to do evil is the evidence of liberty."[20] Grace, therefore, for Pelagius, consists in the gifts of natural creation, including the possibility of sinful choice, the gift of instruction, by law or by Christ, forgiveness given in baptism — all the illumination and "external" help which makes easier the good choice, while leaving the will free, and responsible.

In contrast, Augustine stood for free will in the sense that *nothing outside the will coerced its choices*; it suffered no external constraint, from God, goodness, or evil. But ever since man first chose a lesser good the will has been *inwardly* self-corrupted, and remains free now from external constraint only to express its own evil nature.[21] As we have seen,[22] no nature created by God is evil, nor if it became totally corrupt would it continue to exist. "No person is evil by nature, but whoever is evil is so because of a fault,"[23] a fault which so corrupts the will that it can no longer choose freely between real alternatives of good and evil. Adam's original wrong choice left the will free only to express its sinful self — free still from outward constraint but not from its own, now evil, nature. Augustine does greater justice than did Pelagius to the real dimension of human responsibility. Complete indeterminism does not belong to man; character, experience, past choices all affect the will with which he chooses. Choice is not unmotivated, nor is any man wholly free from social and inherited influences, though his final reaction to them is his own. Nevertheless, Augustine's doctrine of freedom only to express the self you have become, would be wholly pessimistic, but for his compensating view of grace.

For Augustine, grace is no mere outward influence and opportunity, but an internal dynamic: "it is not by law and doctrine uttering their lessons from without, but by a secret and wonderful and ineffable power operating within, that God works in men's hearts . . . good dispositions of the will."[24] By such internal grace, the will is freed from its tendency towards evil, and enabled to choose the good.

> "The grace of God . . . must be understood as that by which alone men are delivered from evil, and without which they do absolutely no good thing." "Nothing whatever pertaining to godliness and real holiness can be accomplished without grace" . . . "what good work can a lost man perform . . .? Can they do anything by their own will? God forbid. For it was by the evil use of his free will that man destroyed both it and himself . . . He who is the servant of sin is free to sin: he will not be free to do right until, being freed from sin, he shall begin to be the servant of righteousness. This is true liberty — for he has pleasure in the righteous deed. It is at the same time a holy bondage — for he is obedient to the will of God. But whence comes the liberty to do right to the man who is in bondage except he be redeemed by Him who has said, 'If the Son shall make you free, ye shall be free indeed'? Before this redemption is wrought in a man, when he is not yet free to do what is right, how can he talk of the freedom of his will and his good works?" — "For it is God who worketh in you both to will and to do of His own good pleasure."[25]

With the theological accompaniments of this emphasis — "original sin", predestination, the doctrine of the "fall" — ethics is not directly concerned. But the reassertion of moral responsibility, of the possibility of recreating personality at its centre by the free, self-moving grace of God, and of salvation by the work of God alone, was axiomatic in Augustine's moral philosophy. "This emphasis on the will, and its inherent impulse towards self-realisation, is the new and epoch-making feature in the psychology of Augustine. The *good* will realises itself in freedom through the love of God, which is inspired within by grace; the *evil* will also realises itself in freedom, through the love of self, which is characteristic of its fallen state. In this way Augustine replaces the metaphysical dualism of matter and spirit, by the ethical and religious dualism of sin and grace"[26] The Pelagian controversy made clear to Christians for all time that no element in man is untouched by sin, and no good in him is independent of grace.

(C) Against the Donatists, who demanded that the church be holy, those who had proved traitors in days of persecution being excluded, Augustine was compelled (i) to insist that the church was *one* through mutual charity, and holy, not because her members were blameless, but because her purposes are holy. The empirical church contains good and evil men: only at the End will the tares be rooted out, and the distinction of church from world become apparent. Until then, the church remains only partially Christian.[27]

Thus Augustine accepts the Christian double standard. The ideal is perfection, which Christians approach but never reach. Venial sins meanwhile are catered for by penitential discipline, and by attempting more than is required. For the latter, Augustine supports monasticism (though not the idleness it frequently involved), and the imitation of Christ in suffering and humility. The reward was contemplation of the supreme beauty of the divine.[28]

(ii) The Donatist controversy raised also the question of the use of force to suppress heresy. Augustine accepted the civil power as a part of divine providence, and so available to assist the church.

"It is indeed preferable . . . that men should be led gently to the worship of God by teaching rather than forced into it by punishment . . . But I have proved that many people profit by a preliminary dose of fear or force, which makes it possible for them to be taught something . . . While the best men are well guided by love, most men are still goaded by fear."[29]

This, the best justification that can be offered for religious persecution, is supported by the discipline advised in *Proverbs*, the fear often expressed by psalmists, and the phrase in *Luke* concerning those "compelled to come in to the sacred supper". To this is added the explanation that the church's appeal to the forces of the emperor was for protection; it was forestalled by the emperor's making illegal "the very existence of this monstrous heresy, lenience toward which, would be more cruel than their own savage barbarity." That argument has justified every kind of intellectual oppression.

Elsewhere, Augustine pleads for clemency for heretics, urging that the sufferings of God's servants should not be avenged on the principle of an eye for an eye — "not that we would stop you depriving such criminals of the opportunity to do wrong" but they should be curbed by law and reduced to sanity by solitary confinement. "It is more of a kindness than a punishment to hold in check their savage audacity."[30] Augustine deprecated the death penalty, and was glad that he had never inflicted worse than a flogging. So while sitting in judgement on the State, Augustine uses the State's support *when convenient*. Inge says, "Augustine was in favour of liberty of conscience while the Donatists held the ascendancy in Africa, but when the Catholics got the upper hand he frankly changed his mind."[31]

(iii) In this connection was coined one of the most famous sayings of Augustine. Beach[32] gives it in the form "Love God and do what you want", commenting "If one loved God truly, one would be constrained . . . to seek what God willed for the new particular situation." F. R. Barry[33] has the saying in the form "Love and do what you like", and comments that Augustine "could hardly have said anything more dangerous — or, should one say, more authentically Christian? The phrase is now . . . part of the stock-in-trade of the emancipated." Barry adds, that on the strength of "those six blessed monosyllables" Augustine appears to have become the patron saint not only of situation ethics, but of the "new morality" generally.

In fact, when use of State force against Donatists was bitterly criticised, homilies on the epistle of John were interjected into a series of sermons on John's Gospel, contending that it was right, *and loving*, to "compel them to come in" — to use compulsion in the service of love.[34]

"Charity may cause a man to be fierce, and wickedness (may cause him) to speak smoothly. A boy may be struck by his father, and have fair words from a slave dealer — it is charity that strikes, and wickedness that ingratiates. The actions of men are discerned only according to their root in charity . . . Some actions seem harsh, but are performed for our discipline at the dictation of charity. Thus a short and simple precept is given you once and for all: *Love, and do what you will.* Whether you keep silence, keep silence in love; whether you exclaim, exclaim in love; whether you correct, correct in love; whether you forbear, forbear in love. Let love's root be within you, and from that root nothing but good can spring."[35]

A later commentary by Augustine himself is significant:

"Hold fast then to love, and set your minds at rest. You need not fear doing ill to anyone, for who can do any ill to the person whom he loves? *Love, and you cannot but do well.* You may rebuke, but that will be the act of love . . . you may use the rod, but it will only be for discipline . . . hatred may use fair words and love may sound harshly . . . Search out the root from which they proceed."[36]

Burnaby describes this argument as the sad monument of an uneasy conscience, seeking to assure itself that the end justifies the means. Nevertheless, controversy has here thrown up a succinct and powerful statement of the criterion of all Christian action: "Love and do what you will . . . Love, and you cannot but do well." This may appropriately introduce Augustine's own ethical position.

(2) "EUDAEMONISM"

For Augustine makes love central to his moral philosophy. Though he speaks frequently of the eternal law of God, and of conscience as the implanted law of goodness,[37] his approach is not legalist, emphasising duty. The heart of morality is pursuit of what is *good*; and in so far as the attainment of what is good confers happiness, Augustine's ethic may be called "eudaemonistic".

"Morals — what manner of life must be held in order to obtain happiness . . ."[38] "All men love happiness . . . Perverse folk not only want wickedness without unhappiness, which is an impossibility, but they want to be wicked on purpose to avoid being unhappy . . . In all the wickedness men commit, they always desire happiness . . . For the sake of driving away unhappiness and obtaining happiness, all men do whatever they do, good or bad . . ."[39]

What matters is where men seek for happiness: to that extent Augustine sounds hedonist. But he has other criteria for the guidance of the good life: for example —

Seeking to prove that lies are *always* sinful, Augustine argues successively that the lie is a turning away from truth; it kills the soul — the spiritual cost is "destruction"; consequences must be weighed — telling a lie in jest, or breaking a promise to restore a sword when its recipient has gone mad, are admittedly less harmful; yet *accidental* good consequences do not make a lie less sinful; "religious lies", having eternal consequences, are most serious of all; the intention (the purpose to deceive) also affects our judgement of the lie; lies to save others from exposure, lies told out of kindness, are less heinous; but then it is not the action but the motive that can be praised.[40]

Here, considerations of intellectual valuation, spiritual cost, motive, consequences, are all weighed — it is not enough to seek "happiness", or even to "Love, and do what you will". In another passage, on matters which "do not admit of final decision by scripture or by the tradition of the universal church . . . there is no better rule than to conform to the practice prevailing in the church to which it may be his lot to come . . . for the sake of fellowship".[41] Plainly, a great variety of considerations enter into moral judgement. (i) But what Augustine calls "happiness" is spiritual satisfaction, only attainable by ardent love of the highest good. The tendency of the will to seek happiness is itself called "love"; the moral problem is not whether we should love, but what. Virtue lies in loving what one ought to love.[42] There is no happiness in the satisfaction of every random desire, while —

"No one can feel confident regarding a good which he knows can be taken from him . . . how can he be happy while in such fear of losing it?"[43]

But the only permanent object man *can* love is God. To love Him is happiness indeed.

Behind Augustine's exposition of the "scale of values" of objects man can love, lies the "graded order of being" and of goodness which he found within creation.

"All men love happiness . . . But you are a human being; whatever you covet as a source of happiness is inferior to yourself — gold, silver . . . You are more excellent, more important . . . Look for what is better than yourself: (not) physical beauty . . . what you are looking for is in the soul. You want to be happy — look for something better than your soul itself. . . Hence if your body's good is your soul, because it is superior to your body, when you seek your own good, seek that which is better for your soul. What will that be, except your God? You can find no *thing* of more worth than your own soul: higher there is nothing, save the Creator."

"The title 'happy' cannot . . . belong either to him who has not what he loves, or to him who has what he loves if it is hurtful, or to him who does not love what he has . . . The happy life exists when man's chief good is both loved and possessed . . . What is a man's chief good? It cannot be anything inferior to man himself: happiness consists in the enjoyment of a good than which there is nothing better — the "chief good", beyond which nothing remains for us to arrive at.

The chief good of the body, then, is not pleasure, absence of pain, strength, beauty, swiftness, but simply the soul, which supplies all. The soul is not the chief good of man, but . . . anything in following which the soul comes to perfection. The question is, what gives perfection to the soul? No one will question that *virtue* gives perfection to the soul: and that is produced in the soul by following after something. Only God remains, higher than the soul, following after whom we live well: in reaching whom we live happily.''[44]

The argument is close-knit and repetitive, but clear. By a theory of comparative values Augustine reaches what earlier thinkers long sought, the *summum bonum*, ''man's chief good''. A rightly ordered love, a rightly orientated will, depends upon a right judgement of value. ''Augustine examines'' in the *City of God* ''three types of finite good (bodily, psychic, social), and argues that none of these could wholly satisfy man's aspirations . . . God is the only goal worthy of man's efforts. The fitting end of human existence is a loving union with God.''[45] In this way, Augustine reaches the Christian law:

''Let us hear O Christ what chief end Thou dost prescribe to us . . . 'Thou shalt love' He says 'the Lord thy God' . . . What must be the measure of love . . .? — 'with all thy heart'. Nor is it enough yet — 'with all thy mind'. What does Paul say on this? — 'We know . . . that all things issue in good to them that love God' . . . This we must strive after; to this we must refer all our plans. The perfection of all good things, our perfect good, is God. We must neither come short of this, nor go beyond it; the one is dangerous, the other impossible.''[46]

There lies exposed the nerve of Augustine's ethic, and the heart of his religion. Such concentration of soul on God, the highest good, would reproduce the likeness of God in man. It constituted the essence of worship — ''of what is the worship of Him except the love of Him?''[47] Love for God is, again, the meaning of the cardinal Christian virtues:

''I hold virtue to be nothing else than perfect love of God: . . . temperance is love keeping itself entire and incorrupt for God; fortitude is love bearing everything for the sake of God; justice is love serving God only, and therefore ruling well all else; prudence is love making a right distinction between what helps it towards God and what might hinder it.''[48]

Love for God is no less the enjoyment of God — the ''thirst for God'' expressed by the psalmists, and the Platonic desire for the vision of ideal beauty both finding satisfaction in the possession of God. The famous words ''Thou hast created us for Thyself, and our heart knows no rest until it repose in Thee''[49] voice the essence of religion — deep, satisfying enjoyment of God, that sets the soul free from the love of illusory goods, and kindles rapture —

''Late have I loved Thee, O Beauty so ancient and so new, late have I loved Thee! And behold, Thou wert within and I was without. I was looking for Thee out there, and I threw myself, deformed as I was, upon those well-formed things which Thou hast made. These things held me from Thee . . . Thou didst call and cry out and burst in upon my deafness; Thou didst shine forth and glow and drive away my blindness; Thou didst send forth Thy fragrance and I drew in my breath and now I pant for Thee; I have tasted, and now I hunger and thirst; Thou didst touch me, and I was inflamed with desire for Thy peace . . . When I shall cleave to Thee with all my being, sorrow and toil will no longer exist for me, and my life will be alive, being wholly filled with Thee."[50]

(ii) The Christian law does not stop with love to God. "As this divine Master inculcates *two* precepts, the love of God and the love of our neighbour; and as in these precepts a man finds three things he has to love — God, himself, and his neighbour; and that he who loves God loves himself thereby; it follows, that he must endeavour to get his neighbour to love God, since He is ordered to love his neighbour as himself . . ." This pietistic argument for neighbourly love, arises because Augustine's logic leads him first to draw direct inference from the commandment. He soon describes other duties of love. For "wife, children, household, all within his reach" the Christian will do even as he would wish his neighbour to do for him. He will be at peace with all men, so far as in him lies. "And this is the order of this concord, that a man in the first place injure no one, and in the second, do good to every one he can reach." Primarily, his own household are his care but his love goes out to all — even to the evil. "The man who lives according to God will love the good and hate the evil. Moreover, he owes 'a perfect hatred' to evil men; not that he should hate the man on account of his fault, nor love the fault because of the man, but he should hate the fault and love the man. For when the fault is repaired, there will remain something that should be wholly loved and in no way hated."[51]

Augustine knows what "charity" means: an ordered love, in an ordered common life, finding expression in service:

Marrou's account of the astonishing busyness of Augustine's life best illustrates this: endless letters of counsel, innumerable lectures, catechumen-classes, daily celebration of liturgy and sacrament, the direction of works of charity, pleading with magistrates for offenders, care of orphans (including finding them husbands), administration of church lands and treasuries, daily administration of justice (in ecclesiastical, inheritance, wardship and property cases); in travelling, councils, preaching, negotiations, disputes and a truly enormous literary output.[52]

Augustine's "bishop's load" explains how he interpreted love of one's neighbour; why he insisted that it lay within the will (not the impulsive emotion); and why he so sharply criticises the idleness of many wandering monks. It also lends perfect illustration to his own comments:

"You should be thinking all the time, that God is to be loved and your neighbour . . . These are the two things to be thought about, kept in mind, carried out, *every minute of the day*. Loving God comes first in the issue of the order, but loving your neighbour first in carrying it out. He who gave you these two commandments would not of course put your neighbour first, God second. But you cannot yet see God — it is by loving your neighbour that you will first deserve to see Him. It is only by loving your neighbour that you can polish up your eyes to see God with, as St. John says, 'If you do not love the brother you see, how will you be able to love the God you do not see?' So, love your neighbour; then look inside yourself at what you love him *with*; then, as far as you can, you will see God. Begin by loving your neighbour. 'Break your bread to the hungry, bring the needy into your house; if you see him naked clothe him . . . Then shall your light break forth like the dawn . . .'(Isaiah 58:7f.)."[53]

Elsewhere, Augustine spells out the scope of love:

He who loves his neighbour does good, partly to the man's body and partly to his soul. What benefits the body is called medicine — everything that preserves bodily health — the art of the medical man, food, drink, clothing, shelter, covering, protection, taking the stranger into the house, freeing the oppressed, giving the dead burial. Augustine includes also "rare offices of the teacher, counsellor, of restraint and instruction".[54]

Much discussion surrounds the relation, for Augustine, of love of neighbour to love of God. In general, he interprets Christ's command in the light of the hierarchy of being. "Man shall love God alone, for Himself; and all other beings only in the measure that their intrinsic perfection allows them to be used in the service of that love for God. In God alone is it lawful to rest and have joy: all the rest we should only *use*, as instruments to this end."[55] This has been criticised as degrading love for the neighbour into a "means" whereby the individual is aided to achieve his own perfection. But perfection, for Augustine, includes being made like God, sharing in His nature as out-going, self-giving love, in response to love received: this is not to love the neighbour for one's own sake, nor merely "as oneself", but with divine love. In the end, Augustine defines the peace of the heavenly City as "the perfect union of hearts in the enjoyment of God and of one another in God".[56] Ramsey cites:

"(The apostle John) seems to have passed by the love of God in silence; which he never would have done, unless he intends God to be understood in brotherly love itself . . . This same brotherly love . . . (is said) not only to be *from* God but also *to be God*. When we love our brother from love, we love our brother from God. Whence it may be gathered that these two commandments cannot exist unless interchangeably. For since 'God is love', he who loves *love* certainly loves God; but he must needs love *love* who loves his brother'' —

and comments: ''the brother stands forth as a final object of love; he is loved through God, through love; there is here none of that 'loving God in the neighbour' which certain interpreters find in Augustine, and none of that 'loving the neighbour simply for the sake of loving God' which often seems to be Augustine's manner of speaking.''

''Neither let that question disturb us, how much love we ought to spend upon our brother and how much upon God: incomparably more upon God than upon ourselves, but upon our brother 'as much as' upon ourselves; and we love ourselves so much the more, the more we love God . . . We love God for the sake of God, and ourselves and our neighbours for the sake of God.''[57]

In sum:

''The first thing to aim at — be benevolent, cherish no malice, no evil design. As a man may sin against another either by injuring him or by not helping him; and as it is for these things that men are called wicked; all that is required is: 'The love of our neighbour worketh no ill.' If we cannot attain to good unless we first desist from working evil, *our love of our neighbour is a sort of cradle of our love to God* . . .''[58]

For in the end, ''He alone knows how to love who loves God.''[59]

(3) PRACTICAL COUNSELS

From Augustine's voluminous tracts, letters, sermons and treatises it is difficult to cull a representative selection of his practical counsel; but four issues upon which he helped to shape the historic Christian conscience, should be mentioned.

(a) Marriage

Augustine has no doubt that ''to multiply and replenish the earth in virtue of the blessing of God is a gift of marriage as God instituted it before man sinned, when He created two sexes manifestly distinct . . . for the very purpose of begetting offspring . . . It was . . . plainly of the matrimonial union that our Lord . . . said 'They shall be one flesh'.''[60] But virginity is sacred, too, higher than marriage, deserving a greater palm of glory. ''Certainly, neither Augustine nor his friends ever denied the lawfulness of this sacrament (of marriage) nor the possibility of sanctity in the married state,'' says Marrou[61]; ''if they turned from it, it was perhaps . . . because pagan civilisation had so fouled the very notion of sex." It is here that the circumstances of his own conversion, and the ascetic tradition of the church, plainly colour Augustine's thought:

"But I, miserable young man . . . had entreated 'Grant me chastity and continence, but not yet.' For I was afraid lest Thou shouldst soon deliver me from concupiscence, which I desired to have satisfied rather than extinguished."[62]

Burnaby holds that Augustine's theory of the transmission of original sin by way of sexual desire "has had a most disastrous influence upon much of traditional Christian ethics". In Augustine's intention, his great drama of the two Cities was not a conflict between flesh and spirit but between the love of God and the love of self. But it was read as encouraging rejection of this world's good for the sake of the world to come — "a rejection which runs counter to the central principles of Augustinian ethics."[63] Augustine's ambivalence concerning marriage became characteristic of the whole mediaeval church.

For all this, Augustine was aware of "the conjugal honour . . . well ordering a married life and sustaining children":

"Primarily . . . his own household are his care . . . This is the origin of domestic peace, the well-ordered concord of those in the family who rule and those who obey. For they who care for the rest, *rule* — the husband the wife, the parents the children, the masters the servants; they who are cared for, *obey* . . . But in the family of the just even those who rule serve those whom they seem to command; they rule not from love of power, but from a sense of the duty they owe to others — not because proud of authority, but because they love mercy."[64]

(b) Property, wealth

Augustine at sixteen had to interrupt his studies for lack of money until a friend offered assistance. Later, his doctrine of the scale of "goods" ensured that "earthly things" would always be kept in their place; his fundamental distinction between *enjoyment* and *use* defined the place of wealth as, at best, a means only towards the great end of life — the enjoyment of God. A sermon to business men deals forthrightly with the "itch for money-making" and with the perjury and avarice that can demean business life, craftsmanship, farming. Nor are the learned professions free of vice: students break faith with their teachers, and "for the love of money set a small value on justice, . . . not preferring the learning to the money."[65] To the monastery at Hippo Augustine brought "nothing more than the clothes that I wore at the time . . . As I sold my meagre little estate and gave it to the poor, so also did those who wished to live with me . . . In our community no one is permitted to own anything.''[66]

Luthardt summarises Augustine's attitude as recognising the right of private property. The vow of poverty is not essential to salvation. All the same, riches are a chain better shaken off: renunciation of possessions is higher than inward renunciation of the love of possessions — while retaining them.[67] Deane says that Augustine inherited the idea that private property came in with the fall of man. By divine right, the earth is the Lord's; rights of private possession emerge with systems of justice established by earthly rulers — and can be changed. (This strange argument defends the right of the State to confiscate Donatist property in north Africa!) As wealth is a danger, though not necessarily an evil, the most admirable course is common ownership — practicable only for monks and nuns. He who is not called to abrogate all possessions must still use his money in God's service. As to the desire for more, Augustine says, shrewdly, it is better to have fewer wants than greater riches to supply increasing wants. Wealthy Christians must possess their riches, not be possessed by them. Christ condemned covetousness, not wealth. Riches do no good: ''What certainly profiteth is a work of mercy done by a rich man *or a poor man* — one, with the will and the means; the other, with the will only.'' The rich use their riches to accomplish good works, but attribute their good works to the grace of God. Paul's counsel is to ''communicate — not to give the whole away, but to share. How much? — the Pharisees gave a tenth: consider what you do . . .''[68]

The rich man doing good is counted among God's poor: the poor man who is envious is guilty of avarice. Augustine has been criticised for teaching that almsgiving obtained forgiveness of lesser sins, and for the dead, bestowal of alms being placed side by side with the Eucharist for this purpose. But Augustine strictly confines this privilege to those whose lives were acceptable to God; and is especially indignant with those who would use their riches to ''expiate'' continuing sins:

> ''They say, he that hath showed mercy, though he has not reformed his dissolute conduct . . . shall have a merciful judgement. They suppose that by giving to the poor a small fraction of the wealth they acquire by extortion they can propitiate Christ, so that they may with impunity commit the most damnable sins . . . We ought to do alms that we may be heard when we pray that our *past* sins may be forgiven, not that while we continue in them we may think to provide ourselves with a licence for wickedness by alms-deeds.''[69]

Finally, like all the church before him, Augustine denounces usury in the widest sense and in the strongest terms. The whining plea of the money-lender he classes with the blandishments of the bandit, the seducer and the criminal.[70] The only permissible usury is to *give* to the poor and thus to give to Christ, who will repay far more than we have given.

(c) The State

The enthusiasm with which Ambrose had greeted the "Christian" State is modulated in Augustine, by longer experience of its weaknesses and dangers. Augustine held the State to be good, as part of the divine creation — yet only so far as it was just, and that included its worshipping the true God. The truly Christian State, therefore, was good: the State in itself could be evil.

Every ungodly nation "which did not obey the command of God that it should offer no sacrifice save to Him alone, which therefore could not give the soul its proper command over the body, nor reason its just authority over the vices, is void of true justice . . . Justice being taken away, what are kingdoms but great robberies? . . . That was an apt reply . . . given to Alexander by a pirate . . . Asked what he meant by keeping hostile possession of the sea, he answered, 'What thou meanest by seizing the whole earth; but because I do it with a petty ship, I am called a robber, whilst thou who dost it with a great fleet art styled emperor'."[71]

Augustine criticises as unrealistic Cicero's ideal State — "the weal of the people", united by justice and community of interests. There never was such a republic. Men defraud God of His due; Rome ruled only by injustice and subjection. Where there is no subjection to God, all just control is at an end, in individual and society; where there is no faith or love, there is no true "people", and no just society.[72] Natural law and universal reason afford no sufficient basis for peace and justice, because what should rule the body, and vice, and society, is itself not ruled by God; it possesses no authority, seeks only to obtain and keep its own interests, and is inflated with pride.[73] Such a society is ridden with the desire for honour, power, wealth; "justice" becomes the orderly pursuit of these common desires. The Christian, on the other hand, relates justice to man's highest end, love towards God, and so towards one's fellow-man — a higher conception altogether.

"And thus it has come to pass that, though there are very many great nations all over the earth . . . yet there are no more than two kinds of human society, two cities, according to the language of our Scriptures. The one consists of those who wish to live after the flesh, the other of those who wish to live after the spirit; and when they severally achieve what they wish, they live in peace, each after its kind."[74]

The earthly city is formed by love of self to the exclusion of the love of God; it seeks glory from men, is dominated by the lust for power, rejects true wisdom for the folly of idolatry. The city of God is in all particulars the direct opposite of the earthly city — but not its enemy:[75]

"Families which do not live by faith seek their peace in earthly advantages; families which live by faith look for eternal blessings . . . and use as pilgrims such advantages of time and of earth as do not divert them from God . . . the earthly city . . . seeks an earthly peace . . . the combination of men's wills to obtain what is helpful . . . The heavenly city . . . makes use of this peace only because it must . . . until this mortal condition . . . pass away. So long as it lives like a captive in the earthly city, . . . it makes no scruple to obey the laws of the earthly city (for the sake of the common mortal life). But as the earthly city has . . . many gods . . . and the celestial city one God only . . . the two cities could not have common laws of religion. The heavenly city has been compelled in this matter to dissent, and to stand the brunt of hatred and persecutions . . . This heavenly city . . . calls citizens out of all nations not scrupling about diversities in the manners, laws and institutions whereby earthly peace is secured . . . so long as no hindrance to the worship of the one true God is introduced. Even the heavenly city therefore, while in its state of pilgrimage, avails itself of the peace of earth, and . . . desires agreement among men regarding the acquisition of the necessaries of life . . . In its pilgrim state the heavenly city possesses the peace of heaven by faith, and by this faith it lives righteously."[76]

Clearly, the two cities are not to be identified with church and State. The State is not the organisation of sin, but an attempt to control it, to establish relative peace, order and justice; it possesses therefore moral purpose and dignity — though its end is a temporal happiness. The church, on the other hand, is the present appearance of the kingdom of God, transcending earth and time. To it, for the sake of the eternal values it enshrines, the State should be subordinate. Meanwhile, the Christian lives as citizen *both* of the pilgrim heavenly city and of the necessary, temporary earthly city. The memberships of the two cities "overlap".[77]

"Let this city (the pilgrim city of King Christ) bear in mind that among her enemies lie hid those who are destined to be fellow-citizens . . . So, too, the city of God has in her communion some who shall not eternally dwell in the lot of the saints. Of these some are not now recognised; others . . . you may today see thronging the churches, tomorrow crowding the theatres with the godless . . . In truth, these two cities are entangled together and intermixed until the last judgement effect their separation."[78]

Thus, for Augustine, the religious status of the body politic depends upon the extent to which it enshrines the values of the Christian faith. In itself it is earthly, temporal, useful for purposes of justice and peace but no absolute good. When it supports the inner elite community who love God it is good; when it fails to do so, becomes idolatrous, it is "Babylon", a sphere of "bad angels under its king".[79] Bainton remarks Augustine's "mournful" view of coercive activities of State — tortures, punishments, uncertainties of human justice, strife: "If then such darkness shrouds social life, will the wise judge take his seat . . .? That he will, for human society . . . constrains him to do his duty . . ." Like the prophets, Augustine believed in a transcendent, righteous God who would guarantee permanence to no human institution; like the apocalyptists, he centred his hope upon a new order, to be established by God.[80]

(d) Military Service

The attitude of the church towards war, says Inge, was to a large extent settled by Augustine, for both Catholic and major Protestant groups: Moffatt says his was "a steadying verdict", virtually authoritative, expressing the central good sense of the church.[81] Augustine's "moralisation of war" deserves therefore careful scrutiny.

It is wholly wrong to suppose Augustine militaristic. "Few writers in the early church speak more sternly of the callousness, the havoc and the senseless retaliation which war may breed. War for war's sake is wrong . . . ferocity and treachery are inconsistent with a Christian soldier's duty . . ." (Moffatt)[82] Moreover, Augustine ardently craves peace:

> "We may say of peace as we have said of eternal life, that it is the End of our good. For peace is a good so great that even in this earthly life there is nothing we desire with such zest. Even those who make war desire nothing but . . . to attain peace with glory. Every man seeks peace by waging war, but no man seeks war by making peace. *All* seek peace — conspirators, robbers, families, the most savage animals . . . Peace between man and God is the well-ordered obedience of faith to eternal law; peace between man and man is well-ordered concord . . . The peace of all things is the tranquility of order . . ."[83]

Nevertheless, since it is impossible for governments not to use force against invaders as against criminals, perfect peace is reserved for heaven.[84] Bainton cites the pleas of Augustine, faced with invasion, to the Roman general Boniface, who thought to retire and become a monk:

> "Not now . . . Monks indeed occupy a higher place before God, but you

should not aspire to their blessedness before the proper time. You must first be exercised in patience *in your calling*. The monks will pray for you against your invisible enemies. You must fight for them against the barbarians, their visible foes." For similar reasons, Augustine could praise God for military victories of Constantine and Theodosius. "A passion for doing injury, cruel revenge, a fierce and implacable temper, savage fury, the lust of power, and things like these, sum up what is rightly reprobated in war. It is generally to punish these crimes rightly that good men undertake war at all in obedience to God or some lawful authority . . . The Hebrew monarch wielded the sword on behalf of loyal piety, humility and justice . . . Tribute money (to be rendered to Caesar) is . . . for providing pay for soldiers . . . The natural order of things lays it down that a ruler has authority . . . to undertake war. It is wrong to doubt that war is righteous when undertaken in obedience to God, to overcome . . . human arrogance."[85]

"Peace ought to be your desire, war only your necessity, a means to secure peace."[86] The scriptural position is firmly defined: the Baptist did not condemn soldiers who came to him; Joshua was justified in using spies in a righteous war; David, and the centurions whom Jesus and Peter praised, show that military service is not forbidden. Peter was enjoined to put up his sword because he had no right authority to wield it. Gospel injunctions to love, turning the other cheek, refer to inward disposition towards the good of others. Sometimes the real interests of the aggressor require us to resist him. Elijah was warranted in calling down fire from heaven because he had love in his heart; the disciples were rebuked for wishing to do the like because of their vengeful intent. Moses, in putting to death sinners, was moved not by cruelty but by love, as was Paul in committing an offender to Satan. Love does not preclude severity, nor correction, nor wars of mercy waged by the good.

Augustine in no way abates the personal ethic of the sermon on the mount. He distinguishes between murder for selfish ends, judicial execution, self-defence and war. "The private citizen may not defend himself because he cannot do so without passion, and a loss of love": killing to prevent robbery or rape is unjust. "As to killing to defend one's own life, I do not approve, unless one happen to be a soldier or a public functionary acting in defence of others or of the city." Thus, without lowering the standard of individual good will, forgiveness, non-retaliation, Augustine yet makes clear to his own mind that defence of right, of others, of the State, and of God's purposes, may well make military service a Christian vocation. But the monk and the clergyman are not to share this vocation on any account.[87]

Augustine's other contribution concerning military service was to adopt finally into Christian tradition the Platonic and Stoic doctrine of the "just war", as a means of limiting war's evils and bringing justice into its conduct. The "just war" is the nearest Christianity comes to any conception like a "holy war".

The just war must be fought only for defence; as a last resort; it must be declared with adequate warning; the purpose must not be conquest, or power, but a just peace; prisoners and all who surrender must be spared; only soldiers may be involved: so Cicero.[88]

Christian ethics largely accepted this view, discussion focusing mainly upon its basis. In Augustine, several elements receive strong emphasis. "Righteous wars may be defined as wars to avenge wrongs, when a State has to be attacked for neglecting either to make reparation for misdeeds committed by its citizens, or to restore what has been wrongfully seized." A just peace is always desirable, and war may be legitimate to secure it, to reduce injustice. War should be waged only as necessity, and that through it God may deliver men from necessity and preserve them in peace. Even in war, the spirit of the peacemaker must be cherished. Just wars may include wars to defend safety, to avenge injuries, or in face of refusal to grant passage. To be "just", war must be waged only by the proper State authority; and its conduct must be just — keeping faith with the enemy, fulfilling promises, avoiding unnecessary violence, looting, massacre, vengeance, atrocities, reprisals. The temptations of the military life — especially to vengefulness and hate — must be met by deep personal devotion.[89]

The great weakness in every doctrine of "just war" concerns *who decides* what is just, and at what stage of history? Reflection, impartiality and hindsight make what is plainly "just" to one people appear wholly unjust from a wider point of view. War decides the comparative strength and character of peoples, rarely their truth and righteousness. Augustine sought to accept unpalatable realities — the State's necessities and dangers — while not abandoning Christian hopes of peace, mildness and gentleness, nor withdrawing Christian duty from involvement in public affairs. Not surprisingly, Ferguson claims that this case for Christian militarism rejects the pacifist tradition of the church in the first three centuries.[90]

All "summaries" of Augustine must be inadequate. Professor Cock[91] remarks, "St. Augustine represents the climax of Platonic spirituality . . . henceforth knowing and loving are . . . two ways by means of which the Christian soul progresses along the path of beatitude." Harnack finds Augustine's importance to lie "in his giving to the west, in the place of the Stoic-Christian popular morals, a religious, specifically Christian, ethics".[92] Warfield declared the most significant thing about him to be that "he first gave adequate expression to . . . the religion of faith as distinct from the religion of works, the religion which despairing of itself casts all its hope on God . . . religion in the purity of its concept as over against a quasi-religious moralism.''[93] To inward values, religious emphasis, and the necessity of grace, we may add one of the ten aphorisms of Augustine which Cock says have become the inheritance of the whole church: ''the sum of religion is to imitate Him who is the object of thy worship.''

This insight is repeatedly expressed in the long argument about worship in *City of God*.[94] Basic to Augustine's theology is the assumption that within man's soul is the image of God: ''the human mind contains that image; it received it, and by stooping to sin, defiled it; He comes to refashion it, who had first of all fashioned it . . .''[95]

''For man is made in the image and likeness of God — all the thought of the Fathers was as it were inspired by this verse from Genesis (1:26): in the human soul we may learn to discover the presence and the impress of God'' (Marrou).[96]

So, the closing paragraphs of the *Confessions* wind to this passage from Genesis — though here, as in *City of God*, the ''image'' is understood especially of the mind and its power to comprehend God.[97] So with religious exercises and Christian progress: true blessedness is the contemplation of God, the piety that is wisdom, and also worship. ''What is worship, except the love of Him, by which we now desire to see Him, and believe and hope that we shall see Him . . . face to face . . . 'when he shall appear, we shall be like him, for we shall see him as he is'.'' Hereafter, ''we shall see Him according to the measure in which we shall be like Him; just as now, we do not see Him according to the measure of our unlikeness to Him.''[98]

Christian worship, theology, contemplation, and hope, thus assume our approximation to the likeness of God — as known in Christ. It is true that, except in passages on worship, Augustine conceives the theme of the divine image in intellectual terms; but he provides, nevertheless, strong theological support for the mystics' more emotional concentration upon the imitation of Christ.

6

Abelard: Ethical Psychology

THE WAYWARD, BRILLIANT, CONTENTIOUS, ABELARD finds place in the story of Christian ethics partly because "through Peter Lombard's *Sentences*, founded on the model of Abelard's *Sic et Non*, Abelard swayed and moulded the theology of the next three hundred years."[1] Partly, too, because his provocative review of contradictory statements by the church Fathers — "the doctors of the church should be read without the necessity to believe but with liberty to judge" — and his very modern-sounding claim that the interpretation of scripture may err, or the text may be faulty, "had considerable effect in waking people from their dogmatic slumbers".[2] Such vigorous assertion of intellectual freedom affected Abelard's ethical teaching no less than his theology. Though, like Augustine, he faced the challenge of the gospel primarily in the area of sexual morality, his reaction to the traditional attitudes of the church was quite different. Abelard's ethical interpretation of the death of Christ, his commentary on Romans, and especially his treatise *Scito Teipsum* — "Know Thyself" — reveal his departures from conventional, Augustinian, moral philosophy.

Thus Abelard "summed up the spirit of a premature revolt against unreasoning authority . . . So great intellectually, so completely in advance of his age . . . that his positions were bound to seem heterodox to a generation that leaned wholly on the past, . . . Abelard in fact belonged to the future."[3] Of his pupils, twenty-five became cardinals, over fifty became bishops, one became pope; his theory of atonement determined the lines of most subsequent discussion of the death of Christ; while his special emphases in ethical theory have undoubtedly contributed, for good and ill, to the modern Christian conscience.

(1) THE MORAL THEORY OF ATONEMENT

A moral interpretation of Christ's death is certainly to be found within the New Testament and the Fathers, yet because of his concentration upon this theme, it is with Abelard's name that "the moral theory of the atonement" is usually associated. On this view, the death of Jesus saves men by the process of "love enkindling love".

"We are justified in the blood of Christ and reconciled to God by this singular grace exhibited to us, in that His Son took our nature, and in it took upon Himself to instruct us alike by word and example even unto death (and so), bound us to Himself by love; so that, kindled by so great a benefit of divine grace, charity should not be afraid to endure anything for His sake . . ."

"Every man . . . becomes more loving to the Lord after the passion of Christ . . . because a benefit kindles the soul into love . . . Our redemption, therefore, is that supreme love of Christ shown to us by His passion, which not only frees us from slavery to sin, but acquires for us the true liberty of the sons of God, so that we fulfil all things not so much from fear as from love of Him who exhibited so great favour towards us . . ."[4]

"Of this love the Lord says, 'I am come to cast fire on the earth . . .' So does He bear witness that He came for the express purpose of spreading this true liberty of love amongst men." "The apostle clearly expresses the mode of our redemption through the death of Christ, namely, He died for us to no other end than that true liberty of love might be propagated in us, through that loftiest love which He displayed to us."[5]

Abelard's central thesis in Romans, says Cave,[6] "is the cross as the manifestation of the love of God . . . The justification of man is the kindling of this divine love in his heart in the presence of the cross." "The efficacy of Christ's death is now quite definitely and explicitly explained by its subjective influence upon the mind of the sinner. The voluntary death of the innocent Son of God on man's behalf moves the sinner to gratitude and answering love — and so to consciousness of sin, repentance, amendment" (Rashdall).[7] The idea that Christ in His death paid a ransom to the devil is wholly wrong: the devil has no rights over us.[8] Equally wrong is any thought of expiation: "Indeed, how cruel and wicked it seems that anyone should demand the blood of an innocent person as the price for anything."[9]

Abelard reverts to more traditional language, to "sacrifice" and "expiation", only when expounding New Testament terms, or reproducing Origen's thought.[10] His central and characteristic interpretation is that no one has shown greater love than did Jesus in His death for men, that "He might draw our minds away from the will to sin and incline them to the fullest love of Himself." This "exemplarist" *aspect* of the death of Jesus is implied in every challenge to take up the cross with Christ, and to "follow His steps" of suffering. As a theory of atonement, it is insufficient: it fails to show *how* the death of Christ is an exhibition of love unless by dying Jesus accomplished something else for us that needed to be done. As Dale said, "God does not redeem us by revealing His love — He reveals His love by redeeming us."[11] Moreover, Abelard's view scarcely takes account of the guilt of sin, or of its power over many who would love like Christ if they could. Nevertheless, unless the cross of Christ has subjective effects within those who look to it for salvation, the whole concept of redemption, forgiveness, salvation, is emptied of ethical meaning. As R. S. Paul well says, "No conception of the atonement which does not have a central place for the truth that Abelard revealed can be true to the New Testament. We need to see our Lord as the human ideal and example, if only to understand how much we stand in need of grace."[12] And even so great a champion of an objective, Godward atonement as James Denney remarks "Abelard undoubtedly did great service in emphasising the love of Christ and the appeal it makes for love, and in *bringing the discussion back again from the metaphysical to the moral world*."[13]

Thus in Abelard's theology of the cross ethics is given once more its full place, in criticism of doctrine and in defining the meaning of salvation. The force of the example of Christ is likewise re-emphasised, as in the New Testament John and Peter had insisted upon it, and as Christian mysticism had seized upon it. One significant feature of Abelard's presentation was the concentration upon the humanity of Christ. H. R. Mackintosh[14] shows how catholic dogmatic has in the doctrine of Christ's *work* emphasised His humanity, while "practical piety, also, kept a firm grasp on the full manhood of Jesus, as is proved by the immense literature on the imitation of Christ . . . In essence this is true also of Abelard." H. B. Workman,[15] likewise, includes among the doctrines of special interest expounded by Abelard, the essentially real humanity of Christ, even to His sharing the infirmities and defects of ordinary humanity. As Christological doctrine receded into metaphysics, practical faith and piety, in Abelard's ethics, returned the more insistently to the moral example and inspiration of Christ's perfect life and death.

(2) ETHICAL INTENTION

Abelard's originality arose in part from his freedom from the Aristotelian influence, in part from reaction against Augustinianism, but mostly from his deliberate choice of a subjective basis for ethics. Breaking with the whole tradition of authoritative morality which runs through Jewish legalism, the New Testament commandments, the church's canon law, monastic rules, and penitential system, Abelard returned to Christ's appeal to purity of heart, the dedicated spirit, the free love of God; and to Paul's mind refashioned in the likeness of Christ. For Abelard, the underlying *intention* alone determined the moral quality of all behaviour. Outward conformity to social or ecclesiastical patterns may signify nothing of ethical virtue or fault: the subjective attitude is everything, the intensely personal inner discipline in which alone character consists. If an act is good, it is made so by its purpose; if it is evil, its bad intention makes it so: the sole difference between stabbing and surgery lies in the motive. Thus sin consists not in any act in itself, but in the consent of the will to what is done. It therefore becomes supremely important to "know thyself" — to understand one's own motives and inner purposes, upon which the whole quality of life entirely depends.

This principle was by no means peculiar to Abelard. Richard of St. Victor declares "A work without a good intention is like a body without life. That which appears to be good is still not good without this."[16] Anselm held that moral rectitude is a matter of the disposition of the human will; and justice, of "rightness of will".[17] Others had held no less firmly to the internal principle emphasised in the sermon on the mount. But Abelard made "the agent's will-act of consent" central to ethical judgement. The same act may be good or bad at different times in different circumstances by different actors or by the same actor on different occasions, according to the intention then prompting it, and *according to the moral situation*.

> "Morality is only grounded in that which stands within man's power, the *intentio animi*, not in the outward act, the performance or non-performance of which depends on circumstances that do not stand under man's control, so the completed action contributes nothing towards increasing the moral worth, which lies exclusively in the intention." "All actions are in themselves indifferent; the intention, only, gives them moral worth . . . God judges actions by the intention, not by the outward act . . . Two men may do the same thing, and yet it shall be entirely different, considered in reference to the different intentions of the doers."[18]

"It was," says, Neander, "one of Abelard's favourite sayings, that the 'intention' is the 'eye of the mind,' to which he would add that fine remark of Augustine: 'Have love, and do whatever you will.' "[19] This is clearly not far removed from a medieval situational ethic.

Motive being everything, Abelard strongly opposes a merely intellectual Christianity, of orthodox learning. Right understanding proceeds from the Holy Spirit's enlightenment, granted only to the pure in heart. "The more we *feel* of God, the more we love Him; and, with progress in the knowledge of Him, the flame of love grows brighter . . .They who to us seem simple and ignorant, and yet possess piety so much the more fervid, want only the ability to express that knowledge which divine inspiration bestows on them." So Abelard condemns those who set up to be teachers of theology without reforming their own lives: a right feeling, a right attitude, a right intention — these alone make a godly man.[20]

It would be wrong to conclude that Abelard's ethic is entirely subjective — real though that danger is. Abelard is sure that in order to be good and meritorious, an intended act must be in accord with the law of God.[21] Moreover, motive being everything, only God, who knows the heart, can judge men — not the ecclesiastical authorities. It was necessary to distinguish every human tribunal from the tribunal of God:

"Who does not see how impertinent it is for one man to set himself up as judge over the sense and understanding of another, when it is to God alone that the hearts and thoughts of all men lie open; and when He warns us against this arrogant presumption, saying, 'Judge not, that ye be not judged'? And the apostle says 'Judge nothing before the time, till the Lord come, who shall bring to light the hidden things of darkness and make known the secrets of the heart.' "[22]

Doubtless there is something superficially paradoxical in this position. Though a man's motives, alone, determine the moral quality of his acts, yet he is not himself the final judge of his own behaviour. God alone judges both acts and intentions; for He alone knows what they truly are. So the final standard after all is objective, the eternal will of God.

(3) FAR-REACHING CONSEQUENCES

Abelard always maintained that he was "a devoted son of the church"; a later verdict speaks of his humility, devotion, and being "named with honour as the servant of Christ". He himself wrote "I would not be an Aristotle if this should keep me away from Christ."[23] Yet much that he said offended church opinion. If all moral judgement focused upon intention, all quantitative assessment of moral worth — the accumulation of merit to offset vice, the transference of the merits of the saints through prayer and penance — must be rejected. So too, if the essence of true repentance depended on inner disposition, on love of God and pain at having offended Him, then the discipline of external acts of penance, as administered by bishops and priests, was valueless.

Another insight was to re-echo in Protestant ethics: Abelard's insistence that only *disinterested* love of God has any moral value. "The majority . . . had fallen into so wrong a state as to avow that, if they did not hope to obtain some benefit from God, they would cease to worship and love Him. But God, even when He punishes, ought none the less to be loved, since He would not do this unless justice required it."[24]

"Whoever seeks in God not Himself but something else, does not in reality love Him, but that other thing . . . It is only then a pure love to God, when it has for its object only God as He is in Himself, without respect to that which He communicates to us. In this case we shall alike love Him in whatever way he may treat us. Such in fact is the true love of the wife for her husband, of the father for his son . . . Because He is supremely good, He should be supremely loved . . . Fear, and hope of reward, are but the first step in piety . . . the perfection of it is pure love to God for His own sake."[25]

Elsewhere, Abelard spoke of the appeal to fear and reward as characteristic of the Jewish position of servitude, compared with the Christian position of grace and freedom, where love is the motive of all actions.[26] Such protests helped to refine grosser mediaeval concepts of heaven and of hell, but popular religion has never been able to dispense entirely with the motives of hope and fear.

Abelard challenged Augustinianism on two further issues that opened new ground of discussion. Augustine had declared that where there is no true religion there could be no true virtue: "the virtues which the mind ignorant of God seems to itself to possess are rather vices than virtues."[27] With this unjust — not to say uncharitable — judgement, Abelard could not agree. "In life and doctrine," he contended, "the old philosophers came very near to apostolical perfection . . . Christians were so called from Christ, the true wisdom, and they who truly loved Christ might with propriety be called philosophers." Indeed, "philosophy, which represents love to God as the highest motive, was on this point more nearly akin to Christianity than Judaism was." To the objection that the pagan philosophers' goal was not love to God but only love toward what is good, Abelard replied "this amounts to the same thing, since God is the original fountain of all good." This is why the gospel had met with readier reception among the philosophers than among the Jews. "The philosopher of pre-Christian days, by aligning himself with the natural law, could act with the same kind of good intention as the Christian . . . the main difference being that for the Christian good conduct has been more clearly and attractively set forth in the incarnation" (Mechie).[28]

Luthardt thought that for Abelard, this universal, ancient, immutable law of nature was the exhaustive rule of all action, the sufficient condition of salvation. Neander admits that Abelard idealised the ancient philosophers, but denies that they could, without Christ, ever have attained salvation. Faith in the Saviour is a means of salvation necessary for all: Abelard would not allow that this faith was wanting in the divinely-illuminated ancient philosophers.[29]

This follows from Abelard's principle that only intention determines moral quality, though his vehemence in asserting it was motivated in part by the desire to contrast the abstemiousness and self-denial he ascribed to pagan philosophers with the luxury and self-indulgence of contemporary abbots and monks! But a much larger, more relevant, truth is here finding expression. Morality is not a private, domestic concern of Christians only; the moral law is universal. Virtue is *not* confined to the good churchman — it would be unchristian to assume so. Virtue is virtue and vice vice, wherever they are found — and God will not confuse them in order to favour Christians in the final judgement.

The second challenge to Augustinianism concerned the nature of sin. Abelard declared it "inconceivable that God should condemn a man for the sin of his parents"[30] "Original sin" is the penal consequence of wrongdoing: it is not sin in itself. Like Augustine, Abelard had sore experience of the power of the flesh to resist the things of the Spirit: but where Augustine's reaction was to condemn all sexual desire as wholly evil, being inherited original sin transmitted through concupiscence from Adam, Abelard took the view that "it is not the temptations of lust that are sinful. Morality here depends upon whether the ruling bias of the will overcomes these temptations or yields to them. One man has by nature stronger propensities to this sin, another to that: but temptation to sin is not sin — it serves rather for the exercise of virtue in him who victoriously sustains the contest. Sin arises only when one suffers oneself to be drawn by those (fleshly) solicitations into transgression of the divine law: the true merit of virtue consists in this, that in conflict with ourselves we do God's will."[31]

Virtue cannot be attained without conflict — where would greatness lie if our inclinations were always in harmony with our duty? But the conflict, like the inclination, *is not sin*: only consent to transgression, proceeding from a wrong intention, is sin. the original, inherited tendency to sin is not man's guilt but his problem: it becomes culpable when he assents to it, and (in Jewish phrase) becomes the Adam of his own soul. There is little doubt that on this question — and on sexual morality generally — modern Christian sympathy would lie more readily with Abelard than with Augustine.

In appreciation of Abelard's emphasis as a whole it is enough to set beside it the supporting analysis of Kant, in the opening section of his *Fundamental Principles of the Metaphysic of Morals*:

"Nothing can possibly be conceived in the world or out of it which can without qualification be called good, except a Good Will. Intelligence, wit, judgement, courage, perseverance, are undoubtedly good in many respects. But these may also become extremely bad if the will is not good. The same with fortune, power, riches, honour, health, happiness . . . if there is not a good will . . . A good will appears to constitute the indispensable condition even of being worthy of happiness. Some qualities of service to this good will itself may yet have no intrinsic value . . . the coolness of a villain makes him more abominable . . . A good will is not good because of what it performs or effects . . . but simply by virtue of the volition — it is good in itself. Even if this *will* should wholly lack power to accomplish its purpose, and there should remain only the good will (not, to be sure, a mere wish, but the summoning of all means in our power), then, like a jewel, it would still shine by its own light, as a thing which has its whole value in itself . . ."

This is the basis upon which Kant erects the imposing argument for the categorical imperative: it appears that whether or not he had read Abelard, he would have agreed with his main contention.

In criticism of Abelard's position, however, it must be said that the determination of moral quality by intention alone needs to be qualified. It is one-sided: as Kant saw, the good intention may fail through want of resolution, of courage, of patience and perseverance, of ingenuity in overcoming obstacles, of reasonable foresight and attention to the conditions of success — for each of which a man may be justly blamed, however good his intention.

Further it is inadequate: a man is rightly held responsible not only for his intentions but for his actions (or his inaction) in themselves; for being the kind of man which he has allowed himself to become, that he should have such intentions, or fail to have better ones; for the unintended but foreseeable consequences of his behaviour — though he may protest that he never meant things to turn out so, he may well be censured for so acting as to make them inevitable — whatever his motive may have been. Moral judgement, in fact, falls upon far more than professed, or even sincere, intention. Thirdly, Abelard's position is dangerous. From determination of the morality of an act only by its motive, it is a short step to the pernicious doctrine that the end in view justifies the means employed. By this principle almost any cruelty, persecution, fraud, deceit, violence, war, neglect, may be justified on the plea that out of it comes some degree of good to some person or group or cause — and because that "good" may be represented as the ultimate intention, all the cost and wrong, the injustice and suffering involved, may be excused, even approved, against all conscience. The danger is not imaginary: the consequences have sometimes been dire.

A further serious danger to which Abelard's position is exposed is that of moral relativism. It is true that he himself guarded against total subjectivism by his insistence on the law and judgement of God as final arbiter of man's intentions. Nevertheless, Abelard's exclusive reliance upon a man's own motive as the ground of ethical assessment leaves every man the sole judge of his own behaviour, since he alone can know the nature, the purity, the genuineness of his intention. Moreover, since whatever be the ultimate consequences of a man's actions, any good that *he* intended must determine the moral quality of his conduct, a good intention that failed miserably, for any cause, is as meritorious as one that succeeded against all odds. And a result produced by ignorance, immaturity, even foolishness, is no less creditable — the intention is all. Abelard saw this danger, and himself raised the question: "How are we to judge, then, concerning those who persecuted Christ Himself, or the Christians, thinking that they thereby did what was acceptable to God — persons who, from the positions they occupied, from the degree of their knowledge, *could not do otherwise*, or if they had done otherwise, *would have sinned against their consciences*?"[32] Thus an act which all observers conceive to be wrong may, on Abelard's principle, be held not only excusable, but — given the doer's intention — actually right — *for him*. All moral judgement is thus relative to the present condition of the person acting, arbitrary, individualist, and (pending the final Judgement) subjective.

Abelard drew back from this, and with all the church condemned the actions of unbelievers, as in crucifying Christ. This was scarcely consistent. He also sought some safeguard by distinguishing the true from the falsely professed "good intention": "what has been said of good intentions by no means applies to everything a man might *believe* he did with good intention, when this intention itself was a mistaken one, when the eye of the soul was not single, so as to be able to discover clearly, and guard against error." But this helps little, unless Abelard assumes that a true heart — "a single eye" — will always know infallibly what to do. Those situations still remain where the professed good intentions are sincerely held, but are hopelessly mistaken as to facts, or misled by partiality, prejudice, unbelief, propaganda, self-interest, moral or intellectual blindness, inexperience and the like. All such considerations ought to influence our assessment of the degree of responsibility and guilt incurred by the doer; they cannot affect our judgement of the act done, of the consequences that followed, of the principles upon which he acted. Unless the immorality of the thing done is conceded — whatever the intention — we cannot begin to educate the doer to a clearer understanding of the nature of the good, and so to better intentions in the future.

For all that, Abelard unquestionably introduced a new freedom of thought, and returned to genuine insight into the spiritual ethic of the New Testament, by his insistence that conformity to inherited tradition, external standards, and ecclesiastical authority, is *not* the sufficient mark of Christian behaviour. Christ, and not church law, remains the norm. His death for us sets His death within our hearts for example and inspiration; the inward principle is not sufficient, but it is essential — "for the Lord looketh upon the heart".

7

Aquinas: Moral Theology

BY WIDENING THE HORIZON OF ETHICS to include again the insights of pre-Christian philosophy, and by his empirical approach, Abelard had, without knowing it, prepared Christian ethics for a new climate — the revival of learning, the rapid growth of speculation beyond Augustinian boundaries and the rediscovery of Aristotle. The work of redefinition and of synthesis was, however, the phenomenal achievement of Thomas Aquinas, whose prodigious writings reveal immense thoroughness and erudition, who never wrestled with a question without prayer, and whose works were placed on the high table alongside the scriptures, at the Council of Trent. Of his authority in the Roman Catholic church it can still be said, "while contemporary catholicism displays an interesting variety of opinion in moral theory, all of it can be measured by its distance from Thomas Aquinas."[1]

Hitherto Christian teaching had found expression in terms consonant with Plato's ideal world of perfect forms, more real and permanent than this world. The new popularity of Aristotle, with his concentration upon the reality of this world, and the purpose and laws revealed within it, demanded a re-thinking of Christian positions. Aquinas' restatement of Christian teaching "had no rival in coherence, lucidity, reasonableness and sobriety".[2] Nevertheless, though Aquinas approached many ethical questions in Aristotle's way, he owed even more to Augustine, and the whole Christian tradition. "Discussing man's final end, he starts with the Aristotelian conception of happiness and ends with the Christian doctrine of the beatific vision of God."[3] That so much primitive Christian thought and feeling was preserved and mediated to a new cultural milieu in the language of Aristotle is the measure of Aquinas' epoch-making accomplishment.

For example of the kind of translation needed: Aristotle exalted magnanimity — "the great soul," largeness of personality, self-sufficiency. Aquinas struggled to reconcile this with Christian humility, as "holding great honours" within the bounds of reason; as allowing man to "exalt himself'' in consideration of gifts received from God (humility being held to relate merely to one's own defects); as ''feeling contempt towards others'' only as destitute of grace; as ''independent'' only as receiving nothing without full repayment in gratitude. In fact, of course, pagan and Christian ideals are here irreconcilable.[4]

(1) PHILOSOPHICAL FOUNDATIONS

(i) Aquinas inherited the assumption that man is destined for a spiritual end in which he is to find felicity. But he needs a supernatural revelation in order to see that end, and supernatural means in order to achieve it. This ''teleological'' view of man rests upon the nature of every human *act* of will. For every truly human act is rationally directed towards some end or goal thought of as good, as tending to perfect the one who so acts. Such is the purposive nature of will, set always towards the ultimate good of man: and that ultimate good lies in ''the supernatural vision of God which is attainable only in the next life''.[5] Of course, not all realise this; men vary greatly in the good they strive after:

> ''All desire the final end, because all desire their perfection, which is what the final end signifies. But they do not all agree about the concrete nature of that final end.''[6]

Aquinas shows that neither sensual pleasure (which satisfies only the irrational body), nor power (which can so easily serve bad purposes), nor scientific knowledge (which satisfies only the intellect), nor a philosophic knowledge of God, will suffice for that end, but only the vision of God, which includes knowledge, love, blessedness, the ''possession'' of God. Aquinas distinguishes between contemplation of God (mediated through creation, reason, ancient philosophy) and intuition of God's presence, reached by faith.

Every human act, therefore, is good or bad as it tends towards attainment of human nature's true and final goal in God. In so assessing acts, intention is important, but not (as in Abelard) the sole criterion of morality: ''to give alms for the sake of vainglory is bad''; to steal in order to give alms is also bad.[7] The end, therefore, does not always justify the means. What is done, its intention, and the way in which it is done, must all be compatible with the final end, before an act is approved. When an act is wrong, the reason is always its failure to promote the ultimate end in which human nature shall find its fulfilment. Such judgement, however, is never merely upon the act, but upon the agent acting.

(ii) The distinctive human capacity is reason, which enables man to apprehend and seek a chosen end. When the end he seeks is objectively and ultimately good, as well as good in his individual judgement, it is so recognised through *right reason*. The criminal may act rationally, but since crime is not compatible with man's objective good, it does not accord with "right reason". In accord with right reason, subject to its control, emotions too have their place in human fulfilment. Right action may have to be pursued in spite of feeling, but it is better, for example, "to do kindness with pleasure than with set teeth . . . Ideally, the whole man should be attracted by the good."[8]

Aquinas recognises the possibilities of purified passion as instrumental to contemplation; the passionate pursuit of truth, goodness, and beauty, all have part in the attainment of man's chief end. "It is this passion, sublimated and sublime, which makes of Thomas both philosopher and poet, mystic and metaphysician."[9]

Alongside emotion, rationally ordered, are habits, disposing man to act readily and easily in given ways. The effect of virtuous habit is stability — without it we would not act uniformly, readily, in a "quasi-spontaneous" manner.[10] Right reason, ordered emotion, and established virtues all operate to lend strength, the balance of the cultured mean, to the fully matured character.

(iii) Obligation, too, arises in the moral life, although the pursuit of the *good* remains the determinative concept. Obligation originates in God as man's Creator, and is determined by man's nature, as *the law of his being*. On law, says J. M. Heald,[11] Aquinas offers the first scientific discussion of post-classical times, and the best introduction ever written. The *eternal law* in the mind of God furnishes the ultimate distinction between good and evil;[12] it is experienced by man as "an ordinance of reason made for the common good".[13] The moral law is one of the ways by which God guides man towards the fulfilment of his nature. "Hence the eternal law is nothing else than the plan of divine wisdom directing all things to the attainment of their ends."[14] In words of Professor Beach, "the context within which man practises his morality is a law-abiding universe under the sovereignty of God."[15] Inanimate things act necessarily in conformity with their nature; animals are governed by instinct; both participate *unconsciously* in the eternal law. Man, as rational and free, may act out of harmony with eternal law, and needs therefore to know it. He can discern the fundamental needs of his own nature, can reflect rationally on his experience, and reach some knowledge of *natural (moral) law*. "The natural law is nothing else but a participation in the eternal law by a rational creature."[16] But as it is discerned and proclaimed by man's reason, for himself, natural moral law is therefore essentially *autonomous.*

The "primary precept" of this natural law is "that good should be done and pursued and evil avoided: on this are founded all other precepts of the law of nature."[17] To this Aquinas gives clearer content by deducing from man's natural inclinations and tendencies towards self-fulfilment, the moral precepts of self-preservation, self-propagation, and "thirdly, there is present in man an inclination to his good as a rational being — a natural inclination to know the truth about God, and to live in society."[18] Other, secondary precepts can be rationally derived from these more fundamental ones. Not all men can fulfil every precept; no moral ideal is universally applicable. There may be special need, for example, or a special vocation, for celibacy. Nor is "deduction" of natural precepts from general principles an entirely intellectual process: "feelings" (of approval, disapproval), habits of moral judgement, ethical intuition, have their place in morality, as in the perception of facts, and of mathematical relations. Moreover, in perceiving natural law there is room for errors of discernment and of judgement. Hence, in discovering the broader, ultimate ends for man, in forming moral judgements, and in reaching moral decisions, there is need for prolonged and shared reflection, personal prudence, and responsibility.

Because passion and prejudice, false belief, evil custom and corrupting habit, may hide from men even the elementary "natural" precepts discoverable by reason, it was necessary that God should reveal as Commandments what man, unhindered, could have discovered by reflection. Even more, however, is revelation necessary for the discovery that man *has* a supernatural end — the beatific vision of God; and for discovering the means appointed for its attainment — the gospel and the sacraments. To natural law, therefore, is added *divine law,* in the total discipline which leads towards self-fulfilment. Of this divine law, Eenigenburg says, "The Holy Spirit inscribes it on the Christian's heart, creating an inner disposition of love to God . . . The right inner disposition provides the motivation which gives acts their proper virtue; without it, the act is without moral quality."[19]

Human law, enacted by governments, is valid only so far as it is grounded in natural moral law. Because Aquinas sees man as "by nature a social animal,"[20] social order itself is natural, willed by God. Its end is to promote the good life. Its laws, therefore, are intended to define and support the natural moral law: for example, *what* killing is to be considered murder? By what punishments will murder best be stopped? Not all natural moral laws can become legislation; kindness cannot be made mandatory. But no human legislation may oppose natural moral law without becoming a perversion of law.[21] The Christian conscience is thus bound to uphold human laws that embody the moral law; to resist those which by unfairness, violence, oppression, contravene natural moral law; to defy those which, by requiring idolatry (for example), contravene divine law. "Laws of this sort ought not to be obeyed", and tyrants who persist in enacting unjust laws may legitimately be deposed.[22]

(2) THEOLOGICAL EXTENSIONS

(i) The capacity to attain some knowledge of natural moral law by rational reflection, Aquinas called *synderesis* (or synteresis) — moral insight. Application of the principles so perceived to particular situations, Aquinas called *conscientia*.[23] In such application, there is room for ignorance and mistake, though conscience retains its authority nevertheless. There is room also for confusion, so that in some particular situation "we have no conscience in the matter".[24] Thus conscience is no infallible guide or source of general rules: it merely breaks down the moral insights of natural moral law, rationally perceived, into detailed personal directions.

But beyond natural moral law lies divine law. Aquinas employs in the perception and application of this supernatural revelation, the old distinction between evangelical *precepts* — defining what is required to arrive at eternal felicity, and dealing mainly with the right *use* of this world; and the higher evangelical *counsels* — which lead more surely to felicity through complete *abandonment* of this world, the total renunciation of lust of the eyes, lust of the flesh, and pride of life. Where the precepts enjoin right use of property, sexual capacity, and personal freedom, the counsels require voluntary poverty, celibacy, and obedience. Neander sees the essential difference as that between a Christianity that negatively combats the world, and that which positively appropriates the world for God.[25] Luthardt notes that Aquinas perpetuates the old compromise of the double morality.[26]

(ii) By such insight, conscience, precepts and counsels, man is to be guided towards his great end. But since the Fall, man has lost the supernatural gift of blessedness, and become corrupted, blind in reason, stubborn of will. God therefore sent Christ, to break the power of evil and establish the church as a continuing channel of forgiveness and divine sustenance (grace), through the sacraments.[27] Sustained and energised by such supernatural resources, the

Christian is able to make much better use of the principles of natural morality than the non-Christian does.[28] It is essential to the understanding of Aquinas' ethics to appreciate this religious dimension of his thought. The highest intuition of God is not possible to reason alone, reflecting upon creation, but needs *faith*. The object we seek is not sufficiently clear to enforce conviction: the mind is poised, until "the bent of the will" towards belief "tips the scales". Faith is the act by which the mind assents to divine truth, according to the direction of the will moved by grace.

"The impulse which so directs the will to believe is the end which the soul seeks and clasps . . . The motive power behind belief is love of the supreme good — God. Thus it is love of the good — of God — which inclines the will towards believing, so creating faith."[29]

Man's justification consists in this first infusion of grace. In this all is given at once — first, the infusion of grace, then the movement of the free will towards God, the will's opposition to sin, the forgiveness of sin, all moved by God's love turning men to penitence, forgiveness, fitness for eternal life. Salvation depends upon this interior working of grace, producing God's life within the soul, from which faith *follows*. Grace goes before faith: "free will cannot be converted to God unless God converts it to Himself." Grace is, essentially, the supernatural gift creating the new nature, which then believes. Grace precedes merit, also, by moving men to good living — "operatively" (working of itself) and "co-operatively" (working along with man) — so achieving merit.[30]

(iii) Two problems arise from thus ascribing everything in man's ethical salvation to the divine initiative of grace. First, how far is man free and responsible? Man's will stands poised between reason and concupiscence; it can be moved by either.[31] As to whether man *can* will good without grace, previous discussion had emphasised that "the primary ground of all that is done or can be done, by men or angels, is divine providence" (Albert Magnus). So Aquinas: "God knows all things as immediately present: hence things contingent (such as man's free acts) are also known infallibly by God as present." Everything takes place as God wills. But then, He wills that some things should happen through contingent causes, among them man's free will. Through man's free will, *as a secondary cause*, God wills to let His will be done.

"God works in each according to its constitution: in natural things, to give them power for acting; in the free will, to impart to it the power to act. God works in the free will as the nature of it requires: although He changes the will to another direction, nevertheless by His almighty power He causes that man should freely will the change. Thus all constraint is removed. To suppose otherwise, that the man willed not the change which is a change in his own will, would involve contradiction.'' As Wheeler Robinson says, ''we have psychological freedom within metaphysical determination.'' (''What did the first frog say?'' asks Chesterton. ''Lord, how you made me jump!'' — He jumps because God so made him — metaphysical determinism; but he likes it — psychological freedom.)[32]

In the secondary causation allotted to the human will, Aquinas finds sufficient basis for freedom, and so for responsibility, and for merit.

(iv) Ascribing everything in man's ethical salvation to the initiative of grace raises also the question of the origin of evil. Like Augustine, Aquinas held to a ''privative'' definition of evil as the *absence* of good, not in a purely negative sense (in which a man would be evil if he lacked, say, the swiftness of a wild goat), but as lacking something properly belonging to moral fulfilment. This implies no unreality in evil: blindness is none the less real for being a deprivation. Every evil action, however positive in expression and consequences, *is* evil precisely in that it lacks conformity to the moral law, is ''deprived'' of moral value. It follows that God did not create evil: He created only positive good, privation of which constitutes evil. God created beings sensitive to pleasure — which involves capacity to feel pain; to that extent only, God permitted physical evils. God created beings morally free but ''man's power to act morally involves the power to choose immorally''.[33]

The cause of all sin is unrestrained love of self; the result, loss of original righteousness, through withdrawal of grace, and decreased inclination towards virtue. Although the soul sins, not the body, yet the disordered nature and the graceless, mortal body seminally transmit corruptibility to Adam's descendants, resulting in their sin and death. But the *guilt* attached to sin is based — as guilt always is — upon the evil will.[34]

That God foresaw and permitted such evil, for the greater good that might thereby be achieved, must be admitted. Copleston holds that the question why God should, beside this, create a world in which *so much* evil exists, is unanswerable. The Gospel of redemption shows how evil can be made to yield good: but it does not explain evil. Nor does the further fact, that God foresaw, and commands, all man's efforts to diminish its extent.[35]

Yet ''Christian optimism is integral to the ethics of St. Thomas.''[36] Evil cannot be predicated of God; it has no independent reality, no positive ground in being; the evil God permits is over-ruled for ultimate good.[37] ''The universe is better, and more complete, if there are some beings in it capable of falling from goodness . . . in that God does not prevent it. It is in the very nature of things, however, that a being who is capable of falling should sometimes actually fall. Aquinas quotes Augustine's view that God is so mighty that he can make even evil subservient to good, and so much good would be wanting if there were no evil.''[38]

From such extensions of his ethical positions, as from their treatment within a treatise on theology, it is evident that Aquinas' thought on morality is rightly described as moral theology, despite his borrowing from Aristotle. Aquinas is aware of the distinction: ''the theologian considers sin principally as an offence against God, whereas the moral philosopher considers it as contrary to reason.''[39] ''He was convinced that without revelation we can have only an inadequate knowledge of the purpose of human life and of man's supreme good.''[40] The same sense of the need of more than human insight and resources is evident in Aquinas' conviction that man's highest end is a supernatural one; in his addition of precepts and counsels to moral insight and conscience as guides to fulfilment; in his supplementing human and natural law with divine and eternal law as the framework of moral discipline; and in his insistence on the need of divine grace and faith to attain salvation. It is plainly indefensible to dismiss Aquinas' ethics as merely ''baptising Aristotle into Christian respectability''.

(3) SPECIFIC APPLICATIONS

(i) Beside right reason, ordered emotion, divine and human laws, precepts and counsels, man is helped towards the attainment of his true end by the formation of stabilising habits, or ''virtues'' — settled dispositions towards goodness. Man-to-man relationships, especially, are governed by the great natural virtues, temperance, courage, justice, and prudence. To these Aquinas adds endowments given by God through revelation, church and sacrament — the three ''theological virtues'' of faith, hope, and love. ''These seven cardinal virtues are the internal habits of the good life.''[41] But to these Aquinas added three ''intellectual virtues'', which, because ''the supreme and final blessedness of man consists in the contemplation of God'',[42] take precedence.

The intellectual virtues, which perfect man's rational powers, are: *Wisdom*, which enables the mind to assess the highest aims, embracing the goal of all human knowledge; *Knowledge* (or science), which enables the mind to perceive the intellectual goal; *Intuition* (or intellect), which discerns first principles ''at a glance'' — as known of themselves. The acquired moral virtues, habitual acts built into dispositions in accord with natural moral law, are four:

Prudence, in selecting the means best calculated to attain the moral end. Rational good must appear to man as some form of knowledge, which prudence recognises. Prudence includes contempt of worldly things, a mind bent wholly upon good; and it resolves practical moral problems. Prudence, for example, would recognise by reason that lying is an abuse of the capacity to communicate; a less intellectualist viewpoint would see it as injury done to another.

Temperance — reason counteracting the passions — includes every virtue which disciplines feeling, promotes (for examples) fasting, virginity, and withdraws the mind from objects of sense. Its main problem is moderating sensual desire. Again intellectualist; sexual offences, for example, are treated as violations of one's own temperance, not as injustice to others.

Fortitude includes all that makes the soul firm against the passions; resisting every hindrance to the rational life, and strengthening emotional response to danger, opposition, emergency, delay.

Justice includes every disposition to do good as a matter of obligation and of right. It sustains in all relationships the order of reason and equity, reconciling inter-personal claims.

The "infused" virtues, faith, hope, and charity "transcend the human virtues, for they are virtues of man in so far as he is made to share in divine grace."[43] *Faith* completes our moral knowledge with the truths that only revelation discloses; it comprehends the supernatural. *Hope* makes accessible the divine end of all moral aspiration, surpassing the forces of nature; it strives after the supernatural. *Love* is a passion stirred by some good. The "love which is concupiscence", desiring possession, is distinguished from the "love which is friendship", desiring only the good of the one loved. Divine love ("charity") is higher still, the gift of grace, based upon God's self-communication to man. In divine love, God Himself is loved, and for Himself, not for anything to be gained from Him. In such love, the will unites with the supernatural.[44]

In general, Aquinas regards each virtue as the fitness required in a rational being to answer the end for which he is destined.[45] The sevenfold gifts of the Spirit (Isaiah 11:2) aid man in effecting the virtues; the beatitudes of Jesus (Matthew 5) express the blessing of the virtues.[46]

(ii) "It is natural for man to be a social and political animal, living in community;" says Aquinas: "this is more true of him than of any other animal, a fact shown by his natural necessities." On this,

Copleston comments, "Aquinas regarded life in society as prescribed by the natural (moral) law . . . Social life is thus founded on human nature itself, and the family and the State are both natural communities."[47] Man's food, for example, depends upon social organisation; his social nature is shown equally by the natural development of language. Civil society is willed by God, since man could not attain his full stature without it — irrespective of the Fall: "a common social life of many individuals could not exist unless there were someone in control to attend to the common good."[48]

One would not expect a mediaeval Dominican, who exalts virginity and applauds clerical celibacy, to speak of "a fundamental precept of the natural moral law — that the human species should be propagated."[49] Aquinas declares, "the precept about generation bears on the human community, which ought not only to be multiplied corporeally but also to make spiritual progress. So sufficient provision is made if some, only, attend to generation, while others give themselves to the contemplation of divine things for the enrichment and salvation of the whole human race. All things cannot be done by one man."[50] "It is no more incumbent on married people to have as many children as possible, regardless of circumstances," adds Copleston, "than it is for a man to eat as much as possible" because the natural moral law requires that he preserve his own life. Aquinas thought that from the precept regarding propagation and education of children, one could derive the law of monogamy, on the ground (among others) that this is required for their proper care and upbringing.[51] Aquinas' general position concerning family life is that of the earlier double standard: a natural life disciplined by Christian morality and grace, or a higher life which denies nature in the fulfilment of a wholly spiritual vocation.

Within the wider life of society, a career of trade is justified by service of the common good; but taking interest, in any form, is usury, and morally wrong. Community of earthly goods is a natural right: private ownership is so far qualified that a *duty* to share is necessarily implied in any right of property. In dire need, the original and natural right of community of goods asserts itself, and "theft to serve necessity" is justified[52] — presumably by the natural precept that requires a man to preserve his own life.

Since civil and political society is willed by God for the common good, and necessary to the fulfilment of man's social nature, the State possesses its own proper function by its own right:

"For the good life of the community three things are required: the community should be established in the unity of peace; the community should be directed to good action; through the ruler's diligence there should be a sufficient supply of necessities for a good life.''[53]

Though Aquinas thought monarchy the form of government most conducive to unity, the likest to God's, this implies nothing of totalitarian authority. The State exists for the welfare of the community. Man's destiny is supernatural, needing for its fulfilment the independent mission of the church and its sacramental ministry, which the State must respect. Further, the State's enactments must derive from the natural (moral) law, or they become perversions of law, and possess no authority over the Christian conscience. The ruler has a trust to fulfil; he should devote himself and his authority to the objective common good.[54]

On the claim of the State to the Christian's service in war, Aquinas adds little to Ambrose and Augustine. He stresses the necessity of a just cause, but the moral issue concerning war focuses upon rightful intention rather than upon consequences. The intention must be to secure peace, not to kill, conquer, or gain honour. Here as everywhere, justice is determined by law as an ordinance of reason for the common good, derived from natural moral law, and so from the eternal law of God.[55] Aquinas meets "literalist" objections with skilful interpretation. Jesus forbade Peter to take the sword — that is, to use it without warrant: He prohibited only unauthorised persons from drawing the sword. Jesus said "Resist not evil . . . avenge not yourselves:" and such injunctions are fulfilled by a placable spirit; they cannot require us to do mischief by allowing wickedness to go unpunished. To the argument that, if peacemakers are blessed, warmakers are accursed, Aquinas retorts that war may be the best, even the only, means of attaining peace.[56] One object of a just war might be to recover property: the damage that might be done is then relevant to its justice. So with the overthrow of tyrants: recourse to arms would be justified if foreseeable damage would not exceed the injury sustained by submission.[57]

Despite the ascendancy of Aquinas in Roman Catholic ethics, many would find his teaching academic, too dependent upon Aristotle to harmonise with modern thought about life's development, and about man's duty towards society. The basis in natural law implies that Thomist teaching on such topics as family, sex, contraception, remains determined exclusively by the natural purpose of sexual intercourse, understood to be procreation. Abortion, too, for *any* reason, is similarly excluded. On other ethical questions, gambling, drunkenness, perhaps drug addiction, Thomist ethics seem to some Christians somewhat lax. Though in some respects, granted its assumptions, Aquinas' system appears an end-of-the-road for Christian ethical development, from other points of view discussion continues. For example, it is debated whether man's ultimate end can ever be known; whether obligation is not central in ethics, and not merely derived from pursuit of the good; whether ethics should be made so dependent upon theology; and whether an ethic of personal fulfilment (even in Aquinas' high-toned form of it), or one centring in the common good, is the more Christian. Many Roman Catholics have explored the relation of moral theory to the social questions troubling the world today, and some recent papal declarations have shown the same outward looking concern. The current ferment within Roman Catholicism springs from new thinking in ethical and social fields, at least as much as from experiments in liturgy and theology.[58]

Thus despite Aquinas' power, and apparent finality, Christian ethical development did not cease with him, but continued along lines which departed from the whole mediaeval world-view, and sought other theological bases for the concept of the good life.

8

Erasmus: Christian Humanism

THE RELEVANCE OF ERASMUS to the unfolding story of the Christian ethic is clouded by argument over his theological orthodoxy. This depends upon what was "orthodox" in the early sixteenth century; upon how far, in order to be counted Christian, one had to give support to Luther; and upon whether anxiety to reform the church but *not* disrupt it is the craven, time-serving, attitude of a man without principle, or evidence of a Christian love of unity which rejected violence and trusted to moderation, enlightenment, and ridicule.[1]

Of Erasmus' historical importance there is no doubt. His books sold in prodigious numbers — one ran through sixty editions in his lifetime; some set educated Europe laughing. Rupp describes him as the "spiritual father of all the great scholars of the 1530's and '40's."[2] Atkinson says Erasmus "combined high intellect with a vivid imagination, an almost perfect memory, a rapier wit, a sensitive and refined taste, and a genuine faith. In his own field . . . he towered as a sovereign of intellectual Europe . . . Erasmus forwarded the Reformation positively by reviving classical, biblical and patristic studies; negatively by exposing pitilessly, with a mordant wit, the ignorance and bigotry of the monks as well as the obscurantism of the schoolmen."[3] Rupp notes the view put forward by Aleander in 1520 and revived by a modern scholar, that the really dangerous enemy to the church was not Luther but Erasmus; Chadwick recalls a saying of the sixteenth century, "Erasmus laid the egg, Luther hatched it."[4]

It is important, even for Erasmus' ethical teaching, to understand his attitude to the essentially theological Reformation debate. It is often contended that Erasmus was not a theologian — the scholastic theologians were Erasmus' "one very perfect hatred."[5] Erasmus, says Bainton[6], "was desirous of bringing religion itself within the compass of man's understanding . . . by . . . couching Christian teaching in terms simple enough to be understood by the Aztecs, for whom his devotional tracts were translated. His patron saint was ever the penitent thief, because he was saved with so little theology."

It by no means follows that Erasmus questioned fundamental Christian affirmations. Judgements like "Erasmus is basically an ethical humanitarian . . . divorced from a thoroughly Christian foundation"; "a naive secularism", "hero of liberal Christianity", "a heretic", all ignore, as Dolan points out, Erasmus' devotion to the Fathers. The real object of his distaste, was theological dialectic, with its profitless quarrels and abstract speculation, tending away from the spiritual fountains of Christianity.[7] Erasmus did, after all, restore to Europe its Greek Testament, an "erudite and massive edition of the Fathers", and improved tools of biblical scholarship; while his main ethical thrust is fairly described as "Christocentric".[8] Rupp approves P. S. Allen's judgement that the greatness of Erasmus consisted of brilliant intellectual gifts, combined with absolute sincerity and enduring purpose. Atkinson says he was concerned about the church, and a believing man: "he did not mock at religion but at its pompous performers, its obscurantist theologians, its ignorant and irreligious monks . . ."[9] Bouyer calls Erasmus the Christian conscience of his epoch; Bainton says he was closer to Luther than many another figure of the Renaissance, because he was so Christian.[10]

To cite only one confession of faith: "No one will doubt (that the Lord's mercy surpasses all his works) if he considers how much more wonderful the work of redemption is in comparison to creation. It is more marvellous that God was made man than that he created the angels. That He wailed in a stable rather than that He reigns in the heavens. This plan to redeem the human race is Christ's life, Christ's teaching, Christ's miracles, His passion, cross, resurrection, appearance, ascension, the descent of the Holy Spirit . . . The creation of the world was a work of power, but the redemption of the world was a work of mercy."[11]

It is equally important, for Erasmus' ethical position, to understand how he came to offend *both* sides in the Reformation argument.

He was suspected of sympathising with Luther, of writing Luther's *Babylonian Captivity*; all his writings were proscribed by Pope Paul IV. Yet Luther directed his *Bondage of the Will* against Erasmus, was shocked at Erasmus' preference for Jerome over Augustine, and in the end wrote to Erasmus "a final and disgusted letter" — "We see that the Lord has not given you the courage or the sense to tackle these monsters openly with us."[12]

It is true that Erasmus said "Even if Luther had written all things well, I should not have courage to risk my life for the truth. All men have not the strength for martyrdom."[13] He was "leader of the moderates".[14] Certainly, as Chadwick says, "he aimed his most penetrating shafts at the abuses of the church". He hated the vices and follies of the monks and clergy, still more their ignorance and superstition — "those superstitions, cults of statues, visits to Madonnas that rolled their eyes or to bleeding Hosts, seemed to be not harmless vehicles of a rude devotion, but the bane of true religion." He criticised even the papacy for teaching contrary to Christ.

"Perhaps thou believest that all thy sins are washed away with a little paper, a sealed parchment, with the gift of a little money with a little pilgrimage. Thou art utterly deceived." "Christianity," said Erasmus, "has been made to consist . . . in abstaining from butter and cheese during Lent . . . What good are indulgences to those who do not mend their ways? . . . Those who never in their life endeavoured to imitate St. Francis desire to die in his cowl . . ."[15]

Nevertheless, he "could not give Luther unqualified endorsement without a violation of his own integrity."[16] Erasmus was "horrified" to hear personal integrity and decency characterised as "idle and damnable sins". There were deep differences of viewpoint: the law was for Erasmus, outward ceremonial law, custom, and observance: for Luther, the divine imperative; Luther argued theology with a pastor's heart, which Erasmus lacked; they disagreed finally on freedom, and human dignity.[17]

Erasmus' real offence was his attempt to mediate where neither side thought mediation acceptable. "As long as reformation was being *discussed*, Erasmus went along with the idea," says Atkinson; "as soon as Luther burned the papal bull . . . Erasmus began to withdraw." Much later, he still counselled caution, and the calling of a General Council, proposed mediation, urged it was in everyone's interest to give Luther a fair hearing. He exhorted Catholics to abolish abuses, the evangelicals to submit to ecclesiastical authority.[18] Luther himself pays tribute: "You have checked my zeal for battle . . . you discuss the matter throughout with quite remarkable restraint, by which you have prevented my wrath waxing hot against you". Dolan comments that it is a measure of the failure to understand Erasmus, that his book on freedom of the will was attacked because of its very gentleness. Erasmus is sure the great need is for persuasion: "Christ's way of winning men to Himself was persuasion and love." Only so would theologians serve the peace of the church.[19] It was Erasmus' greatest misfortune to be "by conviction a neutral, in an age intolerant of neutrality."[20]

But however Erasmus' true relation to the Reformation of theology, and of the church, is finally assessed, his position as the Reformation's outstanding moralist is not likely to be challenged.

(1) THE HUMANIST CRITICISM

The great significance of Erasmus lies in his position, chronologically and in thought, between the Renaissance and the Reformation, and his leadership of the humanist movement.

Humanism endeavoured to emancipate thought from narrow scholasticism, appealing to the civilising influence of "humane letters" — "disinterring buried classics to recapture an ancient charm of style, and a broader humanity of spirit."[21] It opposed persecution and dogmatism, pleading for tolerance. Humanism was "the good cause which enlisted most of the forward-looking minds in the first half of the lifetime of Erasmus."[22] The revival of Platonism and of Cicero, new methods of criticism, a ferment of discussion and speculation, journeying scholars, book fairs, an extraordinary network of correspondence, fostered a new spirit. Chadwick, remarks that humanists had little in common except a love of classical antiquity. Humanism in Italy was literary, artistic, philosophical; in northern Europe it was more religious, even theological, though sharing literary and philosophical influence.[23] Dickens describes Christian Humanism as "loose, many-coloured, pervasive among both Protestants and Catholics." "Petrarch and his followers transformed . . . education and the art of living: they ended by giving a sense of superiority to . . . the new educated classes, and in this humanist sphere met clerics upon at least equal terms."[24]

Dickens notices also the "secularising of mental interests" even among the clergy.[25] Luthardt spoke of the growing division between sacred and secular, and the discovery of virtues in Islam, loosening of moral dogma. New reverence for ancient ethics, following the movement of scholars westward, and the rise of popular literature advocating free and joyous secular life, shows culture withdrawing from ecclesiastical authority; a new freedom of enquiry was coming to birth which presently would bring the Middle Ages to an end in the new age of science. Reformist zeal like that of the Waldensians, of Wiclif (rejecting a double morality and exalting love), of Hus in Bohemia (making the law of Christ the only standard), of the Brethren of the Law of Christ" (re-establishing New Testament rules as the law of living) nourished a new idealism, and prepared for ethical reformation.[26]

To this new climate Erasmus belonged. He "believed that room could be found within the thought and life of the church for the new learning" (Selwyn[27]). He was educated first in a school of the

Brethren of the Common Life, a movement founded in the fourteenth century as a more liberal and practical monastic sect — "cells of reforming zeal and devotion . . . the milieu from which had arisen the peak of mediaeval devotional writing, the *Imitation of Christ*".[28] These "beneficent and far less cloistered" laymen renounced private property, lived in community, stressed practical piety rather than ritualism and theology, and founded schools which "became justly famous".[29] With this intellectual beginning, Erasmus passed (through poverty) into a monastery, an experience which coloured his attitude towards religious orders, but also gave him opportunity for intensive study. Thereafter, he represented the grace, charm, tolerance, and humanity of the new learning, in most countries north of the Alps.

Nevertheless, as Mann Phillips says[30], "to the humanism which imagines man as supreme Lord of the Universe, needing no God to inspire and no Christ to redeem him, Erasmus was a stranger." He stood firmly for a *Christian* humanism. He wished (he wrote) that literature should "find that Christian character which (it) lacked in Italy, and which as you know ended in glorifying pagan morality"[31] — for the new freedom of thought had some licentious consequences. But it was the attempt at theological simplification, the return to original biblical languages and "the philosophy of Christ", which brought humanism into collision with religious authorities. "Sixteenth-century humanism was the attempt to return to the Bible and the Fathers, and to disentangle the religion of wayfaring Christians from the elaborate subleties of the later schoolmen."[32] One perceptive critic declares, "With Erasmus — not with Luther — the individual conscience comes to its destructive dominance in the modern age."

"Christian humanists . . . tended to regard Christ as an exemplar . . . They saw in Christian life the struggle of an essentially free and dignified being to control his selfhood and his appetites . . . they would seem to represent a cultural trend, not a school of thought, still less a Reformation in its own right . . . " Their most important contribution to the development of Christianity lay in applying strictly historical and philological techniques to the Bible, to rediscover precisely what Christ and Paul had taught, to re-examine the Vulgate, and re-translate tendentious words like *episcopos* and *metanoeite*. Erasmus' edition of the Greek Testament, says Wheeler Robinson, was "epoch-making".[33]

But Christian humanism, in Erasmus, also directed upon prevailing church practices a searching *ethical* criticism. His best known book, *The Praise of Folly* — "a witty sermon, an earnest satire, a joke with ethical purpose"[34] — expresses the whole attitude of the

Enlightenment towards superstition, religious abuses, the avarice of ecclesiastics, the sometimes blasphemous disputations, the widespread intolerance, immorality, false miracles, indulgences . . .

"We kiss," says Erasmus elsewhere, "the old shoes and dirty handkerchiefs of the saints, and we neglect their books, the more holy and valuable relics. We lock up their shirts and clothes in jewelled cabinets, but as to their writings, on which they spent so much pains, we abandon them to mouldiness and vermin."[35]

Erasmus was equally opposed to all means of spiritual oppression —

"Their only weapons ought to be those of the spirit: and of these indeed they are mightily liberal, as of their interdicts, suspensions, denunciations, aggravations, greater and lesser excommunications, and roaring bulls . . . and these most holy fathers never issue them out more frequently than against those who . . . attempt to lessen and impair St. Peter's patrimony."[36]

Theologians, in turn, are pilloried for unbalanced opinions —

"It is a lesser crime to cut the throats of a thousand men than to sew a stitch on a poor man's shoe on the sabbath; it is better to want to perish, body, boots and breeches (as the saying goes) than to tell a single lie, however inconsequential."[37]

Erasmus criticises place-seeking, the purchase of office, holds the disciple under obligation *never* to be ashamed of his Master, and opposes to religious ceremonialism the simplicity of Christ.

Almost invariably the criticisms are ethical. His primary concerns are personal attachment to Christ, the interior life, the return to scripture. Hence Erasmus' strictures upon the monks, not upon the principle of monasticism but upon "their filthiness, their ignorance, their bawdiness, their insolence", mainly concerned with the precise number of knots to the tying of their sandals, the colour and style of their lace, hair of just so many fingers' length. "Nor is it so much their concern to be like Christ as it is to be unlike one another . . . "

"Never recalling that Christ will demand a reckoning of that which He has prescribed, namely charity, . . . rejecting boasts about fasts, ceremonies . . . Christ, interrupting their unending pleas, will ask 'Where does this new race of Jews come from? I recognise only one commandment yet I learn nothing of it. Many years ago in the sight of all men I promised . . . the inheritance of my Father to those who perform works of mercy, not to those who merely wear hoods, chant prayers, perform fasts. Nor those who acknowledge their good works too much . . . "[38]

Erasmus' attitude to the monastic system is best expressed in a phrase that became famous: "*Monasticism is not holiness*, but a kind of life that can be useful or useless . . . I neither recommend it nor do I condemn it. Let me warn you about it, however . . . [39] Nevertheless, daily detailed examination of conscience is good; external discipline has its place — provided always that surrender of freedom is voluntary; devotional rules are valuable, provided they are not imposed, and obedience is not regarded as meritorious. The church has authority over outward obedience: the inner life must be free.[40]

At this point, Erasmus' criticism touches moral theology. "As a good humanist," says Dickens, "Erasmus believed in the basic dignity and goodness of man, in man's ability by the exercise of free will to contribute towards his own salvation."[41] Here Erasmus broke with Luther: his treatise *On the Freedom of the Will* opposed the doctrine of depravity and argued "that freedom was essential if moral responsibility existed; a man was free to heed or to disregard."[42] Atkinson holds that this shows Erasmus had never plumbed the depths of evangelical theology; with equal truth it might be retorted that Luther had not weighed the necessities of Christian ethics. Bainton[43] traces the disagreement to Erasmus' primary interest in morals; the question is, whether the ethical precepts of the gospel have any point if they cannot be fulfilled.

Luther "countered with characteristic controversial recklessness that man is like a donkey ridden now by God and now by the Devil" — having no freedom to decide for good or ill — though that was not Luther's habitual position. Erasmus was concerned for morality in God — "is it not unjust that God should create man incapable of fulfilling the conditions for salvation, and then at a whim save or damn for what cannot be helped?"

Erasmus would rather limit God's power than forfeit God's goodness. And so, probably, would every Christian moralist.

(2) "THE CHRISTIAN SOLDIER"

Erasmus' positive individual ethic is best illustrated in his earnest tract entitled "*Handbook for the Christian Soldier*". Curiously, Russell dismisses this as "a book . . . giving advice to illiterate Christian soldiers"; even Rupp speaks of it as "an armchair study of the Christian warfare."[44] Chadwick sees it as "an attempt to expound the lines of the true theology . . . direct to the human soul."[45] These are cool assessments: Mann Phillips suggested that in modern language it might have ranked beside the masterpieces of the renaissance; a Louvain professor called it "a booklet of genuine gold"; Dolan traces its wide and lasting influence, and describes it as containing "an ethical code founded upon reverence for a divine Person."[46] Erasmus himself says, "I intended to describe a way of life, not a method of learning" and his account of its origin is of the greatest importance.[47]

In a letter, twenty years later, Erasmus speaks of a plea, by a lady of piety, for notes which might call her dissolute husband to some sense of religion. Whatever was prepared for that immediate purpose was evidently much revised and elaborated, but the direct appeal is clearly retained in scores of personal allusions and friendly pleas. Throughout, the argument is interspersed with encouragements to persist in self-conquest. "I pray that Jesus will bless your undertaking." Finally, there is clear warning against those who would exploit "a man returning from vices to virtue".

It is scarcely possible to dismiss all this as a literary device, though obviously the immediate purpose has been generalised, and the argument in places elaborated and polished, for a wider audience. The spirit that breathes through the work is itself a revelation of the heart of Erasmus.

No summary could do justice to the earnest eloquence of the *Handbook*, but the main thought of one of the most impressive ethical treatises of the Middle Ages must be outlined:

Life is warfare, the world vicious; complacent peace with evil betrays our baptismal treaty with God through Christ, who redeemed us with His blood. We need to be ever sensitive to God and rely on the power of our Ally. But it will not be without effort: we must neither presume on divine grace nor become disheartened (34).[48] Our weapons are prayer, knowledge, scripture, referring all to Christ Himself (39).

We need the wisdom that is 'to know oneself' — since the warfare is mainly with ourselves (42). Man is twofold, animal yet capable of divinity, ever at civil war; reason must regain authority and be served by piety, charity, compassion; it cannot be corrupted without protest (44). The opinion that men are compelled to vice is harmful. Some are by nature moderate — for them virtue is little effort. For others, the rebellious body can scarcely be subdued — virtue is not impossible, but a richer victory is offered. Yet all must struggle over some things; weaknesses must be turned to opposite virtues — impetuosity into burning zeal, inflexibility into constancy (46).

Such self-conquest, difficult in our own strength, is easier if mindful of God our helper. The argument is then transposed into scriptural terms. After struggle, we realise that the Lord is sweet (47).

According to traditional Christian psychology, *spirit* argues for obedience towards God, *flesh* warns of displeasure and disinheritance, *soul* wavers between the other two. Those not troubled by flesh are not necessarily virtuous: virtue lies in victory. Attending Mass, or comparing self with others, is not virtue; nor natural love (51).

Virtuous life is accompanied by discipline that the Holy Spirit breathes into those who aim at godliness. Baptism removes stain of original sin; but remnants remain, needing direction, resolve, turning to God — and some practical rules (52), such as: scripture, resolute decision, casting oneself upon Christ, dying to sin, imitation of our Head (55), dealing trenchantly with fears, dedication to Christ, good examples (even of pagans). Worry when you have no temptation. God will never forsake (77).

Make "violent" effort to put sin out of mind. Pray with all your might, have some stirring scripture at hand, seek God's help always. Remember, not the cost of virtue but the bitterness of sin's aftermath: each defeat makes the next conflict harder. What makes a man evil is not that he sins, but that he loves his sin. Bear in mind your gospel privileges, God your friend, the reward of immortality (83).

The final fivefold remedies against sin are most eloquent. A strong plea to fight manfully is set against a strong warning that without such inward struggle the monastic way is mere delusion.

"I have set my work aside, so that I could . . . point out for you a short cut, as it were, to Christ."

The closing plea underlines two characteristics which mark Erasmus' ethical teaching: his insistence that the moral problem lies within the soul — relics, monastic rules, ceremonial, outward conformity, have little to do with it; and his constant appeal to the imitation of Christ. In those two insights lay the new direction of Reformation ethics.

"The aim of Erasmus' theology" says Dolan, "was an interiorization, a spiritualization, of religious practice, a more personal affair between the individual soul and God."[49] His fifth ethical Rule requires that we seek ever the invisible, *internal* world of Christ, turning from things deceptive to those that are real, searching out the unseen meaning in all experience (for example, sickness), and in scripture, and in the sacraments (letting what takes place in the Mass take place also in your heart; letting baptism cleanse the inner filth of your mind). "See in everyone you meet the image of Christ"; above all, have Christ *within your heart* —

"When you venerate the image of Christ in paintings . . . think how much more you ought to revere that portrait of His mind the Holy Spirit has placed in Holy Writ . . . You gaze in silent amazement at the tunic that reputedly belonged to Christ, yet read the wonderful sayings of that same Christ half asleep . . . A particle of the true Cross in your home is nothing compared with carrying the mystery of the Cross in your mind."[50]

The false value set upon such relics and external ceremonies is a reversion to the superstitions of Judaism. Charity does not consist in visits to churches, prostrations before saints, lighting of candles, repetition of designated prayers. Of these things, God has no need: charity is loving one's neighbour as oneself.

God, a spirit, is appeased by spiritual sacrifices; God is mind, and must be worshipped with a pure mind. Of what advantage a body covered by religious habit, if that body possesses a worldly mind? What does it profit to venerate the wood of the Cross and forget the truth of the Cross? . . . You keep the Sabbath, but in your mind permit vice to run rampant . . . If a man's body walks in Christ's footsteps, more to his credit that his mind has followed the way of Christ. If you wish to be forgiven, you must attack the enemy *within*.[51]

Thus virtue and vice proceed from within. Yet with all this inward-looking and heart-searching, Erasmus is by no means subjective in morality: the standard always, in everything, is Christ. "He said on many occasions that to imitate the life of Jesus was far more important than to argue about dogma" (Hyma[52]). "In Christ is the fulfilment of all things . . . Get out of your own self and let Him support you . . . Though all cannot attain the perfect imitation of the Head, all must aim for this . . . Make Christ the only goal of your life."[53]

Dedicate to Him all your enthusiasm . . . don't look upon Christ as a mere word, but as charity, simplicity, patience, purity, everything He has taught us. Our determination to imitate Christ should be such that we have no time for other matters. There is no temptation for which Christ did not furnish a remedy: when ambition pushes . . . think to what extent He lowered Himself; when envy fills your mind, remember how He poured Himself out for us; when lust tempts you, remember how Christ lived . . . "Whatever things you find Christ's image in, join yourself to them."[54]

Such is Erasmus' "biblical piety . . . which gradually permeates the whole of life in imitation of Christ" — the *devotio moderna* of the Brothers of the Common Life rejuvenated by study of the gospels in a new spirit of objectivity (Bouyer).[55]

(3) SOCIAL CONCERN

Erasmus is scarcely less insistent that the individual is firmly set within society, and the church; his life must therefore exhibit a social concern. He is keenly aware of the debt each individual owes to society; and of the extent to which society holds in its own hands the key to its own improvement.[56] In resting his hope for the future on the teachableness of man, Erasmus anticipates the humanist "faith in progress" of the eighteenth and nineteenth centuries.

The link between individual and social morality lies for Erasmus in Christian love: "as Christ gave Himself completely for us, so should we give ourselves for our neighbour." Paul declares charity to be the edification of our neighbour, the attempt to integrate all into one body in Christ, the loving of one's neighbour as oneself. Indeed, for Paul, he is charitable who rebukes the erring, who teaches the ignorant, who lifts up the fallen, who consoles the down-hearted, who supports the needy. The truly charitable devote all wealth, zeal, and care to the benefit of others.[57] "No one prepares to harm another unless he has already far more gravely harmed himself. You cannot inflict a wound, unless you have already received at your own hands a much more frightful hurt."[58]

Let no Christian think to have been born for himself, nor wish to live for himself . . . Let him love the pious in Christ, and the impious also for Christ's sake . . . A man is an adulterer . . . commits sacrilege: let adultery, sacrilege, be despised, but not the man . . . Let him sincerely desire well of all men . . . let him manifest joy over the good fortunes of all as he does over his own.

"It is generous to ignore someone else's mistakes; quite the opposite to imitate them. Injury inflicted is not lessened, only increased, by revenge. To avenge corruption brings self-corruption . . . The only person that can harm a Christian is himself. Pardon your neighbour, that Christ might forgive you your countless thousands of sins. To overcome evil with goodness, malice with kindness, is to imitate Christ's charity.[59]

Nor is Erasmus' social concern expressed merely by a gentle and pious spirit in personal relationships. In the *Adages*, the *Complaint of Peace*, the *Commendation of Marriage,* the *Education of Princes,* he offers a far-reaching social and political programme, of which only salient elements may be noticed.

(i) On Wealth

Erasmus' love of simplicity devalues riches and luxury; despite his attitude towards asceticism, he deeply distrusted affluence and the power it confers. He condemned also all idleness: wealthy families ought to train their sons to useful professions; beggars, pedlars, gamblers, he reprobated, and especially itinerant monks — useless parasites no better than moneylenders and brokers.[60] So, too, he would limit the number of monasteries.

"If you feel your nature tends towards avarice . . . think of the greatness of your value as a human being . . . You are a disciple of Christ, called to a far greater possession than gold . . . Forget gold, and admire something truly great." "A person who strives to be godly will always have enough to get along . . ."[61]

Erasmus was "absolutely in favour of reducing worldly possessions to a minimum, providing meanness be avoided" (Bouyer[62]). He includes among opinions worthy of a Christian the view that "all that he has, he does not credit to himself; he gives credit to God, and considers his goods the common property of all. Christian charity recognises no property." Your brother is in dire need, and you go on mumbling prayers, pretending not to notice his predicament. God will actually despise that kind of prayer.[63]

Nevertheless, "he had no thought of simple common sharing of the goods of society,"[64] though More's *Utopia* had contemplated communism.

"I am not greatly impressed with those who dispossess themselves of everything they have, then run around for the rest of their lives begging shamelessly. It is not wrong to have money. It only becomes wrong when money is loved as an end instead of looked on as a means. If rich, act the generous steward; if poor, do not feel robbed, but rather as though a friend relieved you of a dangerous thing. A person who spends his whole life gathering wealth can hardly be a good Christian. You can neither keep, nor get, great riches without sin . . ."[65]

Instead of total renunciation, Erasmus urged strict discipline in production and distribution of riches; a social hierarchy founded not on wealth, industry, or aristocracy, but on learning and merit. He proposed to *prevent* the concentration of riches in few hands,[66] in order to safeguard spiritual ends. Monopolies should be illegal; so should tax-farming, and taxation of the necessities of life and food-producing land. Erasmus was not sure of the ethical value of free competition; on the whole he approved it, with social safeguards. He condemned profiteering by the raising of prices, and regretted the passing of effective city control of weights, measures, prices, and quality of goods.[67]

Faced with the rise of capitalism, Erasmus chose a middle course. He saw that banking was socially useful, although money-lending and speculation were bad. Priests engaged in usury were especially horrifying! He did not condemn interest on capital invested in a business in which one took no further part: but he saw the tremendous social change it would effect in the enrichment of a new class of middlemen, which he judged a menace to social equilibrium, and to spiritual values. This issue was important, for a great new merchant middle class was already emerging, between the aristocracy and the feudal labourer.

Erasmus held therefore that the public economy should be directed and hedged for the common good, with laws against excessive expenditure. The great increase in wealth, due to overseas discovery and colonisation, seemed to him very close to pillage. Above all, the economy of any morally healthy society must be founded upon peace.

(ii) On Government

Erasmus consistently pressed Christian and humanist ideals upon kings, princes, and popes. His *Education of Princes* challenges comparison, in some degree, with Plato's *Republic*, and challenges contrast with Machiavelli's *Prince*. Erasmus strongly censured the despotism of Europe's rulers. The prince should ever consider himself the first servant of the law, and of the public good. He should be educated to care for his people "with an enlightened love", to impose only fair taxation, to sell no public office, to censure all bribery, to promote schools for girls as well as boys, and to build universities.[68] In dealing with criminals, the prince should not only punish to deter, but diagnose the causes of crime, and remove them.[69] All turns upon the analogy of the wise father, slow to punish, never revengeful, quick to protect, untiringly watchful and active for the common good, doing violence to none.

> So long as individuals seek their own interests, the common good must suffer. No good is achieved by evil methods. The attitude of the ruler towards his subjects should be that of a father towards his family: neither ruler nor subjects should consider private gain.[70]

The folly and callousness of the idle ruler, given to drink and dicing, is castigated severely. The Christian prince must outdo the pagan rulers of the past; his "cross" is, to follow the right at all times, at all costs, in toil and self-sacrifice. Moreover he must remember he rules free people — twice free, by creation and by redemption. The prince may exercise no tyranny: Erasmus' thought is far from "the divine right of kings".

> The ruler must ever remember that he deals as man with fellow men, as free citizen with free citizens, above all as a Christian with fellow Christians. Citizens must show due respect for the king for the sake of the common good. Consent by the citizens will curb the aspirations of the prince. Nothing is more admirable in rulers than imitation of Christ. Erasmus urges the true Christian prince to behold the image of his chief Prince; to play the role of minister among his people, and to surpass others especially in aiding those who need help."[71]

All the same, Erasmus has no high opinion of the masses; he does not credit the people with wisdom to govern themselves.[72] Princes must be endured, lest tyranny give place to chaos: "the insurrection of the German peasants has taught us that the cruelty of kings is better than the universal confusion of anarchy." Government should therefore be directive, though aimed at preserving the people's rights and property. Few laws are necessary: the spread of good principles is the pre-requisite of social order: then "local councils", and common consent, will support princely rule. "All Erasmus' respect goes to an aristocracy of education and intellect: all his pity to the common people."

(iii) On Peace and War

Erasmus opposes war with energy and eloquence. The spirit of the Crusades still lingered but "Erasmus asked cynically whether if a crusade were successful, the pope would be likely to govern the east better than the Turk."[73] The only possible "just" war was one of self-defence, and in his opinion, Cicero was right, "an unjust peace is far better than a just war". He says, "I do not condemn every war; yet it cannot be denied that when war breaks out there is a crime on one side or the other, if not on both;"[74] but he will not condemn those who "undertake legitimate war to repel barbarous invasion, or defend the common good."[75]

Erasmus recounts the pretexts for war to expose behind them all the vanity and unrestrained ambition of princes. Relentlessly, he attacks faithless churchmen for their unreflecting egoism, their fostering of militaristic nationalism, their failure to promote reconciliation. The true causes of war are rival claims to power, private quarrels of ruling houses, nationalism, the desire of tyrants to strengthen their tyranny by weakening their own people, profiteering in weapons and in spoil, and mischievous ecclesiastical exhortations to patriotism and pride. The *Complaint of Peace* is very moving:

War is the destroyer of all things; no greater enemy exists of goodness or of religion.[76] Nature herself preaches peace, yet neither intelligence, education nor necessity seem able to unite men in love, despite human interdependence. Christians are worse than the heathen: yet scripture, and Christ, exalt peace continually. Contrary expressions, "God of armies" and the like, are Judaist — or allegories for *moral* battles. David, being a man of war, was held unworthy to build the Temple.

"With what audacity do you call upon the common Father while thrusting your sword into your brother's vitals!" It is monstrous that Christians fight each other. Dare Christian men, while making war, offer the holy sacrifice? Christ reconciled Pilate and Herod, yet He cannot bring His followers to agreement! He told Peter to put up the sword. We are all the same species, of the same religion, redeemed by the same sacrifice, nourished by the same sacraments. Has Christ accomplished *nothing*?

If war is unavoidable, the misfortunes resulting from it should fall on those who caused it: in most wars the safety of the heads of government is assured, and their captains stand to gain! It is desirable sometimes to *purchase* peace — it is cheap at any price. Trophies in churches suggest it is a work of religion not only to be martyred but to martyr others! War is "the cesspool of all impiety", and immeasurably, endlessly, costly.

Thus war is condemned, by humanity, reason, divine example, scripture, compassion, the gospel, by war's own effects both moral and economic. To avoid it, Erasmus would unite Christians across all frontiers, fix the succession of rulers, take decisions about war from any individual, organise arbitration, mobilise the moral forces of the world, in season and out of season urge the wickedness and folly of international homicide.[77] Predictably, Erasmus was dismayed at the rising violence of the Reformation, and "deplored the disintegration of Christendom".[78] His comments on the Peasants' War in Germany, and on Luther's reaction to it, are sharp: he attributed the violence of the revolt to "the violence inherent in Reformation thinking",[79] and saw the reaction as savage repression, symptom of the materialistic attitude which supposes that right and power belong to brute force alone.[80] Small wonder that he was rejected by *both* sides in the scarcely less savage strife that was to disrupt the church.

(iv) On Marriage

Chadwick[81] suggests that opportunity for legal marriage was the greatest single change that affected the Protestant clergy. Because of the marital irregularities widespread under celibacy, "in judging the Reformation it will not do to forget the burden that poured from so many consciences, or the true and honourable homes and families which thus became possible." Erasmus pleaded permission for clergy to marry. At the request of Queen Catherine of Aragon he also wrote *The Institution of Christian Marriage*, defining marriage as "a perpetual and legitimate union" and elaborating thoroughly the evils of divorce. Wedlock is solemn and binding, sanctified by both law and religion; there are impediments which render null the marriage *contract*, but not the consummated union. The treatise as a whole presents "a well balanced view". The choosing of mates is best left to parents; the nurture of girls requires especial care, to keep them "unspotted from the world" — innocent of romance-reading and lascivious pictures (with which Bibles are often illustrated!).[82]

Like others of his time, Erasmus preferred bigamy to divorce. Some Anabaptists, some Roman Catholics, and some rationalists too, defended polygamy, as common in the Old Testament, not forbidden in the New. Luther, too, is said to have expressed the opinion that polygamy is not prohibited by the New Testament.[83]

In *The Praise of Folly*, it is not always easy to perceive where the irony ends: but sympathy as well as shrewdness underlies —

Marriage is an indivisible joining for life: but what divorces, or even worse, would come about if the domestic life were not upheld by flattery, joking, compromise, ignorance, and duplicity — all satellites of mine (of folly)? How few marriages would be contracted if the husband inquired about what tricks his seemingly delicate and innocent little darling had played before the wedding? And once entered on, fewer still would last if the many tricks of the wife were not kept unknown through the stupidity of the husband . . . But how much happier to be thus deceived, than to wear himself out with unresting jealousy. A people will not long bear with its prince . . . nor a wife with her husband . . . unless they make mistakes, flatter each other, wisely overlook things, and soothe themselves with the sweetness of folly.[84]

Among arguments against lust, Erasmus urges "If you are married, your marriage is the symbol of the union of Christ and his Church"; and discussing the meaning of love and hate, he argues —

When a youth is "out of his mind" over a girl, the common folk call this love. There is in fact no truer form of hate. Love looks to the benefit of another: Whoever seeks his own pleasure loves only himself . . . Is seducing a girl, by flattery and gifts, *love*, or *hate*? Or, what is more *hateful* than neglecting to discipline children, pampering them, to the detriment of their eternal welfare?"[85]

Erasmus assumes a positive valuation of human love, of domestic happiness, and of parental responsibility, essentially different from the grudging attitude of the mediaeval church towards marriage. In another passage, Erasmus returns even more plainly to a view of married love that breathes again the spirit of the New Testament:

You say you love your wife because she is your spouse. Pagans do this: with love based upon physical pleasure. But if you love because in her you see the image of Christ, modesty, and purity, then you love Christ in her. This is spiritual love.[86]

Beyond question, Erasmus set Christian ethical thinking upon lines very different from the whole mediaeval discipline of piety, challenging the separation of religious and secular, rejecting alike the double standard of morality and the dogmatic authoritarianism of the church, yet retaining with renewed clarity the appeal to scripture and the central ideal of the imitation of Christ. The intellectual maturity of the classics, a wide experience of men and affairs, an academic devotion to the original Gospels, and a disciple's devotion to the original Jesus, all produced in him a fresh re-statement of Christian moral principles, making him the unquestioned leader of the age of change, — as Bouyer suggests — "its Christian conscience".

Miss Phillips isolates as essentials of Erasmus' life "his shrewd perception of values; his sense of reality; his individualistic attitude to religion, combining a reasoning knowledge of the scriptures with a simple devotion which led him to the threshold of mysticism; his strong interest in the conduct of the world's affairs; his refusal to join a party or enrol himself under any banner, or accept any ready-made solution to the problems of the spirit; his hatred of war . . ."[87] There might be added, the inwardness of his viewpoint; and the first emergence of a Christian ethic *for* society, as distinct from an ethic of the church's ministry *to* society (the Apologists), or of the church withdrawn *from* society (monasticism). Henceforth, the church will explore the relation of Christian faith to the common life of common men, to government, economics, and social need, as she had not done for a thousand years. At a deeper level, reacting against theology that had become "an intellectual gymnastic", and against dogma that brooked no discussion, Erasmus presented ethics not as "This shall ye do", but as "This in my opinion were the better; this I suppose to be more tolerable."[88] His has been called "an ethics of the preferable" — in his age, a novel approach, significantly approximating to modern "value theory". In so many directions did Erasmus contribute to the conscience of the modern Christian. With all his fun, ridicule, and evasion of strife, he yet presented insights, denials, a sense of priorities, a searching inwardness, a relentless standard of Christlikeness, that even today remain out-reaching in their challenge.

9

Luther: Conservative Reformed Morality

DESPITE THE WIDESPREAD INFLUENCE of Erasmus, the Reformation did not emerge from the circle of the humanists, still less from the more extreme heretics and 'enthusiasts.'[1] "The times called for rougher men and rougher measures" says Inge; "Indeed, on one side the Reformation was a mediaevalist reaction against the Renaissance, which was degenerating into licence."[2] The leader of the Reformation was of another kind, a catholic monk who remained for long obedient to his spiritual superiors, who is sometimes criticised for unclear thinking and coarse language, for narrow attitudes towards sex, inconsistency, naivete, and occasional violence of opinion. Luther's early poverty, legal training, desperate want of assurance, the conflicts focused in his abandonment of his vows for marriage, his moral earnestness, passionate love of the scriptures, reverence for preaching and great personal courage, all helped to shape his ethical attitudes.[3] He rejected humanist support, turning from philosophy to biblicism nourished by spiritual experience.

Luther's many-sided thought invites misconceptions. He remained nearer to the mediaeval mind than to the modern, in his appeal to scripture against reason, in his sacramentalism, and in his basically ascetic outlook. Nor was he a "rugged individualist", the unassailable protagonist of private conscience; he certainly stood alone, but looking back he could say, "Then was I the church."

"These very words show how he understood his aloneness. He did not oppose . . . the corporate body of the church as a single isolated Christian: but he was conscious of his duty as a defender of the true teaching of the real catholic church of all ages . . ." He remained troubled that error might exist on his side too: "Can I believe that all previous teachers were ignorant? would God have allowed His people to remain in error for so many years?"[4]

Thus Luther desired "neither to split the church nor to found a new one;" adopting the language of scholasticism, upholding the law of antiquity, episcopacy, the mass as a valid eucharist, wanting to recall the church to its own true gospel.[5] Though he "individualised piety" as Inge says, yet "Lutheranism belongs to the church type not to the sect type."[6] Luther was "driven into rebellion" although his own bias was in favour of institutions as part of divine order, as his social ethic makes clear.

Troeltsch points out that Protestantism, no less than Catholicism, "emphasised the idea of a church-civilisation in which all departments of life . . . were to be regulated in accordance with the law of God;" Tawney comments, "that conception dominates all the utterances of Luther on social issues."[7]

Nor, again, was Luther an evangelical for whom "works," conduct, ethics, had only consequential significance. Salvation is by faith alone, and faith is God's gift, the work of the Holy Spirit: yet this in no way controverts the need for Christian morality.

"There is no justification without sanctification, no forgiveness without renewal of life, no real faith from which the fruits of new obedience do not grow."[8]

For Luther, the very thought of God is morally disturbing, a cleansing fear, "a consuming fire". But faith kindles love: it receives new power to exercise itself in obedience towards God and effort for the good of men. "It is as impossible to separate works from faith as it is to separate heat and light from fire."[9] Further, much of Luther's antagonism towards the ecclesiastical system arose from moral repugnance:

at the "abysmal spirituality of the church" — dissensions, sensual pleasures, wretched extravagances, the heavy odour of scandals, foul corruption" — the clergy "filled with carnal vice" — "the follies and ignorance of the monks, squabbles between princes and prelates, the sordid materialism of the clergy." And, of the papal curia of Julius II, "the most revolting cesspool of filth, luxury, pomp, avarice, ambition, and sacrilege."[10]

Luther's ethical concern is equally evident in the list of his writings — *On Good Works, Christian Liberty, Secular Authority and Obedience, On Usury, To the German Nobility,* and the expositions of *Romans, Galatians, The Ten Commandments,* and much else. It must be remembered that the brevity and systematisation necessary to introductory exposition cannot but present as separate steps what were originally facets of one integrated, fertile and constantly developing religious insight.

1. THE ETHICAL PROBLEM

The turning point in Luther's experience was doubtless "a discovery in the sphere of exegesis".[11] His religious distress was basically theological in origin: yet since he was wrestling especially with the meaning of *salvation,* it is no serious distortion of his teaching to concentrate upon ethical issues.

(1) Psychological and Moral Assumptions

Richard Niebuhr remarks[12] upon Luther's "voluntaristic, activist understanding of human nature." As Luther says, "the nature of man cannot for an instant be without doing or not doing something, enduring or running away from something, for life never rests." Man's conduct is not so much the reflection of his thought as the expression of his nature, of the disposition of his will. In line with this dynamic view is Luther's insistence that to produce good conduct we must first make the man himself good; and his conception of faith as "a movement, a direction, an activity, a *working out* rather than a static condition."

"Man's existence is always in a state of Non-Being, Becoming, and Being . . . He is always in sin, in justification, in righteousness. Always a sinner, always penitent, always justified." Man exists in movement: "The present life is a kind of movement, passage, transition . . . a pilgrimage . . . constantly a progress from act to act, from potentiality to potentiality, from understanding to understanding, from faith to faith, from glory to glory, from knowledge to knowledge . . . We are always travelling." To the Christian: "Your life does not consist in rest but in moving from the good to the better . . . the whole life of the new people, consists only of longing, seeking, praying . . . to be justified, right up to the moment of death; never standing still, never having apprehended, constantly looking forward to righteousness . . ."[13]

This dynamic view of man raises acutely the question of man's freedom of activity, the nature of will. For Luther, this was "the point on which our disputation turns, the central issue . . ." as he wrote to Erasmus[14]: "our purpose is to investigate what the free will is capable of, and how it is related to the grace of God . . ."[15] Ebeling comments: "Luther himself has no intention of denying . . . that I can choose between different possibilities of action. Least of all does he intend to deny the moral responsibility of man for his action. He can concede without question these obvious manifestations of the freedom of the will, because they fall outside the range of his discussion."[16]

"I know that free will can by nature do something: it can eat, drink, beget, rule . . . I grant that free will can by its own endeavours move itself in some directions, we will say unto good works, or unto the righteousness of the civil or moral law . . . God did not create the kingdom of heaven for geese . . . But we are asking whether he has free will towards God, so that He — God — obeys and does what man wills . . ."[17]

Ebeling adds that this implies no complete distinction between two spheres. Man can exercise his will in things subject to him, and in secular morality; but it is meaningless to speak of free will in relation to God: "here man can only be considered as the one who is acted upon, is subject to judgement, who is accepted or rejected." The scholastic view of man as in principle independent of God, one who makes free decisions, is here set aside. Man is never independent of God; "free will is a divine name and is appropriate to no one, except the divine majesty alone."[18]

But it is not only as a creature, but as a sinner, that man lacks freedom:

"In all his actions, man is subject to an inner bondage, a conflict and a self-contradiction, which does not allow him to live at full capacity" (Niebuhr). "The internal bondage appears in the sense of guilt, in anxiety, in self-centredness, and blindness to the values of others, in compulsive cravings for pleasure, and in abnormal scrupulosity. The fundamental moral problem of man is therefore the problem of *freedom* . . . of achieving liberation from these internal fetters, so that man can serve his good causes without hindrance." "In this fallen world" comments Rupp, "the only true human liberty is the liberty of the Christian man, that glad spontaneous service of God whereby the will is freed from the deadly paralysis of its own selfish preoccupations."[19]

So Luther denies that man is able, in his fallen state, to turn from sin to God; to will, or not to will, to embrace the word of God. The will cannot change itself and turn itself into another way. "The will of man without grace is not free but enslaved": indeed, "no one has the power, of himself, even to think something good or evil . . ."[20]

In part, this means that "everyone who commits sin is a slave to sin"; but it goes deeper. Man is, in Luther's graphic phrase, curved in upon himself.

"The natural man enjoys everything with reference to himself; uses everybody else for the same purpose, even God; seeks himself and his own interests in everything." "Unless faith begins to illuminate, and love sets him free, no man can will anything good; he does evil even when he is doing good." "This is scriptural, which describes a man as curved in upon himself, handing back to himself not only physical but also spiritual goods — a natural crookedness, a natural defect, a natural evil." "Nature . . . sets before itself no object other than itself, sees itself alone. Everything between itself and its own interests, even God, it by-passes, and directs its attention to itself. This is a 'perverse' and 'wicked' heart, its own idol . . . It values only things it can turn to its own advantage . . ." "Man makes himself the ultimate object and idol . . . this crookedness, depravity, iniquity . . . is in the depths of our nature, nay, rather in nature itself, wounded and in ferment . . ."[21]

"In fact", comments Atkinson,[22] "the only path to grace is the broken will, which alone can accept God in Christ . . . The will has no freedom in its salvation . . . The exhortations in scripture to repentance and holy living are calls to convince us we can do neither, meant to convict us of helplessness and hopelessness, and to throw us on the mercy of God." This incurving of the self in helpless self-dependence is described by Niebuhr:

"The self curved in upon itself discovers that instead of loving God it is admiring or grieving over its own measure of love; instead of being concerned for the neighbour it is concerned about its acquisition of the virtue of neighbour-love; instead of being humble it seeks to excel in humility." It afflicts as deeply men who earnestly want to be saints as it does those who are content to be sinners; indeed, the radical change of direction necessary to attain any love of God or neighbour "may be easier in some respects for the profligate than for the self-righteous sinner."[23]

As to what needs to be done to save men, Luther is convinced that neither the church's penitential and ascetic system, nor the rigour of the law, offers any hope: nothing, indeed, but a new man. Man, for Luther, stands ever "before God": "the fundamental situation of man is that of a person on trial."[24] To this situation the whole mediaeval apparatus — the treasury of transferable merit, indulgence, the transformation of penitence into sacramental penance, the threat of purgatory, and the replacement of true contrition (in the scheme of absolution) by fear of consequences without change of life — seemed trivial and irrelevant. Discipline deepened despair, experience did not validate the offered doctrines, asceticism merely deprived Christians of God's gifts, doing nothing to merit salvation.[25]

"Those who think they become pious through works have no regard for fasting but only for the *works,* and . . . sometimes break their heads over it and ruin their bodies."[26]

Neither can law save the soul, though all law, moral, natural and civil, is divine.

(2) The Relevance of Law

Like Paul, Luther strives both to preserve the place of the law and to distinguish it so sharply from the gospel as almost to dispense with it. (a) For the *content of the law* we need look no further than the Ten Commandments, though "the teaching of the law takes place in various forms of jurisdiction, education, instruction, upbringing, learning, civilisation, philosophy and religion . . . making demands on man, challenging him . . ." always confronting him with the difference between good and evil (Ebeling).[27]

"the law is already there . . . without our being necessary to it, even against our will, before justification, at the beginning of it, during it, at the end of it, and after it."[28]

Moreover Luther retained the concept of natural law, that is, the law known by nature, wisdom, personal experience, and in corporate political life:

"God has given to all reason and the law of nature . . . Natural law is reflected in legal systems, in the wisdom of the past, in proverbial wisdom of the people;" — Luther speaks with respect of wisdom in government shown by pagan philosophers, and statesmen,[29] — even though the occasion of natural law is sin. "The political and economic ordinances are divine; God Himself ordained them . . . There was no political organisation before sin — no need of it; a polity is the remedy for corrupt nature. So you may rightly call polity the kingdom of sin. For it is the chief work of political institutions to keep out sin."[30] Luther can add, with refreshing realism, "If natural law and reason were in all human heads alike, then idiots, children, and women, could rule and make war as well as David, Augustus, and Hannibal . . . You will find among those who boast about natural reason and law a good many thorough and big natural idiots!"[31]

(b) In so *defending law,* Luther is concerned with the rule of God over creation. The first use of law is to order human life —

"In the world, law is necessary, forming, ordering, maintaining life, making righteousness possible. This is the civil use of law, irreplaceable so long as it is not misused to provide justification in the sight of God, but intended to lead no further than worldly, secular righteousness, limiting consequences of sin, subduing man."[32]

In divinely ordained "offices" of husband, father, magistrate, teacher, farmer, the Christian man fulfils his vocation within creation; unbelievers, likewise, are within this divinely ordered life of home, society, and State; civil justice is a true righteousness.

(c) Nevertheless, "the law of God . . . *cannot bring a man to righteousness*. It is a hindrance rather than a help" said the Heidelberg thesis. Error arises when the natural man prefers law as a method of justification, a prescription for do-it-yourself salvation.[33]

"Unbelief is man's fundamental sin . . . the principle of self-justification . . . Faith in the law . . . is the common element underlying every kind of unbelief. 'In this respect there is no distinction between the Jews, the papists, and the Turks . . . They say, If I have acted in such and such a way, God will be well disposed toward me.' "[34]

This is atheism, pious or rebellious: refusal to be dependent upon God. At the same time, law's accusations, and the death it brings, constitute the "theological" use of the law (in contrast with the civil use), carrying out God's "strange work" (Isaiah 28:21) and bringing about abandonment of all self-justification. So far from setting man free, the law burdens and imprisons him, accuses, judges him, kills him, drives him to despair. "The law of the Ten Commandments is the strength of sin because it creates knowledge of oneself . . . so God promotes and perfects His proper work by means of His alien work."[35]

Law cannot save because (a) its precepts belong to the realm of flesh: "the law speaks *to* us . . . it abides without; . . . In the law many works are enjoined, all external . . . the sins, righteousness, sacrifices, holy things, promises, doctrines, of the old law all pertained to the flesh. They did not sanctify conscience, but only the body."[36]

(b) Law could not save because none could keep it: "It is not true that works of law can fulfil the law since the law is spiritual, and demands the whole heart and will. It is impossible to have these of ourselves. For this reason they who do the works of the law do not fulfil its intent."[37]

Thus although (as we shall see) law remains binding upon the Christian, it cannot save, nor is meant to. It is essential to distinguish law, in its preparatory, disciplinary work, from gospel, which demands nothing but offers, and effects, everything.

"Virtually the whole of scripture, the whole of theology, depend upon true understanding of the law and the gospel . . . Anyone who can properly distinguish the gospel from the law may thank God, and know that he is a theologian."[38]

Nor is the distinction one merely of intellectual clarity, to be stated once for all: it must be reaffirmed constantly in the exercise of utterly dependent and trustful faith.

2. THE SOLUTION — FAITH ALONE

The only resolution of man's problem which Luther allows is that of faith in the saving initiative of God:

"When it dawned upon Luther that 'the grace of our Lord Jesus Christ' was less an example set for him than a deed done to him and for him, that he was loved and accepted by God prior to any achievement . . . then all his ideas and values were subjected to a sharp change . . . In the dialogue of self and God . . . the self had forever been seeking to make itself heard by God, multiplying its prayers, increasing its efforts so to change itself as to invite divine acknowledgement . . . When at last God's word and deed broke through this self-concentration, the whole situation between God and man was altered . . . Now the self recognised itself as both sinful and beloved, able to live before God in repentance and faith, in daily reliance on forgiveness and in constant gratitude."[39]

(1) The New Posture

One consequence of Luther's representation of religious experience is that the dynamic, activist view of the self is modified, or supplemented, by a new passive *receptiveness,* which comes to mark Christian character.

"Righteousness which derives from us is not Christian . . . we are not justified by it . . . Christian righteousness is the passive righteousness which we merely receive, in which we allow God to work within us. I desire to receive the righteousness of grace, of forgiveness, of mercy, of Christ, which God gives, while we receive, letting it happen to us, as earth receives the rain . . ."[40]

As Niebuhr well says, "man is to be receptive rather than active, *hearing* the word of God, *accepting* His forgiveness. On its active side, this life is one of doing . . . But the man of faith does all these things with a difference — in freedom from anxiety, without self-seeking, for the sake of the objective good, not for the sake of the agent . . ."[41] Christian benevolence is thus purified of that religious self-interest, and spiritual complacency, which so often corrupt religious "good works".

(2) The New Man

No less a change took place in the process by which moral improvement is to be achieved. Luther insisted that the man must be changed before the required change in behaviour can be expected: "good works do not make a good man, but a good man produces good works"; "a man cannot do good before he is made good."[42]

"When a man and a woman love, who teaches them how to behave, what to do, leave undone, say, not say, think? Confidence alone teaches them all this and more." So, Christians given true confidence, not in themselves or any of the imagined securities but in God the Father and Saviour, then "all their actions reflect this fundamental re-orientation . . . set free from concern about themselves their energies are released in the service of their neighbours.''[43]

This fundamental adjustment of method, from the endeavour to become a Christian by doing Christian things, to the acceptance by faith of Christian standing and experience as a gift, and bearing Christian fruit as the natural consequence of thus being *made* a Christian, lies at the very heart of Reformation soteriology and ethics.

(3) The New Faith

This saving confidence, or faith, is not under man's control, as though he can will to believe or will to trust: it is God's gift through the gospel to those prepared (by law and the Spirit) to receive it. By faith, says Dickens,[44] Luther understood no mere intellectual assent to the creeds but rather *''fiducia,* the sinner's mental attitude of childlike trust as he reached for the saving hand of the Redeemer.'' ''It takes root in the soul when the gospel has been declared.''[45] Being thus passively, and continuously, received, faith constantly renews the Christian: ''. . . destroys sin, makes the person pleasing and righteous . . . The Holy Ghost and love are given to it, so that it takes pleasure in doing good.''[46]

''Just as faith brings blessedness so it also brings good works: just as a living person must have something to do, so no one need do anything else to get someone to do good works than to say, 'Only believe.' You do not have to demand good works from someone who has once believed: faith teaches him everything, and everything he does is well done, for faith is so noble that it makes everything good in a man.''

''Faith is a work of God within us which transforms us, slays the old Adam, makes us completely new persons in heart, courage, mind, and all our powers, and brings the Holy Spirit with it.''[47]

Ebeling comments: ''Numerous utterances by Luther seem to be in accord with this interpretation of faith as the 'moral driving force' . . . the image of the tree and its fruits which he uses so often . . . portrays the precedence of persons over works —

'faith is living, busy, active, powerful; it is impossible that it should not unceasingly bring about good. Nor does it ask whether there are good works to be done: — it has done them. One who does not do such works is faithless, groping around himself for faith and works, knowing neither what faith is, nor what good works are . . .'.''[48] Compare Atkinson's summary: ''A Christian's life is made up of faith and love: faith expresses his relationship to God, love his relationship to man. Man is made free by faith, which alone justifies, but faith manifests itself in love to one's fellows and in good works. The person must first be good . . . good works proceed from a good man.''[49] And the good man, for Luther, is a sinner made good by faith in Christ.

Behind this formulation lies the concept of a ''work'' — whether of aesthetics or of ethics — as the expression of the person doing it, a form of self-realisation:

It ''is not that one becomes righteous by doing right . . . but that the righteous man, by being so, does right. God does not accept the person on account of his works, but the works on account of his person . . .''[50]

So, the Christian's virtuous character is not a *habit* acquired through many virtuous deeds: but a new nature given by God through faith, before any virtuous deeds are possible: the new ''habit'' of godliness is created in the changed relation to God which faith in Christ effects. ''Anything . . . done in response to faith . . . is a good work; anything that such a faith does is transformed into a good work'' (Atkinson[51]). Indeed, ''the first, highest, and most sublime good work *is* faith in Christ . . . All works are summed up in this work, and receive from it the influence of their goodness in fief'' — which Ebeling interprets as, ''faith is not the power to act which makes good works; it is the power of the good which makes works good.''[52]

It will be necessary to consider whether Luther's experience (or our own) confirms this optimistic thesis: but that Luther held it is clear. ''It was basic to Luther's theology,'' says Atkinson,[53] ''that if faith and doctrine were sound, then the fruits of morality were secure and prolific.'' In his comment on the First Commandment Luther himself says, ''it is of first importance that a man's head be right. Where the head is right, the whole life must be right.''[54] This view of faith is the heart of Luther's doctrine of justification.

(4) Justification

In his summary of the epistle to the Romans, Luther declares:

''God wants to save us by a righteousness and wisdom which do not come from ourselves, but which come into us from somewhere else . . . from heaven . . . As men without anything we must wait for Him to reckon us as righteous and wise.'' This ''righteousness of God'' is revealed to a man only in the gospel: in other words, *who* is righteous, *how* he is righteous, how he may *become* righteous, in the sight of God. This comes about *only* by that faith with which the Word of God is believed.''

''It is not because a man is righteous that he is reputed to be righteous by God; but because he is reputed to be righteous by God he is therefore righteous . . . Apart from Christ no one is righteous, no one keeps the law . . . ''The good man knows that . . . Christ is his wisdom, his righteousness, his all.''[55]

The implications of this doctrine for Christian ethics must not be minimised. As Sasse[56] points out, this is a righteousness which contradicts all our moral criteria. By our standards the Pharisee, not the publican, should have been justified. We declare a man righteous when he does right, but God calls the sinner righteous. The prodigal is nearer to his father than is the elder brother; there is more joy in heaven over one penitent than over ninety-nine just men; those who labour for only one hour receive full pay; the thief on the cross is saved in a moment; the first are last, the last first; Jesus grants His gracious fellowship to *sinners* — all this is incomprehensible to our rational system of morality. It reverses all ethical judgement, to hold that he who is, and remains, a sinner can in God's sight be held a saint, because the righteousness of Christ is accorded to him. Luther would reply that this is the whole point: God has not dealt with us according to our sins.

It follows, too, that for Luther *justification* is no gradual cleansing of the believer by grace infused within the soul, whether sacramentally or mystically, but an instantaneous conferment of the righteousness of Christ. *Grace* is no bestowed "habit" or disposition towards goodness, but "a personal, living experience of Christ by which divine encounter a new creation is born". *Faith* is no human achievement or effort, but "an opening of the eyes", "a sober trust in God". *Repentance* is not doing penance, but "an inward and continuous dying to self and rising again to righteousness, a whole turning of the entire man to God".[57] Moreover, justification is here not essentially a moral or social condition of character, but a man's position in the sight of God — *"coram Deo."* It is "in God's sight" that man is sinner, judged, condemned, justified, forgiven, freed. "The fundamental situation . . . is existence in the sight of God, in the presence of God, under the eyes of God, in the judgement of God, and in the word of God."[58] It is within this God-orientation that Luther sees all that is important about man, without denying that man is also orientated towards men, and towards the world.

By such passive receptiveness in the presence of the preached word of Christ, transforming the self through faith by an experience of justification in God's sight, the predicament of man was resolved, as Luther believed, and his moral impotence removed.

3. THE MORAL CONSEQUENCES — INDIVIDUAL

Luther thought that the experience of justification by faith actually *solved* the moral problems of men and of society, in numerous interrelated and mutually sustaining ways.

(1) Faith and Works

Luther did not, of course, discourage good works or preach antinomianism; though works availed nothing towards salvation, they must be done, out of love for God and to subdue the flesh. He urges that "faith is always and incessantly in action", and could not understand how people could conceive of faith without works.[59]

"Faith is the first principle of good words" quotes Rupp from Luther's lectures on the Psalms. "With their salvation thus assured in the unmerited forgiveness of Christ, grateful and obedient Christians are free to redirect their reason and good works towards serving their neighbours' welfare" is the summary of Lazareth.[60]

But the good works required of the Christian are often not those he prefers to do — such as fasting — but those which God commends. The first and only work is faith, from which stem all the good works God requires. "Once faith has taken root in the heart, a man never needs any telling as to what work is good and what is not — he knows it intuitively."[61]

"A Christian living in this trust" says Luther "knows everything, is capable of everything, dares everything and does everything joyfully, freely, not to amass merits, but because it is pleasure to him to please God; he serves God gratuitously, content that it pleases God."[62]

As Ebeling points out, this liberates good works from the selfish purpose of providing the doer's own justification, while (in Luther's words) "in this faith, all works become equal . . . great or small, brief or lengthy, many or few. For works are not pleasing on their own account but on account of faith."[63] The calculating "scale of merit" disappears.

(2) Faith and Love

In his *Galatians,* Luther deals at length with the meaning of love as the quality of good works appropriate to the life of faith. Love implies not pleasing ourselves but our neighbour: "ordered love" involves a "hatred of self" — strictly, the denial of any proper self-love — which is important to Luther.[64] Some argue that self-love is basic to moral character, pre-supposed in the golden rule: the earnest and ascetic young Luther had concluded that God's commandments could not be met by a self "incurved" upon itself in self-interest. Luther believed there was no way "from self-love, though it be love of one's best self, to love of God and neighbour, except through a radical change of direction;"[65] through a surrender to grace which transforms the inward-curving to the outward-going, and makes a man love in the way God commanded, selflessly, and (as Bernard had insisted) disinterestedly.

This change of direction affects the nature of love for one's neighbour. The unspiritual man selects the friends he will love, and the qualities in them he will admire, loving the learned, the merry, the attractive, and disliking fools and sinners. "But true charity is universal; without picking and choosing it loves all men in God, and treats its neighbour without respect of persons," or of personal qualities and attractions.[66] Christian charity loves the neighbour as human, as a person, deserving and needing to be loved for that sufficient reason.

It is faith which "gives the power to love" in *this* way. Ebeling's discussion is here particularly enlightening:

> "Just as the person and works, doer and deed, cannot be separated, neither can faith and love . . . clear faith and love have their unity in the fact that they sum up the true life of the saved man." "The formula 'by faith alone', although it excludes love as the basis of justification, is far from excluding love as the consequence of justification . . . Mere faith is a dead faith, and only becomes living and true through the practice of love. It is faith that justifies, but — in this view — not faith alone, but *fides charitate formata* — faith given form by love." As Luther says "Faith is the doer and love the deed."[67]

The example of love is Christlikeness: *"I will give myself as a sort of Christ to my neighbour."* This, says Bainton[68] "ought to be placarded as the epitome of Luther's ethics."

(3) The Unified Standard

Inge summarises the change Luther achieved as involving among other things the fall of dualism. "The Christian is face to face with the world as he finds it, and must conquer it for Christ".[69] Sacred and secular are reconciled, the spiritual pervades the material; the believer is both "spiritual priest" and "spiritual lord" over all things, sanctified to his use and enjoyment. The distinction between commandments universally binding, an ethic for common life, and evangelical "counsels of perfection" to be realised only in monastic life, was to Luther meaningless and harmful. "Luther put the layman on his theological feet", proclaiming "a single human estate and the priesthood of all believers."

> Luther speaks scathingly of the great and difficult tasks our noted saints have invented for themselves: "we shall have our hands full in keeping these Commandments, practising patience, gentleness, love, chastity . . . Is it not detestable presumption in those desperate saints to try and find a higher and

better life than the Commandments teach? They pretend . . . that taught in the Commandments is a simple life, for common men, but that theirs is for saints and perfect men! poor, blind people . . ."[70]

One effect of this unification of moral standards was to devalue special virtues cultivated by the "religious", and accord new importance to the secular vocations of ordinary people.

"Love is all that is necessary . . . It does not belong to the new law to set aside days for fasting . . . certain foods . . . some days as holy . . . certain kinds of church, organs, altar decorations, chalices, images . . . to have religious men wearing tonsures . . . all but shadows of reality. We have outgrown them. Every day is a holyday, every food permitted, every place holy . . . Everything is matter of free choice as long as moderation is kept . . . and love."[71]

Ascetism was not forbidden: "Every one can use his own discretion as to fasting and watching, for every one knows how much he must do to master his body."[72] But ascetic and religious practices have no special merit:

"Good works are not specifically religious . . . A mother washing her baby, the miller's girl putting corn on the mule's back, the farmer ploughing, the cobbler at his last, the scholar with his students, the prince governing his people . . . These are 'good works' . . . God wants His people to do for one another, so that His world may continue in harmony. On this argument, going on pilgrimages, reciting pater-nosters, saying masses for the dead, and other religious 'good works' stand condemned . . ." So Atkinson summarises Luther, and Inge adds "It is better to sweep a room carefully than to fast or flog oneself in a cloister."[73]

Thus a man must serve God in the calling to which God had called him — a view which sounds similar to that of Paul in 1 Corinthians 7, but is in fact substantially different.

The prince's function differed from the peasant's, the potter's from the priest's, but the same God . . . saved them in the same way . . . In the sphere to which he was called a man was to obey God, not in some "holy" performance, useless to God and man. Christian vocation is not religious vocation, though some are called to preach and organise churches. Any useful work is a vocation when carried on with faith and repentance. Some few activities *cannot* be done in the right spirit, (thieves, harlots, would-be "saints"), but no activity carries a guarantee of the right spirit . . . Every vocation "is involved in the constant problems of living as a sinner and yet by grace."

"The labour of the craftsman is honourable", serving the community; the honest smith or shoemaker is a priest. Trade is permissible, when confined to exchange of necessaries: unforgiveable are idleness, covetousness, "Mendicant orders cover the land with a horde of beggars. Pilgrimages, saints' days, monasteries are excuses for idleness. Vagrants must be banished, or compelled to labour."[74]

This doctrine of work as Christian vocation in the secular sphere was to have immense consequences in Protestant countries which witnessed the industrial revolution.

Nevertheless, as Tawney argues,[75] Luther's sharp antithesis between the external order and the inner life itself had dualistic tendencies. The "internalising of faith" shattered the mediaeval concept of the social order as a highly articulated organism whose members, secular and religious, contributed in different degree to one spiritual purpose. Grace no longer "completed" Nature, but was its antithesis. Thus though in one sense the distinction between secular and religious life vanished, and all men stood henceforth on the same footing before God, yet in another sense the old distinction became more profound than ever. For though all might be sanctified, it was their inner life, their attitude, alone which constituted sanctification; the world remained divided into good and evil, light and darkness, spirit and matter, and no human effort could span the chasm.

(4) The Christian's Freedom

For Luther, obedience must spring spontaneously from the heart: this emphasis has been held "the characteristic stress of Luther's ethical teaching" (Sormunen); "freedom is the very essence of salvation" (Ebeling).

"A Christian is free and independent, bond servant to none . . . By virtue of kingship (in Christ) he exercises authority over all things; by virtue of priesthood he exercises power with God . . ." (Yet) "A Christian is a dutiful servant in every respect, owing a duty to everyone." "The freedom which a Christian has through faith is freedom to render the service of love," comments Ebeling, "it is only the service of love if it is carried out in freedom." Love gives rise to a free, eager, glad life of serving one's neighbour without reward."[76]

Luther's leading idea here, says Atkinson,[77] "is a kind of dual paradox . . . the Christian man is the lord of all, subject to none, by virtue of faith; he is also the servant of all and subject to everyone, by virtue of love."

Christian freedom is many-sided. It spells psychological liberation from the "satanic bondage"[78] of incurving selfishness, to serve in gladly accepted obligation, free from any outward "work", save where brotherly love requires obedience. It includes freedom within and above the law, no longer imposed from without but accepted from within — the fruits of the Spirit are beyond legal obligation.

The just man "has not the law", owing nothing to the law; it is of the unjust that we say "he ought": of the good man it is sufficient to say that "he does."[79] Ebeling sees this liberation from the compulsion and curse of law as placing the Christian "above the law and outside the law, so making him lord over the law instead of a slave."[80] So "the law is established, when we do it in will and deed."[81] The law of God remains after all permanent, universal, relevant: but performed "with joyful, unprompted gladness".[82]

Lazareth[83] points out the profoundly "situational" aspect of Christian freedom in Luther. "A Christian ethic based on the 'divine indicative' of God's grace (rather than the 'divine imperative' of God's law) preserves the freedom of the believer, under the guidance of the Holy Spirit through the Bible, the Church and prayer, to discover anew in each concrete situation what the will of God requires then and there." So Luther opposes to all principles, regulative ideals, and ecclesiastical rules, customs, and the like, the biblical pattern of "faith working through love", and finding fresh application in each new circumstance. The church has no power to bring anyone to heel, except the power of the Word.

"Even where the Word of God allows no freedom, we have no right to constrain others by any other means than by the preaching of the Word." "I will preach and talk and write against these things, but no one will I attempt to force . . . The Word that has created the heavens and the earth must do this, or it will be left undone." "I neither am able nor ought to compel anyone to believe; God alone does this. We have to preach the Word, but the consequences should be left to God alone in His pleasure."[84]

Thus Christian freedom implies large intellectual and spiritual tolerance, rejecting spiritual coercion of any kind. "Faith desires to be accepted freely, without constraint."[85]

(5) "The Theology of the Cross"

"True theology and knowledge of God lies in the crucified Christ". To Luther, "the theology of the cross" was the criterion of all theology, focusing upon what God chose to do to save men in the passion of Christ. On its ethical side, it must be distinguished from the mystics' imaginative concentration on the passion story; from the sympathetic veneration of the tortured Christ in art; and from the ascetics' artificial austerities, miscalled the Christian's "cross". Instead, by the "theology of the Cross" Luther denotes the actual solidarity of Christians with Christ in real suffering; the mortification of the old Adam in life-long penitence; the conformity of Christians with Christ as opposed and crucified by sinful men.[86]

The final theses at Wittenberg express this forcibly:

93: "Let all those prophets . . . say to the people of Christ, 'Cross! Cross! when accepted it is no longer a cross'."

94: "Christians must be exhorted to follow Christ their Head with utter devotion, through punishment, through death, through hell."

95: "In this way let them have confidence that they will enter heaven through many tribulations, rather than through a false assurance of peace."

89 — "You can see how . . . the theology of the Cross has been emptied of its meaning . . . The theologian of the Cross (that is, one who speaks of the hidden and unfathomable God) teaches that punishments, crosses, and death are the most precious treasure of all and the most sacred of relics, relics which the Lord Himself, the creator of this theology, has consecrated and blessed . . . Blessed is the man who is considered by God worthy to receive *these* treasures of the relics of Christ!"[87]

The sufferings to be shared with Christ are literal enough: Luther was too aware of psychological and legalistic dangers inherent in any call to 'recapitulate Christ's passion" to give pietistic "imitation of the Crucified" a prominent place. Yet the oldest theme of Christian ethics is here not far from his mind. Dickens notes how Luther replaces the mystics' passive abandonment by a Christocentric emphasis, "the tragic and triumphant sacrifice of Jesus" evoking a "profound anguish both for Christ and for each man chosen to follow him along the way of the Cross." Dickens adds that Luther's *Of the Liberty of the Christian Man* expounds a faith which "begets no mystical quietism but . . . a participation in the battle and the victory of Christ over sin, death, and the Devil."[88] Luther warns the speculator to "purge the eye of his heart in meditating on the wounds of Jesus Christ . . . the *wounds* of Jesus are *safe* enough for us."[89]

Rupp summarises the theology of the Cross dramatically:

"The theology of the Cross means not only that Christ's humanity and extreme humiliation are the way by which we know God: not only that his work 'for us' is the ground of our salvation, and his work 'in us', that we too are to conquer sin, death and the devil. The Christian man and the Christian Church must also share the sufferings of Christ, that 'form of a servant' which brings an ambiguity and contradiction into all their earthly existence." Of the people of Christ — "Theirs does not seem to be a kingdom but an exile, and they seem not to live but always given up to death, not to glory but put to shame." "To have Christ crucified in oneself is to live full of temptations and sufferings, and thus be, in bodily things, 'a sign to be spoken against' . . . For verily Christ always comes in that form which he took when he emptied himself of the form of God."[90]

As Loewenich expresses it, Christian men, the church militant, are called to share this contradiction, of poverty, weakness, shame, humiliation, suffering. The theology of the Cross is a theology of indirect, veiled revelation through receptive suffering — "God is not to be found save in passions and in the Cross". Those who believe are enabled to fight with Christ against sin, death, and the devil: with Him they are united in the church which shares the contradiction involved in "the form of a servant". Life in the church means life "under the Cross".[91]

This is a new interpretation of the imitation of Christ, more literal than mystical, involving actual and deliberate sharing of Christ's rejection in history by the world, rather than the invented austerities, and "empathy" with the suffering Christ, of the ascetic tradition. It is, moreover, more closely related to the actual suffering of Christ for the believer's sin; for here the believer, too, stands under divine judgement, and turns from his sin in penitence to cling to Christ crucified, his only hope.

So rich and varied is Luther's exposition of the individual moral consequences of his gospel. The prevailing emotional tone of Christian character is likewise determined by Luther's emphases. The believer's complete dependence upon Christ alone, by faith alone, for salvation, and the conception of life as lived ever "before God", necessitate a constant "unconditional self-condemnation" — awareness of one's sin and helplessness — which for Luther is true humility, in contrast with the self-generated, self-conscious humility practised by the monks.[92]

> "Unless a man is always humble, always distrustful of himself, always fears his own understanding . . . his passion . . . his will, he will be unable to stand for very long without offence. For truth will pass him by . . ."[93]

Theologically, such humility is discussed as "aptness" (or prerequisite) for grace, as the essence of faith.[94] Humility is therefore entirely compatible with assurance, which relies only on the gracious mercy of God. "A Christian man is always in good heart" Luther once remarked; the wit, humour, and high spirits often ascribed to him were the effervescence of a confident expectancy and gladness, kindled by all God's saving goodness.[95] This, in turn, was nourished by a constant, free, and informal prayer-life. During the first three hours of each day, usually at an open window, Luther talked to God "with as much ease and naturalness as to his dear Philip". An intensely practical exposition of the Lord's Prayer[96] urges that only by constantly seeking the ear of God, learning how and what to pray, can we hope to fulfil the divine Commandments, and sustain the humility of spirit and joy of heart that lend radiance to character.

4. THE MORAL CONSEQUENCES — SOCIAL

Luther's social teaching arouses the strongest partisanship. Tawney can say "Luther's utterances on social morality are the occasional explosions of a capricious volcano, with only a rare flash of light . . . an impression of naivete, of impetuous but ill-informed genius;" Inge's verdict is that Lutheranism had no valuable social message; Lazareth speaks of an "impressive social reformation . . . Luther's contribution to a better world is incalculable."[97] But Luther's deep social concern is not open to debate. His insistence that saving faith works through neighbourly love to manifest itself in works useful to mankind; his hallowing of "secular" vocations; his efforts to make educational reform (for girls as well as boys) a community obligation in every town and village; his establishment of "community chests" to alleviate illiteracy and mendicancy; his protests against economic injustice, against rebellious mobs misusing freedom and arbitrary rulers neglecting public responsibilities — are all of immense significance. Equally impressive is his elaboration of the Ten Commandments in Christian terms as a social code:

The First Commandment (on Luther's reckoning) insists that what you trust in — riches, self-esteem — is your God and makes you what you are. The Second safeguards by the oath the truth professed in society, business, courts of law, pulpits. The Third justifies rest days by bodily necessity and need for worship; the Fourth extends esteem and assistance to parents, masters, rulers, with side-comment upon reciprocal duties. The prohibition of killing does not affect execution; it forbids revenge, and harm done by word, anger, gesture; its purpose is protection, and to refuse help is murder. Prohibition of adultery protects chastity; the ban on stealing protects property against all fraud and unfairness, and requires protection of the neighbour's interests. Prohibition of false witness condemns perjury, heresy, slander, evil-speaking, ill-judgement. The word against covetousness forbids greed, fraud, taking advantage of weakness, "shrewdness" in business, avarice, envy. Such social rules teach us how to please God, provide channels along which good works must flow, and require more than any can give without the faith of the Creed and the power of prayer.[98]

(1) Social Conservatism

In his practical social counsel, Luther is open to the charge of conservatism. Chadwick remarks that "Luther himself believed in gradualness"; Inge, that "Luther was politically a Conservative"; and Tawney, that "Where questions of social morality were involved, men whose names are symbols of religious revolution stood, with hardly an exception, on the ancient ways . . . Of that revolutionary conservatism Luther is the supreme example."[99] Luther certainly hankered after past simplicities. Hating the new commerce and emerging capitalism, he "sighed for a vanished age of peasant prosperity" and suggested that Germans "leave the overcrowded world of trade to rehabilitate agriculture."[100] He condemned the luxury trade with the East, which drained land and people of their money. The reason was partly biblical, partly a wish to return to "natural" ways, from the growing individualism, competition, commercial finance, monopolies, credit, and capital investment for speculative profit. In all such matters, "the eyes of Luther are on the past."

This nostalgic attitude saw *(i) the social orders* — ecclesiastical, domestic, economic, political — as embodying in institutional forms the requirements of divine law; as the Creator's bulwarks against sin. Men should therefore accept the social structures, and act responsibly *within* them; they can be reformed only by law, within the realm of man, whereas *persons* can be transformed by the gospel, in the kingdom of God.[101] The institutions and structures of secular society — justice, education, economic life, government — have no particular Christian "form"; they are infected by sin yet through them the Creator preserves His fallen world from even greater chaos. While the church may hope to "Christianise" politicians and economists, it cannot "Christianise" politics and economics. God ordains that these remain secular: reason and justice, not faith and love, are their foundations.

Hence Luther's response to widespread social protest was reactionary. He was convinced that serfdom was the necessary foundation of society, horrified by the demand that villeinage should end because Christ has redeemed all men equally:

"This . . . would make all men equal and so change the spiritual kingdom of Christ into an external one. Impossible! An earthly kingdom cannot exist without inequality. Some must be free, others serfs, some rulers, others subjects. As St. Paul says, Before Christ both *master* and *slave* are one." Luther "even tells the Christian slaves of the Turks that they must not rob their masters of their bodies, which their masters have bought."[102]

Luther's conservatism affects also his view of *(ii) marriage*. Though his own break with celibacy challenged prevailing thought on who should be allowed to marry, his attitude to marriage in general was traditional. From the form of the Seventh Commandment, Luther argued that God "especially honours and commends wedded life" — establishing it first of all institutions, creating man and woman for it, intending life-long loyalty and family unity. It is the most universal, the noblest, and necessary estate; men and women of all conditions should be found in it, excepting only those specially exempt as unfit, or "gifted to become free to live chastely" without marriage. His dictum, "To unaided human nature, as God created it, chastity apart from matrimony is an impossibility . . . that man might more easily keep his evil lust in bonds, God commanded marriage" directly echoes Paul at his least exalted. The Commandment does however also require a man "to love and appreciate the consort God has given him", and perfect fidelity.

Out of a valued home-life Luther has perceptive counsel to offer; but against marriage "spiritualised" into a sacrament he argues, that marriage belongs to the realm of creation and not to redemption; is ruled by law not gospel; is a temporal remedy against sin, not a sanctifying means of grace. Yet marriage remains among the creative ordinances of God; there is no higher calling in which Christians can exercise faith in deeds of serving love.

"Someone who is married but does not *recognise* married life can never live in it without disgust, and sorrow . .. those who recognise it firmly believe that God instituted marriage, and ordained that man and woman should be joined together and raise children. They have God's word for it . . ."[103]

The "non-sacramental concept of matrimony" says Dickens[104] "involved the possibility of divorce and remarriage if the vows were broken." But already the Pope himself had not infrequently "sanctioned the equivalent of divorce for a first wife".[105] In the difficult case of his friend and supporter, Philip of Hesse, Luther sanctioned a bigamous marriage — bigamy being preferable to divorce."

In *(iii) commercial affairs* Luther sought amid ever-increasing complexity and widening trade to conserve older principles.

"A man should not say 'I will sell as dear as I can' but 'I will sell as is right and proper.' Thy selling should not be within thine own will, without law and limit, as though thou wert a God. Because thy selling is a work thou performest to thy neighbour, it should be restrained within law and conscience, that thou mayest practice it without injury to him."[106]

The Christian trader will observe the price fixed by public authority, or common estimation, or cost plus need and risk, never by scarcity, by cornering the market, by future uncertainties, or by charging more for deferred payment. Cost, labour, and risk, alone regulate the fair price.[107]

Against the charging of interest on borrowed capital, Luther is even more severe than traditional Christian teaching. He would deny to usurers the sacrament, absolution, and Christian burial. Lending ought to be free: investment in rent-charges was forbidden, and even payment of interest as compensation for loss.

"The greatest misfortune of the German nation is easily the traffic in interest . . . the devil invented it; the Pope, by giving his sanction, has done untold evil throughout the world."[108]

In this respect, Luther was in harmony with widespread and vociferous protests against extortion.

A similar loyalty to custom informs Luther's support of *(iv) the established authorities,* though he sets older ideas in radically new context in his doctrine of the two kingdoms. For him, obedience must precede reform:

Expounding the Fourth Commandment, Luther mentions various spheres in which obedience is required to authorities whose *duty* it is to command — masters, princes, magistrates, civil rulers — all *in loco parentis* to their subordinates, and so due the reverence, esteem, and assistance enjoined in the commandment.

It may be supposed that Luther sorely needed the help of German princelings; and so, naturally, opposed reckless mobs who confused Christian freedom with civil freedom. But that his was no merely sycophantic policy is shown by his insistence on the princes' responsibility, under God, for the welfare of their people, and even more by his open criticism:

"A clever prince is a very rare bird, and a devout prince rarer still . . . usually the biggest fools or the wickedest fellows on earth . . . (we) can expect little good of them . . . If a prince happens to be clever, devout, or a Christian, this is a great miracle, and a most precious sign of God's grace upon his country."[109]

Nevertheless, when crisis came he sided with authority.

Much of Luther's language encouraged revolt. He "had been born a peasant . . . hit hard at the oppression of the landlords, agreed with many of the peasants' demands. But he hated armed strife . . . travelled round the country districts risking his life to preach against violence" (Chadwick[110]). Tracing the causes of the Peasants' Revolt, Inge says the oppressed looked to Luther as champion, but when revolt came Luther was divided between genuine sympathy for the poor and extreme respect for authority. Niebuhr speaks of Luther "alarmed by the prospect of anarchy"; Tawney, of his being "terrified" into his outburst — "whoso can, strike, smite, strangle, or stab, secretly or publicly . . . such wonderful times are these that a prince can better merit heaven with bloodshed than another with prayer." Tawney comments that this helped stamp upon Lutheranism an almost servile reliance on secular authorities; Inge says it estranged the "official" Reformation in Germany from democratic sympathies, making Lutheranism a middle-class movement while the artisans became supporters of the Anabaptists.[111]

Atkinson's defence of Luther's position is probably the best that can be offered.[112] He argues that "misunderstanding" leads to use of the above "stock quotation" to condemn Luther, without realising how widespread were the social stirrings of the age, how tragic the mistake which identified the peasants' just economic cause with the religious cause of Luther, how dangerous the teachings (of Carlstadt and Muntzer) with which Luther was confronted. The "cool common sense" of Luther replied that force belonged to civil authority, appointed by God for social order, not to be withstood by mystical enthusiasts or mob law. His *Exhortation to Peace* sought reconciliation, but failed; he therefore counselled firmness, as to "a dog that had run mad", in words that were harsh, but never retracted, against "persistent lawless devilry." "The violence of his language is the measure of the issue that was at stake." Others might see in it the measure of Luther's own inner confusion, or even of his bad conscience.

There was, of course, in Luther's teaching and example, a limit to Christian obedience to authority. The ruled "ought to obey God rather than men". The ruler must prevent the oppression of sound doctrine, and support the Reformation — else Christian obedience might be strained.[113] But the use of force, in itself, constituted no difficulty:

"Christians are rare people on earth. Therefore stern, hard, civil rule is necessary in the world, lest the world become wild, peace vanish, and commerce and common interests be destroyed . . . No one need think that the world can be ruled without blood. The civil sword must be red and bloody."[114]

So the authority which Luther challenged in the papal government is transferred to the secular ruler. "Self defence is a natural right, which the gospel must be understood to presuppose". In general, Luther held that law-enforcement is the ultimate mercy, and Christians should not shrink from it:

"See there is no lack of hangmen, police, judges, lords" . . . and such officers are Christians; because "if the State and its sword are a divine service . . . then that which the State needs to wield the sword must also be a divine service . . ." "Worldly government through the sword aims to keep peace: this God rewards with temporal blessing . . ."[115]

(v) War itself is "justified as legitimate and necessary . . . in a good cause" (Inge[116]). In his *Sincere Admonition to all Christians to Guard Against Insurrection and Rebellion,* Luther argues that the falseness (of the papacy) can only be overcome by truth and exposure, not by force:

"We shall do him no damage by violence, only strengthen him . . . If I had wanted violence I would have brought about a great shedding of blood . . .

But it would have been a game for fools . . . I have let the Word act . . ."[117]

But this relates to religious conflict: in the political field, Luther "held that the gospel presupposes natural rights and duties, and vigorously defended the Christian soldier."[118] According to Bainton,[119] Luther reworked the theory of "the just war" of Augustine and the early middle ages; but he rejected crusading — partly because it was instigated by the Pope, but also because of his doctrine of two kingdoms, one sustained by persuasion through God's Word, the other sustaining order by force. Civil rulers are ordained not only to maintain justice, but to repel invaders from without.

Ministers, armed only with the Word, cannot be executioners, soldiers, or crusaders, and must offer only passive resistance. The soldier, like the magistrate, is God's instrument, regretfully exercising the judgements of God — war being an aspect of the police function of the State. The soldier's calling is therefore legitimate, ordained by God — though Luther approved the desertion of troops used against the Reformation! The object of the just war is always peace, and "where there is peace there is half of the kingdom of heaven."[120] So war is a last resort, engaged upon always with due regard to cost — "like fishing with a golden net". Luther's whole code of the just war was traditional Christian teaching — with its traditional limitations.

(2) The Two Kingdoms

The ethical doctrine behind these practical counsels was far less conservative, even though the basic notion — the "two kingdoms" — resembles Aquinas' "two realms" (nature, redemption), Augustine's "Two Cities", the apocalyptists' "Two Ages", and Paul's "two humanities" (one deriving from Adam, the other from Christ). Traditional doctrine sharply divided the secular State from the spiritual kingdom, as on two different "levels". The "Enthusiasts" repudiated the secular State altogether. Luther thought that the absolute division drawn between the two was false,[121] and its implications — that secular power has no spiritual authority, is independent of divine law; that church and State are rivals or foes; that Christians owe no obedience to the State — were perilous.

Accordingly, Luther *(i) differentiated sacred and secular spheres,* either as two ministries within one Christian community, or as relating to two different communities, Christian and non-Christian within one land.[122]

"We divide men into two parts: those who belong to the kingdom of God are all believers in Christ, subject to Christ . . . all who are not Christians belong to the kingdom of the world and are subject to the law." "The world is a house . . . I am outside the house, on the roof, not yet in heaven but also not in the world. I have the world beneath me and the heavens above me; I am suspended in faith between life in the world and eternal life."

"The State" (summarises Bainton) "goes back to the order of creation and arose in Paradise because of man's urge to association. The coercive power of the State was introduced after the Fall . . . The administration of the State is in accord with natural law . . . and reason . . . In the kingdom of Christ reason does not apply for this is the area of faith. The State rules over things outward — the body, houses, lands and the like — the church only over things spiritual. The State deals with crime, the church with sin."[123]

In the kingdom of men, *God* rules sinful creatures through State, law, civil justice, enforced obedience; in the kingdom of redemption, God rules all regenerate believers through Christ and the gospel of love. Luther carefully defines the responsibility of each: the role of the church is to preach, teach, care for people as Christ had done. "To confuse these roles was disastrous for both."[124]

"Church order had not to be upset . . . secular order must be preserved . . . both are from God." "I must always drum and hammer and force and drive in this distinction between the two kingdoms . . . The Devil himself never ceases cooking up the two kingdoms together: secular authorities seek, in the name of the Devil, to teach and instruct Christ how He should conduct His church; false priests and sectaries, not in the name of God, seek to teach people how they should conduct secular rule. Thus the Devil is unrestrained on either side . . ."[125]

But Luther insisted *(ii) the secular, too, is God's.* The State does *not* stand over against God and church as pagan, godless, outside divine law. "So far from leaving politics to itself, free to make its own laws," says Rupp,[126] "Luther would have regarded the attempt to establish a secular State . . . as the summit of human folly and pride . . . We are not to think that God is only interested in Christians and has left the world to its own devices." As Creator and Redeemer, God is Lord of both kingdoms.

"The secular rule can also be called the kingdom of God. He intends it to stand, and us to be obedient in it. But it is only *the kingdom of His left hand.* The kingdom of His right hand, which He rules himself, not placing in it father, king, executioner and jailer but dwelling in it himself, is that in which the gospel is preached to the poor." Though Luther can also say, of God's secular kingdom, that it may be "poor, wretched, a foul and stinking kingdom", and can become the kingdom of Satan.[127]

Subjects of Christ's kingdom need no secular law, enforced by the sword. If everyone were Christian, there would be no need of prince, law, or sword — the Spirit would teach the right way and ensure it was obeyed. Where wrong is passively accepted, and right passionately pursued, there arises no quarrel, strife, court, punishment, law or sword.[128] But, for the sake of non-Christians, all these are necessary.

"Since few believe . . . God has made for most, instead of the kingdom of God, *another form of rule,* has subjected them to the sword, so that even if they do evil, they may not do it without fear . . . If this were not done, since there is scarcely one true Christian in a thousand, no one could nurture his wife and children, feed himself, serve God; the world would become waste. Consequently, God has set up two forms of rule, the spiritual, which makes Christians through the Holy Spirit subject to Christ; and the secular, which restrains the wicked, so that they have to keep peace outwardly and be silent against their will."[129]

Thus there are "two different ways in which God encounters the sinful world" says Ebeling, "the first, with the gospel, which gives the Holy Spirit, and the second, with the law, which outwardly checks the consequences of sin."[130] Both reactions express the divine will: this would be part of Luther's answer to the charge that he teaches two moralities, one for the Christian realm and one for the secular life of the world.[131]

Luther required, therefore, *(iii) Christian involvement in secular life.* The divine authority behind secular rule held good whether or not the ruler was Christian; it is not confined to a Christian State.

"It is not necessary for the emperor . . . to be a Christian to rule. It is sufficient . . . to possess reason." "God has subjected secular rule to reason because its purpose is not to control the salvation of souls but only temporal goods, which God subjects to man . . . In the gospel we are taught nothing of how this rule is to be exercised, only commanded that it should be honoured. That is why pagans . . . are far more skilled than Christians in such matters . . . Christians seem to be mere children, fools, and beggars by contrast with them."[132]

Nevertheless it is well, for their own good and the public's that the rulers be Christian, for the temptations of power are great:

"Do not blasphemously say that a Christian may not carry out the work, ordinance, and creation of God himself . . . for the service of God befits no one so much as Christians. It would be valuable if all princes were truly Christian, for to wield the sword and authority as a service of God is more fitting for Christians than for all others."

It should be added, with Atkinson, that "when Luther put all power in the hands of the prince, it was of "a 'godly prince' (the great Reformation idea) who respected this distinction'' (between the role of church and State), who granted the church full liberty, and sought to protect the church in her spiritual tasks.''[133]

So Christians are not to hold aloof from secular responsibilities. As the Augsburg Confession insists, they are not so to misunderstand the ''two realms'' as to fall into dualism, but must permeate all society with love and justice, fulfilling social obligation. While there can be no government ruled by the gospel, no *Christian* State, it remains the duty of Christians to serve the State, as God's ordinance. Politics is a legitimate occupation, and Luther urged Christian parents with gifted children to ''keep the best boy for this work.''

The truth is, the two realms are not only under one divine King, but also united in their members. The Christian is subject at once of the realm of creation *and* of the realm of redemption. As citizen, he is compelled by the State, in law-abiding loyalty, to civil righteousness; as saint, he is empowered by Christ, in love activated by faith, to a Christian righteousness. The Christian lives simultaneously before God and the world: not as two persons, but as one person in two ''persona'' or masks — the same person is seen, both publicly and privately, before God as a believer, encountering God's word, and at the same time is seen, before the world, publicly and privately, as husband, father, teacher, prince, judge, maid.[134]

These two relations ''go perfectly well together; you satisfy God's kingdom and the kingdom of the world at the same time: at the same time suffering wrong and yet punishing wrong; at the same time not resisting evil and yet resisting it. In one case, you are paying attention to your own affairs; in the others, to your neighbour and his affairs . . .''[135]

Again, the Christian as a *person* does not need the civil law; as a *person-in-relation* he is under civil law towards his fellows, as they are towards himself. For such reasons, Ebeling well says that the two kingdoms cannot be represented in a diagram, whether of concentric spheres or parallel lines: ''the relationship is one of movement, activity, and conflict.''[136]

Luther, therefore, *(iv) resisted the mediaeval identification of the two kingdoms with two institutions* within society — one ''religious'', the church, that is, the clergy, the ''sacred realm''; the other ''secular'', the laity, forming one ''estate'' with the civil realm. From such identifications had arisen the immense claims of the ruling church: Pope, bishops, priests and monks, as a ''spiritual estate'' possessing ''quasi-divine power,'' ruling Europe in God's name.[137] This ''organisational'' definition of the two kingdoms Luther firmly rejected. The Christian minority cannot expect to rule the non-

Christian majority; every Christian is both righteous and a sinner, needing both forms of rule, gospel and law. The distinction between clerical and lay is a distinction of *calling,* within the one body of Christ:

"To call popes, bishops, priests, monks, nuns, the 'religious' class, but princes, lords, artisans, farm-workers, the 'secular' class, is a specious device invented by time-servers . . . All Christians whatsoever belong to the religious class; there is no difference among them except as they do different work . . . Baptism, gospel, faith, *alone* make men 'religious', create a Christian people . . . Baptism makes us all priests . . . Those who exercise secular authority have all been baptised like the rest of us; therefore they are priests and bishops. They discharge their office as an office of the Christian community and for its benefit."[138]

This destroyed the distinction between "clerical" and "lay" as the basis of rival "ecclesiastical" and "secular" powers. The church *may not* impose its will on the community ("clericalism"): indeed, because of the pride, and greed, of church leaders, "it would be much safer if the temporal affairs of the clergy also were placed under the control of the secular arm".[139] But not, of course, the church's doctrine or her purely spiritual functions, which Luther held to be controlled already by scripture. The State must not interfere in the church's role as prophetic teacher and critic of society, nor seek to silence men of God, nor confiscate Bibles, books, papers, nor "invade the province of a man's soul and his relation to God."[140] Chadwick summarises results of the new system: some ecclesiastical abuses removed, some merely replaced by princely abuses — greed, misappropriation of church funds and misuse of power.[141]

Tawney's reference to a certain naïveté in Luther's social outlook may now be appreciated. For the arts by which men amass wealth, the foresight by which they ensure the future, Luther had "all the distrust of a peasant and a monk". Christians he expected to earn their livelihood by the sweat of their brow, take no thought for the morrow, marry young, and trust heaven to provide. In all temporal transactions, — the golden rule: then everything would arrange itself! No law books, courts, would be required; all things would quietly be set to rights; everyone's heart and conscience would guide him. Tawney comments, few would deny this: but how if everything does not "arrange itself"? Confronted with the appeal of the Danzig civil authorities, whether they should put down usury, Luther retreated into the clouds: "the preacher shall preach only the golden rule and leave it to each man to follow his own conscience." But it is precisely for that confused private conscience that Christian guidance is needed. Luther had shaken the one authority that offered "infallible" — or at least, unchallengeable — counsel: on social and political matters he had nothing to put in its place, save the moral intuitions of such as were godly among the bearers of secular power.[142]

5. *Assessment.*

The history and development of Lutheranism is itself a wide field of Christian scholarship, and the far-reaching *importance* of Luther's thought is immeasurable. He lay the foundation for Protestant-evangelical ethics, yet despite the disruption of the Reformation, he strikingly illustrates the changing continuity of Christian ethics, not only in his personal origins and life-long loyalties, but in his most searching enquiry. His analysis deliberately returns to the ancient formulations of bondage, sin, law, freedom, and unmerited justification. His insistence upon the morality already *given* in faith, as a driving force that works, and works by love, returns likewise to the apostolic emphasis upon the new-made man behind the new code of behaviour. His detailed social counsel, on the orders of society, marriage, usury, obedience, the just war, follows closely lines laid down long before by Christian moralists. His "theology of the Cross" gave a new practical and realist application to the oldest and most central principle of Christian ethics, the imitation of Christ. Indeed, both in its form of biblical exposition, and in its content, Luther's teaching consciously resorted to the original fountains of Christian inspiration as they flowed still through scripture. It is one measure of Luther's achievement that he helped to create a new Christian Europe by returning to the oldest themes of Christian ethics.

Nevertheless, as to the *success* of Luther's ethical endeavours there is room for serious debate. He himself had the gravest misgivings concerning the practical results of his work, and no small disappointment. The abuse of authority by Protestant princes was only one symptom of the disparity between evangelical profession and ethical practice which faced him repeatedly. Atkinson underlines frequently this saddened "concern":

"One sometimes senses in Luther the faith that once the evangelical trumpet had blown loud and clear all the walls of sin and ignorance would fall. In principle he was right, but in actuality many people continued to hold to their old ways . . . Luther showed at this time a marked concern for . . . immorality of the nobility . . . vulgarity of the peasants . . . Drunkenness caused him much distress." His feelings against usury and avarice . . . were strong . . . gluttony and gambling, drunkenness and unchastity, looseness and immorality. He was troubled when scandals kept breaking out within the church: "That God could be so unreal and faith so ineffective in the lives of evangelical men gave Luther much distress of mind." So did "the state of religion and morals at every level of society in Germany . . . He was deeply aware of the feeble root that evangelical religion had taken . . . Spite of clear preaching, the people showed little change in their lives and morals . . .churchmen, princes, and common folk concerned but for themselves. . ."

"He reproached his folk more severely than he did his opponents — peasants were castigated for indifference, stupidity, coarse selfishness; burghers for luxury and worldly values; all for drunkenness, gluttony, immorality, indifferentism; . . . even his students, for living like swine, indulging in loose sexual activity."

"It galled him that Wittenberg, the cradle of the Reformation, should bear such meagre fruits of spirituality and morality. He criticised the provocativeness of the ladies' dress, vulgarity and rioting, loose women hanging round students' quarters; dishonesty of trade and usury. How little changed the human heart, for all the torrents of the gospel that had flowed through Wittenberg!"

"Therefore we would like to let the Pope be over them again . . . such a mob, who will not obey the gospel, deserve nothing more than such a jailer . . ."[143]

But though Atkinson faithfully records so much, he does not discuss its deep significance.

For inevitably, Luther's disappointments raise the question whether his ethical doctrine is *true to experience and to life.* The credo —

"Faith brings with it good works and is irresistible . . . Only believe, and you will be able to do everything . . . You do not have to demand good works from someone who has once believed. For faith teaches him everything, and everything that he does is well done. . . . Faith makes everything good in a man . . ."[144]

is a statement of theological *belief,* which Luther's concern, twenty years later, scarcely validates. To speak of "disillusionment" would be too sweeping: but it is essential that Protestant-evangelical ethics learn the lesson that if — as is so often assumed — a true faith and experience are sufficient to transform a life, without need for ethical instruction, encouragement, or demand, then it is imperative to give "faith" and "experience" their fullest, apostolic, meaning.

Faith, which is no more than orthodox, scriptural, intellectual opinion, even though hardened by habit or dogmatism into "conviction"; and "experience" which is only a mystical emotionalism kindled by the name of Jesus, will transform nothing. An intellectualised gospel misses the truth about human motivation, that it is less rationalist than emotional and intuitive. Evangelical emotionalism misses the point that emotion must be channeled by ideas, goals, and directives, to produce anything at all. A Christian faith which — in Synoptic terms — is the positive side of moral repentance; which in apostolic terms is faith-union with the dying and living Christ, confessed at risk of persecution, *will* transform a life. A spiritual experience born out of deep abhorrence of sin and a consuming sense of guilt, which reaches forth to Christ for moral deliverance, *will* transform the soul. Without such qualifications, the evangelical expectation that "faith alone" will generate Christlike character is always doomed to disappointment.

10

Calvin: Radical Reformed Morality

"THE MOST CHARACTERISTIC FORM OF PROTESTANTISM" and "the most potent religious force in Protestantism" were, according to Tawney and Chadwick, the teaching and the followers of John Calvin. This was partly because Calvin's *Institutes* "took the place of the mediaeval textbooks of theology in the universities"; but as Dakin remarked, the Calvinist attitude to life has been no less fruitful than its theological system.[1] There is no question of Calvin's importance: but there is, in some quarters, serious doubt of Calvin's moral truth and value.

Calvin is often presented as a grim, inhuman figure. Orr says he was a man of naked intellect, conscience, and will; much is said of his legal training, French logic, ruthlessness, austerity, his rigorist discipline of the city-State of Geneva, and his hotly-debated share in the torture and death of the heretic (or libertine) Servetus.[2] It is well therefore to recall that Calvin writes a surprising amount about enjoyment of the world.

"It becomes man seriously to employ his eyes considering the works of God, since a place has been assigned him in *this most glorious theatre* that he may be a spectator of them . . ." "Sculpture and painting are gifts of God . . . manual and liberal arts . . . intelligence in some particular art (is) a special gift of God" . . . "in reading profane authors, the admirable light of truth displayed should remind us that the human mind . . . is still adorned and invested with admirable gifts . . . we will be careful . . . not to reject truth wherever it appears. In despising the gifts we insult the Giver . . ." lawgivers, philosophers, rhetoricians, medicine, mathematical sciences.[3]

On "the proper use of earthly blessings", Calvin argues we must use necessary supports of life, "nor can we shun things which seem more subservient to delight than to necessity. We must observe a mean . . ."

"Let this be our principle: in the use of gifts of Providence, refer them to the end for which their Author destined them . . . If we consider for what end He created food, we shall find He consulted not only our necessity but also our enjoyment . . . (so with) . . . clothing, comeliness, honour, herbs, fruits, gracefulness of appearance, sweetness of smell." The Prophet enumerates among mercies of God, wine that maketh glad the heart, and oil to make the face shine. "Has the Lord adorned flowers with all the beauty which spontaneously presents itself to the eye and the sweet odour which delights the sense of smell, and shall it be unlawful for us to enjoy that beauty and this odour . . .?" (so with) colours, gold, silver, ivory, marble. "Has God not given many things value without any necessary use? Have done then with that inhuman philosophy which . . . cannot be realised without depriving man of all his senses."[4]

Though the discussion continues with the dangers of excess, Calvin clearly must not be credited with the "absurd and unsympathetic attitude towards innocent amusements" of which Inge accuses some of his followers.[5] Friend of humanists, himself "one of the more accomplished young humanists of his day" (Dickens[6]), students of classical literature, Calvin's first book was — significantly — a commentary upon Seneca's *De Clementia.*

Besides, moral rigorism was not confined to Calvinists. "The age was earnestly moral, and the tone of Europe was reforming and therefore strict" says Chadwick. Niebuhr agrees: "rigorousness and severity were part of the temper of the time."[7] But Dickens remarks that Calvin knew when to become flexible, and sometimes "expressed strangely liberal sentiments: 'We cannot but behold our own face in those who are poor and despised . . .' Even a Moor, or a barbarian, 'from the very fact of his being a man' carries about with him 'a mirror in which we can see he is our brother and our neighbour.'"[8]

Where Lutheranism was conservative, Calvinism was radical, intellectual, urban, at home among tradesmen and merchants of the great business and industrial centres, a factor considerably affecting its social ethic.[9] Calvin venerated Luther, and "sought to embody Luther's teaching in a church and in a society which would really put that teaching into practice."[10] The twenty years that separated Calvin's work from Luther's confirmed Luther's view that the Word was anything but irresistible; the papal authority which Luther had destroyed needed to be replaced. "It was a great and necessary work to prove that to adopt the Protestant religion was not to surrender discipline or moral and social obligations" says Inge.[11] And Dickens shows how, inheriting from Luther a religion which could have become merely individualist, Calvin added, from Zwingli, a systematic social discipline through magistrates and pastors. This corporate emphasis of Calvin is clearly expressed in the famous words:

". . . Of the visible church . . . from her title of Mother how necessary knowledge of her is . . . is no other means of entering into life unless she conceive us in the womb, give us birth, nourish us at her breasts, keep us under her charge and government until . . . we become like angels . . . Beyond the pale of the church no forgiveness, no salvation, can be hoped for . . . abandonment of the church is always fatal."[12]

His other emphasis is epitomised by Chadwick: "Calvin's ultimate religious act was the assent of the will to an everlasting Lord; his ultimate text, 'Thy will be done'."[13] Tawney conveniently summarises Calvinism for us in a single sentence:

"For the Calvinist, the world is ordained to show forth the majesty of God, and the duty of the Christian is to live for that end — his task is at once to discipline his individual life and to create a sanctified society."[14]

The premise here, that God is incomparably majestic, sovereign, transcendent, is Calvin's supreme theological principle: the two conclusions form Calvin's essential contribution to Christian ethics.

"The first word in Calvinism is *God*" — "Calvin's sense of divine sovereignty is almost unmatched in Christian literature outside scripture."[15] The world, and all within it, are subject to God's power: the divine will directs every individual event of history. Even in the theory of predestination, Calvin is more concerned with the absolute sovereignty of God, than with the problem of the reprobate and his freedom — which absorbed his followers.[16] Calvin presses God's absolute sovereignty to the exclusion of man's freedom, making all life, salvation, faith, the gift of God's sole initiative. Man *belongs* to God — by creation, redemption, church-membership. "The great point" says Calvin "is that we, who are consecrated and dedicated to God, should not henceforth think or speak, design or act, without a view to His glory."[17]

A. "To Discipline Individual Life" — to God's Glory

The divine sovereignty confronts the *individual,* first as law; secondly, as a divinely appointed salvation-experience, for which man is totally dependent upon divine choice; and thirdly, as a divine requirement that man should respond in obedient self-discipline.

1. THE DIVINE LAW

Calvin gives exceptional place to the divine law and to the Ten Commandments — a "Judaic" tendency which recent expositors have faithfully reproduced. For a Calvinist, one definition of sin is, "any want of conformity to, or transgression of, the law of God''; and of sanctification, ''ever more complete obedience to the Ten Commandments.''[18]

(1) The Meaning of Law

Calvin accepts the basis of morality in natural law:

''By nature a social animal, man is disposed, from natural instinct, to preserve society; the minds of all have impressions of civil order . . . every individual understands how human societies must be regulated by law . . . the seeds of them being implanted in the breasts of all without a lawgiver . . . (and) not affected by wars, thieves . . . quarrels . . . (which) do not destroy the primary idea of justice . . .'' An apostle declares: ''the gentiles . . . show the work of the law written on their hearts'' . . . ''We certainly cannot say that they are altogether blind as to the rule of life. Nothing is more common than for men to be sufficiently instructed in right conduct by natural law . . .''[19]

Clark summarises Calvin's account of divine law as a revelation that came —

''First, in God's act of creating man in His own image so that certain basic moral principles were implanted in his heart; . . . second, special instructions given to Adam and Noah, which overlapped and expanded the innate endowment; third, the more comprehensive revelation to Moses; plus, fourth, the various subsidiary precepts in the remainder of the Bible.''[20]

John Murray reflects the same high valuation of the Decalogue:

''The Ten Commandments . . . furnish the core of the biblical ethic . . . the Ten Commandments as promulgated at Sinai were but the concrete and practical form of enunciating principles . . . relevant from the beginning . . . As they did not *begin* to have relevance at Sinai, so they did not cease to have relevance when the Sinaitic economy had passed away . . . these commandments embody principles which belong to the order which God established for man at the beginning, as also to the order of redemption.''[21]

Such cursory dismissal of the prophetic tradition, the whole teaching of Jesus, and the apostolic didache, as ''the various subsidiary precepts in the remainder of the Bible'' is startling. The implied rejection of the whole biblical presentation of the *development* of ethical vision towards the supreme authority not of Moses but of Christ, gives one pause. The method of exegesis which thus reads *into* the Decalogue all later scriptural insights as already latent, opens the door to almost any extension and re-interpretation of scripture which the taste of later ages might prefer. But there is little doubt that this was Calvin's purpose, to see the Ten Commandments, supplementing natural law, as ''the core of the biblical ethic.''

(2) The Uses of the Law

Calvin's definition of the uses of the law does not, at first sight, make much of law as moral instruction or directive. The demands of the law are "placed far above us, in order to convince us of our utter feebleness":

Since to the commands "promises are annexed which proclaim . . . that our whole power is derived from divine grace, they testify that we are unequal to observance of the law, mere fools in regard to it . . . having so much need of grace . . ."[22] "It is vain to teach righteousness by precept until Christ bestow it by imputation and regeneration . . . In order that a sense of guilt may seek for pardon . . . our being instructed in the moral law renders us more inexcusable . . . in none of us is the righteousness of the law manifested: therefore we again fall under the curse . . . The doctrine of the law transcending our capacity, a man may indeed look from a distance at the promises . . . from their excellence to form a better estimate of his own misery; the result must be despondency, confusion, and despair . . ."[23]

"A succinct view of the office of the moral law: . . . First, by exhibiting . . . righteousness it admonishes unrighteousness, . . . and condemns in order that man . . . may be brought to confess; as a kind of mirror, it discloses our iniquity, (and that) the unrighteous will perish . . . in order that men may take refuge in His mercy. Second, by . . . dread of punishment, to curb those who . . . have no regard for rectitude; such forced righteousness being necessary for society. Third: the principal use of the law has respect to believers . . . enabling them to learn what the will of the Lord is, (and) a constant stimulus . . . a perfect pattern of righteousness . . . even to the end of the world . . . It points out the goal . . ."[24]

Thus, in the end, the law retains its ethical function also, of directing towards moral perfection. Keeping the law does not save — but the saved had better keep the law! In Paul's phrase, the righteousness of the law is after all, "to be fulfilled in us who walk not after the flesh but after the Spirit."

(3) The Exposition of the Law

Calvin therefore devotes much attention to expounding the Ten Commandments as the law for *Christian* life,[25] given to clarify the meagre "law of nature", and to show that nothing is more acceptable to God than obedience, source of all the virtues.

Three rules govern interpretation of the commandments:

(a) Divine law must be "internally" interpreted, God having care for the heart as well as for outward behaviour. So Christ made clear, and Paul declared the law "spiritual".

(b) The *intention* must govern interpretation, though it goes beyond the words. Moreover, a command forbids its opposite.

(c) It is vain to talk of righteousness apart from religion: hence our Saviour summed up the law in two heads — to love the Lord, and our neighbour; and the Decalogue has four religious, and six social commandments.

So Calvin evades the criticism that the ancient commandments were necessarily external, and incorporates into each all that later teachers enjoined in the light of fuller revelation and wider experience. Nevertheless, Calvin's "Exposition of the Moral Law" is obviously important for Protestant Christian ethics, and must be briefly summarised:

Preface: God's authority to command; His kindness already shown, liberating from one bondage that we may submit to Him who makes us free.

1st Commandment: forbids superstition; *requires* that we adore Him only, with pious zeal; our innumerable duties to God reduce to adoration, trust, invocation, thanksgiving. Not enough to refrain from other gods if we do not give ourselves wholly to Him.

2nd Commandment: forbids reducing God to sensible, visible shape, and worship of such images. God is mighty, jealous (as wronged husband) avenging His majesty on following generations, yet showing mercy, also, to thousands.

3rd Commandment: forbids profaning God's name by irreverent, contemptuous use; also forbids perverting God's *word* for avarice, amusement, detracting from God's works, misusing His name in abuse, necromancy, cursing, illicit exorcism, incantation. False oaths are especially detestable: here the prohibition relates to worship rather than to justice; calling God to witness shows veneration of Him as eternal, unchangeable truth: oaths, being a species of worship, must not contain insult, contempt, falsehood; God's name must not be used superfluously, vulgarly, or frivolously. The argument against *all* use of oaths is rebutted with words of Christ, who forbade only those forbidden in the law.

4th Commandment: Purport: that we meditate on the kingdom of God; that Israel might have a type of the believer's rest from works; also to appoint a day for worship and for rest. The sabbath important in the Old Testament: but principally, the mystery of perpetual resting from our own works. Though ceremonial law was abrogated in Christ, the day of worship, and of relaxation for servants, still has place; nothing in Paul's advice against superstitious days contradicts this. Reasons for the Christian change to the first day.

5th Commandment: Purport: to respect dignity appointed by God; we must yield honour, gratitude, obedience, to all whom *God* has set over us: He himself as Father, God, Lord, is reflected in earthly fathers, princes, rulers. Knowing individuals in authority are set there by God, we should pay every duty irrespective of the individual's deserts. 'Honour' — reverence, gratitude, obedience — is specially due to parents. The attached promise originally meant long life in Canaan: for us, long life in God's favour also. The implied warning is elaborated.

6th Commandment: Purport: the race being one, safety of all is entrusted to each, and all violence, injury, prohibited. *Required:* whatever in us lies to defend life, tranquility, safety of our neighbour. *Prohibited* also is the murder of the heart — wrath, hatred; the reason, — the fellowman is the image of God and our own flesh.

7th Commandment: Purport: against all uncleanness, impurity. *Forbidden:* Adultery, lust. Man created not for solitude but for helpmeet — since Fall, need for this provision is increased, and God sanctified marriage. Any other cohabitation cursed. Natural feeling, inflamed by the Fall, makes marriage necessary (save for those exempt). Virginity not to be despised, but is denied to some; incontinence should apply the remedy appointed — to refuse marriage is to oppose God and nature; to the incontinent, marriage is obligatory. Lust *is* fornication; wantonness within marriage is also adultery. The commandment further forbids ensnaring the neighbour's chastity by lascivious attire, gestures, conversation, imagination.

8th Commandment: Purport: God hates injustice. *Forbids* wanting others' goods; *requires* exertion in preserving our own. What each possesses is by God's distribution; misuse involves fraud on divine dispensation. Theft includes violence, plunder, imposture, fraud, litigation, sycophancy, oppressive laws, omission of duties owed, neglect of entrusted property, extravagance, betrayal of secrets. *Requires* further, contentment, seeking only honest gain, helping others to prosperity, assisting the needy, paying one's debts, supporting one's rulers — who likewise care for their people's welfare, pastors for their flocks, parents for their children, servants for masters; let each consider what he owes to his neighbour, and pay it.

9th Commandment: Purport: God abhors falsehood; *forbids* calumnies, false accusation, all untruth, all injury by evil speaking; *requires* we assist everyone in asserting truth and defend his good name. Corrective rebuke, judicial decision, public censure, forewarning of evil consequences, are not forbidden, only malicious slander; the bitter mind, the suspicious spirit, are also condemned.

10th Commandment: Purport: God would have the soul pervaded by love, every adverse feeling banished, no *thought* permitted to inflame concupiscence tending to our neighbour's loss; *forbids* cupidity; *requires* charity.

Any one who exhibits in his actions "this perfect rule of righteousness" would in some measure exhibit a living image of God. For a general summary of the whole moral law as it applies to believers, Calvin turns to *Moses'* exhortation to fear the Lord, walk in His ways, love Him, and keep His commandments, adding *Paul's* "The end of the commandment is charity out of a pure heart, a good conscience and faith unfeigned." "For complete perfection, nothing more can be required than is expressed in these passages of Moses and Paul." Jesus is not mentioned.[26]

2. THE SALVATION EXPERIENCE

The divine sovereignty confronts man not only in moral law but in redeeming grace, as the *sole* initiative that can originate salvation.

"To sins Christ gives the name of *debts* . . . which we could not possibly pay were we not discharged . . . when God freely expunges the debt accepting nothing in return, receiving satisfaction in Christ. Those who expect to satisfy God by merits have no share in this free pardon."[27]

So grace remains sovereign, self-originating; there can be no forgiveness at any time "but by the free and sovereign grace of God in Christ." Calvin rejects Peter Lombard's distinction between the operating grace of God, (by which alone man can will to do good), and the co-operating grace of God (by which the will-made-good is enabled to perform well); for Calvin, to desire good, to do it, and to continue in it, is of God's grace alone.[28]

(1) Man's Moral Helplessness

Adam's sin (essentially disobedience, but implying infidelity, ambition, pride, ingratitude) brought to his posterity estrangement, spiritual death, and hereditary corruption — the depravation of a nature formerly good:

"We bring innate corruption from the very womb" . . . all "come into the world tainted with the contagion of sin." "Original sin . . . hereditary corruption and depravity of our nature . . . first makes us obnoxious to the wrath of God, and then produces in us . . . works of the flesh." It is not that we, being innocent, bear Adam's guilt: through him, *pollution* has been instilled, "for which punishment is justly due. It is Adam's sin and *ours:* it continues to produce evil fruits — everything in man is pervaded with concupiscence . . . a *natural* viciousness, received by hereditary law."[29]

The natural endowments of man are corrupted, the supernatural withdrawn: his rational mind is immersed in darkness, his will so enslaved as to produce nothing but evil . . .[30]

No integrity, knowledge, or fear of God, is in man. Man's *will* is necessarily in bondage, though "voluntarily": conversion's beginning, continuance, completion, faith itself, perseverance in grace, are all the work of grace. The *mind* of man cannot conceive, desire, design anything but what is wicked, distorted, impure; his *heart* can breathe out nothing but corruption and rottenness; if some make show of goodness, their mind is interwoven with deceit, their soul inwardly bound with wickedness."[31]

Such a conclusion would appear to many a gross overstatement of the position which Calvin means to establish: that man certainly needs salvation, and can do nothing to attain it; that to will good, to believe, to be changed in nature, to persevere in Christian life, are all free gifts of divine grace.[32] There is no righteousness in man himself, either as believer or unbeliever; man is received into God's favour "clothed" in the righteousness of Christ, "as if" he were himself righteous.[33] Such emphasis upon utter helplessness and corruption appears to leave no room for moral responsibility before conversion, or for moral endeavour afterwards; yet Calvin insists that man *is* responsible — God is neither the Author of sin, nor tainted with evil[34] — and Calvin fully expects that salvation will totally transform the believer's character. The results of justification are "firstly being reconciled . . . secondly, being sanctified by His Spirit, we aspire to integrity and purity of life."[35]

(2) Man's Moral Response: Repentance

Discussing effects resulting from faith, Calvin names first repentance,[36] so as to demonstrate that holiness of life is inseparable from the free imputation of righteousness.

"That repentance not only always follows faith, but is produced by it, ought to be without controversy: . . . no man can embrace the gospel without betaking himself into the right path and making it his whole study to practise repentance. Those who think repentance precedes faith instead of being produced by it, . . . have never understood its nature . . . " "a man cannot seriously engage in repentance unless he knows he is of God."

The explanation of this doctrine lies in the extent of moral transformation which Calvin includes under repentance: *mortification* (grief produced by conviction of sin and the sense of judgement, hatred of sin, self-dissatisfaction, humility, despair, all comprising "contrition"); and the *looking up to God,* the taking of new courage and joy, the desire of holy living which springs from new birth. Repentance is a real conversion of our life unto God, consisting in mortification of our flesh . . . and quickening of the Spirit.

Thus Calvin can say, "by repentance I understand regeneration" — progressive, continual renewal after the image of Him that created us. Regeneration delivers from the bondage of sin, but there remains a spring of evil which stimulates to sin, and creates conflict to the end of Christian life. So God assigns repentance as the goal towards which believers must keep running all their lives.[37]

Repentance bears numerous fruits — carefulness of conduct, indignation against sin, fear of offending, desire of good, zeal — but piety, charity, purity, are chief. Since it follows faith, repentance, too, is the gift of God — nothing of man's ability. Yet, so analysed to include the total revulsion of the regenerate soul against every form of sin, repentance is plainly the foundation of Calvin's individual ethic.

(3) Salvation and Morality

For there is no doubt that Calvin expects the salvation-experience to produce high Christian morality. "The object of regeneration is to bring the life of believers into concord and harmony with the righteousness of God", so that the image of God is restored in us, "the entire excellence of human nature as it shone in Adam before the Fall", to be fully displayed again only in heaven. To this image God would have us to be conformed. Indeed, "the scripture system" has *innumerable* admirable methods of *recommending righteousness.*"[38]

"We must be holy because God is holy. We are to inhabit the Holy City, and must not defile it. God has shown himself Father — we must exhibit ourselves as sons. Christ purified us, by blood and baptism, and it ill becomes us to remain defiled. As members of His body we must avoid stain; as temples of the Spirit we must guard against being profaned. Soul and body, being destined to heavenly incorruptibility, must here be kept uncorrupted. None has truly learned Christ who has not put off the old man and put on Christ. Doctrine must pass into conduct, not prove unfruitful. Believers are righteous "as exerting themselves in the study of righteousness" for perfection is not yet; it is the goal. "The sense of the divine perfections is the proper master to teach us piety".[39]

Herein lies justification, so far as concerns individual ethics, for including Calvin among Christian moralists. "The doctrines of Calvin" says Chadwick, "clothed the moral idea, embodied it within an atmosphere of scripture and particular forms of devotion and religious customs."[40] The outstanding characteristic of that moral idea was, for Calvin, *discipline:* but four other qualities of Christian morality also found expression in his exposition.
(a) Energy: One unexpected consequence of Calvin's doctrine of God's election to salvation was the release of tremendous moral energy. Though good works contribute nothing to justification, yet — partly because of Calvin's inculcation of discipline, partly because of his valuation of daily work, but mainly for religious and psychological reasons — far-reaching ethical and social activity was evoked. "Energy, rather than deep feeling, was the proof of justification" says Inge,[41] "and the consciousness of being justified was a spur to action." Christians are by divine choice fellow-workers with a trans-

cendent God; election did not paralyse, as fatalism often does, but nourished vigorous dedication. "Calvin found in predestination a religious force, the deepest source of confidence, fearlessness, and a moral power"; life became purposeful; "reconciliation . . . is the beginning of a new and intense activity."[42] In consequence, Calvinism has ever been essentially active, combative and missionary. *(b) Liberty:* Unexpected, too, is Calvin's emphasis upon liberty. Together with Luther, he made it "a great European idea". The Roman yoke, the external law, are replaced by the obedience of sons who delight to please, in response to free forgiveness and favour. In a very significant sentence, Calvin rejects advice to confine enjoyment to necessities, because "it does the very dangerous thing of binding conscience in closer fetters than those in which they are bound by the Word of God."[43] This recalls Calvin's positive and "enjoying" attitude towards God's gifts, and his rejection of imposed celibacy as "impious tyranny". "Men had no title whatever to forbid what God had left free" when God has expressly provided in His Word that this liberty to marry shall not be infringed.[44]

Calvin devotes a whole chapter[45] to Christian liberty "as a subject of primary necessity" if conscience is not to be fluctuating and afraid. It consists of: freedom from the bondage of seeking righteousness by law; voluntary obedience responding to the fatherly kindness of God; freedom to use or omit, as we choose, things in themselves morally indifferent. Where this freedom is wanting, conscience finds no rest:

"When a man begins to doubt whether it is lawful to use linen sheets, shirts, napkins, handkerchiefs, he will not long be secure as to hemp, and will at last have doubts as to tow . . . Should he deem a daintier food unlawful, he will afterward feel uneasy for using loaf bread . . . because his body might be supported on a still meaner food. If he hesitates as to a more genial wine . . . at last he will not dare to touch water if more than usually sweet and pure . . ."[46]

"There is nothing unclean of itself" makes all external things free, provided God approves. We are to use God's gifts, without scruple, for the purpose for which He gave them. Things are "indifferent" when they are used "indifferently", not immoderately, and liberty consists in abstaining, as well as in using. Nor may liberty be paraded to give offence: we conform for the sake of others. Offence thoughtlessly given, and offence needlessly taken, are in fault: freedom must observe consideration for troubled brethren: charity, edification remain paramount.

Remembering how dearly Christ bought our liberty, to insist it shall not be infringed becomes a duty. One danger lies in human authority and mere tradition. This does not mean that all obedience is at once abolished. *Spiritual* liberty must not be transferred or extended to imply *civil* lawlessness — as though Christians were less bound than others by human regulations.

Calvin argues, tortuously, that Christians must obey magistrates for conscience' sake, while yet affirming that conscience is free from human authority. But he is clear that the *general* rule of conscientious obedience to magistrates does not apply to every law enacted; loyalty to worship, and to righteousness, is superior to all human decrees; human laws when just and good are to be obeyed for the general end, but not as binding conscience in detail.[47]

Another danger to Christian liberty arises from "ecclesiastical constitutions . . . without number — innumerable fetters to bind and ensnare the soul". Calvin scorns the many superstitions, ceremonies, traditions, imposed by the mediaeval church: God is our only Lawgiver, His law the sufficient rule. Decency and order, alone, govern ecclesiastical concerns — for the rest, conscience, scripture and charity remain the best guides.[48] It does not belong to faithful ministers to coin new duties, or arrogate to themselves a dominion over their brethren which Paul would not claim. This does not conflict with the church's duty to exercise discipline "by the suffrages of the faithful" over the flagrantly sinful: discipline according to God's Word cannot conflict with freedom of conscience, which delights in God's Word.[49]

The fate of Servetus shows that the full implications of such liberty for religious tolerance were not yet realised. Chadwick remarks[50] that there were plenty to circulate scandalous rumours. So, when Servetus was executed for heresy, Beza (Calvin's supporter), defended the action on the grounds that the magistrate must be concerned with the morals of his people, and heresy undermines morals; that Christian gentleness cannot extend to "murderers", of body or soul; sincerity is no excuse for heresy — the sincere pacifist must not be free to undermine the garrison; the penalty for heresy does not compel to faith, but it prevents others being led astray; the State ought to protect true religion.

Such an argument rested, as Chadwick shows, on twin assumptions: that the truth is known to all sensible men; that the State was endangered if more than one religion flourished. But, clearly, persecution for heresy was already felt to need elaborate defence. After 1600 death for heresy was rare.

(c) Charity: Beside energy and liberty, Calvin expected charity to issue from salvation. He argues minutely against the "Pharisees' " idea that we are justified by charity rather than by faith, and insists

"What the schoolmen say as to the priority of love to faith is a dream: it is faith alone that first engenders love".

— yet he nowhere questions the moral necessity of love. The whole second table of the law is summed up in the command to love one's neighbour; and "neighbour" in the Tenth Commandment is given the full extension of meaning implied in the parable of the Good Samaritan.[51]

"The whole human race, without exception, are to be embraced with charity; here there is no distinction of Greek and Barbarian, worthy or unworthy, friend or foe, since all are to be viewed not in themselves but in God . . . Our first step must be to turn our eyes not to man, the sight of whom might oftener produce hatred, but to God, who requires that the love we bear to Him be diffused among mankind . . . *Let a man be what he may, he is still to be loved because God is loved*."

Nor may the law of love be confined to monks, as a counsel of perfection; it is the Lord's requirement of all Christians, to love the neighbour, and the enemy.[52]

Acutely, Calvin includes love of neighbour among the implications of self-denial. To prefer others in matters of honour before ourselves, sincerely to labour for others' advantage, requires suppression of self-love, the cultivation of modesty, courtesy, friendliness.

Paul illustrates how demanding love is: to seek not our own, yield our right to others; to accept the scriptural view, that gifts are bestowed only for the common good, that we are members one of another, that we are but stewards of God's gifts; to practise almsgiving; and not to grow weary in such well-doing, for charity suffereth long, is kind, is never easily provoked . . .

"The Lord enjoins us to do good to all, though the greater part are most unworthy of it. But scripture subjoins a most excellent reason: we are not to look to what men in themselves deserve, but to the image of God in all, to which we owe all honour and love." This is especially true of those in whom that image is renewed by the Spirit. None therefore may be declined, all are to be loved for *Christ's* sake. "In this way only we attain to what is altogether against nature, to love those that hate us, render good for evil, remembering that we look to the image of God in them, which, obliterating their faults, should by its beauty and dignity allure us to love them." Nor should we forget that the duties of charity are not discharged unless with the purest *feeling* of love, with true pity, humility, kindness, fullest generosity — never with arrogance, pride, reproach, or as conferring obligation.[53]

(d) The Imitation of Christ: There is less in Calvin than in more mystical or emotional writers concerning imitation of Christ. Yet this formulation of the Christian ideal is not wholly absent, having two especial applications. Calvin says much of the aim of regeneration, "to form in us anew the image of God which was all but effaced, by the transgression of Adam", as we put on the new man "which after God is created in *righteousness* and true *holiness*;" and ". . . renewed in *knowledge* after the image of him that created him." This is accomplished slowly: "the nearer anyone approaches in resemblance to God, the more does the image of God appear in him".[54] That image consists in part in "light of intellect, rectitude of heart, and the soundness of every part". But "Paul says that, beholding the glory of Christ with unveiled face, we are transformed into the same image . . . Christ is the most perfect image of God, into which we are so renewed as to bear the image of God, in knowledge, purity, righteousness, and true holiness." "Christ . . . is set before us as a model, the image of which our lives should express . . . If the Lord adopts us as sons on condition that our life be a representation of Christ . . . then unless we dedicate ourselves to righteousness, we . . . abjure the Saviour himself."[55]

The other connection in which the idea of imitation appears is in the sharing of Christ's sufferings. "For if we have true fellowship in His death, our old man is crucified, the body of sin becomes dead . . . If we are partakers in His resurrection, we are raised up by means of it to newness of life."[56]

> "By fellowship with Him, He mortifies our earthly members, that they may not exert themselves in action, . . . An effect of His burial is that we as His fellows are buried to sin . . . By His cross the world is crucified unto us and we unto the world . . . we are dead with Him . . . He not only exhorts us to manifest an example of His death, but declares there is an efficiency in it which should appear in all Christians if they would not render His death unfruitful and useless."[57]

The bearing of the cross is always such imitation of Christ. "He submitted on our account that He might in His own person exhibit a model of patience. Wherefore . . . all the children of God are destined to be conformed to Him. It affords us great consolation in hard circumstances . . . to think we are holding fellowship with the sufferings of Christ." "When Christ was subjected to death, and by rising gained a victory over death, it was not on His own account, but in the Head was begun what must necessarily be fulfilled in all the members."[58]

The thought of imitation of Christ is not one to which Calvin's mind turns easily or eagerly, but it could not be omitted from a system that sought to be so thoroughly in line with the New Testament. It is in fact given, if not extensive place, yet central prominence, in being thus linked to the original creation of man, the purpose of regeneration, and the deepest meaning of the cross.

Yet, even when this dimension is added to the other qualities of Christian morality emphasised by Calvin, it does not convey the depth and power of his individual ethic without his most characteristic contribution — the ideal of the totally disciplined life.

3. CHRISTIAN DISCIPLINE

Balmforth describes Calvin's as "a conversion to obedience" and Tawney said that Calvin gives to discipline the primacy which Luther gave to faith.[59] It is significant of the quality even of earthly obedience that it sprang from inner motivations, rather from approval of those in authority: "this feeling of reverence, of piety, we owe to all our rulers, be their characters what they may".[60] So, God is sovereign, His will supreme: this was the immense strength of Calvinism — its exaltation of mind over body, of spirit over suffering, of resignation over resentment, of inner victory over all allurement, despondency, defeatism. Behind this commitment to obedience lay the thought of eternity: as the throne above is the centre of Christian living, so the world beyond lends it perspective. Disciplined obedience is the path towards the Christian's high, elective destiny.

(1) Self Denial

The basis of all obedience is self-denial, surrender of self-will. Calvin had little use for invented austerities: "false zeal, replete with superstition" set up fasts imitating Christ's, or forbade the eating of flesh while indulging in delicacies. Fasting had value . . . but not "that kind of perfection fabricated by cowled monks in order to rear up a species of double Christianity" by "a more rigorous discipline".[61] Nevertheless we are not our own: we must ever seek the glory of God by obeying His will; we must exercise true self-discipline, towards others and towards God.

Towards others, by sobriety, righteousness, godliness, true humility, honouring good qualities in others, turning from natural self-love, seeking always the good of our neighbours — charity is ever self-mortifying. *Towards God*, by resigning ourselves to the disposal of the Lord, letting Him tame the desire to pursue wealth, intrigue for power. Christians should not contend for prosperity, success, recognition, apart from the blessing of God, on which they should recline, letting the Lord conduct them to whatever lot He has ordained.

"Happen what may, he whose mind is thus composed will neither deem himself wretched, nor murmur against God because of his lot" but will retain a "placid and grateful mind".[62]

Such charitable and contented self-denial, "reaching to every department of life . . . temperate in all things . . . sparing in pleasures . . . "[63] is the secret of the strong Calvinist character, "placid and patient in enduring penury, . . . moderate in enjoying abundance." While the Christian is free of strict rules as to enjoyments, he "will indulge as little as possible, curb luxury, cut off all show of superfluous abundance;" will bear want bravely, and exercise frugality, and charity as one who constantly hears sounding in his ears, "Give account of your stewardship." Yet this is no proud, Stoic indifference, but a humble waiting upon God in cheerfulness and faith, a courageous self-denial inseparable from bearing the cross of Christ.[64]

Calvin's inclusion of humility in self-denial is significant. Self-will is but self-confidence in action: the abandonment of self-confidence which constitutes faith, finds its parallel in the abandonment of self-will, which is obedience. Calvin cites Chrysostom's "the foundation of our philosophy is humility" and Augustine's "if you ask me what is the first precept of the Christian religion, I will answer 'First, second, and third, humility'." "As our insignificance is His exaltation, so the confession of our insignificance has its remedy provided in His mercy."[65] For any intellectual, such an attitude is an exceptional test of self-denial: for Calvin, its depth and sincerity are best revealed in his insistence upon being buried in an unmarked grave.

(2) Vocation

Self-discipline gains added equanimity when applied to social status and opportunity. "The Lord enjoins every one of us . . . to have respect to our own calling. He knows the boiling restlessness of the human mind . . . Therefore He has assigned distinct duties in the different modes of life, distinguished by the name of callings. Every man's mode of life is therefore a kind of station assigned him by the Lord . . . He who is obscure will not decline to cultivate a private life . . . The magistrate will more willingly perform his office, the father confine himself to his proper sphere. Every one in his mode of life will suffer its cares, uneasiness, anxiety, persuaded that God has laid on the burden . . . In following your proper calling, no work will be so mean as not to have a splendour in the sight of God."[66]

This concept of "my station and its duties" is sometimes said to dominate Protestant ethics. Its depth of faith, and humility of spirit, must be fully appreciated before egalitarian, or "fatalistic", criticisms are offered. Calvin himself found no contradiction between contentment with one's vocation and either simple prudence, or hard work:

"The eternal decrees of God by no means prevent our proceeding to provide for ourselves . . . He who fixed the boundaries of our life, entrusted us with the care of it. Our duty is clear: to defend it, to use it: and, since He supplies remedies, not to neglect them."[67]

As to the need for work:

"Augustine strenuously contends that it is not lawful for monks to live in idleness . . . our monks place the principal part of their holiness in idleness."[68]

Inge comments: "All work is taken up into the religious sphere; there is no distinction between sacred and profane. For the first time in the history of Christianity, the dignity and value of work as work are fully insisted on . . . idleness is the worst of sins."[69] Calvin took great interest in the way men earned their living. He opposed minimum wages, and treating of man's work as merchandise; neither, apparently, afforded to daily work its true dignity. Industry and thrift, in the service of God's people, were the normal discipline of the life God had redeemed for His glory.

(3) Marriage: Celibacy

Of more personal self-discipline, much is said in exposition of the Seventh Commandment, to include every kind of physical and mental impurity. The divinely appointed remedy for sexual pressure is marriage; the tempted have a duty to avail themselves of God's remedy. Imposition of celibacy is unnatural, against the divine intention, and morally perilous.[70]

The decision of the Council at Nicea, that "legitimate conjugal intercourse is chastity" was the opinion of the fathers; subsequently, "superstitious" encomiums upon virginity lessened the dignity of marriage and obscured its sanctity, while the effects of enforced celibacy in the priesthood were obvious in the licentiousness that had prevailed. Calvin then quotes as final, Chrysostom's dictum: "a chaste love of matrimony is the second species of virginity."[71]

Marriage is unquestionably "an institution of God . . . a good and holy ordinance of God", though not a sacrament.[72] Equally clearly, it is no mere cloak for sexual license, no abrogation of the paramount need for discipline. Though a main purpose of marriage is as remedy against lust, yet the married must not give way to unrestrained indulgence; wedlock must not become the stimulus to incontinence. Let there be sobriety in the mutual behaviour of husband and wife, with dignity, measure, modesty, not wantonness. Ambrose had described "the man who shows no modesty or comeliness in conjugal intercourse as committing adultery with his wife."[73]

Thus by law, salvation, and self-command, recognition of the sovereignty of God would "discipline the individual life to God's glory". The over-riding ethical category is *law*. It is relevant to ask how far Calvin's individual ethic differs from that of the mediaeval church. Significantly, Dakin[74] compares Calvin with Ignatius Loyola, founder of the Jesuit Order, as exhibiting a parallel emphasis upon self-discipline under God, in the service of a vigorous activity on behalf of God in the world. But with Calvin the Christian does not deny himself in order to become a "religious" but because he is religious, saved, dedicated, accepted through grace. Moreover, Calvin's self-denial is never negative, mere renunciation, but the surrender of life to *do* God's commands (not merely to abstain from things); and the laying aside of regard for oneself, to give oneself to God and one's neighbour — the positive "athleticism" of Paul. Calvin's view is positive in another sense, too: so far from implying a withdrawal from the world into the monastery, Calvin's self-discipline demanded the acceptance of hardship and toil *in* the wide affairs of the world's daily life and business — what Niebuhr calls "intra-worldly asceticism', in distinction from the "extra-worldly asceticism" of the monastery. As others have expressed it, Calvin introduced the rigours of mediaeval "religious" life to ordinary Christians, and made the world one vast monastery, the arena of a strenuous and all-absorbing consecration to the all-embracing will of the sovereign God of grace.[75]

B. "To Create a Sanctified Society" — to God's Glory

The divine sovereignty confronts man also *corporately*, as a theocratic ideal for society. Calvin would have Geneva submit to the rule of God, in all its civic, commercial and political arrangements. Calvin's aim was to make the sovereignty of God tangible and visible in the life of the city as it had appeared to be in the mediaeval church. Where Lutheranism tolerated the world, Calvin sent his followers out to master it, as Dakin remarked. In Rupp's words, the Calvinist "lives by faith for the honour and service of God in a world the whole life of which must be brought from sinful chaos into the ordered liberty of the children of God." In Catherwood's, "the Catholic tended to see the physical world as evil", and the saint had no part in it; "to the Protestant, the evil was within; . . . the natural resources of the world were . . . given to man for his use."[76] Calvin says much, in this positive vein, about the Christian's relation to the world around him.

1. THE COMMERCIAL WORLD

Geneva was a commercial city, producing clothing, leather, watches, jewellery, books, later involved in banking, international loans, industrial finance. Seeking to bring its life under the law of God Calvin recognised the necessity of trade, industry, capital, banking. Faced with the gulf between the church's teaching and the world's practice, where Lutherans sought to return to feudal, rural simplicities, and humanists waited for the slow regeneration of society by reason, Calvin sought to discipline commercial life by those very virtues of hard work, high responsibility, thrift and diligence, which the emerging industrial economy required. Business became, if not a religion, certainly another expression of the religious spirit.[77]

"Feudalism was marching . . . into capitalism. Currency rather than goods was taking pre-eminence in trade. The great banking houses had arisen, trading companies, monopolies, all the machinery of capitalism . . . 'money talked'. A new monied class had come to the top . . .The old leading classes being ousted by merchants and manufacturers. A mysterious . . . rise in prices was taking place all over Europe . . ." everybody blaming everybody else.[78]

(1) The New Temper

All qualities which Calvin inculcated in the disciplined individual contributed towards the new industrial and commercial spirit — self-denial, frugality, honesty, sobriety, devotion to the general good, study, purposefulness, responsible stewardship in the handling of resources, the sense of vocation, the release of energy, the new valuation of work. Actual mental effort and physical toil was a Christian duty, not to be laid aside when physical needs were met. All this generated immense industrial drive. Weber says that when the new spirit took hold of some members of a trade, "leisureliness was suddenly destroyed". The men who so fostered in society stern frugality alongside energetic work "had grown up in the hard school of life, calculating and daring at the same time, above all temperate and reliable, shrewd and completely devoted to their business.[79] "The idea of economic progress as an end . . . found a new sanction in the identification of labour and enterprise with the service of God. The magnificent energy which changed in a century the face of material civilisation was to draw nourishment from that temper."[80]

(2) Wealth: Property: Usury

Public well-being and order, with justice and compassion as guiding principles, promotes the glory of God: and general well-being requires general wealth. To Calvin, prosperity was a sign of God's goodness, though poverty was *not* proof of His displeasure. "Calvinism's ideal is a society which seeks wealth with the sober gravity of men . . . devoting themselves to a service acceptable to God."[81] It no longer distrusts the capitalist, as one grown rich on his neighbour's misfortunes; no longer regards poverty as the badge of sainthood. Wealth is the gift of God entrusted to His stewards, the natural reward of hard work; but none holds his gifts for private use — but shares with others in brotherly love.[82] If this view emphasises the rich man's responsibilities, it still allows him, even encourages him, to be rich, recalling Clement of Alexandria rather than the Gospels.

Private possession is part of the divine ordering of society, protected by the Eighth Commandment. What each possesses has fallen to him by the distribution of the sovereign Lord: no one can "pervert his means to bad purposes without committing fraud on a divine dispensation".[83] Private ownership is necessary for the peace of society.[84] As Dakin says, property comes to "shelter under the protection of a religious idea . . . the inscrutable but unimpeachable will of God."[85] At the same time, Calvin demands compassion for the genuinely poor; he condemned indiscriminate almsgiving, as he did gambling;[86] but concern, stewardship, and responsibility all impose generosity.

One of the most far-reaching of Calvin's newer principles was his concept of usury, for so long under scriptural and ecclesiastical ban. Chadwick says later schoolmen devised formulas to allow interest on public loans; Calvin ended the prohibition entirely, arguing that the Deuteronomic law applied only to the polity of the Hebrews, *not* universally. The sole guide is charity.

"Extortion is always wrong, excessive rates are wrong, lending to the poor is wrong, but normal loans may be to the reasonable advantage of all the contracting parties. Interest is not to be condemned unless it transgresses the law of love."[87]

The rate of interest was officially fixed, not charged to the poor, must benefit the borrower as much as the lender. Lending on interest must not become a regular occupation, but to lend capital was to deserve a share of the profit made possible. Credit is a tool of social effort; payment of interest for capital is as reasonable as payment of rent for land. According to Troeltsch, this break with canon law was "the only form of Christian social doctrine which accepts the basis of the modern economic situation without reserve."[88]

Inge draws attention to the man "who works like a slave accumulating money which his tastes and principles forbid him to enjoy." Weber makes the point that the constraint placed upon consumption of wealth by disapproval of all indulgence, made possible productive investment of capital. It might be truer to say it made investment necessary. When conscience bids you make money and forbids you to spend it, and giving it away only encourages thriftlessness in others, what else can you do with it, but invest it to make more?[89]

With limitation of interest-rate went concern for a just price for goods and a just wage for labour. The Consistory Court at Geneva "censures harsh creditors, punishes usurers, engrossers, and monopolists, reprimands or fines the merchant who defrauds, the clothmaker whose stuff is too narrow, the dealer who provides short measure, the butcher who sells above the rates fixed by authority, the tailor who charges strangers excessive prices, the surgeon who demands an excessive fee."[90]

The mediaeval just price was based upon "exchange of equivalent value", judged by the generally prevailing assessment in a given district. It was laid down as *wrong* to take advantage of urgent need (illness, a starving child), or shortage (a fair price when available is still the just price during bad harvests).

The just wage, being one example of the just price, was likewise a matter of equivalent value; but unless similar employers wished to engage similar workers, general assessment of labour-value was hardly possible. Equal pay for equal *capacity* was sometimes advocated. It was assumed a man should receive enough to maintain himself at the level associated with his status.

(3) Capitalism?

The personal qualities and public attitudes Calvin taught have sometimes been held to imply a close connection betwen Calvinism and capitalism. Weber[91] thought that western Christianity, "in particular certain varieties of it which acquired independent life as a result of the Reformation", had been more favourable towards the capitalist system than had other religious outlooks. This was never intended as explanation of the rise of capitalism; Weber, like his critics, pointed out almost innumerable contributory factors. But the suggestion provoked wide discussion.

Dakin holds the two movements certainly grew together, but capitalism would have arisen in any case. Tawney sees the new attitude to usury, the acceptance of commercial life, and dealing with capital and labour in the light of social need, instead of with texts and traditional doctrines, as a watershed in economic theory. He avoids relating capitalism to Calvinism directly, holding that either an intense individualism, or a rigorous Christian socialism, could be deduced from Calvin's doctrine — depending upon whether Calvinists were a majority who could stamp their ideals on the social order (as in Geneva and Scotland), or a minority on the defensive (as in England). Hill says most historians accept *some* connection between Calvinism and capitalism. Rupp speaks of the theory as "more than a little damaged". Dickens recorded the "collapse" of the "specious" Weber thesis, arguing that business and financial functions of the sixteenth century existed also in Catholic countries; that hard work was preached equally by Jesuits, that Calvin resisted capitalism's abuses. Chadwick sees "the truths behind an alleged connection of puritanism and capitalism" as two: first, Reformed divinity, less chained to precedent, adjusted itself more rapidly to the new economy; secondly, those who practised thrift, temperance, honesty, consideration for others, and who believed an active life to be a vocation for God, were likely to be more successful merchants than those without these qualities.[92]

Such a debate is best left to economic historians. One well qualified to weigh the facts — H. R. F. Catherwood — is content to offer statistical support for the view that Protestant Christianity *provided a necessary element* in what was needed to encourage development of science, commerce and industry.[93] But, as Haroutunian points out,[94] while it may be true that Calvin contributed, at a distance of a century and more, to the development of capitalism, it was by a long process, in course of which Calvinism changed, became secularised, lost much of its self-denial, its dedication to the glory of God. Clearly, Calvin must not be held responsible for a capitalism that in its worldliness, selfishness, and materialism, has departed far from Calvin's principles and ideals.

2. THE POLITICAL WORLD

Dickens contends that "on any showing, the political importance of Calvinism immensely exceeded its economic importance."[95] Its discipline could build communities capable of self-government. It was identified with small independent city-States rather than with autocratic Catholic monarchies, and it possessed the steely qualities of a fighting resistance. Calvin believed in law, in constitutional organisation, in freedom and independence; he managed to combine these in strong support for authority that yet left conscience free.

(1) Authority

Calvin saw civic authority as expressing within its own sphere the "natural" law of God for the good ordering of society. Men, being wicked, need restraint: even rational, sociable men could not live together without leadership, so government must be strong.[96] Calvin therefore devotes an extensive chapter to its discussion.[97]

> Civil institutions regulating manners belong to the order established by God; Christian liberty is not to overthrow courts, laws, magistrates, government, as polluted, no concern of Christians. "To civil government is assigned to foster worship of God, defend sound doctrine and the church, adapt conduct to human society, form manners to justice, conciliate us to each other, cherish peace," — all needful for Christians, as still imperfect. Wickedness desperately requires restraint; government is necessary as bread, light, air, for life to continue, that no blasphemy or idolatry flourish; that peace, property, commerce, modesty, a true public form of religion, and humanity, be fostered: "civil authority is in the sight of God the most sacred, most honourable, of all status." Such considerations inspire magistrates to faithfulness — their tribunal being the throne of God, their mouth the organ of divine truth, themselves vicegerents of God.

As to the *form* of government, Inge notes the individuality and initiative fostered by Calvinism, and says "the natural tendency is towards a conservative democracy . . . Calvin himself was anti-democratic, but the logic of his system favoured democracy." Chadwick declares "there was little that was democratic in Calvin's ideal constitution."[98] Calvin himself defends, as having "the highest testimonial", monarchy — "the power of one" — while himself preferring aristocracy.

> Scripture affirms "it is by divine wisdom that 'kings reign', and commands 'honour the king'. "Monarchy is prone to tyranny. In an aristocracy . . . the tendency is to the faction of a few; in popular ascendancy there is the strongest tendency to sedition . . . the form which greatly surpasses the others is aristocracy, either pure or modified by popular government . . ." Kings often dissent from what is right: "it is safer, more tolerable, when several bear rule."

Argument based upon social utility and moral assessment must affect the Christian's attitude to authority. But Calvin continues: "if it has pleased Him to appoint kings over kingdoms, and senates or burgomasters over free States, whatever be the form which he has appointed in the places in which we live, our duty is to obey and submit."

The power of magistrates extends to both tables of the law. It is necessary that magistrates exert themselves defending Him by whose favour they rule; and that in accord with prophetic teaching they defend the oppressed, the widow, the fatherless, guard the public innocence, honour and tranquility, keep the peace and safety. For this they are armed, since all public discipline depends upon reward and punishment. In punishment and bloodshedding the magistrate acts not of himself, but as executing the judgements of God.

"The law of the Lord forbids to kill: but, that murder may not go unpunished, the Lawgiver himself puts the sword into the hands of His ministers . . ." To avenge the afflictions of the pious at the command of God is neither to afflict or hurt. Examples are added (from the Old Testament) of the unremitting execution of divine justice by God's appointed servants — whom duty called to bloodshedding.

Yet mercy and humanity, not excessive severity, must temper justice. The right to prosecute wars, to raise revenue, follow from the divine origin of authority — but these too require moderation, and concern for the public good.

The law for Christian states originates in the moral law, the true and eternal rule of righteousness. The ceremonial law (of Moses) was tutelage for Israel. The judicial law safeguarded justice and expressed the rule of charity by which all human law must be assessed. The moral law is "natural", the conscience engraven on the minds of men, and contains all equity — again, a test of all laws. The basic prohibitions — of murder, theft, adultery, false witness — are present in all laws, though form and punishments vary with conditions. It follows that the reaction of Christians towards civil law should be positive, using the courts: not, indeed, misusing the law to pursue revenge, but as using a sacred gift of God. Paul so used the Roman courts. Vindictiveness and dishonesty make litigation evil: Christ's forbidding of retaliation does not prevent our using the laws for the preservation of our goods, and for the punishment of the wicked for public good. Paul inveighs against the rage for litigation prevalent at Corinth, and the spirit of their disputes — but not against proper use of law. The test, as of all behaviour, is charity.

Towards rulers, the first Christian duty is honour, not merely accepting their social utility while thinking them necessary evils, but venerating their office for conscience' sake. Christians' second duty is obedience, complying with edicts, paying tribute, undertaking public office, fulfilling orders, not acting to oppose or correct any public ordinance. The Christian must leave to the magistrate the powers that are his, unless he is ordered to act, in which case he comes to be invested with the magistrate's authority.[99] So far, the civil obedience required of Christians would seem to be complete.

(2) Tensions

How far such submission to the State should be carried had troubled the church from the days of Peter, with increasing perplexity since Constantine. Despite Calvin's emphasis on the divine authority of the magistrate, Inge considered that he inculcated *less* of patient submission than did Luther. The "private man" must obey, but (following Beza) the "lower magistrates", as themselves exercising authority and protecting liberty, ought sometimes to resist the "higher", "when misgovernment becomes intolerable, it is justifiable for subjects to rebel."[100]

Calvin describes frankly the shortcomings of some magistrates, and the consequent natural impulse to rebel; nevertheless "one most unworthy of all honour . . . in so far as public obedience is concerned is to be held in the same honour as the best of kings." It is not for us to cure the evils in our appointed rulers: God ever raises up deliverers in His own time. Let princes hear and be afraid, but the people continue to obey.

In spite of all this, Calvin can continue (apparently answering the question, Who are these "deliverers", if all must obey?) — "I speak only of private men. When popular magistrates have been appointed to curb the tyranny of kings" (as in Sparta, Rome, Athens, and perhaps in certain contemporary States) if they then connive at tyranny, "I affirm they fraudulently betray the liberty of the people." Moreover, "in that obedience we hold to be due to rulers, we must always make the exception, that it is not incompatible with obedience to the King of all kings. We are subject to the men who rule over us, but subject only in the Lord. If they command anything against Him, let us not pay the least regard to it. We ought to obey God rather than men: let us console ourselves that we are rendering the obedience which the Lord requires, when we endure anything rather than turn aside from piety."[101]

This is heartfelt: Calvin was familiar with tension between civil and ecclesiastical authority. Geneva's discipline illustrates strains within Calvin's doctrine. Pastors chose pastors, and the city's teachers, — subject to the city council's approval; the councils, consulting the pastors, chose the elders, who exercised moral discipline over the townspeople, the pastors dealt with disorders in the church. This "interference" by the Consistory (pastors plus elders) transferred to the Reformed church an ancient moral surveillance exercised by bishops' courts and city councils. Calvin wanted the church to adjudicate, the civil power to punish. Geneva's council resisted surrendering decisions to the pastors; they also objected to long sermons, licensed theological books, paid the pastors, critically examined their proclamations, limited their exercise of excommunication. Calvin himself was once publicly rebuked, often resisted: "It is correct to speak neither of magistrates dominated by pastors, nor of pastors dominated by magistrates . . . Calvin was not the absolute ruler of Geneva pictured by legend and his enemies" (Chadwick). He never exercised "anything like a dictatorship" (Dickens).[102]

Conceding that on the whole Calvin counselled submission, Dickens[103] draws attention to "the loopholes" left to the political activists. God sometimes commissions avenging prophets, like Moses; inferior magistrates have a positive duty to oppose tyrants; commands contrary to divine law call for passive disobedience. Calvin can speak of a biblical king as having "virtually abnegated his power" by exalting his authority above that of God. In a letter to Coligny he countenances resistance to the king of France, if that is agreed by Princes and Parliament. Chadwick[104] summarises a tortuous correspondence with Huguenot leaders on this question: Calvin agrees that to fight to save a king from his own despotism was permissible. In this imposition of restraint upon the power of unworthy rulers, constitutional and parliamentary government was later to find strong support. Dakin speaks of Calvin always reserving the right to criticise the State; and of the quality of strong initiative, the *duty* to resist misrule, with which Calvinism fostered resistance to oppression.[105]

(3) The Military Demand

The single exception which Calvin allows to the "private" Christian's duty of submission to civil authority — that such obedience shall not transgress the law of God — is crucially tested in time of war, when civic duties imposed may sharply conflict with Christian conscience.

Bainton remarks[106] that the question of war was acute because Geneva was constantly in danger of attack; in France, the Netherlands, Scotland, and England, Calvinism became a militant minority; later, under Conde and William of Orange, actually a recruiting movement. Zwingli had died in battle, bearing arms.

Calvin saw war as merely the extension of the ruler's power of the sword against sedition, violence, and crime, to enemies of the State, whose sedition, robbery and crime being on so much vaster a scale call for the greater armed resistance.

"Natural piety and duty, therefore, demand that princes be armed not only to repress private crimes but to defend the subjects committed to their guardianship whenever they are assailed. Such even the Holy Spirit in many passages of scripture declares to be lawful."[107]

To the objection that the New Testament does not show war to be lawful for Christians, Calvin replies: the ancient reason for war still exists; there is no reason for debarring magistrates from defending those under them; the apostolic writings set out the kingdom of Christ, not civil polity; Christ's coming did not change the situation in this respect — citing Augustine on Christian soldiers in the New Testament. Nevertheless "in taking up arms against an enemy, that is, an armed robber," rulers must especially beware of anger, hatred, implacable severity. They must not catch at opportunity for war, nor take it except under strongest necessity. From this "right of war" follows justification for establishing frontier garrisons, defensive alliances, and "everything pertaining to the military art."[108]

This argument minimises the problem by concentrating on defensive war, assuming the enemy has no more justification than "an armed robber". Elsewhere, Calvin argues from Old Testament teaching: "Was not David, the man after God's own heart, a mighty man of valour?"[109] His concession that opposition to misrule may be required of Christians, also accepts a non-defensive war. Bainton sees Calvinism associated with the Crusade: "the State was ordained of God . . . to support the true religion . . . With such presuppositions, war would have to be the battle of a religious society fought with fervour in the name of the Lord God of Hosts, and the more holy the cause, the less restrained the means. Calvin repeatedly said that no consideration could be paid to humanity when the honour of God was at stake."[110] Later British, and European, wars of religion showed that Calvinism could extract this crusading militarism from Calvin's position. Out of all that followed from that, "the tragedy of the Reformation" was born — the loss of religious vision in the scramble for power.

In Calvin's view church and State are united in seeking to produce a Christian society under God's sovereign law. The State, hardly less than the church, is an instrument in the hands of God to save the world. Yet, since the first task of the State is to maintain true religion, and the State itself comes under the discipline of ideals revealed by the church, the church is seen to possess the paramount authority: the highest role of the State is to support and execute the church's principles.[111] For all that, as Niebuhr says, there is no evidence that Calvin sought *control* of the State by the church: "the Geneva ideal was government by God, not by church, or clergy, or even Bible."[112] The divine sovereignty was all. As "Scotland's Calvin," Knox, said to Mary Stuart, "My one aim is that Prince and People alike should obey God."[113]

It takes more than idealism to sanctify society. "In the typical Calvinist," writes Inge,[114] "we find a vigorous political interest, but not for the sake of the State; a steady diligence in labour, but not for the sake of riches; a careful, often intrusive, social organisation, but not for the sake of increasing human happiness; a zeal for productivity without any great interest in the objects of production . . . There is sometimes a strange blindness to the maladjustments of industrial society . . . and it is assumed rather too hastily that what is good discipline for the individual is good for society; there is great confusion as to the objects of communal life, and its true values." Doubtless that summary judgement expresses twentieth-century hindsight: with that qualification, it remains valid.

Calvin's great scheme, the sovereignty of God reflected in the disciplined individual and the sanctified society, seems simple, and Calvin worked out its implications with immense thoroughness, logic, and moral force. Yet Calvin's answer to Luther's problem, how to make Protestant Christians *good* — the acceptance of discipline, enforced by the church-State — was scarcely more successful than Luther's "transforming faith." The church was too broken, the political tensions were too great, for a new Protestant "canon law" to control either the forces released by the Enlightenment, or the wayward hearts of men.

11

Conservation and Change

WHATEVER THE GAIN OF THE REFORMATION for personal religion, the price paid was high. "The sixteenth and seventeenth centuries saw the break-up of the political, intellectual and ecclesiastical forms in which mediaeval Christianity had expressed itself . . . So great an upheaval . . . tides of disruption . . ." (Selwyn).[1] What began as a movement to reform the undivided church of Christ ended in a divergence of varying patterns so wide that the one church has never reappeared.

Many of the bonds of unity had been severed. Scriptural precedents, for example, had been so manipulated, distorted, reduced to polemic weaponry, that interpretation, and even relevance, were too debateable to unite Christians on any issue. The Reformed churches never replaced the ecclesiastical authority which they destroyed: they remained scattered and divisive, and the very nature of their attack upon the papacy removed all possibility of supplanting it. The appeal to inner experience — to faith, regeneration, the internal witness of truth, or of the Spirit — was too subjective to afford ground for authority, tending instead towards a refined evangelical version of every man's being right in his own eyes.

Intellectually, the renaissance and the Reformation between them disrupted the "mediaeval synthesis" within which all serious thought had been systematised into a coherent world-view. As Russell says, "with very few exceptions, all the men of this period who contributed to the intellectual life of their time were churchmen."[2] Such a synthesis not only unified thought, it tended also to stifle enquiry with an assumption of completeness, finality, and divine authority, denial incurring eternal judgement. By the fifteenth and sixteenth centuries, political changes, the rise of a humanist culture which looked to pagan antiquity for inspiration, the enlargement of men's horizons by the discoveries of Columbus, de Gama, Copernicus, stimulated mental and emotional drives hitherto repressed by dread of excommunication in this world, and of purgatory in the next. "The long centuries of asceticism were forgotten in a riot of art and poetry and pleasure . . . the old terrors ceased to be terrifying and the new liberty of the spirit was found to be intoxicating." Russell finds the two most important differences from the mediaeval period to be, the diminishing authority of the church and the increasing authority of science.[3]

Christopher Hill[4] focuses one far-reaching change upon a sentence of Francis Bacon: "Let us never think or maintain that a man can search too far . . . in the book of God's word or in the book of God's works . . . but . . . let men beware . . . that they do not unwisely mingle or confound these learnings together." This "separation of science from religion, so vital for the future advance of science, was in the best Protestant tradition". Thus "Bacon gave the scientists' activities a moral sanction . . . Religion . . . instead of opposing science should clearly protect all increase in natural knowledge." Such an attitude ended the mediaeval ban upon enquiry; the inventive industrial revolution, and the whole scientific apocalypse of modern knowledge, could proceed unhindered.

So again the church confronted a completely changed intellectual and moral milieu, and Christian morality necessarily shared the general uncertainty.

1. PROTESTANT RE-ADJUSTMENTS

In ethics, as in theology, the field lay open to fullest exploration. Where there is no authority, no consistency of teaching, only experiment and challenge, varying emphases must emerge. Extreme individualism, ever one of the dangers of the Reformation, invites anarchy. In the aftermath of renaissance and Reformation, what had been hailed as liberty, the end of the shackles and obscurantism of the omni-legislative church, appeared to some earnest souls as *lostness* — the lack of all direction, anchorage, and meaning. Some reacted (even in Protestantism) with a longing to return to authority and dogmatism. Christian ethics must ever reckon with that hunger in timid souls for strong leadership, discipline, and authoritative direction. Not all Christians desire to be left without compass or chart in ever-changing "situations".

It is wrong, therefore, to suggest that post-Reformation loss of authority in ethics was simply a revolt. Much serious re-examination of the grounds of ethical philosophy was occasioned by disappointment with the fruits of reform, such as Luther felt. Calvin, too, regretted sometimes the kind of people with whom he had to deal.[5] Some of the barbarities of "religious" wars in France and Britain exposed the hollowness of much "Protestant" morality;[6] later, in the sad hindsight of the industrial revolution and its social cost, deep impatience with theological futilities gave rise to the call for "practical Christianity" and "a social gospel" that would test the truth of "justification by faith" by the fruit of Christian "good works". By that time other influences also had deeply affected Christian ethics, as it sought once more to make adjustment to the changing philosophic climate within which Christians had to witness.

To follow the development of Christian morality in the crowded, kaleidoscopic centuries that followed the Reformation is impossible. Even to introduce adequately the chief among the innumerable writers and schools of thought must overburden an elementary text, and bewilder by the richness and variety of the exploration to be surveyed. Although to summarise is often to distort, the only profitable method of study in so luxuriant a field is to indicate generally those main lines of post-Reformation ethical development which have helped to fashion the modern Christian conscience — facing once more unprecedented situations with few directives from the past.

Even so limited a programme necessitates attention to numerous factors. Arising directly from one major emphasis of the Reformation is a greatly increased reliance upon inward experience, upon the constitution of *human* nature, and the light of faith and truth within the regenerate soul, as a basis for ethics; with a resulting tendency to *internalise* ethics to a degree new in Christian history. Further, as throughout its story, the Christian ethic had to respond not only to its originating impulse within salvation-history, but also to its changing environment (the so-called "adjustment-ethic"): in the ferment of thought that followed the renaissance, that response had to be especially flexible and receptive. Christian thinkers learned much from teachers on the fringes of the church or outside it. Meanwhile, the world changed almost beyond recognition with the coming of industrialisation, scientific inventiveness, materialist, humanist, and secularist fashions of thought, and social revolution. New problems constantly challenged old principles, and found scripture inadequate, tradition confused, and the Christian conscience unprepared.

Another post-Reformation ethical theme is the note of social concern, which sounded so clearly in the patristic church, echoed in the public service offered by the later monasteries, but was heard with altogether new fervour and determination in the Reformed churches. Curiously, in more evangelical circles a trend towards pietistic non-involvement with the world appears to conflict with, but actually seems to stimulate, a deep social compassion: until eventually a "social gospel" with innumerable agencies seeking to alleviate a variety of social ills take prominent place in the work of Protestant churches.

Still another factor influencing post-Reformation developments in ethics arose directly from the new attitude towards scripture, used no longer to justify and supplement church tradition, but as the *sole* authority by which all tradition, doctrine and conduct must be judged. For the following centuries saw a revolution in biblical studies, that could not but affect ethics as deeply as it affected theology. Precisely *how* ancient texts can determine behaviour in the contemporary world has become a central question for Christian ethics: and behind it lies a wholly new understanding of what *is* Christian scripture. Nor can these various themes be kept separate, for trends of thought cross with surprising inconsistency. Not only does intense, other-worldly spirituality manifest a keen social conscience, but Puritans who in Cromwell's time create the efficient Model Army are forerunners, nevertheless, of Quaker pacificists; and philosophers without any apparent Christian presuppositions contribute valuable insights to the expression of Christian ideals. Historical links and intellectual influences are rarely as direct and obvious as the expositor wishes — or pretends.

If there is one consistent impulse to be discerned in Protestant ethics, it may be the desire to re-establish moral authority, whether in scripture, in human nature itself, in the stronger organisation of a Reformed and regenerate church, in the Christian conscience, or in pragmatic social necessity. Some new foundation was certainly needed on which to erect barriers against evil, corruption, violence, fences of discipline within which life might be lived in safety and order. *That the quest for such moral authority has largely failed is the root-cause of the modern church's ethical confusion and moral impotence.*

The search for authority was the explicit purpose of the learned Anglican, Richard Hooker, who in *Law of Ecclesiastical Polity* sought a middle way between the extreme Puritan biblicism and individualism on the one hand, and the rejected authority of the papacy on the other. Hooker attempted a new synthesis by appealing "essentially to reason, to inform men's minds with some method of reducing the laws whereof there is present controversy into their first original causes, that so it may be in every particular ordinance thereby the better discerned, whether the same be reasonable, just, and righteous, or no."[7] To do this, Hooker argued directly for the authority of Bible, church tradition, and reason, *together*.

His theory of law, mainly Thomist, begins with the eternal law of God's own being, in which man participates, so perceiving his own chief moral duties by the law of reason, the natural law implanted by God at creation. This is further amplified and interpreted by the divine law revealed in scripture, without which man cannot reach his eternal destiny. By their approximation to this divine-natural-scriptural law, all human laws (ecclesiastical, civil, international) must be judged.

Here is triple authority for moral judgements and direction, argued with a balanced reasonableness which possessed immense weight for many minds. The assumed consonance of divine, natural, and scriptural law is not, of course, so obvious to all. Acceptance of scriptural authority in matters affecting salvation, while appealing to human reason and natural law for the basis of "polity", might seem a workable compromise between the bibliolatry of Calvinists and the more philosophic judgement of "humanist" minds. But it could also offend both: the assumption that the Bible was insufficient for "novel needs" would upset literalists, while the concession that "the long historic tradition of the church may also contain wisdom for present perplexities" would scarcely satisfy ardent churchmen. Nevertheless, "through the seventeenth and into the eighteenth centuries, the ultimate reasonableness of Christian morality is a note repeated frequently. The Christian life is one of ordered harmony, wherein the master principle of cool reason fits the various demands of the self into a well-regulated whole, where the realms of nature and supernature, body and spirit, are regarded as supplementary, not opposed, and where self-love and benevolence both find their due place in Christian living."[8] This is a note peculiarly impressive for those sufficently cultured to appreciate it. It fails to lend to Christian morality any such authority as would restrain the contentious or redeem the corrupt. The quest for a foundation for moral law was to continue for a long time.

2. CATHOLIC REFORMATION

Meanwhile, in the "unreformed" church of western Europe a significant Counter-reformation was proceeding, outwardly along lines very different from those initiated by Luther, Calvin, and their colleagues, but not without internal parallels to the Protestant search for authority. Inge points out[9] that religious revival had already begun in Papal areas, deriving in part from "the religion of pure inwardness" which mystics had preserved alongside the hierarchical institution: "the numerous religious reforms in the south of Europe were not entirely the work of the Counter-reformation." Dickens[10] argues similarly that "there would assuredly have occurred a Catholic Reformation had Protestantism never developed". Wheeler Robinson[11] speaks of the Council of Trent as itself the outcome in large measure of a genuine Catholic demand for reformation "most emphatically in the morals and organisation of the church."

But as Catholic reform proceeded it was bound to define itself increasingly in contrast with Protestant positions. To this extent Chadwick's repeated remark, that "the only way to counter Protestantism was to reform the church",[12] is justified. Official Catholic moral theology remained that of Aquinas, and the reform of the papal church cannot be said to have contributed greatly to shaping the modern Christian conscience. But it is significant that both wings of the divided church felt the same ethical need; significant also that Catholicism felt the same impulse as prompted Protestantism to look within the soul for new springs of moral understanding and saintliness. The Catholic reform found expression in the social enterprise of new religious orders, in an intensified interest in prayer as the spring of Christian morality, and in fresh concern with problems of moral decision and casuistry.

(a) Chadwick traces in detail movements which enshrined the determination to purify religion:[13]

Cardinal Ximenes of Spain redistributed the wealth of religious houses to support hospitals and better training for clergy, who were enjoined to educate children and expound scripture. The Capuchin Order sought to restore the simplicity of the early Franciscans, devoting energy to pastoral charities, lepers, hospitals, evangelism, while criticising magnificence and depreciating scholarship. A "brotherhood of prayer and pastoral works" in Rome, The Oratory of Divine Love, set a pattern for similar institutions elsewhere, whose members, without withdrawing from the world, lived austerely, established orphanages, hospitals, refuges for fallen women, schools for children, help for the sick and the destitute.

Ignatius Loyola dedicated himself to the religious life with ascetic zeal, and finding little consolation finally achieved escape "through a concentration of his own will upon obedience to the suffering Christ — an obedience formed by . . . the precepts of his church." This set upon his numerous followers — the Jesuits — a character not greatly different from that of Calvinism. Loyola's *Spiritual Exercises* prescribed for thousands a discipline of solitude, self-examination and humiliation, issuing in a voluntary, soldierly submission to superiors of the church. Unquestioning obedience (with sacrifice of personal judgement and initiative), confession, frequent communion, clerical celibacy, fasting, and veneration towards relics, indulgences, scholastic theology, papal decrees and tradition, added up to a new and severe devotion to the *church*, which found its special service — along with preaching, conducting retreats to enthuse the clergy, and hospital chaplaincy — in the education of children, beginning with "the urchins of Rome" and by sheer excellence coming to have charge of the training of aristocrats, princes and kings. Loyola resisted attempts to make the new Order severely ascetic, conventional, or contemplative, requiring his followers to remain in the world, meeting people's needs, in orphanages, refuges for prostitutes, schools, centres for poor-relief; though educational, missionary, and pastoral work remained central. The Jesuits' discipline became proverbial — "the young women are good Jesuits: they go to church first thing in the morning and fast a great deal" — but by 1640, probably because of their intellectual ability and wide influence, the word "Jesuit" came to mean "treacherous".

Pope Pius V added force to reform, especially against simony, blasphemy, sodomy, concubinage, extravagance, prostitution, adultery; he decently clothed the nudes of Roman art, improved the discipline of the clergy, insisted upon religious education and confession, tried to abolish bull-fighting, sought to curtail the expensive administration of the church. It was suggested of Pius (as later of Calvin) that he "wanted to change the whole city into a monastery."[14]

(b) A warmer emotional impulse entered into the Counter-reformation with the increased frequency of communion, more elaborate decoration of churches, the greater use of the Bible in private devotion, and the new adoration of the Virgin. Addleshaw,[15] recalling how the foundations of Christian morality were sapped by the paganism of the renaissance, holds that Christian leaders in Spain, France, and Italy, after Trent, were pre-eminently practical in their approach to the immense problem of rebuilding Christian morality. Their chief contribution to Christian theology "is a detailed examination of the different stages in Christian prayer, which they considered the foundation of Christian character . . . On the basis of prayer they recreated Christian sanctity."

"Realising that only by seeing the Christian ethic in its noblest forms will the world be convinced of its truth, they met the situation not by exhortations to Christian duty, but by teaching people to pray. The galaxy of saints who adorn the period shows how right they were."

Beside Loyola's more intellectual discipline of prayer, Saint Teresa of Avila and Saint John of the Cross brought psychological and mystical depth to the teaching, and Francis de Sales advised *everyone* to make a daily devotion," — a revolutionary idea. Together, these leaders nourished a deeper Catholic piety, which moved from the cloister into secular life. They insisted that perfection is possible for every man; that contemplation, and silent mental prayer, are practicable even for those fully occupied with the world's work; that "the daily round and common task afford ample opportunity for self-abnegation, to him who will seize it."[16]

The place of imitation of Christ in this intensified interest in prayer must not be overlooked. "Saint Teresa emphasised the need of bringing the truths of Christ's life before the mind. To Saint John, contemplation itself with the aridity and desolation of the Nights of Sense and Spirit is nothing but a very real and grim sharing in the Cross." In the French Oratorian school, the incarnation played a central part: "the life of the soul is an extension through grace of the God-man Jesus Christ; it should display the marks of His own humanity . . . the soul must be emptied of all self-longings and be entirely possessed by the Spirit of Christ . . . making its own Christ's interior dispositions as they are manifested in the events of His earthly life . . . resolving to follow His example."[17]

(c) Inevitably, division within the church, widespread religious uncertainty, the changing social situation throughout Europe, created practical problems for ordinary Christians, with their discipleship to fulfil while experts wrangled. The more earnest leaders advised recourse to spiritual directors to ease the consciences of bewildered men: the study of casuistry — the systematic application of moral principles to individual cases of conscience — flourished as a result. Protestantism had its counterpart in numerous books of spiritual guidance and self-examination (Perkins: *Whole Treatise of the Cases of Conscience*; Hall: *Practical Cases of Conscience*; Baxter: *Christian Directory* and many others). The distress of soul occasioned by doubt of the divine will and the clamour of contradictory advice, led to the formulation of a general rule — "Probabilism" — which advised that when any moral principle had, in some particular application, almost as good reasons against it as for it, it could be set aside. The narrow balance of "*probably* right" could not impose weighty obligation, conscience must not be burdened with debateable duties. Misuse of the general rule allowing increasing laxity, and moral principles being set aside for more and more trivial reasons, an older rule was revived — Probabiliorism". This required more careful balancing of reasons for or against a duty, and a much stricter obligation to obey the more probably right injunction — by however narrow margin the probability was measured. That the whole casuistical system eventually fell into disrepute, its name becoming a by-word for insincerity and evasion of plain duty, should not conceal the motive behind its rise — to resolve individual moral problems by serious ethical reflection, and to maintain the importance of conscientious obedience in the Christian life.

The Catholic reformation of morals had considerable success. The

Inquisition of 1542, with the later censorship of books (not confined to the Catholic wing of the church) represent a set-back to reforming influences. But as Chadwick points out,[18] by 1559 the *Catholic* world had greatly changed, "seeking discipline and order, not only admiring the friars but wanting the church to conform to the ascetic and puritan pattern, suspicious of nude and pagan statues, fiercely struggling to diminish or eradicate the veniality of church administration. . . . The wave of moral severity which in another part of Europe was creating puritanism, was now strengthening the hand of the reformers in Italy." Moreover the intensifying of social concern is especially significant: the sick, the poor, the illiterate and the degraded still, as of old, stirred Christian consciences and evoked Christian compassion. And Chadwick notes also that, despite the temptations of extensive colonial discovery and exploitation, "the Popes of the Counter-Reformation . . . steadily condemned the doctrine of slavery for the Indians."[19]

3. EASTERN ORTHODOXY

The churches which looked to Constantinople rather than to Rome, and used the Greek language rather than the Latin, were essentially conservative, both in liturgy, as their preoccupation with service-books and ritual suggests, and especially in faith, as the name "Orthodox" was intended to convey.

"The term . . . is used to indicate the immutable conservatism of the true Christian doctrine . . . inasmuch as it was in the name of this faithfulness that it broke off the connection with the Western church . . . Orthodoxy does not allow of the possibility of dogmatic development."[20] Appeal is generally to the Greek Fathers, and their ethical idealism: modern Orthodox catechists seek still to "remain in the continuity of a timeless orthodoxy."[21]

The same conservatism preserved the *older* monastic ideals. Vows of chastity, obedience, poverty (variously interpreted) remained obligatory; the great monastery at Kiev exercised enormous influence over Russian Orthodoxy, both in setting the tone of its religious devotion, and in providing its leaders.

"Outside the monastery rude passions had full play; within, was quite another world, where the spirit ruled over the flesh, a world of ascetic exploits, visions, miracles, supernatural help in conflict with devils. This explains the desire of the best Russians to enter a monastery . . . Almost all monasteries were also refuges for book-learning. In them lettered men gathered and wrote chronicles, histories, tales, lives of saints; in them schools were founded." Russian monasticism showed two tendencies: one practical and political; the other critical, ascetic, refused all communion with the world. Monastic colonies grew throughout the sixteenth century: "Here, almost alone in Christendom, the primitive ideals of the old Egyptian solitaries continued to be renewed among the forests . . . Cyril of Novoyezersk walked barefoot upon pilgrimage and lived upon pine bark, roots, and grass, spending twenty years among the wild beasts before he decided in 1517 to build himself a cell . . . Nowhere else, . . . might this freshness be found . . . " (Chadwick). Asceticism was indispensable, "not an independent end in itself but as a means for fallen man to reach moral perfection." Despite this, the Orthodox churches did not impose celibacy on their clergy.[22]

On the whole, this attitude left little room for "natural sympathy between Orthodox and Protestants." Chadwick illustrates certain theological contacts, but concludes "It is still a fact of great moment in Christian history that the Orthodox church, despite these various influences, should have missed both the Reformation and the Counter-Reformation."[23] One consequence is that Orthodox theology rejected the Reformation doctrine of salvation by faith alone, requiring also good works; and denied the unconditioned sovereignty of divine grace, insisting that grace works together with man's freedom ("synergism").

Man fell from righteousness, and in Adam all his descendents sinned. Salvation is through the church, established by Christ "for the continual supply of the benefits of the Cross"; it is obtained by true doctrine and the divine sacraments "established by Christ for the sanctification of men . . . spiritual means by which . . . there is granted a . . . saving force of God." Faith and preparation, are indispensable. Original sin, and all pre-baptismal sins, are annihilated in baptism, but their consequences remain, in a tendency to sin, and in suffering. Penitence, including contrition, confession, remission, is taught from the age of seven. Thus "the church is the storehouse of truth and of sanctifying grace." By means of her seven sacraments, the believer is "both justified and edified through faith working by love, in the work of sanctification and in advancement towards all that is good."[24]

Ethical motivation and resource are plainly conceived very differently from the Protestant view; but the emphasis upon Christian morality and obedience is just as firm.

Leading ethical themes discernible within the Orthodox outlook, despite Greek, Balkan, Turkish, and Russian variations, include: (1) the ancient ideal of the "divinisation" of man. This derives in part from "special potentiality for God, as having preserved the *image* of God, though having lost His *likeness*;"[25] and in part from the Eastern

Fathers — Irenaeus, Clement of Alexandria, Athanasius — words of the last-named being often cited, "He became man so that we might become divine."[26] As Ashanin says,[27] "To an Orthodox Christian the human and cosmic world are deeply theocentric, for they proceed from God, and are understood only when approached with the spiritual response of love . . . It is a supremely personalistic world, for in it each one is known as a being for the other, and both for God." Men are thus responsibly inter-related, deeply engaged, seeking fulfilment and reconciliation in God. This is not individualism, but *personalism*, and Ashanin quotes Benz —

> "The Orthodox doctrine of *Sobornost* achieves a nice balance. It avoids the West's occasional over-emphasis on the claim of individuality, which may end by alienating the person from the mystical body of Christ. On the other hand, it also avoids an over-valuation of a collective that kills all individuality . . . " Stahlke says that *sobornost* is untranslatable, and suggests "all for one and one for all".[28]

Such a view of the world demands from each a triple response: the mutual, sacrificial attitude of *love*, a "creative, redemptive effort . . . to restore the world to God and overcome its alienation . . . "; the acceptance of *creative suffering* — seeking another's redemption by personally sharing his suffering, though it be well-deserved; and the discipline of *kenosis*, "the disposition to be sacrificed for all," a readiness to emulate Christ in His self-emptying to reach and reconcile others at the depth of their alienation and emptiness. Behind this typically eastern ideal lies plainly the New Testament's teaching on *agape* and Christlikeness, and a special concern with the deeper ethical implications of the incarnation.[29] The imitation of Christ is here applied at a moral and theological level not at all usual in Christian ethics. "Divinisation" is for most Christians an unwelcome expression, but it must not be confused with "deification"; nor must its exacting and humiliating demand for deliberate self-emptying and personal sacrifice for others' good, modelled on that of Jesus Himself, be under-valued.

(2) Ashanin speaks[30] of a "certain world detachment" in Orthodox ethics, finding its explanation less in ancient Greek pessimism than in primitive Christian eschatology. He links with it the Orthodox stress upon the heart and its penetrating influence, rather than the activist will and its political expression. It stresses also the scriptural basis of ethics, especially in the Ten Commandments and the Beatitudes: "Eastern Orthodox ethics . . . knows of no concept of natural law." The nineteenth century mystical movement under Czar Alexander I, and the creation of the Russian Bible Society, illustrate this aspect of

Orthodox piety.

Nevertheless, though Orthodoxy rejects the "natural law" which earlier western moralists borrowed from pagan thought, it has a clear concept of law at the heart of ethics. "Jesus Christ passed His life on earth in the most perfect fulfilment of the law . . . The divine law is written on the heart of every man, is contained in the Ten Commandments . . . " It is natural, being universally innate; the written law is a facsimile of the natural "as it contains no precept of which the conscience of every man is not convinced."[31] Orthodox ethics thus repudiates non-scriptural, non-traditional sources, but in its own way finds the revealed law of God to be fundamental to human nature, and to deeply personalist relationships.

(3) "Detachment", in this sense of possessing independent origins, does not however for a moment imply carelessness of the world and its needs. Nor must we mistake a lack of theoretical social philosophy for insensitiveness to social problems.[32] Troitsky says that even in the fourth to ninth centuries, as church property and State protection increased, "Christian philanthropy assumed great importance." As Orthodoxy advanced into Russia, from Kiev to Moscow, much of the wealth of the monasteries went to charitable objects, and not only in the founding of schools — their immediate concern. Well before the ninth century, the monastic Orders of Constantinople had adopted the rule of St. Basil, for whom monastic life was life in community, practising the love of one's neighbour — the isolation of the hermit was mere egotism; the monk's duties must include care of children and of the poor. Following Orthodox tradition, and the reforms of Prince Vladimir (937-1015), the Metropolitan of Russia was officially recognised "champion of all the oppressed, protector of the sick, of widows, and of orphans, of liberated slaves, and of prisoners of war . . . " Most Orthodox leaders were zealous for education, not least of the clergy. Following Peter the Great (1682-1725) Russian Orthodoxy was charged with the religious education of the people, the establishment of parish schools, and considerable missionary activity. Ashanin cites the tremendous activity of the Eastern Orthodox church among refugees as typical of the material care of the Russian church for her children; and quotes Benz on the social activities of the Greek church as probably the strongest historical evidence to counter vague charges of "failure in social ethics".[33]

(4) Church-State relationships, for the Orthodox churches, were embraced under the formula of "symphonia". Deriving from the generally "communal" outlook of Orthodoxy is clear recognition of needs in the community which the church, as primarily concerned with the kingdom of God, cannot meet. Such needs fall within a

divinely ordained *diaconate* of the State, alongside the *apostolate* of the church. Their relation is inter-dependent, each assisting the other in its religious task. This has been the Orthodox ideal since Constantine, though it has been given varying interpretation, the emperor sometimes interfering with the appointment of bishops, disposition of church property, or the summoning of councils; the church sometimes influencing civil government, laws, and administration, overseeing legal judgements, and occasionally receiving royal honours.

In Russia, early Metropolitan archbishops were the recognised supporters and guides of the princes, strengthening their authority and upholding the unification of the Russian peoples. Under Mongol rule, a fair measure of religious toleration was met by conciliation from the church. Early in the seventeenth century, Patriarch and Czar were father and son, joint "Great Lords" of Russia, and this close "harmony" continued also through the latter half of the century. Under Peter the Great, the church's "Most Holy Governing Synod" took an oath of allegiance to the emperor and bound themselves to observe all the interests of the State, in exchange for rights equal (in its own field) to those of the Senate.[34]

The doctrine of "symphonia" has sometimes been criticised as excessively submissive and conformist, to which the reply has been made that "the long agony of hostile rule" experienced by Orthodox Christianity under Turks, Mongols, Catholics (in Poland), Muslims, and some Russian princes, explains the stance adopted. "It is no wonder that Orthodoxy has remained more conscious of persecution and Christian resignation, more geared to compulsory compliance."[35] But the idealism of creative suffering and self-emptying, in imitation of Christ, must not be under-estimated. And it must be conceded that Orthodox Christianity never suffered (until the Revolution) the bitter church-State conflicts that have marred the story of the western church.[36]

It was to be expected that the ferment of change would affect the deliberately, eagerly reforming churches more than those anxious to conserve the past and to yield only by necessity. Yet even those groups who sought reform were aware of the obligation of loyalty to their original roots in scripture, and of the compulsions of a saving experience which was patterned upon salvation-history, in the life, death, resurrection and example of Jesus. That tension between conservation and change created the main problems, for the western church especially, for the next three centuries.

12

The Inner Light — Conscience, Reason

THE FORMULATION OF ETHICS which resulted from rigorous application of Reformed principles by followers of Luther and Calvin may broadly be called "evangelical ethics". That phrase serves to describe the moral outlook of several groups for whom the revealed gospel, and personal experience of divine action within the soul, were the primary factors in Christianity — church loyalty, historical continuity, ethical and social obligations being secondary. It is true that "the earnestness engendered by the Reformation epoch thrust morality into the centre"[1] but it was a morality expected to flow spontaneously from faith, justification, regeneration, possession of the Spirit, the light and life of grace within the soul.

The appeal to inner experience characteristic of the Reformation, was consonant with the new interest in psychology shown by Locke and Hume[2], who deeply influenced Jonathan Edwards. The church as a corporate spiritual authority had given place to numerous sects, each a "gathered" company of Christians of like belief and experience, providing social context for this internalised Christian piety. Since the divided church could no longer dominate the ruling powers of the world, Christians tended to withdraw from a society passing out of Christian control, into a more satisfying inner life. Obedience to appointed spiritual directors gave place to an introspective appeal, for instruction and authority, to private judgement informed by the Spirit exercised upon scripture but only validated in the end by individual conscience — Luther set the key:

"unless I am convinced by the testimony of scripture, or by an evident reason . . . I am held fast by the scriptures adduced by me, and my conscience is taken captive by God's Word . . . I neither can nor will revoke anything seeing it is not safe or right to act against my conscience."[3]

This movement inwards had both an intellectual aspect, seeking the inner light of the Spirit upon the Word, or "the light within" without the Word, in order to *know* the will of God; and a dynamic, conative aspect, seeking the motive forces of grace, conversion, sanctification by the Spirit, by which to *do* the will of God. It took psychological form in the appeal to the light of conscience, in Joseph Butler; more philosophical form — somewhat on the fringe of Christian ethics — in Immanuel Kant; a deeply religious form in the Puritans, Baxter, Fox, Barclay, Edwards.[4]

Despite its individualist and introspective tendency, evangelical ethics manifested, paradoxically, a deep concern for social reform — or at least, for social amelioration. A second unexpected result of the appeal to a moral arbiter within the soul was to strengthen the trend towards moral autonomy, and ultimately towards a wholly secular ethic.

1. THE LIGHT OF CONSCIENCE

"Among the greatest exponents of natural theology and ethics in England since the Reformation,"[5] Butler based morality squarely upon the constitution of human nature itself.

Hobbes insisted that man was dominated by desire for pleasure, self-preservation, power, and not by nature a social being; pity is but *self*-pity at the prospect of another's injury happening to ourselves; benevolence is either fear purchasing peace, or delight in power to affect others' welfare; all moral rules arise from a social contract in which rival self-interests are reconciled. In reply, *rational intuitionists* (Cudworth, Charles) held that moral ideas like justice are as universal, unalterable, as intellectual axioms — rooted in the nature of the universe. *Aesthetic intuitionists* held conscience to be a moral sense, analogous to the sense of beauty, passing judgement on acts, thoughts, as our aesthetic sense passes judgements upon objects; there is no general principle of goodness; conscience is not a rational function, applying universal laws, but a kind of tact, taste, a "feeling" for the virtuous or vicious. *Shaftesbury* contended that the moral quality of actions inheres in them — moral distinctions have reality independent of our perception; the characteristic property of the good is to be harmonious with the system of which it forms part — human goodness lies in maintaining harmony with humanity; virtue maintains balance, proportion, between self-affections and natural altruistic affections; the ultimate criterion, the general good, always coincides with private virtue.

Butler wrote in this context. He may have seen that moral ideas are not, like intellectual ideas, logically non-contradictory; and that a moral sense yields no authority. He adopted the intuitionists' psychological approach, Shaftesbury's social nature of man and special moral faculty — but as a principle of *reflection*. Thus his view is intuitionist, in holding that acts are right or wrong by their intrinsic nature, not simply by their consequences, and are assessed by an inward moral faculty. But his intuitionism is partly psychological, partly rational, and certainly religious.[6]

The general tendency of Butler's thought is nevertheless towards an autonomous ethic: "man is . . . by his very nature a law to himself."[7]

"Man cannot be considered a creature left by his Maker to act at random . . . from his make, constitution, or nature, he is in the strictest sense a law to himself: he hath the rule of right within him: what is wanting is only that he honestly attend to it." "Yet it may be asked, 'What obligations are we under to attend and follow it?' I answer: it has been proved that man by his nature is a law to himself . . . The question then carries its own answer. Your obligation to obey this law is its being the law of your nature. That your conscience approves of such a course is itself an obligation . . . Conscience does not only offer itself to show us the way, it likewise carries its own authority with it, that it is our natural guide . . ."[8]

Beach therefore describes Butler as thoroughly rationalist, subscribing to the tenet of the age, the authority of reason. He contrasts Butler with those Christian thinkers who begin with "a truth about God's nature, or the incarnation, or the revealed will of God in church or Bible . . . " to show that in taking human nature as its point of departure, his ethic is "autonomous, not theonomous in its foundation." Because of this anthropocentric approach, Beach asks whether Butler's ethical theory can be called Christian, answering that its theological element is more a supplement than a foundation.[9] Butler himself can say:

"Our being God's creatures, virtue the natural law we are born under, the whole constitution of man plainly adapted to it, are prior obligations to piety and virtue, than the consideration that God sent His Son into the world to save it, and motives which arise from the peculiar relation of Christians, as members one of another under Christ our Head" —

though he immediately adds that Christians could not but insist mostly upon considerations of this kind.[10] Matthews, who accepts that Butler bases morality upon "natural religion" rather than on Christianity, speaks of him as "sternly impersonal and sternly practical", avoiding individual feeling — he explicitly deprecated "enthusiasm", the eighteenth-century word for "fanaticism".[11] Butler also deprecates the confidence of Calvinists —

"Other orders of creatures may perhaps be let into the secret counsels of heaven and have the designs and methods of Providence in the creation and government of the world communicated to them: but this does not belong to our condition . . . "[12]

Yet Butler was fully aware, as Matthews argues,[13] that ethics needs theology as its completion and support. If conscience is our natural guide, it is because it is "the guide assigned to us by the Author of our nature." His belief in Providence convinced Butler that "in the end the dictates of conscience and the demands of self-love will have been found to have pointed to the same conclusion". The moral government of the world and its ultimate happiness is "the concern of Him who is the Lord and the Proprietor of it." "There is seldom any inconsistency between duty and 'interest', happiness, satisfaction." Whatever exceptions there are, "all shall be set right at the final distribution of things. It is manifest absurdity to suppose evil prevailing . . . under the administration of a perfect mind."[14] Butler's view includes ideas of "an authority in the universe to punish the violation of this law" in man's nature — a "divine punishment" — though such beliefs are not necessary to the obligations of morality. He argues that since the good of the whole must be the interest of the universal Being, and "goodness is a fixed, steady, immovable principle of action", the impartial rule of goodness is even more to be feared than the fickle. easily appeased, rule of malice.[15] So in the last resort conscience is not merely subjective, but the voice of God representing in the soul the laws of eternal justice, bearing witness to the supreme Judgement. "It goes on to anticipate a higher and more effectual sentence which shall hereafter second and affirm its own."[16] Always Butler assumes a teleological view of human nature: we are "made for society and to do good to our fellow creatures . . . we were intended to take care of our own life health and private good."[17] The extensive place given to the great double commandment of Jesus is significant; and Butler repeatedly assumes a future life.[18]

There is, therefore. no question that Butler sees ethics within an ultimately religious framework. Nevertheless, reason is held competent to judge both of the evidential value of revelation, and of its morality. Conscience no less than the Bible is a gift of God, and no scripture can offer pretext for evading the moral imperative. Apparent immoralities in the Bible just cannot be real.[19] Butler's fundamental appeal is not to revelation, to Christ, or to the church, but to the constitution of human nature.

Though at least eight of the fifteen famous sermons are upon sayings of Christ, or quotations of Christ by Paul, an occasional reference is made to "our Saviour", and His words are quoted with reverence, yet nothing could be more characteristic of Butler than the remark "I shall close these reflections with *barely mentioning* the behaviour of that divine Person who was the example of all perfection in human nature . . ."[20]

(1) The Appeal to Human Nature

"For Butler, moral excellence consisted in fulfilling the demand made upon us by our whole nature, in . . . concrete situations."[21] (i) That man's nature is essentially moral is assumed. This is supported from experience, in ourselves and in others, of a capacity to reflect upon actions and characters, with approval or disapproval; from the familiarity in all languages of words like *right* and *wrong, odious* and *amiable, base* and *worthy*; from the many systems of morals, which cannot easily be dismissed as meaningless; from the gratitude we feel towards goodness in others; from the distinction we make between accidental injury and deliberate harm, or punishment; and from the general agreement of mankind as to what *is* moral — that which all would publicly profess, which all civilised laws uphold, such as justice, veracity, devotion to the common good.[22]

(ii) Human nature contains many elements within an organised hierarchy. A number of passions, impulses, prompt us to pursue particular objects. These are subordinate to the restraint and direction of a natural principle of benevolence, on the one hand, tending towards compassion, affection, the good of others; and a natural principle of self-love on the other hand, tending towards care of one's own health, life, character, and private good. Further: "there is a principle of reflection in men, by which they distinguish between, approve and disapprove, their own actions . . . This principle is conscience . . . And that this faculty tends to restrain men from doing mischief to each other, and leads them to do good, is too manifest to need being insisted upon . . . "[23]

(iii) To "live according to nature" can have a licentious meaning. It can assume that what is passionate, instinctive, *strongest* in human nature must be obeyed, with vicious results; "following nature" is then equated with acting as we please. But since Paul argues that the gentiles do "by nature" the things contained in the law, being a law unto themselves, it follows that some other meaning of "according to nature" is implied. Indeed, there is in every man, by nature, "a superior principle of reflection or conscience . . . which

> distinguishes between the internal principles of his heart as well as his external actions; which passes judgement upon himself and them; pronounces some actions to be in themselves just, right and good; others to be in them-

selves evil, wrong, unjust: which, without being consulted, without being advised with, magisterially exerts itself, and approves or condemns him . . . It is by this faculty, natural to man, that he is a moral agent, that he is a law unto himself . . . this faculty, I say, not to be considered merely as a principle in his heart which is to have some influence as well as others; but considered as a faculty supreme over all others, and which bears its own authority . . . This prerogative, this natural supremacy, of the faculty which surveys, approves or disapproves the several affections of our mind and actions of our lives, being that by which men are a law to themselves, their conformity or disobedience to (it) renders their actions in the highest and most proper sense *natural* or *unnatural* . . ."[24]

It is, therefore, by living according to that element in his nature which possesses greatest authority, not according to that which possesses the greatest strength, that man fulfils the law of his own being, and "lives according to nature."[25]

(iv) "Thus that principle, by which we . . . approve or disapprove our own heart, temper and actions is . . . superior . . . insomuch that you cannot form a notion of this faculty, conscience, without taking in judgement, direction, superintendency. This is a constituent part of . . . the faculty itself: and to preside and govern, from the very economy and constitution of man, belongs to it. *Had it strength, as it has right: had it power, as it has manifest authority, it would absolutely govern the world.*"[26]

"This gives us a further view of the nature of man; . . . that this faculty was placed within to be our proper governor; to direct and regulate all under principles, passions, and motives of action . . . How often men refuse to submit to it . . . makes no alteration to the natural right and office of conscience . . . Neither can any human creature be said to act comformably to his constitution of nature, unless he allows to that superior principle the absolute authority which is due to it."[27]

Such exaltation of the human conscience was to have far-reaching influence in Protestant circles, turning the Christian's gaze inwards for guidance, and founding Christian ethics upon the innate morality of man.

(2) The Natural Principle of Self-love

Contemporary moralists felt it necessary to reject Hobbes' doctrine that man is governed solely by the desire for pleasure, self-preservation, and power: but the reply of Butler is judicious:

"The nature of man . . . leads him to attain the greatest happiness he can for himself in the present world . . . It deserves to be considered whether men are more at liberty, in point of morals, to make themselves miserable without reason than to make other people so . . . It should seem that a due concern about our own interest or happiness, and a reasonable endeavour to secure it . . . is . . . virtue, and the contrary behaviour faulty and blameable . . ."[28]

Butler illustrates the varying degree in which we blame "thoughtless want of attention to our own happiness", and shows that we approve or disapprove not the consequence only but actions themselves, and the prudence or folly they exhibit.

Such "settled regard for himself", "cool reflection upon what is for our own interest", is one measure suggested in the great Commandment for the required love of our neighbour — "as thyself". We are "in a peculiar manner, as I may speak, entrusted with ourselves . . . care of our own interests, as well as of our conduct, particularly belongs to us."[29]

"Self-love in its due degree is as morally good as any affection whatever . . . Neither does there appear any reason to wish self-love were weaker . . . Men daily, hourly, sacrifice the greatest known interest to fancy, inquisitiveness, love or hatred, any vagrant inclination . . . It is ridiculous to call . . . an abandoned course of pleasure *interested* when the person engaged in it knows . . . that it will be as ruinous to himself as to those who depend upon him. Upon the whole, if the generality of mankind were to cultivate within themselves the principle of self-love . . . it would manifestly prevent numberless follies and vices . . . Self-love is, of the two, a much better guide than passion."[30]

Again, Butler can argue that

"Religion . . . is so far from disowning the principle of self-love that it often addresses itself to that very principle . . . There can no access be had to the understanding but by convincing men that the course of life we would persuade them to is not contrary to their interest . . . Though virtue or moral rectitude does indeed consist in pursuit of what is right and good as such, yet when we sit down in a cool hour we can neither justify to ourselves this or any other pursuit till we are convinced that it will be for our happiness — or at least, not contrary to it."[31]

Butler carefully distinguishes self-love, as a general principle of far-seeing regard for one's own interest, from various "self-regarding" impulses to seek objects outside the self (riches, power, reputation) — impulses which can in fact defeat true self-love. Men too rarely consider wherein their true happiness consists, or else cool self-love is prevailed over by passion and appetite. A very great part of the wickedness of the world is . . . owing to the self-partiality, self-flattery, and self-deceit of men; vice consists in too great regard for ourselves, false selfishness, and partiality, which corrupt character.[32]

Such defence of self-love is rare in Christian ethics. Where it occurs it is usually through the influence of Stoicism, as with Butler's repeated quotation of "Know thyself"; or in opposition to self-abnegation, self-injurious asceticism, or specious self-depreciation. Some regard Butler's view as the consequence of his fundamental error in basing ethics upon human nature; others find in it a return to the biblical valuation of man as made in God's image, superior to the brutes, with capacity for divine sonship and eternal life.

(3) The Natural Principle of Benevolence

Nevertheless Butler also contends, against Hobbes' egoism, for the presence in human nature of a natural impulse towards benevolence, a true concern for the welfare of others, "the seeds of it implanted in our nature by God."

"There are as real . . . indications in human nature that we are made for society and to do good to our fellow creatures . . . There is a natural principle of benevolence . . . Mankind are by nature so closely united . . . that disgrace is as much avoided as bodily pain, and to be the object of esteem and love as much desired as any external goods . . . Relations merely nominal are sought and invented — fraternities, co-partnerships . . . Men are so much one body that in a peculiar manner they feel for each other shame, sudden danger, resentment, honour, prosperity, distress . . . As the nature of man leads him to attain his own happiness, so the nature of man leads him to a right behaviour in society . . . Men follow or obey their nature in both these capacities . . . or they violate their nature, as often in one respect as in the other."[33]

Two sermons (XI and XII) fully expound this principle of benevolence. The former distinguishes benevolence from self-love by precise analysis, and emphasises the special obligation of Christian benevolence; the latter examines in detail the Commandment of love.

"Love thy neighbour" is more concrete than love of "humanity"; "as thyself" may intend the same *kind* of affection, *proportionate* affection, or *equality* between self-love and benevolence. As a principle for reasonable agents it must be directed by reason, taking note of distant as well as immediate consequences, of greater obligation towards family and friends than towards strangers, and of others' judgement. Benevolence nourishes other virtues also — temperance, sobriety, moderation in sensual pleasure; indeed, as including all the virtues it is the pre-eminent precept. It finds its perfection in love of God. Elsewhere, Butler insists that benevolence is not the whole of virtue: morality must consider not only the happiness achieved but the means used: violence, treachery, injustice are bad although they contribute to an individual's happiness; and adultery, murder, perjury are wrong in themselves, apart from their consequences.[34]

Healthy character needs "affections" as well as reason — the *apathy* of the Stoics, suppression of affections, does not increase happiness. Compassion, it is true, creates sympathetic sorrow, but also joy in *being* compassionate, rather than callous. The exercise of the widest social affections certainly contributes to human welfare.[35]

This paradox, that human nature should contain both the principle of self-love and the principle of benevolence, receives considerable attention. To "love thy neighbour as thyself" turns out to be the great Commandment "precisely in that it harmonises private and public interest, self-love and benevolence" (Beach[36]).

"The comparison will be between the nature of man as respecting self, and tending to private good . . . and the nature of man as having respect to society and tending to promote public good . . . These ends do indeed perfectly coincide: they mutually promote each other." "More delight than sorrow arises from compassion" (for example). It serves self-love to be benevolent: neither does benevolence exclude self-love (Butler argues this with copious illustration). "Though benevolence and self-love are different, yet they are so perfectly coincident that the greatest satisfactions to ourselves depend upon our having benevolence in a due degree . . . That we can scarce promote one without the other, is equally a proof that we were made for both."[37]

So neatly may all tension between egoism and altruism, all struggle between private temptation and public morality, all the tragic contrast between human idealism and the wickedness of the world, be resolved into misunderstanding, poor judgement, and a sad want of foresight!

(4) Love towards God

Butler is not content to assert that benevolence finds its perfection in love for God. In two moving sermons he argues that God alone is an adequate *subject* for man's understanding, and the only sufficient *object* of all human affections — of reverence, desire of divine love, delight in divine approbation.[38] Such love, comprehending awe, hope, honour, worship, is the appropriate affection of such a creature as man towards the perfect, infinite Being who is his Guardian, Governor, and Ideal. It includes a love of heart, soul, and mind, as "implied in words of our Saviour, speaking of the love of God and neighbour as containing the whole of piety and virtue."[39] Butler can speak of our being *commanded* to love God, though he argues that "the nature of man is so constituted" as to feel certain affections upon sight of certain objects. So, an affection towards good characters, "reverence and moral love of them, is *natural* to those who have any degree of real goodness in themselves: surely this is applicable . . . to that Being who is infinitely more than an adequate Object of all those affections.''[40]

Analysing the regard due to God as fear, love, hope, Butler unexpectedly proceeds, "There is a temper of mind . . . which follows from all three . . . namely, resignation to the divine will, the whole of piety: it includes all that is good, and is a source of the most settled composure of mind. There is the general principle of submission in our nature.''[41]

> "Human nature is formed to compliance . . . Nature inclines us to take up with our lot: the consideration that the course of things is unalterable . . . appointed and continued by infinite wisdom and goodness . . . hath a tendency to quiet the mind, to beget a submission of temper." Such is "loyalty of heart to the Governor of the universe," the "submission of heart, soul, and mind, the religious resignation naturally produced by our having just conceptions of Almighty God and a real sense of His presence with us.''[42]

It is significant that Butler can find the ultimate springs of such piety in the original constitution of human nature.

(5) Assessment

Of Butler's contribution to Christian ethics there can be no question. Matthews[43] notices the links with one side of Kant's thought; with the Utilitarian doctrine of the common good (though Butler insists that virtue is an end in itself, not only a means to social welfare[44]); and with the modern concept of self-realisation. MacKinnon remarks upon Butler's reactivation of the tradition of natural law, doing justice to its inwardness, recognising the place of general principle and human particularity in framing ethical problems.[45] The weight which Butler lent to the tendency towards an autonomous ethic has already been mentioned; conscience has held higher place in Christian ethics since his age than it ever held before — in some circles it has become the sole ethical guide. Yet even Butler's thorough exposition leaves open serious questions.

(i) Mackenzie[46] thinks that the nature of the authoritative principle is not clear — whether an inexplicable faculty by which laws are laid down, or an intelligible authority whose commands can be understood by rational reflection.

> "The inadequacy of conscience as a basis of morals becomes further apparent when we endeavour to determine definitely what principles are laid down by it." The content of conscience varies considerably, having reference to utility for welfare: the principles laid down can be rationally justified. "Only so can we distinguish what is permanent and reliable in the

decisions of conscience. But when we thus draw distinctions and pass judgement upon conscience itself, it is evident that we must somehow have a conscience behind conscience, a faculty of judgement which stands above the blind law of the heart."

Butler, as we saw, assumed that benevolence must be directed by reason; Mackenzie argues that conscience, similarly, must be rational; but also purposive, since man is a teleological agent:

"It would be unnatural for us simply to follow our appetites and instincts . . . we have definite ideas of ends that we pursue, and know the means that may be expected to secure them. If the authority of conscience is of this nature, it is . . . the authority of reason itself."[47]

This is the insight developed by Kant. But from Butler's own extensive argumentation it is clear that he considered the "principle of *reflection*", the faculty of moral approval and disapproval, to be both analysable and defensible. To it, "the principles of morality were intuitively evident, and errors of moral judgement arose only from superstition and self-deception" (Cross).[48]

(ii) Matthews[49] suggests that Butler too easily assumed that conscience always and everywhere speaks the same. But from the particular deliverances of conscience which Butler names — the basic distinction between right and wrong, a respect for justice, veracity, the common good[50] — it would appear that he thinks of "the conscience of mankind" speaking in general, indeed universal, terms. Detailed application of moral generalities involves much else, knowledge of facts, compromises, habits of mind, assessments of persons, foresight of probable consequences, and the like, which are not matters of conscience but of intelligence, education, and experience. Mackenzie, too, suggests that when intuitionist writers refer to conscience as the supreme principle of morals, what they mean is "the universal conscience . . . that ultimate recognition of the rightness and wrongness of actions which is latent in all men."[51] This is not, however, the way in which conscience is usually understood in Protestant ethics: but rather as individual experience of the voice of God within the pious soul.

(iii) Butler's appeal to human nature for the sufficient basis of morality, also raises questions for the traditional Protestant view. It is evident that for Butler there is in man no such "dark perversion of sin"[52], no such incapacity, total corruption and slavery to sin, no such "depravity", as Augustine, Luther, Calvin, and many other soteriologists had declared. Man, for Butler, is essentially good: "the dictates of the natural conscience are inherently right." Sin is disproportion, lack of harmony, error, disregard of the superior authority of conscience — essentially a failure in reasoned judgement. "Virtue consists in following human nature, and vice in deviating from it": "nothing can possibly be more contrary to nature than vice."[53] Where the Reformers would insist that any good in man must be the fruit not of nature but of intrusive divine grace, Butler looks rather to the divinely created constitution of man himself for the knowledge, obligation, and impulse of morality.

It follows that Christianity is the *natural* ethic for human nature, in which Butler finds foundation for the highest Christian law, love for God and neighbour.

> "The moral theory of the gospels is the fullest and most convincing expression of this natural morality that one could find. The ethical teachings of Jesus Christ are normative for Christians, not because they go counter to human nature but because obedience to them fulfils our true natures and brings the happiness all men seek." (Beach)[54]

Sermon VIII, on the Christian law of love towards enemies, argues that resentment has a natural, advantageous function, in defending the individual against sudden violence, a weapon against injustice and cruelty. It is abuse, excess, of resentment that are forbidden — as human nature itself would require. In Sermon IX, the "specially Christian" virtue of forgiveness of injuries is analysed to show that retaliation and excessive resentment are self-defeating; forgiving love of enemies "is in truth the law of our nature", both practical, and rational.[55]

Despite his own religious presuppositions, therefore, Butler unquestionably contributed to that movement away from Christian foundations towards a secular ethic which was to find its most elegant and persuasive expression in the cultivated Hume, its most influential in the Utilitarianism of J. S. Mill — both building as Butler had done on the analysis of man's own nature, "dispositions", and motivations. Even those who shared Butler's religious assumptions came to look more and more within themselves — to the light of conscience — rather than to scripture or the church for moral direction. The problem of moral *authority* cannot be said to be solved, in Butler's ethics, except for those for whom his highly philosophical approach has compelling appeal.

2. THE LIGHT OF REASON: KANT

As Luther set reason beside scripture as "holding conscience captive", and Hooker combined reason with scripture and tradition in seeking a new base for authority, so the "ethical rationalists" (Clarke, Wollaston, but especially Kant) conceived the basis of ethics as essentially reason applied to conduct. For Kant, conduct is right only in so far as it is dictated by the moral reason.[56]

"The effect upon Kant of the progress of knowledge in the eighteenth century," says Selwyn "was the conviction that new ground must be found for the primary truths of religion . . . in the facts of the moral world alone. The relationship of Kant's 'categorical imperative' to the Christian conscience is a matter of dispute, and he set little store by the Christian metaphysic . . . At the same time, his ethical fervour could not fail to have its influence upon those who regarded Christ as the greatest of all ethical teachers . . ." Matthews sees Kant's practical reason as the lineal development of Butler's view of conscience as a rational principle; and Cock suggested that Kant's ethics are but Christian ethics cut loose from their metaphysical foundations.[57]

Kant's motive was doubtless to establish morality upon more than feeling, taste, external authority, intuition, or numerous "principles" discoverable (or posited) within human nature, by appealing to sovereign Reason itself. The effect was to divorce practical reason from pure reason, value judgements from factual judgements, as clearly distinguishable in nature but in every respect equally valid for understanding experience. From Kant's analysis stems the modern concept of a system of values, parallel to the system of scientific facts, two correlative but different ways of apprehending the world.

(1) The Authority of Reason

Most rigorous of all ethical rationalists, Kant contributed — as a Lutheran — to the later development of Christian ethics a superb emphasis upon the importance, the unshakable authority, of the moral reason. Kant taught Christians in quite a new way that "nothing can possibly be conceived in the world or even out of it which can be called good without qualification except *a good will*". And that is good "not because of what it performs or effects, not by its aptness for the attainment of some proposed end, but simply by virtue of the volition, that is, it is good in itself . . . Its usefulness or fruitlessness can neither add to nor take away anything from this value."[58] Kant reverenced above all things the infinite majesty presented, without any mystic vision or supernatural faith, to reason's own gaze: "Two things fill the mind with ever new and increasing admiration and awe, the oftener and the more steadily we reflect on them: the starry heavens above and the moral law within. I have not to search for them . . . I see them before me, and connect them directly with the consciousness of my existence.''[59]

For a third lesson, Kant wrote into Christian ethics the concept of absolute obligation. The moral law is not, like that of a nation, a law imposed by sanctions, making it *advisable* to obey; nor is it a hypothetical law, as the laws of architecture apply only to those who wish to build, the laws of rhetoric only to those who wish to persuade — laws that apply *if* we seek some specified end; ''the supreme moral principle . . . lays its command upon us absolutely, and admits of no question . . . There can be no higher law by which the moral imperative might be set aside . . . the moral law is unique . . . the only categorical imperative . . . a pure categorical imperative imposed on us by reason.''[60]

In such ways Kant endowed morality with an authority scarcely felt since the Reformation. He believed that he had found certainty, also: ''An erring conscience is a chimera . . . I limit the question suggested to this: Whether it is not of the utmost necessity to construct a pure moral philosophy, perfectly cleared of everything which is only empirical . . . Everyone must admit that if a law is to have moral force, that is, to be the basis of an obligation, it must carry with it absolute necessity . . .'' Kant thus sought in *reason* the moral authority lost at the Reformation: ''the basis of obligation must not be sought in the nature of man, or in the circumstances of the world in which he is placed, but *a priori* simply in the conceptions of pure reason.''[61]

(2) The Categorical Imperative

Kant begins from his principle that only the good will is good without qualification, and that inherently, not because of any useful consequences. To consider the usefulness of actions must introduce questions of intelligent foresight, experience, knowledge of the world, and other matters strictly beyond *moral* judgement. To be good absolutely, the good will must fulfil the fundamental law of morality, which is: ''act in conformity with that maxim, and that maxim only, which you can at the same time will to be a universal law.'' In order to be universal, and categorical, the moral law cannot have specific and detailed content, which depends upon circumstances; it can only have the abstract form of law itself, that is, of complete and universal consistency.

To break a promise is wrong *because* making a promise at all depends on the principle that promises are to be kept — otherwise it is futile to make them; breaking one, then, asserts an exception, an inconsistency. So in lying we at the same time appeal to the universal rule of truth-telling — else the lie will achieve nothing — and yet make an exception for ourselves by telling untruth.

"What sort of law can that be, the conception of which must determine the will, even without paying any regard to the effect expected from it, in order that this will may be called good absolutely and without qualification? . . . There remains nothing but the universal conformity of its acts to law in general, which alone is to serve the will as a principle; that is, I am never to act otherwise than so that I could also will that my maxim should become a universal law . . . It is the simple conformity to law in general that serves the will as its principle."[62]

This is the universal ethical obligation which Kant saw to be absolutely binding upon all men. It is the sum of duty — "Duty is the necessity of acting from respect for the law"[63] — and has been described as "a rational statement of the golden rule".[64] It has been variously criticised: as *formal,* giving no detailed direction; as too *stringent,* requiring duty to be done from rationalist motives, not from virtuous desire, right feeling, good impulse; and as *insufficient,* because in a fallen world, given ingenuity, any maxim could be universalised as "consistent with itself". To understand as "consistent with the self and its universe as a whole" introduces into the imperative much more than the abstract form of self-consistency. Moreover, the authority of reason is not very great or compelling over those to whom "reason" itself is an abstract concept, difficult to grasp. "Kant's categorical imperative carries no terrors."

(3) The Practical Reason

Nevertheless, for those already bound by ethical ideals Kant did offer imposing argument for the absoluteness of moral claims. This was the more acceptable because, having first proved by his analysis of "pure reason" that man could *know* only the phenomenal world as it presented itself to his consciousness, not as it is in itself, and could never know anything that did not so present itself, he then proceeded to argue, from the analysis of the "practical reason" that man *must* postulate the existence of God, the reality of his own freedom, and his own immortality, in order to make sense of his moral experience. Thus although to pure reason the basic religious questions must ever remain open and unanswerable, Kant found a new path to religious confidence, in the necessary postulates without which the *summum bonum* man feels compelled to strive after, and the sense of obligation under which he lives, simply do not make sense.[65] Without such a moral faith, reality would no longer appeal to us as fully rational. The spiritual demands of life, equally with scientific thought, have a right to induce belief, and in the end their claim is the more fundamental one. The truths of pure reason are subordinate to those of practical reason, intellect to moral insight, because man lives under ethical obligation as surely as he lives within intellectual mystery. There is a reason as binding upon the conscience as logic is upon the mind: by one he lays hold upon the *noumenal* world of supra-sensual reality; by the other he apprehends the world of phenomena all about him. Some trace the gulf within modern culture between science and religion ultimately to the gap between Kant's two "worlds' and two "reasons".

Kant's thought was too abstractly philosophical, too little related to historic Christian concepts, too closely involved with Kant's own epistemology, to determine the development of Christian ethics. Yet his emphases were attractive to religious minds, and Kant has rarely lacked powerful Christian expositors. God, freedom, immortality, the "unseen" world, the moral law, were all philosophically respectable again. Moral insight gained a new status in man's interpretation of experience; "reason" was given a new dimension by the addition of the epithet "practical". All this seemed favourable to Christian faith. Yet Kant's ethic was anthropocentric, ultimately secularist. Like Butler and Hume, Kant began with man himself; the resulting morality was autonomous. Mackenzie suggests that since Kant those who acknowledge any moral authority at all see it as the authority of reason;[66] that means human reason — and ethics has a secular basis. In such a scheme, the rational individual is morally sovereign, free to pursue whatever he reasons to be right, uttering the commands of morality to himself, accepting no moral criteria from any divine or other external authority. Neither Butler nor Kant intended such a result: but each clearly contributed to the rise of a humanistic ethic divorced from religion.

13

The Inner Light — The Spirit

THE REFORMATION'S INTELLECTUAL APPEAL to reason and conscience was reinforced by the religious appeal to an inward divine experience, a living faith, an understanding illumined by direct revelation from the Holy Spirit. This approach to moral authority characterised especially the "Puritan" movement, which arose in England in the sixteenth century in attempts to "purify" the English church, and crystallised in the seventeenth century into "Separatist", non-conformist groups. In the eighteenth century, now largely traditionalist, it still contributed much to the Evangelical Revival. In America, through refugee immigration, the founding of trading companies in Virginia, Massachusetts, Plymouth, Rhode Island and elsewhere, and the immense influence of Jonathan Edwards, Puritanism "gave the new world those moral principles in State and society which are the foundations of American life at its best."[1]

(1) THE ENGLISH PURITANS

Puritanism is often misrepresented as stern, narrow, Pharisaical, opposed to all culture, joyless, "puritannical". In truth, as Knox says,[2] Puritans "played a notable part in every country where they were found."

> "The Puritans were not ignorant fanatics; they were university bred men, who could read Latin, Greek, and sometimes Hebrew, and showed in controversy both scholarship and ability. Controversialists like Cartwright and Travers did honour to the university . . . Henry Smith was lauded as the Chrysostom of England . . ."[3]

Puritans opposed the theatre, mainly because of its licentious themes, the impersonation of women by boys, and its desecration of the sabbath: the theatre took revenge by caricaturing Puritans, exaggerating the zealots, cranks and eccentrics of which Puritanism had sufficient.[4] Disliking pictures in churches, as distracting from spiritual worship, they cherished them in their homes. A movement which embraced among its leaders Cromwell the soldier, Protector of the Commonwealth; Milton the poet, and propagandist for liberty; William Law, devotional counsellor to thousands; John Bunyan the religious novelist; the Quakers' pietistic worship and social endeavour; and Richard Baxter, pastor, author, public leader amid much political strife, cannot seriously be said to be narrow. Nor was the Puritan self-righteous: his awe of God, and the habit of self-examination, inculcated humility.[5] Baxter pleads that Christians shall live "much more joyfully than the most prosperous wordlings . . . in that constant cheerfulness and gladness which becometh the heirs of glory."[6]

Despite its tenderness of conscience, Puritanism produced hard and independent men prepared to fight for freedom. The Puritan, says Tawney, "has within himself a principle at once of energy and of order which makes him irresistible both in war and in the struggles of commerce . . . a race of iron." Chadwick summarises: "At best, the Puritan was Mr. Valiant-for-truth; at worst he was a narrow and repellent bigot."[7]

"England refused to adopt Calvinism as an ecclesiastical system while it drank deep of the Calvinistic theology and ethic" (Dakin[8]). Though Puritanism and Calvinism were not identical, Puritans shared the conviction of the sovereignty of God: God is "a living, active, dynamic Will",[9] and man's chief end is to glorify God by being like God in character, obedient to God in the minutiae of behaviour.

Baxter writes: "Let thy very heart be set to glorify God, with the estimation of thy mind, the praises of thy mouth, and the holiness of thy life . . . HOLINESS TO THE LORD written upon all our faculties and affairs . . . It glorieth God . . . when we contemn the riches and honour of the world, and live above the wordling's life . . . when death . . . appeareth as disarmed and conquered . . . It honoureth God when you abound in love and good works . . . (and) study to do good to all and hurt to none . . . The unity, concord, and peace of Christians do glorify God . . . Justice private and public, in bargainings and in government, and judgement, doth honour God . . . when we do to all men as we would they should do to us. That a man's word be his master, and that we lie not (or) . . . take the name of God in vain . . . If you will glorify God . . . you must be intent upon the public good and the spreading of the gospel. A selfish, private, narrow soul brings little honour to the cause of God . . . "[10]

"Their God was their glory" — and their hope. Men are saved only by the electing grace of the sovereign God; this does not undermine moral responsibility, because good works are the fruit of such electing grace, the "signs" to ourselves and to others of our election. Since no one can be confident of his election, "it behoves him to pass his precarious days neither in complacency nor despair, but with the earnestness of moral resolve."[11]

(a) Moral Earnestness

Puritanism's "greatest impact was in the field of moral action."[12] All life must be struggle against evil in the heart and the devil in society. Bunyan's *Holy War* and the struggles of Christian towards the Celestial City in *Pilgrim's Progress* well illustrate the warrior-pilgrim, beset with evils, contending by prayer and vigilance against the flesh, the world and the devil. Moral rectitude, "even-handed justice and open-handed honour" in all dealings with one's neighbours, truth and integrity within oneself, comprised the righteousness of life which God required. Everything a man did deliberately and rationally, not of mere habit, must be *moralised,* "as ever in the great Taskmaster's eye," as service to God after due ethical analysis: "Do nothing, deliberately . . . but God's service in the world, which you can say He set you on."[13]

"Because he saw that Puritan ideas produced good lives" Baxter came to count himself a Puritan; possessing "excessive conscientiousness", with "zeal for goodness born in him" he ever proclaimed himself "a mere Christian". "The Ten Commandments, the creed and the Lord's Prayer were all that were required, a rule under which to live, a faith in which to believe, a hope in which to pray." All stemmed from "his insistence upon goodness as the essential reality in life;" the only compulsion, gratitude. From "interaction of divine love and human obedience it seemed to him there arose that sense of deep and lasting fellowship which is the crown of spiritual experience . . ." (Dickens)[14]

That is the authentic voice of Puritanism: *serious* — life is dedicated, not to be wasted on trivialities; *earnest* — for a man living before God must mind his own spiritual business above all things; *careful* — "Do the best you can to know the will of God and do it" is the summary of Baxter's Directory, full of shrewd wisdom and practical counsel; and *centred upon God* —

"The object of (a holy life) is the eternal God . . . The end, the pleasing and glorifying of our Father, Redeemer, and Sanctifier; the rule, the infallible revelation of God . . . the work, a living unto God and preparing for everlasting life . . ."[15]

From Calvinism, the Puritan inherited his emphasis upon discipline and hard work: "It is will — will organised and disciplined and inspired, will quiescent in rapt adoration or straining in violent energy, but always will — which is the essence of Puritanism, and for the intensification and organisation of will every instrument in that tremendous arsenal of religious fervour is mobilised. The Puritan is like a steel spring compressed by an inner force" (Tawney[16]). Among forces so "mobilised" were meditation, prayer, endless sermonic instruction, self-examination, scripture, shared counsel, external discipline by a Puritan group, careful recording of the soul's progress or failure. At the same time the Puritan toiled industriously. Though often wealthy he cultivated simplicity, frugality, thrift, an "ascetic" attitude towards personal comfort. The Calvinist idea of "vocation" made the daily work of artisan, farmer, tradesman and teacher a religious imperative to the otherwise unambitious Puritan: "Be busy; the soul is at stake, so loiter not" — "They that will not sweat on earth will sweat in hell."

(b) "Vanity Fair"

Austerity, effort, and dedication do not however remove the Puritan from the present secular scene: "The way to the Celestial City lies just through this town, where this lusty fair is kept; and he that will go to the City and yet not go through this town, must needs go out of the world."

> "The world is under a believer's feet . . . He travelleth through it to his home . . . nor doth he make any great matter whether his usage in it be kind or unkind . . . indifferent whether for so short a time he be rich or poor . . . further than as tendeth to his Master's service."[17]

"The Christian must live in the market-place and not the monastery", labouring for his needs, raising a family, maintaining simplicity and self-restraint. It is not the world that is evil, but worldliness; the senses are not evil, sensualism is; drink is a good creature of God to be received with thankfulness, but the abuse of drink is from Satan.[18]

As to worldly wealth, Inge[19] quotes Baxter: "If God show a way in which you may lawfully get more . . . without wrong to your soul or to any other, if you refuse this . . . you cross one of the ends of your calling, and refuse to be God's steward;" and Tawney cites Cunningham:[20] "the triumph of Puritanism swept away all traces of any restriction or guidance in the employment of money." The Puritan "no longer esteems poverty a Christian virtue."[21] But (as Tawney replies), the Puritan erected a more rigorous discipline of his own: critics taunted him with intolerable meticulousness. If he regarded wealth as a sign of divine favour, he accepted it seriously as a stewardship of time, talent, resources, opportunity, for which he must give account.

"The Puritan . . . knows that he holds earthly possessions in trust for God, in stewardship for the good of his neighbour. From the one more blessed with material favour, more is required in philanthropy. Economic duties take priority over economic rights. Nowhere in seventeenth century Puritan writing is Christian sanction given to unlimited gain or *laissez faire;* for the laws of self-denial, scrupulous honesty, and charity, must govern the relations of getting and spending."[22]

How deeply stewardship entered into Puritan thought is illustrated in the very language used by Baxter: Lives must be "laid out" (invested) in God's service; Christians are "engaged to God as servants", "entrusted" with talents, must "give account", "making it the trade and business of their lives"; they must "keep thus a just account of what goods of your Master's is put into your hands; . . . keep an account of expenses . . . bring yourselves frequently to a reckoning, what good you have done".[23]

Chadwick pictures the homelife of a Puritan squire: charitable to his tenants, not exacting high rents, encouraging their labour, buying winter clothes for the poor, visiting the sick, feeding many at his own table, supporting students, generous to the point of debt.[24] Tawney mentions a Puritan consultation which dealt with the cure of vagrancy, universal education, and organisation of hospitality for poorer Christians.[25]

(c) Puritan Economics

The Puritan was as careful of his neighbour as of his own integrity. It was well for Christians to confine their dealings to "the godliest of their trade", but to all they were to be scrupulously honest, fair, and generous. A famous treatise, *De Conscienta,*[26] by Ames, laid it down that to buy cheap and sell dear is common — but a common vice; men must not sell above the maximum fixed by public authority, though they may sell below; they must not take advantage of the necessities of buyers, nor over-praise their wares, nor sell dearer to recoup great expenses or injudicious buying. English Puritans had accepted only hesitantly Calvin's condonation of moderate interest on loans, but still held the usurer should be "thrust out of the society of men". Cartwright described usury as "a heinous offence" prescribing banishment from the sacraments. Ames accepts the impossibility of distinguishing between investment in business and in land; and accepts Calvin's view that interest is not forbidden in scripture or by reason; but he insists that interest shall not be charged to the needy, while the lender should share all risks with the borrower, and receive only a fair share of profit.

Baxter's Directory offers realistic guidance to lawyers, physicians, schoolmasters, soldiers, masters and servants, buyers and sellers, landlords, tenants, lenders and borrowers, rulers and subjects. The appeal is to enlightened common-sense. The Christian is responsible to God: "Business is business" is not a motto for Christians; "it is not lawful to take up any oppressing monopoly, or trade, which tends to enrich you by the loss of the commonwealth or of many". The Christian must carry on his business in the spirit of public service . . . the advantage of his neighbour as much as his own — and more, if his neighbour be poor. He may not get another's goods, or labour, for less than they are worth; nor a good price by working on men's ignorance of the market, or errors, or necessity; he must observe legal maximum prices, or the common valuation; and may not doctor his wares to increase price, nor conceal defects. Baxter repeats Ames' limitations upon usury; and is equally strict about abuse of the ownership of land, and of others' homes: one who oppresses others by such means is "an anti-Christ, an anti-God, the agent of the devil and his image." The Christian must "avoid sin rather than loss", and seek first to keep his conscience in peace.[27] Bunyan's *Mr. Badman* illustrates a very similar conception of economic morality.

On the whole, therefore, Puritanism made a marked contribution to economic and social progress, by making the commercial virtues of honesty, thrift, hard work, consideration for others, into religious duties; by setting strict limits to ambition, selfishness, extravagance, the exploitation of men or markets.

(d) The State: Freedom

Its contribution was hardly less to social and religious freedom. Towards the State, Puritanism took the typically Calvinist attitude. As all things serve God, so the State, while separate from the Church, is itself God's instrument. But the church is primary in God's purposes, and the State should never interfere with her ministry, but serve as her handmaid, punishing all who break the laws of God.[28] The value set upon the individual, and upon freedom of conscience, tended towards democracy, but (confronting Queen Elizabeth) "the Puritans indignantly rebutted the charge of disloyalty . . . They were, they maintained, religious reformers, not politicians."[29] Nevertheless, their appeal to scripture, law, and conscience, against oppression, had far-reaching effects in the struggle for liberty. By the sixteenth century, the new Dutch republic offered refuge, and "thus began that emigration movement for conscience' sake which was destined to such high and mighty purposes in . . . the vindication of public as well as religious liberty.''[30]

It must be acknowledged that at first Puritans did not champion rights of conscience for those who disagreed with them; they freely invoked the law against their antagonists: MacKinnon can even speak of ''their own intolerance.''[31] Even so early, however, a few voices claimed more complete freedom.

Smyth wrote, ''The magistrate is not by virtue of his office to meddle with religion, . . . For Christ only is the King and Lawgiver of the church and conscience.'' Helwys went further: ''Our Lord the King is but an earthly King . . . and if the King's people be obedient and true subjects, obeying all human laws made by the King, our Lord the King can require no more: for men's religion to God is betwixt God and themselves''. The Independent ideal secured genuine toleration for the first time in any large State, says Chadwick. ''Through . . . belief in the independence of the local congregation, the chief stress came to be laid upon liberty . . . Hence that emphasis on private judgement which . . . has had a powerful, and often salutary, influence on English religion and . . . upon the growth of English Parliamentary democracy'' (Balmforth).[32]

Puritan faith in freedom was compounded of resistance to unconstitutional monarchy, the supremacy of law, loyalty to God, longing for reform of the church, and a view of life centred upon salvation of the soul. To men of such outlook, unquestioning obedience to church or State was impossible: they would prefer to lose their personal liberty, their homeland. Sometimes, as in Massachusetts, Puritanism in power tended itself to become autocratic, confining the franchise to church members; but one ''irrepressible and indomitable protagonist of toleration'', Roger Williams, became founder of one new State in which untrammelled liberty of conscience was the corner stone, and religious belief was entirely free.[33]

(e) Authority

Freedom did not mean for the Puritan unbridled individualism. Says Baxter:

''Men reverence that faith and practice which they see us unanimously accord in . . . will despise both it and us when they hear us in a Babel of confusion, one saying This is the way; and another, That is it . . .''(Not that any should say) ''think as I think, and say as I say, or else you are schismatics. But we must all agree in believing and obeying God.''[34]

With agreement must go scripturalness, understood sometimes in literalist and legalist fashion, and with apparent preference for the

Old Testament.[35] Again Baxter defines the position:

"The rule (of a godly life) is the infallible revelation of God, delivered to the church by His prophets, His Son, and His apostles, and comprised in the Holy Scriptures, and sealed by the miracles and operations of the Holy Ghost that did indite them."[36]

Bunyan's incessant, and perceptive, citations of scripture eloquently illustrate the typical Puritan mind.

And in turn, alongside scripture was conscience, illumined by the Bible and also by the Holy Spirit. The criterion for all individual moral judgement was "What would God have me to do?" and the motive in all moral aspiration was the hope of divine approbation — "Expect your reward from God alone" (Baxter). Inward daily experience of the presence of God, a direction of the Spirit within the soul, and the constant endeavour towards "keeping up one's communion with God", provided the basis of Puritan ethics.[37] Much was made of special leadings, particular providences, "motions of the Spirit" in the daily ordering of life: and the ultimate judgement was God's — "An approving conscience is a foretaste of heaven; an accusing conscience is a 'hell-worm' which shooteth like a stitch in a man's side, a kind of private judgement day before the public day of judgement."[38]

Baxter, at any rate, was aware of the dangers inherent in this position:

"Make not your own judgements or consciences your law, or the maker of your duty . . . There is a dangerous error . . . that a man is bound to do everything which his conscience telleth him is the will of God; and that every man must obey his conscience as if it were the lawgiver of the world, whereas indeed it is not ourselves but God that is our Lawgiver. Conscience is not authorised to make us any duty which God hath not made us, only to discern the law of God and call upon us to observe it: an erring conscience is not to be obeyed, but to be better informed."[39]

This sounds like a very direct answer to Butler's moral autonomy, "man a law unto himself". For the Puritan, the inner light was especially the light of scripture interpreted to the soul by the Spirit and binding upon the individual conscience. *Moral authority lay within,* but it was the authority of a given revelation, the light of the Spirit, in the past through scripture, in the present through daily communion with God.

"The growth, triumph and transformation of the Puritan spirit was the most fundamental movement of the seventeenth century" says Tawney[40] . . . Immense as were its accomplishments on the high stage of public affairs, its achievements in that inner world . . . were mightier still." Knox claims the Puritan tradition has been among the most important factors moulding the character of the English-speaking world, imparting especially willpower, personal responsibility, and complete dedication.[41] Even so, the most lasting contribution of Puritanism to the ongoing development of the Christian ideal crystallised in the tenacious and morally powerful group known as "the Society of Friends of the Truth," later "the Quakers."

(2) THE SOCIETY OF FRIENDS

The Friends represent the extreme development of the Reformation, in their repudiation of all inherited forms of worship, ministry, and external authority, civil and ecclesiastical, and in their carrying the idea of inner illumination of scripture and conscience by the Holy Spirit to its furthest conclusion: the supersession of scripture, doctrine, church, tradition and history by "the light that lighteth every man that cometh into the world." Yet the ethical emphasis of Puritanism remained, in a rare combination of deep piety and far-reaching social action.[42]

(a) Man: Sin: Grace

Originating with George Fox, the Society of Friends found its most articulate defender in Robert Barclay, whose *Apology* is still held "the supreme declaration of Quaker belief."[43] Fox found no satisfaction in "steeple houses", doctrines of predestination, an overwhelming sense of sin such as Bunyan experienced. Naturally pious, mystical in temperament, he believed that "all who opened their hearts to the divine Presence would receive guidance and power to overcome." For denying any consciousness of evil, now that he had opened his heart to Christ, Fox was imprisoned — for blasphemy![44] Barclay, however, brought from the Calvinist springs of Puritanism the notion of "natural man", no longer innocent but with appetites which grow with gratification; a natural self whose course is evil until it yields to the divine will, is crucified and buried, and rises a new man — "the Christ within."[45]

"A seed of sin is transmitted to all from Adam, though imputed to none, until by sinning they actually join with it; which seed is the origin of all evil in men's hearts . . . This seed of sin . . . and its product is called the old man, in which all sin is; for which we use this name and not 'original sin', of which phrase the scripture makes no mention . . ." Barclay adds testimonies from Plato (the soul fallen into a dark cave); Pythagoras (man a stranger banished from the presence of God); Plotinus (the soul fallen from God as a cinder, a dead coal); and Genesis (Adam driven out from fellowship). Hence "Whatsoever real good any man doeth, it proceedeth not from his nature . . . but from the seed of God in him, as a new visitation of life."[46]

Such is "man's fallen, lost, corrupted, and degenerate condition."[47] How men are freed from this estate, we know from "the revelation of Christ *in us,* fortified by our own sensible experience, sealed by the testimony of the Spirit in our hearts, according to the testimony of the holy scriptures."[48]

"God has given His only Son, a Light, that whosoever believeth shall be saved — a Light who enlighteneth EVERY man that cometh into the world; and teacheth all, temperance, righteousness, godliness. This light enlighteneth the hearts of all for a time . . . reproves the sin of all individuals, and would work out the salvation of all if not resisted. Nor is it less universal than the seed of sin, being the purchase of His death who tasted death for every man: for as in Adam all die, even so in Christ shall all be made alive."[49]

This is the central and distinctive emphasis of the Friends. The light of Christ is available to all, even to "those living in parts of the world where the outward preaching of the gospel is unknown". Socrates was a Christian, and "all such as lived according to the divine word in them, which was in all men."[50]

Some, "cast by providence where knowledge of the history (of Christ) is wanting" are "made partakers of the divine mystery if they suffer His seed and light, enlightening their hearts, to take place; in which communion with the Father and the Son is enjoyed, so wicked men become holy, lovers of that power by whose inward touches they feel themselves turned from evil to good, and learn to do to others as they would be done by." "This is that Christ within . . . a divine, spiritual, and supernatural light in all men . . . as it is closed with in the heart, Christ comes to be formed and brought forth": not indeed *formed* in all men, or *in* men by union, but *as a seed* — "that holy, pure seed and light which is in all men . . . We have directed all men to Christ in them . . . that they may repent, whereby He that now lies slain and buried in them may come to be raised and have dominion in their hearts."[51]

"This seed is the kingdom of God . . . according as it receives depth, is nourished, and not choked." As the tree is wrapped up potentially in the seed, so is "the kingdom of Jesus Christ — yea Jesus Christ Himself . . . is in every man's and woman's heart, in that little incorruptible seed, . . . Grace and light in all . . . of its own nature would save all: he that resists its striving is the cause of his own condemnation; he that resists it not, it becomes his salvation. The working is of grace, not of the man . . . though afterwards . . . there is a will raised in him by which he comes to be a co-worker with the grace . . . According to Augustine: He that made us without us will not save us without us.''[52]

The first step in salvation is not by man's working, ''but by his *not contrary working.*'' ''Man is wholly unable to work with the grace, neither can he move out of the natural condition until the grace lay hold upon him; (but) it is possible for him to be passive and not to resist . . . Man's nature . . . though of itself wholly corrupted . . . yet is capable to be wrought upon by the grace of God;'' also to ''resist and retire from the grace of God, and return to its former condition again.''[53]

(b) The Inner Light

The doctrine of the inner light is one of Quakerism's two distinctive contributions to Christian ethics. Its basis was a particular translation of John I: 9 — ''the light which lighteth every man that cometh into the world,'' plus promise of the coming of the Spirit, Paul's words concerning the things of God known only by the Spirit of God, and numerous Old Testament references to knowledge of God by means of the Spirit. Barclay argues for the necessity, in any living Christianity, of an ''inward in-being of the Spirit of Christ in the heart.''

''The certain knowledge of God'' is obtained ''by no other way than the inward, immediate manifestation and revelation of God's Spirit, shining in and upon the heart, enlightening and opening the understanding.''[54]

Yet the coming of Christ into the heart, Fox declared, ''was a new birth that came in no miraculous way, but matured in the hours of silent waiting from the seed implanted by God.''[55]

So against Butler, Kant, the inner light ''is not any part of man's nature,'' nor any ''reliques of any good which Adam lost by his fall.'' ''This light of which we speak is not only distinct but of a different nature from the soul of man''. Man has reason, by nature, and can apprehend knowledge *about* God; but the tendency of reason is anti-Christ; it should order man's life only in things natural, though when enlightened by divine light it can assist in spiritual things. Nor may the inner light be equated with conscience, which also man has by nature, and which registers the agreement or disagreement of our actions with already held beliefs: it follows our judgement, and does not inform it. So conscience can be misled, defiled, by wrong belief: a Turk's conscience may smite him for drinking wine while approving his keeping many concubines! The inner light of Christ is needed to illuminate conscience — it then becomes "the seat and throne of God" in man. "The testimony of our consciences in the sight of God" is for Christians a sufficient guard against all calumnies; yet it is not conscience, but "the inner voice of God speaking to the soul" which is the source of truth.[56]

Relying upon this "inward certitude" as "supreme religious and moral authority",[57] the Friends turned away from churches: "being a Christian . . . has nothing to do with formal church practices . . . (but) is a matter of the living allegiance of every man to the Divine Light within."[58] An intuitionist ethic has here become the whole of Christianity.

Says Penn: "Quakers lay down as a main fundamental that God, through Christ, hath placed a principle in every man to inform him of his duty, and to enable him to do it; those who live up to this principle are the people of God; those who live in disobedience to it are not God's people, whatever name they bear . . ." Baptism, the Lord's Supper, the New Testament ministry, are set aside; "God hath dismissed all those ceremonies and rites, and is only to be worshipped in Spirit . . . *all* life is sacramental." The church . . . comprehends all thus called by God . . . out of which church we freely acknowledge there can be no salvation; because under this church . . . are comprehended all . . . though remote from those who profess Christ and Christianity in words, and have the benefit of the scriptures, as become obedient to the holy light and testimony of God in their hearts . . . heathens, Turks, Jews . . . men and women of integrity . . . secretly united to God . . . true members of this catholick church."[59]

Despite their use of scripture in defence of their opinions, the Friends turned away also from the authority of the Bible.

"From these revelations of the Spirit to the saints have proceeded the scriptures . . ." Because they are only a declaration of the fountain, and not the fountain itself, they are not the principal ground of all truth and knowledge, nor yet the adequate primary rule of faith and manners. They are a secondary rule, subordinate to the Spirit, from which they have all their certainty . . . Provided that to the Spirit be granted that place the scriptures themselves give to it, I freely concede to the scriptures the second place . . . Though God doth principally lead us by His Spirit, He sometimes conveys His comfort through His children, whom He inspires to speak a word in season . . ." Significantly, Barclay paraphrases 1 John 1: If: "What I have heard with the ears of my soul, and seen with my inward eyes, and my hands have handled of the Word of Life, and what hath been inwardly manifested to me of the things of God, that do I declare . . .'[60]

One misses, in this exposition, any means of checking what *are* inward motions of the "Spirit of God", and what may be impulses from some less exalted source. The dangers of this extreme subjectivism were illustrated in division which arose in the nineteenth century over the contention of Hicks that "the Christ within" made superfluous not only scripture, creeds, church and worship but also the historic Christ and the atonement. For all that, there was never doubt that, ethically, the Friends expected the highest standards. In those who do not resist the light, "it becomes a holy, pure, and spiritual birth, Jesus Christ formed within us, working His works within us, and so we are justified." "Good works naturally follow from this birth; they are of absolute necessity to justification. Their judgement is false who say the holiest works of the saints are sinful . . . these are not the works of the law . . . but the (necessary) works of grace."[61] Works performed "in man's own will, by his strength, in conformity with outward law," are imperfect, and to these belong all the ceremonies, and traditions of the Jews, against which Paul spoke. "The works of the Spirit of grace wrought in conformity to the inward, spiritual law, not in man's will or power but in the Spirit, are pure and perfect in their kind . . . and may be called Christ's works . . . Such we affirm absolutely necessary to justification . . . all faith without them is dead . . . But faith which worketh by love availeth . . . (and) faith which worketh by love cannot be without works."[62]

(c) Liberty

The Friends shared fully the Puritan passion for liberty:

> "Liberty of conscience from the magistrate hath been of late years largely handled . . . yet few have walked answerably . . . each pleading it for themselves, but scarce allowing it to others. That no man, hath power over consciences is apparent, because conscience is the seat and throne of God, of which God is alone proper and infallible Judge . . ." "We understand by matters of conscience such as relate betwixt God and man, or men and men, under the same persuasion, as to worship God in that way which they judge acceptable unto Him, and not to seek to force their neighbours, otherwise than by reason, or such other means as Christ and His apostles used . . . But not at all for men to do anything contrary to the moral and perpetual statutes acknowledged by all Christians; in which case the magistrate may use his authority; as on those who under pretence of conscience" (would) "destroy all the wicked, that is all that differ from them . . ." "The liberty we claim is . . . for men . . . to profess what they are persuaded is right, and so practice . . ."[63]

Thus liberty of conscience is clearly distinguished from license and from anarchy. The church retains the duty to discipline its members, though not to persecute: later Quakers set the slogan "Keep in the unity" alongside "To your own" (the appeal to individual conscience) in counsel to young converts.[64] The magistrate, likewise, must exercise authority in morals. Barclay repudiates any intention "to destroy the mutual relation betwixt prince and people, master and servant, parents and children," and any tendency towards "levelling" society.[65]

The practical outcome of such freedom within unity and order was an attitude of "selective withdrawal" from the world, believing most of the structures of the world were inimical to the Christian spirit.[66] This moral stance was more significant than Barclay's trivial examples might suggest. He warns against superfluous titles, prodigality in meals and dress, gaming, sport, and all playing. The strain after simplicity, in dress, speech, greetings (refusing to bow, or doff the hat), declining compliments, rejecting feast-days, reducing "entertainment" to such gaieties as "reading history", produced a spiritual elité, separated from the common culture (though not from trade), attractive to eccentrics, and yet serving, as monasticism had done, as protest and example, which might have been ignored had it been less extreme.[67] The prohibition of swearing (both as blasphemy and in solemn oaths) was based partly upon reverence, mainly upon scripture;[68] in place of oaths, Barclay urges "the use of truth", and Friends earned a unique reputation for scrupulous honesty.[69]

Barclay was "perfectionist" in demand: whether he thought obedience to the inner light would produce personal perfection, is doubtful. One Friend, William Simpson, "taught the conviction of moral perfection, present as Christ's perfection, and almost as personal infallibility."[70] But Barclay is careful:

"We do believe that to those in whom this holy birth is fully brought forth, the body of death and sin comes to be crucified and removed, their hearts united and subjected to the truth; so as not to obey any suggestion of the evil one, but to be free from actual transgressing of the law of God, and in that respect perfect."[71]

But this perfection does not preclude growth; nor do Christians share God's attributes, but only a "perfection proportionable and answerable to man's measure, whereby we are kept from transgression . . ." Nor does Barclay assume that such perfection may not be lost. "Nevertheless I will not affirm that a state is not attainable in this life, in which to do righteousness may be so natural in the regenerate soul, that in the stability of that condition he cannot sin." The way to such perfection is to "turn thy mind to the light and spiritual law of Christ in the heart, and suffer the reproofs thereof," so that the old life may die, a new life be raised, and "Christ be alive" in thee: then thou wilt be a Christian indeed.[72]

(d) Social Concern

A social ethic of equally high standard is Quakerism's second contribution to Christian moral teaching. Fox had protested, "How are you in the pure religion when blind and sick, halt and lame lie up and down, cry up and down, in every corner of the city?" His best memorial is "a society that has proved itself one of the greatest forces for social righteousness . . . (whose) tradition of social service won the esteem of the whole world."[73] Social reformer Robert Owen, a century later, acknowledged that Quaker Bellers was father of his own doctrines — especially in poor law reform; Tawney adds, "the Friends, in an age when the divorce between religion and social ethics was almost complete, met the prevalent doctrine that it was permissible to take such gain as the market offered, by insisting on the obligation of good conscience and forbearance in economic transactions, and on the duty to make honourable maintenance of the brother in distress a common charge."[74]

Quaker social compassion extended to many fields. John Woolman (1720-72) campaigned for thirty years against slavery, for negro rights; William Penn applied his enlightened penal code to free men and slaves within his experimental Pennsylvania. By 1758 London Quakers were drawing attention to the iniquities of slavery; in 1774, Quakers persisting in the trade were expelled; two years later, all Friends were ordered to free their slaves. In 1781, Quakers petitioned the English Parliament, and established a committee which became the nucleus of the attack on the slave trade led by Sharp, Clarkson, and Wilberforce. "To the Quakers belongs the honour of being always in the van in a movement which . . .'saved civilisation in three continents.' Their efforts lifted them to a position of leadership, in social service and in matters of conscience, which has never been lost."[75]

Elizabeth Fry brought beside compassion an immense practicality, typical of many Quakers, to her far-ranging work for prisoners and transported convicts. Many members of the later Howard League for Prison Reform, were likewise Quakers. William Tuke and other Quakers made equal strides in treatment of the mentally sick, eventually transforming the whole public reaction to madness from punishment to treatment. Later Quakers have pioneered Christian industrial relations, welfare, housing, pensions schemes for work-people, in numerous investigations bringing new scientific and practical thoroughness to the handling of social problems.

But above all, Quakers have been identified with opposition to war, without losing public approval, partly through the integrity of their pacifist propaganda, but mainly through their fearless devotion in ambulance work on the battlefields and bomb disposal in the cities. Uncompromising opposition to war was an early tenet of the movement: Fox said "I live in virtue of that life and power that takes away the vocation of all wars."[76] Although godly men within the army should stay until bidden by clear directions of the Spirit to leave,[77] the Quaker "testimony" against war was unwavering:

Barclay: "It is not lawful for Christians to resist evil or to fight in any cause . . . (war is) as opposite to the Spirit and doctrine of Christ as light to darkness . . . Strange that men made after the image of God should bear the image of roaring lions; tearing tigers, devouring wolves, raging boars . . ."[78]

Barclay argues it is impossible to reconcile war with the words of Christ, and presses the contradiction in appeals to God by both sides. Christian magistrates exercise their authority in imperfect situations. "We shall not say that war upon a just occasion is altogether unlawful to them" — they being not yet in the patient, suffering spirit, not yet fitted for this "perfection" of Christianity, which would not defend itself but trust to the Lord. Indeed, "only the few 'pure' Christians could follow the way of non-violence:" it is not an ethic the world could adopt, nor could it be "successful". But "Christian warfare" is utterly illogical, indefensible — on many grounds.[79]

A feature of Barclay's argument here is reliance upon scriptural teaching, which elsewhere has but "secondary" authority. Moreover, the distinction between the pacifism of the "perfect" Christian and the acceptance of military responsibilities by "imperfect" Christians involved in the world's duties, unexpectedly reintroduces the ancient double standard into Reformed ethics. Respect for the conscience of the enemy, whose antagonism was equally sincere, and in obedience to his own commanders, was another Quaker objection; so was the soldier's ignorance of the causes, and justice, of the fight. William Penn argued passionately on more prudential grounds, always on the Quaker assumption that practicability and idealism would eventually coincide.[80] One truth stands clear from Quaker testimony and example: to be a Christian pacifist it is *not* necessary to relinquish all social responsibility and involvement.

For strong insistence upon the inner light, as one moral guide and source of authority; and for their splendid record of social initiative and compassion, the Quakers will ever hold honoured place in the unfolding story of Christian idealism.

(3) JONATHAN EDWARDS

In the American Puritan, Jonathan Edwards, most eminent American theologian of his time, and closely associated with the evangelical Awakening, the inner contradictions of the evangelical approach to ethics come to the surface. Calvinist in its emphasis on the majesty of God, the helplessness of man, Edwards' thought was affected also by scientific and philosophical currents: Richard Niebuhr mentions, for examples, his contending with Hobbes on man's self-interest, with "naturalists" who make conscience psychological, with sociologists on the cultural shape of morality.[81] The names, often the words, of Augustine, Newton, Locke, the Cambridge Platonists, Hutcheson, Wollaston and Hume also occur.

In ethics, Edwards held that the source of all action is emotion; man is free from external compulsion but not from self-determination. Created to love God, since the Fall man loves only himself; even his conscience is akin to self-love, partial in its interests. True good will, pure virtue, are beyond him, unassisted by grace. Edwards devotes twenty-four closely printed pages to demonstrating that men are naturally God's enemies; fallen, depraved, more vicious than the animals, man would kill God if he could.[82] Called to repent, he cannot respond, though that does not excuse him. Man occasionally performs deeds of external morality, formally but not materially good — "bad good works", in that they do not meet God's demands; these need repentance no less than his "bad bad works". Man is a rebel, setting up rivals to God, never learning they must fall before divine justice.[83] But God reconciles man to Himself, and to the universe, implanting delight, redeeming him from self-love to "the love of all being." God commands moral perfection from all, but gives grace to achieve it only to the elect, in whom through regeneration a new disposition prevails, and good works follow.

An Enquiry into Prevailing Notions of the Freedom of the Will — directed against Arminianism — asserts man's total depravity and moral helplessness, apart from divine grace. Another, equally thorough, expounds *Original Sin*. Free from all external compulsion, man is morally responsible, though not free to choose his emotions, to select what he hates or turn from what he loves. Trapped since the Fall in self-interest, man depends utterly upon grace to enable him to love God or men for their own sakes, and become virtuous. Once made new in Christ, he becomes obedient, strives to follow all Christ commands, to resist all Christ forbids, never ceasing the endeavour after holiness — though never achieving it.[84]

(a) Religious Affections

Edwards diverges from the intellectualist tendency of Calvinism to emphasise that "the affections, or emotions, directed towards objective goods are the springs of human action."[85]

The *Treatise Concerning Religious Affections* argues that true religion in great part consists in holy *affections*. Beside perception, man possesses inclination, will — by which the soul is inclined towards or away from objects, liking or disliking, approving or rejecting. The affections are the more vigorous, lively, exercises of inclination and will. In every act of will, the soul is thus "affected" with liking or disliking, love or hatred.[86]

True religion consists to large degree in such vigorous actings of inclination and will, fervent exercises of the heart. "The religion which God requires does not consist in weak, lifeless wishes . . . God insists we be in good earnest, fervent in spirit, our hearts vigorously engaged in religion"[87]. Such emotional affection is the true spring of moral living.

"As there must be light in the understanding as well as an affected, fervent heart" (for where there is heat without light there is nothing divine), so "where there is a kind of light without heat, a head stored with notions with a cold, unaffected heart, there can be nothing divine, — that knowledge is no true spiritual knowledge of divine things. *If the great things of religion are rightly understood they will affect the heart.*"

There speaks all evangelical religion. But Edwards warns that the only guarantees that affections are truly of divine grace are: their *origin,* from divine influence; their *object* in divine excellence and high morality; their illuminating quality; the humility and new nature attending them; the Christlike temper they beget; and their fruit in Christian practice. So Edwards conducts the same assessment of religious emotionalism as Paul conducted at Corinth, making the moral and Christlike *value* of emotion sole evidence of its divine origin. But throughout, Edwards is certain that no good at all originates in human nature, in and of itself.

(b) The Meaning of Depravity

At this point the contradiction within Protestantism emerges: that between an optimistic view of man's natural constitution — as bearing the image of God, capable of moral decisions (Erasmus), possessing a natural conscience (Butler), a moral reason (Kant), an inner light which is the Christ in every man (Barclay) and a pessimistic view of man's natural sinfulness, helplessness, blindness, antagonism to God, and total depravity, such as in varying degree Augustine, Luther, Calvin, taught — and Edwards. In two directions especially he expounds the moral incapacity of man. (i) In his account of virtue Edwards has to build upon unexpected definitions in order to preserve the Calvinist emphasis.[88] "True virtue essentially consists in benevolence to being in general — that union of heart to being in general which is immediately exercised in general good will."

The "love of benevolence" (that is, based on benevolence) is that propensity of heart to any intelligent being which inclines to its well-being; the "love of complacence" is simply delight in another's beauty. "Pure benevolence in its first exercise is nothing else but being's propensity to being (in general) . . ." The second object of benevolence is *benevolent being* — (pure benevolence taking delight in benevolence in another. Loving a being on *this* ground necessarily arises from pure benevolence to being in general, and comes to the same thing). In this love of being, and the qualities and acts arising from it, lies all true virtue.

It follows that true virtue must chiefly consist in love to God, since He is the most general Being (the first ground of benevolence), and He is the most benevolent Being (the second ground of benevolence). All affections focused on private, limited being must be subordinate to this general affection toward being itself: "a truly virtuous mind, . . . under the sovereign dominion of love to God, above all things seeks the glory of God."

"So far as a virtuous mind exercises true virtue in benevolence to *created* beings, it chiefly seeks (their) good . . . in (their) knowledge of God's glory . . . love to Him, and joy in Him. That propensity of mind to being in general, is virtue . . . grace . . . holiness . . . Whatever other benevolence or generosity towards mankind, and other virtues (may exist), not attended with a love to God . . . *there is nothing of the nature of true virtue or religion in them* . . . Nothing is true virtue in which God is not the first and the last . . ."

The purpose of these abstruse definitions here comes to light: all lesser beauties of character, all lesser virtues, not being benevolence towards being in general, nor dependent upon such a wider benevolence, *are no true virtue.* Man, unaided, cannot rise to that.

Beauty of form is an agreement of parts, not unlike virtue, and is designed by God as an image of virtue: the beauty of order, and justice, is again a form of balance, an accord with truth, and with the will of God. But the disposition to find pleasure in such lesser beauties "has nothing of the nature of true virtue." "The natural taste for such lesser beauty is not at all a true virtuous principle supposed by some to be implanted in the hearts of all mankind."

The idea is next examined that all love arises from self-love (as Hobbes had suggested): gratitude, love for those who love us, resentment of injuries, hatred for those who hate us, instinctive feelings, pity, parental and brotherly love, friendship, admiration — none of these has the nature of virtue. Even conscience is a private self-love:

"Approving, because we act in agreement *with ourselves,* and being uneasy in disagreeing with ourselves, is quite a different thing from approving or disapproving actions because in them we are united or disunited with being in general. The former principle, an inclination to agree with ourselves, is private, natural; the latter union of heart to 'the great system', and to God the Head of it, is public, truly benevolent, a divine principle."

In natural affections there appears the effect of benevolence, but not the general nature of virtue, the love of being itself, for they are private, and leave the Divine Being out of view. Patriotism, illustrates this love of the part (one's own country) often to the destruction of the rest of mankind. Throughout the argument, true virtue, is something essentially different from the "virtues" which pagan philosophers and the natural man have praised. In chapter IV of "Miscellaneous Remarks" — *Concerning Efficacious Grace* — the full bearing of the discussion is brought out: Edwards replies to Arminians, to Butler and to Turnbull, that pride in one's virtue and achievement is especially forbidden in scripture; that the idea that habits of virtue are in man's power to attain makes for great presumption: and that "saving virtue is *given* by a sovereign operation of the Spirit of God."

"Saving virtue is implanted by divine operation different from the common assistance of God to men." "Sincerity of endeavour" can arise only from the grace of God. Such grace is decisive as to conversion, and the habit of true virtue is immediately implanted or infused. "We are His workmanship." The natural man has nothing of the life, or virtue, of the spiritual man.

(ii) Edwards is equally repetitious about the moral incapacity of man when he writes on natural conscience or religion, with more optimistic views of human nature clearly in mind.

"All that natural men do is wrong" is the title of one sermon.[89] "the innate sinful depravity of the human heart" is the thesis of the most sustained of all Edward's great arguments, *On Original Sin:* "Mankind naturally, universally, run themselves into their own eternal perdition, accursed of God, subjects of His remediless wrath through sin, their nature corrupt with a moral depravity that implies their utter ruin." "All mankind have an *infallibly effectual* propensity to that moral evil which *infinitely* outweighs the value of all the good that can be in them . . ." Hence, "all schemes of moral philosophy which . . . have not a supreme regard to God laid as the *foundation* . . . are not true schemes of philosophy but are essentially defective . . ."[90]

Edwards knew what had been written upon conscience as evidence of innate moral capacity in man, and wrestles with it. He acknowledges, "there is another disposition or principle natural to mankind . . . to be uneasy in a consciousness of being inconsistent with oneself . . ."

"Natural conscience consists in these two things: that disposition to approve or disapprove . . . from a determination of the mind to be easy or uneasy in a consciousness of our being consistent or inconsistent with ourselves; (and) the sense of desert . . ." "The natural conscience, if the understanding be properly enlightened . . . concurs with the law of God, joins its voice with it in every article." When others blame us, we may become conscious that in their place we should judge likewise; our conscience in similar manner may justify *God's* condemnation of us. Sinners, too, may have a sense of the ill-desert of sin, from being aware of the anger which would arise in their own hearts if they were in God's place. "Thus has God established that natural conscience, though it implies no actual benevolence to being in general, yet should approve and condemn the same things that are approved and condemned by a spiritual sense or virtuous taste."[91]

Despite these concessions to conscience, Edwards denies that it is more than a feeling of ease or unease over self-consistency; and contends that it is no proof of true virtue implanted by nature within humanity.

"Approbation of conscience is the more readily mistaken for a truly virtuous approbation because . . . when conscience is well informed and thoroughly awakened, it agrees with (God) as to the object approved though not as to the ground of approving . . . Natural conscience is implanted in all mankind to be as it were in God's stead, as an internal judge." Nevertheless the private and merely natural conclusions (of conscience) are not to be mistaken for genuinely virtuous love . . ."[92]

In the end, therefore, man's moral nature (such as it is), like man's virtue (such as it is), do not at all contradict the essential depravity and helplessness of man. That this was the intended conclusion from *The Nature of True Virtue,* Edwards indicates at the close of the treatise *On Original Sin:*

As to arguments made use of by many late writers, from the universal moral sense . . . to show that we are born into the world with principles of virtue; with a natural . . . love of righteousness, truth, goodness, public welfare, and a native bent to mutual benevolence, those who desire to see them particularly considered, I ask leave to refer them to a treatise on *The Nature of True Virtue* . . ."

The whole discussion suffers from Edwards' polemic intention. The subtlety of definition, and the contradictions to be resolved, show the strain the argument is under: one is tempted often to borrow one of Edwards' own objections — "if the . . . gospel depended only on . . . such reasonings as learned men are capable of, it would be above the reach of far the greatest part of mankind." Protestantism has never truly reconciled moral helplessness with moral responsibility; the effectual election of some to "total and remediless wrath", with the justice of God; the inability of man to repent, with the gospel call to repentance and faith; the total depravity of the whole race *ab initio,* with any distinction of merit or blame between the abandoned wicked and those who are at least striving to be good, or with any incentive so to strive. A conception of man as corrupt, accursed, "more vicious than the animals", does not harmonise with the basic biblical estimate of man as God's creature, "a little lower than the angels", in God's image, utterly dependent upon grace ever available to all, but bearing his own responsibility for use or rejection of that grace, in responding to God's invitation in the gospel. But if Edwards' emphasis raises serious problems, there can be no doubt that the depth of human sinfulness is here being measured realistically, in a way that Butler's and Hume's bland optimism and academic detachment never attempt.

(c) Ethical Expectations

It might be questioned whether Edwards' fundamental positions can be reconciled with Christian ethics at all, so little room does he leave for human choice, moral responsibility, and ethical endeavour. Nevertheless, though far more theoretical than practical, he certainly expects that ethical results will follow from evangelical experience. One sermon[93] argues that the divine light imparted to the soul by the Spirit of God, "changes the nature of the soul . . . assimilates our nature to the divine, changes the soul into the same glory, will wean us from the world and raise the inclination to heavenly things, turn the heart to God as the fountain of good, conforms the heart to the gospel, disposes the soul to give up itself entirely to Christ. It has its fruit in a universal holiness of life; it draws forth the heart in a sincere love to God, which is the only principle of a true, gracious, and universal obedience . . ."

This again is theoretical. Among the few subjects dealt with in detail is *dishonesty,* "the sin of theft and of injustice", which is analysed into withholding what is due to the neighbour (by breaking engagements, neglecting to pay debts), and unjustly taking what belongs to the neighbour (by negligence, fraud, violence, taking advantage of need, or of weak laws, by stealing, extortion, or not warning the neighbour of threatening loss). Various excuses are considered and dismissed, and the lesson is turned to solemn warning *against* unloading bad money in charitable contributions, stealing from orchards, and *for* the more careful restitution of all we have wrongfully taken from others.[94] Another section of a larger work on *Christian Cautions*[95] elaborates the need for constant and conscientious *self-examination,* about discipline of thought, use of the Lord's Day, secret sins, our temper of mind towards our neighbour, our charity, our family life. In such counsel, the widespread habit of evangelical casuistry is turned inward, with mixed results.

A third ethical theme is *Christian Charity.* Edwards says perceptively, "In pure love to others . . . there is a union of heart with others, a kind of enlargement of mind, whereby it so extends itself as to take others into a man's self . . . it implies a disposition to feel, to desire, and to act, as though others were one with ourselves . . ."[96] Edwards' special treatment of the subject is brief, but reveals his usual penetration. The duty of generosity towards the poor is argued from Old Testament law, that giving be bountiful and sufficient (Deuteronomy 15:7-11). We must not snatch at objections, but give freely. Scripture insists upon this duty; reason recommends it, by the present state of mankind, our privileges in the gospel, and the close relationship to others established by redemption. The duty is enforced by consideration of our stewardship; by the reminder that what we do to others we do to Christ; by its being a difficult duty, so needing greater attention; by the warning that God will deal with us as we with others. Generosity is the character of a godly man, as final judgement will reveal. We shall not lose by charity, being rewarded here and hereafter. Another consideration urged is, we might need such help at any time. Objections are then answered: "I am in a 'natural condition' and so would do it in a wrong spirit"; or self-righteously, "I have not found that generosity pays"; the need is not extreme; the needy are not deserving; "I have nothing to spare"; "I have not been asked"; others ignore this duty; public provision for the needy is sufficient. Each objection is analysed, met with scripture, and brushed aside.[97]

Edwards' contribution to ethics is slight, though enough to make one wish he had turned more often to the examination of Christian duties. But even in so little one may discern the typically post-Reformation approach: a true experience of grace is expected to create, of itself, the true Christian attitude — "the inward divine light changes the nature of the soul;" the outworking of that attitude in detailed individual and social duties may safely be left to itself!

The pre-eminent characteristic of "evangelical" ethics is its subjectivity; the appeal to an inner light, in all its forms, inevitably turns man's gaze inwards. The Christian "depends for guidance on the direct instructions of the Spirit; scriptural directives are regarded as insufficient, or even as inapplicable in the age of grace. Therefore a person must receive an answer to prayer in order to know whether a particular action is right or wrong."[98] The ideal is no longer conformity to law, or prescribed discipline, but self-fulfilment, the perfection of the "best self" according to the leadings, impulses and "checks" that issue from within the soul. *In practice* it makes little difference whether the "self" appealed to is called moral reason, conscience, the inner light, the Christ within, or the Holy Spirit: since all external criteria are rejected, nothing remains to identify the source of authority and direction but the individual's own intuitive conviction. The "religion of the heart" beloved of the reformers does approach, in ethics, every man's doing that which is righteous in his own eyes.

One unintended consequence is that ethics moved towards anthropocentric, ultimately secular, foundations. Goodness came to be again, as in pagan eyes, the law of man's own being. Christ is the sample of man at his best; His example and encouragement may stimulate the moral reason, or sensibility, or resolve, may educate the conscience of every man; may even be the inspiration of morality throughout the world — "the Christ in every man" — but in the end the capacity, the criteria, and the resources, for moral life are within secular man himself. By his own moral judgement, in the last resort, he must assess and appreciate the Christ — or reject Him.

A second consequence of the subjective viewpoint was to throw into sharp relief the dilemma of Protestantism. If man is by nature morally capable and responsible (though undoubtedly a sinner) then Christ, and grace, though necessary to salvation, wait upon his acceptance; if man is helplessly depraved, then Christ and grace are beyond his reach; he is saved by miracle alone, and is not responsible if the miracle does not happen. The Calvinist denial of any natural goodness, or capacity for right choice, of any inward light of conscience, or reason, capable of perceiving truth or morality, destroys moral responsibility. Yet the rationalists' insistence upon man's natural moral capacity, through reason, conscience, or the Christ within, destroys the necessity for the gospel. Reformation ethics, like Reformation theology, and so much else in the post-Reformation world, posed with ever greater clarity the fundamental modern question, *What is Man?* Both optimistic and pessimistic replies could argue from scripture; the reply from within depends too much upon individual experience and presuppositions. The Christian moralist has felt bound to cling at all costs to the moral capacity and responsibility of all men, as the sole foundation for human dignity, and the only point of contact with the saving energies of God.

A third consequence of post-Reformation subjectivity was the lure of pietism, tempted to concentrate upon devotional life of prayer, Bible-study, personal discipleship, leaving the world and its problems far behind. It testifies to the persistent strength of the Christ-ideal, as enshrined in the gospel-portrait, that the historical movements associated with pietism — in Germany, Moravia, among the English Puritans — found it impossible, in spite of the temptation, to withdraw from the world. The impulse both to world-wide missionary expansion, and to far-reaching social reform, actually arose from within a "pietist" devotion to Christian obedience and pursuit of Christlikeness. Already the Puritans' political involvement, still more the Quakers' social concern, provided evidence of the direction which evangelicalism would take. In the event, the appeal to the inner light did not retreat from ethical responsibility, but remained a powerful force within western society.

14

The Social Gospel in Action

OUT OF PURITANISM EMERGED the social gospel. Though the term *Puritan* fell into disrepute, the movement's emphasis upon Reformation principles — the fact of sin, the need of individual salvation, the hope of redemption through grace and the Spirit, granted to personal faith in the atoning death of Christ and personal commitment to Him as Lord — endured in the "Evangelical" tradition, which (as the name implies) made more of the gospel than of the church and its disciplines.

"The evangelical party" within the Church of England (Fletcher of Madeley, Venn, Newton, Simeon), the evangelical revival (a movement in England parallel to the Great Awakening in America), the Evangelical Alliance (1846, "seeking to promote the interests of a scriptural Christianity"), and numbers of smaller evangelistic sects, all shared something of the outlook, and zeal, of German Pietists, and Moravians, and inherited much of the Puritan and Quaker immediacy of spiritual experience, their high sense of discipline, vocation, and service for others. True religion, the Evangelicals taught, is "the life of God in the soul of man bearing fruit in every good work for human betterment."[1] One typical English group of evangelical peers, statesmen, business men, bankers, dubbed "the Clapham Sect", well illustrates the amazing generosity, wide vision, far-spreading influence, and social initiative, of evangelicalism. For all his journalistic eulogy, Bready compiles a formidable list of literary giants, social reformers, powerful preachers, and missionary explorers, kindled by the evangelical faith in two continents.

A persistent, but inexcusable, blunder identifies evangelical piety with neglect of social problems. Philanthropy had always been an essential part of Puritan virtue, and the frugality, dedication, and social responsibility which harnessed all Calvinism's drive to "good works" had had considerable impact on social evils. Already the Quakers had transformed this consequential social good into a primary social aim: but through the eighteenth and nineteenth centuries the "socialisation" of the Christian ethic proceeded with both practical and theoretical power.

It is however crucial to the discussion to bear constantly in mind the *developing* meaning of words like "socialisation". Essentially, socialism is the opposite of individualism, and the "social gospel" merely the application of "the" gospel to society and its needs. Socialisation then means an increasing persuasion to look upon truths and problems from the point of view of society.

In the background are Adam Smith's free individualism and unfettered *laissez faire* (without his more social qualifications); Ricardo's uncontrolled "laws" of rent, value, wages; J. S. Mill's equally uncontrolled "law of supply and demand"; Malthus' doctrine of the natural checks upon population exercised by hunger and misery; the Darwinian thesis of a struggle for existence which ensured the survival of the fittest — all implying that the elimination of the needy and the weak was both a natural and a moral law. In reaction, Spencer, T. H. Green, Ruskin in various ways emphasised the organic nature and responsibility of society in such matters; T. H. Huxley, Thomson, Geddes, found room for ethical struggle, sacrifice, sociality, among the factors making for survival; while in law, enactments of the latter half of the nineteenth century "were definitely collectivist." By "socialism", F. D. Maurice meant that a society or "Association" of workers should no longer wait upon the initiative and control of individualistic enterprise, but should undertake production and ownership among themselves, sharing risk, management, and profits. The main purpose of his "Trade Association" was to demonstrate "how working men can release themselves from the thraldom of individual labour under the competitive system; or at least how far they can at present by honest fellowship mitigate its evils" (Ludlow). Political, often unchristian, forms of socialism came later in England, partly from Europe, adopting the definition of socialism as "State (or social) control of the means of production, distribution, and exchange."[2]

Some of the tensions which inevitably emerged as words became more sharply defined in controversy are expressed in the protest of Ludlow (1908) against any narrowing of the large word "socialism" from its original meaning — "the faith which brought men together in one common force." Similarly, the later League of the Kingdom of God defined its object as "a Christian sociology consonant with the needs of the age", which one of its sponsors elaborated later: "no longer content to select from among contemporary social programmes the one that most attracts them, and endeavour to enlist for it the support of organised religion . . . (but) looking to their own movement to supply something which, in a society not acknowledging Christ's inspiration and sanctions, they cannot hope elsewhere to find." Such semantic changes must be remembered when we read of Headlam's "distinctively socialist" Guild of St. Matthew (1877); of Dr. Clifford's "Christian Socialist League" (1856); of H. Price Hughes founding a Christian Socialist Journal, *Methodist Times*

(1890); of Gore and Scott Holland founding the Christian Social Union (1890); and of Flint nevertheless arguing that the "Christian socialism" of Maurice was not socialist at all but pure Christianity.[3] Of the American evangelical social movement, Sherwood E. Wirt says frankly: "Until Timothy L. Smith wrote *Revivalism and Social Reform,* it was generally assumed that the Social Gospel was an American theological aberration . . . the product of preachers who had strayed from the gospel of the grace of God . . . Yet Smith has shown that the preoccupation with social problems that later dominated a large segment of American Protestantism actually stems from the zeal and compassion which revivalists in the mid-nineteenth century awakened for sinning and suffering men. The social theories of the evangelists became the working basis of the Social Gospel."[4]

Something of this socialising movement — in its most general meaning — was due to a changing intellectual climate. For some, ethics came to displace dogma as the essence of Christianity; proof of the gospel was to be seen in its practical outcome; truth was to be validated pragmatically rather than logically; the emphasis of philosophy moved from the ideal world of the rationalists to the "real" world of the empiricists, and that of ethics from obedience to utilitarianism.[5] The increasingly anthropocentric tone of ethics, together with Kant's rejection of metaphysics and his exposition of "faith" as practical reason, helped to concentrate attention on man in society. The rise of natural science; excesses and cruelties of the industrial revolution, with its urbanisation, steep rise in population, overcrowding, leading to creation of slum-areas ("rookeries"); destruction of rural patterns of life, relationships, and leisure — all produced a situation in which, if Christianity was to survive at all, it must exhibit its truth and prove its value in *this* world. A "practical" Christianity was demanded by intellectual and social circumstances, and the demand was spurred by the rivalry of non-Christian dreams of revolution and reconstruction. Nevertheless, the most powerful motives of the Social Gospel came from within evangelical faith: sometimes from severely practical and ethical interpretation of the evangel itself, coupled with circumstances which evoked Christian social activity to give any value or permanence to *evangelism* (as with Wesley); sometimes from a mixture of compassion, guilt, and social idealism (as with the "outburst" of evangelical social activity in the nineteenth century); sometimes from the search for a new Christian theory of society, either through criticism of the existing order, or through radical re-thinking of the Christian ethic (as in Maurice, Holland, Gore, Temple, in England; Gladden, Rauschenbusch, Mathews, Reinhold Niebuhr, in America; Bonhoeffer in Germany).

1. PRACTICAL CHRISTIANITY: WESLEY

Foremost among eighteenth century examples of social endeavour stirred by simple, practical Christianity was John Wesley, contemporary with Jonathan Edwards, and sharing so fully in the same spiritual renewal as to transform the face of England. Less Calvinistic than Arminian (especially as to man's freedom of will), Wesley retained much of Puritanism — its inner asceticism, its individualism, its fervour — but was less other-worldly, essentially earthly and practical. He and his followers strove to be "total Christians", to achieve scriptural holiness, to share the warmth of spiritual experience learned from the Moravians, to practise "methodical" self-discipline, biblical morality, a weightily scriptural manner of preaching. "I take religion to be . . . a constant ruling habit of soul, a renewal of our minds in the image of God, a recovery of the divine likeness, a still-increasing conformity of heart and life to the pattern of our most holy Redeemer."[6]

(i) The significance of Wesley for Christian ethics lies in the link he forged between seventeenth century Puritanism and the "social" Christianity of the nineteenth century. For him, "social activity" was but the application of the Christian ethic. "The only sure hope of a better age was a better man . . . A scheme to reconstruct society which ignored the redemption of the individual was unthinkable . . . A doctrine to save sinning men, with no aim to transform them into crusaders against social sin, was equally unthinkable." "Christianity is essentially a social religion; to turn it into a solitary religion is indeed to destroy it." Reinforcing this ethical interpretation of redemption were the ignorance, poverty, drunkenness, degradation of the masses who came to respond with pathetic eagerness to Wesley's gospel. Here lies the motive of that tireless, detailed passion for social "salvage", the organisation of far-seeing ameliorative work, in assistance-funds, institutions, and habits of personal discipline, which made his campaign so powerful a lever to uplift the people. A "passion for moral righteousness and inward freedom was the centre and essence of the evangelical crusade . . . the very foundations of the movement were ethical, practical, and experimental, rather than doctrinal, theoretical, and metaphysical." For Wesley, creative faith must issue in works of service and love. He disliked the cant phrase "gospel sermons", preferring those on good works and good temper. Converts "were to help each other work out their salvation, doing no harm, avoiding all evil, doing good and being merciful in every possible way to all possible men . . ." The faith of the Evangelical Revival was supremely ethical, and in consequence, reformatory.[7]

So for Wesley, an individualist gospel and a socialised gospel were scarcely distinguishable. He evangelised England challenging all to individual faith in Christ, *at the same time* proclaiming the need for charity, feeding the hungry, clothing the naked, helping prisoners, tending the sick, educating children, social amelioration of all kinds. He instructed his preachers to "Keep out of politics . . . You have nothing to do but to save souls": yet himself set an example in passion for public righteousness.[8]

Methodism's ideal disciple "loves every man as his own soul . . . his enemies, yea, the enemies of God, the evil and the unthankful . . . As he has time and opportunity he does good toward all men . . . not only to their bodies by feeding the hungry, clothing the naked, visiting those who are sick or in prison, but much more to their souls. Love to God and all men is the centre of religion . . . the never-failing remedy for all the evils of a disordered world . . ." Social and brotherly love must "express itself in every kind of beneficience, spreading virtue and happiness all around it." Wesley asks his congregation to "survey this strange sight — a Christian world! — from which injustice, inequality, hatred, vice, and war were forever banished."[9]

(ii) Wesley's personal ethic, his doctrine of holiness, follows Barclay's, and has often been criticised because of his use of the word "perfection". Wesley had greater assurance than many Calvinists that the individual could know himself saved now, already, by the power of Christ within him: in this sense he was "made perfect in Christ". Wesley did not mean that Christians were incapable of misjudgements, free of infirmities, insulated against temptation; nor that the saved man was insured against losing his new life. Whether he thought the true Christian *incapable* of sin is doubtful; he is "perfect" as not actually committing sin, being purified, delivered cleansed.

"Christ's blood cleanses from all sin: if the cleansing . . . is from the guilt of sin, then we are not cleansed from guilt . . . unless on condition of 'walking in the light as He is in the light.' Christians are saved in this world from all sin, from all unrighteousness; they are now in such a sense perfect as not to commit sin, and to be freed from evil thoughts and evil tempers."

Wesley implies that the Christian has still to maintain discipline — and must still grow:

"There is no perfection . . . which does not admit of a continual increase . . . how much soever any man has attained . . . he hath still need to grow in grace and daily to advance in the knowledge and love of God his Saviour."

Perfection, in Wesley's thought, lies in the right will — "perfection of intention." It is Christlikeness: "all the mind which was in Christ, enabling us to walk as Christ walked . . . a renewal of the heart in the whole image of God, the full likeness of Him that created it." And "it is the loving God with all our heart, and our neighbour as ourselves."[10]

Hall traces the Christian doctrine of perfection to certain biblical references to "perfect men"; notices some patristic expressions (Justin, Irenaeus, Origen) do not go beyond asserting obligation to avoid sin and live by the Spirit and by love. Jesus' words "If thou wouldest be perfect" and the "Counsels of Perfection", created for monasticism the double standard, reserving perfection for the "religious", Augustine, Aquinas, identified perfection with the beatific vision of God — though Aquinas spoke also of Christian perfection as "the removal from man's affections of all that is contrary to love . . . and also whatsoever hinders the mind's affection from tending wholly to God" — a negative definition. After the Reformation, Fénelon identified perfection with pure love; Zinzendorf, with fullness of faith; Wesley, with entire sanctification as a normal experience for every Christian subsequent to conversion (so Hall) — "a loving God with all your heart, mind, soul, strength, that implies that no wrong temper, none contrary to love, remains in the soul; and that all the thoughts, words, and actions are governed by pure love." Methodism continued to teach entire sanctification, but perfection as an experienced fact has not become a main theme of Christian ethics. It remains of course the "impossible ideal" towards which Christians strive and by which they are judged.[11]

(iii) On details of dress, comfort, personal expenditure, Wesley required Puritan simplicity, austerity, avoidance of delicacy, ostentation, discontent. "Every shilling which you save from your own apparel you may expend in clothing the naked and relieving the necessities of the poor." "But I can afford it!" — ". . . No Christian can afford to waste any part of the substance which God has entrusted to him."[12]

Wesley's famous sermon on the use of money elaborates first the importance of the theme; insists that money is not to blame for evil, unless it has been used ill; argues that the value of money lies in charity. Three plain rules guide the Christian: *Get all you can* — not at the expense of life, or health (there are numerous unhealthy employments); nor by hurting your mind (by cheating, lying), or hurting your neighbour (in his substance, or in his body as by over-working him, nor by offering him strong drink, or any other temptation). Gain all you can by diligence, wisdom, application. *Save all you can:* — not to serve luxury, gratifying the senses, wasting substance in gluttony, idle expenses, costly paintings, books, superfluous furniture, elegant gardens. *And give all you can* — in Christian stewardship, as not a proprietor of possessions but a trustee; we must make ourselves friends of the mammon of unrighteousness, providing for others — to the household of faith, and all men. In doubt whether expenditure is justified, we ask, Am I now acting as steward of this wealth? obeying my Lord?

It is wrong to forget for whom such a sermon was mainly intended — for the poor, for those unskilled in husbanding their resources: it is *not* a charter for economic capitalism, but counsel for the feckless.

"Snatching to hoard, hoarding to snatch" is insanity: "Give me neither riches nor poverty, but enough for my subsistence", the law of reason. "The poor are the Christians" — though he was too practical to under-rate money: "it is unspeakably precious if we are wise and faithful stewards of it." "First supply thine own wants together with those of thy family; then restore the remainder to God through the poor." "Give all you can — hoard nothing. I defy all the men upon the earth, yea all the angels in heaven, to find any other way of extracting the poison from riches." To pile up treasures upon earth is to flout a command as plain as "Thou shalt not commit adultery".[13]

"All cheating and over-reaching in business, all pawnbroking and usury" are forbidden; "we cannot, consistent with brotherly love, sell our goods below market price; we cannot study to ruin our neighbour's trade to advance our own. None can gain by swallowing up his neighbour's substance without gaining the damnation of hell."[14] The sight of poverty, and the assumption that poverty was always due to idleness or thriftlessness, deeply angered Wesley. He warned, "Give none that asks relief either an ill word or an ill look. Do not hurt them . . . Treat every poor person as you would God Almighty should treat you." "The rich consume so much they leave nothing for the poor" — Wesley would abolish large estates, and tax gentlemen's horses. Yet "the mercy of God is boundless: it can save even a rich man."[15]

It may be that Wesley was self-congratulatory about his own unworldliness: "For upwards of eighty-six years I have kept my accounts exactly; I will not attempt it any longer, being satisfied with the continual conviction that I save all I can, and give all I can — that is *all I have.*" Receiving an enquiry concerning tax on plate, he replied "I have two silver spoons at London and two at Bristol. This is all the plate I have at present, and I shall not buy any more while so many around me want bread."[16] But he had some justification. Bready recounts instances of Wesley's initiative in organising work, and obtaining capital, to enable the poor to begin earning again. High tribute was paid to the success of a Loan Fund organised to help poor "Strangers" (not of the Methodist Society, whose poor were otherwise assisted) take opportunity of employment. But there must be no usury: "we cannot devour the increase of our neighbour by requiring such interest as even the laws of our country forbid. Hereby all pawnbroking is excluded, seeing that whatever good we might do thereby, all unprejudiced men see with grief to be abundantly over-balanced by the evil.''[17]

(iv) Concern about poverty naturally focussed upon one symptom, the use of liquor, and one possible means of cure, education. Evidence of the liquor problem, moral, economic and social, in England at the time is abundant — though Wesley had opposed trade in gin formerly in Georgia. Kathleen Heasman[18] says the seeds of the nineteenth century temperance movement can be traced to Wesley, who in 1743 advised his followers to avoid buying or selling spiritous liquors, or drinking them except in extreme necessity. Beach says ''he fought hard liquor as much for economic as for moral reasons'', advising his hearers ''to buy books instead of gin.'' His preachers were ''commanded'' to preach the necessity of education, and Wesley himself supervised their training, insisting that they spend at least five hours in twenty-four reading, for the sake of their preaching and their Christian maturity. The preachers became travelling salesmen, Wesley himself producing books and other literature for his converts — he edited fifty volumes of extracts to form the ''Christian Library'', and many local Methodist Societies established lending libraries. Wesley himself, too, created a school for poor children. ''No man in the eighteenth century did so much to create a taste for good reading, and to supply it with books at the lowest price.''[19] ''The local preacher and not the secularist lecturer has formed the mind of the miner and the labourer.''[20]

Wesley's compassionate initiative included also prisoners and prison conditions — ''nurseries of wickedness'' — and also the ''bedlams'' established for seclusion of lunatics. In nine months he preached at least sixty-seven times in gaols, being eventually (as he said) ''forbidden to go to Newgate gaol for fear of making them wicked. and to Bedlam for fear of driving them mad!'' Bready thinks that Wesley prepared the way for John Howard and Elizabeth Fry, ''his spiritual children'', and Mrs. Heasman agrees that ''the beginning of systematic prison visiting can probably be traced to the Methodists: Whitefield, Wesley and his followers prayed, preached, and distributed alms in all gaols, bridewells, and bedlams within the circuits.''[21] The health of the poor, again, stirred Wesley's interest: his handbook of simple home remedies saw twenty-three editions and his free medical dispensary set a pattern others copied. ''Some employments,'' he warns ''are absolutely and totally unhealthy, as those dealing with arsenic, or other equally hurtful minerals, or the breathing an air tainted with streams of molten lead . . . Others may not be absolutely unhealthy, but only to persons of a weak constitution . . . "[22]

(v) Always a supporter of "the powers that be", Wesley could be no radical pacifist, yet considered war a foul curse, enemy of all civilisation, rebellion against humanity and God. "War is a horrid reproach to the Christian name, yea to the name of man, to all reason and humanity. In all the judgements of God the inhabitants of the earth learn righteousness: famine, plague, earthquake, the people see the hand of God. But when war breaks out God is forgotten."[23] "So long as this monster stalks uncontrolled, where is reason, virtue, humanity? They are utterly excluded."[24] On America's war of Independence he wrote, "Countrymen, children of the same parents, are to murder each other with all possible haste — to *prove* who is in the right. What an argument is this! What a method of proof! What an amazing way of deciding controversies!"[25] In such an aversion to war, at that time, Wesley had support only from the Quakers.

(vi) With the Quakers, too, Wesley spoke boldly against slavery, in Georgia, England, and elsewhere. His last letter speaks of the oppression of the negro as "villainy"; his *Thoughts upon Slavery* (1774) argues:

> "Give liberty to whom liberty is due, that is, to every child of man, to every partaker of human nature. Let none serve you but . . . by his own voluntary choice. Away with all whips, all chains, all compulsion. Be gentle toward all men."

A book by "an honest Quaker", Benezet, brought this "execrable sum of all the villainies" to Wesley's shocked attention, but two years gathering further evidence ensured that his own book would be "perhaps the most far-reaching treatise ever written against slavery" (Bready). With moving eloquence he reviews the story and conditions, arguing against calling the trade "legal" — "I absolutely deny all slave-holding to be consistent with any degree of even *natural* justice." Its excuses were hypocritical: "a man can be under no necessity of degrading himself into a wolf!" — "Men-buyers are on a level with men-stealers" — "the spring that puts all the rest in motion, captains, slave-owners, kidnappers, murderers . . . — "Thy brother's blood crieth unto thee . . . thy hands, thy bed, thy furniture, thy house, thy lands are stained with blood . . . Whether Christian or not, show yourself a man" — Some judges are "the slaves' greatest tyrants" — The grand idol of the whole traffic "was the god of gain" — It was the work of all true Christians "to proclaim the Liberty of Heaven, and act as instruments of God for the suppression of slavery."[26]

(vii) In all moral pressure towards social reform, Wesley presupposes the power of the State to right wrongs and the duty of the Christian citizen to move the State to do so. Townsend suggests this stance was possible only because Methodism inherited freedom dearly purchased by earlier nonconformists who through one hundred and fifty years had battled against political oppression. In the nineteenth century, when nonconformity was growing conscious of new freedom and power, "its application of evangelical principles to politics and social problems would have been far more fruitful in the life of the nation if official Methodism had thrown its weight into the struggle for religious equality."[27] Economically, Wesley's ethic is sometimes judged naive though it was not intended as economic policy for the nation, but as prudent counsel for ordinary Christians, many of whom through frugality, sobriety, integrity and education, became increasingly affluent and influential. Beach holds, "there is partial truth in the claim often made that Wesley saved England from such a revolution as tore France asunder . . . quenching any politically revolutionary sparks that might have ignited in his Societies . . . removing the economic ceiling put upon the poor, thus counteracting the polarisation of classes which was in part the source of the revolution of the French proletariat."[28]

The emergence of "working class" leaders as personalities of integrity, self-education, and social drive, the creation of Societies in which such found opportunity for action on moral and religious issues, contributed enormously, as Bready shows, to movements of liberty and reform in the nineteenth century, and to the "democratisation" of England. The conclusion of Bready is not too enthusiastic: "the much neglected and often lampooned Evangelical Revival . . . was the true nursing-mother of the spirit and character-values that have created and sustained Free Institutions throughout the English-speaking world . . . Wesley opened springs of human sympathy and understanding, which in turn inspired and nourished a glorious succession of social reforms." Bready then quotes Ostrogorski on the evangelical reformers: "they appeal always and everywhere from the miserable reality to the human conscience. They make one see the man in the criminal, the brother in the negro . . . (they) introduced a new personage into the social and political world . . . *the fellow man,* (who) never more will leave the stage."[29]

That comment, evoked by Wesley's achievement, fittingly defines the link he forged between evangelicalism and social reform, and his contribution to the new social dimension of the Christian ethic.

2. CHRISTIAN SOCIAL ACTIVITY

In Christian history, action frequently outruns theory. In the nineteenth century, especially, the inheritors of Puritan, Quaker, and Wesleyan tradition, and of sporadic efforts like the Friendly Societies, Savings Banks, agitation for "a living wage" and unemployment insurance, the Chartist Movement (1837-1842), and the first Trade Union "martyrs" (1834), gave a wholly new impetus to post-Reformation ethics, reminiscent of the second and third centuries and the Christian impact upon the Graeco-Roman world.[30] Of the Victorian age in England it has been said, "Evangelicals are remembered for what they did rather than their theology" — or, it might be added, "their sociology." They were not alone in Christian concern; the Anglican High Church party, and the Unitarians, shared in many schemes of social amelioration and compassion; but as "only a rough generalisation" it appears that "as many as three quarters of the total number of voluntary charitable organisations in the second half of the nineteenth century can be regarded as Evangelical in character and control."[31] Such societies, "movements" and initiatives "exploded" into church life on all sides almost simultaneously: "scarcely a human contingency was not met and publicised."

(1) In Britain

Even the chapter-headings of Mrs. Heasman's *Evangelicals in Action,* taken alone, reveal the astonishing scope and variety of evangelical social activity in Britain:

"The Great Christian Missions" ("for the general benefit of the poor") — "The Social Work of the Churches and Chapels" — "The Ragged School Movement" — "Children's Homes and Orphanages" — "The Teenager' — "Gospel Temperance" — "The Reform of the Prostitute" — "Help for the Prisoner" — "The Blind and the Deaf" — "The Unsound in Mind and Body" — "The Care of the Sick and the Aged" — "The Sailor and the Soldier" — "Some Other Groups of Working People" — and Mrs. Heasman marshals hundreds of names, organisations, dates and other details to support her case. The example of one London church is typical: at Metropolitan Tabernacle, the Victorian Puritan, C. H. Spurgeon, made the church the centre of social service, rebuilding almshouses, organising classes, clubs, and numerous other societies, free evening schools, "provident" (loan) societies, benevolent societies, maternal societies, supporting temperance work, work for the blind, and the Ragged Schools, very actively assisting Lord Shaftesbury's factory reforms, and Dr. Barnardo's work among homeless children, establishing hostels and a registry for domestic servants, later creating the Stockwell ("Spurgeon's") Orphan Homes. In Scotland, Thomas Chalmers pioneered popular education and poor relief, followed by James Begg with his "Social Charter" and the Scottish Social Reform Association (1850); Patrick Brewster at Paisley Abbey preached "Chartist" sermons.

Among motives behind "such a vast number of voluntary charities" Mrs. Heasman mentions — growing awareness of social problems (evidenced by several government investigations, and by creation of The National Association for the Promotion of Social Science (1857)); deepening guilt at prevailing inequality of wealth, and the appalling conditions in which many lived; desire for publicity and power on the part of some benefactors. Conversion from self to Christ, from self-centredness to charity, at first towards Christian neighbours but then beyond the Christian circle, encouraged by examples of Puritans, Quakers, Methodists, German Pietists (as at Halle and Kaiserswerth), led increasing numbers to attempt the relief of suffering. Despite some debate whether evangelism or social aid should have priority, the basic concept of "the infinite latent value of even the downmost soul" in the eyes of the Redeemer prompted compassion as well as zeal, even while it imposed an over-individualistic approach on methods and on aim. Unexpectedly, social concern was fed also by revivalist movements: "this connection between revivalism and social service seems first to have been made by Charles G. Finney in America, where he preached that 'conversion' meant not only a fitness of the individual for a future life, but some attempt to make the world a more suitable place to which Christ should return."[32] Finney's visits brought this view to England, and from revivalist campaigns new workers were fed into social charities. D. L. Moody, likewise, urged his converts to seek out and help, on every level, the poor, the immoral, the drunken, and criminals. Numerous organisations, "Christian Unions" for mutual support and active service, sprang from counsel given in evangelistic meetings to express the new Christian life in Christian usefulness. The *duty* of philanthropy became, Mrs. Heasman argues, a more mellow and active benevolence towards all in need.

There was much over-lapping; too much concern with amelioration, too little interest in underlying causes; in consequence, no social policy, no wish to interfere by legislation with freedom of action of employers, investors, the free play of market forces which produced such conditions. Few, like Lord Shaftesbury, architect of so many reforms, sought to deal with governments and to transform society by legislation affecting the roots of the tragic conditions which Christian pity sought to alleviate.

Miss Constance Smith remarks, "an awakened public conscience, if it is not to spend itself in futile emotion, must find a channel of expression. Shaftesbury taught it to speak with the voice of law . . ." Reckitt thought Shaftesbury stood outside of, temperamentally and religiously opposed to, "the Christian social movement" — meaning, apparently, that socialising movement which led towards Trade Associations and economic reform. Miss Smith also says that "by temperament, tradition, education, he remained an aristocrat; to the end he worked *for* rather than *with* the people whose cause he championed." To some degree, this serves to underline the religious and conscientious motive, free from personal interest or inclination, which drove Shaftesbury to become involved in factory legislation. Southey described the factory system as "this most hellish of all slaveries"; even "if the organised church did not rise against (its evils), Christian men did in numbers — the factory agitation (1802-1847) may be said to have been a definitely Christian agitation". Parallel movements towards State education, and towards legal protection of Trade Unions, likewise had active Christian support.[33]

But despite weaknesses, evangelicals did focus attention upon social problems, document the facts (as in Charles Booth's massive surveys), stir the public conscience, initiate many methods and explore many areas of social concern later to be widely developed by professional training, and adopted by official agencies when the whole task of social organisation in England passed increasingly into government hands.

Nor were Christian philanthropists always neglectful of underlying causes. The Quaker, George Cadbury recognised the difficulty of nurturing sound character and outlook in the grim back streets of an English midland city, and set about designing factory premises, working conditions, workers' homes in a garden village, schemes of training broadening into general adult education, higher wages, pension schemes, medical care, and Trade Union representation. Cadbury was "convinced that sound ethics would prove to be true economy". With typical Quaker practicality, he did not argue between evangelism and social service: "to change men's hearts and to change their homes were parts of the same task, and the Christian has not to ask which comes first or is the more important, but to take his share in either line of work as he may be guided."[34]

Bready tells his own story, parallel to that of Miss Heasman, of "the expression of voluntary benevolence and social service" which in no other age has "reached such proportions and exhibited such virility as during the last century and a half among the Anglo-Saxon peoples". 'Whence this . . . passion for social justice and sensitivity to human wrongs? — it derived from a new social conscience . . . nurtured by the Evangelical Revival of vital and practical Christianity — a revival which illumined the central postulates of the New

Testament ethic, which made real the Fatherhood of God and brotherhood of man, which pointed the priority of personality over property, and which directed heart, soul, and mind toward the establishment of the kingdom of righteousness on earth."[35] Bready's examples include extending concern for education, increasing care for children, for health, for animals, and for victims of alcohol, organisations like the Young Men's Christian Association for young business men friendless in the cities, Salvation Army, with its worldwide, measureless toil for the destitute, homeless, ignorant, deserted, aged, prisoners, and all "the hopeless". Bready also traces the manifold contribution of evangelical Christians to the rise of Trade Associations, later the Trade Union Movement. More was involved here than compassion, and amelioration of intolerable, or dangerous, working conditions: as Charles Raven said, "democracy was inevitably changing the whole social tradition of mankind" — was moving over, in fact, from politics into economics.[36]

(2) In America

Evangelicalism was no less socially fruitful in the United States. "The American expression of the Evangelical Revival . . . finally . . . was to affect profoundly the whole republic's life and destiny . . . The heroic labours of such tireless Methodist pioneers as Asbury and Coke were to leave an abiding concern for righteousness."[37] As early as 1823 opposition to slavery was expressed by ministers in St. Clair County — "the clergy of Illinois . . . exerted great influence in securing rejection". The American Anti-Slavery Society was founded in 1833 by William Lloyd Garrison, who had earlier declared —

"I call upon the spirits of the just made perfect in heaven, upon all who have experienced the love of God in their souls here below, upon the Christian converts in India and the isles of the sea, to sustain one in the assertion that there is power enough in the religion of Jesus Christ to melt down the most stubborn prejudices, to overthrow the highest wall of partition, to break the strongest caste, to improve and elevate the most degraded, and to equalise all its recipients."[38]

Henry Ward Beecher of Brooklyn declared the Fugitive Slave Law a "mandate of Satan" to be obeyed at the peril of one's soul. Lincoln, says Bready, was as much a product of the revival's impact upon America as was Wilberforce of its impact in England; and he draws a remarkably close parallel between the American President and Lord Shaftesbury.[39]

A. L. Drummond[40] vividly describes "the gilded age" of unparalleled opportunity, affluence, moral decline, too rapid immigration, and poverty, that followed the Civil War. Personal morality was often much higher than political and commercial standards — "Men should make money according to the laws of business and spend it according to the laws of God." Not many in the churches supported "The Knights of Labour" (1869) or the later American Federation of Labour, while fierce competition, speculation, cheap immigrant workers, and depression, often inhibited benevolence.

Most of the new millionaires had a church connection, and lavishly endowed universities and colleges. So-called "institutional churches" provided clubs and societies for the unprivileged — as at St. Georges, New York, where D. W. S. Rainsford "brought the church close to the working life of a great city", and at Elvira, where gymnasium, library, theatre, creche, and consulting rooms surrounded the church. Palatial "parish houses" provided by the wealthy catered for the poor. Armour built cheap model tenements in Chicago; C. H. Parkhurst, "a minister of the gospel who took social problems seriously", led public protest against corruption in New York. Crusades against drink, gambling, vice, were frequent, though not always with understanding of the conditions that produce such problems. Theodore Parker was an outstanding exception in tracing most evils to low wages, high rents, irresponsible management and exploitation. Though nothing like English "Christian Socialism" had yet appeared in America, Parker could speak of "socialising Christianity." Drummond refers also to the social gospel reflected in fiction — in Sheldon's *In His Steps,* Mrs. Ward's *Robert Elsmere,* and Churchill's *Inside of the Cup,* the last blending theological liberalism with social concern.

The close connection of evangelicalism with "apostolic concern for the poor" in America in the 1920's is emphasised also by Morris L. Stevens,[41] adding that by 1840 the revival movement had brought with it "a corresponding resurgence of evangelical social service." In the 1850's five thousand volunteers from one hundred and fifty churches were working in charitable activities in Philadelphia alone. In New York's slums, within ten years, the evangelical leadership of Phoebe Palmer achieved extensive relief projects, boarding houses, a young women's home, refuges for young delinquents, an asylum for the deaf and an orphanage for five hundred negroes. Work among seamen, the poor, the unemployed, the uneducated, flowed from evangelical groups elsewhere. The Pacific Garden Mission (1827) maintained "prodigious work" among alcoholics. Sherwood Wirt adds that evangelists and revivalists who "roamed the frontier" in the nineteenth century not only preached the gospel of inner salvation, but championed the friendless, jobless, illiterate, drunken, widows and orphans, the Indian and the negro. Evangelist D. L. Moody, conducting personal work in Chicago's slums, would often enquire, "Do you have food, clothing, fuel?" — and provided such necessities as part of his evangelistic effort.

Bringing the story up-to-date, W. Stanley Mooneyham[42] explains the motives of the American National Association of Evangelicals (1942). These included recapturing the compassion of Jesus; desire for a positive Christian programme alongside the protective withdrawal from society of previous years; desire to reflect "renewed awareness of the social implications of the gospel, and the commitment of an increasing number of evangelicals to give arms and legs to their faith through meaningful social action." He instances the 1944 Committee for Post War Relief to aid victims of war in Europe, the expanded humanitarian ministry in Korea, the later World Relief Commission which today (meaning 1973) "maintains a world-wide outreach, with projects in the disaster and poverty-stricken areas of the world, including Korea, Vietnam, Pakistan, India, China, Peru, Nigeria, and other places — covering orphanages, schools, vocational centres, leper colonies, refugee programmes, hospitals, and agricultural development."

Such summaries are necessarily selective, and hopelessly incomplete, just because the efforts themselves were so numerous, varied, and self-propagating; while all such conscientious compulsions appear sporadic, ill-organised, and superficial. Yet they were genuine and spontaneous expressions of the essential Christian spirit, entirely consonant not only with Puritan altruism, but also with much mediaeval charity, with the monastic service to the community, with the ancient patristic ethic of social witness, and with the New Testament portrait of Him who went about doing good.

Nevertheless, the "socialisation" of the Christian ethic needed to go much further than impulsive, sporadic goodwill — and did so.

15

Christian Social Theory

ONE STRONG ELEMENT IN the changing Christian outlook of the nineteenth century was an altogether new prominence given to the idea of the kingdom of God. In Europe, Ritschl and Harnack saw the kingdom, ethically conceived, as the goal of the church's activity, though wider than church life itself. It represented a kingdom of brotherhood, the moral unification of the race, towards which Christians work and move by neighbourly love, and by diligent obedience to the teaching of Jesus.[1] But European social movements tended towards anti-clericalism and atheism; whereas in Britain attention to the kingdom of God produced various forms of "Christian socialism", and in America, "the Social Gospel". In Germany more recently the outcome has been almost an inversion of all that Christians had understood by the kingdom of God.

(1) BRITAIN

In Britain the development of Christian social theory was marked by gradualness, compromise, and varied contributions by several outstanding figures.

(i) Maurice

Theologian, prophet, perhaps saint, "certainly one of the most significant figures in the history of English religion", F. D. Maurice was the main inspiration of the deliberate application of Christian ethics to society.[2] Moved by Coleridge and Carlyle to think of social reform, and by Ludlow, expert in economics and acquainted with French socialism, Maurice became convinced of the need for Christian interpretation of industrial and economic relations, and together with Ludlow, Kingsley, Hughes, Neal, and others, founded Christian socialism. The initial impetus was short-lived (1848-1854), but the consequences immense. The movement sympathised with the aspirations of the disenfranchised working class, as set out in the

People's Charter (1838), but held "socialism" to mean simply "the science of partnership", men working with, not against, each other. Competition they held not a law of the universe but a blasphemy.[3]

(a) Maurice's whole approach was theological, never far removed from evangelical valuation of personal piety, inner experience, and complete dependence upon God.

Raven insists that the work of these early Christian socialists had an avowedly spiritual basis, drawing attention to the weekly Bible class under Maurice's leadership, focus of their fellowship. Maurice himself declared, "I have no vocation except for theology . . . To preach the gospel of the kingdom, that it is amongst us, and not to be set up, is my calling . . . Let us not try to sever principles which affect the problems of earth from those which affect the kingdom of heaven. All unrighteous government that sets itself against the order and freedom of man is hostile to Christ's government . . ." Flint, not altogether sympathetic, speaks of Maurice and Kingsley as faithful and fearless in rebuking evils and indicating the requirements of their time . . . "from the very heart of the gospel, for they believed the distinctive truths of Christianity were wonderfully adapted to the wants of human society."[4]

Maurice's central thesis was the already existing kingship of Christ: "I was sent into the world that I might persuade men to recognise Christ as the centre of their fellowship with each other." "The quest for unity haunted Maurice" (A. M. Ramsey): Christ's universal headship and kingship was the unifying principle of his message.[5]

Maurice proclaimed it his mission, says Reckitt, "to show that economy and politics . . . must have a ground beneath themselves, that society is . . . to be regenerated by finding the law and ground of its order, the only secret of its existence, in God." "The kingdom of heaven is to me *the great existing reality* which is to renew the earth . . ."[6]

J. E. Symes says that Maurice invented the phrase "Christian socialism" in protest against unsocial Christians and unchristian socialists; disliking the Chartists' use of force, and distrusting "democratic ideals", Maurice believed the will of God, expressed in the kingdom, was the sole uniting centre of a socialised community life — not only common self-interest.[7] But Maurice and his friends were by no means only theoretical idealists: their scheme for Working Men's Associations in tailoring, building, ironfounding, printing, with a view to co-operative production, management, and profit-sharing, was a large step towards Trade Unionism. Their recognition that working people need to be educated to such wider responsibility, leading to the Working Men's College (London), set a pattern long followed in workers' re-education. The journal *Politics for the People,* and the *Tracts for Priest and People,* express the same confidence that ordinary men can grasp the nature of social problems and effectively influence them.

The root of such schemes and such faith was Christian theology. "Beneath all distinctions of property and of rank," said Maurice, "there lie the obligations of a common creation, redemption, and humanity; . . . all our doings must be witnesses to them." The church "can scarcely make her voice heard against schemes for reducing all things to a common stock, establishing fellowship upon a law of mutual selfishness, because she has not believed that . . . the law of love, the polity of members united in one Head, of brethren confessing a common Father, was a real one . . . She has left people to fancy it was only a dream, a cruel mockery . . ."[8] The Fatherhood of God, and Christ's teaching about the kingdom, indicate that human brotherhood is not a distant ideal but a present fact. It is the church's task to help men see, and become, what they are already.[9]

Selwyn comments that Maurice held, against dualism, that nature itself was spiritual, all creation the work of God, indwelt by His Spirit. This conviction enabled Maurice to claim humanity, the social order, secular history, physical science, for Christ: "This is God's world, men are God's children, and so brothers". "That the sharp cleavage between organised religion and the social movement, so common on the Continent, has scarcely existed in England . . . is traceable in large measure to the influence of Maurice."[10]

Maurice therefore joins the optimists in regard to human nature:

"Men feel they are not merely lost creatures: they look up to heaven and ask whether this is the whole account of their condition; that their sense of right and wrong, their cravings for fellowship, their consciousness of powers no other creatures possess, are all nothing . . . If religion will give us no explanation of these feelings, if it can only tell us about a fall for the whole race and an escape for a few individuals of it, then our wants must be satisfied without religion. Then begins Chartism . . ."[11]

Maurice holds (with Barclay) that the immanence of God is a moral and educative influence in human existence: Christ is the revelation of the light that lighteth every man. Men *are* in the divine image, *are* members of a redeemed race, are one in God's sight and law. To Maurice, says Kerr Spiers,[12] "the form of Christ to be encountered daily were the poor who lived in the environs of Lincolns Inn Fields, or the sick to whom he ministered in London's Guy's Hospital. Such as these, impoverished of body and indeed of mind and spirit, were not 'unsaved' or 'lost' — they were incorporate in the *all* of *Colossians* whom God had reconciled to Himself through the incarnation of Christ, and it is from this theological perspective that he saw the multiform Christ incarnate again in the least of his brethren."

(b) It was however supremely in the theology of the kingdom that Maurice found his social principles. His best-known book, *The Kingdom of Christ* (1838), set beside the Quaker doctrine of the inner light the visible forms and channels of the Spirit, especially the church, as a spiritual kingdom; to confront the individualism which uncontrolled would destroy society, with the law of human brotherhood. The book expounds the "theocratic principle", seed of all Maurice's later thought. The best human ideas could not refashion society: God had acted before man and for man; "through creation and redemption, His kingdom, the universal community of Christ our Head, was already 'the great practical existing reality' which is to renew the earth." The kingdom has been "planted by the great acts of God . . . in the very nature of things;" it is not that life ought to be founded on mutual helpfulness — it is so. Competition was not the law of the universe: "Christian socialism is to my mind the assertion of God's order."[13]

Maurice's later commentary on Luke's Gospel, *The Gospel of the Kingdom of Heaven* applies his theses to exegesis: "the life of Christ can only be contained in a Gospel of the kingdom of heaven" (xxxvf). Luke presents the birth, temptations, acts, spirit, glory, limitations, agony and triumph "of the *King";* the announcement, laws, signs, subjects, parables, life, feast, joy and coming of the *kingdom* — as already in operation, embodying the laws under which all men actually do live, or rebel against to their cost. "Your faith does not make Me your Lord; you do not elect Me to be your sovereign." *The contrary assertion, that all the kingdoms of the world belong to Satan, is a temptation and a lie.* Christ *is,* and ever will be, King.

Flint found the views of Maurice and his friends — all social disease caused by disobedience to divine law; Christianity the power of God unto social salvation — excellent, but *not* socialism. They contain no specific socialist tenet; while the demand for individual reform, the ideas that trust in State aid was superstition, that co-operation should be voluntary, that private possession was not robbery but stewardship, that brotherhood was not common selfish interest but relation to a common Father, struck at the very roots of Socialism.[14] In such a judgement, the developed, technical understanding of "Socialism" is clouding Maurice's meaning: but it serves to underline what Maurice did, and did not, stand for; and to emphasise how firmly Maurice had turned Christian ethics towards a social theory that was at once sympathetic to, but essentially different from, the democratic trend of the late nineteenth and early twentieth century.

(ii) Headlam, Holland, Gore, Temple

Among Maurice's successors, S. D. Headlam founded the Guild of St. Matthew (1877) to remove the prejudices of secular socialists against the church, by showing how faith, gospel and sacraments were related to social justice.

It did not interest Headlam to further political reforms but to persuade Christians to recognise the implications of their religion. "Baptism was the entry to the greatest democratic society in the world. The mass was the weekly meeting of a society of rebels against a mammon-worshipping world order. Let the working men of England . . . do their duty as Christian soldiers, and the present order would crumble."[15]

Headlam illustrates the socialising of Christian ethics within the High Church wing of the English church — he "blended with the message of Maurice the Catholic heritage restored by the Tractarians."[16] The Guild of St. Matthew, though never large, lasted into the new century and shocked many within the church into new awareness of the social problem.

Stronger High Church support came through one "whose whole soul beat in tune with the great theology of the creeds", Henry Scott Holland, brilliant spokesman for the "Christian Social Union" (1890, later the Industrial Christian Fellowship).[17] Holland saw political problems yielding place to economic and industrial problems, and declared "the ultimate solution of the social question is bound to be discovered in the person and life of Christ. He is 'the Man' and He must be the solution of all human problems ..."[18] The church should consult *experts* in business and economics, but solutions lay in"the unfaltering assertion of moral as supreme over mechanical laws; "the vacillation of Christians between economic laws and Christian morality attempted to evade trouble which their own "miserable double-mindedness" had caused. Holland's task was to persuade the Church of England that the Christian community is responsible for its own economic and social order.[19] He insisted that within a democracy "State interference" is the people's own intervention in their own social affairs: "the State which imposed the law is our social self." He also supported energetically the growing demand for "a living wage."

The "living wage" replaced a "just wage", calculated not now upon equality of exchange but on *need* of the wage earner, generously understood. "The first charge upon every industry should be the payment of a sufficient wage to enable the worker to maintain himself and his family in health and honour, with such a margin of leisure as will permit reasonable recreation and the development of mind and spirit."[20]

Holland, most patient seeker of facts, framer of proposals, leader of deputations, investigator of "the sins of trade" included shareholders in the moral responsibilities borne by firms, demanded united church action, not merely individual charity, and helped to ensure that the atheism of European socialists was little known in the British movement.

"From over the sea we began to be aware of a Social Philosophy which . . . took its scientific shape in the hands of Karl Marx, but floated across to us . . . using our own Christian language, and invoking the unity of the Social Body and the law of love . . . It read out the significance of citizenship in terms spiritual and Christian. It challenged us to say why we were not bringing our creed into action as the true secret of all social well-being . . . in the form of Christian Socialism . . . We woke up to Maurice . . . Christian doctrine showed itself the very heart of a social gospel!"[21]

Holland's Christian Social Union was more academic than the Guild of St. Matthew, claiming for the Christian law the authority to rule social practice, and patiently building up theological scholarship and episcopal authority behind it.

The Church Socialist League (1906), embracing responsibilities from which the Christian Social Union shrank,[22] and adopting the slogan "Christianity is the religion of which Socialism is the practice", illustrates another temptation facing the Christian social ethic — that of facile identification with a ready-made social programme. Democratic, humanitarian, optimistic, the League suffered heart-searching when individual freedom was seen to be threatened by Socialist thinking, even more when Marxism in eastern Europe gave new colour to terms like "revolution", "new social order;" and when the kingdom of God was regarded as an earthly paradise to be built by socialistic legislation. One result was renewed search for theological foundations, and the concept of the kingdom as "the regulative social ideal"; Maurice would have said, "the ever-present reality."

Another High Church leader, with "permanently troubled conscience" was Charles Gore,[23] less hopeful of the secular prescriptions then in vogue, more suspicious of the "collectivist" trend, but deeply concerned about social questions.

"What I complain about . . . is not that commercial and social selfishness exist . . . but that its profound antagonism to the spirit of Christ is not recognised; that there is not . . . an adequate conception of what Christian morality means . . . We must identify ourselves with the great impeachment of the present industrial system."

Gore's final work, *Christ and Society,* draws summary lessons for his own time:

Because of "the emancipation of commerce and industry from the control of religion at the Renaissance it was no longer possible to insist upon just price or fair wage. (Reckitt held later that "failure to master the problem of usury in an expanding economy went far to wreck the church's traditional sociology".[24]) No new Christian sociology emerged, the church became individualistic, falsely other-worldly. This world-order is not the goal; but one day Christ is visibly to reign, we are to see the City of God; the church of here and now, the vestibule of the kingdom, will pass into the kingdom in perfection. Meanwhile, the wise will lay up treasure in heaven, but heaven is not merely individual union with God, but perfected *fellowship,* the City of God. So, *the Christian ethic is a social ethic through and through.* Social requirements guard the entrance to the final kingdom — "Inasmuch as ye did it not to one of the least of these . . . Depart . . ." The church is building a fabric which only eternity can complete, but meanwhile she must build the fabric of the true humanity, within *this* world. The urgent question: does the religion of fellowship permeate all human relations?

The church, existing to "regulate human life in accordance with God", cannot stand outside politics or economics, but must insist that all develop the full richness of personality — *in industry,* where absentee owners and wholly dependent workers create an unjust, unnatural situation, which must give way to workers' participation; *in education,* where for many, opportunity ends too soon; *in law,* which is too concerned with protection of property of one class; *in international and in Commonwealth relations,* where democracy, equality, the divine right of all races to fair opportunity, must be accepted.

William Temple, in the tradition of Maurice and Scott Holland, rejected division of the world into spiritual and material, which undervalues the "secular". An incarnational, sacramental theology gives spiritual significance to the material, concreteness to the spiritual; so a high faith is realised and expressed within home, economics, and politics. In the sacramental view of the universe, hope is given of making human both politics and economics, and of making effectual both faith and love.[25] Temple saw the world consisting "in turn" of matter, life, intelligence, spirit, the higher existing only by means of the lower, yet taking control of the lower. So we interpret the lower by the higher, the whole in terms of spirit. Thus the transcendent is immanent within the actual world — the "secular" has sacramental character — and an "incarnational, sacramental ethic" must follow.[26]

Christianity has, during the greater part of its existence, set itself to influence the political and social ordering of men's lives. The nineteenth century recovered a forgotten part of Christian belief and practice, as religion became less individualistic.

It is the Christian's duty to be active in all enterprises of neighbourly love —

seeking fairer opportunities, better housing for all; modifying the social and industrial order to assist formation of good character; rejecting the idea that economic "laws" are beyond human modification; and applying to the world at least four Christian principles — the sacredness of personality; the fact of fellowship (community); the duty of service; the power of self-sacrifice.[27]

In 1936 Temple presided at a church conference which pledged itself to combat malnutrition, bad housing, unemployment, and "secure for our fellows their birthright as children of one Father." Five years later, another Conference showed "a more pervasive belief that the evils of society arise from our desertion of an ascertainable order for society which springs from . . . Christian faith in God as Creator, Redeemer, and Sanctifier".[28] The echo of Maurice is unmistakable.

But by Temple's time, Christian social concern and theory in Britain were giving way to secularist sociology on the one hand, and to a Christian Right and Christian Left on the other. Christian protest against social evils was meeting a secularist protest against "religious interference" in affairs deemed the private province of government, political parties, or radical worker-movements. In *Christianity and the Social Order,* Temple argued that "the church is bound to interfere" as agent of God's purpose, outside which no human interest can fall. Reckitt comments:

It was largely owing to his own work that Temple could say that "among Christians who have seriously and thoughtfully faced the historical situation with which we are dealing (1944), there is . . . an observable convergence." Reckitt summarises that "convergence": "It is 'for God Who has spoken', for Neighbour; for Man as rooted in Nature; for History; and for the Gospel and the Church. In several of these respects the social outlook of the Christian community today is notably different from that of previous decades. It is more consciously theocentric; it sets more store upon man's immediate environment and his functional associations, home, community, and workplace; it has recovered some understanding of the idea of Natural Law; it apprehends that the truth about society is not primarily to be discovered in abstractions but that 'it is in history that the ultimate meaning of existence is both revealed and actualised'; it founds itself not on a sanctified humanism but on the revelation of God in scripture and on the redemptive function of the Church."[29]

That paragraph might well summarise the findings of one hundred years of Christian social theory.

The contrast between the manifold activist labours of the evangelicals and the more academic work of the Anglicans arose in some measure from the different opportunities open to dissenting sects and the established national church. In part too, perhaps, from differing intellectual capacities and backgrounds. But something was due also to the differing Christian ethos. For evangelicals, as in part for Maurice, the spur to Christian social action was the gospel itself, with its compassion, the command to love, and the Christ-ideal. For the Anglicans, an incarnational and sacramental emphasis, and a definition of the kingdom of Christ as a present reality, the inner truth about all men and all society, was the premise for a theological approach to problems on which the "keepers of the nation's conscience", felt bound to offer advice.

(2) AMERICA

Beach distinguishes the "doctrinal seriousness" of Christian social ethics in England from one type of Social Gospel in America, preoccupied with humanitarian reform and unconcerned with orthodox theology.[30] Nevertheless, American social theory, like American social activity, had evangelical inspiration. Macquarrie dates American concern with social application of the gospel in the early twentieth century; Shailer Mathews places it earlier. Richard Niebuhr thought the kingdom of God had always been central to American Christianity, but in modern times has been identified with a social order, mainly under the influence of secularism, immigrant problems, and national sentiment.[31]

Parker of Boston recognised the interlocking of social, economic, and moral problems — hence his "socialising Christianity"; J. R. Lowell explained that socialism was not necessarily atheistic, but "the practical application of Christianity to life . . . secret of orderly and benign reconstruction." By 1892, Bushnell was teaching "constructive civics"; C. R. Henderson, was appointed Professor of Ecclesiastical Sociology at Chicago. In 1900, Harvard's F. G. Peabody produced one of the most influential books on the social gospel, *Jesus Christ and the Social Question*.[32]

From its beginning in 1908, the Federal Council of the Churches of Christ in America emphasised the social bearing of Christianity, and published the Social Creed of the Churches, a statement of principles and social ideals (formulated by Frank Mason North) — abolition of poverty, curbing of divorce, labouring men to share in determining working conditions, abolition of child labour, arbitration, application of the teaching of Jesus to family, State, international affairs. Christian activity must remove causes of social injustice and evils; "opposed to revolution, it must be interested in reconstruction."[33]

Dean Sperry considered these "outposts held by more advanced persons" had "educational" value.[34]

Among those who helped to formulate Christian social theory in America Washington Gladden, Walter Rauschenbusch, Shailer Mathews, and Reinhold Niebuhr, chiefly influenced contemporary Christian ethics.

(i) Gladden

Approaching social questions from pastoral experience, Gladden crusaded "to capture the imagination and conscience of churchmen not for doctrinaire Socialism but for social justice." To questions like, Is human personality a mere commodity on the labour market? Do laws of political economy exclude protection of the poor man? he gave a forthright negative in *Working Men and Their Employers,* and *Applied Christianity.*[35] Gladden "thought in social categories" but retained a strong evangelical faith: social redemption is reconciliation to God restoring the unity of society; God's work in Christ effects social transformation; the kingdom of God, here on earth steadily widening its borders, is traceable directly to Christ. Spearhead of the kingdom in 'Christianising' society, the church should reconcile all classes — though Christianity does not cancel natural differences between men, nor inequality of gifts, work, and resulting rewards.[36]

In *The Christian Pastor,* Gladden insists that a church include rich, poor, learned, unlearned, with no distinction of caste or colour. "The Christian church is on trial before this generation . . . whether there exists within it genuine brotherhood . . . The separation of classes threatens the disruption of existing society . . . If the church is true to the principles of its Founder, we may escape revolution." Capitalist elements, labouring classes, *are* members one of another. Industrial society is on something like a war basis; it is the business of the church to bring all together in fellowship, as the church once brought Jews and Gentiles together.

"The sacredness of all life, the essential religiousness of every kind of work, are not to be gainsaid:" the whole community of Christian people, in State, church, art, education — is the kingdom of God. Within the kingdom, is the church, organised for worship, training people for the life of the kingdom. By its fruits in the community, the success of a church must be judged. The problem is to make all life religious: *special* associations are needed to cultivate religious ideas and feelings: that religion is for all life and all society must not disparage the function of the church. To nourish a church while the community deteriorates in corruption, frivolity, bitterness, would be futile — and impossible: the church is not in the world to save itself but to save the world. Either the church must pour a steady stream of saving power into the community, or it will receive a steady stream of poisonous influence from the community. The minister must include social questions among his studies; the individual cannot be saved without consideration of the social forces that bear upon him. Each pastoral duty is then examined in social light.[37]

(ii) Rauschenbusch

More radical than Gladden, Rauschenbusch sought not merely the reconciliation of different classes but the alliance of the church especially with the working class.

"Ameliorative measures and piecemeal reforms cannot bridge the cleavage in modern society between labour and capital, and if we are in earnest about overcoming the evils of industrial society we cannot, he argues, stop short of socialism" (Macquarrie[38]).

It is especially important to understand Rauschenbusch's approach. Brought up in a German pietist tradition, a "convinced believer in personal Christianity", and translator of Moody-Sankey revivalist hymns, he combined deep personal piety with concern for the community in *"Prayers of the Social Awakening"* (1910). During pastoral experience on the edge of "Hell's Kitchen" on New York's West Side, he met at first hand the "terrible effects of poverty, unemployment, malnutrition, disease and crime." Social concern pressed on him "from the outside" —

"When I saw how men toiled all their life long . . . and at the end had almost nothing to show for it; how strong men begged for work and could not get it . . . how little children died — Oh the children's funerals! They gripped my heart . . . Why *did* the children have to die? — In that way, gradually, social information and social passion came to me."[39]

Nor was this only a passing youthful protest: at 31 he warned that "Many of us, through ease of life . . . are prone to sag down from evangelical religion to humanitarian morality, from spiritual fervour to altruistic earnestness," while from a hospital bed near the end he wrote —

Lonely, often beset by conservative antagonism, "I have been upheld by the comforts of God. Jesus has been to me the inexhaustible source of fresh impulses, life, and courage. My life would seem an empty shell if my personal religion were left out of it."

"His liberalism," said Handy, "was evangelical, not humanistic." "Although Rauschenbusch gives a this-wordly turn to Christian theology," says Macquarrie, "he still retains like Gladden an evangelical faith, and insists on the supernatural character of the kingdom." Drummond adds: "he did not over-rate environment and minimise sin;" and he never forgot the struggles of his fellow immigrants.[40]

Nevertheless, Rauschenbusch's great theme was the Social Gospel;

"Christ's conception of the kingdom of God came to me as a new revelation. Here was the idea and purpose that had dominated the mind of the Master Himself. All His teachings centre about it. His death was suffered for it . . . The spiritual authority of Christ would have been sufficient . . . But in addition I found this new conception . . . strangely satisfying . . . The saving of the lost, the teaching of the young, the pastoral care of the poor and frail, the quickening of starved intellects, the study of the Bible, church union, political reform, the reorganisation of the industrial system, international peace — it was all covered by the one aim of the Reign of God on earth . . . the divine transformation of all human life."[41]

So Rauschenbusch became major spokesman of the kingdom of God ideal, relating his profound evangelical faith to his passion for social reform. The realisation of the kingdom on earth must be made central in theology, as it had been with Jesus. The church however had become preoccupied with adventism, then dogma, then monasticism, and with herself. The sociological interpretation of Christianity had had a long time to wait! Now, the kingdom on earth was "the fundamental purpose of the church's existence."[42]

In *Christianity and the Social Crisis* (1907) a review of the prophets, the life and teachings of Jesus, and dominant tendencies of primitive Christianity establishes that the purpose of Christianity was to transform human society into the kingdom of God, regenerating all relations in accordance with the will of God. The church, now more fit for her social mission than ever before, faces an urgent call from the world itself for salvation. The present crisis is complex — industrialisation, the expropriation of land, little work and low wages, poor morale, widespread physical decline, inequality, the crumbling of democracy, undermining of family loyalties, an anti-Christian atmosphere of greed and competition, loss of faith in justice, goodness, and God. The world sits in judgement upon "Christian civilisation" and its response to legitimate hopes of working people; *this* is the church's stake in the social crisis.

There is need for *social* repentance, the rejection of entrenched interests; for a vision of Christ's service that embraces all life; for multiplication in society of socially enlightened Christians; for the valuation of people above things, profits, organisation; for good social customs as well as laws; for stewardship of rights, property, on behalf of people; for rediscovery of the ideal of communism in property — as family, school, and church, are communistic. Christianity has more affinity for a society based upon solidarity, fraternity, than for one based in selfishness, antagonism. Competition is selfish, covetous, unchristian. Socialism would overcome the division inherent in capitalism, make the workers owners again of their vaster tools, and evoke a new morality.

In *Christianising the Social Order* (1912) Rauschenbusch judged that though domestic, educational, and political institutions had been in some degree Christianised, to bring big business under the law of Christ was the next task. With great foresight, he spelled out the application of Christian ethics to labour unions, health legislation, fairer distribution of wealth, democratisation of industry, extension of consumer co-operatives, socialisation of production and resources, insurance covering unemployment, illness, old age, and graduated income tax.

It was, however, in *Theology for a Social Gospel* (1918) that the American Social Gospel reached clearest theological expression.

(a) *Sin:* natural sensuousness, ignorance, become guilt when asserted against the higher self, the neighbour and God (or the common good). The definition of sin as selfishness reveals the social spirit of Christianity. Sin is usually against people: the sinful is the anti-social, rebellion against the kingdom of love. Hence evil is corporate. "Original sin", transmitted biologically is less significant than sin perpetuated through social tradition, as past wrongs govern present attitudes, and individual acts of sin contribute to the solidarity of evil.

(b) *Salvation* is likewise social: individual conversion to religion can make men worse (as Pharisees) unless it turns them outward to God and humanity. Salvation is *the voluntary socialising of the soul.* Saving faith is seeing God at work in the world and co-operating with Him for the kingdom. Redemption by Christian values must affect the super-personal forces (companies, industry, the State).

(c) *The Kingdom of God* must become central, is divine, founded by Jesus, miraculous all the way, a revelation of God's love and power, uniting religion and morality; present and future, always pressing in, inviting action and faith: "by accepting it as a task we experience it as a gift." The kingdom is "humanity organised according to the will of God", implying the freest development of personality, the progressive reign of love — abolishing coercion, penalties, want, war, exploitation, private ownership, monopoly. All theology must be reinterpreted with the kingdom as the theme, "the Christian transfiguration of the whole social order"; the church conserves religion only with a view to the wider kingdom of God in the larger life of humanity.

Despite the evangelical origin, and insistence upon the teaching of Jesus, one senses sometimes in the writing that something has been lost from the kingdom as Christ preached it. "Humanity organised according to the will of God . . . Christianity transfiguring the whole of the social order" are doubtless true and important definitions of the kingdom. Yet in Christ's presentation there was a personal relationship with a King who was also Father, obedience inspired by joyous, untroubled trust; faith resting not on an immanent force of righteousness making for socialisation, but in the personal care and providence of One who knows that we have need. In Jesus' thought of the kingdom, the love of neighbour remained secondary to love of God, and was not identified with it; the kingdom which would transform society began "within you". This is not to deny the truth which Rauschenbusch presses, but only to set it in context. The worship and spiritual training of the church is not only with a view to better economic arrangements in society. But it must be agreed, with Handy, that "no interpretation of Rauschenbusch can be adequate if it misses the fact that the centre of both Christian and socialist faiths was for him the life and teachings of Jesus Christ".[43]

(iii) Mathews

The suspicion that the Social Gospel had obscured the Christian message is levelled more often at Shailer Mathews, for whom (says Macquarrie[44]), the prophetic evangelical faith is replaced by "a sophisticated evolutionary theology." The individual is incomplete; he seeks union therefore with others, and with God, made possible by fundamental brotherhood, Fatherhood. Union with God works a moral change, the basis for progress towards brotherhood: Jesus is the decisive expression of these relations. Religion is social behaviour in which men seek to extend the kind of relations they have with each other to forces in the cosmic environment. The idea of God arises in this behaviour, and changes necessarily with social advance. But *God* is not a name for human ideals; He is a cosmic reality, and the right ordering of society depends on a true relation to Him; though the idea of God as Sovereign gives place to the idea of an immanent "power" in the universe which brings forth personality. Our relation with this God is not subjection, but co-operation. God becomes contemporary, and democratic. To be properly adjusted to "these cosmic activities we know as God," as "fellow workers in the process" is to be rightly adjusted to our fellows, and forward the ideal society.[45]

Later,[46] aware of criticism, Mathews finds the origin of the Social Gospel not only in the rise of sociology and in environmental, economic, insights but in "the application of the teaching of Jesus, and the message of salvation, to society, economic life, and social institutions." In New Testament times, the gospel promised membership in a social order, the kingdom of God, transcendental yet real: the pre-requisite was the social attitude of love.

The Social Gospel is opposed by those who merely wait for the Advent, those who think Christianity concerned only with abstract virtue, individual morality, atonement, salvation into heaven. "However, confidence in the ability of the gospel to present a way to social as well as individual salvation is rapidly increasing . . . The heart of the Social Gospel is in the teachings of Jesus as to the Fatherliness of God, the brotherhood of men, and the supreme worth of personality. It holds to the practicality of these truths: it believes God is working in human history. It does not forget that individuals need saving, but holds the gospel is equally applicable to group activities. Never a merely sociological presentation of humanitarian principles, the Social Gospel is the social application of the gospel of Jesus Christ.

Mathews appears to illustrate simultaneously the deviationist dangers and the genuinely evangelical motive of the Social Gospel.

(iv) Reinhold Niebuhr

"Heir to the prophetic and social passion of Rauschenbusch", "a child of the Social Gospel, though indeed a rebellious child"[47] Reinhold Niebuhr turned theology outwards upon the world, retaining social concern while rejecting optimistic liberalism (Macquarrie)[48].

Says Harland: "Niebuhr's entire thought has been motivated by one passionate concern — so to understand and present the historic Christian faith that its insights and resources might bring illumination and healing to the frightening problems and perplexities of our age." Much American theology was so exclusively about the situation addressed that it became part of the situation, lacking a transcendent vantage point from which to speak its judgement: Niebuhr achieved relevance by throwing the "offence" of the gospel into bold relief.[49]

As Rauschenbusch had found pietism inadequate to the slum life of New York, so Niebuhr, facing industrial depression in Detroit, turned from naive liberalism "to counter it with what came to be known as Christian realism."[50] Of the "coldly analytic approach" of *Moral Man and Immoral Society* (1932), Daniel Jenkins says: "In these bewildering times, when we have had to face so many cruel dilemmas . . . we have come to prefer our morality as untinged with emotion as possible. This makes us the more ready to discern a Christian objectivity, patience, and realism in these astringent pages."[51]

(a) Niebuhr is realistic about man, opposing to the current optimistic view the Christian doctrine of sin, which he sees as basically pride. Exaggerating his powers and status, man usurps the place of God, assuming himself secure against vicissitude, self-sufficient, judge of his own values, master of his own destiny. Sin is verifiably universal; the universal tendency to sin makes sin inevitable, though not *necessary* — man sins in freedom, and is responsible. Niebuhr denies that man is totally corrupt, which would make sin man's fate, destroying responsibility. Though finite, creaturely, sinful, man is a free spirit, able to transcend nature, to make history. As Selwyn says, Niebuhr "underlines the tragedy of man's predicament . . . and goes on to claim that Christianity alone can supply man's mundane activities with the principle of integration which they so manifestly need." Beach similarly describes Niebuhr's startingpoint: "it is in the Pauline-Augustinian description of the human predicament that Niebuhr finds the clue to the right reading of current human events."

Niebuhr thought the environmentalist and Marxist analyses less acute than the theological interpretation, which locates the fatal fault in the heart of man, in his proud attempts to order his universe around himself; and he spells out this classical view of man's situation with historical, political, and economic illustration. The Fall is a mythical expression of the deep sources of pride and self-centredness on every level of cultural, moral, and religious advance.

It is wrong, Harland argues, to hold that Niebuhr is "obsessed with sin" but he is clear-eyed, unsentimental. Bennett too points out that beside this emphasis, Niebuhr has a strong doctrine of the *imago Dei* and the availability of divine grace and forgiveness.[52]

(b) Niebuhr is realistic about society. "A sharp distinction must be drawn between the behaviour of individuals and of social groups", necessitating political policies which individualistic ethics must find embarrassing. Individuals may consider interests other than their own with sympathy, consideration, reason, objectivity. Such achievements are difficult, if not impossible, for social groups. In every group there exists less reason to check impulse; less capacity for self-transcendence; more unrestrained egoism. The book may be said to answer moralists who disregard political necessities in the struggle for justice; fail to recognise in man's collective behaviour elements which can never be brought under reason or conscience; and forget that collective power may be qualified by reason or conscience, but can never be dislodged except by power raised against it.[53]

Niebuhr's conclusion is sobering:

"The moral obtuseness of human collectives makes a morality of pure disinterestedness impossible. There is not enough imagination . . . (nor any) possibility of persuading any social group to make a venture in pure love . . . In such a situation (as ours) all the highest ideals and tenderest emotions . . . will seem . . . something of a luxury . . . Yet we are at least rid of some of our illusions . . . We cannot build our individual ladders to heaven and leave the total human enterprise unredeemed".

In that redemption the effective agents will be men who have substituted new illusions for abandoned ones: the most important, that collective life can achieve perfect justice. It is a valuable illusion for the moment; for justice cannot be approximated if the hope of perfect realisation does not generate a sublime madness in the soul; the illusion is dangerous because it encourages terrible fanaticisms. It must be brought under control of reason: "One can only hope that reason will not destroy it before its work is done."[54]

Scarcely the hope that has sustained the Christian generations.

(c) Niebuhr is realistic, therefore, about possible cures of society's ills. He emphasises the severe limits of *moral* choice in the international sphere; we must accept "proximate" solutions. Christian civilisation is beyond us: we must steer between a naive hope of reaching ideal society simply by persuading people to love, and the cynical rejection of love in favour of power or self-interest.

"Amid the moral ambiguities and power collisions of life on earth, the Christian can expect at best only a rough justice;" but responding to God's love in contrition, he can "make his way in faith through the traffic of compromised decisions with less self-righteousness, but no less conviction," to witness for the kingdom of God.[55]

Crucial among "proximate solutions" is acceptance of justice as the best possible expression of love. Society cannot live by absolute ideals: the "actualities" of group behaviour limit possibilities to practical options to which majorities can be persuaded or coerced. So, says Bennett,[56] "the key to Niebuhr's ethics is the dialectical relation between love and justice: justice embodies, but never completely fulfills, the requirements of love. Love widens the idea and application of justice, but it cannot be substituted for the institutions of justice". As Harland neatly summarises — love demands justice, negates justice, transcends justice, fulfills justice: justice without love ceases to be justice.[57] But to say that love is an impossible ideal for society is not to say it is superfluous; an impossible ideal retains relevance as the one inspiration which causes Christians to strive for maximum social justice.[58]

(d) Niebuhr is realistic about Christianity itself. Love is the Christian law of life, but not a programme for achieving an ideal social order. It is by the suffering love of the cross that man's pride, idolatry, even his "partial realisations of good", are to be judged. The cross of Christ is for Niebuhr the supreme revelation of grace, and of the sacrificial love which is the pinnacle of ethics. The love so shown illumines all experience; sacrificial, heedless, uncalculating, disinterested love is the norm of man's life. Man cannot make himself his own end: love, by including others, is his norm; it is *commanded* because it is not by nature his possession. "We see in the crucified Christ our own essential nature." In this way Jesus is the "key of meaning" to human experience, a symbol of the enduring power of love. Christianity itself is not a metaphysic, but a dramatic representation of abiding truth.[59]

But more: "It is in history that we meet the Christian revelation pointing us beyond the immanent factors of history to the divine grace that can overcome sin, complete what man cannot of himself complete, and make available new resources. God's gracious personal action in history cannot be demonstrated or analysed, but known only in personal encounters and their creative consequences. The humility and charity of true repentance, the absence of pride and pretension, must be the proofs that there has been an encounter with the only true God."[60]

Thus in the name of realism and experience, rather than of dogma, the more pessimistic estimate of man, especially of "man in the mass", survives in Christian ethics. The reality of sin finds emphasis in Niebuhr hardly less than in Jonathan Edwards. Nevertheless the world is neither to be abandoned nor despaired of: the Social Gospel remains the crown of Christian ethics, eclipsing merely personal perfection. The kingdom of God on earth remains the ideal — impossible of achievement, but essential as criterion, inspiration, and goal of all Christian endeavour.

(3) GERMANY

The application of the Christian message to social need, which marked a full century of Christian ethical thought, can of course be represented from the opposite point of view as an invasion of the pure gospel by earthly, materialist considerations: Kierkegaard warned that "what looked like 'Christianising' of the culture might also be conceived as a secularising and attenuating of true Christianity."[61] Secularism has since spread widely in theology, but the plea for a secularised ethic, a "religionless Christianity", is usually associated with Dietrich Bonhoeffer. Here again, the original approach was evangelical: but Bonhoeffer's passionate involvement with the social and political situation in Germany lent to his thought first a social emphasis, later a secularism, more thoroughgoing than any predecessor's. Bonhoeffer asks whether individualistic concern for personal salvation has not disappeared: righteousness, the kingdom of God on earth, is the focus of everything now. Whatever is above the world exists *for* this world; "no man has the mission to overleap the world and to make it into the kingdom of God."[62]

Bonhoeffer is not of course the only German Christian concerned with social ethics: Piper[63] mentions Martensen (1808-84) applying love and conscience to social problems; Wichern (1808-81) "proclaiming the church's inescapable obligation to come to the rescue of its needy, neglected, and sick members", and others. Both Brunner and Barth discuss social institutions that go back to creation. But Bonhoeffer most clearly presses the social gospel to its logical conclusion.

The orientation of Bonhoeffer's thinking constantly towards the contemporary situation in Germany, the fragmentariness of his surviving papers, and a stylistic obsession with paradox, all make interpretation difficult. He confesses of his *Ethics*, "my ideas were still in a raw state, anyhow" and elsewhere he admits that he is only "thinking aloud."[64]

What remains is but unrevised materials for a book; the editor arranges the latest edition under four possible "starting-points". Bonhoeffer lays down several different "points of departure" for Christian ethics.[65]

How Bonhoeffer would expect ordinary Christians to grasp his involved argumentation, and exactly how his own actions followed from his insights into the will of God, can only be conjectured.

Piper says Bonhoeffer's aim seems to be a Christian existentialism: "Ethical life is not so much a compliance with general principles . . . (as) life with God as He encounters us in our daily contact with non-Christians." Bonhoeffer shows an existentialist's abhorrence of abstractions (*goodness, principles*); an insistence that only life itself is good; that ethics has to do with real man, the real world, reconciled in the real Christ; Christian life is "real" life (one expects "authentic"), of "responsibility". Bonhoeffer, as Burtness says, was a situationist in that he saw the command of God as always concrete; but differed from some situationists in grounding his position specifically in Christ, and "building structures which . . . would provide corporate and historic dimensions to personal decision-making."[66]

(i) An "evangelical" trait is evident in four elements of Bonhoeffer's thought. (a) In his demand for discipleship costly in its obedience, utterly loyal to Christ, which shall attain true grace in becoming truly new — contrasted with discipleship loyal only to the church-institution, knowing only the "cheap grace" in orthodox belief and ritual. Within this demand is sounded already a call to secularisation, to a searching *reality* of experience, which all evangelicals understand.[67] (b) The same trait appears in a glowing passage of self-revelation:

"All we rightly expect from God is to be found in Jesus Christ . . . We must persevere in quiet meditation on the life, sayings, deeds, sufferings, and death of Jesus in order to learn what God promises and what He fulfils. One thing is certain: we must always live close to the presence of God, for that is newness of life: and then nothing is impossible . . . no earthly power can touch us without His will; danger can only drive us closer to Him . . . Our joy is hidden in suffering, our life in death. But all through we are sustained in a wondrous fellowship . . . that is the firm ground on which we stand."[68]

(c) Bonhoeffer shares the evangelical's concern to know the will of God. He contrasts the knowledge of good and evil which resulted from the Fall with the knowledge of God's will possessed by the "new" man, "the child of God living in unity with the will of the Father." No system of rules, or impulse of the heart, is sufficient: only in a knowledge, a life, continually renewed every morning, can I know the will of God, which is new in each situation.[69]

This "proving" of God's will springs from our being sustained, guided, within the union with God regained in Christ. To discover what pleases God in any situation, intelligence, discernment, attentive observation of the given facts, all come into lively operation, pervaded by prayer, with lofty self-control and careful assessment of possibilities and of consequences. No direct inspirations are expected: but "the belief that if a man asks God humbly, God will give him certain knowledge of His will". The "proving" must be accompanied by the doing — also only in Christ, without whom we can do nothing.[70]

(d) The evangelical trait is clearest in Bonhoeffer's penetrating treatment of the imitation of Christ — "undoubtedly of fresh and great significance."[71]

Bonhoeffer speaks much of man's being "conformed to the form of Christ" as that "form takes form in the world." Macquarrie interprets as "the form of Jesus Christ itself works upon us in such a manner that it moulds our form on its own likeness." Bonhoeffer wishes to avoid "efforts to become like Jesus;" to reject any thought of a system of rules, principles, examples, to which we must conform our outward life; and to insist upon a situational, existential discernment of what the "form" of Christ implies in any given circumstance. His view of imitation by "conforming to the form of Christ" is in fact very close to Paul's "having the mind of Christ."[72]

Bonhoeffer argues that amidst the complex relations of modern life, theoretic principles, duties, conscientiousness, are insufficient: only simplicity of vision and love for God will serve. To see with simple, undivided wisdom God and the world of reality, simultaneously, means seeing God and the world not as torn asunder but as one, *reconciled* in Jesus Christ. "Whoever sees Jesus Christ does indeed see God and the world in one. He can henceforward no longer see God without the world or the world without God."[73]

There follows an eloquent portrayal of Christ, as sole and living Redeemer, overcoming the world by love, willing to be guilty of our guilt; becoming *real* man, so rebuking both scorn of men and idolisation of men, and enabling us to become real men. He was sentenced, judged, executed — and ourselves in Him: for only as those upon whom sentence has been executed, do men achieve *their true form*, sentenced, executed, yet awakened by love stronger than death. Humanity *has been made new* in Jesus Christ: "mankind is still living the old life, but it is already beyond the old, already beyond death and sin." The man whom God has taken to Himself, sentenced, and awakened, is Jesus Christ, but in Him is all mankind: "only the form of Jesus Christ confronts the world and defeats it . . . From this form alone comes the formation of a new world, reconciled with God."[74]

"The formative forces in the world do not arise from Christianity . . . Practical Christianity is unavailing . . . (to reform the world). The word *formation* must be taken in a different sense. Scripture is not primarily concerned with forming a world by means of plans and programmes . . . only with the one form which has overcome the world, the form of Jesus Christ. Formation can come only from this form, so it is not a question of applying . . . the teaching of Christ: formation comes only with being drawn into the form of Jesus Christ — formation in His likeness — conformation with the unique form of Him who was made man, crucified, and raised again . . . Thus it is not Christian men who shape the world with their ideas, but it is Christ who shapes men in conformity with Himself."[75]

To be conformed with the Incarnate, transformed in His image — that is to be a real *man*. So the form of Jesus Christ takes form in man: what gives him the new form is always solely the form of Jesus Christ Himself. It is no vain imitation or repetition; nor is it a form alien to man; but the form Christ took in becoming man. It remains a mystery that only part of mankind recognise the form of their Redeemer; He bore the form of men as a whole, yet He can take form only in a small band — His church, hence called His body.[76]

The church is not a religious community, but Christ Himself who has taken form among those taken up by Him, and in them all humanity: "the church is nothing but a selection of humanity in which Christ has really taken form." She has essentially nothing to do with the "religious functions" of man, but with the whole man in his total existence in the world . . . with the form of Christ and its taking form amidst a band of men . . . To lose sight of this is inevitably to lapse into programme planning for the ethical or religious shaping of the world.[77]

So the point of departure for Christian ethics is the Body of Christ, and formation of the church in conformity with the form of Christ, the true form of mankind. The church is not the model for the world but, so to speak, the *anticipation* of the form of Christ intended for the whole world.

Christ is not a principle, or a legislator, but a real man like ourselves. Christ did not love a theory of good, but *men*; and God did not become an idea, programme, law, but *man*. So the form of Christ takes form in man, in many guises . . . Formation in conformity with Christ implies both that the form of Christ remains the same, and unique, as the incarnate, crucified, and risen God; and that the form of the real man is preserved, to receive the form of Christ.[78]

Such an emphasis leads away from abstract ethics to concrete situations and real men. Generalising Christian ethics has always failed. The "concretely Christian ethic" starts from the already accomplished reconciliation of the world, from the man Christ Jesus, and from the acceptance of real men by God. The west received the form of Christ as its spiritual heritage and basis of unity, but the Reformation broke the historical order asunder, resolving European unity into its constituents — the Body of Christ and the world.

The "two kingdoms" — the church ruled by the word, and the world ruled by the sword — should neither be mixed nor torn apart: the Lord of both is the God made manifest in Christ. But in Protestant Europe, this doctrine was taken to justify the autonomy of the "secular" kingdom; God was removed from the real world, and man "emancipated". In Roman Catholic Europe (through the French Revolution) anti-Christian "emancipation" produced rationalism, "The Rights of Man" (liberty, equality, fraternity), government by the "masses" and nationalism. In America, Puritanism, and the "kingdom of God" theology, created a "Christian" democracy. Failure to distinguish the offices of church and State led to secularisation; by "the loss of the unity possessed through the form of Christ, the western world is brought to the brink of the void." The only way back is by confession of the "defection from Christ, from the form which was ready to take form in us and to lead us to our own true form." Justification consists in the individual, and the church, becoming partakers of the form of Christ, judged, sentenced, awakened to new life, reconciled; and in the church, the whole western world.[79]

Here, clearly, the indestructible theme of the imitation of Christ is explored with new thoroughness, and used in a totally new and far-reaching way. Precisely *how* the uncomprehending world can be conformed with the form of Christ "through" the conformity of the church, and what the process yields for daily discipleship, is not in these draft papers made clear. But there is no question that Bonhoeffer has brought the original and unique element in Christian ethics back into the centre of modern discussion.

(ii) Bonhoeffer's second emphasis is very different. He felt keenly the gulf that divided the faith from the course of events in Europe — "the formative forces in the world do not arise from Christianity at all." One reaction was to blame the church for making Christianity a matter of "religious" experience, duty, preoccupation, separate from all other human concerns. The other reaction was to proclaim a secular "religionless" Christianity. Bonhoeffer refused "to carve up reality" — he would not let even "imitation of Christ" separate a man from "involvement in the pains and promises of God's world", which he so often described as "earth in which the cross of Christ is planted."[80]

Three fundamental insights control Bonhoeffer's thought about "secular Christianity".

God must no longer be dragged in to explain whatever scientific investigation has failed to elucidate — a deduction, a mere appendage to the world. He is the transcendent God who through Christ grasps men . . . at the centre of their lives. Man has learned to cope without recourse to God as a working hypothesis. Efforts made to prove to a world come of age that it cannot live without the tutelage of "God", Bonhoeffer considered pointless, unchristian. We have to live in the world as though God were not given — God is teaching us that we must live as men who can get along without Him. Man's religiosity makes him look to the power of God in the world; the Bible directs him to the powerlessness and suffering of God. God cannot be used as a stop-gap: He must be found at the centre of life, in *health, vigour, activity* — in no sense did Christ come to answer our unsolved problems: He is life's *centre.* "This must be the starting point for a worldly interpretation."[81]

The world must no longer be conceived as separate from God. In the New Testament, not man's falling apart from God is the basis of discussion, but the rediscovered unity, the reconciliation. The form of Christ overcomes the form of Adam. "It is precisely this 'disordered' world that in Christ is reconciled with God and that now possesses its true reality not in the devil but in Christ. The world is not divided between Christ and the devil, but solely and entirely the world of Christ." In Jesus Christ God and man, "secular" and "Christian", become one: in Christ, we see *humanity* as that which God has accepted, and see *God* in the poorest of our brothers. There is no relation to man without a relation to God, and no relation to God without a relation to man. "The really salient ethical fact for Bonhoeffer", says N. H. G. Robinson, "and the absolute centre of gravity for the Christian life . . .

are to be found . . . in the fact . . . that the world is always sustained, accepted, and reconciled, in the reality of God''.[82]

Goodness must no longer be divorced from the world, from life. To understand "good" as certain moral ideas to be applied to "life" destroys the unity: it is life, itself, which *is* good. And it suggests the existence of autonomous domains of life outside of goodness, and of Christ — which Bonhoeffer denies. "Good" is *reality itself*, seen in God. "The will of God is none other than the becoming real of the reality of Christ, in us and in our world." In Christ we are offered the possibility of partaking in the reality of God and the reality of the world, but not in the one without the other. Christian ethics enquires how the reality in Christ is taking effect; its purpose is, participation in the reality of God and the world in Jesus Christ today — such that I can never experience the reality of God without the reality of the world, nor the reality of the world without the reality of God.[83]

This view of God, the world, and goodness, is the basis of Bonhoeffer's insistence upon a "wordly", "religionless" Christianity. The "religion" here rejected is that in which the "sacred" is set apart from the rest of life, the "secular". The "world" here affirmed is the world already loved, judged, crucified, awakened to life, reconciled, in the incarnation, death and resurrection of Christ. "There is no part of the world, be it never so forlorn and never so Godless, which is not accepted by God and reconciled with God in Jesus Christ". Christ's Lordship sets creation free for the fulfilment of its own law, already inherent in it by virtue of its origin, goal and being in Jesus Christ.[84] So, *in a world which is Christ's*, "worldliness" is the Christian way. To regard Christianity as a religion of salvation *from* this world is a cardinal error: "this world must not be prematurely written off."[85] But the "worldliness" of Christianity is not "the shallow this-worldliness of the enlightened, the busy, or the lascivious . . . It is something in which the knowledge of death and resurrection is ever present . . . This is what I mean by worldliness, taking life in one's stride, with all its duties and problems, its successes and failures, its experiences and blessings. It is in such a life that we throw ourselves utterly into the arms of God and participate in His sufferings in this world . . . That is faith, that is repentance . . . what makes a man a Christian."[86]

Such "worldliness" gives no support to pious indolence which abandons the wicked world to its fate. Man is appointed to the concrete, limited responsibility which knows the world to be created, loved, condemned and reconciled by God, and acts within the world accordingly. Bonhoeffer elaborates this concept of responsible living within the world as living on behalf of others ("deputyship"), living in close correspondence with reality, and accepting the guilt and freedom of Christians within God's world.[87] At the same time, such "worldliness" does imply a "secular", "religionless" Christianity. The time of inwardness, of religion as such, is over; men cannot be religious any more. Religion is but the garment of Christianity; no *religious* act makes a Christian what he is, but participation in the suffering of God in the life of the world — that is, "to plunge himself into the life of a godless world, without attempting to gloss over its ungodliness with a veneer of religion; he must live a 'worldly' life, not being religious in any particular way, as sinner, penitent, saint, *but a man.*"[88]

For all this, it would seriously distort Bonhoeffer's position to forget how often in *Letters and Papers from Prison* he speaks of spiritual help afforded by "Paul Gerhardt's wonderful hymns"; of constant reading of the Bible, and his use of the text for the day and the Book of Prayers; of longing to share the eucharist with his friend; and of observance of the church calendar. If his Christianity did not consist in such things, it was certainly nourished by them.

The secular understanding of Christian life finds expression in living for others. The church must learn to lose itself in service, find itself in the salvation of the world. The Christian, looking to God for his inner life, must live in the world, like Jesus a man for others. "Whoever professes to believe in the reality of Jesus Christ as the revelation of God must in the same breath profess his faith in both the reality of God and the reality of the world, for in Christ he finds God and the world reconciled."[89] This is not to apply Christian principles to secular problems: it restores secularity to Christianity itself, seeking to recapture the original faith, as a way of life immersed in all the complex concerns of this material world.

How Bonhoeffer might have developed this radical restatement of Christian ethics must be gathered from brief summaries of certain other themes.

(a) Bonhoeffer rejects the tradition which divides reality into *two spheres* — nature and grace; the orders of this world with their own autonomy, and the law of Christ; sacred and profane. Such a view makes the cause of Christ one part within a total reality, other parts of which are outside the reality in Christ. Ethics then concerns the relation of these two spheres. In truth, the reality of Christ comprises the reality of the world *within itself:* there is only one sphere in which the reality of God and the reality of the world are united. That which is Christian is to be found only in that which is of the world; the "supernatural" only in the natural, the holy only in the profane. When the secular stands by itself, it falls victim to license and self-will; when Christianity withdraws from the world it falls victim to unnatural, irrational, presumption and self-will. All created things are through and for Christ, reconciled in Christ: all secular institutions (State, economy, family) are subject to Christ — but only *as secular,* in their genuine worldliness. The dominion of Christ over the secular is not an *alien* rule, but the true character of the secular within a world created, loved, and reconciled, through Him. In Christ the secular receives its rightful place, and is emancipated to be itself. "The purpose of the dominion of Christ is not to make the worldly order godly, or to subordinate it to the church, but to set it free for true worldliness."[90]

(b) Bonhoeffer distinguishes the *ultimate,* in which alone true Christian life, the life of Christ, is found; and the *penultimate,* where discipleship must be exercised, here, and now, where the preservation of order, and preparation for the coming of Christ, are provisional guide-lines. These guide-lines assume concrete form in certain moral orders or "mandates" of God imposed upon all men:

the mandate of labour, man's participation in the creation; human work, preparing for Christ;
the mandate of marriage, again sharing creation; also, in the family, the task of education; preparing for Christ;
the mandate of government, preserving what is created by human law, enforcing obedience, for the sake of Christ;
the mandate of the church, which enables Christ to become real in the preaching, organisation, and Christian life.

The mandates are divine in their origin and goal in Christ, not in themselves. (If any particular marriage violates the divine intention, it lapses into "relative justification.") Such mandates, preserving the order of the world for the sake of Christ, until the coming of Christ, will continue until the end of the world.[91]

(c) Bonhoeffer notes how loss of the concept of "natural", either to original sin, or to humanism, left Protestantism unable to offer counsel about the natural life; in a totally "fallen" creation natural and unnatural are equally damned. Yet "the natural is the form of life preserved by God for the fallen world and directed towards . . . redemption and renewal through Christ." In the living race, with its *natural reason* to guide, and its innate *will to preservation,* life is its own physician, in individual and community, and wards off the unnatural as always destructive of life in the end. "So long as life continues, the natural will always reassert itself." Life is both a means, serving other lives, and an end in itself. Attempts to make it only a means (to the social collective), or only an end, are alike destructive.

As an end, life possesses inherent *rights;* as a means, it bears also *duties.* The most general formulation of its rights is the law "to each his own" — the inherent right of each to what is natural to him, subject only to the rights of others. Bodily life has the natural right to —

preservation (housing, food, recreation, play, sex, joy);
safeguard from "arbitrary" killing (that is, of innocent life: the soldier, the

criminal, forfeit this by attacking other lives; the right of safeguard excludes euthanasia, suicide);
propagation (including choosing one's partner; the right of marriage is original — arbitrary limitation is unnatural; this right involves the right also of the life that is to come into being, a right not at the disposal of the married couple but inherent in life; this precludes abortion, deliberate childlessness, and sterilisation);
freedom of the body (precluding rape, torture, and slavery). Had Bonhoeffer's analysis been pursued, natural rights of mental life would have included the right to work, property, fellowship, piety, happiness, self-defence, and culture.

Bonhoeffer thus views nature as instinct with something very like "natural law", not in any autonomous fashion, but because nature is created and reconciled by *Christ*. Even in a fallen world it makes a difference whether a man observes or violates the order of marriage, acts justly or arbitrarily. "Whatever humanity and goodness is found in this fallen world must be on the side of Jesus Christ." Bonhoeffer can even take comfort in a natural law of righteousness: "The immanent righteousness of history rewards and punishes the deeds of men;"[92]

(d) To base the State *on the nature of man* destroys its authority over man. To hold that the State is *necessitated by the Fall,* to ward off chaos, precludes a Christian State. Both theories make the State a self-contained entity. Bonhoeffer asserts the basis of the State is Jesus Christ, as possessing authority over all things, reconciling all things (including the State). Government is divine in its being (however it came to be), and in its task (wielding the sword, executing justice). By its work, life is held open for Christ. It is divine also in its claim upon conscience (except where government invades Christian belief). Even an anti-Christian government is still in a certain sense *government* — but the ensuing discussion, against the background of German church-State relationships, is especially tortuous.[93]

Bonhoeffer manifestly leaves far behind the Calvinist dualism, and the "total depravity" of the world without Christ. We are to take with perfect seriousness the fact that Christ *did* reconcile the world to God. *It is therefore reconciled.* In it, here and now, we are to see the form of Christ taking form. Living responsibly *in* the world in "Christian worldliness", we are to be conformed to that form, within a world that has come of age within the total reality of Christ who loved, came, died, rose again, and is here, now, in the real world. We do not need to Christianise society after all: we must secularise Christianity.

How far Bonhoeffer's insights and challenges become part of the inheritance of the modern Christian, remains to be seen. N. H. G. Robinson[94] has suggested that one way forward from Bonhoeffer is that of Harvey Cox, in *The Secular City*. Cox sees in the emergence of the "technopolis", marked by anonymity, mobility, pragmatism and profaneness, an outlook authenticated in the Bible, a stage of liberation, maturity, responsibility, an adulthood to which Jesus calls men, "freed from infantile images . . . to face the world matter-of-factly." Robinson comments, the thesis is "that man has taken control of his own destiny, creates his own values, and tackles with his own technological skills his own problems; he is master of his fate . . . captain of his soul; to attempt to give to that thesis a theological grounding and authentication is simply to contradict it." The other way of developing Bonhoeffer's "worldliness" is in "situational ethics," which sees the modern Christian confronted by infinitely varied situations without rules, laws, principles, guide-lines or directions from the past, with only unfettered and unlimited openness to "love" to distinguish his response from that of other men.

Christian ethics during the modern period has travelled a long way from the position summarised by J. C. Wenger,[95] "*Evangelism* is the greatest commission Christianity can undertake in the area of social concern." With Puritans, Quakers, Wesley, the English evangelicals and American "Social Gospel" preachers in mind, it would be hard to justify the claim that such a stance, thus unqualified, was ever characteristic of evangelicalism. As the sixteenth and seventeenth centuries sought in a new direction for the gospel's moral authority in an inner light, so the nineteenth and twentieth centuries sought in a new direction for its application and expression, and found it in the life of the community. To a considerable extent, the social gospel represents an adjustment ethic, an adaptation of the New Testament, patristic, and mediaeval emphasis upon charity and Christlike service to the new political opportunities of democracy, and the new economic system of industrial capitalism. But there was also something new: the social gospel revealed a developing breadth and strength of conscience, and eventually a theology, of its own.

"As one group after another of the victims of social conditions and economic laws claimed the attention of Christian people, these have refused to allow such conditions and such laws any longer to operate . . . First of all, conscience insists upon providing all kinds of ameliorative measures, and utters itself in spasmodic protests against social evil. Next we have more positive and constructive attempts to reach a condition in which evils will not arise. Then follows a third period, of more deliberate thought and educational effort to grapple with the problem scientifically all along the line social evils begin to be felt as matters for deep penitence and reproach, and the possibility of social progress is increasingly identified with positive Christian faith and practice."[96]

Meanwhile, as Beach says, the "social gospel" came to mingle prophetic ideas of the Lord of the earth and of righteousness with immanentist and evolutionist ideas of God and of human progress. The "kingdom of God" theme conceived Jesus as Initiator, the church as means, Christian life as unflagging effort for its realisation. As to man, it recovered the solidaristic view of society, an optimistic view of human nature. A gradation between a *less* and a *more* Christian society replaced the dualism of City of God or City of Satan, sacred or profane, the saved or the world. The collective destiny of society replaced personal immortality as the goal ahead.[97] This trend is later countered by the attempt to restate theological concepts in *secular* terms.

Socialisation thus represents a wide, deep, far-reaching, shift of concern in Christian ethics. Doubtless something is lacking here of the personal warmth and joy of individual piety. As Piper says, part of the influence behind the shift of emphasis was Utilitarianism — "the overwhelming portion of ethical literature is now devoted to particular problems of social and international reforms, rather than to the problems of man's place in the world and its relation to God's Spirit."[98] Macquarrie's criticism is that in the end "we have not been given any single convincing answer to the question of what precisely is the relation of a religion to the society in which it is practised"; and he suggests that though religion is certainly a social activity, and socially conditioned, it is not to be identified with sociology.[99] Nor is a warning sounded by the Church Union in 1946 altogether out-of-date:

"The church is God's appointed instrument for saving mankind: but it is not her mission, nor within her power, to save the world on its own terms. She cannot offer salvation to nations or to individuals except upon the conditions of repentance. She cannot get society out of trouble which it has brought upon itself by its refusal to acknowledge the standards which she exists to proclaim. Nor is it her vocation to add moral force to social purposes in which religion is regarded as merely instrumental."[100]

That is well said. All the same, Christian ethics can never again forget the social implications of the gospel, even if changing political conditions should make Christian witness on social matters dangerous and costly. Christianity has finally left behind the ascetic repudiation of society; the indifference to social problems which is content to enjoy benefits without acknowledging responsibility; the naivety which proposes some single spiritual panacea for all the world's ills.[101] The Christian now recognises that this world, all human affairs and relationships, comprise the theatre in which he must work out his discipleship and live under the divine rule. He knows, once and for all, "that the one purpose worth striving after is the kingdom of *God,* and that no region of life . . . can be excluded from His sovereignty."[102]

16

Extraneous Influences

THE SOCIAL AND CULTURAL CHANGES of the last century have been so vast, rapid, complex, that merely to isolate those directly relevant to Christian ethics, as helping to shape the modern Christian conscience, is bewildering. It is *the* problem of twentieth century morality that the whole world has changed from that in which the Christian tradition was formulated. Christianity's ethical development has shown one element in its ideal derived from a revelation historically conditioned, divinely initiated, and to that extent absolute; and another element contributed by each generation's adjustments to current circumstances and to that extent relative. Already within the New Testament such an adjustment-ethic is plain, in changing attitudes towards slavery, marriage, mixed marriages, the State. The pagan environment, the "conversion" of the Empire, the break-up of Europe, the rise of industrialism, all wrought far-reaching changes in Christian emphases, while Justin, Clement, Ambrose, Aquinas, Erasmus, Calvin, Butler all sought to restate Christian morality in terms of prevailing intellectual fashion. Such continual re-adjustment is essential if Christian ethics is to remain relevant, as continual reformulation is essential if it is to remain intelligible: and such power of adaptation is the best evidence that at its heart lies enduring truth and the direction of the living Spirit.

1. THE SOCIAL CLIMATE

(i) Just how powerful is this adjustment-impulse within Christian ethics may be illustrated by its effect upon the most tenaciously conservative church, the Roman Catholic. The ill-effects of industrialisation upon the working classes, which stirred Protestantism's social conscience, evoked also one after another Papal Encyclical, from that of 1891, concerned with "the misery and wretchedness which press so heavily at this moment on the large majority of the very poor," through that of 1931 defending a controlled and charitable capitalism, to that of 1936 which condemned Communism as atheistic, materialistic, and destructive of personal freedom.

Private ownership was defended as a necessary incentive to work, and demanded by human need and dignity; but God's beneficence is for all; the social purpose of wealth must direct its distribution. Christian love demands united action to cure the malfunctioning of the socio-economic order, and to defend the lonely and the poor. Leo XIII expounded the principles of the living wage, the protection of child-labour, and Trade Unionism. Pius XI explored the Christian limitations of capitalism, demanding charity as well as justice; he also (against collectivism) argued that the State, based on man's social nature and God's authority, must never become an end in itself, depriving individuals of God-given rights. John XXIII urged the church is concerned with the temporal order, and drew attention in detail to areas especially depressed; the need for international action in technical and financial aid; problems of world peace, on the bases of the inviolable rights of persons, and international brotherhood. The rights include: life, bodily integrity, things requisite to truly human existence, respect, freedom, truth, culture, opportunity, work, economic initiative, worship, assembly and association, freedom of movement, public action, justice, social and racial equality — with corresponding duties towards others. The divine authority and moral order of the State are again defended. Political unities must likewise manifest truth, justice, liberty, equality. The common good of individual States cannot be divorced from the common good of all men; there is need for wide collaboration in problems of population, land, capital, and the diverting of arms expenditure towards constructive purposes. World community, and the universal common good, are the ultimate goals pursued by men "acting in the light of faith and with the strength of love."[1]

In such reaction to contemporary circumstances the Roman church shows perhaps more awareness of the external world than at any time since the Counter-Reformation; nor is this sensitiveness seen only on social issues. J. P. Scull SJ speaks[2] of extensive "renewal and reform" in Catholic moral theology, with emphasis no longer upon outward observance but upon "the inner dynamism of God personally coming to us and being one with us in forgiving love"; and on morality as not an obedience to impersonal regulations but personal dialogue between God and the individual in concrete situations. Sin is failure of response to God's love; and conscience resumes its traditional place in Christian ethics, for by it God's requirements are known, as the individual forms his judgement according to objective Christian truth. God speaks to conscience as *the God Who made man* in His own image, through the law of nature; as *the God of salvation,* through the teaching of Christ in scripture, and the church; and as *the God who through the Spirit guides* each individual, by "movements of the Spirit in the depths of each person as he faces the unique moments and situations of his life." The law of Christ is primarily internal, too, as God's love given us through Christ tends to express itself in our love to God and men.

The external laws of Christian life direct that internal, spontaneous love towards desirable ends. If the inner life be egoist or sensual, we experience external law as restrictive, contrary, the occasion of temptation, sin, and death. Valid moral laws express God's nature and win the Christian's consent. Natural law is the demand arising from the dignity of one made in God's image. Divine positive law is direct revelation; human positive law (liturgical and disciplinary laws, for example, of relative value, and civil justice) is made by a human legislation, with divine authority. All laws need concrete application: it is necessary to evaluate by conscience the good intended by the law, and how in given circumstances that good will best be achieved. All ethical relationships, with Christ and with Christians, flow from the dynamic of personal faith, animated with love directed by inner grace, nourishing prayer, meaningful participation in the sacraments, and obedience to the church as to Christ — though with "varying degrees of certitude."

It is not hard to recognise here, in the most "institutional" of churches, the modern preoccupation with psychological processes, a reaction parallel to the Protestant search for inward authority; and democratic emphasis upon discipline by consent. In the same way, the long-held tradition of "the just war" has yielded to soul-searching and disagreement in the face of nuclear weapons — which Pope John XXIII condemned. The whole of "Roman Catholic social doctrine . . . in face of modern dilemmas in regard to world peace, demands that Christians strive . . . for an international world organisation." Even the Roman doctrine of sacramental marriage, based upon thorough analysis of man's sexual nature, human love, family life, natural law and revealed intention, has yielded to modern pressure "now through the aid of the new knowledge provided by science in union with theology and philosophy, the church is seeking a deeper understanding of . . . possible legitimate means of birth-regulation."[3]

(ii) No less significant, as illustrating the adjustment-motive in unlikely places, are changes in Orthodox ethics. Already in the early twentieth century some relaxation was accepted in Orthodox marriage laws, especially with regard to the "prohibited degrees" and the possibility of divorce.[4] Stahlke recalls[5] that history had taught Orthodoxy both endurance and compliance, and adds that the

Russian church has been subjected to "persecution as massive as earlier catastrophes." Yet Berdyaev opposed the reduction of individual personality to the mere instrument of policy, the sacrifice of justice to power. Ashanin holds[6] that to oppose this Communist view "which disregards man as . . . a self-motivating agent . . . whose inherent value and justification for existence lie within himself" and sees him only as the "instrument of a social system", is the most important concern of contemporary Orthodoxy.

Such opposition reaches a climax in relations with the Soviet State and its claim, not to the divinely ordained "diaconate status" afforded in traditional Orthodox doctrine, but to absolute value and power. At one time the Russian church reacted by excommunicating Communists; the prevailing adjustment is to assert once more the doctrines of *kenosis* and willing acceptance of oppression, in the deep faith that "the gates of hell shall not prevail" against the church: her duty is not to fear, or to fight, but to convert the State to its diaconal character. "The novel thing in the modern Eastern Orthodox approach to the problem of the State is that it has ceased to look upon any particular form of government as the one to which the church should be committed . . . Any form of government could receive the charisma of the diaconate, so far as the church is concerned, provided the State divest itself of the myth . . . of absolute power." The eastern church has learned that "demonic elements" may infect any form of government — even monarchy, which, traditionally, Orthodoxy supported. The acceptance of a diaconal role under God is more important than the pattern of government itself.

(iii) Meanwhile, with widening democracy, one side-effect of the Social Gospel has been the emergence of the "political Christian." Men and women who first learned their social idealism, ability to persuade, first lessons in organisation, within the churches carried social concern beyond amelioration and protest to agitation and political involvement, sometimes losing patience with the churches, sometimes using labels like Christian Socialist, Christian Democrat, to witness to their deepest motivation. The significance of this development for Christian ethics lies in the absence of traditional directives for the unprecedented opportunities afforded by universal franchise and representative democratic decision. For such responsibilities Christians have on the whole been unprepared. The role of an "elite minority" is hardly more effective than an aloof separation from public life, but the strong suspicion entertained by Christians towards political methods and manipulation of power, together with the necessity of appeal to the widest taste and opinion if any policy is to succeed, inhibit more active participation in politics. Few are happy at attempts to impose Christian ethical standards by law upon the unchristian majority. If government by Christians only is mere wishful fantasy, there appears no alternative but unworthy compromise of Christian with non-Christian in a scramble for power. Many Christians remain conscious, nevertheless, of a real share in blame for the deterioration of social life, persuaded that within democracy all — Christians included — eventually get the kind of government the majority deserve.

(iv) Scientific advances likewise create for the Christian conscience, along with innumerable and invaluable benefits, a whole series of unprecedented problems. Medical science has presented immeasurable posers in the development of organ transplantation with its attendant problems of the determination of death, the right to one's own bodily organs, the source of authority for decisions involving life or death — with another individual's life at stake. Another facet of the same issue is the heart-breaking responsibility of euthanasia, and the withdrawal of life-support from the senile. The prolongation of life by medical prowess has complicated the imbalance of population and resources, creating new problems of family limitation, whether by birth-control or by abortion, with a score of ethical and social difficulties implied in each. Various methods of contraception, of abortion, and of genetic manipulation, have raised a host of novel moral questions for which, again, neither scripture nor Christian tradition offers any direction, other than a tentative and debatable extrapolation from "general Christian principles" to totally untried ethical situations.

Other scientific achievements have accompanied much good with new challenges to the Christian conscience related to conservation and weaponry. Industrial exploitation of limited natural resources, and consequential spoliation of natural beauty and other living species, for the sake of material progress, pose new, far-reaching questions about comparative human values, and the kind of world — the kind of life — one generation bequeaths to its successors. New, too, is the difference made for Christian ethics by the development of modern scientific weapons, a difference well expressed by Bonhoeffer:

"Total war makes use of all conceivable means which may possibly serve . . . national self-preservation . . ." Western wars have always distinguished means which are permissible and those prohibited and criminal. Belief in a just, divine government of the world made it possible to dispense with unchristian practices. "War remained a kind of appeal to the arbitration of God . . . When Christian faith is lost, man must himself make use of all means, even criminal ones, in order to secure by force the victory of his cause." In place of chivalrous war between Christian peoples, directed towards unity in accord with God's judgement in history, there comes total war, in which everything is justified, and the enemy is treated as a criminal.[7]

Many who, reluctantly, found complete pacifism difficult to maintain in a world where evil arms itself efficiently, have now become persuaded that no consideration of "the lesser of two evils," "the balance of justice," "holding back another Dark Ages that the light of reason and truth may yet have a chance," can justify aerial bombardment of open cities, nuclear, bacteriological, nerve-destroying arms, or the various other refinements of cruelty which science has placed at the disposal of modern "civilisation". Adjustment of the Christian ethic in this realm is confused, uncertain.

R. H. Bainton says that when we appraise the traditional Christian ethic of war we must remember that the situations in which it was conceived no longer exist. "The development of technology and the dehumanising of war have progressively excluded middle courses and narrowed the range of choice." Bainton then gives examples of hesitant, contradictory, unrealistic statements of Christian commissions and spokesmen since 1950.[8]

But this confusion is only one example of the whole urgent problem facing modern Christian ethics — the disclosure, by the current explosion of knowledge, of the inadequacy of its traditional positions, in scripture and in theology, to provide solutions to problems wholly new.

(v) Behind political and scientific changes lies the cultural atmosphere of the modern world. Already in 1912 Rauschenbusch complained that the Darwinian theory had proved welcome justification of things as they were —

"It is right and fitting that thousands should perish to evolve the higher type of the modern business man! Those who are manifestly surviving in the present struggle for existence can console themselves . . . they are the fittest, there is no contradicting the laws of the universe. Thus an atomistic philosophy crowds out the Christian faith in solidarity. The law of the cross is superseded by the law of tooth and nail. It is not even desirable to 'seek and to save the lost,' because it keeps the weak and unfit alive."[9]

Nothing that has happened since 1912 has undermined that popular assumption of evolutionary determinism, materialist mindlessness plus chance — an amoral universe which denies all meaning in nature and history. We are required to assess each individual solely by his contribution to the wealth of the collectivist whole, in the long march towards an ideal future which no actual generation must ever suppose they shall see.

One insidious element in this new climate of culture has been the dwarfing of man. "The universe in which man lives has withdrawn its roof and walls at the magic touch of astronomy; a not less bewildering perspective of man's origin in opened up by the combined labours of geology and biology."[10] Even man's space-triumphs, while adding considerably to human pride, have not left him feeling any more at home in the vastness of the galaxies, nor renewed at all his lost sense that his life, behaviour, and struggle *matter* to the destiny of the cosmos. Meanwhile, the growth of the collective State — "the insect society" — and the deterministic view of man's inner life adopted by much modern psychology, have helped to reduce still further man's sense of dignity, responsibility, and freedom, and to release a naturalistic sensualism which threatens to engulf his spiritual capacities.

A second insidious element in the new climate is secularism, naturalistic in outlook, neglecting the super-natural, usually anti-religious in tone, anthropocentric in concern, impatient with long views either backward or forward. The so-called "secular theologies", advocating a secular Christ, secular salvation, a secular conversion, and a secular future, were symptomatic of a tone of society that has become general, almost unconscious. On Christian ethics, it had the effect on the one hand of isolating Christian moral standards from those prevailing in society — especially concerning sex, marriage, divorce, homosexuality, gambling, alcohol and drugs, business ethics, and the use of violence to obtain political ends. On the other hand, in the secular climate Christians themselves have been forced to re-examine the grounds of their own morality, and have been surprised sometimes to discover how *religious* those grounds are.

The usual designation of secularist ethics — "Humanism" — is appropriate just so far as it indicates its concern with human interests only, with man as the measure of things, and with forces of redemption and progress within man himself. The popular definition of Humanism — "human control by human effort in accordance with human ideals" — is both over-optimistic and plagiarist. After the experiences of the twentieth century it is futile to ask modern men to place their faith in man: "few pages are more tragic, or more grotesque" wrote De Burgh, "than those which record the effort of civilised Europe during the last two centuries to wrest the idea of humanity from its other-worldly foundations and to base a humanistic gospel on the progress of civilisation and the perfectibility of human nature."[11] Maritain summarises the Humanist generation's sad experience, "To offer man only what is human is to betray him . . . for by the principal part of him, which is the mind, man is called to something better than a purely human life;" and Berdyaev warns, "Human life becomes truly terrible when there ceases to be anything above man . . ."[12]

Experience apart, the so-called "human ideals" turn out to be, not "human" but *Christian* — with Christ subtracted. Humanism originates no new ethical vision, no new moral goal, no new virtues, no new ethical resources. When it is not merely reiterating ideals patently borrowed from the gospel, without their theological or historical validation, it reduces "virtues" to "the specifically human qualities of strength which are implicit in man's psycho-social evolution." Thorough-going Humanism regards morality as essentially "the cruel conscience, the moralistic Super-Ego" — "a makeshift developmental mechanism" — and holds that "to the evolutionist, ethics can no longer be regarded as having any absolute value."[13] Faced with such a rival, Christian ethics need only accept with gratitude this fresh testimony to the intrinsic humanness of Christian ideals, and demonstrate ever again its unique superiority among all ethical systems — its power to regenerate and sustain the ethically desperate.

Secularism, however, has discovered that it has not the last word. The twentieth-century resurgence of older faiths, and the increasing intermingling of races from Africa and Asia in the society of Europe and America, have evoked new awareness of religion itself, as an ancient and varied phenomenon of human life; and with that, growing understanding that the ethical teaching of all faiths is not after all the same. Moreover, while the "grey and colourless world of secularism" (Inge) is ever unfriendly to Christian morality, signs are accumulating that society's confusion, helplessness, and fear, are causing second thoughts about the supposed "irrelevance" and "obsolence" of religion. The widespread call for better moral education of the young, for a moral basis for social control, and for a new quality of life with moral foundations and goals, has found both science and political wisdom wanting. Some educationists, psychologists, even politicians, have begun publicly to include "the decay of religion's hold upon the people" among the causes of contemporary social malaise. In so short a time is secularism already proving ethically bankrupt: therein lies some hope of a new evaluation of Christian ethics.

Meanwhile, adjustment of Christian ethics to prevailing conditions reaches its limit here. Neither scientific materialism, evolutionary naturalism, nor atheistic secularism, are compatible either with the presuppositions or with the goals of Christian ethics. The contrast is too violent, the contradiction too obvious. The Christian moralist must in the end show not only adaptability but fidelity, conviction, and patience.

The same must be said (equally summarily) of those philosophical theories which have not so much influenced Christian ethical thought as collided with it. Modern empiricism, finding all truth only in what may be verified (at least in principle) by sense experience, reduces all ethical statements either to anthropological statistics ("most people have admired, or do admire, justice; most people have rejected, or do reject, cruelty"); to emotional reactions ("justice — clap! clap! cruelty — tut! tut!"); or to propaganda ("justice — let all practise it! cruelty — let all avoid it!") On this view, no ethical statement expresses a fact, or makes any contribution to knowledge. Since it cannot "predict" the *sense* experience by which such a "factual meaning" could conceivably be verified, as a factual statement it would be literally meaningless — since the meaning of a statement (on this view) lies in the means by which it could be verified. With this, as with all its positivist, linguistic, elaborations, Christian ethics cannot adjust, but only reject the subjectivist presuppositions entirely. To other philosophic developments over the last two centuries, however, Christian moral theory owes much that has helped to shape the Christian conscience, and Christian ethical language, sometimes quite unconsciously.

2. THE ETHICAL CLIMATE

(i) As Rauschenbusch remarked,[14] "the Reformation began to free the mind and to direct the force of religion towards morality": the former effect may be seen in the rise of secular philosophy; the latter, in the emergence, for the first time in Europe for over a thousand years, of a non-religious ethic. The exploration of human nature as the basis of autonomous morality, that appealed in Kant to moral reason, in Butler to natural conscience, in Hume to a natural propensity towards benevolence, in Hobbes to the principle of self-love, all in place of scripture, evangelical experience, or divine law, influenced Christian ethics deeply. Partly, by provoking reaction, but in part also by contributing analyses and concepts which Christian morality borrowed, adjusted to, or sometimes rediscovered within itself. In particular, the Christian conscience, as it faces the problems posed by the last quarter of the twentieth century, has absorbed something, at least, from each of five different "schools" of secular ethics.

Hedonism has usually repelled moralists, the search for "pleasure" scarcely yielding a moral ideal; yet as Sidgwick recognised, it is an inevitable element in any complete system of ethics that the end at which we aim should offer some satisfaction.[15] Unlike mediaeval Christians and extreme Puritans, most contemporary Christians are hedonist enough to expect happiness, joy, "the highest satisfaction" as reward for dedication — even if they translate "pleasure" into "bliss" or "blessing." R. W. Dale's stern insistence that "God's great end is not our happiness but our perfection" shocks modern Christians, who interpret the love of God as divine concern to shelter, comfort, and reward the good, unaware how heretical such an idea would seem in the age of martyrdoms or the theology of the cross.

As *Utilitarianism,* for which morality lies in seeking the greatest happiness for the greatest number, hedonism has provided intellectual support for social concern, and a new definition of sin as "anti-social behaviour". It also engendered a pragmatic view of morality — what is claimed as right, good, obligatory, must be justified by its fruits, the removal of some evil, the increase of some "satisfaction". Truth, beauty, Christianity itself, must be seen to "work", must be proved "relevant" by social usefulness, by increase of wealth, welfare, or enjoyment. Nothing henceforth is intrinsically good: it has to be good "for" someone or something.

Despite continuing suspicion of *evolutionary theory* as sufficient explanation (or even description) of the processes of life, or of the emergence of ethics within human culture (Spencer), the notion of development has entered deeply into Christian ethics. Some such view as that of Julian Huxley,[16] that the process of biological evolution becomes self-consciously purposive in the ethico-social striving of personality and community, would probably be shared, in vague half-conscious ways, by most modern Christians. But for Christians, the "current of things" is the immanent purpose of the living God; the end-stage is the goal which God has set; the stages on the way are by no means inevitable steps in automatic progress, but gains painfully, falteringly made by costly commitment, agonising decisions, struggle and sacrifice, sustained by the grace of Christ. Even so, the forward look is inherent now in Christian ethics, together with the assumption that man is part of nature (with all that implies, for example for sexual morality), one with the evolving world, participating in the unfinished creation of the world, himself still uncompleted.

Consonant with this notion of an end-result was the idealist *perfectionism* which saw mind or "spirit" as the clue to the nature of reality, and the "realisation of the highest self" — "working out the brute" — as the goal of ethics. Lower, narrower selves must give place to the more rational, more inclusive, self in its moments of deepest wisdom and insight. To become what implicitly we already are, is to achieve self-fulfilment. It is not far to the Christian theme of the old man's dying in order that the new man might come to life.

Consonant too with the teleology implicit in evolutionary ethics is the emphasis upon the purposive nature of human behaviour.[17] All truly human conduct is directed towards ends which are pursued for the *value* they possess. The values which direct behaviour form a system or "hierarchy" in which the narrower, more temporary, more limited and superficial, are subordinated to the wider, more permanent, inclusive, and intrinsically more human or spiritual — a scale of values according to which all actions and decisions may be "evaluated" ethically. It is not difficult to transmute this scale of values, also, into a gradation of Christian duties, virtues, or fruits of the Spirit of steadily widening, more spiritual, and more demanding, importance as they move from personal to social goals, and culminate in the kingdom and the glory of God.

(ii) Something of each of these secular themes has been adopted by Christian ethics, if only to rephrase its own insights. It might appear that Christianity would find nothing at all in *existentialism* sufficiently compatible to make borrowing possible.[18] Complete openness to the future, "nihilating" (suspending) the past with its traditions and directives, so as to leave absolute freedom to create — "invent" — the future by new, unguided decisions, as each situation reveals its need, appears to imply an ethic without law or principle — a freedom whose only norm is the transcendence of all rules — acknowledging neither status, function, or authority in Christian tradition and the Christ-event. Some existentialists, moreover, gained a reputation for defiant atheism and libertinism. For all that, existentialism has contributed to the modern Christian conscience, and its main inspiration, Kierkegaard, for all his independence and his criticism of the church, was a Christian.

Kierkegaard defies brisk summary.[19] Emphasising the distinctiveness of Christian morality, he sought to define Christianity in ethical rather than theological categories. "The only reality that exists for an existing individual is his own ethical reality" — to every other reality he stands in but a *cognitive* relation, and man is more than cognitive. A "believer" is one who is infinitely interested in another reality — God's reality as a particular, individual, human being — named in Christ. Only by being *before God* can a man entirely come to himself.

Kierkegaard distinguished *(i) aesthetic life,* marked by self-interest, happiness, pleasure, security, following the crowd, speculation, and drifting — which is inauthenticity; *(ii) ethical life,* marked by decision, earnestness, concern, freedom, relation, responsibility; *(iii) religious life,* marked by the sense of sin, and estrangement from God, suffering, forgiveness, faith, which place aesthetic and ethical living into a new perspective.

Only life in accordance with truth is authentic living; and to *be* the truth is the only true explanation of what truth is. Christ was the truth; not a sum of sentences, a definition of concepts, but a *life.* Always the truth consists not in knowing but in being: the truth becomes a life in me. Hence Christ wants not admirers, or adherents of a doctrine, but followers of a life. The follower aspires to *be* what he admires: thus only followers are Christians.

So, Christianity's requirement is. "Thy life shall, as strenuously as possible, give expression to works, and then admit, 'None the less, I am saved by grace'." God desires to be in relation to me, and so desires the thanks and adoration which are "in spirit and in truth": namely, imitation. Imitation must be introduced to induce humility; everyone must be measured by the Pattern, the ideal standard, never to be lowered. To be a disciple, imitation, not merely instruction, is required. Christ Himself lived in humiliation lest any should say that our Pattern possessed earthly advantages, placing the imitation-ideal beyond our reach.

In essence, such faith imitating Christ will be known by love. Love is neither feeling, nor "a full heart", but *work* — "sheer action", grounded in God's love. Christianity requires such love towards the neighbour, the whole race, enemies, without partiality or dislike. Only in loving the neighbour does one learn what is meant by loving "as thyself". But love to God is the decisive issue: if you love God above all else, then you also love your neighbour, and in your neighbour every man. Christianity always turns attention inward, making each relationship with other men a God-relationship. From the Christian standpoint, a man has ultimately to do only with God; when you love your neighbour, you resemble God.

From such emphases, upon "authentic" living, and truth known only in life, as before God — among many others — sprang most existentialist insights, whether atheistic or religious in tendency. Existentialism rejected the abstract theorising of philosophic schools to affirm the priority of "real life", authentic existence, in contrast with the shadowy thought-existence of mere spectator-philosophers. "Man is nothing else but what he makes himself: that is the first principle of existentialism" (Sartre).

Things exist only chaotically, and for man, when man experiences them; *man* begins to exist, "lives existentially", when he faces life's inevitable choices with fundamental earnestness, confronting each crucial situation as free, alone, responsible, choosing his own set of values and his own goals in the full freedom of self-determining spontaneous decision, totally engaged and committed to the fullest possible personal action. Man is nothing else but what he purposes, chooses, makes himself by his decisions, creating himself moment by moment, unbound by past or future, by systems, rules, obligations. To have to choose thus, without guidelines, is absurd, but life *is* absurd: that is man's anguish, creatureliness, and doom.

So man is not to be fitted into moulds that abstract philosophising constructs for him, or social convention, or (so especially Jaspers) industrialisation, or the collectivist State. He must continually realise himself in free, responsible decisions, refusing to be generalised, or submerged. Though this may tend towards an extremely subjectivist, individualist, attitude, in practice either theological or Marxist presuppositions form a bridge to social ethics.[20]

Such emphasis upon absolute freedom of choice represents autonomy in ethics at its highest: the individual "authenticates himself by a bare act of will," compelled to choose for himself even the ends, rules, and obligations with which he freely consents to be bound — or to ignore: and to do this afresh in each decision.

Kierkegaard stressed that a man should act responsibly apart from the crowd, as an individual hearing the eternal voice of conscience. Heidegger saw man finding authenticity by assuming responsibility for direction of his own life rather than permitting himself to be determined by external factors, Kuhn comments that authenticity, seems to connote individual integrity, self-reliance. Sartre stressed man's contingency, futility, disposability, absurdity: but the man who accepts the anguish of unguided free choice may achieve himself and his values. Sartre accepts responsibility: the norm of freedom is so to act as to let others be free while oneself remaining free. Existentialists make much of the anguish of finiteness, the certainty of death, the futility of hope: life is contradictory, paradoxical — rational systems of thought are useless academic exercises. Man in authentic existence faces "the sting of the real." Heidegger insisted man is "thrown into" the world lacking cosmic meaning, finite, vulnerable, mortal; he must accept anxiety, ambiguity, estrangement, especially mortality, without complaint or self-deception, and "live towards death." Camus and others place the absurdity in man's own moral folly.[21]

In such an outlook, ethical decision has become the very meaning of existence. The individual discovers his own authenticity by involvement, commitment, which is not theoretical or credal only, but a subjective, inward engagement of the responsible self, in which thought, decision, action interpenetrate, and man affirms his values through free creative self-assertion. That such a view is open to damaging criticism is clear; but that it has deeply infiltrated Christian ethical thought is equally plain. W. W. Paul mentions Jaspers, Marcel, Barth, Brunner, Bonhoeffer, Bultmann, Tillich as in various ways influenced by Kierkegaard, in particular by his making central "the Christ who becomes contemporary in man's act of existential faith".[22]

The existential emphasis upon commitment, engagement, involvement — upon active participation contrasted with merely holding religious opinions — is now a Christian commonplace. It is wholly biblical. Detached observation of life, the spectator-role, is promised no discovery of truth, or blessing; Christ is much more concerned with man *being* than with man *thinking,* and Christian truth is revealed in encounter and action, not in argument. It is equally scriptural to see man as not merely a reflective mind but a responsible agent acting in spiritual freedom, making himself what he becomes as he chooses right or wrong in each ethical confrontation of daily life. It is no less true that man is finite, creaturely, mortal, vulnerable, lost in his aloneness; and that it is the beginning of moral wisdom to accept that predicament and fashion in it a way to victory and to God. Biblical, again, is the contention that God is encountered in experience, not contemplated afar off — He is met as Subject, not studied as an Object, and known not by intellectual analysis but in obedience. If these insights have been reiterated in mid-century Christian ethics until they now seem obvious, that is a measure of the influence which existentialism has wielded, countering the comarative detachment of Kant, Butler, Hume, and even of Maurice and Rauschenbusch. In so many directions has Christian ethics come to terms with the changing climate within ethical philosophy.

(iii) Nevertheless, perhaps the greatest change has been the new status accorded to ethics within Christianity itself. In place of the doctrinal preoccupations of the early centuries, the ecclesiastical and political struggling that ensued, the concentration upon soteriology that followed the Reformation, in the late nineteenth century ethics moved to the very centre of the stage, not only as the inspiration of the social gospel, but as itself the essence of the Christian message, the strongest basis of theological faith. Followers of Kant centred interpretation of religion on the idea of moral value, seeing in "axiology" — the science of values — the true field of philosophy. Following this clue, Ritschl built Christian theology on a philosophy of value, for example substituting for the traditional affirmation of the Godhead of Christ the proposition that "Christ has for us the value of God." Metaphysics, dogma, Ritschl held, were distortions of religion, which was concerned essentially with ethics: theological statements are not assertions of fact but value-judgements.[23]

"The religious estimate of the historical Christ as God perfectly revealed arises from the ethical estimate of Christ's moral perfection; the aim of the Christian religion is the realisation of the kingdom of God, both the highest religious good and the moral ideal for men." Christianity is the highest form of religion because it is absolutely ethical. Ritschl sees Christ especially as Founder of the kingdom, which comes into being wherever Christlikeness prevails. The goal of Christianity, the purpose of the church, is the *transformation of society* by love — the highest form of righteousness.[24]

Among Ritschl's considerable followers, some were prepared to dismiss as fictions the *statements* of Christianity about Christ, the kingdom, immortality, believing that their value as ethical incentives would remain unimpaired.

For Hoffding the function of religion is to encourage the moral life; religious ideas are not explanations but evaluations. Religion is based upon ethics, conservation of value is the axiom, of which all dogmas and myths are but symbols. Herrmann followed Ritschl in repudiating metaphysics, laying all stress upon moral values: "Christian doctrine is only understood as the expression of a new personal life", the "inner life" of Jesus laying hold on us. It is our inner moral conviction realised in Christ that finds expression in the confession of Christ as God.[25]

But probably the greatest disciple of Ritschl was Harnack.[26] Harnack retained his hold upon the historical revelation of God in Christ, but still saw religion as essentially practical, a holy life its chief aim, doctrine best reduced to a minimum. By concentrating on dogma, the church obscured the heart of Christianity, which in Jesus' own teaching consists of the Fatherhood of God, the infinite worth of the soul, the ethical ideal of the kingdom. "The essence of Christianity is therefore the ethic of Jesus in its theistic setting." Christ is Example and Hero; Christian life is achieved by following His teaching, realising the kingdom of brotherhood and love.

Here, for the first time in Christian history, ethics, not doctrine, is made fundamental. Before long, the basic doctrines were being deduced from the ethic. Kant set the example, insisting that belief in God, freedom, immortality, found justification in the *practical* reason, as necessary postulates without which the moral imperative is unintelligible. Following Ritschl's contention that our recognition of the divinity of Christ was itself a value-judgement, the argument broadened into a general approach to problems of theism from the facts of moral experience and the insights of the moral consciousness.

Rashdall defends the validity of moral *knowledge* (as more than feeling, taste) and the implication that the universe in which this knowledge arises must therefore have moral quality; a moral ideal must objectively exist, in God. Only so could varying moral opinions be tested; and only upon such an objective moral standard could *obligation* rest.

Sorley analysed purposive behaviour as implying a scale of values rational and objective — "Both postulates (the objectivity of reason and the objectivity of value) proceed from the purposive life of man as demands of the will" if life is to be coherent. We apprehend the world by reason *and* value: only as we posit a mind behind nature which is the source alike of reason and value is man's rationality and value-judgement vindicated. Such a source is "a personal God, who is both the creator of the universe and the . . . bearer of value . . ."

Taylor held likewise that in the concretely experienced world, facts and values are never separated. The moral life implies an eternal, not a temporal, good; but man cannot attain such: only the "initiative of the Eternal", the divine grace which reaches out to man, can enable its achievement. In fact, the moral life implies God, grace, and immortality, though it needs the concreteness of a historical revelation to complete such moral theology.

De Burgh argued from the "antimonies" in morality (the free pursuit of the good *versus* the obligation of duty; the universal failure of man *versus* the universal ideal, for examples), that only the perfect vision of God and the will of God, resolve the first; and only the intervention of God's grace resolves the second. Thus morality without religion is incomplete, its inner contradictions remaining unresolved.[27]

It has not been contended that such an argument from the theological implicates of morality is sufficient to establish the central Christian convictions: but the method itself is remarkable, reversing the assumption of centuries that Christian ethics was the consequence, the "application" of the Christian creed. Now, ethics becomes part of the *data* of philosophy, not its appendix; and the Christian ethic takes on a new role in apologetics, an unprecedented status within theology.

3.THE THEOLOGICAL CLIMATE

Theology in the twentieth century has suffered many "revolutions". It would be profitless, even were it possible, to outline all the "consequences" for Chrsitian ethics of the various schools, "approaches", fashions that constitute the current "debate", but certain broad changes have affected deeply the theological climate in which Christian ethics has to grow. One of the most far-reaching is undoubtedly the new attitude towards scripture.

Of the crucial importance, to almost all ethical schools, of this appeal to scripture, the whole story of Christian ethics is sufficient illustration.

However eager the first moral apologists to placate pagan contemporaries, Tertullian, Clement, Origen, Ambrose, Augustine, all accepted the necessity to expound, and argue their positions from the Bible. Republication of the Greek Testament, the expository work of Luther and Calvin, the Protestant search for biblical authority and the Catholic assertion of it are essential to the story. N. H. G. Robinson says, "Within Protestantism perhaps the earliest type of treatment which morality received involved collection and systematic presentation of practical injunctions and exhortations to be found in scripture. This . . . even Calvin appears to have had in mind when he said, 'it will be useful to collect from various places of scripture a rule for the reformation of life, that they who cordially repent may not be bewildered in their pursuits'."[28]

Puritan biblicism traced its influence back through Tyndale to the Lollards, as well as to Reformation emphasis on scripture: "By their vernacular Bibles," says Chadwick, "the Protestant churches thrust into the popular consciousness a religious dynamic . . . The England of the middle seventeenth century was to test what happened when the "mechanick', the brazier, the feltmaker, and the coachman went into the Bible to fetch their divinity for themselves."[29] Barclay repeatedly defended his basic principles from selected scripture verses. Butler published ethical philosophy in the form of sermons upon scripture texts, taking care to expound their biblical settings, however briefly. Edwards was a meticulous expositor; Wesley scarcely less so. Maurice, troubled by technical criticism of the Bible, insisted that scripture was record of divine revelation, and relied on the general sense of scripture in speaking of a "loving and redeeming God" as sufficient certificate of inspiration. Maurice's fullest exposition of the kingdom of heaven is in fact a commentary on Luke's Gospel.[30] Rauschenbusch begins *Christianity and the Social Crisis* with detailed examination of the prophets, the synoptic Gospels, the apostolic church, and confesses "I had to go back to the Bible to find out whether I or my friends were right."[31] Bonhoeffer, too, reveals traditional dependence on scripture in much of his *Ethics,* appealing to Genesis for the "mandates" of marriage, labour, government, for the explanation of shame, and conscience; analysing constantly words of Jesus, describing in detail the story of Christ.

Such instances are mere illustrations: while philosophic climate and social milieu have always formed the matrix in which Christian ethics took shape, its skeleton-structure, heart, and genetic drive have always been drawn directly from the Jewish-Christian scriptures.

Yet, as clear as the reliance upon scripture for illustration, authority, and defence, is the growing unease about the use made of biblical precedents. That *both* sides in the Reformation struggle could claim biblical support was disturbing, but not new: the church had never failed to find scriptural justification for opposite views on slavery, military service, wealth, persecution, as well as doctrine. Blake's sharp comment was justified —

> Both read the Bible day and night
> But thou read'st black where I read white[32]

Calvin confessed himself unable to understand Revelation, as Luther expressed doubts about the Epistle of James, and placed "an evident reason . . . my conscience" alongside the scriptures as his final court of appeal.[33] Dickens[34] links with the slow decline of reverence towards Aristotle in Protestant circles a "weakening of biblical fundamentalism." Butler had argued in the *Analogy*[35] that reason judges the evidential value of revelation, and its morality; no scripture can offer pretext for evading the moral imperative; apparent immoralities in the Bible just cannot be real. Butler's fundamental appeal was not to revelation, but to the constitution of human nature, while at the opening of the famous *Sermons* he says, very significantly,

"The epistles of the New Testament have all of them a particular reference to the condition and usages of the Christian world at the time they were written. Therefore as they cannot be thoroughly understood, unless that condition and those usages are known and attended to, so further: though they be known, yet if they be discontinued or changed, exhortations, precepts, and illustrations of things which refer to such circumstances now ceased or altered *cannot at this time be urged in that manner* and with that force which they were to the primitive Christians."[36]

Such an assertion of the historical relativism of the scriptures is commonplace among serious Bible students now: in 1726 it must have startled many.

From a very different angle of approach, Barclay likewise made the authority of scripture only relative and "secondary":

"From the revelations of the Spirit . . . have proceeded the scriptures — a declaration of the fountain, not the fountain itself — not the principle ground nor adequate rule . . . but a secondary rule, subordinate to the Spirit . . . they testify that the Spirit is the guide by which the saints are led into all truth . . . Therefore according to the scriptures, the Spirit is the first and principal leader . . ." This is said to remove difficulties concerning scripture: some who could not read them, being pressed by adversaries with awkward citations, and "finding them to disagree with the manifestation of truth in their own hearts, have boldly affirmed the Spirit of God never said so, and that it was certainly wrong" — things found afterwards to be indeed errors of the English translators. The Spirit gives second place to the scriptures, though they are useful for comfort, encouragement, to make wise, and to reprove, those led by the Spirit.[37]

This asserts a yet more serious relativism, the subordination of scriptural authority to subjective intuitions of divine revelation.

Of deliberate misuse of scripture, Kingsley had said that the Bible had been used as an opium dose for keeping beasts of burden patient while they were being over-burdened; and Rauschenbusch complained that —

"The sermon on the mount, in which Jesus clearly defines the points of difference between His ethics and the current morality is always praised reverently but rarely taken seriously. Its edge is either blunted by an alleviating exegesis, or it is asserted that it is intended for the millenium and not for the present life."[38]

Rauschenbusch states the whole changing attitude to scripture in one eloquent protest:

The church had always had a literature which might have opened its eyes to social facts; every time the Bible was freshly comprehended the social leaven began to work. But the social enlightenment was numbed by dogmatic and ecclesiastical interests. Theologians hunted for proof-texts of dogma; churchmen were interested in the tithing system but not in the land system of the Mosaic law. The allegorical method neutralised the social contents of the Bible by spiritualising everything: "the emancipation of the Israelite slaves from galling overwork and cruelty in Egypt . . . is a striking story of social revolt, but it was turned into an allegory of the exodus of the soul from the world . . . The great social parable of the good Samaritan was spiritualised into an allegory of humanity . . . It was an ingenious way of getting ready-made doctrinal results . . . But it never took anything out of the Bible that was not already in the mind of the interpreter, and it learned nothing new from the Bible . . ."[39]

In such a paragraph, a long tradition of evasion and manipulation stands arraigned. Rauschenbusch understood equally well the historical retranslation which responsible exegesis demands:

"It is futile to attempt to reform modern society on biblical models. The principle underlying the Mosaic land system is wholly right. The spirit . . . protecting the labourer and the poor is so tender and noble that it puts us to shame. But these legal prescriptions . . . would be wholly unworkable under modern conditions. It is rather our business to catch the bold and humane spirit of the prophetic tribunes of the people and to do as well in our day as they did in theirs . . . to understand the social contents of the Bible in their historical setting and press home on the Christian church the essential purpose of its own inspired book. But here, too, the letter killeth; it is the spirit that quickeneth."[40]

Bonhoeffer was still urging the same need forty years later, but with clearer awareness of the tensions involved:

"In ethics, as in dogmatics, we cannot simply reproduce the terminology of the Bible; the altered problems of ethics demand an altered terminology. But it must be remembered that an extension of the terminology involves the risk of slipping away from what is essential; also that the use of the biblical terminology is not without its dangers."[41]

As an ethical source book the Bible has always been historically conditioned. Not only does it offer little direction on slavery, economic ethics, political participation in community life, nothing at all on the host of entirely new problems that face modern men; its perspective has always been backward-looking. Parallels between Bible situations and our own inevitably grow fewer and fainter with the passing centuries. The blunt truth is that no "documentary ethic" could ever satisfy conscience in a world whose sum of knowledge redoubles at ever shorter intervals — in which as much new experience is crammed into a decade as filled a century in earlier times. Nevertheless, the Bible retains its hold upon Christian hearts, largely because strenuous effort has been made to liberate the "timeless" message from the historical documents.

Men like George Adam Smith served Christian ethics far better than they knew, by pioneering interpretation of the Hebrew prophets as messengers to their contemporary situations in Israel, so revealing depths of moral and social insight never more powerfully expressed. The analysis of documentary sources set oft-quoted verses against the background of their time and the purpose of the original writers, providing a *control* for exegesis by insisting that every passage means what it was intended by the writer to convey to the original readers, in their terms and for their immediate need. A further consequence of historical exegesis was abandonment of one-level application of passages of all kinds and dates to modern situations: what was said by Jews like Moses, David, Zephaniah, 'Malachi', could no longer be addressed indiscriminately to Christians of Europe, Asia, America, in the third, tenth, seventeenth, or nineteenth centuries. Implied in the new exegesis, too, was a more flexible doctrine of revelation, recognising *development* through the centuries of preparation for Christ. In such ways there emerged a supreme norm for testing all inspiration, in the revelation of God in the person of Christ, who becomes Himself the acknowledged Lord, Judge and criterion of the word of God in Old and New Testaments. For Christian ethics, this was revolutionary.

Whatever emotional loss may appear to be involved in the surrender of one-level, equal-all-through revelation within the Bible, for ethics at any rate the recognition of historical relativity within scripture brought enormous gain. No longer need the Christian moralist devise tortuous arguments to defend the test by poison-cup for adultery, the child-sacrifice apparently required of Abraham, the bloodthirsty wars of Canaan, the extermination of witches, the divine vengeance of bears savaging "children", or indiscriminate punishment of whole families for the sin of one man. In the same way, some of the "scriptural" arguments put forward to perpetuate war, capital punishment, slavery, racial apartheid, social and religious devaluing of women, torture of heretics, compulsory conversion, are seen now to be, sometimes deliberate misapplication of "sacred oracles"; oftener, merely stages, or obstacles, on the way towards the perfect ideal of Christ, before whom all attitudes, beliefs, customs, laws, tabus, alien to His spirit, however ancient, *must give place*. Christ's "But I say unto you . . ." was liberation indeed.

Alongside historical interpretation went intensive literary, historical, textual, and theological scholarship devoted to the scriptures: throughout, the court of appeal for consensus results has been, not theological dogma or ecclesiastical authority, but reverent judgement informed by reason and by facts. The day has gone when the recitation of texts could resolve ethical dilemmas, and "It is written" be used indiscriminately to impose upon tender consciences.

Setting Calvin's recommended method of reaching "evangelical" decisions ("collecting from . . . various scriptures a rule of life"), alongside that of A. A. Hodge ("to deduce from the doctrines and precepts of the Bible rules . . . for the guidance of the individual Christian"), N. H. G. Robinson[42] urges two serious objections. First that this procedure presupposes a "propositional" view of revelation, as concerned to convey information, commandments, an external and (to the recipients) arbitrary truth presented for acceptance. Robinson prefers the "personal" view of revelation, as the reconciliation of God with men in fellowship, God revealing not ideas or commands but Himself in communion — scripture being the instrument used by the Spirit, not the foregone conclusion of His leading. Secondly, on man's side, settlement of ethical questions by biblical texts would make the human response an automatic, submissive, external obedience to presented, alien commands, instead of a clean heart, a right spirit, and a deep love towards God, in which Christ lives in the believer — the resulting life infinitely richer than subjection to external, written law could ever be. "This does not mean that scripture has no place in Christian life . . . That life would be inconceivable without it . . ." But its function is not "precepts out of a book" to direct daily living: the value of scripture lies in "pointing beyond itself to the sovereign centre of Christian life."

Robinson might have added (and probably implied) that in practice it is scripture that has conducted men into that "sovereign centre" of Christian life where the indwelling Spirit directs the heart; that has illumined the whole of experience; that led the first, faltering steps of faith, warned, instructed, inspired, rebuked, nourished, and guided towards that Christian maturity in which the actual written words come eventually to count for less than the communion with God which they have created within the soul, in the daily obedience of a loving heart.

The adjustment of the Christian ethic to modern circumstances, to the changing cultural climate, to alien influence from secular ethics, most of all to the new understanding of scripture, has confronted the modern Christian with a *radically* new situation. Here, the whole issue of the relation of a long-past revelation to present moral decisions — *the relevance of heritage to situation* — is brought to sharp focus. In current debate, the proffered solutions are three. In place of infallible written words is offered the Word, the timeless meaning within the historical documents; or, the all-sufficient, intuitive, spontaneous impulse to attain the self-evident ethical "norm", namely Love; or, the Figure of the historical-and-living Christ, Exemplar and Lord of the Christlike life. And each is offered on the clear understanding that moral truth and duty are discoverable, not by abstract intellectual grasp of ethical rules, principles, programmes, but *only* in existential response to unique, given, concrete situations.

17

Heritage — Threshold of Debate

BEFORE EXPLORING THAT MODERN debate on the relevance in Christian ethics of ancient heritage to today's situations, it is well to recall what that heritage has been, to seek coherence in the long story, and to distinguish perennial from ephemeral elements. The biblical heritage focussed upon the religious root of morality, its objective source and obligation, and — from the nature of God as love — an obedience that is spontaneous and inward. Yet the biblical ethic is never wholly individual: "from the first pages of the Bible to the last duty is extended beyond the individual's own concerns to involve all that is implied in being his brother's keeper"; nor is the biblical ethic ever wholly other-worldly: the earth is the Lord's, and the ideal became incarnate within earthly conditions. The unique contribution of biblical ethics, however, was the embodiment of the Christian vision in the figure of the Christ, the secret of Christianity's constant power of adaptation and timeless appeal. It is needful now to enquire how far the biblical emphases have survived the ensuing centuries.

1. THE HISTORICAL HERITAGE

(i) Major adjustments of the ideal to circumstances certainly occurred. Standing within the New Testament, it would be impossible to foresee a Christianity that would counsel war, defend usury, assimilate slavery, establish political concordat with the varying State, defend the use of force, create power bases within democracy, train members for responsible posts of civic government, or come to comfortable terms with affluence. Yet the church did all these things, not carelessly, but under leadership of men of the calibre of Clement, Ambrose, Luther, Calvin, Maurice. Some adjustments may fairly be regarded as experiments, long tried but mainly abandoned. The theory of the double standard lost its hold when philosophic dualism declined and the notion of secular vocation grew in Christian minds.

Extreme asceticism is never likely to trouble the church again, if only because of Freud — though the church did learn from Erasmus that "monasticism is not holiness." One exception is Christianity's ambiguous view of marriage, which many still hold a sacrament and yet forbidden to Christian leaders and impossible to the mother of our Lord. Experiments with limited, and voluntary, communion of goods have persisted within the church, but have not created a conviction that communism is required of Christians, practicable without celibacy, or wise for society. Similarly, concerning pacifism the old doctrine of the just war and the State's claim would be thought irrelevant by many Christians in the twentieth century. Overlong tolerance of slavery has surely given place finally to true appreciation of the value and cruelties of human toil, and recognition that "the workers of the world" are the children of God. It is significant that Christianity has bred not a few critics and satirists — Tertullian, Erasmus, Fox, Bonhoeffer are but examples — whose vigorous and eloquent ridicule have aroused first anger, and then admiration.

(ii) On the whole, history has confirmed the biblical insight that disciples would be known by their fruits. The first *apologia,* and the earliest impact of Christianity upon paganism, were predominantly ethical. In the late nineteenth and the twentieth centuries, the church has realised again that her chief hope of making any impression upon her contemporaries depends upon demonstrating a superior quality of life and greater effectiveness in social reform — dogmatically at a loss, Christianity must once more woo the unbeliever by ethical excellence. As to Christian social morality, the church has through the centuries explored every possible formulation: an ethic for a church *within* society (New Testament); an ethic for the independent church *towards* society (Apologists, Augustine); an ethic for a church withdrawn from society (monasticism); an ethic provided by the church for a society becoming liberated from ecclesiastical control (Erasmus); an ethic of the church differentiated from society but holding that "the secular too is God's" (Luther); an ethic for a church working to Christianise society (Calvin); an ethic for a church in harness with society (Greek Orthodox); an ethic for the Christian "against" society in inner, selective withdrawal, combined with scrupulous participation (Puritan); an ethic for a church serving as almoner for society (Wesley and the English Evangelicals); an ethic for the church as mentor and inspiration of society (Maurice, Rauschenbusch); an ethic for a church which, realistically, no longer expects society to be Christian (Reinhold Niebuhr); an ethic for a church that respects the autonomy of society and no longer attempts to Christianise it (Bonhoeffer).

Variety of approach is here the struggle to remain relevant to ever fluctuating circumstances, but several motifs persist. Christ's law of love is never far from the Christian mind, engendering compassion. The vision of the kingdom of God recurs constantly, both as an eternal standard by which to assess life on earth, and as a blueprint for Christian activism. The earthly ministry of Jesus towards the sick, the needy, and the unprivileged, has always nourished Christian social concern, and in the missionary expansion of the western church in the nineteenth century this combined fruitfully with the impulse of mission.

The historical church has been faithful to the biblical insistence that religion is essentially corporate, and must be corporately expressed in love and service. The social emphasis within the gospel is more in line with current conceptions of social control for social ends than individualism would be. Nevertheless, as the twentieth century enters its final quarter, it seems probable that the church will face a situation resembling that of the second century. Scientific, cultural, and political developments are tending to isolate the Christian community anew; the gulf appears to be widening between idealism and actuality, between the Christian faith and the centres of political power, as more States declare for "the secular society", as nationalism again confronts the internationalism of the gospel, as social welfare passes out of voluntary into official hands, as — even in Catholic Europe — democracy is ranged behind non-religious and anti-religious movements. It may well be that, shorn of institutional and political influence, Christianity will once again bear witness within society as an ethically elitist community whose purity of life and social vision beckon and encourage the well-disposed and the disillusioned, but coerce no-one. But despite narrowing opportunities, and some contrary trends in evangelicalism and mysticism, Christianity has never long forgotten, and still will not forget, its social conscience.

(iii) With equal thoroughness historical Christian ethics has explored the psychology of Christian morality, seeking the motivation and resources which may sustain the vision inherited from Jesus. While the impulse of gratitude, obedience, and Christ-idealism, have never been totally spent, their power over Christian hearts has been especially strong at certain periods — in the ages of persecution, in mediaeval mysticism, and again in the devotion of Puritanism. Augustine examined the nature of man's freedom, and its perfection in pursuit of the *summum bonum,* which for men made in the image of God must be God Himself. The mystics explored the inner life of the soul in pilgrimage towards the perfect vision of God. Abelard examined with new care the place of intention in the determination of virtue, the good life, and personal merit; Aquinas turned for deeper motivation to "right reason", emotion, habitual virtue, faith, as fruits of infused grace. Erasmus reacted against superstition and formalism by seeking the "interiorisation" of ethics. Luther saw, as the answer to the broken will and incurved nature of man, moral faith creating a new man to whom obedience was true freedom; Calvin saw the new man created by the gospel under the discipline of the divine Sovereign whose will was expressed in church and State. Butler's appeal to the natural "principles" constitutive of human nature under the supreme principle of conscience, Kant's appeal to reason, the Friends' appeal to the inner light of Christ in all men, and Edwards' to the religious emotions created by grace in an otherwise totally depraved human nature, are all attempts to find within man — or within the Christian man — that authority and resource which the "catholic" Christian possessed in the sacramental life of the church. It cannot be said that recent thought has carried this investigation much further; the Social Gospel took a natural incentive of compassion in the Christian somewhat for granted. While it seems improbable that Christian ethics will ever lose the conviction that morality proceeds from within, and again become simply the discipline of the Christian institution, nevertheless the appeal of absolute loyalty and absolute obedience, freeing the individual from the torment and uncertainty of personal decision, must not be underestimated. Human nature is so varied, the appeal of the gospel so many-sided, that it is probably futile to try to catalogue all the motives and incentives that move Christian hearts to ethical endeavour.

(iv) On the deeper question of the precise relation of faith to ethics, the church has, through the generations, sought a clearer answer. The two emphases discernible in the New Testament resound in later writers: on the one hand the confidence that a right faith, a true relation to God, will of itself bear fruit in right qualities of character and a correct pattern of living; on the other hand the conviction that — since this does not always happen — some pressure is necessary upon the Christian conscience, and some effort by the Christian soul, to see that right conduct accompanies right belief. Jesus' conception of sonship as the basis of likeness, Paul's view of faith, Peter's of love for Christ, and John's of the inherent ethical quality of eternal life, all find echo in Augustine's view of the direct effect of grace upon original sin, in Aquinas' confidence in the gifts bestowed by infused grace, in Luther's and Calvin's high expectations from the man renewed by the gospel through faith alone, in the Quaker's belief in the moral efficacy of the inner illumination, and the Puritan's energy of dedication so well expressed in Edwards' "If the great things of religion are rightly understood they will affect the heart."

In support of the opposite conviction — that some further pressure and effort are needed — the church could appeal to the challenge of Jesus that disciples take up the cross, follow steadfastly, count the cost, obey the great commandment; to the sub-apostolic requirement that right conduct shall accompany sound doctrine in the "exercise" of godliness; to the constant warnings and exhortations of the Fathers, inculcating moral heroism out-doing Jewish and pagan standards. In Aquinas, Luther, Calvin, recurs the emphasis upon the Commandments; both Luther and Calvin were disappointed with the ethical results of Reformation theology — Calvin, especially, underlining the place of discipline in Christian life. Butler urged, as few have done, the necessity of obedience to conscience. Most of the argumentation in theology about law and grace, about predestination and free will, turns so far as ethics is concerned upon this moral dilemma: if the good life depends wholly upon man's effort, he is found morally *incapable;* if it depends wholly upon divine grace, man is left *irresponsible.* To assert that it depends upon both effort and grace is, in this context, to solve nothing. Here, too, modern thinking has not added greatly to the historical discussions — perhaps because the necessity of grace through faith, and the necessity of effort in faith, have both been demonstrated to the point of impasse. Perhaps, too, because what is difficult to express precisely in words is sufficiently clear in practice: that without faith in God's ever-available grace we could do nothing at all; but the essence of that faith *is* the constant struggle to cast ourselves wholly upon God in a living, transforming relationship that makes obedience a delight.

Doubtless other persistent themes could profitably be identified, but the terminus of an introductory text is the threshold of current discussion, and the chief recurring factors in the history of Christian ethics are precisely those which underlie the "proffered solutions" which preoccupy the modern debate — the appeal to scripture for authority and objectivity, in the ethic of the timeless Word; the longing for a simple, unquestioned moral directive, in deference to man's "adulthood" and autonomy, in a spontaneous impulse towards a single, self-evident *norm* of love; and the return to Christian origins in the rediscovery yet again of the "imitation" of Christ. It is no accident that these "growing points" are also the chief threads of continuity which identify the Christian ethic as one enduring vision and loyalty throughout all its manifold adjustments and far-reaching development.

2. THE ETHIC OF THE WORD

H. R. Mackintosh coined the title "theology of the Word" to describe the work of Karl Barth; J. Macquarrie adopted it to cover the whole "revolution" in philosophical theology which has turned from seeking the truth of religion in the customs, traditions, and cultus of many peoples to listen only to the Word of God in Christ.[1] Within this theology of the Word much attention is necessarily given to the "ethics of the Word", though the precise meaning of "the Word" in this connection is not always clear.

(1) Karl Barth

Reacting against the subjective "religion of experience", Barth set himself to reassert the transcendence of God, the absolute lordship of Christ, the objective "givenness" of revelation. There is no way from man to God, no capacity in man to discover God, no revelation save that of the Word incarnate. That Word is *given,* essentially alien to man's thoughts: man cannot comprehend it, except by illumination of the Spirit. Originally, Barth held the image of God in man utterly destroyed by sin; later he concedes that the image survives in man's *relationship* to God and to humanity, though to God only in election and response; to humanity only as a fact of life, not an ethical norm. As Reinhold Niebuhr said: "Man is convicted . . . of being human and not divine."[2]

Barth emphasises this "givenness" of revelation especially by rejecting all human ethics as merely the "prolongation of the Fall." True ethics is completely dependent upon Christian theology — God's offer of salvation by grace alone is as opposed to man's ethics as it is to man's sin. Once, perhaps unguardedly, Barth classifies morality with chance as an arbitrary factor in human experience, and describes non-Christian ethical systems "the people of Canaan, their culture and their cultus" with whom "there must be no armistice." Barth sees in secular ethics only hypocrisy, self-justification, failure: man's sole hope is to give up the struggle and accept divine grace. By insisting that "ethics has its basis in the knowledge of Jesus Christ", Barth at least in his earlier work, in effect denied any distinction between good and bad in secular experience. God Himself, by vertical intervention and absolute miracle "creates within man all the psychological and critical conditions required for us to make the response of faith," with which alone morality begins.[3]

Hence Barth's uncompromising "theology of the Word" seeking objective authority in revelation which is always active — God seeking us in grace — and continuous, through the "kerygmatic" proclamation of the truth and each generation's fresh hearing of it, not a once-for-all event of ancient history. Christians find for themselves that the Bible "lights up" by the inner witness of the Spirit: this self-authenticating power lies at the heart of the conviction that the Bible is the Word of God.[4] Neill asks "When is the Bible the Word of God?" and says we get the impression that Barth would answer, "When the Reformed preacher preaches it" — which is not entirely caricature, for in the "kerygmatic" theology emphasis falls upon the timeless gospel heard within the documents.[5] "The Word is conceived" says Macquarrie, "as the living incarnate Word Jesus Christ, to whom indeed the human words of the Bible bear witness, but cannot express the fullness of the divine Word."[6] Thus Barth refuses to appeal to words and injunctions of scripture as rules of conduct, external prescriptions entitling the conformist to self-righteousness: "the Christian life is given over in faith to the over-lordship of Christ, as containing within himself the whole duty of man."[7]

> The Word is that which God speaks to man; only secondarily the word which man speaks to man, as prophets, apostles, the church, speak on God's behalf. This justifies "Barth's threefold distinction (of) the Word preached, the written Word, and the revealed Word, and his clear consistent contentions that 'revelation engenders the Bible that attests it', that prophets and apostles are 'journeymen of revelation' . . . What man says now in the church, and what man has already said and written in the Bible, are significant only in so far as they echo and are the vehicles of what God says, the Word of *God*."[8]

On this foundation rests the ethic of the Word, a morality strictly *given,* authoritative, rejecting man's autonomy, self-discipline by laws inherent within man's nature, or self-realisation as a moral being. Man is utterly helpless, even to hear the Word which God speaks to him in Christ. N. H. G. Robinson speaks of Barth's "heteronomous determinism", faith being "first and last the determination of our nature by the Word of God." In faith, it seems, "we are not only confronted by God in Christ, but are completely determined by His grace on every side of our being, including our reason." Both revelation and our response to it are *given,* created by God; "faith is bare openness, an empty space, a blank page, pure receptivity".[9] Man thus is wholly passive. Bultmann criticised this as "inculcating an attitude of blind surrender at the price of intellectual suicide." Niebuhr spoke of Barth's "transcendental irresponsibility", leaving man nothing he can do towards leavening society with good, except only in bearing witness to what has happened to himself, since others cannot respond to his testimony. H. D. Lewis has inveighed against the trend in current Protestant theology, at variance with elementary ethical principles, denying that man's will is free, that men vary widely in moral character, that each is responsible only for what he himself has done or failed to do — theology allied with "the darker forms of reaction . . . in the repudiation of that most treasured and significant feature of civilised life, the sense of responsibility."[10]

If this seems overstated, Barth does give room for it:

> "What right conduct is for man is determined absolutely in the right conduct of God . . . We cannot even incidentally make it the object of our choice . . . This good is chosen only in obedience, that is, in the choice in whose making we have no choice because we are chosen ourselves and can only make this one choice."[11]

Barth pays "lip-service to the notion of moral responsibility and self-determination": "The Word of God is not addressed to beasts, plants, or stones, but to men;" but "the concept . . . never appears in Dr. Barth's theological system as more than an island lying off the continent of his more characteristic thought."[12]

If all human responsiveness be denied, there is an end of ethics in Christianity; faith as trust, loyalty, obedience, love, becomes impossible. So does faith as "knowing" — which requires discrimination and appropriation. In believing I am *not* just passive, but spiritually alert: there is in man addressed by the gospel a "destination of communication" to make the coming of the Word of God conceivable. "Nothing is taken from the generosity of the giver if a man has hands to receive" (N. H. G. Robinson): moreover, man's ability to refuse, even to obduracy, seems obvious. God is not dealing with creatures as with property, but seeking to love undeserving children back into sonship; revelation is not blinding, overwhelming light — but the wooing invitation to *believe*.

Barth was right to emphasise that the Word which saves is *God's* Word, and the opportunity to accept is of divine mercy: but unless the reality of human response and of responsibility for rejection are also safeguarded, it is hard to see how any ethical meaning can be left, either as the presupposition of religious persuasion, or as the fruit of Christianity itself.

Yet Barth certainly contends for the moral implications of his theology. "Ethics so-called I regard as the doctrine of God's

Command and do not consider it right to treat it otherwise than as an integral part of dogmatics . . ." "The doctrine of God is at every point ethics".[13] So, in *Church Dogmatics,* the doctrine of election is followed by the divine Command, the doctrine of Creation by the ethics of creation, and doubtless the projected doctrines of Reconciliation and Redemption would have been followed by ethical expositions. In the divine Covenant, man becomes a covenant-partner in the manner which the conditions of his life may require.[14] Grace and law coincide in Christ: the law's content is conformity to Christ, its fulfilment is made possible by Him.[15]

In *Church Dogmatics* II 2 God takes man into responsible relation to His own will: ethics is this "Command of God" for men called to covenant-partnership with God. God's purpose is to rule, as our "Commander". This Command is the Word of God in creation, reconciliation and redemption — in Nature, grace, and glory. The *basis* of the divine Command is not power but grace, the foundation of His authority. The name of Jesus designates the *content* of the divine claim as obedience to Christ.

The *form* of the claim is freedom — in response to grace "ought" takes on the character of privilege. We "have to do" what corresponds to grace, living as those who *accept as right everything God does for us.* Thus the divine Command is a permission, a freedom, saying "Do this, freely, *because* in so doing you will live by My grace." Thus freedom and obligation meet in the obedience of Jesus. The obedience commanded is essentially decision for Christ. God's Command is not to be ignored: it includes our decisions within itself — "it is our own free decisions whose character God decides even as we ourselves take them." This is our responsibility, asking *"What — ought — men — to do*?" The answer is given in Jesus Christ.

God's Command is concrete, individual, not a general rule. It comes with specific content embracing momentary decision (though this "momentary concreteness" is illustrated profusely from scripture, the Decalogue, the Sermon on the Mount). It is one command, not many rules, and unites men in Christ as Lord. It also judges us, by Christ, "the image to which we have to conform ourselves".

In III 4 ethics is the Command of the Creator. The meaning of man the creature is revealed in the incarnation: ethics can therefore be treated only in relation to Christ, true ground of creation, and in the world of Nature, history, work. In creation, too, the Command is always concrete: Barth rejects casuistry as destroying the immediacy of divine commanding in personal, daily encounter. Yet Barth expounds at tremendous length the responsibility of man in *freely* acknowledging that God is right in all He does.

Freedom before God is considered under the holy day (covenantal and eschatological), witness to faith, and prayer. *Freedom in the fellowship of humanity* is considered under male and female — wide-ranging discussion of sexuality, homosexuality (a "moral malady"), marriage (a divine calling to lasting, exclusive life-partnership); parents and children (a social and religious relationship), duties of children towards parents, childlessness, birth control, duties of parents towards children; of near and distant "neighbours". *Freedom for life* means man is commanded to live, as individual, in time, free, in community. So God commands *respect for life* in wonder, affirmation; for primitive impulse (hunger, sex, sleep, regulated by spirit); for humanity; for community; for natural life (a strong protest against wilful killing); for health; for joy; for oneself, for power to live effectively. God commands *protection of life:* life being God's excludes suicide (but not sacrifice), all lust to kill, abortion (permissible only to protect life), euthanasia (an unqualified No!), self-defence (*not* a natural, or a Christian, right), capital punishment (except for treason, or in tyrannicide), and war (with many qualifications). God commands *the active life* of usefulness, achievement, service of the world (to love as God has loved), and work (ordered, self-supporting, striving after good ends, honest, with due relaxation).

Freedom in limitation recognises one's special situation appointed by God. As to *time* — one life, set within history — the time in which we live is our stage; accept its rightness, opportunity, and mortality. As to *vocation:* to each God appoints his age, situation, aptitude, sphere. As to *honour:* God seeks our elevation, valuing each in His invitation to serve. Let God choose its form — whether public recognition, or abasement (which may serve the cause).

In IV 2 xv Barth discourses on Christian love. Under *the problem of love* Barth defines love as the act of pure, total giving. Faith and love, reception and surrender, are indivisible moments of Christian existence. Love turns to others unseeking, to give what it has, and itself, in contrast with self-interested "love".

Under the *origin of love,* Barth denies (against Luther) that Christian love is God's love "downstreaming and outstreaming to the neighbour". The Christian loves because God loves *him,* electing (the free act of God); purifying (God's reaction towards sin); creative (causing those loved to love); liberating (man to love).

Under *the act of love,* love is new, free, an impartation on all levels, bringing joy. In content it is determined by the one loved: by God, man's hostility being replaced by love; by man (not "humanity" but those "near") in witness to each other of the love of God, guaranteeing to the neighbour that God loves him too. Under *the manner of love* Barth urges that love alone determines life in the Christian community: "love alone counts, love alone triumphs, love alone endures" — the heart of 1 Corinthians 13, which Barth expounds at great length.

Bromiley comments[16] that Barth is conservative in conclusions, particular in application, constantly biblical. Barth's exposition is curiously biblicist, not to say Pentateuchal; Genesis, the Decalogue, are regulative, though he blames Brunner for "abstract Old Testament thinking".[17] He draws immense implications from the story of "the rich young ruler". As illustrations, his biblical examples are apt: as arguments, often artificial. One wonders what Barth thinks *is* the Word of God within these stories, and is disconcerted to read (against sophistries supporting euthanasia) that "their derivation is obviously from another book than that which we have so far consulted."[18] West thinks Barth, on Nazism, insists on the rights of theology in political and social questions, though the church may await events, reserving judgement. He rejects Luther's two realms, placing the State firmly in the order of reconciliation, under the control of Christ.[19] W. W. Paul notices how often (as on abortion) dialectic dominates Barth's treatment: "on the one hand" the sixth Commandment yields a decisive divine No! — "on the other hand" A divine Yes! if the life of the mother be endangered . . .[20]

No summary can do justice to the thoroughness of Barth, nor to the unity of his thought. Equally impressive is his constant insistence, not on ideas but on existential confrontation of the living Christian with the living God in Christ. The Word of God comes here and now in daily discipleship, upon this and that moral problem; the Christian's obligation in the last resort is to his divine Commander. Whether or not Barth's presuppositions will be widely shared in future, it is certain that Christian ethics for a long time will reckon with Barth's searching discussion.

(2) Emil Brunner

At first a leading exponent of Barthianism, Emil Brunner[21] strongly defended Reformation emphases. The Good is not what is well adapted to human nature, but what *God* wills; the way is not by human striving but in union with God; God's will must be asserted not only in the cloister but in the community; sinful man is totally dependent on the *givenness* of revelation and of grace. Brunner therefore rejected all "natural" ethics, as marked by sin, merely illustrating how "man in revolt" seeks to establish independence.[22] Autonomy is "the devil himself"; "it is precisely morality which is evil"; "the worst state of man is complete confidence in himself." The concept of natural law merely conceals "great confusion of thought".[23] Philosophical ethics knows only two systems: the *naturalistic* says men should follow their natural desires — though wisely; the idealistic says men should obey a law "which commands only obedience as such". Hence natural ethics is "a heap of ruins" presenting the dilemma, "life without law, or law without content".[24]

Nevertheless Brunner defended man's responsibility before God as a *person,* although as a *sinner* he is in revolt. Again and again Brunner posits man's "ability to respond".[25]

The significance of the revelation given in creation is that man is a person, responsible, "standing before God", "inexcusable". This is the presupposition of the *saving* revelation in Jesus Christ . . . a decisive once-for-all act of God in history, which becomes personal in the divine-human encounter where God in Christ meets man.[26]

The Christian faith makes responsibility (ability to respond) the heart of personal existence, although the sense of responsibility *for sin* is a result of the false autonomy man sinfully claims. The sense of obligation, likewise, is the result of sin: "If I feel that I *ought* to do right, it is a sign that I cannot do it . . . The sense of *ought* shows me the Good at an infinite impassable distance from my will."[27] Robinson thinks this "rigoristic"[28]; it might be asked whether it is true — whether the sense that any Good is quite impossible does not destroy all sense of oughtness in relation to it. Brunner is right that willing obedience is never the fruit of the sense of ought, but only of love, the *desire* for goodness; but this does not affect my responsibility.

Man does not cease to be man because of the existence of sin: he has become neither animal nor devil, but remains a responsible person,[29] "created in the image of God, which is not to be narrowly conceived as rationality, but is rather man's full answerability before God." A "broken natural revelation" in the heart of sinful man provides the point of contact for the gospel: there survives in man the bare form of the image of God, the formal possibility of being addressed, the formal ability to respond. "Not even as a sinner does he cease to be one with whom . . . God can speak."[30] No "point of contact" dictates the form of God's revelation, but (as N. H. G. Robinson argues[31]) God, the *Source* of moral distinctions, will not ignore them when He approaches man. In His parables, His questions, and His reply to the enquiry of John Baptist, Jesus assumed His hearers possessed sufficient moral understanding to assess His claims. Besides, natural morality is *not* evil, but good: "otherwise it would be immorality".

Notwithstanding this assertion of man's answerability, Brunner has no doubt of the *givenness* of God's saving act and word. "All have sinned": man remains helpless, utterly dependent upon grace. Hence the contention against legalism, which distorts ethics; for to seek to attain God by our own effort is the very root of sin. This is "the great inversion": previously, life at its best is directed *towards*

God; now life is lived *from* God as its centre.[32] This must be "heard, known, recognised" through *faith,* not in striving but in knowing that one's life is a gift of God. This "inversion" is new birth, conversion, redirection of the self; henceforward, goodness is *what God does in us,* not what we do. God has really come to man. "God reveals Himself in His Word — which is at the same time a deed — an actual event, in Jesus Christ; and He reveals Himself operatively in His living Word, which is now taking place — in the Holy Spirit."[33] The New Testament proclamation of the Word of God makes no distinction between "dogmatic" and "ethical" elements.

Jewett remarks that Brunner offended by refusal to identify the Word of God with scripture. Brunner said, "there is obviously a great deal written in the Old Testament as divine law which no Christian can regard as binding upon himself unless he ceases to be Christian." "When we wish to know what is just in the State, economics, society, marriage, the family, we receive no help from the Decalogue, but can only attach to its Commandments what we have learned in other ways." Brunner, says W. W. Paul, "makes his appeal not directly to the commands of God in scripture, but to imperatives received from God afresh each time through the voice of the Spirit . . ."[34]

It is this emphasis on the living Word of God, which is first an act, an event, in Christ, then a record in scripture, then a proclamation, and finally a continuing Command of God in each new situation, voiced by the Spirit, which places Brunner beside Barth within the ethics of the Word.

The saving action of God, the foundation of Christian ethics, both shows what Good is, and achieves it. (a) The Bible's message is the revelation of the Good, "that which God does"; the goodness of man lies in letting himself be placed within the activity of God. The Good is God's will: in the Old Testament, theocracy; in the New, the kingdom. Union with the sovereignty of God involves fellowship with man — men are bound to God, and to each other, by *God's* love. Thus the will-of-God-for-community is the final meaning of life, revealed now in the Deed-Word of God as the meaning of the Good.[35] Christian ethics, therefore, is "the science of human conduct as it is determined by divine conduct." We may think of the abstract "idea of good", but we can only know *the Good,* the will of God, by His revelation.[36]

Brunner thinks this revelation — "what God does and wills is good; all that opposes the will of God is bad" — overcomes all dilemmas of natural ethics; also that nothing is good save obedience. The content of the command is irrevelant: "the form of will, obedience, is all." This, Robinson thinks, is formalistic, and untrue; from what we already know of

God, He could not command *hate* and remain the God and Father of our Lord Jesus Christ. The content of His Command *is* relevant.[37]

"As it happens", however, what is revealed as the Good, the will of God, is *love*. This is clear, not only in the will-of-God-for-community, but in His giving of Himself, which redefines the Good as unconditional self-giving; God manifests Himself as disinterested, generous love.[38] Thereby He claims us for that love. His giving Himself to us becomes His Command to us to give. "He who lives by the generosity of God becomes Himself generous."[39] The right act, as Jewett summarises,[40] is one saturated by love, and the Spirit illumines the moment of decision so that one knows what love requires at each moment.

What love demands cannot be predefined; "I cannot know beforehand the content of the Command . . . I can only receive it afresh each time through the voice of the Spirit . . . God is always bidding us do some particular thing, something which cannot be done at any other time, something quite new."[41] The right decision cannot be looked up in the ethical law-book; the whole responsibility rests on the individual himself. This kind of love alone is free from heteronomy as well as from autonomy: — back of its decisions is a discovery; but each discovery is something *given*.[42]

"That which ought to be done in love, in the freedom of the Spirit, that love alone, or the Spirit, can teach . . . God's Command can only be perceived in the actual moment of hearing it . . . The record of God's love in the historic Christ is only known to me *now,* as living and active, through the Holy Spirit . . . God's Command is concrete, known through His present speech — in the Holy Scriptures, as Creator (speaking from the past) and as Redeemer (speaking from the goal, the future), but addressing *(me)* on the border-line of the present."[43]

Here, plainly, Brunner approaches the main contention of "situation ethics."

For all that, what love means can be considered. "Love means the acceptance of love's bonds . . . we are united to our neighbour by only the one duty — to do to him what the love of God wills . . . here and now. Love does not steal, kill, lie, commit adultery, but does its best for its neighbour."[44] The Command of God the Creator will, in general, be to accept what is, and to conserve; the Command of God the Redeemer will, in general, be to change, to recreate: so love accepts a man as he is, and yet seeks to lead him to the goal in Christ. God's Command is one — to know God as Love, and so to love Him: this "means" — loving the neighbour: it is one duty: "He wills that we should love Him in our neighbour," though our neighbour is not God, and the God-man, Christ, is not our neighbour.[45]

Such love is only possible when we accept our neighbour as he is, as given to us by God — "in a relatedness": "Jesus Christ revealed this as the true norm, and gave it back to us". Love, again, means regarding the other man as a whole, as an individual (desiring him as he is); as a knowing being (willing to listen to what he knows, and always speaking in truthfulness); as a willing being (meeting his will-to-power with more than justice, ourselves intent upon the best for him).[46]

Elsewhere, Brunner relates love and justice —

"Love establishes no order: it transcends all orders. It enquires neither into its own right, nor into those of others, for to all it gives itself, whole, and undivided, beyond all limits". Compared with Aristotle's distributive justice, "to each according to his contribution", Brunner (says Ramsey) prefers the "Christianised" form, "What is due the labourer, the expectant mother, the little old crippled lady standing in line . . ." The accent falls on inequality of *need* and *difference* of function. "Love can only do more, it can never do less, than justice requires."[47]

Such emphasis upon love is plainly perennial in Christian ethics: but Brunner draws one unexpected conclusion: the distinction between an individual and a social ethic is "disastrous" — "a Christian individual ethic is a thoroughly monastic idea, and wholly unscriptural."[48] *All* Christian law is fulfilled in love; the individual out of community just does not exist; a Christian cannot possibly be an isolated individual. This suggests that the traditional emphasis (as in the Sermon on the Mount) on purity of *heart,* integrity, faithfulness, humility, and other "internal" qualities of personality, is mistaken. Brunner even suggests that "He who loses his life . . . shall find it" is an argument against an individual ethic. But when Brunner goes on to show that love to God, prayer, Bible-meditation, are not "duties" to God, while purity, self-cultivation and the like are only an education for life in community, one suspects that the contention is about definitions. Brunner plainly values the qualities which an individual ethic inculcates: indeed he says, "Certainly the self must be made fit for service, must get rid of whatever would make it unfit."[49] Most of Christian individual ethics lies in that concession.

(b) But the saving action of God, the foundation of Christian ethics, not only shows man what the Good is, it operates to *achieve* the Good in men who believe. As "the Good is that which God does (in us), not that which man does", the goodness of man can be no other than letting himself be placed within the activity of God.[50] Faith in Christ, creating a new relation to God, in turn empowers a new kind of conduct.[51] The power to do right comes from the . . . Spirit of Christ Who makes a man a new creature by faith: so "God gains a foothold in the heart."[52] So, too, we can love only "through the

Holy Spirit,'' only when God Himself takes possession of us, by His love, and does His work through us.''[53]

> Robinson finds here a ''heteronomous determinism'' in Brunner, one-sidedly emphasising God's action within the soul. Both divine act and human response are essential — ''else no *fellowship* in faith.'' Certainly man's part is only to respond to the initiative of grace: but it is none-the-less a reality. Man is unable to release himself from bondage, but he is still a self-determining being; ''while lumps of lead may be salvaged, only men may be redeemed.''[54]

Yet Brunner does give large place to faith, ''operative'' faith, as the ''principle of ethics''. ''To let God have His way with me means to base my life on Jesus Christ; it *means* believing in the gracious divine Word uttered in Jesus Christ; it *means* to be 'crucified' and 'raised' with Him.''[55] And this does not mean that nothing remains to be done. ''Faith exists only in the actuality of decision,'' constantly reaffirmed; though to faith law has been abrogated, yet for the believing man, ''round whose neck there still hangs the old Adam'', there remains the *demand* of God. Within the encouragement of justification the Word of God becomes the claim to sanctification: ''the indicative of the divine promise becomes the imperative of the divine Command.''[56]

> ''Faith does not consist simply in passive acceptance; it always means . . . an act of 'pulling oneself together' . . . even in His love He remains our *Master* and our Lord . . . There is no faith, as such, apart from conduct. Real faith always means obedience to God . . .''[57]

Thus Brunner resolves the obstinate problem of the relation of religious faith to ethical obedience — by simply identifying them.

While so much of Brunner's ethic turns upon the intervention of God in Christ, much also rests upon divine creation, and what it reveals of God's intention, beside the ''general'' Command to appreciate, and conserve what God has made.[58] A ''preparatory'' revelation in creation yields guidance to the saved man ''whose eyes have been opened by the historical Word of God'': the divine Command cannot be understood apart from ''the ordinances of creation'', the given structures of life.[59] Brunner appeals therefore in part to ''a naturalistic basis'' — as when he founds the argument for monogamy on the facts that every child has *one* father and mother, and two people in love always resent third parties![60] In consequence, *The Divine Imperative* is organised around two fundamental themes: the divine Command, revealed in Christ and momently by the Spirit; and the Orders of Creation — ''a framework for Christian life''[61] — seen in marriage, the family, labour, economic life, the State, culture, and the church.

Man is constituted by community, not set over against it: any conflict between love's requirements can arise only from multiplicity of neighbours — which is community. Resolution of such conflict only requires understanding of the bases of life in community. *Community of Life* is fundamental, affecting marriage, monogamy (based on nature), love (insufficient basis for marriage, though essential); marriage should be fruitful as possible, (but not unrestrictedly so — birth control is necessary); divorce may be required by the Command of love.

In *the Community of Labour* man should work to use creation and serve his fellows; man needs also rest and enjoyment, and to beware of materialism and acquisitiveness. Mass unemployment is especially challenging to Christian love. Economics is part of God's order, though basically autonomous: there is no Christian economics, yet the economic order is a sphere of Christian service. The weaknesses of capitalism suggest the church's duty to seek a better order. Though civilisation is not the kingdom of God, the Christian can make constructive contribution by personalising it.

The Community of the State is a God-given order for a sinful world, resting on power, law, force, not love. The State, too, is autonomous: no *form* of government is Christian above others. The danger for the State is pride of power, which only fear of God can curb.[62] As international law develops, war becomes outmoded. Penal law rests (with grave qualifications) on expiation (including for *society's* sins); capital punishment is excluded. Christians should be politically active.

The Community of Culture (Art, Science, Education) is a gift of God to reason, self-culture, freedom; and also autonomous. Christian duty is to criticise its self-sufficiency, serve its good ends, help shape public opinion. *The Community of the Church,* is both human and divine, the community of the Word wherever God chooses to speak through Bible, doctrine, or sacraments. The relation of church to churches, State, and world, is critically analysed. As in *Christianity and Civilisation,* Brunner makes many suggestions how Christianity can mould the institutions of society.

Brunner's ethical thought is positive, thorough, based firmly upon the objective, given Command of God, and equally firmly, for moral attainment, upon divine grace which that Command offers and conveys to faith. What is less clear is the source and verification of that Command, since the Bible, creation, the historical Christ, and the voice of the Spirit within the soul, are all appealed to. It is that uncertainty, together with a conservative, Lutheran, tendency to support the established condition of things, that prevent Brunner's being the final word on contemporary Christian ethics.

(3) Rudolf Bultmann

Three powerful features of the changing cultural climate converge in the work of Bultmann.[63] The critical method, which liberated progressive revelation, went further in Bultmann's "form criticism" to undermine confidence in the Gospels. Empiricist investigation of the nature of the world presented a challenge to Christian faith in incarnation, miracle, demonology, resurrection, which Bultmann strove to meet. Existential philosophy insisted that man's chief concern was not with doctrine, or institution but with authentic living in the day-to-day situation of a creaturely, anguished, meaningless, mortal existence: Bultmann followed Heidegger. Moreover, "this was the period in which Karl Barth and his friends were emphasising the Word of God".[64]

Bultmann's anxiety was to reinterpret the Jewish, or gnostic, "mythological" terms used by the first Christians to express that experience of encounter with Christ by which they had passed from meaningless, anxious, drifting, enslaved, "inauthentic" life, to free victorious existence. Bultmann distinguished the "merely historical" facts about the life and death of Jesus, from the "significantly historical" acts of God in grace, forgiveness, the gift of new life; and from the existential appropriation of those acts of God in succeeding generations as men receive the church's proclamation.[65]

According to the "subjective view" of Bultmann's meaning, "the saving event takes place in the actual encounter of faith, in the new knowledge of ourselves which God's action gives us."[66] According to the "objective view",[67] he does not sever salvation-experience from the story of Christ. The crucifixion is still history, but "the interpretative faculty of faith" has already in the New Testament woven around the story its mythological explanations. Jesus was real man, but the Palestinian community, convinced that encounter with him had brought them to the threshold of the kingdom, expressed this by messianic presentation, pre-existence, virgin birth. The cross was enacted "under Pontius Pilate", but acquires its saving meaning in the heart that accepts it; is made contemporary, in preaching, as an "eternal act of God". Responding in faith we find liberation, forgiveness, authentic existence. The resurrection-story expresses mythologically this experience of liberation. Christology expresses in mythological language the church's corporate experience, that in Jesus they had "encountered God"[68]

Such retranslations, of "mythological" into "existential", attempt to disentangle the "merely historical" events from the contemporary saving acts of God within the believer's experience. "The inescapable problem," as Neill says, "is that Jesus of Nazareth remains obstinately and irrevocably in the past . . . How then are we to make Him present?"[69] Bultmann replies:

"What I am concerned with is the permanent 'historic' significance of the unique event of past history . . . in virtue of which . . . it is an ever-present reality . . . on the one hand the kerygma and the sacraments (both of which are forms of personal encounter), and secondly in the concrete expressions of faith in our life. It is only through the preaching of the Word that the cross can become a personal encounter and so an ever-present reality. But this is not to deny the uniqueness of Christ . . . 'the Word made flesh' in which alone the proclamation of the Word has its origin and its credentials."[70]

Thus the "significant history" is equally present at every subsequent moment where the message is proclaimed. In the message of the church the divine event continues, the Word extends the incarnation: "He that heareth you heareth me."[71] In all succeeding generations the transforming encounter recurs as the Word of salvation is reiterated by the church and received in faith by the individual.

It is at this point, the prolongation of the decisive divine act through preaching, that Bultmann's thesis begins to determine Christian ethics. For one thing, the preaching brings home to man his condition, which "far from throwing man back upon himself . . . forces him to renounce the security of human values and . . . abandon himself to God". For another, "it is not the historic Christ who is the Lord, but Jesus Christ as encountered in the proclamation." "It is in the Word of Jesus Christ, in the preaching of the Christian message, that this encounter takes place." Faith understands "that here we are in the presence of the eschatological proclamation, of the saving act of God, of the risen Christ. *These three expressions are after all really synonymous* . . . For Christians of successive generations, *the act of God takes to itself reality in the preaching of the church, in which Christ lives again as interpreted by faith.*"[72]

Here precisely is the significance of the whole existentialist emphasis for Christian ethics, its bearing upon the relation of the Christian affirmations to the Christian imperatives. For Bultmann, history, doctrine, tradition, *have no meaning* apart from their existential impact, their value for authentic experience. All turns upon what happens to, and within, the believing recipient of the kerygma. The proclamation is "a decisive word", challenging decision: bidding man come to the knowledge of himself.[73]

It is impossible (summarises Malavez) for man to apprehend in faith the love of God if he remains what he is: "we do not believe it, or perceive it, save in the act in which we consent to be set free from ourselves and led into a new understanding of our existence." "Paul is not in the least interested," says Miegge, "in the earthly life, the death, the resurrection of Christ on the level of mere history." "It is in presenting (the cross) to us in the concreteness of preaching that God gives (it) the value of a divine gift, of a transcendent summons . . ." Faith confesses quite simply, "God judges *me,* God crucifies *me,* by revealing to me my powerlessness to liberate myself from myself, and by inviting me to accept this. It is precisely by this confession, understood in this sense, that I reach authentic liberation." As Macquarrie represents Bultmann's thought: "The cross and resurrection are experienced as atonement and new life when we take them into our own existence, when we give up all wordly security for a new life . . ."[74]

So the proclamation of the cross *is* the message of dying to sin, and the proclamation of the resurrection *is* the message of freedom and victory for the believer. "The Word of reconciliation places men at the point of inescapable decision, whether they will or will not understand that they have been crucified with Christ and are risen again with Him."[75]

"To believe in the cross means to take upon us the cross of Christ as our own cross; it means to allow ourselves to be crucified with Christ . . . The proclamation of the cross as saving event challenges the hearer to make up his mind whether he is willing to make (its) significance his own — whether, that is, he is willing to be crucified with Christ." To believe in the resurrection "means of course in the resurrection as it is manifest in the potency of life." There is no divine event save within personal commitment at the present moment, no effective salvation apart from the man who is actually united to God by faith.[76]

All this clearly implies that to receive the proclamation of the death and resurrection of Christ is to *be* changed — to encounter God, to *be* liberated, forgiven, raised to authentic existence, made victorious. "When the believer . . . says 'Yes' to the divine Word, when he accepts the revelation of his nothingness and of his own sin, then the believer finds that the cross is the act of God."[77] To believe is to participate in the saving event, and participation *means* obedience and love:

". . . participation in the death of Christ, in the judgement of God which condemns sin, consists in being crucified with Christ. We not only renounce our passions and our greed, but we accept ourselves as we are, as fallen human beings incapable of setting ourselves free . . . we renounce all pharisaical self-confidence, all trust in our own efforts; similarly, participation in the resurrection of Christ, which is an experience of liberation, will consist in 'rising again' with Jesus: that is, we shall believe not only that God sets us free, but also that we *are* truly liberated; this liberty is not only expressed in the indicative of love but also in the imperative: raised to the level of authentic existence, we shall love others with the love with which God loves us, that is to say, with a free and generous love . . . The whole of salvation consists in this."[78]

Such a summary finds most of the major themes of Christian ethics already *given* in the meaning of faith. The whole ethical and religious significance of the death of Jesus lies in its being entered into by believing hearts. Christian morality is not a duty consequent upon Christian profession; nor an obedient gratitude responding to what Christ has done for us: it is the unfolding of faith itself. The essential relation between true faith in Christ and moral transformation is as radical and unbreakable in Bultmann as in Paul.

In his analysis of the concrete expression of Christian morality, Bultmann emphasises autonomy, obedience, and love. Human freedom and decision are afforded large place, since all turns upon man's self-understanding through Christ, upon the authentic life into which Christ ushers him, upon faith, and upon decision for God against the world. Christian morality arises from the believer's confrontation with God's saving act and his resulting *freedom to obey*. The Christian owes his "authentic existence" wholly to God, but "there is continuity and self-identity between man prior to faith and man under faith, between Saul and Paul."[79] The gulf between inauthentic and authentic existence is bridged by a human decision: "wholesale determinism here is quite unthinkable." Certainly, too, "It is God who works in the Christian both to will and to do of His good pleasure," but decision is still demanded of the believer "in the concrete encounter of each moment."[80] It is here that Bultmann criticised Barth for inculcating "an attitude of blind surrender."

But the content of each crucial decision is "primarily and fundamentally obedience, a decision against self-will, self-seeking, and self-pleasing, a decision of obedience — as the freedom Christ bestows is freedom to obey."[81]

> "Genuine freedom is not subjective arbitrariness. It is freedom in obedience . . . Freedom is obedience to a law of which the validity is recognised and accepted, which man recognises as the law of his own being. This can only be a law which has its origin and reason in the beyond . . . It is the Word of God which calls man into genuine freedom and into free obedience . . . "[82]

And obedience, in turn, takes the form of "openness to the demand of love in the immediate situation or encounter." Bultmann insists that love knows "no precise definable content, no law, no preformulation." What love is, and involves, is discovered in the moment of encounter; "faith 'realises itself' in knowledge of what one has to do, or not to do, in the specific instance."[83] Nevertheless, for further definition Bultmann cites "a man is to love his neighbour as he himself would wish to be loved . . . the little words 'as yourself' in the love commandment pre-indicate both the boundlessness and the direction of loving conduct.''[84]

Robinson thinks that by insisting that love knows no definable content, Bultmann empties love of all moral understanding and clarity of purpose, reduces love to isolated situations and encounters, ignores the uncertainties, the conflict of values, in which love may find itself in any unpremeditated encounter. Bultmann's own attitude to the ''mythological'' story of Jesus precludes any appeal to a ''love commandment'', and to any connection between my decision to love and what ''God did''. My decision to love seems now to arise out of deeper self-understanding, evoked perhaps by the story of Jesus, but not necessarily related to it.[85]

The ''norm'' of love, assumed by most existential situationists, is especially difficult to justify on Bultmann's demythologising premise. Nevertheless Bultmann's emphasis upon the moral decision of faith and obedience, responding to a contemporary confrontation with the saving act of God, and worked out in concrete situations of daily life moment by moment, defines an approach which no truly Christian ethic may ignore.

So, despite the critical and philosophical reformulation of the ancient appeal of Christian ethics to scripture, although the biblical history-of-salvation is here seen only as the first occurrence of a confrontation that recurs whenever the gospel is received in faith — yet the insights essential to a scriptural ethic are preserved. Christian ethics is still presented as objectively *given,* upon divine authority, to be accepted or rejected by man at his own risk. The meaning of the Christian ideal is still closely associated with the biblical story, even though the relation of present situational demands to the written Word requires further clarification. And Christian morality still arises within a personal encounter of the sinner with God, as faith transforms the penitent and redemption proves to be a moral renewal and endowment. To this extent, the first persistent ''growing-point'' of modern ethical debate remains basically scriptural, though ''the ethic of the Word'' is not at all what Calvin (for example) would have understood by that phrase.

18

The Christian Norm

WHAT "THE KINGDOM" OF GOD was to the nineteenth-century version of Christian ethics — the seminal idea of the social gospel — that the love-commandment has become in twentieth-century debate, the universal criterion, the "norm", of all ethical decision. For all its ambivalence towards the written Gospels, even the ethic of the Word returns in the end to the age-old demand for *agape*. In Barth, love is one with faith in the response due to God's electing, purifying, creative, liberating love. In Brunner, the nature of the good is revealed in "the will-of-God-for-community", the final meaning of life, and God's self-giving becomes to us the command to love. In Bultmann, the authentic life born in confrontation with God expresses itself in obedience, "which is openness to the demand of love"; the divine love which we encounter is both indicative and imperative, and though love is not preformulated, the great Commandment is our guide. Writers less bound by critical presuppositions reach the same point more directly.

There is little doubt that this concentration upon love is consonant with other trends of the twentieth century — the search for some principle of social cohesiveness, as our world becomes at once smaller and more obstinately divided; the collectivist reaction against excessive individualism of the nineteenth century; the exploration of the nature of man, which finds the truest meaning of "personalism" in interpersonal relationships. It would be wrong, however, to speak of a "re-emergence" of love in Christian ethics as merely an adjustment to external influences, for this emphasis has been native to biblical and historical Christian ethics, from "my brother's keeper", *hesed,* and the corporate dimension of the Old Testament, through the sufficient love-commandment of Jesus, Paul and John, to the compassion of the Apologists, the "charity" of the Middle Ages, and the social concern that developed after Wesley. It was, nevertheless, underlined with new force in numerous studies of the early twentieth century, among the most penetrating and influential being that of Anders Nygren, *Agape and Eros* (1930-36).

Nygren examines thoroughly the meaning of love in Christian thought. He shows that *eros,* commonly understood as sensual desire, had in Plato included desire for the vision of the ideal beauty, "stretching upwards to the intelligible world of ideas, away from the world of the senses." Thence, in Neoplatonism, and in the Christian mystical tradition based upon it, *eros* became desire for union with God, the longing for God as the soul's highest goal. So Augustine saw *eros* "spiritualised" as the search for God as the only worthy and ultimate satisfaction. Aquinas distinguished "love of concupiscence" (desire to possess, stirred by something lovable in its object), from "love of friendship", which seeks only to give itself to its object in outgoing good will, seeking nothing. The latter is the New Testament's *agape,* and Nygren argued that the gulf between ego-centric *eros*-love and theo-centric *agape*-love, uncaused, unselfseeking, is never bridged. Augustine saw *agape* as God's own love, bestowed by the Spirit and flowing through the Christian heart; whereas *eros* was always human in origin, however exalted its desire. We would not know *agape* but for divine revelation: Luther branded *eros* -love — seeking God by human "ascent on the wings of desire" — as mere "works-religion". Nygren concludes that man cannot love God in the sense of *eros.* But neither can he "seek the good of" God, in the sense of *agape.* Thus the first part of the great Commandment is simply a call to faith, to belief in the love of God; the second part requires us to let the divine love in which we believe flow through us to our neighbours.

But in summarising Augustine, Nygren had said,

> "Caritas, love to God, is not merely the religious but the ethical centre of Christianity . . . Only one thing is really enjoined upon the Christian — namely love. *Where love is, no other precepts are requisite.* So he can say: 'Love, and do what thou wilt'."[1]

Those words define the second profferred solution to the problem of the relation of heritage to situation in Christian ethics — the isolation of a single, all-sufficient "norm", hallowed by long tradition but adequate for every modern circumstance. This is the position of "situation ethics".

1. THE SITUATION AND THE NORM

Existentialist emphasis upon immediacy of experience and concreteness of decision depreciates all abstract "moral principles", laws, rules, traditions, and insists upon the freedom and spontaneity of every truly moral reaction to the situations life presents. General rules of behaviour applicable to every conceivable situation and to every type of person are impossible to frame, impracticable to fulfil. Ethical law has always necessitated casuistry — the adjustment of "universal" rules to the infinitely varied complexities of daily life, even as pietism sought the direct instruction of the Spirit in answer to prayer, to discover the "immediate" will of God. Conscience, too, has often been regarded as interpreting the bearing of general moral principles upon personal circumstances. That "circumstances alter cases", that "the Spirit teaches what love requires at the moment of decision" (Brunner), that we must follow Christ "concretely" (Bonhoeffer), that every ethical decision must be fully personal, uncoerced, and relevant to actual circumstances, few would deny. "There must be a situationist element in every worthwhile ethic."[2] But when Joseph Fletcher is said to urge us "to break every one of the Ten Commandments . . . insists that Jesus had no ethics if ethics is a system of values and rules intelligible to all . . . even the most revered principles may be thrown aside if they conflict in any concrete case with love . . . "[3] — the situationist element seems to have cancelled the ethical.

Neither papal condemnation of situationist "subjectivism",[4] nor Fletcher's defects of presentation, should be allowed to obscure his contentions. His examples are often offensive ("those who break the seventh commandment, even whores, could be doing a good thing . . . killing innocent people might be right . . . Whether any form of sex (hetero-, homo-, or auto-) is good or evil depends on whether love is fully served . . . No unwanted or unintended baby should ever be born . . . Baby-making can be (and often ought to be) separated from love-making . . . Getting a divorce is what Christ would recommend").[5] This is propaganda, as is the journalistic style (" 'Christian' sex relations — marital monopoly . . .", "Situationism cutting itself loose from the dead hand of unyielding law");[6] and some of the "logic" — "love is the Holy Spirit", "Christian love and Christian prudence are one and the same, since they both go out to others" (so do a kiss and a slap in the face!).[7] The book is full of exceedingly hard cases (Hiroshima, the fugitive slave law, espionage emergencies) — notoriously unreliable bases for wisdom. Even more indefensibly, the whole thesis is that only the individual in the situation can possibly know what is right, and *not* the professor writing his sweeping generalisations, and innumerable "situationist rules", half the world away. Nevertheless, the argument itself remains debateable.

That argument runs: only one thing is intrinsically good — love, a way of relating to persons and using things; the ruling norm of Christian decisions is love, nothing else — the only law is Christ's law of love; love and justice are the same — justice is love calculating good between neighbours; love wills the neighbour's good irrespective of feeling, attraction; only the end justifies the means — the end sought in love is the sole criterion of morals, and whatever is successful in love's sight is justified; love's decisions are situational, not prescriptive — there are no prescribed rules other than love. Presuppositions implied are a pragmatic assessment of moral truth; positivist assertion of faith and moral value, beyond all argument; relativist, never absolute, decisions; an ambiguous, highly independent attitude towards traditional Christian ethics. Much is attractive to Christian minds — the supremacy afforded to love as the "master criterion", statements like "we understand love in terms of Jesus Christ", the insistence upon concrete and practical reactions in place of abstract moral "principles" and ideals.[8] But the vagueness, and the exclusiveness, of the chosen norm — displacing all other Christian instruction and discipline; the assumption that what love requires of us will always be self-evident; the replacement of all sense of *obligation* by a single, spontaneous, loving *impulse*; and the paradoxical illustrations of the principle that are offered ("A young unmarried couple might decide 'if they make their decision Christianly' to have sexual intercourse . . ."), must give Christians pause.

Defending a "normative" approach to ethics as inescapable, since judgement by foreseen consequences is so fallible, N. L. Geisler analyses alternative attitudes towards behavioural norms. We can accept no norms at all (nothing is objectively right or wrong — Kierkegaard, Sartre, Ayer); or no universal norms (there are always exceptions — Bentham, Moore); or one universal norm (love, truth, beauty, pleasure — avoiding conflict between them — which almost denies ethics by asserting individual caprice); or we can assert many conflicting norms, choosing the lesser evil and excusing contravention of the lost norm; or many non-conflicting norms, ("there is always a way out, for God sees that ideals never contradict — if you think hard enough!"); or a scale of norms, the "higher" taking priority and sacrificing lower norms when necessary.[9]

Such an analysis underlines the necessity to examine the origin, meaning, and sufficiency, of any suggested behavioural norm.

(1) The Origin of the Norm

Fletcher frequently states his case for "*Christian* situationism" in Christian language: "Christian situationism has only one norm . . . the *agape* of the summary commandment to love God and the neighbour". To this are appended eight "proof-texts", including Jesus on love of enemies, the great Commandment, the Samaritan parable,

Paul on love fulfilling the law. "We are always commanded to act lovingly . . ."[10] But when P.H. Nowell Smith, setting out to show that religious morality is infantile, lists among his premises, "Love, I shall assume, is the supreme virtue, because the life of love is in the end the only life that is fully rational, fully social,"[11] Fletcher would see nothing strange in Christian and non-Christian adopting the same norm *as sufficient*. There is for him "nothing particularly different or unique in a Christian's choices — except as to motive . . . But even here . . . lovingness is often the motive at work with full force behind the decisions of non-Christian and non-theological, even atheist, decision-makers . . . Love is not peculiar to Christians". Fletcher continues with the denial that even responsive, *grateful* love is exclusively Christian: "not even the gratitude is unique".[12] This may be true: but it reveals that in Fletcher's thought the love-norm is *not* dependent upon the Christian sources which he quotes.

Indeed, it is not at all clear why Fletcher chooses this norm among those available — "hate, compassion (as in Buddhism), the negative golden rule (as in Judaism)" as Geisler suggests; why not truthfulness, consistency (as in Kant), or simply regard for consequences? Fletcher implies that the norm arises out of the situation itself: "There is nothing outside a situation which by going into it can prejudge it"[13] — which again denies its *Christian* origin. But in fact each situation cannot determine the meaning of love, nor impose it as a norm — for then it would cease to be truly *normative* at all. While if scripture be appealed to, it is never explained why one group of passages should be determinative while so much else (the Ten Commandments, the New Testament interpretation of the law) is discarded.

Fletcher says explicitly that situation ethics "accepts revelation as the source of the norm while rejecting all 'revealed' norms or laws but the one command to love". He denounces Paul's views on the law, holds (against the Gospels) that Jesus would recommend divorce, and insists that Jesus never said anything like "You always have the poor with you" — Jesus was wrong and the disciples right. Even when "quoting" Jesus, Fletcher misuses: for Jesus never spoke of "loving God in the neighbour." G. H. Clark concludes that Fletcher treats scripture as if it were a verbally inspired revelation to himself alone. What Jesus said, or what is important in what Jesus said, is a matter of subjective opinion, to be tested by the love-norm, whose real origin lies elsewhere.[14]

Nor is the basis of the love-norm the social nature of man, which would involve an appeal to "natural law" — which Fletcher abhors.[15]

In the end, the norm appears to be simply *a decision,* resting upon a prior decision: "Any moral or value judgement in ethics . . . is a *decision,* not a conclusion . . . Aesthetic and ethical propositions are like faith propositions, they are based upon choice and decision . . . The key category of love (agape) . . . is established by *deciding* to say 'Yea' to the faith assertion that 'God is love' and thence by logic's inference to the value assertion that love is the highest good."[16] "The basic challenge offered by the situationist has nothing to do in any special way with theological over against non-theological faith commitments." "We love because he first loved us . . . obviously a faith foundation for love." Paul's phrase, "faith working through love" is "the essence and pith of Christian ethics." But this is not in any way essential to the observing of the norm: "a perfectly sincere man, in any way as intelligent and wise as any Christian might be, can refuse to put any stock whatever in Christ, in which case he might in all seriousness also doubt the hope and love that Paul linked to faith . . . " — without, apparently undermining the love-norm. It is not that God *is* love, or *has* first loved us: all depends on our decision to think so.

But the Christian can hardly be content with a "faith" that consists simply in his own "deciding it shall be so;" he believes that what Christ did, said, suffered, and achieved *is so.* For him, the rule of love derives from a whole tradition which reaches him with scriptural and historical authority, as one main consequence of God's character as revealed in His intervention into history in Christ. The Christian loves because he earnestly believes as a fact, not as a position he has chosen to adopt, that Christ loves him. Without that belief he would not love, for there is nothing in the state of the world, in the scientific account of the struggle for existence, in the psychological analysis of human nature, or in the record of man's inhumanity to man, on which to base a love-commandment, but only on the Christian apprehension of Christ as Teacher, Lawgiver, Saviour, and Lord. So Paul Ramsey finds in the fact that God was in Christ reconciling the world, the source and sanction of the Christian ethic of unlimited and unrequited love in a world gone radically wrong.[18]

Though Fletcher appeals to the *teaching* of Jesus, he rejects the consequences of that appeal. If it is love as taught by Jesus that is the norm, then consistency demands it be kept in closest relation with other qualities and virtues which Jesus commended. It will not do to base the all-important norm upon one thing Jesus is reported to have said, and then show (as Fletcher seeks to do) how wrong Jesus was on chastity, divorce, self-discipline — according to the same record. Claiming His authority for the norm, we are obliged to accept the norm as He defined it, and it would be hazardous in the extreme to claim His authority for Fletcher's approval of extra-marital sex, abortion, lies, murder — on whatever loving excuses. Further: if it is love as seen in Jesus which is the norm, then it cannot be set so enthusiastically over against law as Fletcher loves to show. For Jesus certainly did not see love as the compendium, or distillation, of the law in such sense as to be law's replacement or successor, so that the law is *done away.* Jesus explicitly reaffirms love of God and neighbour as the greatest *commandment,* as the fulfilling, not the abrogating, of law. This is Paul's point, both in the passage which Fletcher quotes (Galatians 5:14) and in the one he does not (Romans 8:1f): that the requirements of the law *are* fulfilled in us. This presentation of love as law, as commanded, is of the deepest ethical significance. It means that the norm of Christian behaviour is after all an objective standard to which we are obliged to conform, and not one we decide, or choose, or happen to prefer, because it appeals to cultivated minds. If we ascribe the origin of the love-norm to Jesus, we must keep it what He made it — in context and in meaning.

(2) The Meaning of the Norm

"To act in every situation spontaneously as the free self exercising responsible love" is a sophisticated notion which calls urgently for explanation. *Situation, self,* and *love* are heavily-laden words. To the Christian, the *situation* in which he finds himself is not accidental: "we do not fall like pebbles on the beach." Each situation is "structured by God's great redemptive acts of the past and . . . directed by God's providence towards final consummation . . . The most important factor in the present situation is the ever-living God . . . "[19] As Brunner says, God "is not One who comes on the scene after all that has been done previously has been done without His knowledge. He Himself places you where you are;" and Barth: "The individual moments at which, as Commander, He encounters individual men . . . owe their particularity and concreteness not to any natural process, fate, or chance, but to a particular purpose and disposition of God."[20]

So, too, each situation is but part of a total situation, not only of the individual life but of society, and of the ongoing life of the world. Woods argues that to take truly responsible action we need reasonable knowledge of the situation, of our power of affecting the situation, and of the change in the situation which we hope to effect: and here we are assisted by all kinds of standards, maxims, principles, laws.[21] To the Christian, each situation shaped by providence, redemption, his own experience, by God's call at that moment and

His purpose for the future, is fraught with opportunity for discipline, education, obedience, and service. It is a serious distortion to isolate any decision from the whole background of belief, training, commitment and conditioned emotion, which affects how the individual sees the situation and will help to determine his response. From another side, N. H. G. Robinson objects[22] to the particular moment of decision being "so packed with meaning that it becomes transformed into a mythico-mystical reality" in which are compressed the entire meaning of Christian theology, ethics and destiny — packing the discrete moment "beyond bursting point".

So with the *self* presupposed by situationist ethics. A considerable maturity of moral experience is assumed in one expected to make immediate, responsible decisions undirected by moral rules. Human conduct is not "a series of individual decisions . . . each in isolation . . . It is always the action of the same subject" (Barth[23]), whose past choices, failures, triumphs, endurance, experience, training, hopes, memories and loyalties are all part of each decision. As Ferguson says[24]: "I do make general moral decisions. I do not, for example, ask in relation to every woman I meet, 'Shall I commit adultery?'" A predictable consistency of character is a significant factor in every separate moral response, even in unprecedented circumstances: Fletcher's own phrase, "the responsible self", presupposes such qualitive self-understanding.

In the Christian, especially, this self which responds consistently in successive situations has a distinctive nature. Ferguson mentions the Christian's commitment; C. F. D. Moule says that Christian moral judgements, "however much they may vary with changing circumstances, are by definition the judgements of those who believe the major affirmations of the Christian faith to be true." Brunner, too, describes the Christian confronted with the necessity of moral decision: "Something has happened to him within the sanctuary of faith . . . There he stands, as one who has been touched by God, whose heart has been pierced by Him, as one who has come under the stern judgement of God and has tasted the divine mercy . . . there he stands, this weak human being, in the midst of life, among other people; but because he comes 'from thence' he has now another 'position' in the world, and it is this which makes him a Christian."[25] Clearly, far more is implied than a naked individual confronting a novel situation with only a single norm to influence his response.

The meaning of *love* likewise, is far from simple. Fletcher asserts that love may murder, drop atomic bombs, commit deliberate human sacrifice (to preserve war secrets), falsehood, unchastity, divorce, theft, adultery, homosexuality, extra-marital intercourse, abortion, whoredom, apparently gambling, even polygamy.[26] As G. H. Clark says,[27] Fletcher never reasons out what love requires, but merely asserts (for example) that "no unwanted or unintended baby should ever be born" as though that were self-evident. It may be that love does not exclude any of these modes of behaviour, but the *assumption* that it does not raises a serious question as to what love means. "Loving one's paramour is one thing, and loving one's persecutor quite another" as N. H. G. Robinson remarks. "To do the loving thing in all cases" leaves wide open the question what, in any one case, *is* the loving thing.

Fletcher seeks to give definition to the norm by asserting that love always puts people first: "Love is of people, by people, for people . . . " But there is nothing in this to prevent a Trade Union "loving" a Corporation, a city "loving" the nation — which seems seriously to qualify the personal character of "love".[28]

Sometimes Fletcher speaks as though love *itself* were the moral goal: "One's duty is to seek the goal of *the most love possible* in every situation . . . Our task is to act so that more good (that is, lovingkindness) will occur than any possible alternatives; we are to seek an optimum of lovingkindness . . . the hedonistic calculus becomes the agapeic calculus — the greatest amount of neighbour welfare for the largest number of neighbours possible."[29] Despite the sudden introduction of "welfare", this will hardly serve. It would be unforgivable to postpone help to a neighbour until his need is more desperate, until his enmity is more intense, or to prefer helping my enemy to helping my child, all in order that my help when it comes shall show *more love* on my part. G. H. Clark notes that if Bentham could not calculate pleasures, Fletcher has no easier problem. Should an adulterer seek to maximise his own feelings of love, those of his paramour, those of his paramour and his wife, or those of the whole human race? How *can* love, in itself, be measured?

Even more important, how can love, by itself, be shown? Love needs to know how persons *ought* to be treated, how they *desire* to be, how they *need* to be. Knowing these things, love still does not treat the libertine as he desires to be treated; nor the enemy as we desire to treat him, nor yet as he desires to be treated; nor the child as he wants, but as he "ought" to be treated. Once that is said, we have stepped beyond love as the single, sufficient norm. To speak of love's conferring *good,* or "welfare", is to introduce a further criterion by which to recognise love itself, and a whole class of questions beyond the simple disposition of good will. To acknowledge, for example, that persons *deserve,* or *ought,* or *need* to know the truth, is to throw great doubt on the claim that love may justify lying. The moral life cannot be defined in terms of love until we know what love properly requires: by itself, love offers no direction, content, or criterion of conduct: but only a norm of *motive.*

(3) The Sufficiency of the Norm

That the love-norm is insufficient for moral guidance might be illustrated from Fletcher's numerous qualifications of it: he certainly does not trust to the agapeic "master criterion" alone.

"Moral choices need intelligence . . . concern, sound information . . . more critical intelligence, more factual information, and more self-starting commitment to righteousness, than most people can bring to bear . . . Love must figure the angles — it needs prudence — and imagination . . . breadth of vision, imagination, foresight . . . Love uses its head, calculates its duties, obligations, opportunities, resources . . . calculates immediate and remote consequences, is discerning and critical . . . It is love's business to calculate gains and losses . . . " After this, we are not surprised to learn that situationism has its *strategy:* its one and only law, *agape;* the *sophia* (wisdom) of the church and culture, containing many "general rules"; the *kairos,* or moment of decision whether the *sophia* can serve in the given situation; and its multiple questions — what is the end sought, by what means, for what motive, with what foreseeable consequences?[30]

Nothing here is objectionable, but it adds up to considerable elaboration of the one sufficient criterion. An attitude or disposition of good will is not in itself a knowing, calculating, discerning "entity". The single, simple love-norm turns out to be a compendium of many intellectual, moral, social, judicial, utilitarian, empiricist and religious considerations. For the elaboration of love continues:

"*Agape* is an active determination of the will . . . benevolence . . . a phenomenon of strength . . . We have to add an 's' to neighbour in (Christ's) distillation of the law — We must sophisticate the childish notion that love is only for people one at a time . . . Love does not permit us to solve our problems or soothe our wounds at the expense of innocent third parties. The enemy-neighbour has no stronger claims than the friend-neighbour . . ." "One's *duty* is to seek the goal of the most love possible, and one's goal is to obey the *command* to do just that." So again the highly intellectual consideration of equity is smuggled in — "a just interpretation of the law with due reference to the circumstances"; equally suddenly we come upon the standard what is "fitting, expedient, edifying, constructive . . . with some sense of causation"; while "the situationist enters into every decision-making situation fully armed with ethical maxims of his community and its heritage . . . as illuminators of his problems."[31]

Plainly, *any* single behavioural norm will be sufficient basis for a theory of ethics, if one first makes that norm include every other.

Other criticisms of the single "sufficient" love-norm urge, for example, its lack of consistency, the need of at least something like the Golden Rule, to give good intentions safe direction.[32] The intuition of what is right in every changing situation is "a remarkable gift", not possessed without long experience, struggle, experiment. Many earnest Christians never reach the maturity which can take in its stride all problems of insight and foresight, of priorities and balanced judgement; the just estimate of consequences, of rightly analysed motives; the dangers of emotional enthusiasm out-running wisdom; the difficulty of reconciling rival claims, say of mother and baby, of wife and paramour. Very few are capable of the momentary, spontaneous intuition which reaches wise and right decision at once, often with urgency, and often under stress. Situationism does not take seriously either the necessity of ethical growth, or the fact of sin. For one need, the "bank of experience" summarised in precepts, warnings, guidelines, rules, is an invaluable educator; for the other, the law with its injunctions and warnings, is an immense restraint and safeguard. Fletcher dismisses the need as temporary and "neurotic";[33] yet, as Macquarrie points out[34], life is too short for innumerable agonising appraisals, undertaken each time *de-novo* — rules, customs, habits, save effort, capitalise experience, while prohibitions can save us from our worst selves. Certainly the early church was far too wise to thrust out her new converts mentally naked and spiritually unprepared into moral situations of great complexity and immense danger, armed only with "the agapeic intuition." There is little evidence that for young Christians in the modern world the complexity, or the danger, is really any less.

(4) Some Larger Issues

Three larger issues affect the search for an authoritative, and truly sufficient, ethical norm. (a) As in Brunner's thought, so in agape-situationism, there seems little place for any *personal* ethic. The sole rule is good will towards neighbours: "a solitary man is no man at all . . . the Christian is neighbour-centred first and last . . . the man for others."[35] No room seems left for the man himself, the man before God: all morality lies in relationship, and in *act:* "love is not something we have or are, it is something we do . . . Love does not say to us, Be like me; it says, Do what you can where you are."[36] It follows, negatively, that "pride, covetousness, lust, envy, gluttony, anger, sloth" are no longer seven deadly sins but seven trivial details of psychological make-up: only when they overflow in acts unloving towards a neighbour are they to be deplored — a judgement directly contradicting the Sermon on the Mount. Positively, personal integrity, purity of motive, honesty of mind, humility, are no longer virtues. A doctor will not seek a reputation for truth-speaking, but only for saying what *he* thinks each patient will be the better for hearing. The business man will not cultivate a reputation for personal reliability, but will deal with each customer and situation individually, and "intuitively". Nor will a minister care to be known for consistent kindliness, approachability, just judgement, loyalty to truth — unpredictability will be the proof of his competence! Each individual is reduced to his *public* self, and consists, ethically, of visible reactions provoked momentarily by external situations and other people.

(b) Situationists can never pass beyond immediate assessments of their own conduct to assessments of social attitudes, obligations of social reform, the definition of social goals. Traditionally, the Christian ethic has considered more than individual encounters with neighbours: it has shown concern for the life of society, for social causes and consequences, for social justice, and the protection of the overborne and the minority. It has sought to influence *society,* and the development of morality in history, not by persuasion only but by law. All this, situation ethics with its exclusively personalistic approach and its abhorrence of law, rule, and sanction, must abrogate.

It is urged, "There is nothing individualistic about personalism, nor in situation ethics";[37] but Macquarrie can quote Ramsey's dictum "No social morality was ever founded upon a situation ethic", in support of his own criticism that a purely situation ethic does less than justice to man as a member of a community. So many of the "situations" which Fletcher envisages as examples of the sufficiency of the love-to-neighbour norm — abortion, pre-marital sex, divorce, military murder, and numerous others — have implications that affect the standards, tone, example and moral development of society itself, beyond the intimacies and independence of one-to-one, or one-to-several, relationships. Despite its protestations, situationism appears incurably individualistic, unless Christian ideas like the divine family, the body of Christ, the Christian *summum bonum* as essentially fellowship, can be injected into its conception of love.

(c) In Christian ethics, the love-norm is firmly combined on the one hand with the conception of commandment and law, and on the other hand with the goal of the kingdom of God. In situationism, as law is dissolved by the insistence upon autonomy, so the divine kingdom seems totally eclipsed by the exclusive role given to spontaneous love. So are lost the sense of *obligation*, and also (as N. H. G. Robinson notes[38]) openness to "the inbreaking of a new order," which extends every situation, and my response within it, "back and forwards to Christ come and coming". Not only do the immature need rule before they are ready for autonomy, but so long as man remains a sinner — even a forgiven sinner — the life of love is also a life of obedience, imposed upon him with obligation and authority, by the King who is also Father, Redeemer and Friend.

Such is the "obedient love" of which Paul Ramsey makes so much: "The central notion or category in Christian ethics is obedient love — the sort of love the Gospels describe as love fulfilling the law . . . " Obedient love is shown emerging from Judaism, kingdom-expectation, and legalism, and brought more clearly to light at the Reformation. "Love for neighbour comprises the full meaning of absolute, unhesitating obedience to God . . . Love was for Jesus *obedient* love, not simply some humanitarian ethic. It arose from His prompt and total response to the demands placed on Him by God's inbreaking kingdom."[39]

Obedience, law, are required, not only to enlarge private love-responses into a social ethic, but to bring recalcitrant human nature, *ever and again,* under the yoke of Christ's rule, to love God and thy neighbour at His word and for His sake — whatever the neighbour thinks, however the neighbour reacts. And since the divine kingdom is established first within the soul, such a conception of Christ's command of love ensures that the norm which governs the public life shall govern also the secret places of the heart.

Paul Ramsey argues[40] that Christian love cannot be defined in terms already familiar, but only as all basic and primitive concepts are defined, by *pointing* to their meaning. Of 1 Corinthians 13 he declares, "this classic statement of the meaning of Christian love defines by *indication,* pointing not to anything generally experienced by all men everywhere . . . but . . . to Jesus Christ." In the end, Fletcher reaches the same insight. "What is precisely and exactly and starkly unique about Christian ethics is Christ . . . Take away the doctrine of the incarnation and the Christian ethic is nothing special whatsoever . . . We understand love in terms of Jesus Christ . . . "[41]

The love-norm, illuminating, commanding, inspiring, in every concrete decision-demanding situation, is essential to any ethic claiming the epithet Christian. But before that norm can be held the sufficient master criterion of all morality, it needs considerable enlargement, exposition, and definition. Attempting that, we are led at once, irresistibly, to the image of Him who alone is its source, its embodiment, its only adequate definition.

2. THE CHRISTIAN NORM

So, at the end, we are brought back to the one constant, the one unvarying compass bearing, of Christian morality amid all the changes and adjustments, the development and diversity, of twenty centuries: the imitation of Christ. In Henson's self-evident definition, "Christian morality *is* the morality inculcated by Jesus Christ and illustrated by His example."[42] Although differently interpreted from time to time, that is the one feature never for long lost sight of, or wilfully neglected, throughout the long saga of piety, apologetic and martyrdom, of mysticism, eclecticism and compromise, of heroism and experiment, that is the story of Christian ethics.

The background lies in "Be ye holy, for I am holy, says the Lord", and the synoptics' "resemblance proves relationship." In Paul, the imitation of Christ, as possession of Christ's mind, is the goal of redemption; imitation is scarcely less emphasised in John, and Peter. "Assimilation to Christ" was a formative idea in patristic ethics; a different interpretation exercised powerful influence within mediaeval mysticism and asceticism. Abelard and Erasmus brought the theme into the common life of Christians again; Luther gave it new expression in "being a Christ to my neighbour" and the "theology of the cross"; Calvin, too, from the very different angle of man's recovery of his creation-image. Counter-Reformation emphasis upon prayer looked to the imitation motive, while the "self-emptying" of Christ inspired Orthodox Christianity to heroic endurance. Protestantism found the notion too mystical until Quakerism reasserted "the Christ within". The theme moved into focus again as Ritschl "centred attention on the historic Christ", and Harnack made the teaching of Jesus determinative; later, Maurice and Rauschenbusch worked out the social significance of Jesus' example as Founder of the kingdom. Different again was Herrmann's treatment, concentrated upon sharing the inner spirit of Jesus.[43]

Not less significant is the inability of modern writers, even the more radical, to keep far from this theme.

(1) The Return to Imitation

As we saw, Fletcher is driven by the insufficiency of his own criteria to close his essay with the traditional idca of *Christus Exemplar* — "love is the master criterion . . . (and) we understand love in terms of Jesus Christ."[44] Bonhoeffer, too, made much of the "form of

Christ" as the only mould of Christian morality[45]. Barth appeals to the implications of the incarnation: "Jesus is a valid model for the general relationship of men to the will of God . . . The image to which we have to conform ourselves."

"Jesus never exists alone and for Himself, but always as the firstborn among many brethren . . . " Barth expounds five Pauline passages on imitation, appeals to bear others' burdens, to edify others, to be forgiving, to "live in the mind which is in Christ Jesus" — "What is required of us is that our action should be brought into conformity with His action."[46]

In Paul Ramsey's view, Christ is central for understanding the image of God in human nature. He is perfect man: the fullness of His stature "recreates that image in which man was originally created". Similarly, the idea of love can be "adequately defined only by indicating Christ Jesus;" while sin, too, can be "Christianly taught" only if sin is given a Christocentric definition: "Jesus Christ is the standard for measuring the reign of God among men . . . Not only in what He said but in what He did and in what He was, Jesus placarded before men 'the righteousness of God'." "Think this in you which also in Christ Jesus . . . being changed into His likeness from one degree of glory to another."[47]

"The Christian ideal for human character is summed up in the person of Jesus Christ . . . How men need to measure themselves by the stature of the fullness of Christ can best be seen by acknowledging what narrow specialists in virtue we all are . . ." incomplete, unbalanced. We need to "grow up in every way into Him who is the head, into Christ, into the stature of His fullness." Christianity begins "wholly outside of ordinary human nature . . . and suggests that (it) be made to conform to the Christ-standard. It aims to cut man to fit the pattern, not the pattern to fit man . . . Christianity does not compose its conception of maturity out of available cultural values; it points maturity out . . . citing the Man, Christ Jesus."[48]

Yet another modern writer, Ninian Smart, argues,[49] "This seeming paradox that Christ is both God and man brings new light to the religious demand for humility. Christ himself seems to exhibit the most profound humility: and He is, because divine . . . the central model for imitation. We too must take up our Cross . . . the belief that a human is divine, and uniquely so, implies that there is one supreme life to model our conduct on (models are one main method of inculcating moral insight). This, incidentally, has both an advantage and a defect: for while it harnesses the resources of worship and meditation to the task of self-improvement, a single main model is likely to be hard to apply to the varied circumstances of many lives . . . While the main point of Christ's career is His specifically religious role as Saviour of men, His words and conduct illustrate in a profound manner the way numinous religion and morality hang together."

To cite only one more instance, not less impressive for being critical, N. H. G. Robinson in a chapter entitled *The Imitation of Christ,* examines with great acuteness "that representation of the Christian ethic which fundamentally accepts Jesus Christ as the ultimate pattern in the moral sphere and which thus concentrates attention upon Him as a unique authority in the realm of morals and religion." Though not satisfied with this account of the place of Jesus in Christian ethics, Robinson presents it sympathetically as "a view which has commanded the assent of many who are not professional theologians . . . many have recognised in Jesus a moral genius who contrived to confront the world with a new and unsurpassable ideal . . . the fundamental affirmation seems to be that He is our final authority . . . " Robinson reproduces a discussion by Hastings Rashdall as an "argument of the highest value". His own disagreement is certainly not on the ground that it says too much for Jesus, but that it does not say enough.

Such illustrations suffice to show that the age-old theme of *Imitatio Christi* still holds its place in current expositions of Christian morality.

(2) The Quest for Christ

Returning interest in the imitation of Christ has wider significance however: the inner logic of the Reformation is here working itself out. Just as, with the loss of the "infallible" church, Protestant thought turned with eagerness to the infallible scriptures, so with the rise of biblical criticism Protestant thought turns to seek again the infallible Christ — Lord of scripture and of conscience — for its authority in ethics. Inevitably, the Figure of Jesus has moved firmly again to the centre of theology, of biblical study, of apologetics, and of ethics, and with astonishing emphasis and unanimity.

The "Theology of the Word" shows the living message of God through Christ replacing written scripture as centre of attention. In ethics, Ritschl sought in the life of Jesus, seen as revelation of God and realisation of the moral ideal, a clue to transpose theology into ethical terms; rejecting this, J. Weiss began the process of *historical* study to rescue Jesus from abstractions of theology. Herrmann built upon objective, historical fact though interested mainly in Christ's spiritual development. Albert Schweitzer summarised a whole century's search and gave the movement its name, *The Quest of the Historical Jesus.* Reviewing eighty-six "Lives of Jesus" (or contributions thereto) Schweitzer concluded that a biography of Jesus in the modern sense is impossible: the permanent element in the story is "a spiritual force — the religion of love — a world-affirmation which centres in reverence for life."

The "quest" has continued: a thorough historicism in New Testament studies hunts every archaeological, literary, linguistic, cultural clue to what HE was like, and what He actually said. Schurer, Edersheim, Guignebert, Goguel, Kahler, Gloege, Zahrut, Bousset, Sanday, Borchert and others joined the search, with Farrer, T. R. Glover's *Jesus of History,* David Smith's *In the Days of His Flesh,* Fosdick's *Manhood of the Master,* Seeley's *Ecce Homo,* J. S. Stewart's *Life and Teaching of Jesus Christ* — "an extraordinary stream of popular books . . . by theological scholars, literary men, journalists, poets, novelists" as D. M. Baillie described them, adding that "the very phrases 'the Jesus of History' and 'the historical Jesus' would have been unintelligible to earlier generations." Baillie also quotes D. S. Cairns' verdict on the "recovery of the Jesus history" as "one of the greatest spiritual events in the story of Christianity." Still more recently, T. W. Manson, A. M. Hunter, Dibelius, Bornkamm, Kaseman, Fuchs, J. M. Robinson (*New Quest of the Historical Jesus),* Althaus, W. Barclay, have contributed to "the impossible task". Towering over all are Bultmann's indefatigable researches into Christian origins. H. K. McArthur's *In Search of the Historical Jesus* summarises mid-century discussion.[50]

By no means all of this quest for Christ has had in view the ethical imitation of His example. But the multiplication of our modern problems, the confusion produced by our specialisations, perhaps something of nostalgia for simplicity and certainty, the shallowness of our agnosticism, the timeless fascination of that superb Figure and His "impossible dream", all combine to keep active the search for the ultimate truth about Jesus, and the significance of His ethical vision for our own time. Of that larger hunger for certainty, authority, clarity, and an objective basis for hope, the rediscovery of the *Imitatio Christi* is a significant part.

Ethical and spiritual need does not, however, prove that the desired end is possible, or even that the method is valid. Schweitzer's doubt of the possibility of recapturing the authentic portrait of Christ was strongly reinforced by Bultmann in words that have become famous:

"I do indeed think that we can now know almost nothing concerning the life and personality of Jesus, since the early Christian sources show no interest in either, and are moreover fragmentary and often legendary; and other sources about Jesus do not exist . . . We can strictly speaking know nothing about the personality of Jesus."[51]

N. H. G. Robinson warns of the consequences for ethics:

"It must be stressed that what confronts us is not the career itself, the actual words and deeds of Jesus, but the record of the career . . . a record that must constantly be subjected to literary and historical criticism, and does not provide an unchanging yardstick. Ethical fundamentalism, even when restricted to the Gospels, is no longer a live possibility."[52]

And D. E. Nineham presses the warning home:

"It is idle to deny that some real loss is involved in our conclusions. If they are right, it is illegitimate to press the details, and many of the personal traits, in the stories . . . not only in an historical interest (but) for devotional purposes not directly envisaged by the evangelists. A question mark is clearly set against some forms at least of *imitatio Christi* devotion, and also against the practice, which still largely governs the life of the churches, of quoting individual sayings and incidents from the Gospels as precedents."[53]

That twofold caveat against a naive Jesus-cult is forthright enough!

On its historical side, it is possible to indicate some reaction against earlier scepticism. After a life-time's work on the *Gospel of Mark,* fundamental to our knowledge of Jesus, Vincent Taylor could say:

In Mark we have an authority of the first rank for our knowledge of the story of Jesus. Separated at the time of writing by little more than a generation from the death of Jesus, its contents carry us back farther into the oral period before Mark wrote to the tradition first of the Palestine Community and subsequently that of the gentile church at Rome . . . here is a writing of first-rate historical importance. . . . Without this Gospel . . . invaluable in itself . . . it is impossible to account for the history of primitive Christianity . . . it sets at the centre the personality of Jesus Himself and His redemptive work for men."[54]

To that judicious opinion others may be added, equally weighty:

T. W. Manson, a meticulous scholar of unarguable common-sense: "I am increasingly convinced that in the Gospels we have the materials — reliable materials — for an outline account of the ministry as a whole. I believe it is possible to produce such an outline, and that when produced it will dovetail into the rest of the picture . . . And it will give an adequate explanation of the existence of the church. But we have *some* details; and I think it is true to say that these short stories, parables, sayings, poems and so on, which go to make up the Gospels themselves, epitomise the whole story. The quest of the historical Jesus is still a great and a most hopeful enterprise."[55]

A. M. Hunter summarises his conclusion in words of A. E. J. Rawlinson: "The Gospel record is rooted in history. 'Record and revelation, history and interpretation, cannot in the Gospels be separated; but the control of history is everywhere present . . . The earliest witnesses to Jesus of Nazareth were no followers of cunningly devised fables. They were men who were set to bear witness to the truth.' "[56]

Stephen Neill, reviewing a century of New Testament scholarship, says "It is the view of many competent scholars today that all the fragments of Christian tradition which we possess in the New Testament bear witness with singular unanimity to one single historical figure, unlike any other that has ever walked among the sons of men; and that . . . though an immense amount of work has still to be done . . . he is even now not so much the unknown, the problem, as the one who to the believer is well known . . . the one 'whom we have by heart'."[57]

And William Barclay, concluding a wide-ranging review of modern debate about the historicity of the gospel record, makes two confessions of faith: "The fact is that from the Gospels a recognisable person emerges, and it is equally true that the personality there depicted is in accordance with the facts . . . This does not mean that I must literally and exactly and mechanically accept everything: but it does beyond all doubt mean that I must be able to regard the picture of the Gospels as historically and factually reliable in general . . . The Gospels are certainly the product of the faith of the early church; but the Gospels are equally certainly the reliable record of the events on which that faith is founded . . . no matter what historical research and analysis can do to that record, they cannot alter the historical rightness of its total impression on the mind and heart."[58]

Such a consensus of positive opinion on the historicity of the Gospels' portrait is the more reassuring for being stated with due qualifications and caution. Whether those qualifications justify fully D. E. Nineham's warning against "some forms at least of *imitatio Christi*" depends upon the meaning ascribed to conformity to Christ, how the appeal to Christ's example is handled in Christian ethics.

(3) The Meaning of Imitation

For citation of words and deeds of Jesus, as a preformulated prescription for all situations and problems — quite simply — *has not been the classic understanding of imitatio Christi*. Against a literalist biblicism which quotes reputed words and acts of Jesus to foreclose discussion of all moral questions, Nineham's warning is salutary. But it was not so that Paul understood "conformity to Christ", nor Peter, nor John.[59] Only a partial, and oral, tradition was then available; and the most urgent problems facing the apostolic church were not those upon which Jesus had pronounced. To "possess the mind of Christ" included much more than acquaintance with the story of His life and words, as Paul makes clear. In the patristic period, assimilation to Christ meant emulation of the purity, peaceableness and charity of Jesus. In the middle ages the imitation theme was variously interpreted[60] but acquaintance with the Gospel documents was in all schools less important than inward "experiences". Abelard's appeal is to the humanity of Christ and His example of love in the atonement, not to specific acts or sayings; Erasmus comes nearer to objective study of the Gospels for the content of Christ's example; Luther returns to the general pattern of Christ's love and suffering, Calvin to the explication of the image of God in man, and the sharing of Christ's righteousness, self-discipline and mortification.[61] The Quakers' inner light, and the Orthodox church's self-emptying again rest little upon historical details of Christ's ministry. This is not to suggest that imitation was compatible with ignorance of the matchless story: only that citation of sayings and precedents as rules of behaviour was not of the essence of the Christian ideal. Not until the rediscovery of the Gospel of the Kingdom, and the aptness of many of Christ's words to social problems of the nineteenth century, did the habit grow of weaving reputed utterances and incidents from Christ's own life into ethical doctrines.

If the functions of an ethical exemplar may be described as proving the possibility of a given ideal and inspiring others to emulate it; providing instruction on the nature and conditions of the ideal, and a standard by which to assess all that falls below it; pioneering new ideals and new frontiers where the ideal has not yet been applied; and inculcating and nourishing the imagination and the spirit which attainment of the ideal will demand — then for countless men and women of all generations and all races Jesus has fulfilled all that, without any insuperable difficulties either of historical accuracy, of exact translation, of literary criticism of ancient documents, getting in His way. This, again, is not to suggest that precise scholarship is not an invaluable aid, illuminating dark places, clarifying puzzles, correcting misjudgements, sharpening ethical insight: but only that detailed palaeological accuracy is not essential to Christlikeness — because the *imitatio Christi* proceeds upon another level.

Paul's "having the mind of Christ," almost interchangeable with "the new nature", "the new man in Christ", "possessing the Spirit of Christ"; the mystics' union with the interior Christ; Calvin's image of Christ as a recapturing of an original nature lost in the Fall; the Quakers' "Christ within the soul", are all in a sphere of interest distant from pious antiquarianism. So was Herrmann's contention that the revelation of God lies in the inner life or spiritual consciousness of Jesus, and not in such biographical details about Him as the virgin birth, the miracles, the resurrection. The inner life of Jesus, preserved in the New Testament, *lays hold on us* as on the first disciples — makes an "impression" on us, bringing us into communion with God. "The inner life of religion is a secret in the soul": but its grounds are, the objective historical fact of Christ as it is enshrined within the New Testament and still lays hold of us; and the way our inner moral convictions are realised in the life of Jesus.[62] So again — far removed from antiquarianism — was Bonhoeffer's interpretation of the imitation of Christ as the "form" of Christ to which we are to be conformed: "it is not a question of applying the teaching of Christ . . . It is Christ who shapes men . . ."[63]

In a remarkable way, recent study of the Gospels itself witnesses to a Christlikeness deeper than external duplication of the words and deeds of Jesus. There are a few places in the record where the most reverent student must pause, and cast about for possible explanations. The cursing of the fig-tree, the cleansing of the Temple, the method proposed for finding money for the Temple-tax, the unexpectedly "mercenary" promise to Peter of "thrones . . . houses, brothers, sisters, lands a hundredfold . . . " are points where piety becomes ingenious, or humbly refuses to pronounce. It is the process of maturing Christian judgement that is here significant. We come at first with naive wonder and uncritical mind to every word of the Gospel record; but it is part of the wonder, part of the power of that record, that with growing understanding and increasing experience of fellowship with Christ, we return in time, with the sharpened sensibilities, the clearer discernment of values, *which we owe to Christ Himself,* to read again, and to discriminate, to compare, to seek fresh insight about some details which seem just possibly to obscure the glory of that perfect life. It is so that the apocryphal gospels are assessed and rejected as "out of character" for Him. So far from adhering slavishly to all available written documents about Jesus, the *internal* imitation of Christ — "the mind of Christ" — becomes the best equipment for evaluating the documents themselves, testing all things and holding fast to that which is Christlike.

(4) The Religious Context

Such considerations carry imitation of Christ beyond the sphere of Christian ethics into distinctively religious areas of Christian life and thought. To hear the Christian message powerfully expounded, illustrated and applied to daily life, by faithful preaching within the context of worship; and to study humbly, diligently and repeatedly, the story of Jesus' life and work as given in the Gospels, are undoubtedly major steps in the pursuit of Christlikeness. Yet it is not alone by ceaselessly filling the mind with sayings and deeds of Jesus, that inner likeness matures: the whole sacramental life of the church is designed to the same end. In baptism once for all, and in the Lord's Supper again and again, the individual places himself within an inherited pattern of thought, action and emotion in which great moments of the life and death of Christ are re-enacted. In such objectively disciplined sacramental encounter with the living Christ, the individual's inchoate faith is filled with meaning, rooted in the historic events of man's redemption; while the responding soul is drawn again to die with Christ to sin, and live with Christ in continually renewed commitment to all Christ represents.

Similarly, any progress in Christlikeness will certainly presuppose our being possessed, renewed, "filled" with the Spirit of Christ Himself. The very uncertainties of historiography, the difficulties faced by historical imagination in making its transition from the first century to the twentieth, the complications involved in total commitment to a Christ portrayed long ago in a frame of reference inappropriate to our time, emphasise the need for a more dynamic, developing interpretation of what loyalty to Jesus entails. This is where the situationist approach, the existentialist's insistence upon immediacy amd spontaneity of response, meet the Christian doctrine of the Spirit as personalised, moralised, and universalised in the apostolic faith. It is in the better understanding of the experience of the Spirit, rather than in more erudite criticism, that the deepest meaning of the *imitatio Christi* will probably be found. Though we shall always need the written record of Jesus by which to "test the spirits" and evaluate what is genuinely Christian inspiration, we need equally the direct experience of the Spirit of Christ, by whom the things of Christ are mediated to us in our own time and our own terms. It is in the imitation of Christ under the continuing inspiration of His Spirit, guided by the timeless word enshrined within the scriptures, that the tensions are resolved between commitment to the past and openness to each changing situation in each new age, between the objective, authoritative moral ideal which confronts us in Jesus and the free, unconstrained idealism of hearts that love Him.

In this religious context, moreover, we quickly realise that the category of exemplar, moral authority, moral genius, is scarcely adequate to express the true status of Jesus in the moral realm. Unless this be admitted, the idea of imitation is open to serious misconception. Immediately upon introducing the *imitatio Christi* Barth warns —

"there can be no question of a conformity which means equality, of anything in the nature of a deification of man, of making him a second Christ . . . Jesus Christ will reign, and men will be subject to Him, and they will always be different in, and in spite of, the closest fellowship between Him and His imitators. There will be no more Christs . . . the Unique will always be unique, and the distances will remain . . . "[64]

The point is well taken. Beside it may be set Paul Ramsey's splendid epigram: "In 'imitating Christ' one thing the Christian never attempts: he never imitates the fact that Jesus had no Christ to imitate."[65] But something similar must be said from another side. The idea of imitation of Christ may be seriously misconstrued as implying some native ability on man's part to attain to His perfection, given only sufficient aspiration and strength of purpose. That implication all experience of man's sinfulness and need of redemption flatly denies. To avert this travesty of truth, N. H. G. Robinson argues strenuously and acutely against representation of Christ as moral genius or supreme moral authority. It is difficult to see how his argument can be improved:

> The idea of Jesus as moral genius or exemplar involves three-fold relativity. The moral exemplar must keep well within sight of his followers: to be too far ahead is to invite rejection. But Christ is ethically transcendent, worthy of unquestioning obedience — an incomparable claim. The moral exemplar must aim to make himself superfluous as his followers attain maturity; whereas Christ remains King, Lord; He does not point out moral truth, but embodies it in His will and judgement. Finally, the recognition of a genius is a provisional, empirical judgement; at any time a greater may arise; but Christ's supremacy is inherent, inalienable, not the greatest so far, but finally and unalterably so. Such assertions are based on revelation; they constitute the moral meaning of that revelation. All three assertions about Jesus — His transcendence, sovereignty, finality, are in fact one, and *theological.* "So far from being on the same road as we are, ahead but not too far, and for the time being only, Christ is the object of Christian worship and transcends the religious experience of all his followers . . . transcends also the category of religious genius . . . Christ is Mediator and Redeemer, not only the sovereign but the saviour of men."[66]

That is excellently said. Christian ethics is not Christianity, nor the Christian moral life the whole of Christian discipleship. The gospel and the moral ideal are separable in thought, not in experience. But when, with whatever qualifications, and only for the sake of study, the separation *is* made, the ultimate word to be spoken about Christian ethics is — the imitation of Christ. "He predestined us to be conformed to the image of his Son . . . We are changed into the same image . . . We shall be like him" — in that vision, promise and hope, lies the central unchanging continuity of Christian ethics.

BIBLIOGRAPHY

(and key to references)

Abbott T. K. *Kant's Metaphysic of Ethics*, Longmans Green, London 1907
Addleshaw G. W. O. *"Writers of the Counter-Reformation"* in Selwyn: *Short History . . .*
Ashanin C. B. Art: *"Orthodox Church Ethics"* in Macquarrie *Dictionary*
Atkinson J. *The Great Light,* Paternoster, Exeter 1968
Martin Luther and the Birth of Protestantism, Penguin Books, Harmondsworth and Baltimore 1968
Bainton R. H. *Christian Attitudes to War and Peace,* Hodder and Stoughton, London 1961
Here I Stand, Hodder and Stoughton, London 1951
Baker (pub.) *Dictionary of Christian Ethics,* ed. C. F. Henry, Grand Rapids 1973
Balmforth H. *"Developments in England"* in Selwyn: *Short History . . .*
Barry F. R. *Christian Ethics and Secular Society,* Hodder and Stoughton, London 1966
Barth K. *Church Dogmatics,* T. and T. Clark, Edinburgh 1970 impression
Beach W. and Niebuhr H. Richard *Christian Ethics,* Ronald Press, New York 1955
Bennett J. C. Art: "Niebuhr, Reinhold" in Macquarrie *Dictionary*
Bonhoeffer D. *Cost of Discipleship,* SCM Press, London 1948
Letters and Papers from Prison, Collins/Fontana, London 1953
*Ethics,*Collins/Fontana, London 1964
Bourke V. J. *The Essential Augustine,* Mentor Books, New American Library, New York 1964
Art: *"Medieval Ethics"* in Macquarrie *Dictionary*
Bouyer L. *Erasmus and the Humanist Experiment,* Chapman, London 1959
Bready J. W. *England Before and After Wesley,* Hodder and Stoughton, London 1938
Bromiley G. W. Art: *"Karl Barth"* in Baker *Dictionary*
Bruce F. F. *The Spreading Flame,* Paternoster, Exeter 1958
Brunner E. *Divine Imperative,* ET Olive Wyon, Macmillan, New York and Lutterworth, London 1937
Justice and the Social Order, Harper Brothers, New York 1945
Bultmann R. *New Testament Theology,* ET K. Grobel, SCM Press, London 1952

Burnaby J. *Amor Dei,* Hodder and Stoughton, London 1938
St Augustine — Later Works (Library of Christian Classics) SCM Press, London 1955
Art: *"Augustine of Hippo and Augustinian Ethics"* in Macquarrie *Dictionary*
Burtness J. H. Art: *"Bonhoeffer"* in Baker *Dictionary*
Catherwood H. F. R. *The Christian in Industrial Society,* Tyndale, London (2nd edition) 1966
Chadwick O. *The Reformation,* Penguin Books, Harmondsworth and Baltimore, 1964
Chesterton G. K. *St Francis of Assisi,* Hodder and Stoughton, London 1923 (1951 edition)
Clark G. H. Artt: *"Augustine," "Calvinistic Ethics," "Kant,"* and *"Situation Ethics"* in Baker *Dictionary*
Cock A. A. *"St Thomas Aquinas and Scholastic Theology"* in Selwyn: *Short History* . . .
COPEC Commission Report xii: *Historical Illustrations of the Social Effects of Christianity,* for Conference on Politics, Economics, and Citizenship, Longmans Green, London 1924
Copleston F. C. *Aquinas,* Penguin Books, Harmondsworth and Baltimore, 1955
Cross F. L. *Early Christian Fathers,* Duckworth, London 1960
Ed. *Oxford Dictionary of the Christian Church,* Oxford University Press, London, New York 1958 edition
Dakin A. *Calvinism,* Duckworth, London 1940
Dickens A. G. *Reformation and Society in Sixteenth Century Europe,* Thames and Hudson, London 1966
Dolan J. P. *The Essential Erasmus,* Mentor Books, New American Library, New York 1964
Drummond A. C. *Story of American Protestantism,* Oliver and Boyd, Edinburgh 1949
Ebeling G. *Luther,* Collins, Glasgow 1964
Eenigenburg E. M. Artt: *"Aquinas & R. C. Ethics", "R. C. Ethics"* in Baker *Dictionary*
Feinberg P. D. Artt: *"Harnack",* and *"Ritschl and Protestant Ethics"* in Baker *Dictionary*
Ferguson J. *Politics of Love,* James Clarke, Cambridge nd
Fletcher J. *Situation Ethics,* SCM Press, London 1966
Flint R. *Socialism,* Pitman, London and New York 1908
Frame J. M. Art: *"Reformed Ethics"* in Baker *Dictionary*
Geisler N. L. *Ethics: Alternatives and Issues,* Zondervan, Grand Rapids 1974
Gerstner J. F. Art: *"Edwards, Jonathan"* in Baker *Dictionary*
Glover T. R. *Influence of Christ in the Ancient World,* Cambridge University Press, Cambridge 1929
Hall B. H. Art: *"Perfectionism"* in Baker *Dictionary*
Hamilton K. M. Art: *"Niebuhr, Reinhold"* in Baker *Dictionary*

Handy R. T. Art: *"Edwards, Jonathan"* in Macquarrie *Dictionary*
Art: *"Rauschenbusch in Historical Perspective"* in Baptist Quarterly, London July 1964
Hardy E. R. Art: *"Asceticism"* in Macquarrie *Dictionary*
Harland G. *Thought of Reinhold Niebuhr,* Oxford University Press, New York 1960
Harnack A. *Expansion of Christianity in the First Three Centuries,* Pitman's Sons, New York, Williams and Norgate, London 1904
Haroutunian J. Art: *"Calvin, and Calvinist Ethics"*, in Macquarrie *Dictionary*
Hastings (Ed) *Encyclopaedia of Religion and Ethics,* T. and T. Clark, Edinburgh 1908-21
Heald J. M. Art: *"Aquinas"* in Hastings, *ERE* vol i
Heasman K. *Evangelicals in Action,* Bles, London 1962
Henson H. H. *Christian Morality — Natural, Developing, Final,* Oxford University Press, London 1936
Higham F. *Faith of our Fathers: Men and Movements of the Seventeenth Century,* SCM Press, London 1939
Holmer P. *"Soren Kierkegaard",* chapter 14 in Beach
Holmes A. F. Art: *"Just War"* in Baker *Dictionary*
Inge W. R. *Christian Ethics and Modern Problems,* Hodder and Stoughton, London 1930 etc.
Christian Mysticism, Methuen, London 1899 (1925 edition)
Jacobs H. E. Art: *"Luther"* in Hastings, *ERE* vol viii
Jewett P. K. Art: *"Brunner, Emil"* in Baker *Dictionary*
Kirk K. *Conscience and its Problems,* Longmans Green, London 1927
The Vision of God, Longmans Green, London 1931
Knox S. J. Art: *"Puritanism"* in Macquarrie *Dictionary*
Kuhn H. B. Art: *"Authenticity"* in Baker *Dictionary*
Lazareth W. H. Art: *"Luther"* in Macquarrie *Dictionary*
Lecky W. E. H. *History of European Morals,* Longmans Green, London 1905 edition
Lewis H. D. *Morals and Revelation,* Allen and Unwin, London 1951
Morals and the New Theology, Gollancz, London 1947
Luthardt C. E. *History of Christian Ethics,* 1888-93 (ET of vol i only)
Mackenzie J. S. *Manual of Ethics,* London University Tutorial Press, London 1920 edition
MacKinnon D. M. Art: *"Butler, Joseph"* in Macquarrie *Dictionary*
MacKinnon J. *History of Liberty,* Longmans, London 1906
Macquarrie J. Ed. *Dictionary of Christian Ethics,* SCM Press, London 1967
Twentieth Century Religious Thought, SCM Press, London 1963
Three Issues in Ethics, SCM Press, London 1971
Malavez L. *Christian Message and Myth,* SCM Press, London 1958
Marrou H. *St. Augustine,* (ET P Hepburne-Scott) Harper Bros, New York 1957
Marshall I. Art: *"Personal Ethics"* in Baker *Dictionary*

Marshall L. H. *Challenge of New Testament Ethics,* Macmillan, London 1946

Martin H. (Ed) *Christian Social Reformers of the Nineteenth Century,* SCM Press, London (2nd edition 1933)

Mather E. P. *Barclay in Brief,* Pendle Hill Pennsylvania studies nd

Mathews S. and Smith G. B. (Edd) *Dictionary of Religion and Ethics,* Waverly Book Co/Macmillan, London 1921

Matthews W. R. (Ed) *Butler's Sermons,* Bell, London 1967

Maurice F. D. *Gospel of the Kingdom of Heaven,* Macmillan, London 1893

Mechie S. Art: *"Abelard"* in Macquarrie *Dictionary*

Michalson C. Art: *"Existentialist Ethics"* in Macquarrie *Dictionary*

Miegge G. *Gospel and Myth in the Thought of R. Bultmann,* Lutterworth, London 1960

Moffatt J. Art: *"War",* Hastings *Dictionary of the Apostolic Church,* vol ii

Mooneyham W. S. Art: *"National Association of Evangelicals"* in Baker *Dictionary*

Moule C. F. D. Art: *"New Testament and Moral Decisions"* in Expository Times, Edinburgh, September 1963

Mueller W. A. Art: *"Rauschenbusch"* in Baker *Dictionary*

Murray J. *Principles of Conduct,* Tyndale Press, London 1957

Neander A. *Church History,* vol viii Bohn edition 1852

Niebuhr H. Rd in Beach

Niebuhr Reinhold *Moral Man and Immoral Society,* SCM Press edition, London 1963

An Interpretation of Christian Ethics, SCM Press London 1936

Norris R. A. Artt: *"Patristic Ethics," "Ambrose," "Clement of Alexandria"* and *"Gregory the Great"* in Macquarrie *Dictionary*

Nygren A. *Agape and Eros,* SPCK/Macmillan, London 1941

Oden T. C. *Radical Obedience,* Epworth, London 1965

Orr J. Art: *"Calvinism"* in Hastings *ERE* vol iii

Packer J. I. Art: *"Puritan Ethics"* in Baker *Dictionary*

Paterson W. P. Art: *"War"* in Hastings *ERE* vol xii

Paul W. W. Artt: *"Dialectical Ethics"* and *"Existentialist Ethics"* in Baker *Dictionary*

Peabody F. *Jesus Christ and the Social Question,* Macmillan, London and New York 1900

Phillips M. M. *Erasmus and the Northern Renaissance,* Home University Library, Oxford University Press, London 1950

Pinnock C. H. Art: *"Autonomy"* in Baker *Dictionary*

Piper O. *Ethics,* Nelson, London 1970

Porphyrios Art: *"Eastern Church"* in Hastings *ERE* vol v

Ramsey I. T. *Christian Ethics and Contemporary Philosophy,* SCM Press, London 1966

Ramsey P. *Basic Christian Ethics,* SCM Press, London 1950

Rashdall H. *Idea of Atonement in Christian Theology,* Macmillan, London 1925

Rauschenbusch W. *Christianity and the Social Crisis,* Macmillan, New

York 1907
Raven C. E. *"Ludlow, J. M."*, chapter vi of Martin (ed) *Social Reformers . . .*
Reckitt M. B. *From Maurice to Temple,* Faber and Faber, London 1947
Robinson H. W. *Christian Doctrine of Man,* T. and T. Clark, Edinburgh third edition 1926
Robinson N. H. G. *Groundwork of Christian Ethics,* Collins, London 1971
Christ and Conscience, Nisbet, London 1956
Rupp E. G. *The Righteousness of God,* Hodder and Stoughton, London 1953
Russell B. *History of Western Philosophy,* Allen and Unwin, London 1946
Sasse H. *"Luther and the Teaching of the Reformation"*, in Selwyn (ed), *Short History . . .*
Scull J. P. Artt: *"Pontifical Social Encyclicals"* and *"Roman Catholic Moral Theology (Contemporary)"* in Macquarrie *Dictionary*
Selwyn E. G. Ed: *Short History of Christian Thought,* Bles, London 1949
Smart N. *"Gods, Bliss, and Morality"* in I. T. Ramsey (ed) *Christian Ethics . . .*
Smith C. *"Lord Shaftesbury"*, chapter iii of Martin (ed) *Social Reformers . . .*
Smith P. *Erasmus — A Study,* Ungar Constable, New York 1962
Smith R. G. Art: *"Bonhoeffer"* in Macquarrie *Dictionary*
Sorley W. R. *Moral Values and the Idea of God,* Cambridge University Press, Cambridge 1935
Stahlke O. Art: *"Orthodox (Eastern) Ethics"* in Baker *Dictionary*
Symes J. E. Art: *"Maurice"*, Hastings *ERE* vol viii
Tawney R. H. *Religion and the Rise of Capitalism,* Penguin Books, Harmondsworth and Baltimore 1926 (1942 edition)
Taylor A. E. *The Faith of a Moralist,* Macmillan, London 1937
Teaching Symposium *Teaching Christian Ethics,* SCM Press, London 1974
Temple W. *"The Christian Social Movement in the Nineteenth Century"*, in Martin (ed), *Social Reformers . . .*
Tepker H. W. Art: *"Asceticism"* in Baker *Dictionary*
Thielicke H. and Schrey H.-H. *Faith and Action,* ET Oliver and Boyd, Edinburgh 1970
Thomas G. F. *Christian Ethics and Moral Philosophy,* Scribners, New York 1955
Tindall F. C. *"St Augustine"* in Selwyn (ed) *Short History . . .*
Tinsley E. J. Art: *"Mysticism and Ethics"* in Macquarrie *Dictionary*
Troeltsch E. *Social Teaching of the Christian Churches,* ET Olive Wyon, Allen and Unwin, London 1931
Troitsky S. V. Art: *"Greek Orthodox Church"* in Hastings, *ERE* vol vi and art. *"Russian Church"* in vol x
Trueblood D. E. Art: *"Quakers"* in Baker *Dictionary*
Urquhart W. S. *Humanism and Christianity,* T. and T. Clark, Edinburgh 1945
Warfield B. Art: *"Augustine"* in Hastings *ERE* vol ii
Watt H. Art: *"Humanists"* in Hastings *ERE* vol vi
Weber M. *Protestant Ethic and the Spirit of Capitalism,* ET by Talcot

Parsons, Allen and Unwin 1930
Wenger J. C. Art: *"Evangelical Social Concern"* in Baker *Dictionary*
West C. C. Art: *"Barth"* in Macquarrie *Dictionary*
White R. E. O. *Into the Same Image,* Marshall Morgan and Scott, London 1957; Broadman, Nashville 1957
Wirt S. E. Art: *"Social Gospel"* in Baker *Dictionary*
Wood H. G. *"George Cadbury",* chapter viii of Martin (ed) *Social Reformers . . .*
Wood T. Artt: *"Christian Social Movement," "Hooker, Richard,"* and *"Maurice F. D."* in Macquarrie *Dictionary*
Woods G. *"Situational Ethics"* in I. T. Ramsey (ed) *Christian Ethics . . .*
Woolley P. Art: *"Patristic Ethics"* in Baker *Dictionary*
Workman H. B. Art: *"Ambrose of Milan"* in Hastings *ERE* vol. i
Zockler O. Art: *"Asceticism"* in Hastings *ERE* vol. ii

SOURCE — REFERENCES AND ACKNOWLEDGEMENTS

(for full titles, see Bibliography: *Op cit* = work *just* cited)

FOREWORD
The Question is . . .
(pages 9—12)

1. See foreword to vol i, whose argument and viewpoint the present Foreword is intended, in part, to recapitulate and carry forward.
2. See Foreword to vol i
3. Foreword to vol i, *ad finem*

CHAPTER 1
(pages 13—25)

1. W. E. H. Lecky vol i 256ff
2. W. Barclay "*Hellenistic Thought in New Testament Times*" in Expository Times, T. and T. Clark, Edinburgh lxxi-lxxii
3. H. H. Henson ch. 5
4. E. F. Scott *Varieties of New Testament Religion* Scribner's Sons, New York, 1947 217; cf T. R. Glover *Influence* . . . 69
5. R. Law *The Tests of Life*, T. and T. Clark, Edinburgh, 1909 37
6. See vol i ch ll, citing *adv Haereses* 1 xxiv 5, 1 vi 2, 3. Irenaeus, "the most considerable theologian of the second century", originated in Asia Minor but ministered in Gaul, so representing East and West: c 130-200 A.D.
7. Clement of Alexandria (c 150-213 A.D.) with immense learning and acumen presented Christianity as the fulfilment of pagan insights. Stromateis III i, iv
8. Ignatius (c 35-107 A.D.) bishop of Antioch; writing (probably) seven genuine letters in early second century; ad Smyrnaeans vi 2
9. Clement: *Stromateis* II xx
10. *Refutatio* VI xiv; Hippolytus (c 170-236 A.D.) was the most prolific writer of the Roman church for three centuries.
11. Caius, presbyter of Rome in early third century, with Dionysius, bishop of Alexandria (died 264): Eusebius: *History of the Church* iii 28, vii 25; cf R. Law *The Tests of Life* (above) 37
12. Tertullian (c 160-220 A.D.), lawyer by training, zealot by temperament, rigorist in approach.
13. W. R. Inge *Ethics* . . . 136
14. L. H. Marshall 172
15. H. H. Henson ch v
16. For Luthardt, see bibliography
17. Tacitus *Annals* XV 44 3 and 5; cf F. F. Bruce 163f
18. Celsus in Origen *Contra Celsum* iii 59; translation in T. R. Glover 74. For atheism, incest, cannibalism, see Lechy vol i 414 and cf F. F. Bruce 165

19. W. E. H. Lecky vol i 390f
20. W. E. H. Lecky vol i 391. Origen (c 186-252 A.D.) first pupil and then successor of Clement as head of the Christian school at Alexandria; a rigorous Christian and prolific writer.
21. Epictetus *Arrian* IV 7 (just possibly said of the followers of Judas of Galilee)
22. Marcus Aurelius *Meditations* XI 3
23. Lucian *Death of Peregrinus* 13; see J. Stevenson *A New Eusebius* SPCK London (5th impression) 1970 135
24. H. H. Henson chapter v
25. W. R. Inge *Ethics* . . . 86
26. T. R. Glover 67
27. J. Orr *Neglected Factors in the Study of the Early Progress of Christianity* Hodder and Stoughton, London, 1899 200; cf C. Bigg *Christian Platonists of Alexandria* Oxford University Press, Oxford (2nd edition) 1913 23
28. J. S. Stewart *A Man in Christ* Hodder and Stoughton, London, 1935 57
29. The correspondence is conveniently reproduced in F. F. Bruce 169; see J. Stevenson *New Eusebius* (above) 13, 14
30. J. Orr devoted the second and third of his lectures, *Neglected Factors* (above) to illustrating this point. Cf Pliny *Epistles* X 96, Tertullian *Ad Scapulam* 5
31. Minucius Felix, apparently an African, was author of a (probably) early-third-century defence of Christianity, in form a conversation between a Christian, Octavius, and the pagan Caecilius: *Octavius* viii 31
32. Aristides wrote (c 140 A.D.) an impressive *Apology* for Christianity, dedicated to Hadrian (so Eusebius) or to Antoninus Pius, and based upon the moral character of Christians.
33. Athenagoras wrote (c 177 A.D.) a "*Supplication*" on behalf of Christians, addressed to two emperors, emphasising the moral sublimity of the gospel.
34. Justin (Martyr) "prince of apologists", martyred 163/167 A.D. wrote at least two "*Apologies*" — possibly parts of one treatise — and a *Dialogue* with a Jewish objector, Trypho, emphasising the moral and civic virtues of Christians.
35. Tatian (fl 165), pupil of Justin Martyr, (though later he founded an extreme ascetic sect, the Encratites), wrote a "*Discourse to the Greeks*".
36. Celsus wrote (c 177-180) "*True Word*", a studied and serious attack on Christianity, now known through extensive quotations in Origen's reply, half a century later.
37. W. E. H. Lecky vol ii 3; cf T. R. Glover 74, 75
38. J. Orr *Neglected Factors* (above) 222f
39. Pliny *Epistles* 5f; J. Stevenson *New Eusebius* (above) 13, 14
40. Justin Martyr *Apology* I 14, cf 15, II 116; Dialogue with Trypho 110
41. Justin Martyr *Apology* I 16; J. Stevenson *New Eusebius* (above) 61
42. Aristides *Apology* xv, xvi: J. Stevenson *op cit* 56; W. R. Inge *Ethics* . . . 83
43. Anonymous *Epistle to Diognetus* (? second century) v, vi; J. Stevenson *op cit* 58 (translation from J. Donaldson *History of Christian Literature and Doctrine* Macmillan, London, 1864). Hermas *The Shepherd* (which probably spans the end of the first to the early-second century) reflects a similar practical and outgoing idealism. e.g. Book III 8th 'Mandate'.
44. W. E. H. Lecky vol i 415 citing Lucian *Death of Peregrinus* and Pliny *Epistles* X 97, Julian Epistles ii
45. Lucian *op cit* 11-16 describes how Christian generosity could be imposed upon by charlatans
46. Minucius Felix *Octavius* (above) xxxviii 6 and cf ix
47. Tertullian *Apology* 42-46; *Ad Nationes* I 4, 5; W. R. Inge *Ethics* . . . 84
48. Eusebius *History of the Church* VI 43
49. L. H. Marshall 1f
50. Julian *Epistles* 49: *Ad Arsacium* (in Sozomenus *History* V 16)
51. Eusebius *History of the Church* IX 8
52. Dionysius of Alexandria, in Eusebius *History of the Church* VII 22; Cyprian's *Life* by Pontianus ixf; cf A. Harnack vol i 213 f
53. E.g. Hermas *The Shepherd* Book III 'Similitude' i; A. Harnack vol i 184, 190, 192

54. *Didache* I 5, IV. This anonymous "Teaching of the Twelve Apostles" is variously dated 60 A.D. (F. L. Cross and others); 50-70 A.D. (J. P. Audet); c 100 A.D. (Woolley); 140-150 A.D. and artificially archaic (if Didache uses Barnabas) (Beach). It may be based upon an older Jewish original. Eusebius and Athanasius considered it to be on the fringe of the New Testament canon.
55. Polycarp *Epistle to the Philippians* 10. Polycarp was born c 70 A.D. and martyred 155/6 A.D.
56. Barnabas *Epistle* xix 10: a strongly evangelical work, c 100/150 A.D.
57. Hermas *The Shepherd* 'Similitude' i, ii
58. *"2 Clement"* XVI. *"2 Clement"* is the oldest surviving Greek sermon, variously associated with Rome, Corinth, Alexandria, and dated "mid-second century" by J. Stevenson *New Eusebius* (above)
59. Cyprian *De Opere et Eleemosynis* i, ii, v, xxi. Cyprian (c 200/210-258 A.D.) was bishop of Carthage and church statesman.
60. Ambrose *De Elia et Jejuniis* xx quoting (like Polycarp) Tobit xii 9; *Sermo de Eleemosynis* 30, 31. Ambrose (c 340-397) was an outstanding bishop of Milan. His *"On the Duties of a Minister"* is the first handbook of Christian ethics, epitomising the thought of the first three Christian centuries.
61. Details here are gathered from: Ignatius *Ad Smyrnaeans* vi; *"Epistle of Clement"* (pseudo-Clementine homilies, 2/3 century) *Ad Jacobi* 9; Aristides *Apology* xv; Tertullian *Ad Martyras* 1; Hippolytus *Philosophumena* ix 12; *"Apostolical Constitutions"* (probably late fourth century, but incorporating early third century material) v 1, iv 9. For Phaeno, see A. Harnack vol i 203. Also, Hermas *The Shepherd* 'Similitude' i; Clement of Rome *Epistle to the Corinthians* lv 2; Eusebius *History of the Church* v 8. For burials: Tertullian *Apology* xxxix; Aristides *Apology* xv and Lactantius *Institutes* vi 12. (Lactantius, c 240-320 A.D., was called "the Christian Cicero", as — like the great Roman — exploring ethical "Duties" in his *"Divine Institutes"* and a later *Epitome*). For the attitude towards slaves: Ignatius *To Polycarp* iv; for the care of the workless: *Didache* xii; Cyprian *De Opere et Eleemosynis* ii; pseudo-Clementine *Epistles* viii; Justin Martyr *Apology* II xii; Tatian *Oratio* ("Discourse to the Greeks") xxix; and Cyprian *Ad Donatus* passim.
62. A. Harnack vol i 200
63. A. Harnack vol i 264f
64. W. E. H. Lecky vol i 386-394
65. W. R. Inge *Ethics* . . . 42
66. Irenaeus *Against Heresies* V preface, and i
67. Clement of Alexandria *Exhortation to the Heathen* (at end); *The Instructor* I iii, xii; *Exhortation to the Heathen* xi (at end); *The Instructor* I xii (twice); *Stromateis* ("Miscellanies") II xix, xxii (at end); VI ix, xiv (at end); *The Instructor* I ii (at beginning). Also: *Stromateis* II xx; IV vi, xxii (twice), xxiii, xxvi (twice); VI vii, xii, xvii; VII i, iii (twice), xiv.
68. Ambrose *Duties* (De Officiis Ministrorum) I xxviii, xlix, III iii
69. T. R. Glover 67 citing Epictetus *Manual* 33, 50 and *Discourses* ii 18
70. W. E. H. Lecky vol ii 8. For Lecky's own tribute to the place of Jesus in Christian ethics, recall vol i of the present work, ch 6 *ad finem*
71. Aristides *Apology* XV 1,3

CHAPTER 2
(pages 26—53)

1. R. A. Norris Art *"Patristic Ethics"* 245
2. P. Woolley 489f
3. *Didache* xvi 2, vi 2
4. Quoted in Luthardt I 1. c (1); cf Clement *To the Corinthians* II 4, 16
5. F. L. Cross *Fathers* . . . 13

6. P. Woolley 489f
7. Clement *op cit* xxi, xxxv, xix, xx, xxi, xxxii, xlix
8. "2 Clement" iv, so also vi, xi
9. Justin Martyr *Apology* I x, xii
10. Hermas *The Shepherd* II iv 3, 4
11. P. Woolley 489f
12. Ignatius *To the Ephesians* iii, iv, v; *To the Magnesians* vi, vii; *To the Trallians* ii, iii; *To the Philadelphians* ii, vii; *To the Smyrnaeans* viii, ix; *To Polycarp* vi
13. Hermas *The Shepherd* II iv 3; cf iv 1 — "There is but one repentance to the servants of God"
14 Tertullian *On Penitence* 7-12; *On Modesty* 1, 21, 22; cf 19
15. See F. L. Cross *Fathers* . . . 97. *"Didascalia Apostolorum"* ("the Teaching of the Twelve Holy Apostles and Disciples of Our Saviour") is a rambling compilation by a north-Syrian bishop of early-third century
16. Polycarp *To the Philippians* viii, iii, x
17. Barnabas *Epistle* v, ii, iii, xvi, vi, xvi, xix
18. *Ad Diognetus* vii, v (see note 43 to chapter 1)
19. Justin Martyr *Apology* I lxi, lxv, lxvi, xiv, xv, xvi etc.
20. Tatian *Oratio* xv, xi, xiii (see notes 35 and 61 to chapter 1)
21. Irenaeus *Against Heresies* V preface; V i 1, vii passim, xvii 1; IV xiii 3, xxviii (at end)
22. Clement Alexandria *The Instructor* I ii; *Exhortation to the Heathen* x (at end), xi (at end), i; *The Instructor* (closing hymn); *Stromateis* ("Miscellanies") II vi (at end); *The Instructor* I vi (twice); *Exhortation to the Heathen* i. Cf W. Beach *Christian* . . . 79 (? alluding to Stromateis II vi)
23. Origen *Contra Celsum* III lxii, lxix, lxii, lxiii, lix-lxi, lxvii-lxviii, lxxi, VII xlviii-xlix; *Treatise on Prayer* passim
24. F. L. Cross *Fathers* . . . 25
25. Justin Martyr *Dialogue with Trypho* xi, xii, xv, xxii, xxiv, xxx
26. Barnabas *Epistle* xiv, xv, xvi
27. Irenaeus *Against Heresies* IV xii 2, 3; xiii 1 (repetition at end of 3), 2, 4; xvi 5
28. Tertullian *Against the Jews* ii (twice), iii, iv, v, vi; iii (middle); *Against Praxeas* xxxi
29. Origen *Contra Celsum* I iv, VII li; Clement Alexandria *Stromateis* II xviii, VI xvif
30. Novatian *De Cibis Judaicis*. Novatian, a rival pope, martyred 257/8 A.D. wrote also against theatres and on the value of chastity; after his sect the Katharos ("Clean") Schism was named.
31. W. Beach *Christian* . . . 72f
32. Justin Martyr *Dialogue with Trypho* ii (iii-vi), vii
33. Justin Martyr *Apology* I lxi; II x, xiii
34. Tatian *Oratio* ii, iii, xxvi (twice), xxix, xxxi, xxxv, cf xlii
35. Clement Alexandria *Stromateis* I v; VI xvii; *Exhortation to the Heathen* xi; *Stromateis* I xiii, xvi, xvii. That all philosophy is God-given is argued fully in vi, vii and xvii
36. Clement Alexandria *Stromateis* II ii-iv, vi, xi, xii, V i, ii
37. Clement Alexandria *op cit* VII iii; II xix, xx; IV xxi, xxii, xxiii (twice: citing Psalm 82:6); *On Contemplation* VII iii etc. xii; VI ix; VII xi, xiii; *Stromateis* IV v etc.
38. T. R. Glover 76f
39. W. Beach *Christian* . . . 77f
40. R. A. Norris *Art "Clement . . ."* 60
41. Pfleiderer *Das Urchistentum* II 701, quoted in W. H. Robinson *Christian Experience of the Holy Spirit* Nisbet, London, 1928 42
42. Tertullian *Prescription against Heresies* vii
43. Tertullian *op cit* vii
44. Tertullian *Apology* xlvi, xlvii; *To the Nations* II ii
45. Tertullian *Apology* xvii
46. F. L. Cross *Fathers* . . . 134
47. Origen *Contra Celsum* VII xlvii
48. Origen *op cit* III lxvi, lxvii
49. J. Chapman Art *"Mysticism: Christian, Roman Catholic"* in Hastings ERE vol ix 91a, b; O. Zockler Art *"Asceticism . . ."* 75b citing Origen *Homily in Leviticus* 10, 11 and

Exhortation to Martyrdom
50. Origen *Contra Celsum* III lvi, VII xxxix; cf *In Joannes* xiii 24, *De Principiis* III ii, iv, vi
51. Lactantius *Institutes* V v, vi (twice), vii (see note 61, chapter 1)
52. Lactantius *op cit* VI x
53. Lactantius *op cit* VII; VI iv; III xii, xiii; IV xxix (at end)
54. Ambrose *Duties* I vii, viii, ix — the Christian judging "by the rule of things future," not by present advantages only, "by eternal life and blessedness". (See note 60, chapter 1)
55. Ambrose *op cit* II ii. Similarly with the discussion of anger, I xxi
56. Ambrose *op cit* I v
57. Ambrose *op cit* I xviii, xlvi, xxvii; III iii; I xxviii; *On the Decease of Satyrus* II 4, 6, 130, 45, 46
58. Ambrose *Duties* I xx, xxiv, xxv
59. Clement Alexandria *Stromateis* II ix, xii, xviii
60. Ambrose *Duties* I xxiv, xxv
61. Ambrose *op cit* I xxv, xliii, xxix (at end). l; II ii (at end). Prudence: I xxv, xxvi; justice: I xxvii, xxviii; fortitude I xl-xlii; temperance: I xliii, xlv; happiness: II iii-v; the "useful": II vi, vii and III ii; love (etc): II xi, xii, xvf, xxi
62. W. Beach *Christian* . . . 47
63. Tertullian *Apology* 39; W. R. Inge *Ethics* . . . 84
64. Tertullian *On Prayer* iii; *On Resurrection* xxii 2; *On Spectacles* xxviii. xxix; *"2 Clement"* 6; see also Justin Martyr *Apology* 1 66, Irenaeus *Against Heresies* i 10, Clement Alexandria *Stromateis* vi 12; and cf J. Donaldson *History of Christian Literature and Doctrine* vol ii (Apologists) 259f. (I owe some of these eschatological references to Dr. Gordon W. Martin of Glasgow)
65. *Didache* ii, v; Barnabas *Epistle* 4
66. Athenagoras *"Supplication"* xxxii, xxxiv, xxxv (see note 33, chapter 1); cf Tatian *Oratio* xxiii, xxiv, xxxiii, xxxiv
67. Clement Alexandria *The Instructor* II and III passim; note III xi
68. Tertullian *Apology* vi, ix, xi-xv; *On Spectacles* iv, iii, v-xxviii
69. See F. L. Cross *Fathers* . . . 183; see also Novatian (probably) *On Spectacles* vi (sometimes ascribed to Cyprian)
70. Cyprian *To Donatus* I viii, xiv
71. Lactantius *Institutes* V ix, VI xx
72. W. R. Inge *Ethics* . . . 94, 91, 100
73. Ignatius *To Polycarp* v
74. Justin Martyr *Apology* I xxix; cf *Dialogue with Trypho* 134
75. Athenagoras *"Supplication"* xxxiii
76. For Tatian's attitude, Irenaeus *Against Heresies* I xxviii; cf Clement Alxandria *Stromateis* III xii; for Marcion, Tertullian *Against Marcion* I xxix, IV xi
77. Clement Alexandria *op cit* II xxiii passim, and III; cf *The Instructor* II x
78. Origen *Contra Celsum* I xxvi (at end), VIII lv; cf O. Zockler Art *"Asceticism . . ."* 75b
79. Tertullian *Against Marcion* I xxix, V xv; *To His Wife* I i, ii, iv, vi, vii, viii; II ii-vi, viii; *Exhortation to Chastity* i, v
80. Cyprian *Dress of Virgins* iii, v and passim; *Against the Jews* III xxxii
81. W. R. Inge *Ethics* . . . 99
82. Methodius *Banquet* I i, III viii, VIII i. Methodius was probably Bishop of Olympus (Lycia) and martyred 311 A.D.; his *Banquet* is also called *Symposium*
83. Novatian (probably) *The Advantage of Chastity* iv, ii (sometimes ascribed to Cyprian)
84. Lactantius *Institutes* VI xxiii
85. Ambrose *On Widows* XII 72, 73; *On Virgins* I vi 24, vii 3; *On Widows* XII 72; *On Virgins* I iii 10, iv 14, *Letters* lxiii 40; *Duties* I l 258; *On Virgins* I v 21, 22; viii 51, 52; *Letters* lxiii 33; *On Virgins* II ii 6, 7
86. W. R. Inge *Ethics* . . . 100
87. Cf W. R. Inge *op cit* 101
88. W. R. Inge *op cit* 125 so cites Eusebius *Apodeixis*
89. Jerome *Against Jovinian* I xlvii, xlviii (cf *Perpetual Virginity of Blessed Mary against Helvidius* xxii); *Against Jovinian* I xl (cf *Perpetual Virginity* xxiii); Letter xxii (*"To Eustochium"*) xx. W. Beach *Christian* . . . 144. Jerome Letter xxii (*"To Eustochium"*)

xxii, vi, xx, xxv; Letter cxxx (*"To Demetrias"*) vf. Jerome (c 342-420 A.D.) possessed unrivalled scholarship, administrative skill, almost unique influence in the western church through his Vulgate translation of the scripture; but he was an extreme ascetic.

90. Athanasius *Letter xlviii.* Athanasius (c 296-373 A.D.) was bishop of Alexandria from 328, champion of orthodoxy against Arian and first to introduce monasticism to the western church.
91. F. L. Cross *Fathers* . . . 97. Cf Jerome *Perpetual Virginity of Blessed Mary against Helvidius*
92. *Didache* vi
93. Hermas *The Shepherd* "Similitudes" V iii
94. See notes to section three, above
95. C. Bigg *Origins of Christianity* Clarendon Press, Oxford, 1909 437, citing Origen *In Ioannes* I 18 (20)
96. Origen *Principles* Preface 3; *Contra Celsum* I vii
97. B. J. Kidd *History of the Church to 461* Clarendon Press, Oxford, 1922 vol i 409 citing *In Ionannes* xx 26
98. Origen *On Romans* III 3
99. Tertullian *Against Marcion* I xxix; *To His Wife* I iii, II i; *On Modesty* xvi
100. Ambrose *Duties* I xi, III ii; *On Widows* XII 73; *Letters* lxiii 35
101. Eusebius *Apodeixis* quoted by W. R. Inge *Ethics* . . . 125

CHAPTER 3
(pages 54—80)

1. R. H. Bainton *Attitudes* 66 notes this common opinion
2. Ambrose *Duties* II xxv 128
3. E. Troeltsch vol i 115
4. *Didache* i, ii, v, iv
5. Barnabas *Epistle* xix 10
6. Hermas *The Shepherd* II "Mandate" viii; III v, iii, i
7. Justin Martyr *Apology* I xiv
8. Lactantius *Institutes* V xvi, VI xi, xii
9. E. Troeltsch vol i 184
10. W. Beach *Christian* . . . 75
11. Clement Alexandria *Rich Man's Salvation* ii-xvi
12. W. Beach *Christian* . . . 79
13. Clement Alexandria *The Instructor* III vi
14. Ambrose *Duties* II xxvi, I xxxix, II xiv, xxv
15. Ambrose *Letters* lxiii 85, 86, 89, 91, 92; *Duties* I xlix; III xxii; II xvi, xxv, xv
16. H. B. Workman 376a, citing Ambrose *Elia et Jejuniis* xx, *Sermo de Eleemosynis* xxx, xxxi
17. Ambrose *Duties* I xxviii
18. Lactantius *Institutes* V xvi; *Didache* iv; A. Harnack vol i 187; Justin Martyr *Apology* I xiv; Barnabas *Epistle* xix 8; Troeltsch vol i 115; Harnack vol i 187; Tertullian *Apology* xxxix; Lactantius *Institutes* III xxi, xxii; W. R. Inge *Ethics* . . . 213
19. Deuteronomy 15:2, 24:12f; Ezekiel 18:8 etc; Luke 6:35f
20. Tertullian *Against Marcion* IV xvii; Clement Alexandria *Stromateis* II xviii; Lactantius *Institutes* VI xviii; Ambrose *The Advantage of Death* xii; *On Tobias* is chiefly directed against the practice; Augustine on Psalm 128; Cyprian *Against Jews* III xlviii; J. Dow Art *"Usury — Christian"* in Hastings ERE vol xii 550b
21. Exodus 20:10, 21:26f, 23:12. Deuteronomy 12:12. Job 31:31f
22. Philo *Quid Ominis Probus Liber* 12
23. P. Schaff *History of the Christian Church* — Ante-Nicene Age vol i 348
24. A. Harnack vol i 207f
25. Lactantius *Institutes* V xvi

26. Ignatius *To Polycarp* iv; *Didache* iv, ii; Aristides *Apology* xv; Irenaeus *Against Heresies* IV xxi 3
27. Tertullian *On Idolatry* xvii
28. P. Schaff *History of the Christian Church* (above) 350
29. P. Schaff *op cit* 351; H. L. Gwatkin *Early Church History* Macmillan, London, 1909 vol ii 128; Origen *Contra Celsum* III xlix, liv; for Roman bishops formerly slaves, see L. D. Agate Art *"Slavery — Christian"* in Hastings ERE vol xi 603b, A. Harnack vol i 209
30. Ignatius *To Polycarp* iv
31. Ambrose *Duties* II xv
32. Ambrose *op cit* II xxviii
33. P. Schaff *History of the Christian Church* (above) 353
34. P. Schaff *op cit* 353
35. Clement Alexandria *Stromateis* IV viii
36. Ambrose *On Noah and the Ark* 26
37. *R. A. Norris Art "Ambrose"* 9; Augustine *The City of God* xix 15; Jerome on *Psalm 81* iv; P. Schaff *History of the Christian Church* (above) 353
38. Didache i; Clement *To the Corinthians* lxi (see L. H. Marshall 347); Ignatius *To the Ephesians, To the Romans*; Polycarp *To the Philippians* i, xii, ii,viii, ix
39. See chapter 1 (1) (iii); Ignatius *To the Romans* passim; Hermas The Shepherd II "Mandate" x i, "Similitude" viii, ix and passim; Tertullian *Apology* xxxvii; Clement Alexandria, in many places but especially *Rich Man's Salvation*; Origen *Contra Celsum* III ix; Eusebius *History of the Church* VIII ix; Dionysius in Eusebius *op cit* VI xli 2; Minucius Felix *Octavius;* on Valerian, Eusebius *op cit* VII x and Cyprian Epistle 1xxx i; Irenaeus *Against Heresies* IV xxx i; Ambrose *Letters* xvii; Eusebius *op cit* VIII xi
40. A. Harnack vol i 300f; Origen *Contra Celsum* VIII lxxv citing Hermas *The Shepherd* II iv 1; Barnabas *Epistle* V 7 VII 5; Aristides *Apology* xvi; cf J. Stevenson *A New Eusebius* SPCK, London (5th impression) 1970 58; Justin Martyr *Apology* II vii
41. Justin Martyr *op cit* I ii — iv, vii, xi, xii, xiv, xvii, i
42. Melito of Sardis (prominent 160-175 A.D.) quoted in Eusebius *History of the Church* IV xxvi 7f; cf A. Harnack vol i 329
43. Origen *Contra Celsum* II xxx; VIII lxviii; II lxx; VIII lxxiii, lxxiv, lxxv
44. Origen *op cit* III xxix, xxx
45. Origen *op cit* VIII lxviii, lxii
46. Clement Alexandria *Stromateis* IV xii, vii, viii, ix, x
47. Tertullian *Apology* xxx 1-4, iii 2, 1
48. Tertullian *op cit* xxxiii i, 2
49. Tertullian *To Scapula* 2
50. Ambrose *Letters* xvii, xli, xx (repeated in sermon against Auxentius), xxi xl
51. Ambrose *Duties* I xxvii; *The Christian Faith* I prologue; *Letters* xviii; sermon against Auxentius
52. Ambrose *The Christian Faith* II xvi; *Letters* lxi
53. Lactantius *On the Manner in which the Persecutors Died*
54. J. Moffatt 635ff
55. Justin Martyr *Apology* I xxxix; *Dialogue with Trypho* I x; Irenaeus *Against Heresies* IV xxxiv 4; J. Moffatt 662a
56. R. H. Bainton *Attitudes . . .* 68; J. Ferguson 63; Origen *Contra Celsum* VIII lxviii; Clement Alexandria *Discourse to the Greeks* x (see discussion in R. H. Bainton *op cit* 80); for the Twelfth Legion, Eusebius *History of the Church* V v; Tertullian *To Scapula* IV iv; cf A. Harnack vol ii 209, 213f who names one, Polyeuctes. The forty martyrs at Sebaste, also, are said to have belonged to this Legion; J. Moffatt 664a; Tertullian *On Idolatry* xix, *On The Crown* xi; cf R. H. Bainton *op cit* 68
57. Tertullian *Apology* xxxvii, xlii; *On the Crown* i; *On Idolatry* xix. For Odessa etc., cf R. H. Bainton *op cit* 70; Eusebius *op cit* VII xxx 8, VIII i 8, V v; for Basilides *ibid* VI xii 16 and Cyprian epistle "*Concerning Celerinus*" xxxiii (Besas etc); cf Eusebius *op cit* VI xli 22, VII xi 20 (for Valeria/Decius see McGiffert's footnote); VII xv (Marinus). For Diocletian, Lactantius *On the Manner in which the Persecutors Died* x, Eusebius *op cit* VIII i and iv; for the "vast number" *ibid* VIII iv 3. Cf C. J. Cadoux in R. H. Bainton *op cit* 69; and J. Ferguson 63. For Licinius, Eusebius *op cit* X viii; for Galerius *ibid* VIII xvi;

cf A. Harnack vol ii 213f with R. H. Bainton *op cit* 274 note 15 and also page 69

58. R. H. Bainton *op cit* 85; F. L. Cross *Dictionary* . . . 334f; J. Ferguson 65; for Arles see W. R. Inge *Ethics* . . . 300. Cf Ambrose *The Christian Faith* II xvi 136, 139, 142; Theodoret *History of the Church* II xxvi; Eusebius IX viii 2-4; on Martin, Sulpicius Severus *Life of Martin* I i-iv; *Acts of Archelaus and Mani* I; for Basil, J. Moffatt Art "*War*" 671b, J. Ferguson 63, Firmicus Maternus *De Errore Profanum Religionem* 16ff; for St. Louis see W. R. Inge *Ethics* . . . 300
59. Ignatius *To the Ephesians* xiii
60. Justin Martyr *Apology* I xxxix
61. Tatian Oratio xi
62. Athenagoras "*Supplication*" xxxv
63. Clement Alexandria *The Instructor* I xii; *Dsicourse to the Greeks* ("Protrepticos") x, xi
64. Minucius Felix *Octavius* xxx 6
65. J. Moffatt 664a
66. Origen *Contra Celsum* II xxx. III vii, V xxxiii, VII xxvi, VIII lviii, lxx, lxxiii
67. Tertullian *Against Marcion* III xiv; *On Patience* iii; *Apology* xxxvii; *On the Crown* i, xi; *On Idolatry* xix
68. See F. L. Cross *Fathers* . . . 95, 157 (on Egyptian Church Order) and 94f (on the Hippolytan Canons)
69. Cyprian *On Patience* xiv; *On the Dress of Virgins* xi; *To Donatus* vi
70. J. Ferguson 64 holds that The Canons of Hippolytus, (c 500 A.D.) preserves older material; and cites also "a church order from Egypt statute 29"; later "statute 28"; J. Moffatt 671a
71. Arnobius *Against the Nations* I vi
72. Lactantius *Institutes* I xviii, V x, xviii, VI xx, V xx
73. Ambrose *Duties* I xxxv, xl, xli, xxix; III xiv; I xxv; *Letters* lxi, lxii, li; for Basil: Letter clxxxviii (To Amphilocius) xiii; Ambrose *Duties* I xxxv; *Sermon against Auxentius* ii, ix, xi; *Letters* xx; *Duties* III iv; *On the Christian Faith* II xvi
74. R. H. Bainton *Attitudes* . . . 91
75. Eusebius Apodeixis lviii (in W. R. Inge *Ethics* . . . 125
76. Origen on Matthew 24:7f; *Contra Celsum* VIII lxx, lxxii, lxxv
77. Tertullian *Apology* xxxviii, xxx
78. Tertullian *On Idolatry* xix; Eusebius *History of the Church* X viii 10; A. Harnack vol ii 213; R. H. Bainton *Attitudes* 78f
79. Tertullian *op cit* xviii; Irenaeus *Against Heresies* IV xxx 3; Origen *Contra Celsum* II xxx; Tertullian *On the Pallium* i; J. Ferguson 57, 67
80. Tertullian *On Modesty* xii
81. Origen *Contra Celsum* IV lxxxii; Clement Alexandria *Stromateis* II xviii
82. Tertullian *On Idolatry* xix; Tatian *Oratio* passim
83. A. Harnack 214f
84. J. Moffatt 661b
85. Justin Martyr *Apology* I xv
86. Eusebius *Church History VII xv*
87. Athenagoras *"Supplication"* xxxv; Origen *Contra Celsum* VII xxvi Tertullian *On Idolatry* xix; Lactantius *Institutes* VI xx; Ambrose Letters xxv; see E. Troeltsch vol i 125
88. See W. R. Inge *Ethics* . . . 214f
89. Tertullian *On The Crown* vi citing 1 Corinthians 11:14, Romans 2:14
90. Clement Alexandria *Stromateis* V xiv; Tertullian *On The Crown* v, vi
91. Ambrose *Duties* III iii 21; I xviii 78; *Decease of Satyrus* i 45, 46; *Duties* III iii 23; III iv 24, 25, 28; I xlvi 232
92. Tertullian *On The Crown* vii
93. Lactantius *Institutes* V x (at end)

CHAPTER 4
(pages 81—92)

1. See Luthardt vol i section II

2. Luthardt II 8 D
3. For Alcuin (735-804 A.D.), Jonas (bishop, 821-843 A.D.), and Hincmar of Rheims (806-882 A.D.) see Luthardt vol i II 1 (4)
4. W. R. Inge *Ethics* . . . 114
5. Jerome *Letters* cxxv 12, 13; xxii 7, xvi 2
6. W. E. H. Lecky vol ii 107
7. W. R. Inge *Ethics* . . . 110f, 117
8. See P. Woolley
9. G. K. Chesterton *St. Francis of Assisi* Hodder and Stoughton, London, 1923 (1951 edition) 29-41
10. W. Beach *Christian* . . . 142
11. Luthardt vol i II 5 (3) 8 (c)
12. R. A. Norris Art *"Patristic Ethics"* 245
13. Basil cited in W. Beach *Christian* . . . 143
14. G. K. Chesterton, *St. Francis* (above) 65f, 123
15. Cf Thomas à Kempis *Imitation of Christ* (Chalmer's translation) I ix 1
16. St. Benedict *Rule* prologue; (Benedict 480-543 A.D.)
17. "Little Flowers of St. Francis" (translated Dom Roger Hudlestone) quoted in W. Beach *Christian* . . . 146
18. For Benedict see W. Beach *op cit* chapter 5; for Gregory "the Great" (540-604 A.D.) see R. A. Norris Art *"Gregory the Great"* and Luthardt vol i II 5 (7); for Francis of Assisi (1181-1226 A.D.) see W. R. Inge *Mysticism* 302f, E. R. Hardy Art *"St. Francis of Assisi"* in J. Macquarrie (editor) *Dictionary of Christian Ethics*, G. K. Chesterton *St. Francis* (above) 70, 139 and *"Little Flowers of St. Francis"* xvi (W. Beach *op cit* 173f)
19. E. R. Hardy Art *"Monasticism"*; see W. Beach *op cit* 147
20. For Hugo St. Victor (martyred 1141), Richard St. Victor (martyred 1173) and Bonaventura (1221-1274 A.D.) see Luthardt vol i II 5 (4), 6 (2); cf W. R. Inge *Mysticism* . . . 140ff; A. A. Cock 63. St. Bernard in *Sermons on the Song of Songs* lxxiv
21. Eckhart (1260-1327 A.D.) cited in W. Beach *Christian* . . . 175
22. E. J. Tinsley Art *"Mysticism and Ethics"* 223
23. For Bernard of Clairvaux (1090-1153 A.D.) see A. A. Cock 62, Luthardt vol i II 5 (3), W. Beach *Christian* . . . 177f, 183f. For Anselm (1033-1109) see Luthardt vol i 5 (1). For Eckhart, W. R. Inge *Mysticism* . . . 148, 159, 162, W. Beach *op cit* 182, Luthardt vol i II 6 (6); Eckhart *Sermons* 4
24. For Thomas à Kempis (1380-1471 A.D.) see E. R. Hardy Art *"Monasticism"* in Macquarrie *Dictionary* 217, W. R. Inge *Mysticism* . . . 194
25. For Tauler (1300-1361 A.D.), Suso (1295-1366 A.D.) see Luthardt vol i II 6 (6) and fully in W. R. Inge *Mysticism* . . . Lecture v
26. Cf E. J. Tinsley 222
27. Bernard *Sermons on the Song of Songs* xlvi; see W. Beach *Christian* . . . 179f
28. W. R. Inge *Mysticism* . . . xi-xii
29. E. J. Tinsley 223; W. Beach *Christian* . . . 180
30. Eckhart *Sermons* 3

CHAPTER 5
(pages 93—113)

1. H. Marrou *St. Augustine* 147 (Augustine 354-430 A.D.)
2. D. Mackenzie Art *"Ethics and Morality — Christian"* in Hastings ERE vol v 468a
3. The description rests upon Jerome, Salvian (400-480 A.D.) and *Apostolical Constitutions* (probably 350 A.D.); cf W. E. H. Lecky vol ii 149f
4. J. Burnaby Art *"Augustine of Hippo . . ."* 22
5. F. L. Cross (editor) *Oxford Dictionary* . . . 106
6. J. Burnaby Art *"Augustine of Hippo . . ."* 22b
7. On Psalm 32, sermon 3 15f; *Moral Behaviour of the Catholic Church* 3-8; cf V. J. Bourke *Augustine* . . . 151f, 153f

8. Augustine *City of God* xxii 24
9. Augustine *Confessions* x 6 8; H. Marrou 63f
10. Augustine *Christian Doctrine* I xxii; P. Ramsey 117
11. Augustine *op cit* I i 4; H. Marrou 79f; Augustine *Confessions* x 33, 49, 50
12. H. W. Robinson 176
13. Augustine *Handbook on Faith, Hope, and Charity* ("Enchiridion") 12
14. H. W. Robinson 176; Augustine *Confessions* vii 16
15. Augustine *City of God* xii 6
16. H. W. Robinson 190
17. J. Burnaby Art *"Augustine of Hippo"* 23b
18. See H. W. Robinson 183f
19. Quoted by Augustine *On Grace of Christ* I 19
20. See H. W. Robinson 180f
21. Augustine *Against Two Letters of the Pelagians* I 2; see H. W. Robinson 181
22. Above (a) (ii)
23. Augustine *City of God* xiv 6
24. Augustine *On Grace of Christ* c 24
25. Augustine *On Admonition and Grace* 2.3; *On Grace of Christ* 26.27 *Handbook* 30-32
26. H. W. Robinson 160f
27. F. C. Tindall 47f; Luthardt vol i I 3 (10); cf F. L. Cross (editor) *Oxford Dictionary . . .* 107
28. Cf Luthardt I 3 (10)
29. Augustine *Letters* xcv 3, 4
30. Augustine *Letters* — To Marcellinus, cxxxiii
31. W. R. Inge *Ethics . . .* 172
32. W. Beach *Christian . . .* 108
33. F. R. Barry 93
34. J. Burnaby *Later . . .* 316
35. Augustine *Homilies on 1 John* VII 8
36. Augustine *op cit* X 7
37. V. J. Bourke *Augustine . . .* 150, citing Augustine on Psalm 57 1, and *On Order* II 8 25
38. Augustine *Moral Behaviour* (above) V
39. Augustine *Psalm 32* sermon 3. 15
40. Augustine *Handbook* (above) 18, 19, 22
41. Augustine *Letters* liv 1-4; *To Januaris* 2, 3
42. Cf G. H. Clark Art *"Augustine"* 46b
43. Augustine *Moral Behaviour* (above) III
44. Augustine *Psalm 32* sermon 3. 15, 16, translation of J. Quastern (ed) *Ancient Christian Writers* Newman Press, Maryland; *Moral Behaviour* III-VI
45. V. J. Bourke *Augustine . . .* 149 citing Augustine *City of God* xix
46. Augustine *Moral Behaviour* (above) VIII
47. Augustine *Psalm 32* sermon 3. 16; *On the Trinity* XII 14 22
48. Augustine *Moral Behaviour* (above) XV
49. Augustine *Confessions* I i 1
50. Augustine *op cit* X xxvii 38, xxviii 39, translation of R. J. Deferrari (ed) *Fathers of the Church* Catholic University of America Press, Washington
51. Augustine *City of God* xix 14, xiv 6, translation of V. J. Bourke
52 H. Marrou 38ff
53 Augustine *On the Gospel of John* 17. 8
54. Augustine *Moral Behaviour* (above) 27f
55. H. Marrou 79
56. Augustine *City of God* xix 13; see J. Burnaby Art *"Augustine of Hippo"* 23 and Art *"Love"* (J. Macquarrie, *Dictionary)* 199
57. P. Ramsey 118f citing Augustine *On the Trinity* VIII viii
58. Augustine *Moral Behaviour* (above) XXVI
59. Quoted by E. H. Blakeney in E. G. Selwyn 56
60. Augustine *City of God* xiv 22
61. H. Marrou 24

62. Augustine *Confessions* VIII i 2, vii 17; cf VII xv 25, xi 20, xii 21 etc.
63. J. Burnaby Art *"Augustine of Hippo"* 23b citing Augustine *City of God* xiv 28
64. Augustine *Confessions* VI xii 22, *City of God* XIX 14
65. Augustine *Psalm 70* sermon i 17; *Confessions* V xii 22
66. Augustine *Sermons* 355 2 (translation V. J. Bourke)
67. Luthardt vol i I 3 (10)
68. — Deane *Political and Social Ideas of St Augustine* Colombia University Press
69. Augustine *On Faith and Works* 26; *Handbook* (above) 110; *City of God* xxi 27; cf C. T. Dimont Art *Augustine* in Hastings ERE vol iii 384a
70. Augustine *On Psalm 128*
71. Augustine *City of God* xix 24, iv 4
72. Augustine *op cit* xix 21, 23
73. Augustine *op cit* xix 25
74. Augustine *op cit* xiv 1
75. Augustine *op cit* xiv 28
76. Augustine *op cit* xix 17
77. See V. J. Bourke *Augustine* . . . 198
78. Augustine *City of God* i 35
79. Augustine *On Psalm 64* 2; *Literal Commentary on Genesis* xi 15 20
80. R. H. Bainton *Attitudes* . . . 98 citing Augustine City of God xix 6
81. W. R. Inge *Ethics* . . . 300; R. H. Bainton *Attitudes* . . . 99; J. Moffatt 672a,b
82. J. Moffatt 672a
83. Augustine *City of God* xix 11-13
84. Augustine *op cit* xvii 13; *On Psalm 147* 20
85. Augustine *Letters* ccxx (To Boniface) 3; R. H. Bainton *Attitudes* . . . 93; Augustine *City of God* iii 3, v 19, 25, 26; *Treatise against Faustus* cited by J. Moffatt 672b
86. Augustine *Letters* clxxxix (To Boniface) 6
87. This summary is gathered from: Augustine *Commentary on Joshua* 6 10; *Letters* clxxxix; *Treatise against Faustus* xxii 70, 75; J. Ferguson 62 citing *Letters* cxxxviii 14, 15; R. H. Bainton *Attitudes . . . 92 citing Sermon on the Mount* 1 xx 64; *Treatise against Faustus* xxii 76, 79; *Letters* cxxxviii 11, 14; *Sermon on the Mount* I xx 64; R. H. Bainton *op cit* 97; *Letters* cliii 17; R. H. Bainton *op cit* 98 citing *On Free Choice* V ii; *Letters* xlvii 5; J. Moffatt 672b; R. H. Bainton *op cit* 98
88. Cicero *On The Republic* iii 22-25; *On Duties* i 11-12; See A. F. Holmes 359
89. Augustine *Commentary on Joshua* 6 10; *Letters* clxxxix 6; *On Free Choice* v 12; *Answers to Seven Questions for Simplicianus* IV 44; *Treatise against Faustus* xxii 70, 75; J. Moffatt 672a
90. J. Ferguson 62
91. A. A. Cock 58
92. A. Harnack, quoted by B. Warfield Art *"Augustine"* in Hastings ERE vol ii 222b
93. B. Warfield *op cit* 223a
94. Augustine *City of God* ii 4, 5, 6, 7, 9, 12, 13, 26, 27, 29; iv 27, 32
95. Augustine *On Psalm 32* 16
96. H. Marrou 77
97. Augustine *Confessions* XIII xxii; *City of God* xii 23
98. Augustine *On the Trinity* XII 14 22

CHAPTER 6
(pages 114—123)

1. H. B. Workman Art *"Abelard"* in Hastings ERE vol i 17b (Abelard 1079-1142 A.D.)
2. Abelard *Sic et Non* ("Yes and No") Prologue (J. P. Migne Editor, *Patrologia Latina* Paris 1844-1864; Abelard in vol clxxviii) 1347, *Christian Theology* II 3 (Migne 1050); cf B. Russell 458
3. H. B. Workman Art *"Abelard"* (above) 17a
4. Abelard *Opera* (ed Cousin) ii 766f, 207 cited in H. Rashdall 359 (see 358, 363)

5. Abelard *op cit* 3 26 (on Romans 5:5) (Migne 836)
6. S. Cave *Doctrine of the Work of Christ* University Tutorial Press/Hodder and Stoughton, London, 1937 104
7. H. Rashdall 358
8. Abelard *Christian Theology* xxiii
9. R. S. Paul *Atonement and the Sacraments,* Hodder and Stoughton, London, 1961 81; Abelard *Romans* 11 (Migne 835)
10. See S. Cave *Doctrine of the Work of Christ* (above) 109, H. Rashdall 359 n 2
11. R. W. Dale *Christian Doctrine* Hodder and Stoughton, London, 1894 221
12. R. S. Paul *Atonement and the Sacraments* (above) 193
13. J. Denney *Doctrine of Reconciliation* Hodder and Stoughton, London, 1917 82 (present author's italics)
14. H. R. Mackintosh *Person of Christ* T. and T. Clark, Edinburgh, 1912 226f
15. H. B. Workman Art *"Abelard"* (above) 18a
16. Richard St Victor *Of the Interior State of Man* Tract. i c vi (in A. Neander vol viii 46)
17. V. J. Bourke Art *"Mediaeval Ethics"* 209b (citing Anselm *On Free Will* and *On Truth*)
18. See A. Neander vol viii 26, 47 citing "often in Abelard's lectures" and naming especially *Romans, Dialogue between Philosophers*, and *Scito Teipsum*
19. A. Neander 52f
20. A. Neander 43 citing *Christian Theology*
21. See V. J. Bourke Art *"Mediaeval Ethics"* 209b
22. Abelard *Sic et Non* (above) prologue
23. See H. B. Workman Art *"Abelard"* (above) citing Peter the Venerable *Letter to Heloise* (Migne PL clxxix 347f) and Abelard *Letter to Heloise* (Migne clxxviii 375)
24. Summary by A. Neander vol viii 44
25. Abelard *Romans*; see A. Neander vol viii 44f
26. Abelard *Christian Theology*; see A. Neander 41
27. Augustine *City of God* xix 25
28. Abelard *Christian Theology*; see A. Neander 41 and S. Mechie 1b
29. Luthardt vol ii 11 5 (2) 1; cf A. Neander 34f
30. Abelard *Romans* (Migne 866f)
31. See A. Neander 49
32. See A. Neander 48

CHAPTER 7
(pages 124—135)

1. Aquinas (1225-1274 A.D.) deals with ethics mainly in *Summa contra Gentiles* 3rd book (SG) and *Summa Theologica* (ST) 2nd part. See E. M. Eenigenburg Art *"Roman Catholic Ethics"* 593f
2. A. A. Cock 68
3. F. C. Copleston 193. The first part of the following exposition owes much to this brilliant treatment.
4. Cf A. Neander vol viii 242f
5. F. C. Copleston 197
6. Aquinas *ST* (above) Ia IIae 1.17
7. F. C. Copleston 199f
8. F. C. Copleston 206
9. A. A. Cock 73
10. F. C. Copleston 208
11. J. M. Heald 658b
12. E. M. Eenigenburg Art *"Aquinas"* 34b
13. Aquinas *ST* Ia IIae 90.4
14. Aquinas *ST* Ia IIae 93; F. C. Copleston 213
15. W. Beach *Christian* . . . 206
16. Aquinas *ST* Ia IIae 91.2

17. Aquinas *ST* Ia IIae 94.2
18. *ibid*
19. E. M. Eenigenburg Art *"Aquinas"* 34b
20. Aquinas *ST* Ia 96.4
21. Aquinas *ST* Ia IIae 95.2
22. Aquinas *ST* Ia IIae 96.4
23. Aquinas *ST* Ia 79.12f
24. F. C. Copleston 220
25. A. Neander vol viii 240f
26. Luthardt vol i II (6) 4
27. Cf W. Beach *Christian* . . . 206f
28. Cf E. M. Eenigenburg Art *"Roman Catholic Ethics"* 594a
29. A. Neander 221f, citing Aquinas *ST*
30. A. Neander 221f; Aquinas *ST* Ib 109.6; cf H. W. Robinson 207
31. Aquinas *ST* IIb 155 3
32. A. Neander 172f, 178 citing Aquinas *Sentences* Bk I 38 Qu i Art x and 25 Qu i art iii; cf H. W. Robinson 204f
33. F. C. Copleston 148
34. H. W. Robinson 205f
35. F. C. Copleston 143f
36. A. A. Cock 73
37. H. W. Robinson 205 citing Aquinas *ST* Ib Qu 79 2, 4
38. A. Neander 176
39. Aquinas *ST* Ia IIae 7.6 ad 5
40. F. C. Copleston 193
41. W. Beach *Christian* . . . 206
42. J. M. Heald 657a
43. Aquinas *ST* Ia IIae 58 3 ad 3
44. On virtues, see W. Beach *Christian* . . . 210f and cf J. Burnaby Art *"Love"* in Macquarrie *Dictionary of Ethics* 198b
45. A. Neander 234
46. Luthardt vol i II (6) 4
47. F. C. Copleston 228
48. Aquinas *ST* Ia 96 4
49. F. C. Copleston 216
50. Aquinas ST Ia IIae 152.2 ad 1
51. F. C. Copleston 218 citing Aquinas *SG* (above) 3 124
52. Luthardt vol i II (6) 4
53. Aquinas *On the Rule of Princes* 1.15 (F. C. Copleston 230)
54. See F. C. Copleston 232f
55. Aquinas *ST* II IIa 40 22 Qu 57-61
56. Aquinas *ST* II 11 Qu 11 art 1
57. Aquinas *On Sovereignty*; see R. H. Bainton *Attitudes* . . . 106
58. See E. M. Eenigenburg Art *"Roman Catholic Ethics"* 593f; J. Pelikan *Riddle of Roman Catholicism* Hodder and Stoughton, London, 1960 145ff

CHAPTER 8
(pages 136—152)

1. Erasmus 1466-1536 A.D. See J. P. Dolan 12f
2. O. Chadwick 31; G. Rupp 262
3. J. Atkinson *Great Light* . . . 78
4. G. Rupp 26; O. Chadwick 39
5. G. Rupp 82 and cf 262; J. P. Dolan 12; J. Atkinson *Great Light* . . . 79
6. R. H. Bainton *Here I* . . . 127
7. J. P. Dolan 9f; cf A. G. Dickens 146
8. G. Rupp 261; R. H. Bainton *Here I* . . . 125; J. P. Dolan 16

9. G. Rupp 261; J. Atkinson *Great Light . . .* 79
10. L. Bouyer 150; R. H. Bainton *Here I . . .* 125
11. Erasmus *On the Immense Mercy of God* (ET J. P. Dolan) J. P. Dolan 231f
12. J. Atkinson *Great Light . . .* 71, 25, 111, 80; G. Rupp 268f; O. Chadwick 271; A. G. Dickens 58
13. Erasmus *To Richard Pace*; J. P. Dolan 8; R. H Bainton *Here I . . .* 192
14. R. H. Bainton *op cit* 170
15. O. Chadwick 32, 38f; J. Atkinson *Great Light . . .* 79; R. H. Bainton *op cit* 126
16. R. H. Bainton *op cit* 128
17. G. Rupp 264, 285; R. H. Bainton *op cit* 226
18. J. Atkinson *Great Light . . .* 80, 111, 63; R. H. Bainton *op cit* 169, 253
19. J. P. Dolan 14f, citing Luther *On the Bondage of the Will*
20. R. H. Bainton *Here I . . .* 128
21. See F. S. Schiller Art *"Humanism"*, and H. Watt Art *"Humanists"* both in Hastings ERE vol vi, 830a and 831a respectively
22. G. Rupp 261, cf 81f, 263
23. O. Chadwick 30
24. A. G. Dickens 30
25. A. G. Dickens 196
26. Luthardt vol i II 8
27. E. G. Selwyn in Selwyn (editor) 78
28. O. Chadwick 32
29. A. G. Dickens 42
30. M. M. Phillips xxiv
31. This sentence is so translated in G. Rupp 261 citing Epistle 1581 113-118; its intended meaning is nevertheless clear, and significant
32. G. Rupp 82, see 262, 26
33. A. G. Dickens 30, 32f; see H. W. Robinson *Ancient and English Versions of the Bible* Clarendon Press, Oxford, 1940 75
34. P. Smith 117
35. From the Preface to Erasmus' edition of Jerome
36. Quoted without source in B. Russell 536
37. Erasmus *Praise of Folly*, cited in J. P. Dolan 144
38. J. P. Dolan 148ff
39. Erasmus *Handbook of the Christian Soldier* at end, see J. P. Dolan 92
40. Cf L. Bouyer 190
41. A. G. Dickens 58
42. See J. Atkinson *Great Light . . .* 80
43. R. H. Bainton *Here I . . .* 253f
44. B. Russell 537; G. Rupp 284
45. O. Chadwick 38
46. M. M. Phillips 46f; J. P. Dolan 24, 20
47. Erasmus *Handbook of the Christian Soldier* I 2 (J. P. Dolan's translation); see J. P. Dolan 38f, 27
48. The page references are to Dolan's translation
49. J. P. Dolan 27
50. See J. P. Dolan 66f
51. See J. P. Dolan 68-71
52. Albert Hyma, in J. P. Dolan 10
53. J. P. Dolan 54-58
54. J. P. Dolan 58f, 61, 71, 73, 80f, 87ff, 91f
55. L. Bouyer 125
56. M. M. Phillips 122
57. Erasmus *Handbook of the Christian Soldier* 5th rule (see J. P. Dolan 68)
58. J. P. Dolan 72
59. J. P. Dolan 73f, 90f
60. See M. M. Phillips 136
61. J. P. Dolan 86

62. L. Bouyer 196
63. J. P. Dolan 73, 51
64. L. Bouyer 195f; cf M. M. Phillips 137
65. J. P. Dolan 86f
66. M. M. Phillips 137; L. Bouyer 196
67. M. M. Phillips 139
68. See L. Bouyer 119; M. M. Phillips 123f, 136
69. M. M. Phillips 136
70. Erasmus *The Complaint of Peace*, see J. P. Dolan 193f
71. Erasmus *op cit, ibid; Handbook of the Christian Soldier* J. P. Dolan 74; *The Complaint of Peace* at J. P. Dolan 183, 185
72. See P. Smith 201; M. M. Phillips 135
73. O. Chadwick 348
74. P. Smith 198
75. Erasmus *The Complaint of Peace*; J. P. Dolan 195
76. Erasmus *op cit;* J. P. Dolan 177
77. See P. Smith 198
78. R. H. Bainton *Here I* . . . 253
79. J. Atkinson *Great Light* . . . 86
80. See L. Bouyer 121
81. O. Chadwick 409, 412
82. See P. Smith 279
83. P. Smith 281f, citing Amerbach on Luther
84. Erasmus *Praise of Folly* (Dolan's translation); J. P. Dolan 113
85. Erasmus *Handbook of the Christian Soldier* (Dolan's translation) J. P. Dolan 85, 72
86. *ibid* 51
87. M. M. Phillips xxi
88. J. P. Dolan 13

CHAPTER 9
(pages 153—183)

1. H. Sasse 80 (Luther 1483-1546)
2. W. R. Inge *Ethics* . . . 223
3. Cf O. Chadwick 45f; J. Atkinson *Great Light* . . . 13
4. H. Sasse 82
5. J. Atkinson *Great Light* . . . 22; H. Sasse 83
6. W. R. Inge *Ethics* . . . 224f
7. R. H. Tawney 79 citing E. Troeltsch *Protestantism and Progress* 44-52
8. Quoted by H. Sasse 89
9. H. E. Jacobs 201b; Luther *Romans* Introduction
10. See J. Atkinson *Great Light* . . . 26, 33f
11. H. Sasse 87
12. In W. Beach *Christian* . . . 239
13. Luther *Works* (Weimar edition) 56: 422.15 (see J. Atkinson *Great Light* . . . 33); 4: 362.35-363.2; 4: 319.8-10; 56: 441,15f; 56: 264.16-21. Cf G. Ebeling 161ff
14. G. Ebeling 221
15. Luther *Works* 18: 614.1-16
16. G. Ebeling 218f
17. Luther *Works* 18: 781.6-13; 18: 767.40; 18: 636.18 See G. Rupp 275
18. Luther *Works* 18: 636.28-30 Cf G. Ebeling 224f
19. R. Niebuhr in W. Beach *Christian* . . . 240; G. Rupp 276
20. Luther *Works* 18: 634.30; 1: 147.38; 1: 146.4-8; Cf G. Rupp 276; J. Atkinson *Great Light* . . . 37
21. Luther *Works* 56: 361.13f; 56:355.23-26; 56: 356.4ff; 56: 356-7 (J. Atkinson *MLBP* 120f); 56: 361.15 (cf G. Rupp 165f)

22. J. Atkinson *MLBP* 121, 233f
23. R. Niebuhr in W. Beach *Christian* . . . 237
24. G. Ebeling 197
25. J. Atkinson *Great Light* . . . 40f, 15f
26. Quoted in H. W. Tepker citing Luther *Works* (Erlangen edition) xxvii 27.190
27. G. Ebeling 135f
28. Luther *Works* (Weimar edition) 39: I 477.7; 39: I 353 37f
29. G. Rupp 297f
30. Cited in W. R. Inge *Ethics* . . . 226
31. G. Rupp 299
32. G. Ebeling 139
33. J. Atkinson *Great Light* . . . 32
34. G. Ebeling 138 citing Luther *Works* 40: I 603.5-11
35. Luther *Works* 57: 211.9f; 57: 128.13f Cf G. Ebeling 137f and J. Atkinson *MLBP* 130
36. Luther *Works* 4: 9.28; 57:113.27f; and on Hebrews 2:3, 9:8f; cf J. Atkinson *MLBP* 103, 129f
37. Luther *Works* 56: 264.31
38. Luther *Works* 7: 502.34f; 40: I 207.17f
39. R. Niebuhr in W. Beach *Christian* . . . 237f
40. Luther *Works* 40: I 41.2 to 40: I 44.2
41. In W. Beach *Christian* . . . 242
42. J. Atkinson *Great Light* . . . 23
43. R. Niebuhr in W. Beach *Christian* . . . 241 citing Luther *Works* in Philadelphia edition (Holman 1915) 1: 191, and summarising Luther's *Treatise on Christian Liberty*
44. A. G. Dickens 57
45. J. Atkinson *Great Light* . . . 56
46. Luther *Works* (Weimar edition) 17: II 97.7-11; cf G. Ebeling 159
47. Luther *Works* 12: 559.20-31; and from *German Bible* 7: 10.6-9
48. G. Ebeling 166 citing (from *German Bible*) 7: 10.9-15
49. J. Atkinson *MLBP* 192
50. Luther *Works* 56: 3.13f; 56: 4.11; 56: 268.4-7
51. J. Atkinson *Great Light* . . . 56
52. G. Ebeling 168f citing Luther *Works* 6: 204.25f, 31f
53. J. Atkinson *MLBP* 307
54. In W. Beach *Christian* . . . 246
55. Luther *Works* 56: 157.9; 56: 169-172; 56: 22.5f; 56: 226.7; Heidelberg Theses (cf J. Atkinson *MLBP* 159)
56. H. Sasse 88
57. Cf J. Atkinson *MLBP* 82f; *Great Light* . . . 42 citing Luther's Wittenberg Theses 1-4; O. Chadwick 64
58. G. Ebeling 199
59. Cf A. G. Dickens 58
60. G. Rupp 153 citing Luther's second course of lectures on Psalms; W. H. Lazareth Art *"Luther"* 200
61. J. Atkinson *MLBP* 184
62. Luther *Works* 6: 207.26-30
63. G. Ebeling 169f; Luther *Works* 6: 206.33-36
64. G. Rupp 201f citing Luther *Works* 57: 100.25
65. Cf R. Niebuhr in W. Beach *Christian* . . . 237
66. Luther *Works* 57: 101.23; 57: 102.1
67. G. Ebeling 159ff, 172f, 266f, citing Luther *Works* 17: 2; 98: 5.25; 36: 425.13
68. R. H. Bainton *Here I* . . . 231 citing Luther *Liberty of the Christian Man*
69. W. R. Inge *Ethics* . . . 224
70. J. Atkinson *MLBP* 86; A. G. Dickens 65; the exposition is quoted in W. Beach *Christian* . . . 261
71. Luther *Works* 56: 493.15ff
72. Luther *Works* (Erlangen edition) xxvii 27.90 quoted by H. W. Tepker
73. J. Atkinson *Great Light* . . . 56, *MLBP* 184; W. R. Inge *Ethics* . . . 122f

74. See J. Atkinson *MLBP* 86; R. Niebuhr in W. Beach *Christian* . . . 242f; R. H. Tawney 80f citing Luther *Works* (Erlangen edition) vi 381f (*"To the Christian Nobility"*)
75. R. H. Tawney 81
76. Sormunen in G. Rupp 155; Ebeling 212, citing Luther *Works* (Weimar edition) 7: 21.1f; 7: 28.14-16; 7: 21.3f; 7: 36.3f
77. J. Atkinson *MLBP* 192; *Great Light* . . . 61
78. W. H. Lazareth 200
79. Cf G. Rupp 201 citing Luther *Works* 57: 63.25; 57: 105.21
80. G. Ebeling 213 citing Luther *Works* 40: I 42.11; 47: I 204.6
81. Luther *Works* 56: 263.17ff
82. Luther *Works* 3: 17.1
83. W. H. Lazareth 200
84. H. E. Jacobs (see above note 9) 201b; Luther *Eight Sermons*, Lent, Wittenberg (Erlangen edition xxviii 219); Weimar edition 10: III 15.6-12
85. Luther *Works* 10: III 18.11f
86. Luther *Works* 1: 362.18f; cf G. Ebeling 226f, 240; J. Atkinson *MLBP* 43, 159
87. Luther *Works* 1: 613.21ff
88. A. G. Dickens 55, 65
89. Luther *Works* 59: 400.1
90. G. Rupp 208, citing Luther *Works* 57: 107.17, 57: 122.18
91. Loewenich quoted in G. Rupp 223; cf Luther *Works* (Erlangen edition) V 389
92. Cf J. Atkinson *MLBP* 42, 83
93. Luther *Works* (Weimar edition) 4: 83.3f
94. Luther *Lectures on Romans*; G. Rupp 149f citing Luther *Works* 3: 429.9; 56: 471.17
95. See J. Atkinson *MLBP* 83
96. See W. Beach *Christian* . . . 262f
97. R. H. Tawney 77f; W. R. Inge *Ethics* . . . 229; W. H. Lazareth 201
98. Luther's full exposition may be seen in W. Beach *Christian* . . . 244-265
99. O. Chadwick 64f; W. R. Inge *Ethics* . . . 227; R. H. Tawney 73, 78
100. A. G. Dickens 64
101. W. H. Lazareth 201
102. R. H. Tawney 81 citing Luther *Works* (Erlangen edition) xviii 327; W. R. Inge *Ethics* . . . 229
103. See Luther's exposition of the "Sixth" Commandment: *Works* (Weimar edition) 10: II 294.21-23, 27-29
104. A. G. Dickens 65
105. O. Chadwick 72
106. Luther *Works* (Erlangen edition) xv 295 (in R. H. Tawney 82)
107. See discussion in R. H. Tawney 82
108. Luther *Works* (Erlangen edition) vi 466 (*"To the Christian Nobility"*) in R. H. Tawney 82; and for background, see 41-54
109. Luther *Works* (Weimar edition) 11: 267.30f
110. O. Chadwick 60
111. W. R. Inge *Ethics* . . . 227f; R. Niebuhr in W. Beach *Christian* . . . 243; R. H. Tawney 73 citing Luther *Works* (Erlangen edition) xviii 357-61
112. J. Atkinson *MLBP* 236f
113. Cf R. Niebuhr in W. Beach *Christian* . . . 243; J. Atkinson *op cit* 262
114. Luther *Works* (Erlangen edition) xv 302 (in R. H. Tawney 87)
115. Luther *Works* (in a Philadelphia edition of 1943) 3. 239, 241, 249 also, in Weimar edition, 51: 203.26; so cited by G. Rupp 297
116. W. R. Inge *Ethics* . . . 300
117. Luther *Works* 10: III 18.8 to 10: III 19.7. 11-13; see Ebeling 64, 67
118. W. P. Paterson 679a
119. R. H. Bainton *Attitudes* . . . 136f
120. Luther *Works* 30: 1 202
121. Cf G. Ebeling 181f
122. For the first formulation, cf Luther *"To the Christian Nobility"*; for the second, *"On Secular Authority"*; see G. Ebeling 183

123. Luther *Works* 11: 249.24-27; 11: 251.1f (G. Ebeling 183); 1: 199.3f; R. H. Bainton *Attitudes* . . . 137f
124. J. Atkinson *MLBP* 125
125. Luther *Works* 56: 124.9f; 51: 239.22-30
126. G. Rupp 297
127. Luther *Works* 52: 26.21-27; 32: 467.15; cf G. Ebeling 190
128. Summarising Luther *Works* 11: 249.36 to 11: 250.7
129. Luther *Works* 11: 251 2-18 (G. Ebeling 184)
130. G. Ebeling 185
131. See R. H. Bainton *Attitudes* . . . 138
132. Luther *Works* 27: 417.13 to 27: 418.14; 51: 242.1-8, 15-19
133. Luther *Works* 11: 257.19-23; 11: 257.32 to 11: 258.3; J. Atkinson *MLBP* 125; *Great Light* . . . 34
134. Discussed fully by G. Ebeling 197-201
135. Luther *Works* 11: 255.12-21
136. See G. Ebeling 177
137. J. Atkinson *MLBP* 187
138. Luther *Works* 6: 407.10-15, 17ff, 22f; 6: 408.8-11; see G. Ebeling 180f; J. Atkinson *op cit* 188
139. Luther *Works* 56: 478.30f
140. See J. Atkinson *MLBP* 224
141. O. Chadwick 69f
142. Cf R. H. Tawney 85f
143. J. Atkinson *MLBP* 296, 306f, 317, 319, 328; Luther *Works* 30: I 234.21-26
144. Luther *Works* 12: 559.20-31

CHAPTER 10
(pages 184—211)

1. R. H. Tawney 88; O. Chadwick 96; A. G. Dickens 172; H. Balmforth 107; A. Dakin 208 (Calvin 1509-1564)
2. J. Orr Art *"Calvinism"* 148a; O. Chadwick 88f; A. G. Dickens 84; W. R. Inge *Ethics* . . . 181. Inge says, Calvin caused Servetus' death; Orr, that Calvin thought Servetus a libertine, but did not want him killed, the trial being taken out of his hands.
3. Calvin *Institutes of the Christian Religion* (Beveridge translation) I vi 2; I xi 12; II ii 14f
4. Calvin III x 1-3
5. W. R. Inge *Ethics* . . . 332
6. A. G. Dickens 151
7. O. Chadwick 176; R. Niebuhr in W. Beach *Christian* . . . 268
8. A. G. Dickens 155, 165
9. R. H. Tawney 88f; W. R. Inge *Ethics* . . . 229f
10. A. G. Dickens 155, 159; cf O. Chadwick 83
11. W. R. Inge *Ethics* . . . 230
12. Calvin IV i 4
13. O. Chadwick 93
14. R. H. Tawney 93
15. J. Orr Art *"Calvinism"* 148b; R. Niebuhr in W. Beach *Christian* . . . 271
16. Cf A. G. Dickens 156f; O. Chadwick 93; A. Dakin 209
17. Calvin III vii 1
18. The definition is not Calvin's but summarises *Institutes* II i 4; cf G. H. Clark Art *"Calvinistic Ethics"* 81b
19. Calvin II ii 13, 22
20. G. H. Clark Art *"Calvinistic Ethics"* 80a
21. J. Murray 7
22. Calvin II v 6, 7
23. Calvin II vii 2-4

24. Calvin II vii 6-13; cf J. Haroutunian 43; R. Niebuhr in W. Beach *Christian* . . . 280f
25. Calvin II viii 1-50
26. Calvin II viii 51
27. Calvin III xx 45
28. Calvin III iv 26, II ii 6
29. Calvin II i 4-6, 8f, 11
30. Calvin II ii 10, 25, 27
31. Calvin III iii and iv and v passim; II v 19
32. Calvin II vii 5, III i 1, 4, III xi 23
33. Calvin III xi 2, III xiv 1f, 9
34. Calvin I xviii 4, II iv 5
35. Calvin III xi 1
36. Calvin III iii 1f
37. Calvin III iii 9
38. Calvin III vi 1, I xv 4, III vi 3, 2
39. Calvin III vi 3-5, III xvii 15, 10, IV viii 12, I ii 1
40. O. Chadwick 176
41. W. R. Inge *Ethics* . . . 230
42. O. Chadwick 94, R. Niebuhr in W. Beach *Christian* . . . 272
43. Calvin III x 1
44. Calvin IV xii 23
45. Calvin III xix
46. Calvin III xix 7
47. Calvin III xix 15f, IV x 5
48. Calvin IV x 6-32
49. Calvin IV viii 9f, IV xii
50. O. Chadwick 367, 399f
51. Calvin III xviii 8, III ii 41, II viii 55
52. Calvin II viii 56
53. Calvin III vii 4-7
54. Calvin III iii 9
55. Calvin I xv 3f, III vi 3
56. Calvin III iii 9
57. Calvin II xvi 7
58. Calvin III viii 1, III xxv 3
59. H. Balmforth 87; R. H. Tawney 98
60. Calvin IV xx 29
61. Calvin IV xii 20f (cf 14-18), IV xiii 11f, 14-16
62. Calvin III vii passim
63. W. R. Inge *Ethics* . . . 123
64. Calvin III vii 8-10, III viii 1-4, 8f
65. Calvin II ii 11
66. Calvin III x 6
67. Calvin I xvii 4
68. Calvin IV xiii 10
69. W. R. Inge *Ethics* . . . 232
70. Calvin II viii 41-43, IV xii 23-28
71. Calvin IV xii 26f, cf IV xiii 18f
72. Calvin IV xix 34-37
73. Calvin II viii 44
74. A. Dakin 208
75. R. Niebuhr in W. Beach *Christian* . . . 272f; R. H. Tawney 97
76. A. Dakin 218; G. Rupp Art in the *Times* of London, 1964 quoted in H. F. R. Catherwood 126; H. F. R. Catherwood 1
77. See R. H. Tawney 93f
78. J. Atkinson *MLBP* 30
79. M. Weber 69
80. M. Weber 247

81. R. H. Tawney 90
82. Calvin IV i 3
83. Calvin II viii 44
84. Calvin III iv 2
85. A. Dakin 225
86. R. H. Tawney 97
87. O. Chadwick 183
88. See A. Dakin 226; R. H. Tawney 92
89. W. R. Inge *Ethics* . . . 234; M. Weber 172
90. Words ascribed to E. Choisy in R. H. Tawney 100
91. M. Weber, as summarised in R. H. Tawney vii
92. A. Dakin 223; R. H. Tawney 96; Hill, and G. Rupp, as quoted in H. F. R. Catherwood 117 and 125 respectively; cf A. G. Dickens 178, O. Chadwick 184
93. H. F. R. Catherwood 119-125
94. J. Haroutunian 42
95. A. G. Dickens 180
96. Calvin IV xx 2 16
97. Calvin IV xx
98. W. R. Inge *Ethics* . . . 233; O. Chadwick 83
99. Calvin IV xx 23
100. W. R. Inge *Ethics* . . . 233, 306; cf R. H. Bainton *Attitudes* . . . 146 quoting the *Confession of Magdeburg*
101. Calvin IV xx 24-32
102. Cf O. Chadwick 84, 87f, 90, 392; A. G. Dickens 154, 163
103. A. G. Dickens 162
104. O. Chadwick 159f
105. A. Dakin 230
106. R. H. Bainton *Attitudes* . . . 145
107. Calvin IV xx 11
108. Calvin IV xx 12
109. See W. R. Inge *Ethics* . . . 301
110. R. H. Bainton *Attitudes* . . . 145
111. Cf R. H. Bainton *op cit* 145
112. R. Niebuhr in W. Beach *Christian* . . . 269
113. E. Troeltsch Vol ii 634
114. W. R. Inge *Ethics* . . . 123f

CHAPTER 11
(pages 212—224)

1. E. G. Selwyn (editor) 77, 9
2. B. Russell 323
3. B. Russell 509ff
4. Cited in H. F. R. Catherwood 118
5. See A. G. Dickens 154
6. See R. H. Bainton *Attitudes* . . . 147
7. See H. Balmforth 107f; T. Wood Art *"Hooker, Richard"* 154f. (Richard Hooker 1554-1600)
8. W. Beach *Christian* . . . 328f
9. W. R. Inge *Ethics* . . . 165
10. A. G. Dickens 189
11. W. H. Robinson 209f
12. O. Chadwick 264
13. O. Chadwick 251
14. See O. Chadwick 314f, 283

15. G. W. O. Addleshaw 92f, 100
16. O. Chadwick 298
17. G. W. O. Addleshaw 97f
18. O. Chadwick 272f
19. O. Chadwick 328
20. S. V. Troitsky Art *"Greek Orthodox Church"* in Hastings ERE vol vi 425a, 432a
21. O. Stahlke Art *"Orthodox (Eastern) Ethics"* 478b
22. S. V. Troitsky Art *"Russian Church"* 868 ab (and vol vi 432b); O. Chadwick 361f, 409
23. See O. Chadwick 356, 360; A. G. Dickens 189
24. See Porphyrios 134b; S. V. Troitsky Art *"Greek Orthodox Church"* 433ab
25. S. V. Troitsky *op cit* 433a
26. See O. Stahlke 478; cf. above, chapter 1, at end
27. C. B. Ashanin 241f
28. O. Stahlke 479
29. Cf S. V. Troitsky Art *"Greek Orthodox Church"* 433a
30. C. B. Ashanin 243
31. O. Stahlke Art *"Orthodox (Eastern) Ethics"* 478b citing Archbishop Platon (died 1812)
32. Cf C. B. Ashanin 243
33. S. V. Troitsky Art *"Greek Orthodox Church"* (above) vol vi 426b; Art *"Russian Church"* (above) vol x 868ab, 873, 874a; C. B. Ashanin 243
34. See C. B. Ashanin 242; S. V. Troitsky Art *"Greek Orthodox Church"* 426a; Art *"Russian Church"* 868a, 869b, 871a, 873a
35. O. Stahlke 479
36. Cf S. V. Troitsky Art *"Russian Church"* 868a

CHAPTER 12
(pages 225—240)

1. O. Chadwick 444; see note 4 below
2. Locke 1632-1704; Hume 1711-1776; the latter's *Enquiry concerning the Principles of Morals,* about 1740
3. At the Diet of Worms: B. J, Kidd *Documents Illustrative of the Continental Reformation* Clarendon Press, Oxford, 1911 85
4. Bishop Butler 1692-1752; Kant 1724-1804; R. Baxter 1615-1691; G. Fox 1624-1691; R. Barclay 1648-1690; Jonathan Edwards 1703-1758
5. F. L. Cross (editor) *Dictionary of the Christian Church* 211
6. See W. R. Matthews xiii, xvii, xx, xxi
7. Butler *Sermons* Preface 29
8. Butler III 3; cf II 9, III 5
9. W. Beach *Christian . . .* 328f, 333
10. Butler I 2
11. W. R. Matthews xi; Butler XIII 1
12. Butler XV 16
13. W. R. Matthews xxvif
14. Butler III 5; see F. L. Cross (editor) *Dictionary of the Christian Church* 211; Butler *Dissertation upon Virtue* 10; *Sermons* III 8
15. Butler Preface 29, 30
16. Butler II 8; see W. R. Matthews xxiv
17. Butler I 5, and passim
18. Butler XI-XIV XIII 3, 14; XIV 8, 15, 16
19. Butler *Analogy of Religion* chapters 3 and 4; cf F. L. Cross (editor) *Dictionary of the Christian Church* 47
20. Butler *Sermons* V 13 (present author's italics)
21. D. M. MacKinnon 41
22. Butler *Dissertation upon Virtue* I
23. Butler *Sermons* I 4-7, 8

24. Butler II 3-9
25. Butler II 9-14
26. Butler II 14
27. Butler II 15, Preface 24
28. Butler I 15; *Dissertation upon Virtue* 6
29. Butler XII 15, 17
30. Butler Preface 39, 41
31. Butler XI 20
32. Butler XI 7, 8; Preface 35-37; I 14, V 9-12; Preface 18; X 6, 11
33. Butler I 6, 10, 15
34. Butler XII 25-33; *Dissertation upon Virtue* 8, 10
35. Butler V 10-15, VI passim
36. W. Beach *Christian* . . . 331
37. Butler I 4; V 1, 7, 9, 12; XI 11-16; Preface 38f; I 6
38. Butler XIII 3, 11, 14; XIV 6, 9 (at end), 16f and passim
39. Butler XIII 2
40. Butler XIII 3
41. Butler XIV 2, 3
42. Butler XIV 3-5
43. W. R. Matthews xxvi
44. Butler Preface 42
45. D. M. MacKinnon 42
46. J. S. Mackenzie *Manual* . . . 185f, 188f
47. J. S. Mackenzie *op cit* 294
48. F. L. Cross (editor) *Dictionary of the Christian Church* 211
49. W. R. Matthews xxv
50. Butler *Dissertation upon Virtue* 1
51. J. S. Mackenzie *Manual* . . . 187
52. W. Beach *Christian* . . . 332
53. Butler *Sermons* Preface 13, 15
54. W. Beach *Christian* . . . 331
55. Butler IX 18, 20
56. J. S. Mackenzie *Manual* . . . 189f, 198. Immanuel Kant 1724-1804
57. E. G. Selwyn 115f; W. R. Matthews xxvi; A. A. Cock 72 quoting M. Gilson; cf D. M. MacKinnon 42
58. T. K. Abbott 10, 11
59. T. K. Abbott 260 (at end)
60. See J. S. Mackenzie *Manual* . . . 171-4, 265
61. See J. S. Mackenzie *op cit* 187; T. K. Abbott 4
62. T. K. Abbott 21, cf 46; J. S. Mackenzie *op cit* 192
63. T. K. Abbott 19
64. C. H. Pinnock 48
65. See A. K. Rogers *Student's History of Philosophy* Macmillan, London 412f; G. H. Clark Art *"Kant"* 366; J. S. Mackenzie *Manual* . . . 205
66. J. S. Mackenzie *Manual* . . . 294; see C. H. Pinnock 48

CHAPTER 13
(pages 241—265)

1. Cf S. J. Knox 284; W. Beach *Christian* . . . 327; A. G. Dickens 181; O. Chadwick 208f
2. S. J. Knox 285
3. J. MacKinnon vol ii 349
4. O. Chadwick 178f
5. S. J. Knox 284
6. R. Baxter *Christian Directory* Grand Direction xv. Baxter 1615-1691
7. Cf A. G. Dickens 180; R. H. Tawney 180, 95; O. Chadwick 180

8. A. Dakin 166
9. W. Beach *Christian* . . . 299
10. R. Baxter *Christian Directory* Grand Directions xv, xvi
11. W. Beach *Christian* . . . 299
12. S. J. Knox 284
13. R. Baxter *Christian Directory* Grand Direction x
14. A. G. Dickens 179; F. Higham 93, 98, 100, 107
15. R. Baxter *Christian Directory* Part i chapter ii
16. R. H. Tawney 157f
17. R. Baxter *Christian Directory* Grand Direction xv
18. Cf W. Beach *Christian* . . . 303f
19. W. R. Inge *Ethics* . . . 234
20. R. H. Tawney 166
21. W. Beach *Christian* . . . 306
22. W. Beach *op cit* 305
23. R. Baxter *Christian Directory* Grand Direction x
24. O. Chadwick 180ff (Squire Bruen of Tarvin, near Chester, England)
25. R. H. Tawney 170
26. R. H. Tawney 169f
27. R. H. Tawney 168-175
28. Cf S. J. Knox 284
29. J. MacKinnon vol ii 330
30. J. MacKinnon vol ii 357
31. J. MacKinnon vol ii 343, 362
32. John Smyth *Confession of Faith* (1611) art 84; Thomas Helwys *The Mistery of Iniquity* (1612) 69; cf O. Chadwick 238, H. Balmforth 112
33. See J. MacKinnon vol iii 376f, 188, 474f
34. R. Baxter *Christian Directory* Grand Direction xv
35. See *S. J. Knox* 284
36. R. Baxter *Christian Directory* Part i chapter ii
37. See J. I. Packer 557f
38. See O. Chadwick 180, W. Beach *Christian* . . . 303
39. R. Baxter *Christian Directory* Grand Direction x
40. R. H. Tawney 156
41. S. J. Knox 285
42. Cf D. E. Trueblood 560
43. E. P. Mather 7; George Fox 1624-1691; Robert Barclay 1648-1690
44. See F. Higham chapter viii
45. So E. P. Mather 12f
46. Barclay *Apology* IV (at end); V-VI xxviii; IV ii
47. Barclay V-VI Introduction
48. Barclay V-VI x (at end)
49. Barclay V
50. Barclay V-VI xxv, xxvii
51. Barclay VI; then on V-VI xiii, xv fifthly
52. Barclay V-VI xxiv, xvii
53. Barclay V-VI xvii
54. Barclay V-VI xxi; II x secondly, thirdly; I at end
55. F. Higham 170
56. Barclay V-VI xvi; XIV ii; XV vi thirdly
57. W. Beach *Christian* . . . 307
58. W. Beach *op cit* 308
59. W. Penn *Primitive Christianity Revived* I 1 (quoted in W. Beach *op cit* 308); Barclay X, XII, XIII, X ii
60. Barclay III; then III v; and Foreword *"Address to the Friendly Reader"*
61. Barclay VII; then VII iv thirdly; x secondly
62. Barclay VII x secondly
63. Barclay XIV ii, i, vi

64. Barclay XIV i; F. Higham 179
65. Barclay XV ii
66. W. Beach *Christian* . . . 307
67. Barclay XV passim; cf W. Beach *op cit* 321; Barclay XV ix; cf O. Chadwick 241; F. L. Cross (Editor) Dictionary Art *"Friends"*
68. Exodus 20:7, Matthew 5:33, James 5:12
69. Barclay XV xii eleventhly
70. O. Chadwick 243
71. Barclay VIII
72. Barclay VIII ii thirdly, fourthly, lastly, viii secondly
73. F. Higham 170, 174, 184
74. R. H. Tawney 211f
75. E. A. Payne *Free Church Tradition in the Life of England* SCM Press London 1944 86f
76. R. H. Bainton *Attitudes* . . . 157f
77. R. H. Bainton *op cit* 158
78. Barclay XV ii xiii
79. Barclay XV xv sixthly
80. See R. H. Bainton *Attitudes* . . . 157f, 159
81. W. Beach *Christian* . . . chapter 13
82. J. Edwards *Works* (edited H. Rogers) vol ii 130-141; J. F. Gerstner 200 citing J. Edwards on Romans 4:10
83. Cf W. Beach *Christian* . . . 389
84. Edwards *Works* vol i 3-86; 143-227; cf R. T. Handy Art *"Edwards, Jonathan"* 102 J. F. Gerstner 200
85. R. T. Handy *op cit* 102
86. Edwards *Works* vol i 234-343; see Preface, and Part i section i
87. Edwards *Works* vol i 234f, Part i section ii
88. Edwards *Works* vol i 122-142
89. Edwards *Sermon* cited by J. F. Gerstner 200; *On Original Sin* in *Works* vol i 146-233
90. Last quotation is from Edwards *Nature of True Virtue* chapter II corollary, *Works* vol i 127
91. Edwards *op cit* chapter V
92. Edwards *op cit* chapter VII
93. Edwards Sermon i of *Five Sermons on Different Occasions (Works* vol ii)
94. Edwards *Works* vol ii 220f
95. Edwards *Works* vol ii 173f
96. Edwards *Nature of True Virtue* chapter V
97. Edwards *On Christian Charity, Works* vol ii 163-169
98. Cf G. H. Clark Art *"Calvinistic Ethics"* 81

CHAPTER 14
(pages 266—281)

1. Quoted in J. W. Bready 296, 302f
2. *COPEC* xii 133-137, 144
3. M. B. Reckitt 87, 152, 197; *COPEC* xii 154f; R. Flint 293
4. S. E. Wirt 637
5. See chapter 16
6. John Wesley 1703-1791; cf E. A. Payne *Free Church Tradition in the Life of England* 77; F. L. Cross (editor) *Dictionary* 1446; W. Beach *Christian* . . . 353f, 357f, 364f, citing a private letter
7. Cf J. W. Bready 200-203; Wesley *Works* (1872 edition) vol V 296
8. Cf W. Beach *Christian* . . . 361
9. Culled from J. W. Bready (summarising Wesley) 200f
10. W. Beach *Christian* . . . 359f; Wesley *Sermon on Christian Perfection; Plain Account of Christian Perfection* section 27

11. B. H. Hall 498, citing Wesley *Plain Account of Christian Perfection*
12. See J. W. Bready 259f
13. See J. W. Bready 234f
14. Wesley *Sermon on the Use of Money*
15. J. W. Bready 249f, 237
16. J. W. Bready 238
17. Wesley *Sermon on the Use of Money*
18. K. Heasman 127, W. Beach *Christian* . . . 362
19. Encyclopaedia Britannica (11th edition) Art *"John Wesley"*
20. J. W. Bready 265 ascribes these words to "Fairburn"
21. J. W. Bready 247; K. Heasman 171
22. Wesley *Sermon on the Use of Money*
23. Wesley *Works* (as above) vol XII 327
24. Wesley *Works* vol IX 221
25. Wesley *Works* vol XI 122
26. F. L. Cross (editor) *Dictionary* 1446; E. A. Payne *Free Church Tradition in the Life of England* (above) 86; W. Beach *Christian* . . . 362; J. W. Bready 226f, 336
27. H. Townsend *Claims of the Free Churches* Hodder and Stoughton, London, 1949 219f, 221
28. W. Beach *Christian* . . . 364
29. J. W. Bready Part iii; also, 13, 252
30. See *COPEC* xii 129, 132
31. K. Heasman 15, 13f
32. K. Heasman 26
33. C. Smith 107, 83; M. Reckitt 108; *COPEC* xii 138, 140f
34. See H. G. Wood 191; George Cadbury 1839-1922
35. J. W. Bready 405
36. J. W. Bready 389f; C. E. Raven 148f
37. J. W. Bready 343
38. See J. W. Bready 345, citing Johnson's *Life of Garrison* 106
39. J. W. Bready 346, 388
40. A. L. Drummond 305f
41. M. L. Stevens Art *"Social Service"* in Baker (pub.) *Dictionary* 641; cf W. S. Mooneyham 442f, and S. E. Wirt 637
42. W. S. Mooneyham 442f

CHAPTER 15
(pages 282—311)

1. See W. Beach *Christian* . . . 445; J. Macquarrie Art *"Ritschl and Ritschlianism* in J. Macquarrie (editor) *Dictionary of Christian Ethics* 301f; P. D. Feinberg Art *"Harnack"* 282, and Art *"Ritschl and Protestant Ethics"* 592. see chapter 16.
2. F. D. Maurice 1805-1872. Cf C. E. Raven *Christian Socialism 1848-54* 1920 134f; M. Reckitt 19; *COPEC* xii 142
3. Cf T. Wood Art *"Christian Social Movement"* 56
4. C. E. Raven *Christian Socialism 1848-54* (above) 134f; M. Reckitt 20; R. Flint 321
5. Quotations from Rev T. Kerr Spiers B.D. B.Phil in an article privately circulated.
6. M. Reckitt 85
7. J. E. Symes 499b; cf M. Reckitt 86
8. F. D. Maurice *Sermon* on "Give us this day our daily bread"
9. T. Wood Art *"Christian Social Movement"* 56
10. E. G. Selwyn 120, 126f
11. F. D. Maurice *Kingdom of Christ* (Everyman edition) ii 321
12. Rev T. Kerr Spiers in an article privately circulated
13. See J. E. Symes 499b; T. Wood Art *"Christian Social Movement"* 208; M. Reckitt 84f quoting Carpenter

14. R. Flint 292f
15. J. Adderley, cited by M. Reckitt 135
16. M. Reckitt 120
17. H. Scott Holland 1847-1918. See C. Gore in M. Reckitt 145
18. Quoted by J. Adderley, in chapter on H. Scott Holland in *Christian Social Reformers of the Nineteenth Century* (H. Martin editor) SCM Press, London, 1933 edition, 207f
19. See J. Adderley *op cit* 210
20. M. Reckitt 173
21. Quoted in M. Reckitt 120f
22. See M. Reckitt 142
23. Charles Gore 1853-1932. See M. Reckitt 146f
24. M. Reckitt 207
25. W. Temple 1881-1944. See J. Macquarrie Art "Temple" in Macquarrie (editor) *Dictionary* 341
26. See J. Macquarrie *Thought* . . . 270
27. W. Temple 9f, 15-18
28. Cf M. Reckitt 182, 186
29. M. Reckitt 195
30. W. Beach *Christian* . . . 481
31. J. Macquarrie *Thought* . . . 162; S. Mathews and G. B. Smith (editors) *Dictionary of Religion and Ethics* 416
32. A. L. Drummond 314f, 317
33. S. Matthews in Mathews and Smith (editors) *Dictionary* (above) 416b
34. See A. L. Drummond 317
35. See A. L. Drummond 316
36. See J. Macquarrie *Thought* . . . 162f
37. W. Gladden *The Christian Pastor* T. and T. Clark, Edinburgh, 1901 29f, 34f, 38, 41, 47
38. J. Macquarrie *Thought* . . . 164; cf S. Mathews and G. B. Smith (editors) *Dictionary* (above) 363. W. Rauschenbusch 1861-1918
39. Cf A. L. Drummond 317; W. A. Mueller 566; W. Rauschenbusch in *Clevelands Young Men* xxviii (January 9 1913) quoted by R. T. Handy Art *"Rauschenbusch . . . "* in *Baptist Quarterly,* London July 1964
40. R. T. Handy *op cit;* J. Macquarrie *Thought* . . . 165; A. L. Drummond 317
41. W. Rauschenbusch *Christianising the Social Order* Macmillan, New York, 1912 93f
42. R. T. Handy Art *"Rauschenbusch, Walter"* in J. Macquarrie (editor) *Dictionary* 288; J. Macquarrie *Thought* . . . 164
43. R. T. Handy Art *"Rauschenbusch . . ."* in *Baptist Quarterly* (above)
44. J. Macquarrie *Thought* . . . 165. Shailer Mathews 1863-1941
45. J. Macquarrie *op cit* 165f citing S. Mathews *Social Teaching of Jesus* 54, *Growth of the Idea of God* 210
46. S. Mathews in Mathews and Smith *Dictionary* (above, note 31) 416
47. See J. Macquarrie *Thought* . . . 340, W. Beach *Christian* . . . 482
48. J. Macquarrie *op cit* 344
49. G. Harland 21f. Reinhold Niebuhr 1892-1971
50. K. M. Hamilton 458f
51. D. Jenkins in Foreword to 1963 (British) edition of R. Niebuhr *Moral Man and Immoral Society* viii
52. R. Niebuhr *Nature and Destiny of Man* vol i 201, 346; cf E. G. Selwyn 133, W. Beach *Christian* . . . 482; cf K. M. Hamilton 458f; J. C. Bennett 232f; G. Harland xf
53. See R. Niebuhr *Moral Man and Immoral Society* xi-xiii
54. R. Niebuhr *op cit* 272, 277
55. Cf W. Beach *Christian* . . . 482f
56. J. C. Bennett 232f
57. G. Harland 24f
58. See R. Niebuhr *Interpretation* . . .
59. Cf W. Beach *Christian* . . . 482f; J. C. Bennett 232f; G. Harland 3-13; K. M. Hamilton 459
60. J. Macquarrie *Thought* . . . 346f

61. Cited in W. Beach *Christian* . . . 420
62. D. Bonhoeffer *Letters* . . . 94f; *Ethics* . . . 232. Dietrich Bonhoeffer 1906-1945
63. O. Piper 18f
64. D. Bonhoeffer *Letters* . . . November 18 1943; July 8 1944
65. See Preface to the English (Fontana) edition of D. Bonhoeffer *Ethics* . . . based upon the 6th German edition; also 17, 84, 86, 189, 263 for examples
66. O. Piper 19; D. Bonhoeffer *Ethics* . . . 214f, 222; J. H. Burtness 67
67. See for example D. Bonhoeffer *The Cost of Discipleship*
68. D. Bonhoeffer *Letters* . . . August 21 1944
69. D. Bonhoeffer *Ethics* . . . 17f, 37f
70. D. Bonhoeffer *op cit* . . . 39f, 41, 43f
71. R. G. Smith 34
72. J. Macquarrie *Thought* . . . 331f citing D. Bonhoeffer *Ethics* . . . 80f
73. D. Bonhoeffer *op cit* 64f
74. D. Bonhoeffer *op cit* 78f
75. D. Bonhoeffer *op cit* 80f
76. D. Bonhoeffer *op cit* 82f
77. D. Bonhoeffer *op cit* 83f
78. D. Bonhoeffer *op cit* 85
79. D. Bonhoeffer *op cit* 93f, 97f, 104; 88-109; 110f
80. J. H. Burtness 67
81. See J. Macquarrie *Thought* . . . 331f; D. Bonhoeffer *Letters* . . . 107f, 114f, 118, 122; 104
82. D. Bonhoeffer *Ethics* . . . 17-26, 38, 204, 220f; N. H. G. Robinson *Groundwork* . . . 191f; D. Bonhoeffer *op cit* 212
83. D. Bonhoeffer *op cit* 214, 216f, 220; 192f, 212; 195; 122f
84. D. Bonhoeffer *op cit* 205
85. D. Bonhoeffer *Letters* . . . 112
86. D. Bonhoeffer *op cit* 124f
87. D. Bonhoeffer *Ethics* . . . 233ff
88. D. Bonhoeffer *Letters* . . . 91f, 122f
89. D. Bonhoeffer *Ethics* . . . 202, 70, 201
90. D. Bonhoeffer *op cit* 196-201, 320-328f
91. D. Bonhoeffer *op cit* 133; Part I: iv; 133f, 139, 207-213, 329f, 344f
92. D. Bonhoeffer *op cit* 139f, 142ff, 145, 149, 156f, 186; *Letters* . . . 120f, 142
93. D. Bonhoeffer *Ethics* . . . 323f; 341, 343f
94. N. H. G. Robinson *Groundwork* . . . 242f, 244
95. J. C. Wenger 224
96. *COPEC* xii 157
97. W. Beach *Christian* . . . 446f
98. O. Piper 16f
99. J. Macquarrie *Thought* . . . 166f
100. *"A Christian Realism":* see M. Reckitt 39
101. Cf R. H. Tawney 16f
102. *COPEC* xii 158. For the social conscience of the Roman Catholic Church, see chapter 16 1:(i)

CHAPTER 16
(pages 312—333)

1. See J. P. Scull Art *"Pontifical Social Encyclicals"* 260f
2. J. P. Scull Art *Roman Catholic Moral Theology (Contemporary)"* 302f
3. J. P. Scull *op cit* 302f, 305
4. S. V. Troitsky Art *"Greek Orthodox Church"* 434b
5. O. Stahlke 479f
6. C. B. Ashanin 241f
7. D. Bonhoeffer *Ethics* . . . 93

8. R. H. Bainton *Attitudes* . . . 230, 234f
9. W. Rauschenbusch *Crisis* . . . 315
10. H. W. Robinson 233f
11. W. S. Urquhart 56, citing W. de Burgh *Towards a Religious Philosophy* 161
12. W. S. Urquhart 24, 54, 8 citing A. Huxley *Ends and Means* 268, J. Maritain *True Humanism* 11, and N. Berdyaev *Freedom and the Spirit* 96
13. E. H. Erikson *"The Roots of Virtue"* contributed to J. Huxley (editor) *The Humanist Frame* Allen and Unwin, London, 1961 150, 147f, citing J. Huxley *Evolution and Ethics,* and T. H. Huxley
14. W. Rauschenbusch 421
15. See J. S. Mackenzie *Manual* . . . 218
16. J. Huxley in foreword to J. Huxley (editor) *The Humanist Frame* (above)
17. See W. R. Sorley chapter 2 and following
18. See C. Michalson 124
19. See P. Holmer, chapter on *Kierkegaard* in W. Beach *Christian* . . . 414f, 429; W. W. Paul Art *"Existentialist Ethics"* 230
20. See W. W. Paul *op cit* 230f; C. H. Pinnock 48
21. H. B. Kuhn 47
22. W. W. Paul Art *"Existentialist Ethics"* 233
23. For Ritschl (1822-1889) see J. Macquarrie *Thought* . . . 75f, 77f; & Art *"Ritschl and Ritschlianism"* in J. Macquarrie (editor) *Dictionary* 301; W. Beach *Christian* . . . 445; E. G. Selwyn 116
24. J. Macquarrie *Thought* . . . 76; P. D. Feinberg Art *"Ritschl and Protestant Ethics"* 592
25. J. Macquarrie *op cit* 82f, 84f
26. A. Harnack 1850-1931. See P. D. Feinberg Art *"Harnack"* 282; J. Macquarrie *op cit* 89
27. H. Rashdall 1858-1924; W. R. Sorley 1855-1935; A. E. Taylor 1869-1945; W. G. de Burgh 1866-1943; W. R. Sorley *Moral Values and the Idea of God;* A. E. Taylor *Faith of a Moralist;* W. G. de Burgh *From Morality to Religion;* cf J. Macquarrie *Thought* . . . 69ff
28. N. H. G. Robinson *Groundwork* . . . 21, 162 citing Calvin *Institutes* III chapter vi
29. O. Chadwick 204
30. See E. G. Selwyn 123f; J. E. Symes 500b; F. D. Maurice *The Gospel of the Kingdom of Heaven*
31. W. Rauschenbusch *Rock Theological Seminary Bulletin* November 1918 51 quoted by R. T. Handy Art *"Rauschenbusch . . ."* 316
32. Quoted in M. Reckitt 84
33. See chapter 12
34. A. G. Dickens 194
35. Butler *Analogy of Religion* Part II chapters 3, 4 (Macmillan edition 1900) 153, 174ff, 177
36. Butler *Sermons* at the beginning (present author's italics)
37. R. Barclay Propositions II and III; see E. P. Mather 27f
38. T. Wood Art *"Christian Social Movement"* 56; W. Rauschenbusch 314
39. W. Rauschenbusch 196f
40. W. Rauschenbusch 345
41. D. Bonhoeffer *Ethics* . . . 223
42. N. H. G. Robinson *Groundwork* . . . 152f, 316; C. Hodge *Outlines of Theology* New York 1900 51

CHAPTER 17
(pages 334—355)

1. K. Barth 1886-1968. K. Barth *Dogmatics in Outline* ET SCM Press, London, 1959 5; see N. H. G. Robinson *Conscience* . . . 85; J. Macquarrie *Thought* . . . 321
2. R. Niebuhr *Moral Man* . . . 68; Cf K. Barth *CD* I 2 255f; G. W. Bromiley Art *"Karl Barth"*; also L. Malavez 122, 192f; N. H. G. Robinson *Conscience* . . . 113, 132f; 105, 126f; J. Macquarrie *Thought* . . . 321

3. K. Barth *CD* II 2 520; see N. H. G. Robinson *Groundwork* . . . 132, 50f, 32; 16f, 295; C. C. West 27a; L. Malavez 49, 122f
4. Cf S. Neill *Interpretation of the New Testament 1861-1961* Oxford 1966 206, 211; L. Malavez 206; J. Macquarrie *Thought* . . . 319
5. S. Neill *op cit* 208
6. J. Macquarrie *Thought* . . . 320
7. N. H. G. Robinson *Conscience* . . . 163; *Groundwork* . . . 181
8. N. H. G. Robinson *Conscience* . . . 92f
9. N. H. G. Robinson *Groundwork* . . . 178, 295; *Conscience* . . . 99, 159, 161, 167 citing K. Barth *Doctrine of the Word of God* ET T. and T. Clark, Edinburgh, 1936 18
10. R. Bultmann in article cited by L. Malavez 49; R. Niebuhr's phrase is quoted in J. Macquarrie *Thought* . . . 324; cf H. D. Lewis *Morals and the New Theology* Gollancz, London, 1947 8, 97f
11. K. Barth II 2 538, 536
12. N. H. G. Robinson *Conscience* . . . 98, 101f; *Groundwork* . . . 180
13. K. Barth *Doctrine of the Word of God* (above) xiv; cf N. H. G. Robinson *Groundwork* . . . 102, 132
14. See C. C. West 27
15. See G. W. Bromiley 51f
16. G. W. Bromiley 52
17. K. Barth III 4 266
18. K. Barth III 4 425
19. C. C. West 27
20. W. W. Paul Art *"Dialectical Ethics"* 182; K. Barth III 4 421
21. Emil Brunner 1889-1966
22. E. Brunner *Imperative* . . . 57f, 69; N. H. G. Robinson *Groundwork* . . . 44, 49; cf Brunner's *Man in Revolt* Lutterworth, London, 1939
23. N. H. G. Robinson *op cit* 237; E. Brunner *Imperative* . . . 71, 269
24. E. Brunner *op cit* 62f, 76, 61; cf N. H. G. Robinson *op cit* 49
25. Cf P. K. Jewett 73; N. H. G. Robinson *op cit* 216, and *Conscience* . . . 129
26. E. Brunner *Revelation and Reason* SCM Press, London, 1947 76; cf N. H. G. Robinson *Conscience* . . . 107, J. Macquarrie *Thought* . . . 324, 326, citing E. Brunner *The Mediator* Lutterworth, London, 1934 201
27. E. Brunner *Christian Doctrine of Creation and Redemption* Lutterworth, London, 1952 54-59; 87, 61; *Imperative* . . . 74; cf N. H. G. Robinson *Conscience* . . . 129
28. N. H. G. Robinson *Groundwork* . . . 97
29. E. Brunner *Imperative* . . . 155
30. J. Macquarrie Art *"Brunner"* in Macquarrie (editor) *Dictionary* 36; P. K. Jewett 72, E. Brunner *"Nature and Grace"* in E. Brunner and K. Barth *Natural Theology* Bles, London, 1946 23; cf N. H. G. Robinson *Groundwork* . . . 177
31. N. H. G. Robinson *Groundwork* . . . 136, 47f; cf *Conscience* . . . 72f, 105
32. E. Brunner *Imperative* . . . 70ff, 76f
33. E. Brunner *op cit* 76f, 84
34. P. K. Jewett 72; E. Brunner *Justice* . . . 123, 122; W. W. Paul Art *"Dialectical Ethics"* 182
35. E. Brunner *Imperative* . . . 53-56f
36. E. Brunner *op cit* 114f, 72, 56, 85f
37. E. Brunner *op cit* 53, 59; N. H. G. Robinson *Groundwork* . . . 133f, 177, 184, 186, 233f
38. E. Brunner *op cit* 115
39. E. Brunner *op cit* 116, 79
40. P. K. Jewett 73
41. E. Brunner *op cit* 111, 134
42. E. Brunner *op cit* 134f
43. E. Brunner *op cit* 79f, 117f, 122
44. E. Brunner *op cit* 134, 83f
45. E. Brunner *op cit* chapter xii; 132f with Brunner's note, 603f
46. E. Brunner *op cit* 133, 296, 300f; chapter xxix
47. E. Brunner *Justice* . . . 50; P. Ramsey 14; E. Brunner *op cit* 129

48. E. Brunner *Imperative* . . . 308f, 189, 300
49. E. Brunner *op cit* 190
50. E. Brunner *op cit* 79, 76
51. J. Macquarrie Art *"Brunner"* in Macquarrie (editor) *Dictionary* 36
52. P. K. Jewett 73; E. Brunner *Imperative* . . . 77
53. E. Brunner *op cit* 77, 133
54. N. H. G. Robinson *Groundwork* . . . 176, 295, cf 183, 185, 189
55. E. Brunner *Imperative* . . . 55 (present author's italics)
56. E. Brunner *op cit* 80f
57. E. Brunner *op cit* 81, 118, 133
58. E. Brunner *op cit* 122-126
59. E. Brunner *Revelation and Reason* SCM Press, London, 1947 76; cf P. K. Jewett 74
60. E. Brunner *Imperative* . . . 345f
61. E. Brunner *op cit* 197
62. See also E. Brunner *Justice* . . . 74, 213, 129
63. R. Bultmann 1884-1976
64. G. Miegge 19
65. See L. Malavez 19, 22 (citing Bultmann), 33, 97; S. Neill *The Interpretation of the New Testament 1861-1961* 225-228 and following; J. Macquarrie *Thought* . . . 362
66. L. Malavez 67, 112 citing J. Hamer, R. Prenter
67. Defended by L. Malavez 68 and passim; G. Miegge 46, 143f, F. Gogarten (in L. Malavez 108f); see J. Macquarrie *Thought* . . . 364
68. G. Miegge 23f, 39, 46f; S. Neill *The Interpretation of the New Testament 1861-1961* 249; see L. Malavez 68, 75, 78, 82, 85f, 101, 116; R. Bultmann *Theology of the NT* SCM Press,London, 1952 vol i 27
69. S. Neill *The Interpretation of the New Testament 1861-1961* 233
70. R. Bultmann *Kerygma and Myth* ET by R. H. Fuller cited in Malavez 106
71. See L. Malavez 108; F. Gogarten *Demythologising and History* ET SCM Press, London,1955 7, 66
72. Cf S. Neill *The Interpretation of the New Testament 1861-1961* 271, 234; L. Malavez 24, 95, 88ff (present author's italics); similarly, G. Miegge 48f, 89
73. G. Miegge 14
74. G. Miegge 19, 41f L. Malavez 24f, 101, 115; 76; J. Macquarrie *Thought* . . . 364
75. See G. Miegge 40, 46f
76. R. Bultmann *Kerygma and Myth* (above) 35ff; Cf G. Miegge 43f, 48; L. Malavez 102
77. L. Malavez 79, 115
78. Summarised in L. Malavez 87
79. N. H. G. Robinson *Groundwork* . . . 184
80. Cf N. H. G. Robinson *op cit* 269
81. R. Bultmann *Theology of the NT* (above) vol i 314, 317; vol ii 203
82. R. Bultmann *Jesus Christ and Mythology* SCM Press, London, 1960 41, 43
83. R. Bultmann *Theology of the NT* (above) vol i 325
84. R. Bultmann *Jesus Christ and Mythology* (above) 36
85. See N. H. G. Robinson *Groundwork* . . . 182, 185f, 223, 238f, 269, 273, 277, 327

CHAPTER 18
(pages 356—378)

1. A. Nygren 454; cf *Teaching* . . . (symposium) 43ff; J. Macquarrie *Thought* . . . 329f; J. Burnaby Art *"Love"* in J. Macquarrie (editor) *Dictionary* 198f
2. J. Macquarrie Art *"Situation, Situation Ethic"* in *op cit* 320; cf *Three Issues* . . . (cited in *Expository Times* Edinburgh March 1971 161). On Pietism, see G. H. Clark Art *"Calvinistic Ethics"* 81a
3. G. H. Clark Art *"Situation Ethics"* 623f; see J. Fletcher 31-33, 74
4. See J. Ferguson 99f; cf J. Fletcher 34; G. Woods 331

5. See J. Fletcher 38f, 65, 68, 75, 104, 139, 148; also 140, 131, 133
6. J. Fletcher 80, 120, 135
7. J. Fletcher 51, 89, Proposition III, 135
8. J. Fletcher passim; cf N. H. G. Robinson *Groundwork . . .* 247f
9. The theme of N. L. Geisler *Ethics: Alternatives and Issues* Zondervan Press, Grand Rapids, 1974
10. J. Fletcher 30, 43, 45, 65, 69
11. Reproduced in I. T. Ramsey 95
12. J. Fletcher 155f
13. J. Fletcher 74
14. J. Fletcher 26, 133, 97; G. H. Clark Art *"Situation Ethics"* 623f
15. J. Fletcher 21, 75f
16. J. Fletcher 47-49
17. J. Fletcher 15, 49
18. Summarised in N. H. G. Robinson *Groundwork . . .* 253
19. J. M. Frame 571f
20. E. Brunner *Imperative . . .* 200; K. Barth III 4 16; cf G. Woods 333
21. G. Woods 336
22. N. H. G. Robinson *Groundwork . . .* 239f
23. K. Barth III 4 17
24. J. Ferguson 100
25. J. Ferguson 101; C. F. D. Moule *"NT and Moral Decisions"* (in *Expository Times* Edinburgh September 1963) 370f; and *Birth of the NT* A. and C. Black, London and New York, 1962 212; E. Brunner *Imperative . . .* 9
26. J. Fletcher 20, 98; 37, 65, 124, 133, 135, 139f; 126; 124, 163
27. G. H. Clark Art *"Situational . . ."* 623f citing J. Fletcher 39
28. J. Fletcher 31, 50f, 90; 61
29. J. Fletcher 96, 129; 61, 95f
30. J. Fletcher 114, 137; 81; 69, 90, 92, 95, 98, 103, 117, 118, 127f; 33
31. J. Fletcher 104f, 107, 114; 91, 97, 115; 43, 50; 96, 150; 27, 122, 125, 131; 31; 26
32. G. Woods 337; J. Macquarrie Art *"Situation, Situation Ethic"* in Macquarrie (editor) *Dictionary* 321; N. H. G. Robinson *Groundwork . . .* 237
33. J. Fletcher 82; cf N. H. G. Robinson *Groundwork . . .* 238; G. Woods 377
34. J. Macquarrie *Three Issues . . .* cited in *Expository Times* Edinburgh March 1971 161
35. J. Fletcher 50; 31
36. J. Fletcher 62
37. J. Fletcher 50; for J. Macquarrie, see above, note 34
38. N. H. G. Robinson *Groundwork . . .* 276f
39. P. Ramsey xif, 34, 57, 128f
40. P. Ramsey xvi
41. J. Fletcher 155f
42. H. H. Henson 32
43. This summary reviews parts of vol 1, chapters 4, 6, 8, 11, and 10; vol 2, chapters 1, 3, 4, 6, 8, 9, 10, 11, 16, 12 and 14 in that order. For Herrmann, see O. Piper 18
44. J. Fletcher 157
45. See chapter 15 (3) (i) (d)
46. K. Barth II 2 562, 571, 575, 578, 737
47. P. Ramsey 23, 258f, 288; 44, 259
48. P. Ramsey 193-198
49. N. Smart 25f
50. See J. Macquarrie *Thought . . .* 93, 144; 84; S. Neill *The Interpretation of the New Testament 1861-1961* (above) 194f; J. Macquarrie *Thought . . .* 146f; D. M. Baillie *God Was in Christ* Faber, London, 1961 edition 30f; D. S. Cairns *The Faith that Rebels* SCM Press, London, revised edition 1929 200, H. K. McArthur (editor) *In Search of the Historical Jesus* SPCK, London, 1970
51. R. Bultmann *Jesus and the Word* Charles Scribner's Sons, New York, 1934, Collins/Fontana 1962 11
52. N. H. G. Robinson *Groundwork . . .* 105f

53. D. E. Nineham, quoted from Journal of Theological Studies October 11 1960 254-6 by I. T. Ramsey 395f
54. V. Taylor *Gospel of Mark* Macmillan, London, 1952 148f
55. T. W. Manson *Studies in the Gospels and Epistles* (editor M. Black) Manchester University Press/Westminster Press 1962 11f
56. A. M. Hunter *Interpreting the NT* SCM Press, London, 1951 48, citing A. E. J. Rawlinson *Christ in the Gospels* 118f
57. S. Neill *The Interpretation of the NT 1861-1961* (above) 291
58. W. Barclay *Gospels and Acts* SCM Press, London, 1976 17, 23
59. See chapters 8 (3) iv (c-e); 10 (2); 11 (2) (c) of vol 1
60. See chapter 4 (3) (ii)
61. See chapters 6 (1); 8 (2); 9 3 (2) and (5); 10 2 (3) (d)
62. See J. Macquarrie *Thought* . . . 84; O. Piper 18
63. See chapter 15 (3) (i) (d)
64. K. Barth II 2 577f
65. P. Ramsey 24
66. N. H. G. Robinson *Groundwork* . . . 102f, 117

Index of Scripture References

APOCRYPHA

Index of Other Ancient Sources

Index of Modern Authors

Index of Subjects